The Encyclopedia of
WORLD RELIGIONS
Revised Edition

This book was developed and written by DWJ BOOKS LLC.

General Editor:
Robert S. Ellwood
University of Southern California

Associate Editor:
Gregory D. Alles
McDaniel College

Advisers and Consultants:
Dr. Robert T. Anderson
Department of Religious Studies, Michigan State University

Dr. Frida Kerner Furman
Department of Religious Studies, DePaul University

Dr. Azim A. Nanji
Institutes of Ismaili Studies

The Encyclopedia of
WORLD RELIGIONS

Revised Edition

ROBERT S. ELLWOOD
Distinguished Professor of Religion Emeritus
University of Southern California
General Editor

GREGORY D. ALLES
McDaniel College
Associate Editor

Facts On File
An imprint of Infobase Publishing

For my family and the future
—*Robert S. Ellwood, General Editor*

To my children
—*Gregory D. Alles, Associate Editor*

The Encyclopedia of World Religions, Revised Edition

Copyright © 2007, 1998 by DWJ BOOKS LLC

Facts On File, Inc.
An imprint of Infobase Publishing
132 West 31st Street
New York NY 10001

Library of Congress Cataloging-in-Publication Data

The encyclopedia of world religions / Robert S. Ellwood, general editor; Gregory D. Alles, associate editor. — Rev. ed.
p. cm.
Includes bibliographical references and index.
ISBN 0-8160-6141-6 (alk. paper)
1. Religions—Encyclopedias. I. Ellwood, Robert S., 1933– II. Alles, Gregory D.
BL80.3.E54 2006
200.3—dc22
2005056750

Text design by Erika K. Arroyo
Cover design by Ana Ple

Printed in the United States of America

VB SG 10 9 8 7 6 5 4 3 2 1

This book is printed on acid-free paper.

∞ CONTENTS ∞

LIST OF ~ ILLUSTRATIONS ~

LIST OF MAPS AND TABLES

PREFACE TO THE REVISED EDITION

Gratified by the response to the initial publication of *The Encyclopedia of World Religions,* the editors have prepared a revised and much enhanced edition of this work. The new edition contains 100 new articles on as many fresh topics, from ACTS OF THE APOSTLES to VIETNAMESE RELIGIONS. Numerous suggestions for further reading have been added throughout. Many articles have also been updated and expanded. The entire encyclopedia has been carefully scrutinized to ensure accuracy, to include the latest scholarship and information, and to adequately represent recent world events involving religion.

The early years of the 21st century have turned out to be a time in which religion is much in the news, often in very controversial ways. Once again, faith has shown itself to be a major force behind political and international events, as well as within the hearts of individuals. Regardless of how one feels about religion's role in society, now more than ever, reliable and in-depth information about the world's religions—an understanding of its role both today and throughout history—is essential to responsible modern citizenship. It is hoped that this encyclopedia will contribute to that vital understanding.

—Robert S. Ellwood
General Editor

PREFACE TO THE ORIGINAL EDITION

Religion is one of the most important areas of human life. It has caused wars, inspired great acts of compassion, and produced some of the most exalted literature and philosophy known to humanity. Yet it is often difficult to get information on the world's religious traditions, information that is not only simple and interesting to read but also objective, not partial to the point of view of one religious tradition or another. The purpose of *The Encyclopedia of World Religions* is to help you find this kind of information.

We need always to recognize that religion can be looked at in two ways, from outside and inside. The "outside" point of view means identifying some basic facts—for example, the history, teachings, practices, and organization of a religion, facts that can be called out during research. The "inside" point of view means taking a close look at the people who live and worship in that tradition. To truly understand a religion as it exists for real people, then, you need to be able to get inside—to begin to understand the feelings of a religion's believers, their ways of looking at the world, and the things that are most important in their religious lives. Gaining inside understanding does not mean you have to agree with believers or even accept the representations of their beliefs; it just gives you the ability to empathize with, or have a feeling for, other peoples' values.

Although an encyclopedia like this one can easily provide material for the outside point of view, it is hoped it will make you interested enough to want to also gather some inside perspectives through further reading, especially in the sacred songs and scriptures of religions, and above all by meeting and talking with people of various religious backgrounds. In the United States today, people of almost all backgrounds are accessible because temples of nearly all the world's religions can be found in most large cities. The religious world, in other words, not only is found in books but is also a living reality all around us.

As you use *The Encyclopedia of World Religions,* you will find that you often need to go from one entry to another to find certain new words or ideas explained. To assist you in locating information on topics related to the entry in which you begin to read, you will notice that some words within an article serve as cross-references and appear in SMALL CAPITAL LETTERS. A word in SMALL CAPITAL LETTERS indicates that there is an entry within the encyclopedia for that word, an entry to which you can refer for additional information. Be sure to look up any other words you do not understand in a dictionary or other reference book. Best wishes, and welcome to the wonderful and fascinating realm of the world's religions.

—Robert S. Ellwood
General Editor

Editor's Note: In this encyclopedia, Japanese names are written in the Japanese manner, with the surname first; the surname is also in small-capital letters in cross-references. Terms derived from the Chinese language are transliterated according to the Wade-Giles system; when they appear as headwords in an entry, the Pinyin is also given.

INTRODUCTION

What Is This Encyclopedia About?

Adolescence is a time of curiosity—about one-self, one's friends, one's world. *The Encyclopedia of World Religions, Revised Edition,* aims to help young people satisfy their curiosity about a very important aspect of their world: religions.

Today more than ever young people in North America encounter a variety of religions. Because of changes to immigration laws made in 1965, it is now possible for people from what had previously been "barred zones" to settle in the United States. This includes a large number of people from places where religions such as BUDDHISM, CONFUCIANISM, HINDUISM, ISLAM, JAINISM, Parsiism, SIKHISM, SHINTO, and TAOISM are practiced. Students today are much more likely to have friends who practice these religions or even to practice them themselves than American students would have been in their parents' and grandparents' days.

In addition, and significantly, after the terrorist attacks on the World Trade Center and Pentagon on September 11, 2001, the religions of the world have received a great deal of public attention. It is crucial for students to learn about these religions if they are to become responsible citizens. For example, a couple of years ago, at a Sikh *gurdwara,* I met a priest who was run off an interstate highway after 9/11 by a truck driver who thought he looked like Osama bin Laden. Ignorance about religions and the people who practice them is something that the United States can no longer afford.

Unfortunately, opportunities for young people to learn about religions are limited. Much education in the United States does not include religious studies. (On the difference between religious studies and theology, *see* THEOLOGY and RELIGION, STUDY OF.) Fortunately, though, educators have begun to see the need for such education. For example, the American Academy of Religion now has a special committee devoted to teaching about religions in secondary schools, and first-rate publishers have begun to publish books in religious studies designed to meet the needs of secondary school students. In this climate, it seemed only fitting to update this encyclopedia.

The aims of *The Encyclopedia of World Religions, Revised Edition,* remain unchanged. It aims to address students directly. It provides them with accurate information about religions that they are likely to encounter. It also provides them with information that they can use and understand. Generally speaking, it contains three kinds of entries: historical entries, comparative entries, and theoretical entries.

Historical entries discuss features of specific religions. The most basic historical entries are those on the major religions: BUDDHISM, Chinese religions (*see* CHINA, RELIGIONS OF), CHRISTIANITY, HINDUISM, ISLAM, JUDAISM. Where appropriate, the editors have also included major entries on the persons who started or "founded" the religions: the BUDDHA, JESUS, MUHAMMAD. Many other religions have their own entries, too; for example, AZTEC RELIGION, CELTIC RELIGION, GREEK RELIGION, MANICHAEISM, NATIVE AMERICAN RELIGIONS, and PACIFIC OCEAN RELIGIONS. In addition, more specific entries generally supplement the broader ones. Thus, in addition to an entry on ZOROASTRIANISM, there are entries on the PARSEES, ZARATHUSTRA, and the ZEND AVESTA.

Comparative entries discuss features that appear in several or in all religions. They introduce students to many standard topics in the study of religions. Examples include entries on GOD, GODDESSES, MAGIC, MYSTICISM, RITES OF PASSAGE, SACRIFICE, and SCRIPTURE.

But religions are not simply facts to be recounted and compared. They are topics about which to think. Here is where the **theoretical entries** come in. The most basic theoretical entry is the one on the Study of Religions (*see* RELIGION, STUDY OF). Several more-specific entries discuss theories and movements in religious studies, for example, ANIMISM, DYNAMISM, FEMINISM, FUNCTIONALISM, and TOTEMISM. Other entries discuss major thinkers and their ideas: Émile DURKHEIM, Mircea ELIADE, J. G. FRAZER, Sigmund FREUD, C. G. JUNG, Bronislaw MALINOWSKI, Karl MARX, Rudolf OTTO, and Max WEBER.

In selecting entries, the editors have kept in mind that young people are especially interested in topics that address the world in which they live. Therefore, this encyclopedia supplements the general entries on Buddhism, Christianity, Hinduism, Islam, Judaism, and PROTESTANTISM with entries on these religions in America. It also gives preference to topics that young Americans are most likely to encounter, for example, the Christian theologian Thomas Aquinas but not the influential Buddhist philosopher Nagarjuna, who currently is less often studied in American schools, a situation that may change. In addition, for the revised edition, we have updated key entries to take into account changes in the world and its religions since the first edition appeared. For example, *The Encyclopedia of World Religions, Revised Edition,* includes entries on COMPUTERS AND RELIGION and BRAIN, MIND, AND RELIGION, among 100 others. It also devotes more attention to Christianity in Latin America, Africa, and Asia and to the Pentecostal movements that have recently met with some success in these parts of the world.

The basic structure of many of the entries goes back to the ideas of Joachim Wach. These ideas are certainly not beyond criticism. For example, Wach related experience and expression in a way that opens up all sorts of thorny philosophical problems. But Wach did identify three modes of religious expression—the theoretical, the practical, and the sociological—that are helpful in organizing material for beginning students. Although our major entries use simpler words, Wach's three basic divisions remain. Moreover, entries generally discuss a religion's history before considering its theoretical, practical, and social aspects.

Finally, a few other useful distinctions should be noted. For example, throughout most of the entries, readers will find themselves directed by cross-references to related entries or entries that offer additional information of interest. These cross-references appear in SMALL CAPITAL letters and will serve to extend the scope and depth of the encyclopedia.

Also, usually within the initial definition of an entry, readers will sometimes find references to Sanskrit, the ancient Indo-European language sacred to or influential among Hindus and Buddhists. Other references throughout, often found in parentheses without explanation, constitute references to the Bible.

I want to close on a more personal note. Two groups of young people have inspired my work on this volume.

The first group comprises several generations of students in the SUMMERSCAPE program at Drury College, Springfield, Missouri. During the 15 years that I taught in this program, I was amazed and impressed by the number of gifted and talented sixth to ninth graders who were willing to spend two weeks of their summers taking what amounted to introductory courses in religious studies and philosophy. These students consistently gave me more than I gave them. This volume is a testimony to our time together.

The second group includes my nieces, nephew, and children. I was particularly gratified several years ago to receive a call from a niece who lives in Houston. A friend had shown my niece her favorite book in the school library. It turned out to be the first edition of *The Encyclopedia of World Religions.*

Apparently it took considerable conversation afterward to convince the friend that my niece and I were related.

I do not expect, of course, that this volume will be every student's favorite book. But I do hope student readers will find the revised edition even more helpful than the first one. I also hope that in its own small way *The Encyclopedia of World Religions, Revised Edition* helps them grow into informed and responsible citizens.

—Gregory D. Alles
Associate Editor

WORLDWIDE ADHERENTS OF ALL RELIGIONS, MID-2004

Religions	Africa	Asia	Europe	Latin America	Northern America	Oceania	World	percent	Number of Countries
Christians	401,717,000	341,337,000	553,689,000	510,131,000	273,941,000	26,147,000	2,106,962,000	33	238
Affiliated Christians	380,265,000	335,602,000	531,267,000	504,747,000	223,994,000	21,994,000	1,997,869,000	31.3	238
Roman Catholics	143,065,000	121,618,000	276,739,000	476,699,000	79,217,000	8,470,000	1,105,808,000	17.3	235
Independents	87,913,000	176,516,000	24,445,000	44,810,000	81,138,000	1,719,000	416,541,000	6.5	221
Protestants	115,276,000	56,512,000	70,908,000	53,572,000	65,881,000	7,659,000	369,848,000	5.8	232
Orthodox	37,989,000	13,240,000	158,974,000	848,000	6,620,000	756,000	218,427,000	3.4	134
Anglicans	43,404,000	733,000	25,727,000	909,000	2,986,000	4,986,000	78,745,000	1.2	163
Marginal Christians	3,269,000	3,083,000	4,425,000	10,352,000	11,384,000	650,000	33,143,000	0.5	215
Multiple Affiliation	-50,562,000	-34,528,000	-10,021,000	-80,962,000	-23,217,000	-2,252,000	-201,542,000	-3.2	163
Unaffiliated Christians	21,437,000	5,734,000	22,395,000	5,384,000	49,947,000	4,153,000	109,050,000	1.7	232
Muslims	350,453,000	892,440,000	33,290,000	1,724,000	5,109,000	408,000	1,283,424,000	20.1	206
Hindus	2,604,000	844,593,000	1,467,000	766,000	1,444,000	417,000	851,291,000	13.3	116
Nonreligious	5,912,000	601,478,000	108,674,000	15,939,000	31,286,000	3,894,600	767,184,000	12	237
Chinese Universists	35,400	400,718,000	266,000	200,000	713,000	133,000	402,065,000	6.3	94
Buddhists	148,000	369,394,000	1,643,000	699,000	3,063,000	433,000	375,440,000	5.9	130
Ethnoreligionists	105,251,000	141,589,000	1,238,000	3,109,000	1,263,000	319,000	252,769,000	4	144
Atheists	585,000	122,870,000	22,048,000	2,756,000	1,997,000	400,000	150,656,000	2.4	219
New-religionists	112,000	104,352,000	381,000	764,000	1,561,000	84,800	107,255,000	1.7	107
Sikhs	58,400	24,085,000	238,000	0	583,000	24,800	24,989,000	0.4	34
Jews	224,000	5,317,000	1,985,000	1,206,000	6,154,000	104,000	14,990,000	0.2	134
Spiritists	3,100	2,000	135,000	12,575,000	160,000	7,300	12,882,000	0.2	56
Baha'is	1,929,000	3,639,000	146,000	813,000	847,000	122,000	7,496,000	0.1	218
Confucianists	300	6,379,000	16,600	800	0	50,600	6,447,000	0.1	16
Jains	74,900	4,436,000	0	0	7,500	700	4,519,000	0.1	11
Shintoists	0	2,717,000	0	7,200	60,000	0	2,784,000	0	8
Taoists	0	2,702,000	0	0	11,900	0	2,714,000	0	5
Zoroastrians	900	2,429,000	89,900	0	81,600	3,200	2,605,000	0	23
Other Religionists	75,000	68,000	257,500	105,000	650,000	10,000	1,166,000	0	78
Total Population	**869,183,000**	**3,870,545,000**	**725,564,000**	**550,795,000**	**328,932,000**	**32,619,000**	**6,377,643,000**	**100**	**238**

A

Aaron Brother of MOSES in the Hebrew BIBLE. According to the Bible, GOD appeared to Moses in the desert and appointed him to free the people of Israel from slavery in Egypt (*see* EXODUS). Moses objected that he had no public speaking abilities, so God appointed his older brother Aaron as his assistant (Exodus 4).

Aaron was instrumental in bringing about the various plagues that eventually convinced the king of Egypt to release the enslaved Israelites (Exodus 5–12). On a less positive note, he is said to have manufactured a calf of gold for the people to WORSHIP when they feared that Moses had perished on Mt. Sinai (Exodus 32).

Tradition holds that Aaron was the first high priest of Israel. A group of priests associated with the Temple in JERUSALEM (middle 900s to 586 B.C.E.) claimed to be descended from him. They are known as Aaronides or Aaronites.

abortion and religion The intentional destruction by medical means of a human fetus in the womb prior to birth—a highly controversial ethical issue for many religious people since it means the taking of present or potential human life. On one side are those, calling themselves "pro-life," who hold that a fetus is a person and that abortion therefore is murder. This is the view officially taken by, among others, Roman Catholics, many conservative Protestants, and Orthodox Jews. However, unlike ROMAN CATHOLICISM, Orthodox JUDAISM permits abortion if the mother's life is at stake.

Others, calling themselves "pro-choice," contend that an unborn fetus is not a person and that abortion is not, therefore, murder. Liberal religionists believe that abortion is always a serious moral decision, but that it can be justified for such reasons as saving the life or health of the mother, or the prospect of the child's being born seriously deformed. In the great majority of cases, abortion as a means of birth control, that is, as a means to terminate unwanted pregnancies, usually does not have the approval of religious authorities.

Moreover, the issue is one not only of whether abortion is intrinsically right or wrong, but also of who has the right to decide. Is it the mother's right alone to decide if she will have a child? Or do others—the state, the medical profession, the father, the church—have the right to make that decision? It is a complex and wrenching issue that many persons, religious and otherwise, continue to wrestle with.

Abraham (Arabic, Ibrahim) Legendary ancestor of Jews and Arabs, also revered by Christians and all Muslims. The BIBLE presents an image of Abraham that roughly corresponds to the way of life common in Canaan between 2000 and 1600 B.C.E.

According to the Bible, Abraham left the city of Ur in Mesopotamia and traveled to the land of Canaan. In fulfillment of a promise from GOD, he and his wife SARAH had a son, ISAAC, despite their advanced age. (The Bible says Abraham was 100 years old [Genesis 21.5]. Isaac's son JACOB became the ancestor of the Jewish people. Arabs trace their descent to Abraham through Ishmael (Arabic, Ismail), the son of Abraham and Hagar. Muslims consider Hagar Abraham's first wife. They attribute the building of the most sacred of all Islamic shrines, the KAABA in Mecca, to Abraham.

A well-known story relates how God commanded Abraham to SACRIFICE his son. Jews tell this story about Isaac. Muslims tell it about Ishmael. Abraham obeyed God without question. He stopped only when an ANGEL informed him that God's command was merely a test. Abraham's faith as seen in this incident is the theme of a book, *Fear and Trembling*, by the Danish philosopher, Søren Kierkegaard.

Abraham is a very important religious figure. Three of the world's most prominent religions, JUDAISM, CHRISTIANITY, and ISLAM, are often called "Abrahamic religions" because they see themselves as worshipping the God of Abraham.

Acts of the Apostles

The fifth book of the NEW TESTAMENT. The Acts of the Apostles—commonly referred to simply as Acts—continues the Gospel of Luke. Together, they make up a two-part work. The gospel tells the story of Jesus; Acts tells the story of the early Christian church from Jesus' resurrection to the arrival and missionary activity of the Apostle PAUL in Rome. The first part of the book is about Christians at JERUSALEM. Memorable events include the receiving of the Holy Spirit at Pentecost, the stoning of Stephen, and Peter's vision, which justified preaching about Jesus to non-Jews. The second part of the book tells the story of Paul: his conversion and his journeys in what are now Turkey and Greece, spreading the message of Christianity. In portions of this second part the writer uses the first-person plural pronoun, "we" (16.10–17, 20.5–15, 21.1–18, 27.1–28.16). It is possible that these passages are from a diary that Luke kept. The tradition that Luke wrote the Gospel of Luke and Acts does not go back further than the end of the second century C.E.

Some scholars think that the story Acts tells is somewhat artificial. According to these scholars, the author of Acts presents as united two independent and separate Jesus movements—one in Jerusalem, the other in Antioch (Paul's home base). The author also ignores other Jesus movements

that were active at the time. Traditionally, however, Acts has been taken as the first accurate historical account of the early Christian church.

See also APOSTLES.

Adam

The first human being in Jewish, Christian, and Islamic tradition. The name *Adam* may also be translated simply as "the man." The BIBLE seems to link this name to *adamah,* Hebrew for ground (Genesis 2.7). As told in the second chapter of Genesis, the Lord GOD formed Adam from the Earth's dirt, breathed life into him, and placed him in the garden of Eden. After a futile attempt to find a companion for him among the animals, God put Adam into a deep sleep, took one of his ribs, and fashioned a woman from it, whom Adam eventually named EVE. In Genesis 3 God expelled Adam and Eve from the garden because they disobeyed God's command not to eat from the tree of knowledge (*see* FALL, THE).

Jewish philosophers have seen Adam and his story as symbolizing all human beings. Christians used the image of Adam in defining the special role of JESUS. For example, PAUL saw Jesus as the second Adam, undoing the consequences of the First Adam's sin (1 Corinthians 15.22, 45). For Muslims, Adam is the first in the line of prophets that culminates in the prophet MUHAMMAD.

Adi Granth

Punjabi for "first book"; the sacred book of the Sikhs. It is also known as the Guru Granth Sahib.

The Adi Granth contains almost 6,000 hymns written by Sikh GURUS and other SAINTS (*see* SIKHISM). The hymns are mostly arranged according to the musical modes in which they are sung.

The first and third gurus, NANAK and Amar Das (1479–1574), made collections of their own hymns and those of earlier religious poets. In 1604 the fifth guru, Arjan (1563–1606), added other hymns to the earlier collections to make the first version of the Adi Granth. He installed it in the most sacred Sikh shrine, the Golden Temple at Amritsar. In 1704 the last guru, Gobind SINGH, completed the Adi Granth by adding hymns by his father, Guru Tegh Bahadur, to the earlier version. Before Gobind Singh died, he established the book as the guru of the Sikhs. It is the ultimate authority on religious matters.

Sikhs in fact treat the Adi Granth as their guru. Copies of the book are enshrined in Sikh houses of WORSHIP, known as gurdwaras. There they are unwrapped in the morning and wrapped up at night according to set RITUALS. During worship, the sacred book is fanned, just as if it were a living dignitary, and hymns from it are sung. In the presence of the Adi Granth, one should have one's head covered and remove one's shoes.

Adonis An ancient Greek god. The Greeks knew Adonis as a god who was imported from the ancient Near East. His name seems to bear out this idea. It seems related to the Semitic word *adon,* which means "lord."

Adonis figured prominently in *The Golden Bough,* a well-known collection of mythology by James George FRAZER. According to Frazer, Adonis was a typical god of vegetation. He died and rose again in imitation of plant life. The ancients did indeed know some stories about Adonis being restored to life. But these stories were told about Adonis only at a very late period.

According to some myths the GODDESSES Aphrodite and Persephone struggled over Adonis. As a result, he spent part of the year with each of them in turn. According to another famous myth, told by the Roman poet Ovid in his *Metamorphoses,* Adonis was a favorite of Aphrodite who was killed by a wild boar while hunting.

The women of Athens worshiped Adonis by planting gardens on their rooftops during the hot summer months. When the plants died, they mourned the god's death.

Africa, new religious movements in Religious movements that have arisen in Africa starting in the late 19th century. In the past one and a quarter centuries Africans have started thousands of religious movements.

Reverend John Chilembwe, a Baptist minister in Nyasaland (present day Malawi), is seen here performing a baptism ceremony about 1910. The leader of one of the many Christian movements that arose in Africa during the colonial period, he was killed in 1915 during an uprising. *(Library of Congress)*

The name "new religious movements" may give the wrong impression. Most African new religious movements are actually forms of CHRISTIANITY. North Americans and Europeans have called them "new" because Africans who rejected European and North American control developed and led them. In fact, however, the African movements often resemble the early Christianity described in the BIBLE more than Christianity in North America and Europe does. For example, like the earliest Christians, members of these movements often believe in spirits, whom faith in JESUS allows them to control, and they often heal by the power of PRAYER. Some of these movements are now members of the World Council of Churches (*see* ECUMENICAL MOVEMENT). Other African new religious movements build upon indigenous or native African traditions. A few have arisen within ISLAM.

ETHIOPIAN AND SEPARATIST CHURCHES

Compared with activities in the Americas and Asia, European colonization of Africa began relatively late, in the 1870s. In the 19th century, North

American and European, especially British, Christians took missionary work very seriously (*see* MISSIONARIES). They also took their own superiority for granted, and they acted in ways that made their racist attitudes and presuppositions all too apparent.

Many Africans found the message of Christianity attractive, and some of them joined missionary churches. But many also found the subordination that they experienced in these churches intolerable. For example, in 1890, the first African Anglican bishop, Samuel Crowther (*c.* 1807–91), suddenly and unjustifiably lost his position. As a result of such treatment, many Africans left the churches run by Europeans and North Americans and started their own churches. They called some of these churches "Ethiopian." Ethiopia provides a powerful symbol of African independence, because it has an ancient Christian church and was only briefly colonized. The first Ethiopian churches began in South Africa and Nigeria in the 1890s. Prominent among their founders in South Africa are an uncle and niece: Mangena Maake Mokone (1851–1931), originally a Methodist, and Charlotte Manye Maxeke (1874–1939), originally a Presbyterian. Both of them founded Ethiopian churches related to the African Methodist Episcopal (AME) churches in the United States.

INDIGENOUS AFRICAN CHURCHES

Another set of churches had no historical relationship with previously established Christian churches. African prophets started them. They go by various names: African indigenous churches, African independent churches, African-initiated churches, and African-instituted churches.

The prophets who started these churches emphasized the ability to control spirits and heal by the power of Jesus. They offered protection against witchcraft. They also urged people to abandon traditional African religions and to destroy their traditional religious images (*see* IMAGES, IDOLS, ICONS IN RELIGION). Some who heard them, such as followers of the Congo prophet Simon Kimbangu (1889?–1951), built large bonfires to do just that. Members of these churches also often wear white as a symbol of purity.

Many African prophets made colonial authorities nervous. As a result, some of the most famous spread their messages for only a short time, until the government stopped them. Nevertheless, their churches often continued. Several churches are now quite large and well known.

The prophet William Wade Harris (early 1860s–1929) (his middle name is an African name pronounced way-day) received his revelations from God while in prison for political activities. Although he was from Liberia, his most effective preaching was done in the Ivory Coast. Instead of founding churches, he told his followers that missionaries would come bringing the message of Christianity. In 1924 Methodist missionaries did come to the Ivory Coast for the first time, but the Methodist Church in the Ivory Coast dates its founding to 1914, the year of Harris's missionary activity.

The relationship between Harris and the Methodist missionaries was not always good. For example, following the example of ABRAHAM, JACOB, and others in the Bible, Harris allowed polygamy; the Methodists did not. Some of Harris's followers formed their own churches. Two churches in this tradition are the Church of the Twelve Apostles in Ghana, founded by Grace Tani (d. 1958), who thought of herself as one of Harris's wives, and the Deima Church in the Ivory Coast, founded by Marie Lalou (d. 1951).

A prophet in the Belgian Congo who had a similarly short career but left a lasting legacy was Simon Kimbangu. After less than a year of ministry, which included healing, the government threw Kimbangu in jail, and he stayed there for decades. His church, however, eventually received official government recognition. Named L'Eglise de Jesus-Christ sur la terre par le prophete Simon Kimbangu (The Church of Jesus Christ on Earth through the prophet Simon Kimbangu), it is the largest independent church in Africa.

Some indigenous African churches have emphasized fervent prayer, fasting, dreams, visions, and healing. These features characterize the Aladura churches of Nigeria. (*Aladura* is a Yoruba word meaning "Owner of Prayer.") An example of the Aladura churches is the Christ Apostolic Church, begun in the 1920s. It rejects the use of either traditional or scientific medicine. The same features also characterize the Zionist churches of South Africa. Zionist churches get their name because their inspiration originally came from the Evangelical Christian Catholic Church of Zion, Illinois. Both *Zionist* and *Aladura* refer to groups of churches rather than to a single church.

While some founders of African churches have been prophets, some have been more than prophets: They have been Messiahs. A famous example is the Zulu religious leader, Isaiah Shembe (1867–1935). He received a call from God in a vision and founded a church in the Zionist tradition known as the amaNazaretha Church. In 1912, after an experience similar to the temptation of Jesus in the wilderness, he received the power to heal and cast out demons. He saw himself as a Messiah sent to the Zulu, as MOSES and Jesus were sent to the Jews. His church's worship practices include dances in traditional Zulu style and hymns that Shembe himself wrote.

OTHER AFRICAN NEW RELIGIOUS MOVEMENTS

A large proportion of Africans practice Islam. New religious movements among African Muslims have, however, been relatively rare. Possible examples might include the rise of new brotherhoods within SUFISM.

Other African movements, however, have rejected Christianity and Islam altogether and have attempted to revitalize indigenous traditions. One example is the movement led by Alinesitoue Diatta (1920–44), a Diola woman of Senegambia in West Africa. She resisted the influence of both Christianity and Islam, as well as that of the French colonial government, by calling upon people to revive rain rituals and observe a traditional day of rest every sixth day. Because of her success, the colonial government arrested her in 1943. She disappeared and died in exile, though her death was kept secret for more than 40 years.

Another indigenous revival movement goes by the name of Bwiti. It arose among the Fang people of Gabon at the beginning of the 20th century. It built upon traditional cults of ancestors (*see* ANCESTOR WORSHIP) but has changed over the years by the addition of various beliefs and ritual systems. In some circles it is best known for its ritual use of the plant *iboga,* a nonaddictive hallucinogen.

SIGNIFICANCE

Africa is, arguably, the most vibrant home of Christianity today, and the so-called African new religious movements contribute to that vitality. Some have begun to spread beyond Africa to North America and other places. It remains to be seen what kind of impact they will have worldwide in the 21st century.

Further reading: Kwame Bediako, *Jesus and the Gospel in Africa: History and Experience* (New York: Orbis, 2004); *Christian History* 22, no. 3 (2003) [issue on African Christianity]; Elizabeth Isichei, *A History of Christianity in Africa* (Grand Rapids, Mich.: W. B. Eerdmans, 1995); Philip Jenkins, *The Next Christendom: The Coming of Global Christianity* (New York: Oxford University Press, 2002); Jacob K. Olupona, ed., *Beyond Primitivism: Indigenous Religious Traditions and Modernity,* (New York: Routledge, 2004); Frederick Quinn, *African Saints: Saints, Martyrs, and Holy People from the Continent of Africa* (New York: Crossroad, 2002); Bengt Sundkler and Christopher Steed, *A History of the Church in Africa* (New York: Cambridge University Press, 2000).

African-American religions The religions of people of African descent living in the Western Hemisphere. African Americans have had and continue to have a vibrant and rich religious life.

African-American religions in the Caribbean and South America often preserve and adapt African traditions (*see* AFRICAN RELIGIONS). Good examples are VOODOO from Haiti, SANTERÍA from Cuba, Candomble in Brazil, and Winti in Suriname. They often combine African and European practices. This combining is sometimes called "syncretization" or "creolization."

Many traditional religions interact loosely with ROMAN CATHOLICISM. Those who practice them WORSHIP African deities and spirits in conjunction with Catholic SAINTS. All traditional religions expect the deities and spirits to help with problems and difficulties in everyday life. The deities and spirits may reveal themselves through a medium. Worshippers may also seek advice from a diviner.

The religions of African Americans in the United States developed differently. There the dominant religious tradition was PROTESTANTISM. Unlike Catholicism, Protestantism does not venerate saints who can be identified with African gods and spirits. (In Africa, the high god is usually distant and as a result not worshipped.) In addition, African Americans enslaved in the United States often did not have the opportunity to form their own relatively isolated communities, as they did in the Caribbean and South America.

By 1800 many African Americans in the United States were turning to Protestantism. They tended to favor forms that emphasized conversion experiences rather than a LITURGY. As a result, they became Methodists and Baptists (see METHODISM and BAPTIST CHURCHES). On occasion these African Americans founded their own denominations. For example, several black Methodist congregations formed the American Methodist Episcopal Church in 1816. In smaller numbers, African Americans in the United States also joined the more liturgical churches, such as the EPISCOPALIAN or ANGLICAN and Catholic churches.

African Americans obviously benefited greatly from the movement to abolish slavery. Black as well as white ministers were abolitionists. After the Civil War and Emancipation, African Americans participated in the Holiness movements. Like prewar Baptists and Methodists, these movements emphasized religious experience. Then, at the turn of the century, African Americans were instrumental in forming PENTECOSTALISM. Gospel music is a well-known product of these movements. In the mid-20th century, the Southern Christian Leadership Conference, led by a Baptist minister, Martin Luther KING Jr., helped end legal segregation in the southern United States.

Traditional Christianity did not meet the needs of all African Americans in the United States. Some rejected it because of its connection with the former slave owners. African nationalist movements provided one important alternative. After Emancipation some African Americans called for a return to Africa. In the early 20th century, Marcus Garvey (1887–1940) emphasized black separatism and pride. The best known black nationalist movement is the Nation of Islam (see ISLAM, NATION OF). It was organized in the 1930s by Wallace Fard and Elijah Muhammad. Until a visit to Mecca in 1964, MALCOLM X was its most effective spokesperson. Rastafarianism, a movement from Jamaica, is famous for its music, reggae. It saw the former emperor of Ethiopia, Haile Selassie (1892–1975), as a savior for African Americans. Before his coronation, Haile Selassie was called Ras Tafari.

Other African-American alternatives to traditional Christianity have also emerged. JUDAISM has attracted some African Americans. They identified with the story of the EXODUS, in which the Hebrew slaves were freed from captivity in Egypt. Some have founded Jewish sects. Other African-American movements have borrowed and adapted elements from Christianity. A good example is Father Divine (c. 1880–1965), who used elements of traditional Christianity while preaching that he himself was God. African Americans have also found religious inspiration in traditional African religions. A good example is KWANZAA. Created in 1966, it is a year-end festival that celebrates family values from an African perspective.

Further reading: Taylor Branch, *Parting the Waters: America in the King Years, 1954–63* (New York: Simon & Schuster, 1988); Taylor Branch, *Pillar of Fire: America in the King Years, 1963–65* (New York: Simon & Schuster, 1998); Eric C. Lincoln, *The Black Muslims in America*, 3d ed. (Grand Rapids, Mich.: W. B. Eerdmans, 1993); Albert J. Raboteau, *Canaan Land: A Religious History of African Americans* (New York: Oxford University Press, 2001); Cornel West and Eddie S. Glaude, Jr., eds., *African American Religious Thought: An Anthology* (Louisville, Ky.: Westminster John Knox, 2003).

African religions The indigenous religions of Africa. This entry discusses African religions south of the Sahara Desert. North of the Sahara ISLAM has been the dominant religion since the 600s C.E.

People have lived in Africa for tens, if not hundreds, of thousands of years. Indeed, many believe that the genus *Homo* first evolved in Africa. Hominid bones found at Olduvai Gorge in Kenya from 1959 on seem to confirm this belief. Some are over two million years old.

The history of Africa south of the Sahara is not known as well as we would like. That is true of the history of African religions, too. African religions do have venerable pasts. For example, African rock paintings often have mythological and religious significance. Some rock paintings date as far back as 26,000 B.P. (before the present). It would be a mistake, however, to think that traditional African religions were static and never changed, as was commonly thought in the late 1800s. Like all religions, they changed and developed. For example, in the last 500 years, many African peoples acquired kings. They often thought these kings were sacred.

There are thousands of African cultures, languages, and religions. Obviously, it is impossible to describe them all. But some features of African religions appear fairly frequently.

Many traditional Africans know about a "high god" who created the universe. This god is distant and unconcerned with daily life. Africans tell many different stories to explain why. They also tell stories about the beings who first invented cultural products and social institutions. Other stories tell about figures known as TRICKSTERS.

Some superhuman beings have a more direct impact on human life. They include beings sometimes called gods and sometimes called spirits. They also include the souls of the dead. These souls may be venerated as ancestors. They may also be considered to be GHOSTS. Traditional Africans interact with these beings by means of RITUALS.

Healing plays a large role in most African religions (*see* HEALING, RELIGIOUS). Traditional Africans often attribute sickness and misfortune to WITCHCRAFT and sorcery. In some cases witchcraft may cause disease without any conscious intention on the part of the supposed witch. Traditional Africans may consult specialists who know how to counteract these forces. Sometimes traditional Africans attribute diseases to "affliction," that is, to a spirit that is possessing a person. In these cases the spirit needs to be expelled.

African religions generally have RITES OF PASSAGE to make a transition from one stage of existence to another. INITIATION rituals are particularly well developed. SACRIFICES and offerings are very important components of African ritual practice. Music, dancing, and arts, such as mask-making, also make major contributions to the practice of African religions (*see* MUSIC AND RELIGION, DANCE AND RELIGION, ART, RELIGIOUS, and MASKS AND RELIGION). Many African religions also assign special roles to chosen people. Such religious leaders include priests (*see* PRIESTS AND PRIESTHOOD), prophets, mediums, diviners, and kings.

At the end of the 20th century, only about 10 percent of Africans practiced traditional religions. Roughly 50 percent practiced CHRISTIANITY and 40 percent practiced Islam. During the late 19th and 20th centuries, Africans also developed "new religions." Many of these new religions were indigenous Christian churches. They either broke away from mission churches or were founded by African prophets. Often they combined traditional African themes with Christianity or Islam. Examples include the Aladura ("praying people") churches of Nigeria, which eventually broke away from their American parent church, and the amaNazaretha Baptist Church, founded by the Zulu prophet Isaiah Shembe (d. 1935). Other new religions fit traditional religious practices into the organizational forms of Christianity and Islam. An example is the Bwiti Church of Gabon.

Further reading: Noel Q. King, *African Cosmos: An Introduction to Religion in Africa* (Belmont, Calif.: Wadsworth, 1986); John S. Mbiti, *African Religion and Philosophy,* 2d ed. (Oxford; Portsmouth, N.H.: Heinemann, 1990); Benjamin Ray, *African Religions: Symbol, Ritual, and Community,* 2d ed. (Upper Saddle River, N.J.: Prentice Hall, 2000).

Afro-Brazilian religions See AFRICAN-AMERICAN
RELIGIONS; BRAZIL, NEW RELIGIOUS MOVEMENTS IN.

afterlife in world religions Belief in continuing life after death. Most religions hold that there
exists an afterlife. The way in which this afterlife
is pictured varies greatly among the world's religions. Some envision a shadowy other world or
one similar to this one; some see eternal reward
or punishment in HEAVEN or HELL; some believe in
REINCARNATION (or coming back to be born again)
in human or animal form; some envision ultimate
absorption into GOD or eternal reality.

Many of the world's early religions held that
the afterlife was about the same for almost everyone. The Ainu of northern Japan considered it a
world that was just the opposite of the present
world, so that when it was day here it was night
there; one alternated between the two. Native
Americans often viewed the world of departed
spirits as being like this one but better; it was
a place where crops and the hunt were always
bountiful and the weather mild. Among them,
as among many primal peoples, the shaman (*see*
SHAMANISM) was an important religious figure
who was believed able to travel between this
world and the next, bearing messages, invoking gods and spirits, and guiding the souls (*see*
SOUL, CONCEPTS OF) of the departed to their eternal
home.

For the ancient Egyptians (*see* EGYPTIAN RELI-
GION), the afterlife was very important, above all
for the pharaoh as the supreme human being in
charge of all others. The soul's journey after death
required elaborate preparations, such as making
the body into a mummy. It was said that the soul
would be weighed against a feather to see how virtuous it was.

In ZOROASTRIANISM it is believed that after death
the soul crosses a bridge to the other world, which
becomes a wide highway for the righteous but narrow as a razor for the wicked. The latter then fall
off into hell to be temporarily punished. On the
last day God will resurrect (raise up and restore to
life in their bodies) all persons and create a fresh

and beautiful Earth where they all will live joy-
ously forever.

The same themes—an individual judgment
after death, then a general resurrection and new
Heaven and Earth at the end of the world—can
be found in the Western family of monotheist
(believing in one God) religions besides Zoroastrianism: JUDAISM, CHRISTIANITY, and ISLAM. In
the Hebrew scriptures (Old Testament to Christians) there is little reference to the afterlife until
the last few centuries B.C.E., after the Jews had
encountered Zoroastrian or similar concepts during their exile in Babylon. Modern Judaism has
not emphasized the afterlife as much as some
other religions. It is more concerned with the
good life in this world and the survival of the
Jewish people. Many Jews acknowledge, however, that the righteous continue for all time to
live in the presence of God. Jews have held dif-
fering emphases, some stressing the immortality (undying nature) of the soul and its reward
or punishment after death; others believe in the
RESURRECTION of the body; a few have believed in
reincarnation; still others have just emphasized
life in this world.

Christianity, influenced by both Jewish beliefs
and Greek concepts of the immortality of the soul,
has given great importance to heaven as a place of
eternal reward and happiness, and hell as a place
of eternal punishment for the wicked. In ROMAN
CATHOLICISM there is a third state, purgatory, where
those neither ready for heaven nor bad enough
for hell can suffer temporary punishment to purge
away their sins and finally enter heaven. Christianity traditionally speaks of an individual judgment
of the soul at the time of death, and then a bodily
resurrection of all the dead at the end of the world
with a final judgment. Islam affirms a day of judgment, when the righteous will be assigned to a
paradise filled with wonderful delights, and there
is a more vaguely described place of punishment
for the wicked.

In the East, HINDUISM emphasizes reincarnation based on KARMA, or cause and effect; for every
thought, word, and deed there is a consequence.
One can be reincarnated as an animal, human, or

in a heavenly or hellish state that will last until the good or bad karma is exhausted. The ultimate ideal is to become one with God, and so go beyond death and rebirth altogether.

BUDDHISM is similar to Hinduism. There are six places of possible rebirth, depending on karma: the hells, the realm of the hungry ghosts, the realm of the asuras or titans (fighting giants), as an animal, as a human, or in one of the heavens. These too last only as long as the bad or good karma, and the supreme achievement is to become a Buddha and enter NIRVANA, unconditioned reality beyond life or death. In one important form of Buddhism, PURE LAND BUDDHISM, those who express faith in AMIDA Buddha will be reborn after death in the Pure Land, a paradisal realm from which entering into Nirvana is easy.

In China, TAOISM speaks of becoming an immortal, a deathless one, in this world or a heavenly realm. There are ways to attain immortality through YOGA or MEDITATION, through taking medicines of immortality made by ALCHEMY, and through virtuous living. CONFUCIANISM, because of its emphasis on the family, makes much of ancestral spirits that continue to bless the living. They are venerated at ancestral tablets in the home, in family temples, and at the grave.

Although images of the afterlife in the world's religions are varied, many of these images have in common three features. First, the afterlife is a place of judgment in which the injustices of this world will be corrected; the wicked will be punished and the good rewarded. Second, the world religions' concepts of the afterlife see it as—at least for the righteous—a place of ease and beauty that compensates for the hardness of this world. Third, whatever its form, the belief means that there is more to the fullness of human life than just this world, that our lives are lived out on a larger stage.

Further reading: Mircea Eliade, *Death, Afterlife, and Eschatology: A Thematic Sourcebook* (New York: Harper & Row, 1974); Hiroshi Obayashi, ed., *Death and Afterlife: Perspectives of World Religions* (New York: Greenwood Press, 1992); Richard C. Taylor, *Death and the Afterlife: A Cultural Encyclopedia* (Santa Barbara, Calif.: ABC-CLIO, 2000).

Aga Khan Persian for "great commander", the title of the leader of the Nizari Ismaili community in ISLAM. The Aga Khan is the IMAM or inspired leader of a community in SHI'ITE ISLAM known as the Nizari Ismaili community. Aga Khan I (1800–81) received the designation from the shah of Persia in 1817. Later he rebelled against one of the shah's successors and immigrated to India. There he assisted British military efforts and won British favor.

The title has been passed down to successors of the first Aga Khan: His son Aga Khan II (d. 1885), his grandson Aga Khan III (1877–1957), and his great-grandson Aga Khan IV (b. 1937). In addition to overseeing their community, the Aga Khans have been active in politics and business. For example, Aga Khan III, a philanthropist and statesman, led the All-India Muslim League in its early years. In 1937 he was elected president of the League of Nations.

Agni God of fire in the VEDA. Vedic HINDUISM— a form of Hinduism that scholars often suggest entered India from the northwest around 1500 B.C.E.—centers upon performing SACRIFICES. As a result, the fire into which sacrifices are made assumes tremendous importance. It is worshipped as the god Agni. In the sacrificial grounds three fires represent Agni in the three levels of the universe: HEAVEN, atmosphere, and earth.

As the "oblation-eater" (the one who devours sacrifices) Agni is the divine equivalent to the priest. He is responsible for purifying the gifts of human beings and bearing them to the gods. He also brings the blessings of the gods to human beings. In the sacred collection of hymns known as the Rig-veda, he is praised more than any god but INDRA.

agriculture and religion See PREHISTORIC RELIGION.

ahimsa Sanskrit word for "non-injury"; a central ethical principle in the religion of JAINISM. Many Hindus and Buddhists also teach ahimsa.

Jains believe that any injury to another being produces KARMA and binds people to the world of rebirth. Therefore, Jains avoid injuring others as much as possible. As a result, they act out of a supreme respect for life.

At a minimum Jains adopt a vegetarian diet, because plants are thought to suffer the least injury of all living things. Jains also care for sick and dying animals in sanctuaries. Some Jains filter their water, wear a mask over their mouth and nose, and sweep their path as they walk to avoid accidentally injuring unseen creatures. The most austere Jains end their lives by giving up food and water altogether.

In the early 20th century Mohandas GANDHI made ahimsa a central idea in his teachings.

Ahura Mazda *See* ZOROASTRIANISM.

Akhenaton (ruled approx. 1350–1334 B.C.E.) *a king of Egypt* He is remembered for changes he made to EGYPTIAN RELIGION.

When Akhenaton came to the throne, Egyptian religion focused on the WORSHIP of the god AMON-Re. In the sixth year of his reign, however, Akhenaton made the Aton or sun's disk the central god of Egypt. He changed his name from Amenhotep to Akhenaton, "Servant of the Aton." He also moved his capital up the Nile from Thebes to a place he named Akhetaton, known today as Amarna. Akhenaton and his wife Nefertiti worshipped only the Aton; the people worshipped Akhenaton and Nefertiti.

Akhenaton's changes did not last long after his death. His successor, Smenkhkare, destroyed the settlement of Akhetaton and moved the capital back to Thebes. The next king, Tutankhamen, restored the cult of Amon.

Many have seen Akhenaton as the first monotheist (*see* MONOTHEISM), but that claim is too bold. Some have even speculated that MOSES learned monotheism from Akhenaton. There is no evidence to support such an idea.

alchemy The practice of using chemical experiments or processes for such purposes as making potions of immortality or transmuting commoner metals into gold. Alchemy was widespread in the Middle Ages and early modern times in Europe, China, and elsewhere. In Europe a supreme goal of the practice was isolating what was called the "philosopher's stone," which was believed to give eternal life. Alchemy was intertwined with the origins of modern science, and even as great a figure as Isaac Newton was involved with it. As alchemy sought to transmute "base metals" into nobler ones like gold, create better medicines, and fashion the "elixir of life," some fundamental discoveries about chemistry and medicine were made. Even with these discoveries, alchemy itself fell out of favor by the end of the 17th century. Chinese alchemy, which flourished from the fifth to ninth century, was largely focused on the quest for immortality. Scholars of alchemy, such as Carl Gustav JUNG and Mircea ELIADE, have shown that alchemy often had a profoundly religious or psychological significance, in which various elements and chemicals were seen as symbolic of spiritual qualities, and a whole procedure was like a religious rite.

Allah The Arabic word for GOD; specifically, the designation for God in ISLAM. The basic Islamic attitude to God is given in the profession of faith: "There is no god but God [Allah]." Islam emphasizes the unity of God. In doing so, it explicitly rejects as polytheistic Christian notions that God is a TRINITY and that JESUS was divine.

In Islam, God is the creator of the universe and its eternal ruler. It is the duty of all creatures, including human beings, to submit to his will. (Muslims speak of God in the masculine.) God has revealed his will through a line of prophets. This line culminates in the prophet MUHAMMAD. Islam also looks forward to a RESURRECTION of the dead.

At that time God will welcome the righteous into the gardens of paradise.

Allah is not the only designation for God in Islam. Muslims also recognize 99 "most beautiful names." One of them, al-Rahman, occurs at the beginning of almost every *sura* or section of the QUR'AN: "In the name of God, al-Rahman [the merciful], al-Rahim [the compassionate]."

The highest form of art in Islam is calligraphy, artistic writing. Ideal subjects for this art include verses from the Qur'an about God and his most beautiful names.

al-Qaeda *See* QAEDA, AL-.

altar A place, usually elevated, on which people offer SACRIFICES. Altars vary greatly. There are home altars, public altars, portable altars, stationary altars, freestanding altars, and altars associated with temples. Roman Catholic, Orthodox, and some Protestant Christians call the table on which the EUCHARIST is celebrated an altar, too. At times this altar has been shaped like a sarcophagus and required to hold a RELIC.

Many altars have been quite simple. The first Greek altars were simply piles of ash from previous sacrifices. Other altars have been great works of art. The Pergamum Altar to ZEUS (164–156 B.C.E.), now in a Berlin museum, measures roughly 100 by 100 feet wide by 30 feet tall; its seven-foot-tall marble frieze shows the battle of the gods and the giants. Some classic early European paintings are altarpieces. A good example is the Isenheim altarpiece by Matthias Grünewald (c. 1455–1580). Vedic Hindus constructed elaborate altars, too (*see* VEDA). The scholar Stella Kramrisch once suggested that piled Vedic altars provided the models for Hindu temples.

Amaterasu SHINTO goddess associated with the sun and believed to be the ancestress of the Japanese imperial house. In mythology, she is said to inhabit the High Plain of HEAVEN. There she once hid in a heavenly cave as protest against her brother Susanoo, a storm god, when he desecrated her celebration of the harvest festival. She was enticed out when another GODDESS did a comic dance and the gods laughed uproariously, making her curious. Amaterasu's primary place of WORSHIP is the Grand Shrine of Ise, where her chief symbol, an ancient mirror, is enshrined.

Amida Japanese name of Amitabha, a cosmic BUDDHA. Amida is best known as the principal figure in the form of BUDDHISM known as PURE LAND BUDDHISM (Jodo in Japanese), which is very popular in East Asia. It tells us that many aeons ago on becoming a buddha, Amida vowed that, out of compassion, he would bring all who called upon his name in simple faith to his HEAVEN or Pure Land, also known as the Western Paradise, after death. Temples in the Pure Land tradition generally have an image of Amida in MEDITATION as a central object of WORSHIP, and often works of gold and jewels to suggest the wonders of the Pure Land.

Amish Particular groups of MENNONITE Christians. The most traditional Amish are the Old Order Amish. They are probably the most visible and best known Mennonites. That is because, paradoxically, they are so assiduous in avoiding the ways of the world.

The Amish split off from other Mennonites in the 1690s. The issue was discipline. All of the "plain people"—conservative Mennonites, Amish, and Brethren—observe a strict discipline. It covers many areas of life, such as dress and the use of modern inventions. In observing the discipline they claim to practice what the BIBLE teaches, especially Romans 12.2: "Do not be conformed to this world."

In the 1690s Jakob Amman (c. 1675–1725), a Mennonite elder, disagreed with other elders over how to enforce the discipline. Following certain verses in the Bible, he taught that those who violated the discipline should be shunned. That is, no member of the community should associate with them. Other Mennonites thought that shunning was too harsh. It meant, for example, that one might have to avoid one's own children.

At one time Amish Mennonites lived in several parts of Europe: Switzerland, Alsace (eastern France), southern Germany, Holland, and Russia. Today the Amish live in North America, where they began to settle around 1720. The earliest immigrants settled in Pennsylvania, especially Lancaster County. Amish immigrants also settled in western Pennsylvania, Ohio, Indiana, Illinois, Missouri, and Kansas. In the last years of the 20th century many Amish were leaving Lancaster County, Pennsylvania, and moving farther west, some to the Midwest. Land in Lancaster County had become too expensive. (It is traditional for Amish families to purchase farms for their sons when their sons become adults.) Many Amish also found the publicity they were receiving in Lancaster County distasteful.

Amish beliefs and practices are very similar to those of other Mennonites. The Old Order Amish conduct their WORSHIP services in a dialect of German known as Pennsylvania Dutch; this is the language that they ordinarily speak. Other Amish conduct their services in English. Old Order services are known for the slow, prolonged manner in which they sing in unison; a single hymn may take as much as half an hour. Other Amish sing more quickly; like other plain people they sing without instruments and often in four-part harmony. Old Order Amish worship in homes. Other Amish have constructed church buildings. Men and women sit separately. Like other plain people, the Amish celebrate the EUCHARIST in the context of a "love feast." At this special service, often held in the evening, participants not only partake of the Eucharist but also wash each other's feet. In doing this, they follow the example of JESUS, who washed his disciples' feet at their last meal together (John 13.3–15).

The Amish have traditionally shied away from Bible study and THEOLOGY. In their eyes, study symbolized the sin of pride. But in the late 20th century many Amish were finding EVANGELICAL CHRISTIANITY attractive (*see* EVANGELICAL CHRISTIANITY; FUNDAMENTALISM, CHRISTIAN). They liked its emphasis on the Bible and on cultivating a personal relationship with GOD. Amish groups have bishops, preachers, and elders, all of whom must be men. To avoid pride, these leaders are chosen by lot from candidates recognized as worthy of the office.

A person becomes Amish by being baptized, generally around the age of 15 or 16. Once baptized, a person is subject to the community's discipline or way of life. Technically, unbaptized children are not subject to the discipline's rules, and many teenagers from Amish families experience the wilder aspects of life before being baptized. For example, some keep cars "hidden" in distant pastures on their parents' farms. Nevertheless, an Amish childhood does not simply conform to what is common in the surrounding society. For example, the Amish do not think a modern education is necessary for those who drive horses and buggies, do not use public electricity or telephones, use horses to pull ploughs, and insist that men wear untrimmed beards. In cases of need they may ask their non-Amish neighbors for rides or to take telephone messages. All plain people are strict pacifists; because soldiers in Europe wore mustaches, their men are not allowed to have them.

Despite the extremely plain lifestyle of the Old Order Amish, it would be a serious mistake to see them as unchanging. They change in different ways. Many Old Order Amish own tractors. They use them for power. Amish farmers have invented many pneumatic (air-driven) farm tools. Amish buggies may look plain and old fashioned on the outside. But within the limits of the discipline, the interiors of many buggies are plush. Some even have special sound systems.

Further reading: Carl F. Bowman and Donald B. Kraybill, *On the Backroad to Heaven* (Baltimore: Johns Hopkins University Press, 2001); John A. Hostetler, *Amish Society*, 3d ed. (Baltimore: Johns Hopkins University Press, 1980); Lucian Niemeyer, *Old Order Amish* (Baltimore: Johns Hopkins University Press, 1993); William I. Schreiber, *Our Amish Neighbors* (Chicago: University of Chicago Press, 1978).

Amon Also spelled Amun; the chief god of Egypt in the New Kingdom. At first Amon was only the god of a small place. Around 2000 B.C.E. his cult was brought to Thebes, the capital of Egypt. He became identified with Re, the sun god. When the New Kingdom began in 1570 B.C.E. Amon-Re became the god of the kings and the king of the gods.

Egyptian gods are sometimes shown with the heads of animals; Amon had the head of a ram. His major temples sat on the east bank of the Nile at Karnak and Luxor near Thebes. During festivals Amon went visiting. During one festival a procession carried him from Karnak to Luxor. During another he visited the tombs on the west bank of the Nile. As Egypt's wealth grew, Amon's temples became immense, and his priests became extremely powerful.

Amon had a consort, Mut (mother), and a son, Khonsu (the moon). Some later thinkers claimed that all the gods were his manifestations. Others claimed that he was JUPITER. Ruins of Amon's temples still stand at Karnak and Luxor. They attract hundreds of thousands of tourists each year.

Amos (active mid-700s B.C.E.) *a prophet of ancient Israel* Amos is also a book in the BIBLE containing the sayings of this prophet. Amos was a shepherd who lived in the town of Tekoa in Judea during the reigns of Uzziah, king of Judea (783–742 B.C.E.), and Jeroboam II, king of Israel (786–746 B.C.E.). He claims to have received messages from the GOD YHWH ("the Lord") that foretold the destruction of Israel's neighbors: Damascus, Gaza, Tyre, Edom, Moab, and the Ammonites. They also foretold the destruction of Judah. But most of the messages were about the coming destruction of Israel. At the time that probably seemed unlikely.

The Israelites were worshipping YHWH with lavish SACRIFICES and offerings. According to Amos, however, God rejected these. He also faulted Israel for its failure to repent. The book is not very specific about what Israel has done wrong. Some verses hint that Israel had offended YHWH by worshipping other gods. A few verses explicitly condemn Israel for social injustices. They condemn rich Israelites for taking advantage of and cheating the poor.

The book of Amos is relatively short; it contains nine chapters. It belongs to the portion of the Hebrew Scriptures (*see* SCRIPTURES, HEBREW) known as "The Twelve," which Christians call "the minor prophets." It mostly prophesies destruction, but the final few verses promise that after the destruction, YHWH will restore his people.

Analects of Confucius The most important book containing the teachings of CONFUCIUS (551–479 B.C.E.), the founder of CONFUCIANISM. Confucius was one of the most influential teachers who ever lived. But he did not actually write down his teachings. After his death, his followers gathered his sayings. They were eventually collected into a book, the Analects. The Analects was put together perhaps in the third century B.C.E.

The Analects does not expound Confucius's ideas in a neat, orderly sequence chapter by chapter. It also does not contain stories about Confucius's birth, activities, and death, as, for example, the GOSPELS do about JESUS. Instead, the Analects contains short statements, sometimes no more than a single sentence long, unconnected with one another. These statements claim to present Confucius's teachings in his own words. The following saying is typical: "Tzu-kung asked, 'Is there a single word which can be a guide to conduct throughout one's life?' The master said, 'It is perhaps the word "*shu* [reciprocity]" Do not impose on others what you yourself do not desire'" (Analects 15.24 [Lau tr.]).

In the Analects, Confucius instructs his students, who were male, on how to become gentlemen. To Confucius a gentleman was more than someone who is courteous and polite. He was someone with moral depth. Confucius considered the gentleman to be the ideal of what it means for most people to be human. (A few go beyond being gentlemen. They are sages.)

In Confucius's eyes, what characterizes a gentleman is humaneness. Humaneness has two parts. One part is the golden rule: As Confucius formulated it, do not do to someone what you would not wish them to do to you. The other part talks about how one should conduct oneself: One should always strive to do one's best.

Confucius believed that people had to work hard to realize virtue to the fullest. Virtue had to be cultivated through a process that lasted a lifetime. The process began at home, with obedience and respect—the "filial piety"—that children showed their parents. If one did not love one's parents, Confucius asked, how could one love other members of society? The process of cultivating virtue continued in society as a whole. It did so as people observed the rules of proper behavior. Confucius believed that one nurtured virtue, which is ultimately an internal quality, through one's external behavior. (Compare some North American parents, who teach their children gratitude, an internal quality, by telling them to say "thank you," an external act.)

Confucius expected his gentlemen to be members of the government. He had a very specific idea of how it was best for them to rule. By passing laws and meting out punishments, Confucius said, one could maintain order, but one would not make people more virtuous. The better way to rule was by being virtuous and observing proper behavior oneself. That way, people would develop a sense of shame and as a result govern themselves. These ideals of government often strike North Americans as unrealistic. It is good to remember, then, that for centuries the Chinese government ruled a very large territory at least in part by putting Confucius's ideals into practice.

ancestor worship Rituals directed to relatives who have died, based on the belief that the spirits of the dead continue to influence the living. Ancestors are concerned with the well-being of their descendants, but also with upholding traditional morality and the traditional family structure. They will bless those who keep traditional sacred values, but they may turn malevolent against unworthy descendants.

This entry uses the term *ancestor worship* because it is in common usage, but many scholars find the term misleading. For one thing, the word *worship* does not reflect the wide variety of ritual acts that the living direct toward their dead relatives. For another, not every society distinguishes between the living and the dead the way North Americans do, so not every society thinks of dead relatives as ancestors. The classic examples of this second point are people known as the Suku, who live in Zaire.

The practice of ancestor worship is ancient. Perhaps the best known example of ancestor worship in the ancient world comes from China, where ancestor worship is still strong today. Bronze vessels from China survive that were used in making offerings to the ancestors almost 4,000 years ago.

Ancestor worship is widespread. It is especially practiced in China, Korea, and Japan. It is also practiced in HINDUISM, to some extent in BUDDHISM, and in the indigenous religions of Africa, the Americas, Australia, and Oceania. Not every religion, however, worships ancestors. Jews, Christians, and Muslims today remember their ancestors but do not worship them. A ritual example is the Jewish custom of lighting the *Jahrzeit* candle or light on the anniversary of a person's death. But those who engage in such activities do not give dead relatives gifts or expect benefits from them.

Ancestor worship often begins with the funeral. In societies that worship ancestors the funeral is not simply a way that the living deal with grief. It is a RITE OF PASSAGE by which a dead or dying relative becomes an ancestor. In some cultures these funerals, reserved for older relatives rather than children who die, are joyous occasions. Some cultures also pay special attention to the treatment or placement of the physical remains. For example, the Chinese use FENG-SHUI to determine the location for a tomb that will make the ancestor's existence as beneficial as possible.

People worship ancestors by giving them gifts, sharing a meal with them, and recalling them through RITUALS, among other means. Hindus present rice balls known as *pindas* to their ancestors at several special occasions. They also sponsor feasts in which the ancestors participate, although priests known as BRAHMINS actually eat the food. In traditional Chinese communities, the ancestors are honored at three places: at a household shrine, where simple offerings may be placed daily before a tablet bearing the names of the recently deceased; at an extended family shrine, where large tablets bearing the names of male ancestors for six generations back are set up on tiers and honored; and at the cemetery, where the family traditionally cleans the graves and sets out offerings twice a year, in spring and fall. While Christians today do not engage in ancestor worship in a strict sense, archaeology seems to indicate that the earliest Christians did. They visited the graves of their ancestors and enjoyed a meal there with them.

Many people believe that neglected ancestors have the power to cause illness and misfortune. Especially in these cases it is important to be able to communicate with the ancestors: to learn what has offended them and what one can do to stop their anger. In Korea SHAMANS traditionally consult the ancestors in an effort to alleviate the sufferings of their clients. In parts of Africa people use various methods of divination to determine what is troubling the ancestors.

People also expect the ancestors, if they are treated properly, to help them. Such help often includes health and material well-being. The so-called CARGO CULTS of Melanesia are based on the belief that the spirits of the dead will eventually return and distribute riches among the living. In one cargo cult people used telephones to communicate with the ancestors. In another they built a landing strip for the ancestors to use when they return in airplanes. The cults began in the 19th century when European explorers distributed gifts to the islanders.

There may be more to ancestor worship than first meets the eye. One scholar has argued that for one group of people in Melanesia ancestor worship was actually a way by which the people, perhaps unknowingly, maintained a balance between yams and pigs in their diets. Such an

The Shang rulers of China had ritual vessels cast in bronze to feast the ancestors. This example was decorated with *taotie* (*t'ao t'ieh*) mask images, representing either a flesh-eating monster or a celestial being. (© *Asian Art & Archaeology, Inc./CORBIS*)

ecological explanation is intriguing, but not all scholars accept it.

angels Pure spirits devoted to the worship and service of GOD. Most developed religious traditions have a class of beings that range between the human realm and the supreme God or Ultimate Reality. They include lesser gods, SAINTS, ancestral spirits (*see* ANCESTOR WORSHIP), BODHISATTVAS, and today even aliens from other planets. Angels are among the most prominent, especially in monotheistic (believing in one God) religions. They are believed to be pure spirits created directly by God to praise and honor him in HEAVEN and to serve as his messengers (the word angel comes from the Greek *angellos*, messenger) on Earth.

Angels are important in the Western religious traditions, JUDAISM, CHRISTIANITY, and ISLAM. Here they have several roles. A hierarchy, including the mighty archangels Michael, Gabriel, Raphael, and others, is believed to praise and serve God in heaven. According to ancient sources, there are ranks of angels, in descending order known as Seraphim, Cherubim, Thrones, Dominations, Virtues, Powers, Principalities, Archangels, and ordinary angels. A well-known story, hinted at in the Bible but developed by the poet John Milton and others, says that SATAN, the devil, was once a very high angel, Lucifer (Lightbearer), but rebelled against God and was cast out of heaven and into hell.

Second, angels are messengers of God. Archangels and angels have performed missions for God crucial to the central narratives of these three faiths. In the Hebrew Scriptures (Old Testament to Christians) angels guarded the Garden of Eden after ADAM and EVE were driven out of that garden. They visited ABRAHAM with the promise of a son, and the prophet ISAIAH saw a six-winged cherubim, a kind of angel, in the temple. In Christianity, it was the archangel Gabriel who visited MARY to inform her she would become the mother of the Savior, JESUS, and angels appeared singing in the skies at the time of his birth in Bethlehem. In Islam, the same archangel, Gabriel, delivered the sacred scriptures, the QUR'AN to the prophet MUHAMMAD. On a more personal level, these faiths have traditionally believed that each individual has a guardian angel who guides and protects him or her. There is some popular belief that the departed become angels after death, but this is not considered orthodox.

Third, angels are pictured as protectors. Great archangels are patrons of nations and cities; lesser angels of individuals are "guardian angels," designated to help those persons and fend off temptations from the demons.

Angels have traditionally been portrayed as beautiful human-like figures with wings. They often appear female but are said to be sexless, although the greatest archangels are often represented as male. The wings are partly due to the influence of ancient Greek and Roman art, which

The Annunciation by Botticelli. The archangel Gabriel announces to the Virgin Mary that she is to bear the son of God. *(Alinari/Art Resource, N.Y.)*

pictured various spirits in this way, although some ancient Hebrew angels, like the one Isaiah saw, were also winged. Historically, angels may have been a way to bring popular belief in many gods and spirits into harmony with belief in one God, by making them all his servants. But belief has certainly been reinforced by accounts from numerous ordinary people who report angelic help and encounters. One such account is from the founding of the Church of Jesus Christ of LATTER-DAY SAINTS, the Mormon Church, by Joseph Smith (1805–44). Beginning in 1823, the angel Moroni is said to have visited Smith in upstate New York, and directed him to the golden plates containing the Book of Mormon, scriptures supplemental to the Bible in Mormonism. Moroni is often portrayed atop Mormon temples.

In HINDUISM and BUDDHISM, the equivalent of angels are beautiful figures, *apsaras* or *yaksas* in India, *tennin* or *tennyo* in Japan, said to inhabit the heavens of the gods, the Pure Land, and even mountains and forests as playful or mysterious spirits. Some may tempt holy men, but in their most exalted conceptualization, as in the Pure Land, they represent the wonderful joy of the world of gods and buddhas. The Taoist (*see* TAO-ISM) immortals also have some angelic characteristics, and live in beautiful places in heaven or Earth accompanied by other worldly beings of angelic character.

Lately there has been a renewal of interest in angels in popular culture in the United States. These beautiful beings appear to have meaning to many moderns, just as they did for people of the past.

Further reading: Gustav Davidson, *A Dictionary of Angels* (New York: Free Press, 1971); Rosemary Guiley, *Encyclopedia of Angels* (New York: Facts On File, 1996).

Anglicanism   The form of CHRISTIANITY represented by the Church of England and churches in other parts of the world in "communion" or official association with it. In the early 1530s King Henry VIII (1491–1547) of England wanted to annul his marriage to Catherine of Aragon (1485–1536). The pope refused to grant him an annulment, so Henry and Parliament, in the Act of Supremacy of 1534, declared the English church to be independent of the PAPACY and the King to be the earthly head of the church, with the Archbishop of CANTERBURY remaining its ecclesiastical leader. Henry preserved Catholic teachings and practices. After Henry's death, strong forces favored the more radical changes of the Protestant REFORMATION. Henry's daughter Elizabeth I (1533–1603) mediated between Catholic traditionalism and Protestant reform. Under her the Church of England as we know it took shape.

Anglican churches see themselves as pursuing a middle way between ROMAN CATHOLICISM and PROTESTANTISM. Since Elizabeth's time several movements have stressed one side or the other of its rich heritage. In the 18th century the Church of England experienced revivals that emphasized conversion experiences. A leader in this movement was John WESLEY (1703–91). He never actually left the Church of England, but his followers established an independent METHODISM. In the 19th century the Oxford Movement sought to reaffirm the Catholic identity of the Anglican tradition.

English colonization from the 17th through the 19th century helped spread Anglicanism overseas. Originally Anglicanism was the established or official religion of the American colonies of Virginia, the Carolinas, and Georgia. After the Revolutionary War, American Anglicans formed an independent Episcopal Church (*see* EPISCOPALIANISM). This church was in communion with the Church of England but did not pledge allegiance to the British throne. Since then other Anglican churches have arisen throughout the world. They are referred to collectively as the Anglican Communion. The churches of this communion are independent but recognize the Archbishop of Canterbury as "first among equals." Their bishops meet roughly every 10 years, in what are called Lambeth Conferences, after the name of the Archbishop of Canterbury's headquarters in London.

Anglicans have not defined themselves by a detailed set of beliefs, as some churches have. They do, however, generally respect a set of Thirty-Nine Articles adopted in the 1560s. According to these and other statements, Anglicans acknowledge the BIBLE as the ultimate authority in matters of faith. Unlike adherents of FUNDAMENTALISM, they have generally been open to modern methods of biblical interpretation. They also acknowledge the Apostles' Creed and Nicene CREEDS, and they teach the views of the TRINITY and the INCARNATION developed in the ancient church.

Anglicans have defined themselves much more by practice than by belief. In doing so, they have emphasized WORSHIP as central to the church's work. The most important document of the church has always been the *Book of Common Prayer.* Renowned for its beautiful language, it translates into English revised versions of the worship services used before the Protestant Reformation. It has forms for the administration of the traditional seven SACRAMENTS, of which BAPTISM and the EUCHARIST are said to be most important.

Another distinctive mark of the Anglican churches is their emphasis on bishops. They have preserved the apostolic succession of bishops. That is, their line of bishops is claimed to extend without a break back to the APOSTLES. Besides bishops the Anglican churches have both priests and deacons. Since the 19th century they have also had their own MONKS AND NUNS.

One question sparked much controversy in the late 20th century: Could women be priests and bishops? The majority of Anglicans decided that they could. In the United States the first woman priest was ordained in the 1970s and the first woman bishop in 1989. In England the first woman priest was not ordained until 1994.

More recently, the questions of ordaining homosexuals and of blessing same-sex unions or performing marriages for such couples have divided the Anglican Communion and several churches within it. At the 1998 Lambeth Conference, difference of opinion on the role of women and homosexuality, and on liberal versus conservative doctrinal and moral questions generally, were evident between Anglican churches in Western and developing countries. Churches in Britain, North America, Australia, and New Zealand tended to be liberal on such matters, though there were significant conservative factions within them. Churches in Asia, Africa, and Latin America tended, like their societies, generally to be traditional in their values regarding gender and family. The latter churches were largely founded by missionary outreach from the older churches in the 19th century, but they are now growing far more rapidly than the parent churches under their own indigenous leaders. At the conference, exchanges on gender and sexuality were sometimes heated, and resolutions favoring the more liberal attitudes often failed.

Since 1998, the division has become more pronounced. After the consecration of an openly homosexual priest, the Reverend V. Gene Robinson, as bishop of New Hampshire in the United States in 2003, talk began of a possible split in the Anglican Communion.

However, the Anglican Communion has historically found ways to embrace a variety of points of view and forms of practice. Its 21st-century situation is significant for several reasons, above all because the Anglican Communion, more than most denominations, now includes as equal partners sizable national churches in diverse parts of the world. It can serve as a sort of laboratory illustrating the tensions and prospects in what has been called the "New Christendom." More and more in the 21st century, the demographics of the Christian religion are changing, so that its real center of vitality and numerical strength is not in Europe and North America but instead in Asia, Africa, and Latin America. Clashes are bound to occur because of the different values and cultural background of the older versus the younger but maturing wings of the religion. The test for Anglicanism, as it experiences these conflicts, will be to show whether common bonds can be found that are stronger than the differences.

Further reading: Paul D. L. Avis, *Anglican Understanding of the Church: An Introduction* (London: SPCK, 2000); Susan Dowell and Jane Williams, *Bread, Wine, and Women: The Ordination Debate in the Church of England* (London: Virago, 1994); Hugh G. G. Herklots, *Frontiers of the Church: The Making of the Anglican Communion* (London: Benn, 1961).

animals and religion The symbolism and role of animals in religion. Animals have had a profound significance for religion as far back as religion can be traced. The famous Old Stone Age cave paintings of game animals undoubtedly had some kind of spiritual meaning. But meaning and attitude have varied greatly from one religious culture to another. In hunting cultures, where animals are a major source of food and their killing a mark of human prowess, hunting is a religious activity, involving spiritual preparation by such means as fasting, performing sacred dances before setting out, and observing taboos in the field. PRAYERS may also be addressed to the animal to be killed, and petitions made to a "Master of Animals" deity believed able to give or withhold game.

In many societies, especially early agricultural or pastoral (herding) ones, animals have often been the subjects of religious SACRIFICE. One example is the religion of the ancient Hebrews. The rationale is varied. It is believed that the savor of the offered meat pleases GOD or the gods; that the sacrifice to the highest of something economically valuable, as animals certainly were, indicates faith and devotion; that the life of the animal goes into the crops and the community; or that the spirit of the animal is a messenger on behalf of the people to the gods. If the flesh, after being offered, is then consumed by the community, that sacred meal can be like a holy communion with the gods and a way of reaffirming their identity.

On the other hand, the protection of some animals, or of all animals, can also be viewed as a religious obligation. In JAINISM, AHIMSA, or harmlessness toward all animate life, is a way of affirming the sacred character of such life and the souls within it. Many Hindus and Buddhists also practice such harmlessness for spiritual reasons (see HINDUISM and BUDDHISM). Sometimes certain animals are protected and not killed because of their meaning as the "totem," the emblem or animal protector, of a community. Hindu India's well-known "sacred cows" suggest compassion and the sacredness of motherhood and all life to its people.

Animals also have widespread symbolic meanings in religion. Religious art is full of animals. Sometimes gods are portrayed as animals, or as half-animal and half-human, like many Egyptian deities (see EGYPTIAN RELIGION) or the Hindu GANESA, with an elephant head and a human body.

For Hindus cows have special status. This one is shown walking in the streets of Nepal. *(Getty Images)*

In CHRISTIANITY, the Holy Spirit is often portrayed as a dove. Many gods and Christian SAINTS have an animal companion or symbol: the bull of SIVA, the owl of ATHENA, the eagle of St. John. In such cases the animal is usually said to embody a particular virtue important to that figure: the bull as a token of fertility, the owl of wisdom, the eagle of soaring to the heights.

Animals are our companions and relatives here on Earth. Yet because they cannot speak or think exactly as we do, they are always objects of mystery to humans. Given this, it is inevitable that religion would make much of animals.

animism   Belief in spirits. Strictly speaking, the term *animism* refers to a theory about the origin of religion. The theory is now widely rejected. Some still use the word to refer to the religious beliefs and practices of indigenous peoples. But the beliefs and practices to which animism refers vary widely. As a result, what animists believe and do must be determined on a case-by-case basis.

In 1871 the English anthropologist Edward Burnett Tylor (1832–1917) published an epoch-making book, *Primitive Culture.* In it, he developed the theory that animism—the belief in spirits—was the origin of religion.

At the time Tylor was writing, many authors were developing evolutionary theories of religion (*see* EVOLUTION AND RELIGION). They assumed that evolution always moved in one direction: from the simplest to the most complex forms. Therefore, to find the origin of religion, all one had to do was identify its simplest form. Tylor thought he had found it: the belief in spirits.

Tylor suggested how people first came to believe in spirits. A corpse is strikingly different from a living human being. But what makes it different? Tylor said that "primitives" attributed the difference to a spirit that animates the body, that is, that makes the body alive. Tylor also pointed to the difference between dreaming and waking. He said that to explain the experience of dreams, "primitives" hypothesized that the spirit left the body. Once the idea of spirit was born, it was just

a short step to apply it to the world of nature. Spirits explained the growth of trees and animals, the roar of the thunder, anything unusual. Indeed, for Tylor's "primitives" the whole world was full of spirits. Tylor buttressed his account with numerous references to reports about the religion of living "primitives."

There were, however, competing theories. The anthropologist R. R. Marett said that there was a stage even earlier than animism: not so much belief as emotional awe in the presence of an impersonal force, something like religious electricity. Marett called this religion preanimism or DYNAMISM. Prominent thinkers like Sigmund FREUD and Émile DURKHEIM picked up on an idea of W. Robertson Smith. He had suggested that TOTEMISM was the earliest religion. James George FRAZER hypothesized that a stage of MAGIC had preceded religion. Wilhelm Schmidt said all these theories were wrong. The first religion had been the belief in a high god, "primal MONOTHEISM."

There was really no conclusive evidence for any of these views of religion's origin. Furthermore, Tylor treated religion as if it were nothing more than a set of beliefs. As anthropologists spent time with peoples outside of Europe, they began to realize that Tylor and others had used their evidence in crude and misleading ways. They gave up the search for the origins of religion and culture and studied contemporary religions and cultures instead.

But Tylor's influence had been enormous. "Animism" had become a polite term for what people used to call "paganism," "heathenism," and "savagery." At the end of the 20th century some still used the term.

Anselm (*c.* 1033–1109) *a medieval Christian thinker* Anselm was a BENEDICTINE monk (*see* MONKS AND NUNS) who rose to become archbishop of CANTERBURY, the most important Christian leader in England. After he died, the Roman Catholic Church officially declared him a SAINT. He is venerated on April 21, the date of his death.

Anselm is remembered most for the way he tried to prove that GOD exists (*see* GOD, THE EXISTENCE OF). He defined God as "the greatest object that can be thought of." Then he argued that, given this definition, God had to exist: A God who actually existed would be greater than any God who was only imagined. Anselm also claimed that no one could know what the word "God" means and still doubt that God existed.

Some people have rejected Anselm's proof. Among them are the great Christian theologian Thomas AQUINAS and the important philosopher Immanuel Kant.

Antichrist

Antichrist In Christianity, a figure opposed to CHRIST. The Antichrist is expected to come at the end of time.

In the NEW TESTAMENT (*see* BIBLE, BIBLICAL LITERATURE) only the letters of John mention the Antichrist. In these letters the Antichrist is the person "who denies the Father and the Son." Furthermore, John's letters suggest that many Antichrists are already in the world. That, the letters say, is a sign that the last days have already arrived (1 John 2.18–25).

Although other New Testament writers did not use the word "Antichrist," they shared the belief in a being or force opposed to JESUS. The book of REVELATION has been particularly influential. Christians have often taken one of the beasts in Revelation to be the Antichrist. (See also 2 Thessalonians 2, which anticipates the coming of an unnamed, lawless opponent to Christ.)

Speculation about the identity of the Antichrist has been rampant throughout Christian history. At one time or another, Christians have identified Simon Magus (a miracle-worker in the book of Acts), MUHAMMAD, particular popes and Byzantine emperors, Napoleon, Adolf Hitler, institutions such as the PAPACY, and ideologies such as communism with the Antichrist.

Some who have opposed Christianity and its values have seen the Antichrist as a positive, not a negative figure. The best example is the German philosopher Friedrich Nietzsche, who wrote a book entitled *The Antichrist*.

anti-Semitism Words, actions, and attitudes directed against Jews because they are Jews. The term was actually coined in 1879 by Wilhelm Marr, a German conservative politician, to identify an anti-Jewish racial policy that he and his fellow conservatives advocated. In the 20th century anti-Semitism led to the murder of roughly 6 million Jews in the HOLOCAUST.

ANTI-SEMITISM IN THE ANCIENT WORLD

Although the word was first coined in 1879, anti-Semitism is by no means new. After the conquests of Alexander the Great (d. 323 B.C.E.), Greek-speaking or "Hellenistic" culture became the norm throughout the eastern Mediterranean region and the Near East. Those who favored Hellenistic culture at times looked down upon Jews. Many Greeks valued reason in pursuit of the truth. Some of them saw the Jews' reliance upon God's revelation (*see* TORAH) as superstition. Even more Greeks saw the practice of CIRCUMCISION, an important sign of identity for Jewish males, as a distasteful mutilation of the body.

Hellenistic culture was not, however, the primary source of anti-Semitism in the ancient world; CHRISTIANITY was. Some see evidence of anti-Semitism in the most sacred writings of Christianity, the New Testament. Pertinent passages include Matthew 23, John 8.34–47, and, most fatefully, Matthew 27.25, in which "the Jews" proclaim themselves and their descendants guilty of JESUS' death. Many biblical scholars see these and other passages as motivated by fierce competition between Jews and early Christians. They do not consider them historically reliable.

On the basis of such passages, ancient Christian teachers could utter fiercely anti-Semitic statements. For example, John Chrysostom (*c.* 347–407), a leader of the Orthodox Church in Asia Minor (now Turkey), taught that Jews were viler than wild animals and that all Christians had an obligation to hate them. AUGUSTINE, bishop of Hippo and one of the most influential Roman Catholic thinkers, wrote a "Tractate against the Jews." He taught that Jews should be humiliated in punishment for rejecting Jesus.

ANTI-SEMITISM IN THE MEDIEVAL AND REFORMATION PERIODS

During the Middle Ages, anti-Semitic activity shifted from the regions around the Mediterranean Sea to Europe.

Jews were systematically barred from many economic institutions. The theologian Thomas AQUINAS taught that because Jews were guilty of deicide ("killing God"), princes were permitted to take their property whenever they wanted. Especially from 1200 on, Jews were required to live in separate areas, sometimes surrounded by walls. In Italian these areas were called ghettos.

In the same period rumors about Jews abounded. They were said to conspire against Christianity, deliberately to desecrate the host (communion bread) as they had desecrated Christ's body, and to kill Christian children and use their blood for RITUAL purposes. Some European Christians used the last charge to justify lynching Jews for over 800 years. Also during the Middle Ages, Jews were expelled from every country in Europe except Poland. They fell victim to pogroms or massacres, for example during the CRUSADES and the Black Death (1348–50). In addition, some Jews were severely pursued by the Spanish INQUISITION.

The Protestant REFORMATION (the 16th century) brought more of the same. For example, Martin LUTHER thought he had purified Christianity of every impediment that had prevented people from becoming Christian. He was offended that Jews did not convert. In 1543 he wrote a book, *Against the Jews and Their Lies.* In it he encouraged his followers to burn down synagogues and steal land owned by Jews.

ANTI-SEMITISM IN THE MODERN PERIOD AND THE PRESENT

The movement of thought known as the Enlightenment (the 17th century to the 18th century) changed the position of Jews in European society. It taught that all human beings, by virtue of being human, enjoyed certain basic civil rights. According to the American "Declaration of Independence," these rights included "life, liberty, and the pursuit of happiness." Influenced by this kind of thinking, one European country after another removed legal restrictions that had been placed on Jews. Especially during the 19th century Jews began in theory to participate equally as full members of European society.

In the late 19th century, however, a backlash arose. Some politicians used ideas about race and genetics to develop an anti-Semitic program. They attributed a barrage of vices to Jews and lobbied for the reimposition of traditional restrictions. In the 20th century this backlash attained horrid proportions in the Nazi HOLOCAUST.

Anti-Semitism persists today, but among Americans and Europeans overt anti-Semitism is generally confined to marginal groups such as the Ku Klux Klan and the neo-Nazis. The establishment of the state of Israel in 1948 has prompted the rise of anti-Semitism in the Islamic world, where it had previously been less prevalent. In the United States, anti-Semitic statements by leaders of the Nation of Islam (*see* ISLAM, NATION OF) have contributed to tensions between the Jewish and African-American communities.

CONCLUSION

Anti-Semitism has a long history. It has been especially common among European Christians and their descendants. At least for the last 1,000 years, this history has included severe atrocities. At the same time, it would be very wrong to think of all Christians and Muslims as anti-Semites. Especially since World War II, many Christian churches and denominations have worked hard to develop an appreciation and respect for JUDAISM.

Further reading: David Cook, *Contemporary Muslim Apocalyptic Literature* (Syracuse, N.Y.: Syracuse University Press, 2005); Edward H. Flannery, *The Anguish of the Jews: Twenty-three Centuries of Antisemitism,* rev. ed. (New York: Paulist Press, 1985); Rosemary Ruether, *Faith and Fratricide* (New York: Seabury, 1974); Meyer Weinberg, *Because They Were Jews: A History of Antisemitism* (New York: Greenwood, 1986).

Aphrodite   *See* VENUS.

apocalyptic literature   Λ kind of literature in JUDAISM, CHRISTIANITY, and GNOSTICISM. An apocalyptic book is called an apocalypse. The best known apocalypse is the NEW TESTAMENT book of REVELATION.

The word "apocalyptic" comes from a Greek word that means "to uncover," thus "to reveal something that is hidden." The second meaning is a good indication of what apocalyptic literature does.

Apocalyptic literature provides knowledge to which people otherwise would not have access. It generally claims that its knowledge comes from one—or both—of two sources. One source is a vision that a person on Earth has of the spiritual realm. A good example is the second half of the book of DANIEL in the Hebrew BIBLE (Daniel 7–12). A second source for apocalyptic knowledge is a journey into HEAVEN. Beginning in chapter four, the author of the New Testament book of Revelation is basically taking a guided tour of the spiritual realm.

Whether they see visions or journey to heaven, those who are privileged to have these experiences need help in understanding what they encounter. That is because what they encounter combines natural features in unusual and obscure ways. For example, Daniel sees a ram with horns of different sizes and a goat with one horn. The goat defeats the ram, loses its horn, and gains four more horns. A little horn grows out of one of the four horns. Then it disrupts the SACRIFICES to "the prince of the host" (Daniel 8.1–14). Daniel says that the ANGEL Gabriel helped him understand this vision (Daniel 8.15–17). Indeed, the authors of apocalyptic literature often claim that spiritual intermediaries, such as angels, helped them understand what they encountered.

Many Jewish and Christian apocalypses provide a special look at the course of world history. They often talk about periods of history, and they associate these periods with fantastic symbols, such as the horns in Daniel 8. They also envision a time when the present world of suffering and

misery will be transformed or obliterated and a new world of joy and bliss will take its place. From such apocalyptic expectations, Jewish people in the late Second Temple period (200 B.C.E.–70 C.E.) began to hope for a MESSIAH.

Gnostic apocalypses are somewhat different. That is because of the way Gnostics think of the world and SALVATION. Like Christians, Gnostics envision a liberation from the present existence. But they do not connect that liberation with the course of history. They envision it as a freeing of elements of light and goodness that are mixed up with darkness and evil. Gnostic apocalypses, then, tend to talk not about history but about metaphysics. They describe the hidden world beyond the world in which we live, and they describe what happens to the liberated soul.

Almost all apocalypses are "pseudonymous." That means that, although they claim to be written by famous people in the past, they are not so. The book of Daniel is one example. Although Daniel claims to live during the Babylonian exile, his book's content makes it clear that it was actually written about the time of the Maccabean revolt (167–164 B.C.E.). Many apocalypses outside the Bible claim to be written by such famous figures as ADAM, Enoch, NOAH, ABRAHAM, MOSES, or, among the Gnostics, PETER, PAUL, and James. The New Testament book of Revelation is an exception. Its author actually identifies himself as John. Scholars debate whether this John had any relation to the apostle John.

The prophecies that apocalypses contain are very helpful in showing when they were written. Apocalypses often describe in very figurative language the recent history of the people among whom the writer of the apocalypse lived. The book of Daniel provides a good example. The ram in Daniel 8 is probably the Persian Empire, made up of Persians and Medes (the two horns). The goat is probably Alexander the Great. Alexander's empire split into four parts (the four horns). From one of the horns, the Seleucids, came Antiochus IV. In 167 B.C.E. Antiochus outlawed traditional Jewish sacrifices and built an ALTAR to ZEUS in the Temple ("the abomination that desolates" of Daniel 9.27).

That sparked the Maccabean revolt. Daniel's vision predicts this abomination will last only 1,150 days. Indeed, after about three and a half years the Maccabeans expelled the Seleucids and rededicated the temple. That event is celebrated in the Jewish festival of HANUKKAH.

Some scholars speculate that apocalyptic literature has roots in ZOROASTRIANISM. Zoroastrianism was the official religion of the Persians, who freed the Jewish people from exile in Babylon. It envisions a final battle in which good defeats evil. Apocalyptic literature also has its roots in the visions of ancient prophets. A good example is ISAIAH's vision of GOD's heavenly throne (Isaiah 6).

The earliest apocalypse may be as old as the 300s B.C.E. But most Jewish apocalypses addressed the uncertain time from the Maccabean revolt to the destruction of the Temple in 70 C.E. Apocalyptic thinking assured people whose political fortunes were uncertain that God was on their side. After 70 C.E. rabbinical Judaism largely rejected apocalyptic thinking.

Apocalyptic thinking also appealed to a different movement that grew out of late Second Temple Judaism: Christianity. The GOSPELS of Matthew, Mark, and Luke ascribe a minor apocalypse to Jesus himself (Mark 13.5–37 and parallel passages). It seems to refer to the siege of JERUSALEM and the destruction of the Temple. The New Testament book of Revelation is only one of several apocalypses that the earliest Christians used. Ancient Gnostics also wrote apocalyptic literature. Three of them—the apocalypses of Peter, Paul, and James—were found among the Nag Hammadi Codices in 1945.

At the end of the 20th century apocalyptic literature still exercised its fascination. It did so in several ways.

Many fundamentalist Christians adopted a point of view known as "dispensationalism" (*see* EVANGELICAL CHRISTIANITY and FUNDAMENTALISM, CHRISTIAN). They divided history into several "dispensations" and read biblical prophecies, especially the book of Revelation, as predicting current events. Some recent popular literature has made much of the RAPTURE, an apocalyptic motif.

Apocalyptic ideas and images are not, however, limited to these Christians. A popular book about indigenous Americans, *Black Elk Speaks,* records a great vision that resembles ancient apocalyptic literature in many respects. Science fiction also develops apocalyptic themes.

Further reading: Paul Boyer, *When Time Shall Be No More: Popular Belief in Modern American Culture* (Cambridge, Mass.: Harvard University Press, 1992); Stephen Cook, *The Apocalyptic Literature* (Nashville: Abingdon, 2003); Amy Frykholm, *Rapture Culture: Left Behind in Evangelical America* (New York: Oxford University Press, 2004); D. S. Russell, *Divine Disclosure: An Introduction to Jewish Apocalyptic* (Minneapolis: Fortress Press, 1992).

Apocrypha   Books that Protestants do not recognize as part of the Old Testament but that Roman Catholics and some Orthodox churches do. *Apocrypha* is a Greek word meaning "hidden." Protestants use it for several books that they do not accept as biblical. Catholics prefer the term *deuterocanonical.* This term means that although the books were not part of the first canon of the Old Testament, they are still authoritative. The books in the Apocrypha are Tobit, Judith, the Wisdom of Solomon, Ecclesiasticus (also known as the Wisdom of Jesus, Son of Sirach), Baruch (including the Letter of JEREMIAH), and 1 and 2 Maccabees, along with additions to the book of ESTHER and three additions to the book of DANIEL (The Prayer of Azariah and the Song of the Three Jews, Susanna, and Bel and the Dragon). Other apocryphal books that the Roman Catholic Church does not accept as deuterocanonical are: 1 and 2 Esdras, 3 and 4 Maccabees, The Prayer of Manasseh, and Psalm 151.

WHY IS THERE AN APOCRYPHA?

CHRISTIANITY came into existence before the content of the Hebrew scriptures had been fixed (*see* SCRIPTURES, HEBREW). Because the earliest Christians spoke Greek, they used as their Old Testament a Greek version of Hebrew writings known as the

Septuagint. This version contained more material than what eventually became the Hebrew Bible. Some church leaders were always aware of the difference between the Old Testament and the Hebrew Bible. It did not become important, however, until the Protestant REFORMATION. At that time the Protestants decided to recognize only the books in the Hebrew Bible as having authority. In response, the Council of TRENT declared in 1546 that the deuterocanonical books were just as authoritative as the books in the Hebrew Bible.

CONTENT OF THE APOCRYPHA

Regardless of whether one believes that the books of the Apocrypha have authority, some of them are remarkable. Some books tell folk stories. Judith is the story of a woman who saved her people when the Babylonian army was laying siege to her city. She entertained the general of the opposing army, got him drunk, and then, when he was sleeping, cut off his head with his own sword. Susanna is the story of a woman whom two old men falsely accuse of adultery because she has refused to have sex with them. Daniel, still a boy, proves that the two old men were lying. They are put to death. Tobit tells of a man who is blinded for doing a righteous deed but recovers his sight.

Two books of the Apocrypha, the Wisdom of Solomon and Sirach, are considered WISDOM LITERATURE. They touch upon a great variety of topics, but some people find them to be not so profound as wisdom books in the Hebrew Bible, such as Job or Ecclesiastes. For example, Ecclesiasticus assumes that people can choose to be good all the time: "If you choose, you can keep the commandments, and to act faithfully is a matter of your own choice" (15.15). It also does not seem to recognize, as Job does, the problem of undeserved suffering: "everyone receives in accordance with his or her deeds" (16.14). These books do, however, celebrate Wisdom personified in highly poetic terms, as in this passage from Wisdom of Solomon: "[Wisdom] is a reflection of eternal light, a spotless mirror of the working of God, and an image of his goodness. Although she is but one, she can do all things, and while remaining in herself, she renews all things;

in every generation she passes into holy souls and make them friends of God, and prophets, for God loves nothing so much as the person who lives with wisdom."

1 and 2 Maccabees are about the sufferings of the Jewish people under Persian rulers in the early 100s B.C.E. and how the Maccabees led them to independence in 164 B.C.E. Perhaps the best-known story in these books is the story of the rededication of the Temple. Jews celebrate this event at HANUKKAH.

INFLUENCE OF THE APOCRYPHA

Although Protestants have rejected the Apocrypha, these books have had a major influence on European culture. For example, the composer Georg Friedrich Handel (1685–1759) wrote two oratorios based on the Apocrypha: *Susanna* and *Judas Maccabaeus*. European painters often painted scenes from Susanna, Tobit, and Judith. A striking example is *Judith Slaying Holofernes* by Artemisia Gentilleschi (1597–1651). The Apocrypha even played a role in the European discovery of the Americas. After reading a verse in 2 Esdras, Christopher Columbus (1451–1506) reasoned that the distance across the Atlantic from Europe to Asia could not be very far. He was wrong, but he discovered the Americas as a result.

Further reading: R. H. Charles, *Apocrypha and Pseudepigrapha of the Old Testament* (Oxford: Oxford University Press, 1998); Michael D. Coogan et al., eds., *The New Oxford Annotated NRSV Bible with the Apocrypha,* 3d ed. (New York: Oxford University Press, 2001); Daniel J. Harrington, *Invitation to the Apocrypha* (Grand Rapids, Mich.: W. B. Eerdmans, 1999); Otto Kaiser, *The Old Testament Apocrypha: An Introduction* (Peabody, Mass.: Hendrickson Publishers, 2004).

Apollo An ancient Greek god of social order and law. Artwork shows Apollo as an ideal young man, just reaching maturity, often holding a bow or a lyre. He seems especially to have been the protector of young men as they became old enough to enter public life. More broadly, Apollo was a god of order and justice. As such, the Greeks routinely consulted him when they were thinking of establishing colonies. In addition, Apollo was associated with herding, music, and prophecy. It has been popular to suggest that Apollo was a god of the sun. That view was common among Hellenistic and Roman writers. (Hellenistic literature is Greek literature after Alexander the Great [d. 323 B.C.E.]) But Apollo's connections with the sun always played a very minor role in his worship.

Apollo had two important sanctuaries. The first was the sacred island of Delos in the Aegean Sea; the ancient Greeks said that Apollo and his sister ARTEMIS were born there. The second was the sanctuary at Delphi in central Greece, the site of a famous oracle, that is, a means of consulting the god. Apollo shared the sanctuary at Delphi with the god Dionysos. At Delphi, individuals or communities would put questions to the Sybil, a priestess of Apollo. According to legend, she would breathe vapors, enter a trance, and provide an answer. Then Apollo's priests would communicate the answer in the form of ambiguous poetry. A famous example is the oracle given to Croesus: "If you go to battle, you will destroy a great kingdom." Encouraged by these words, Croesus attacked Persia—and lost his kingdom. Scholarly research suggests that the procedures and responses at Delphi were actually more mundane. Questioners manipulated black and white beans, and the god supposedly used them to reveal yes and no answers.

Europeans and North Americans commonly see Apollo as a god of enlightenment and reason. A good example is the German philosopher, Friedrich Nietzsche (1844–1900). This image of Apollo derives largely from Hellenistic and Roman mythwriters. Nevertheless, many see this Apollo as embodying distinctively Greek characteristics.

apostles From a Greek word meaning "sent out"; the earliest leaders of the Christian church. The word apostle often refers to the 12 special disciples whom JESUS "sent out" into the world. Judas Iscariot, who betrayed Jesus, was originally one of

the 12; according to the NEW TESTAMENT (see BIBLE, BIBLICAL LITERATURE), GOD chose Matthias to take his place (ACTS OF THE APOSTLES 1.15–26).

The word apostle, however, does not refer only to the 12 disciples. PAUL, the early missionary to the non-Jews of the Roman Empire, calls himself an apostle. He also calls James, the brother of Jesus and one of the most important leaders of the Jewish Christians in JERUSALEM, an apostle. Other writers refer to other persons as apostles. Taken most broadly, apostles are the most prominent leaders of the earliest Christian communities, regardless of whether or not they were among the original 12.

Apostles' Creed   See CREEDS.

Aquinas, Thomas (c. 1224–1274) *the most important Christian theologian of the European Middle Ages* Thomas was the son of an Italian count. He became a Dominican friar (see DOMINICANS) and devoted his life to teaching and writing THEOLOGY. His greatest book was the *Summa Theologica* (1266–73), "the summary of all theology."

In Thomas's day western Europeans were just discovering the ideas of the Greek philosopher Aristotle (384–322 B.C.E.). Thomas found these ideas very attractive. He insisted that truth was one, because GOD was one. Therefore, he argued, what human reason said was true could not be opposed to what God's revelation said was true. The two were compatible. But human reason could not discover everything. Therefore, God finished what reason began by revealing the fullness of truth.

Thomas included God's existence among the truths that reason could discover. In fact, he provided several classic proofs for the existence of God (see GOD, THE EXISTENCE OF). He also felt that although all human beings had a natural sense of right and wrong, reason alone could not discover truths such as the INCARNATION of God in JESUS and the triune character of God (see TRINITY). Eventually Thomas's teachings became more or less the official teachings of the Roman Catholic Church.

archaeology and religion   The study of objects that human beings made and used in the past, and the ways in which that study affects scholars' understanding of religions and the claims religions make.

WHAT IS ARCHAEOLOGY?

Religious people have been interested in artifacts from the past for a long time. For example, in the eighth century B.C.E. people in Greece began to WORSHIP heroes (*see* HEROES AND HERO MYTHS) at tombs from the Mycenaean period (ended roughly 1100 B.C.E.). But archaeology is the systematic, scientific study of the things people made and used in the past. It has roots in grave-robbing and treasure-hunting. It also has roots in the sensational excavations of Pompeii and Herculaneum, Italy, that began in the 18th century, and of Troy and Mycenae in the 19th century. In the 20th century scientific archaeology came into its own.

Archaeologists study artifacts in several different ways. Sometimes they make field surveys, that is, they note what kinds of remains are visible on the Earth's surface. Often archaeologists undertake limited excavations. They dig trenches at places where they know or suspect human beings lived. To excavate an entire site is costly and time-consuming. It may also be a bad idea. Such excavation destroys evidence that later archaeologists, with new and better tools, might also be able to study.

The first archaeologists were interested in art treasures, valuable materials such as gold, and sensational headlines. With time, archaeologists learned that careful study of the simplest remains might teach them more. Remains are most significant if the precise location where they were found is known. As a result, archaeology is not the random digging of treasure hunters. It is a painstaking removal of detritus. The site and its objects are carefully mapped every step of the way.

In analyzing the materials uncovered, one of the first questions archaeologists must answer is, "How old is it?" Several methods help them. Unless a site is disturbed, more recent material lies on top of older material. Identifying the different layers of material in a site is known as stratigraphy. It provides a relative chronology—an idea of what is older and what is younger. Analyzing tree rings from wooden objects can provide a relative chronology, too. In the second half of the 20th century archaeologists developed sophisticated physical tests for establishing actual dates. The most widely known is radiocarbon dating. It dates items that were alive within the last 40,000 years by measuring the amount of radioactive carbon they contain.

In the first half of the 20th century archaeologists were interested in major artifacts such as temples and palaces. Besides developing methods of dating, they classified material remains according to types, for example, types of jars and oil lamps. Their ideas about religion generally reflected the ideas of the time, such as DYNAMISM; many scholars today question those ideas. In the 1960s a so-called "new archaeology" arose. This kind of archaeology used statistics to analyze material remains, often those associated with everyday life. In doing so, it applied models of religion and society that sociologists and anthropologists had developed. The results were intriguing, but sometimes controversial.

ARCHAEOLOGY AND THE STUDY OF RELIGIONS

Archaeology provides the only hard evidence available for PREHISTORIC RELIGIONS. That is because prehistory is defined as "before the invention of writing."

It is possible to read too much into this evidence. In 1956, Horace Miner published a good example in the journal, *The American Anthropologist*. He claimed to be analyzing the "We'uns." They lived in a place called "Nacirema." What he actually did was apply archaeological language to artifacts common in American society at the time. ("Nacirema" is American spelled backwards.) The results were amusing. They also pointed out a very real danger: People of today may seriously misinterpret artifacts from the past because they make assumptions about them that simply do not hold.

Despite the dangers, archaeologists have provided a wealth of information about prehistoric religions. They have shown that religion goes back at least to the Neanderthal people, and perhaps even further. From the Paleolithic period they have discovered evidence of religion that includes cave paintings, statuary, and burials. Marija Gimbutas and others have studied the religious significance of Neolithic figurines from eastern Europe. "Archaeoastronomers" have examined megalithic monuments like Stonehenge as well as temples in Mesoamerica. They note the way these monuments relate to the sun, moon, stars, and planets. Some scholars, inspired by the geographer Paul Wheatley, have explored the role religion played in the founding of cities. In south Asia archaeology has uncovered a massive, early civilization known as the Indus Valley or Harappan civilization (see INDUS VALLEY RELIGION). Its writing remain undeciphered. In China archaeologists have unearthed massive, early tombs (see CHINA, RELIGIONS OF).

Archaeologists have also made tremendous contributions to the study of historical religions. One way they have done so is by discovering ancient texts that were previously unknown. Such texts include the hieroglyphs and calendars of the Maya (see MAYA RELIGION), texts from ancient Egypt and Mesopotamia (see EGYPTIAN RELIGION and MESOPOTAMIAN RELIGIONS), and texts that have transformed the understanding of the BIBLE and its world. The last include Canaanite texts from Ugarit and Ebla (see CANAANITE RELIGION), texts from Qumran known as the DEAD SEA SCROLLS, the Nag Hammadi Codices of ancient Gnostics (see GNOSTICISM), and texts of the Bible itself.

ARCHAEOLOGY AND RELIGIOUS CLAIMS

Because religions make claims about the past, archaeological discoveries may have something to say about those claims. Sometimes archaeology raises questions about religious claims. An example is the story of the universal FLOOD. Television stations occasionally show programs in which "archaeologists" are searching for NOAH's ark. In fact, archaeology has made it virtually certain that a universal flood never occurred. On the one hand, archaeologists have uncovered documents that make it possible to trace in a general way where the writers of the Bible got the story. On the other, there is no evidence for the kind of cataclysmic flood that the Bible records. Evidence of such a flood should be everywhere, and it should be unmistakable.

It is worth pointing out that archaeology does not question claims only of JUDAISM and CHRISTIANITY. Some indigenous North Americans think that human life originated in the Western Hemisphere. However, evidence from archaeology and other sources, such as comparative anatomy, make this extremely unlikely. Hindus have traditionally traced sacred events to times in the very distant past. They have dated the events of the *Mahabharata* to roughly 3000 B.C.E. and the events of the *Ramayana* to roughly 867,000 B.C.E. (*see* RAMA, *RAMAYANA*). The first date is unlikely; the second is inconceivable.

Archaeology does more than raise questions about religious claims. It also makes those claims more vivid and meaningful. For example, archaeology has provided an understanding of cities and ways of life pictured in the Hebrew Bible. It has also provided a more accurate and detailed image of what crucifixion was like at the time of JESUS. At the same time, archaeology can say very little about some very important religious claims. These include claims such as the following: GOD wants Jews to live according to the TORAH; Jesus is the son of God; the prophet MUHAMMAD received the QUR'AN by divine revelation; the BUDDHA discovered the path to NIRVANA.

SIGNIFICANCE

Archaeology has transformed the way people think about religions. It has also transformed the way people think about religious claims. Some religious people have reacted negatively to these developments, but others have seen them as an opportunity to rethink and reformulate religious truth.

Further reading: Glyn E. Daniel, *A Short History of Archaeology* (London: Thames and Hudson, 1981);

Marija Gimbutas, *The Goddesses and Gods of Old Europe* (Berkeley: University of California Press, 1982); Charles Keith Maisels, *Early Civilizations of the Old World* (New York: Routledge, 1999); P. R. S. Moorey, *A Century of Biblical Archaeology* (Louisville: Westminster John Knox, 1991); Harvey Whitehouse and Luther H. Martin, eds., *Theorizing Religions Past: Archaeology, History, and Cognition* (Walnut Creek, Calif.: Altamira Press, 2004).

archetype Pattern or model. Two important 20th-century thinkers about religions developed the term *archetype* in very influential ways: Carl Gustav JUNG and Mircea ELIADE.

Jung was a psychologist. He believed that all human beings shared a certain kind of unconscious, the "collective unconscious." In his eyes, the collective unconscious contained fundamental symbols or archetypes necessary to personal well-being. One example is the MANDALA, a geometric diagram of squares, circles, and other designs around a center point. One of his followers, Erich Neumann, developed an archetype that he called the "Great Mother" (*see* GODDESSES). Among other places, Jung thought archetypes could be seen especially in dreams and myths.

Mircea Eliade was a historian of religions. He divided human beings into two general classes: "archaic man" and "modern man." Eliade considered archaic man to be *homo religiosus*. That is, religion defined the way archaic people looked at and lived in the world. In particular, archaic people lived their lives according to archetypes. These archetypes were revealed at the beginning of time and recorded in myth (*see* MYTH AND MYTHOLOGY). By contrast, Eliade considered modern people to be secular. But they have not lost the archetypes completely. They have simply become unaware of them. As a result, Eliade said, religious archetypes recur in cultural forms such as art, literature, music, and film.

architecture, religious The design of buildings for specifically religious purposes. Religious traditions have always wanted to set aside sacred places for WORSHIP, seeing them as dwelling places of gods or as locations where the presence of the divine could be especially experienced. The caves of the Old Stone Age from as far back as 35,000 years ago, with their wonderful paintings of animals located almost inaccessibly deep in the Earth, were clearly sacred sites of some kind. As soon as developing technology enabled human beings to do so, religious shrines were among the first and grandest structures to be built.

From the temples and pyramids of ancient Egypt (*see* EGYPTIAN RELIGION) to the cathedrals and temples of the Middle Ages and today around the world, these buildings have often employed the richest materials and called forth the finest skills of architects and artisans. People have thought that only the best is worthy of GOD or the gods, and because such places are usually community centers as well as places of worship, they reflect the pride and common purposes of a town or society. In many places today, the church or temple is the oldest and most central building in a community, and one that in its history, design, and artwork is best thought to reflect the culture as well as the faith of the community.

Buildings intended for worship provide a space, or total environment, in which the religious reality believed in by these people comes alive through the use of symbols and the evocation of memories. Everywhere one looks there may be a symbolic reminder of some truth of the faith, or scenes that recall previous times of worship or sacred events participated in by oneself or one's people. Often, it has the special feel of sacred space; one may instinctively talk in hushed tones and act differently in a religious building than one does outside. This may particularly be the case during rites or services.

Religious buildings are basically of two types: those that are seen primarily as the House of God, and those that are planned primarily for congregational worship, an assembly place for the People of God. SHINTO shrines, Hindu temples, some Buddhist temples, and many of the ancient temples are chiefly homes of the deity. They are built as one would, in the respective culture, construct the palace of a king or other great figure who is venerated and honored. They present courts where visitors may come to pay respects and present petitions, as if in homage before such a personage. Food offerings and other services are presented regularly as in a royal court. But there is no room for an entire congregation to gather in the temple, for that is not the purpose of the divine house. At times of festival, persons may file by the divine presence in a steady stream, or gather in a courtyard to watch the ceremonies.

Today Muslim MOSQUES, Christian churches, and Jewish SYNAGOGUES are primarily places for congregational worship. The architectural emphasis is on providing facilities for large meetings, with good acoustics for music and sermons, and an inspirational atmosphere for corporate worship. Some churches in the Roman Catholic and Orthodox traditions, and some Buddhist temples, find ways to combine both the House of God and People of God emphases, with shrines or ALTARS for individual devotion and a sense of divine presence, but also room for larger services. The many different styles of architecture found throughout the religious world each have their own messages. The visitor to Japan, for example, will be struck by the contrast between the plain, rustic, understated Shinto shrine, and the more massive Buddhist temple, perhaps with its skyward-reaching pagoda. The Shinto structure tells of its roots in the simplicity of ancient Japanese culture and of the reserved, hidden nature of its KAMI or gods, who are seldom portrayed in images or pictures. The Buddhist temple, on the other hand, representing a faith imported to Japan from the Asian mainland, retains a touch of Chinese influence in its architecture, and through the dark mysterious feel of its interior a sense of the philosophical depths plumbed by BUDDHISM.

Many Hindu temples, especially in the south of India, have high facades (*mandir*) so richly carved they seem overflowing with gods and mythological beings, hinting at the richness of religious creativity in this tradition. Others are open to birds and troops of monkeys that share in the offerings along with the gods. These temples suggest the Hindu themes of the intermingling of life and the divine presence in all creatures. In the interior of the temple, often reached only after passing through outer chambers watched by guardian deities, one comes to the *garbha* ("womb"), the place of the principal deity, suggesting that reaching it is like finding one's way to the ultimate mystery and source of life.

The Islamic mosque, domed, spacious, and austere, with the upward-reaching minaret beside it, fulfills its religious function excellently. It is a meeting-place for the House of ISLAM and a place where the faithful are called to PRAYER, and it bespeaks with its clean empty space the infinity of the One God, Creator of the worlds, who cannot be represented by any form or image made by human hands.

Christian churches in western Europe have adopted several architectural styles through the centuries. First was the basilica, an oblong building with a central passageway or nave and a raised platform in front, based on the Roman court of law. It suggested the church as a place for important meetings and proclamations. Then came the Romanesque church, a squarish domed building with high narrow windows that, in the Dark Ages when it flourished, strongly told of the church as a fortress, a place of refuge both physically and spiritually in a troubled world. In the high Middle Ages came the Gothic cathedral, whose high pointed ceilings and spires and wonderful stained-glass windows spoke instead of aspiration heavenward. In the Renaissance and early modern period the ornate baroque style, found in churches from St. Peter's cathedral in Rome to the Spanish missions of the southwestern United States, suggested richness of depth and texture. The simpler Georgian or Palladian style, with its careful proportions of plain white interiors and exteriors, found in many colonial American churches, reflects Protestant restraint. In the 20th century churches have been built in new styles made possible by new technologies for building as well as by new concepts of worship. There are churches made of poured concrete to resemble ships or tents, churches in the round with the pulpit or altar in the center, churches underground or atop skyscrapers.

The Jewish temple or synagogue also basically adopted the model of the Roman basilica, because its primary function after the Diaspora or dispersion of Jews throughout the world was to serve as a place of meeting for worship and study. Features of the ancient temple at Jerusalem, however, have also been used, along with other reminders of Near East origins such as domed windows and doors. In recent times Jewish temples and synagogues, especially in the United States, have experimented with modern architectural forms.

Throughout history architecture has been one of the most important of all forms of religious art, capable of conveying messages as profound as any other art about the nature of the human relation to the divine.

Further reading: J. G. Davies, *Temples, Churches, and Mosques: A Guide to the Appreciation of Religious Architecture* (New York: Pilgrim Press, 1982); Mircea Eliade, *The Sacred and the Profane* (New York: Harcourt Brace Jovanovich, 1959); Edward Norman, *The House of God* (New York: Thames and Hudson, 1990); Phyllis Richardson, *New Spiritual Architecture* (New York: Abbeville Press, 2004); Harold Turner, *From Temple to Meeting House: The Phenomenology and Theology of Places of Worship* (The Hague: Mouton, 1979).

Arctic religions The religions of the far northern regions of Europe, Asia, and North America. The term *Arctic religions* usually refers to the traditional religions of Arctic peoples. Today, most of them practice CHRISTIANITY. For example, the Inuit (formerly called Eskimo) of North America mainly practice ROMAN CATHOLICISM and ANGLICANISM. The Saami (formerly called Lapps) in Norway, Sweden, Finland, and Russia practice LUTHERANISM and EASTERN ORTHODOX CHRISTIANITY. The former Soviet Union tried to make the peoples in its far northern territories, such as the Samoyed, into atheists (*see* ATHEISM). They had only limited success.

As the names just mentioned indicate, the Arctic is a large region. As one would expect, the traditional religious practices of the Saami in far northern Europe differed from those of the Inuit in Alaska, as well as from other peoples who lived closer to them. But Arctic religions show some striking similarities, too.

In the Arctic it is not possible to grow plants. The people who live there have to get their food from animals or import it. Traditionally, they have hunted and fished. In Europe and Asia they have also kept herds of animals, such as reindeer among the Saami. (Recently Inuit in northern Canada have also experimented with herding caribou.)

Much of the religious life of Arctic people focused on the animals. They believed that animals, like people, had souls. Hunters performed rituals addressed to the souls of the slain animals. Some scholars think that they were giving the souls of the animals gifts so that they would be happy and return again. Especially important for most Arctic peoples were rituals for slain bears. They treated the bear as an honored guest and carefully disposed of its bones. The Inuit in Alaska treated whales in a similar way.

Arctic peoples believed that there were many spirits in nature, not just the souls of animals and people. Some spirits connected with features of the landscape, such as mountains and lakes. Arctic peoples often believed that special spirits controlled animal life. Each species had its own protector; in addition, a special protector, whom modern scholars sometimes call the Master or Mistress of Animals, had charge of many animal species. A good example of such a protector is Sedna, whom the Inuit thought of as the mistress of sea animals. Many Arctic peoples also assigned a special role, such as the role of creator, to the Sun, the Moon, or both.

People everywhere in the region had the same kind of religious leader, the shaman (*see* SHAMANISM). Some shamans inherited their positions; others received them as a result of special experiences that they had. Shamans were healers. They often healed by traveling to the realm of spirits, as the Arctic peoples thought, trying to bring back the soul that had left the sick person. In addition to healing, shamans performed hunting and fishing rituals, helped people find objects that they had lost, and performed funerals. They had relationships with special animals, such as birds or fish, who helped them do these things.

It is hard to know to what extent any of these practices continue today. Many seem to have disappeared completely, but occasionally researchers find that some people continue a practice that was thought to have vanished. In the territories of the former Soviet Union, people preserved some traditional religious practices as a way to resist unwanted pressure from outsiders. Still, religious people in the Arctic today often have other concerns besides preserving traditional religious practices. For example, many are working hard to combat various social ills found in the far north, such as alcoholism, sexual abuse, and suicide (*see* SUICIDE AND RELIGION).

See also NORDIC RELIGION.

Further reading: Ronald Hutton, *Shamans: Siberian Spirituality and the Western Imagination* (London: Hambledon and London, 2001); Juha Pentikäinen, *Shamanism and Culture,* 3rd ed. (Helsinki: Etnika, 1998); Harold Seidelman and James Turner, *The Inuit Imagination: Arctic Myth and Sculpture* (New York: Thames and Hudson, 1994).

arhat   A Sanskrit word meaning "worthy, venerable"; a person who has attained enlightenment by following the path of the BUDDHA. The arhat is an important figure in THERAVADA BUDDHISM, the form of BUDDHISM found in southeast Asia. Theravada talks about four stages leading to enlightenment: the stage of the stream-winner (one who will attain enlightenment in a future life), the once-returner (one who will attain enlightenment in the next life), the nonreturner (one who will attain enlightenment in the present life), and the arhat.

The first arhats were the five ascetics who heard the Buddha's first sermon. (Ascetics are persons who deprive themselves of luxuries and even of necessities for religious purposes.) Many others became arhats in the Buddha's day. After the Buddha died or, as Buddhists say, entered the ultimate NIRVANA, it became harder to become an arhat.

In time arhats became objects of popular WORSHIP. In some Buddhist countries today influential monks are still said to be arhats.

Armenian Church   The distinctive Christian institution of Armenia. Armenia is a region in northeastern Turkey and northwestern Iran, and includes an independent commonwealth between the Black and the Caspian Seas. No one knows exactly when CHRISTIANITY first arrived there. In 314 C.E. Tiridates, the king of the country, converted to Christianity. Armenia then became the first nation in which Christianity was the established or official religion. Armenian Christianity took distinctive form in the fifth century. At that time the BIBLE and many church writings were translated into Armenian.

The most distinctive feature of the Armenian Church is its view of JESUS. In technical terms, the Armenian Church is "monophysite." That is, it rejects the teaching of the Council of Chalcedon (451) that Jesus had two natures, divine and human, united in one person. It teaches instead that the incarnate Word of GOD has only one nature.

Armenian worship practices closely resemble those of the Orthodox churches (*see* EASTERN ORTHODOX CHRISTIANITY). So does the organization of the Armenian Church. The head of the Armenian Church is known as the "catholikos." He resides in Echmiadzin near Yerevan, the capital of Armenia. A smaller group of Armenians recognize as their head a patriarch who now resides in Beirut, Lebanon.

art, religious   Painting, sculpture, architecture, music, dance, poetry, drama, and stories that are created for religious purposes. In its broadest sense, art refers to all that is made by human beings to convey beauty, pleasure, and meaning through its form, whether that be in matter, words, or sound. It even includes such "minor" arts as garden landscaping and jewelry making. All these arts have been given religious significance and have had roles, often very important ones, in communicating religious truths and inducing religious experiences.

These arts can be thought of as stained-glass windows. If ultimate religious reality is like pure light, for us truly to be able to understand it, it needs to take color and shape. This is what religious art tries to do. The greater the art, the more it is able to give meaning to the light without weakening it.

At the same time religious painting and sculpture have performed several different functions, sometimes separately and sometimes in combination. One is to tell the narratives of the religion. Art illustrates important scenes from the faith's myths, histories, and visions of the future. Think of all the pictures and statues of the BUDDHA at the moment of his enlightenment or of JESUS as an infant in the manger or on the cross dying for the sins of the world. Paintings and statues may also be of other events or figures: the lives of SAINTS, prophets, reformers; important shrines or places. As for the future, consider scenes of the Last Judgment in European cathedrals, or of Maitreya, the Buddha to come, in Eastern temples. In times past, when the great majority of people were illiterate, these pictures—in stained glass, in sculpture, in paintings—were, together with the spoken word, literally the storybooks and Bibles. But even those who were able to read frequently found that a visualization helped them hold the scenes of faith in mind.

Another role of art is to serve as a focus for DEVOTION. Paintings and statues are treated as divinity. The devout kneel before them, burn candles or present incense, and pray to the saint or deity represented as though present in the object. While few would perhaps think that the spiritual entity is solely contained within the form, the latter does serve as an effective focus for concentration of mind, and is like a window into the heavenly or divine world wherein the sacred being dwells.

In EASTERN ORTHODOX CHRISTIANITY, for example, icons or paintings of saints are highly venerated. They are thought of as openings into HEAVEN; the background will be the gold of eternity, and the eyes of the saints will be large to represent their spiritual, all-seeing quality.

In ROMAN CATHOLICISM, statues of the Virgin MARY and other saints are worshipped with adoration. In HINDUISM and BUDDHISM, images of gods and buddhas similarly help concentrate the meditative PRAYERS of temple-visitors and provide insight into the splendor of the heavens and the spiritual riches they give the world (see IMAGES, ICONS, IDOLS IN RELIGION). Sometimes art can also represent desired answers for prayers and aspirations. The paintings of animals on the walls of prehistoric caves may have been a form of hunting magic used in rituals to help men slay those same animals in the world above. Some later art offers scenes of heaven, the Buddhist Pure Land (see PURE LAND BUDDHISM), or an ideal city as a focus for hope.

Finally, religious art can portray the world the way the religion wants to see it. An outstanding example is the art of ZEN BUDDHISM. Many of the ink-wash paintings associated with it are not of buddhas or even Zen masters, but of scenes of nature: a mountain reaching into empty sky, a bird on a bamboo branch. Yet these are done with a light touch suggesting that although all things are continually changing, nonetheless they all manifest the buddha-nature. Some Hindu sculpture, like the famous portrayals of the god KRISHNA playing his flute, or the god SIVA dancing, suggest that the creation and activity of this world may be viewed ultimately as divine LILA, the dance or play of GOD.

Religious art takes many different styles. Most often, especially when it is art intended to be used in churches or temples as a part of WORSHIP, it follows certain conventions of style and incorporates standard symbols. Some religious art is more realistic than others. There is, of course, a religious place for decorative art, for abstract art, for art based on symbols, like the Christian cross or the Jewish star of David, rather than living forms. Some Hindu gods and Buddhist BODHISATTVAS have many arms to symbolize their ability to do numerous acts of mercy at once. Some Egyptian and Hindu deities (like the Hindu elephant-headed god GANESA) are in animal form or combine animal and human elements to symbolize certain qualities, like Ganesa's wisdom. With the exception of the Eastern Orthodox icon, Christian art tends to be realistic when dealing with CHRIST or the saints.

In some religions, believers object to certain religious uses of art, usually on the grounds that they represent idolatry or the representation of the infinite God in a particular form at a particular place. JUDAISM, for example, employs decorative art and art for educational purposes but avoids sacred statues or paintings in places of worship. ISLAM rejects any attempt to portray God or the Prophet in art, and in MOSQUES there is only abstract ornamentation, often calligraphed lines from the Koran (see QUR'AN). Protestant churches may have stained-glass windows and prints or paintings, less often statues, as storytellers and reminders but not as objects of devotion in the Catholic or Eastern Orthodox sense.

The use or nonuse of forms of art in worship has been a heated issue in religious history, the subject of fierce argument and even violent persecution. But for all the conflicts, few things have brought more joy to religious believers than the best of religious art within its tradition.

Further reading: S. G. F. Brandon, *Man and God in Art and Ritual* (New York: Scribner, 1975); Jane Dillenberger, *Image and Spirit in Sacred and Secular Art* (New York: Crossroad, 1990); Albert C. Moore, *Iconography of Religions: An Introduction* (New York: Thames and Hudson, 1990); Gerardus Van der Leeuw, *Sacred and Profane Beauty: The Holy in Art* (New York: Holt, Rinehart & Winston, 1963).

Artemis An ancient Greek GODDESS. In mythology she is APOLLO's twin sister. Among other functions, Artemis presided over the rituals that marked a young woman's coming of age.

In character, Artemis is a virgin and a huntress. In the battle of the gods in book 21 of the *Iliad,* she comes off poorly. In effect, Hera disciplines her physically, and she runs to ZEUS for comfort. But Artemis is not always such a weakling.

Some myths tells how she killed the mighty hunter Orion after he had insulted her. In an indirect way she was responsible for another death. Hippolytus, the son of Theseus, was devoted to Artemis. Jealous, the goddess Aphrodite engineered an amorous intrigue that eventually resulted in Hippolytus's death. The playwright Euripides made this story famous in one of his plays.

Artemis watches over the young from birth to maturity. Ancient Greek girls would dance in choruses in her honor as part of their rituals of growing up. Girls of Athens served Artemis at the sanctuary at Brauron. They were known as *arktoi,* bears, apparently after a bear whom myths said the Athenians had once killed.

ascension, of Christ *See* JESUS.

asceticism Self-denial and living a very simple life for religious reasons. Seriously religious people in virtually all traditions have given up things, especially things that appeal to the senses, for the sake of religion. They have given up food by fasting, or by subsisting only on coarse and tasteless food. They have worn only rough clothes, or even gone without clothes at all. They have lived in cold caves or hard monastic cells. They have foregone marriage. They have meditated for hours under a hot sun, or in freezing mountains. They have deliberately induced discomfort by wearing hair shirts or chains, sleeping on beds of nails, and standing under waterfalls. A few have even mutilated themselves.

These states of self-denial are called asceticism—abstention from the natural pleasures of life for religious reasons. It ranges from what may be called "normal" asceticism, that of, say, a monk or nun in an austere order with long hours of prayer or meditation and a sparse but wholesome diet, to the greatest extremes of self-inflicted pain. Ascetics are found in the spiritual traditions of most religions. Examples would include the MONKS AND NUNS of ROMAN CATHOLICISM and EASTERN ORTHODOX CHRISTIANITY, of BUDDHISM and of TAOISM, the Sufi mystics of ISLAM, and the often more individualistic SADHUS or "holy men" of HINDUISM. All traditions have included both "normal" and sometimes very saintly ascetics, and "extreme" ascetics. All religions have also included devout lay men and women who, sometimes very quietly and privately, have practiced various forms of self-denial and asceticism in the midst of an "ordinary" life.

What are the religious reasons for asceticism? First, it can be an aspect of the love or compassion that is the great virtue of most faiths, for what one denies oneself one can give to the poor. In this way it not only does good, it also sets an example to others. Second, it is a form of self-discipline, and to learn to discipline oneself is basic to following any spiritual path. It can be seen as a rejection of the physical body, viewed as the "lower" part of one's nature, or even as a source of temptation and evil, in favor of the spiritual dimension of life (see CELIBACY). Third, it is seen as a way of doing repentance for one's SINS, to work off the punishment or "bad KARMA" they have accrued, and so to set oneself right. Finally, asceticism is believed to enhance religious experience. Fasting can help one to see visions, and a light diet can lead to effective MEDITATION; even pain can alternate with religious rapture. There are psychological and physiological reasons for some of this. Most importantly, though, asceticism always sends a religious message: GOD takes priority over the pleasures and entanglements of this world.

Asoka (early third century B.C.E.–c. 232 B.C.E.) *the third and last great emperor of the Maurya dynasty in India* He is known for propagating DHARMA (Sanskrit for "right order") throughout his realm.

Asoka distinguished himself early in his career by conquering the Kalingas, a people living in northeast India. The conquest of this people gave him sovereignty over almost the entire Indian subcontinent and ushered in an era of peace.

Asoka inscribed a series of edicts on pillars, rocks, and cave walls throughout his realm. A continuous theme runs through them all: dharma. The edicts outlawed the killing of most animals. They urged various religious groups and orders to live together in peace. They also promulgated the virtues of dharma throughout the realm.

Asoka is particularly remembered as a patron of BUDDHISM and its order of monks (see SANGHA). He is said to have called a Buddhist council at his capital, Pataliputra, to settle disputed questions. He is also said to have sent his son to Sri Lanka to promote BUDDHISM.

Most Indians revere Asoka as an ideal ruler. For that reason, the lions atop Asoka's pillar at Sarnath in north-central India are a widely used symbol. They appear, for example, on Indian money.

assassins Popular name for a medieval Shi'ite Muslim community more properly known as the Nizari Ismailis. The Nizari Ismaili community is a group within SHI'ITE ISLAM about which much imaginative lore has circulated. Europeans called them "assassins." Arabs called them *hashishiyah,* that is, "marijuana smokers." Travelers such as Marco Polo (c. 1254–1324) spread rumors that the assassins were incited to murder by being drugged, taken to gardens, and thus given a foretaste of paradise. These rumors remain entirely unsubstantiated.

The Nizaris broke away from the Fatimid Ismaili community of Egypt in the late 1000s. As so often in Shi'ite Islam, the dispute concerned who should be the next IMAM. They established a state in parts of Syria and Iran, which continued in existence until the 1250s. The rumors about them certainly derive from military and guerrilla actions taken in defending and extending this state.

The Nizari Ismaili community still exists, but the name "assassins" is not associated with it. In the early 1800s, the community's imam received the title of AGA KHAN.

Assemblies of God An American denomination in the PENTECOSTAL tradition. The church was founded in 1914 under the leadership of Eudorus Bell (1866–1923), formerly a Southern Baptist and then a Pentecostal preacher who believed, with many others, that the diverse and largely independent Pentecostal churches formed since the movement began in 1906 should come together. Beginning with 531 groups and 6,000 members by the end of 1914, the Assemblies of God have grown rapidly to embrace some 2.3 million members in the United States in 2004 and more than 30 million worldwide. The movement has been particularly successful among Hispanic populations. Headquarters are in Springfield, Missouri.

The Assemblies believe in the divine inspiration of the Bible (*see* BIBLE, BIBLICAL LITERATURE) and traditional Christian teachings about the TRINITY and JESUS Christ as Savior. As a Pentecostal group, they put special emphasis on a BAPTISM of the Holy Spirit, which they believe follows conversion and baptism with water. The coming of the Spirit is made known by the believer's ability to "speak in tongues," that is, utter words in unknown languages held to be divinely inspired.

In church, the "tongues" are usually interpreted by others who can understand them. WORSHIP consists not only of hymns, scripture reading, PRAYERS, and sermon in the usual Protestant manner but typically also includes spontaneous "amens," prayers, tongues, interpretations of tongues, and even dancelike body movements. Spiritual healing is also important. The power to heal is considered a significant gift of the Spirit. These spiritual endowments are thought to be clearly demonstrated in the ACTS OF THE APOSTLES and other NEW TESTAMENT sources. As in Pentecostalism generally, the revival of such powers and practices in the church today is widely regarded as a sign we are entering the End Times, that is, that the Second Coming of Christ and the Final Judgment will occur in the near future. The vitality and rapid growth of the Assemblies of God can be taken as an example of the dynamic of Pentecostalism worldwide in the 20th and 21st centuries.

astrology The belief that the position of the stars and planets in the sky affects the destinies of individuals, and of larger human units such as cities and nations, and even the entire world, is the basis of astrology. Over centuries it has developed into complex methods of determining that influence in particular cases, combining precise calculations with intuitive insight. Astrology is not an essential component of any major religion, but has had relationships with most of them. Sometimes, as in the case of HINDUISM, the Chinese religions (*see* CHINA, RELIGIONS OF), and in some eyes JUDAISM and CHRISTIANITY, especially in the Renaissance, the relationship has been relatively positive. Astrology has been viewed as a confirmation of the orderly working of the universe as a divine system or as GOD's creation, and a legitimate way of divining its secrets. Others, such as the Hebrew prophets, the Puritans (*see* PURITANISM), and many recent Jews and Christians—not to mention most scientists—condemn astrology as worthless, as destructive to the free will of both God and humans, or as an entry into dangerous aspects of occultism. But astrology has retained numerous believers today.

Astrology is thought by most scholars to have originated in ancient Egypt and Mesopotamia, and to have then been developed into a thorough system by Greek thinkers during the Hellenistic period (approximately 300 B.C.E.–300 C.E.). It spread from the Mediterranean world to the Arab lands, India, and China, acquiring many distinctive elements from those cultures so that now Indian and Chinese astrology have important differences from Western astrology. All astrology, though, is based on the zodiac, the path through which the sun, moon, and planets move through the sky. That celestial band is divided into 12 "signs" or constellations. Each of them have particular traits or qualities, such as the balance or equanimity of Libra, or the secretive yet passionate nature of Scorpio. So do the sun, moon, and planets: the emotional moon, warlike Mars, and others.

Figuring the total impact of all these elements as they were configured at the time of one's birth, or at important moments in personal or national or world history, is the task of the astrologer. Many astrologers today say that the art only determines, so to speak, the hand one is dealt by fate; how one plays it is left up to the person, and so it does not

A zodiac shown in an Italian manuscript page from the portolan of Admiral Coligny *(Erich Lessing/Art Resource, N.Y.)*

compromise free will. They also say it shows there is a fundamental pattern to the universe, and that astrology demonstrates that our human lives have cosmic meaning because we are interconnected parts of that cosmic pattern. Others say the basis of astrology is false and that true religion has no need of it.

atheism   Denial of the existence of any GOD or supreme supernatural being. Atheists have long been around. In ancient India, China, and Greece a few philosophers said that the gods were only figments of human imagination, and everything that happens in the universe could be given a natural explanation. Religionists have also accused one another of atheism. Christians have sometimes said that Buddhists are atheists because they do not have a personal God as God is understood by the Western religions, even though BUDDHISM has most other features of what they would call a "real" religion. Atheism has probably grown in the modern world with the rise of science, and

through its association with powerful ideologies like communism. But though many people may be nonreligious for all intents and purposes, atheism as a deeply-felt personal commitment remains a minority stance.

Athena   The most important GODDESS of the ancient Greeks. Athena was a warrior goddess renowned for her intelligence. In that regard she contrasts with Ares, the god of military chaos and unthinking violent rage. According to myth Athena was born from the head of ZEUS. She herself remained always a virgin. Thus, the name for her most famous temple, the Parthenon in Athens, derived from the Greek word *parthenos*, "virgin."

Many cities worshipped Athena, but she was especially the goddess of Athens. At Athens the major festival in her honor was the Panathenaia. During this festival an enormous procession paraded through the city. It accompanied a newly made *peplos* or embroidered robe, which was suspended from the masts of a ship-like cart. Then the Athenians presented the robe to the image of Athena on the Acropolis.

Because of her intelligence, Athena was the goddess of all skillful undertakings, especially spinning and weaving. In myth she was the patron of many heroes, especially the crafty Odysseus. Her special animal was the owl. Images also show her with the aegis, a mythical object shown as either a cloak or a shield (interpretations vary). The aegis is decorated with the head of Medusa. Later generations have seen Athena, like APOLLO, as embodying characteristics distinctive of the Greeks.

atman   A term used for the inmost self in the VEDANTA schools of Hindu philosophy. The Sankhya and YOGA schools have a similar concept. They call it *purusha*, "person." Others, such as the Jains, talk about the *jiva*, that is, the living component of human beings and animals, as opposed to inert matter.

The UPANISHADS are the last layer of the sacred writings known as the VEDA. For that reason they are called Vedanta, "end of the Veda." Among other topics, the Upanishads are particularly interested in BRAHMAN, the reality that underlies the world that we perceive, and atman, the reality that underlies the human person. The sages of the Upanishads wanted to know what the "self" was. They did not have a single answer. Indeed, they did not even use a single word for this self. Sometimes they called it purusha. Nevertheless, the discussions in the Upanishads laid the foundations on which much later Hindu thought arose.

One of the most important discussions took place between a father named Aruni and his son, Svetaketu. It is recorded in the *Chandogya Upanishad.* Aruni asks Svetaketu to open up a seed-pod from a banyan tree, and then to open up a seed. He asks his son what he sees. Svetaketu answers, "Nothing." That is the point. The atman, like the essence of life at the heart of the seed, is imperceptible. Yet from both impressive living beings grow. Similarly, Aruni asks Svetaketu to dissolve salt in water. Svetaketu can no longer see the salt, and he can no longer separate it from the water. The atman resembles salt dissolved in water. It is distinct from a person's body, senses, mind, and desires, but it pervades them all and cannot be separated from them.

The sages of the Upanishads had several ideas of what the atman might be. Some said the sun, others air, others ether, others breath (*see* PRANA). Most important for later thought, some sages identified the atman as consciousness. There are, however, many kinds of consciousness. Not all of them are atman pure and simple. In waking consciousness the atman interacts with a world of material objects. In dreaming consciousness it interacts with a world of subtle objects. Deeper than either of these is sleep without dreams. But according to the *Mandukya Upanishad* deeper still is a fourth, nameless state. That is the atman.

In some passages the Upanishads seem to equate the atman—the reality underlying the human person—with the brahman—the reality underlying the world that we perceive: "This atman is brahman"; "I am brahman"; "All this is indeed brahman"; "You are that." But other passages seem to disagree. Different schools of

Vedanta took different positions. In any case, they agreed that the atman had three basic characteristics: *sat, chit,* and *ananda*—being, consciousness, and bliss.

Ideas about the atman profoundly influenced Hindu teachings about life and death. According to the sage Yajnavalkya, the atman is reborn at death. It takes along with it the fruits of the actions done in this life. This process is known as SAMSARA. According to the BHAGAVAD-GITA, samsara does not alter the atman: "It is never born; it never dies. It does not, nor has it, nor will it become. Unborn, eternal, perpetual, primal—it is not killed when the body is killed" (2.20).

Freeing the atman or purusha from continual rebirth came to be the ultimate goal of some influential forms of Hindu religious practice.

atonement *See* SALVATION.

Augustine of Hippo (354–430) *one of the most important theologians of the ancient Christian church* Aurelius Augustine was born and raised in North Africa. His mother, Monica, was a staunch Christian, but Augustine did not at first practice CHRISTIANITY. He received an education in rhetoric and taught it in Carthage. Later he moved to Rome and then to Milan, where he held a prominent post as an orator. These skills served him well when he eventually became a spokesperson for Catholic Christianity (*see* ROMAN CATHOLICISM).

In matters of religion, Augustine first inclined to MANICHAEISM. This religion taught that two opposed forces, light and darkness, created the world when they somehow came into contact. In time, Augustine abandoned Manichaeism and toyed with the ideas of ancient philosophers known as Skeptics. They took a cautious attitude toward the ability of human beings to know things for certain. In Milan, Augustine came under the influence of Bishop Ambrose. From Ambrose he learned the ideas of Plato and Plotinus. Plotinus had taught that the many things of the world had all emanated from "the One."

In August 386 Augustine had a profound experience. He heard a voice like that of a child saying, "Pick it up and read." He picked up the BIBLE and read a passage from PAUL's letter to the Romans. He was so moved that he renounced his previous life-style (characterized by sexual immorality), adopted celibacy, and was baptized the next EASTER. In 391 the people of Hippo in North Africa convinced him to become a priest. In 395 he became their bishop. He spent the rest of his life administering the church at Hippo, heading a monastery, preaching, teaching, and writing. His highly influential books include the *Confessions* (*c.* 400), an account of Augustine's long road to Christianity, and *The City of God* (413–426). The second book attempts to show that Christianity did not cause the decline of the Roman Empire.

As a thinker, Augustine grappled with questions that became classic in the history of European and North American THEOLOGY. Where does EVIL come from? If GOD already knows what human beings will do, how can they freely choose their own acts? What must people do in order to be saved? Augustine developed his answers to questions like these in the course of attacking three different groups: Manichaeans, Donatists, and Pelagians. Donatists taught that members of the church must be pure and that SACRAMENTS administered by sinful priests were invalid. Pelagians said that human beings could and should try to be morally perfect.

In attacking these ideas, Augustine combined biblical teachings, especially teachings of the apostle Paul, with Greek philosophy, especially the ideas of Plato and his many followers. God, Augustine insisted, is absolutely good. Evil comes into the world because God creates human beings who are free to choose. Since human beings are free to choose, they will not always choose good. In fact, once ADAM sinned, his transgression was handed down to all of his descendants as original SIN. Original sin makes it impossible for human beings to be perfect on their own. They need the gift of God's GRACE before they can do good. One way they receive grace is through sacraments like BAPTISM and the EUCHARIST. Sacraments are effective because God is at work in them.

Augustine wrote in his letters that he was "an African, writing for Africans . . . living in Africa." But he also defined the terms that future European theologians, Catholic and Protestant, would use in trying to express their faith. His ideas influenced Protestant reformers like Martin LUTHER and John CALVIN tremendously. At the same time, the Roman Catholic Church considers him a SAINT. It celebrates his feast on August 28, the date of his death.

Australian religions The traditional religions of the indigenous people of Australia. These people are generally called Aborigines. Human beings seem to have settled in Australia as long ago as 40,000 B.P. (before the present). They developed complex cultural and religious traditions. An example of both are their rock-paintings. Some of them are perhaps 15,000 years old. Traditional Australians lived in local groups that had their own languages, cultures, and territories. They supported themselves by gathering and hunting. Complex trade networks covered the entire continent.

In 1788 Europeans arrived. Many aboriginals died from warfare and disease. Many others gave up their traditional cultures and religions. They assimilated into European society and adopted CHRISTIANITY. Today, traditional aboriginal ways continue only in northern and central Australia.

A major feature of Australian religion is the Dreaming. The name is not aboriginal; it was given by scholars. Traditional Australians believe that at first the world had no form and content. But in a time known as the Dreaming, spirits appeared. They, too, are known as Dreamings. Their activities gave birth to human beings, other forms of life, and features of the natural landscape. Traditional Australians believe further that these spirits did not simply cease to exist. They are still present at specific locations. They are responsible for flourishing in the world of nature. They also give life to a fetus in the womb. Therefore, traditional Australians believe that each person has a share of spirit. At death, this share returns to the spirit realm and waits to be reborn.

Traditional Australians have identified several extremely important spirits. Scholars sometimes call them All-Father, All-Mother, and Rainbow Snake. All-Father was important in southeast Australia. All-Mother is still important in northern Australia. She often has a male spirit as her associate. Rainbow Snake is connected with the fertilizing rains. Some groups thought of it as male, some as female, and still others as both male and female at the same time. Some groups also identified Rainbow Snake with All-Mother.

The purpose of aboriginal religious practices is to foster life. They do so by establishing contact with the spirits and events of the Dreaming. The spirit is often present in the form of an image or emblem. A well-known example is the *tjurunga* of the Aranda people. It is a board, sometimes plain, sometimes decorated. Songs and acting recall the events of the Dreaming.

Life-cycle rites are important religious practices. These include INITIATIONS for both males and females. Most major ceremonies have two distinct components. One component is public; everyone in the community participates. The other component is secret; only initiates into a group can be present. The secret groups are divided according to gender. In most places women as well as men have secret groups and rituals. In most places, too, religious and social power resides with the men.

In Africa, Oceania, and the Americas indigenous peoples developed religious movements to resist European colonization. One example is the GHOST DANCE of North America. Indigenous Australians did not generally develop such movements. But in the latter part of the 20th century, strong movements did arise that pressed the government to recognize their rights to land. In conjunction with these movements, some took a new interest in traditional aboriginal religion and culture.

Avalokitesvara   One of the most important BODHISATTVAS in BUDDHISM, known especially for compassion. Originally Avalokitesvara was male, but in east Asia Avalokitesvara became venerated in female form. She is known in Chinese as Kuan-yin and in Japanese as Kannon.

Avalokitesvara is celebrated in two Buddhist scriptures, the *LOTUS SUTRA* and the *Pure Land Sutra*. He—or she—is a supreme example of the bodhisattva ideal. According to this ideal people should not seek NIRVANA for themselves. That would be selfish. Instead, they should donate whatever good they have acquired to help all beings achieve release.

Many myths connect Avalokitesvara with the Buddha Amitabha, known in Japanese as AMIDA. Pure Land Buddhists say that Avalokitesvara is one of Amida's attendants in the Pure Land (*see* PURE LAND BUDDHISM). Others say he is Amitabha's son. In any case, Avalokitesvara is often worshipped separately. He is said to dwell on a mythical mountain known as Potala or Potalaka. From there he looks after the world during the time from the BUDDHA Siddhartha Gautama (*c.* 560–*c.* 480 B.C.E.) to Maitreya, the Buddha who is yet to come.

Avalokitesvara is the epitome of virtue and compassion. He devoted eons to meritorious efforts. As a result, his ability to help beings who are suffering knows no bounds. Worshippers call upon him—or her—for help in any number of situations. They may desire release from the three traditional Buddhist poisons of lust, anger, and ignorance. Or they may want protection in times of danger, protection for travel on the sea, or long life. Especially as Kuan-yin, this bodhisattva protects women and oversees childbirth.

All Buddhists venerate Avalokitesvara. Buddhists in southeast Asia known as Theravadins call upon him as Lokesvara, "lord of the world." This bodhisattva also has close ties to Tibet. He is said to have revealed the mantra *Om mani padme hum* (literally, "Om the jewel in the lotus hum"), one of the most important mantras in Tibetan Buddhism (*see* TIBETAN RELIGION). He is also said to take human form as the DALAI LAMA, the leader of Tibetan Buddhism.

There are several common images of Avalokitesvara. One shows him resplendent with jewels, wearing a tall crown, and holding a lotus in his left hand. On the crown is the Buddha Amitabha.

Another common image shows Avalokitesvara in female form with 11 heads and a thousand arms. The 11 heads may recall one of the meanings of Avalokitesvara's name, "lord of what is seen." The thousand arms represent the bodhisattva's limitless ability to shower her worshippers with benefits. An image very common in China shows Kuan-yin dressed in flowing garments, a serene, motherly expression on her face; in her arms she holds a jar the way a mother might hold a baby, and from the jar she pours water into a pond, a sign of her beneficent gifts.

avatar A Sanskrit word for "descent"; in HINDU-ISM the appearance of a god on Earth, especially the appearance of the god VISHNU. The BHAGAVAD-GITA says that whenever evil waxes and virtue wanes, Vishnu appears on Earth to restore order. There are many avatars of Vishnu, but ten has become the standard number. Temples in India are often dedicated to Vishnu's "ten avatars."

Ideas vary about who these ten avatars are. The list often includes a tortoise on whose back the gods churned the ocean of milk; a one-horned sea creature who saved MANU, the ancestor of all human beings, from the FLOOD; a boar who raised the Earth on its tusks when it sank into the oceans; a dwarf who rescued the three worlds from an evil ruler; a man-lion who defeated an enemy immune to most creatures; Parasurama ("Rama with the axe"); RAMA; KRISHNA; the BUDDHA; and Kalki, the avatar who will come on a white horse and begin a golden age. Some Hindus think JESUS was an avatar of Vishnu, too. This is an identification that Christians generally reject.

Avesta *See* ZEND AVESTA.

ayatollah Also spelled ayatullah; religious scholars of highest rank in a branch of SHI'ITE ISLAM. Ayatollah is an Arabic and Persian word that means "light of GOD." It denotes the religious scholars who lead a branch of Shi'ite Islam.

Shi'ites maintain that, when MUHAMMAD died in 632 C.E., the leadership of the Islamic community passed to his male descendants. They call these leaders IMAMS. Shi'ites known as "twelvers" maintain that there was a line of 12 imams. The twelfth imam has been in hiding since 874 C.E. The community is now led by ayatollahs, religious scholars who speak on his behalf.

The ayatollah best known in North America at the end of the 20th century was Ruhollah Khomeini (1900–89). In 1979 he instigated the overthrow of the shah of Iran, became the head of state, and led Iran in an aggressively anti-American direction.

Aztec religion The religion of the people who ruled the valley of Mexico (the region around present-day Mexico City) when the Spanish conquered it in the 16th century. According to legend, the Aztecs migrated to the valley of Mexico from the north. Around 1325 C.E. they settled a marshy island in the middle of Lake Texcoco. Their patron god, Huitzilopochtli, had pointed the site out to them. By reclaiming land from the lake, they built a major city named Tenochtitlán (Mexico City, today). Three causeways connected it to land. By the time the Spanish arrived in the 1520s, Tenochtitlán had perhaps half a million inhabitants. By that time, too, the Aztecs had established their dominance over the entire region.

The Aztecs had elaborate views of time and space. Good examples of these are the famous Aztec calendar stone and illustrations from ancient pictographic books known as codices. The Aztec views were very similar to those of the Maya (*see* MAYA RELIGION). The Aztecs resembled the Maya, too, in believing that they were living in the fifth world or, as they called it, the "fifth sun." A famous story, the "Legend of the Suns," relates the fate of the previous four worlds and predicts the fate of the fifth.

The Aztecs worshipped several deities. Huitzilopochtli, "the Hummingbird of the Left," was one of two deities worshipped at the great temple in the middle of Tenochtitlán.

Construction workers in Mexico City discovered the temple by accident in 1978. The other deity worshipped there was Tlaloc, the god of rain. A third god, Quetzalcoatl, the feathered serpent, had a temple nearby.

The Aztecs knew Quetzalcoatl in several forms. One was a priest-king of the ancient city of Tula. This Quetzalcoatl diligently performed rituals. For example, he offered blood from the calves of his legs and he bathed ceremonially. As a result, Tula prospered. At the same time, Quetzalcoatl refused to perform certain rituals, such as human sacrifice. According to one text, he sacrificed only snakes, birds, and butterflies. Because of indiscreet behavior, Quetzalcoatl was forced to abdicate his throne. He traveled to the east and burned himself. His spirit arose to the sky to become the planet Venus. Another legend said that he sailed off into the east.

At first the ruler of the Aztecs mistook the Spanish warrior, Hernán Cortés, for Quetzalcoatl returning.

Like virtually all ancient peoples, the Aztecs practiced RITUALS in their homes. In these rituals they used small figurines and incense burners. They also had a religion associated with ceremonial centers. It consisted of SACRIFICES, often human sacrifices. For the Aztecs, the human body contained the sacred forces that made order and life possible. These forces were especially concentrated in the heart and the head. As a result, sacrifices paid particular attention to hearts and heads.

The Spanish conquerors considered Aztec religion to be the work of devils—literally. They tried to obliterate it. Nevertheless, elements of Aztec religion survived. They combined with the religion of the conquerors to produce a distinct tradition of ROMAN CATHOLICISM.

B

Baal The most important god of the ancient Canaanites. The Bible records conflicts between the priests of Baal and prophets of the Israelite god YHWH ("the Lord"). Texts from ancient Ugarit discovered in the 20th century present the god in a more positive light.

Baal is actually a general word meaning "lord." In religious contexts, the specific lord in question is usually the Canaanite god of rain, dew, and fertile fields (*see* Canaanite religion). This god is said to ride on the clouds. He is also called "Prince Baal." In Semitic languages, the phrase is *Baal zebul.* From it the New Testament derived the term "Beelzebul" (e.g., Matthew 10.25; Mark 3.22; Luke 11.15, 18–19). But it used the term simply to refer to the chief demon; any reference to the Canaanite god had been lost.

Baal was the king of the gods, a position that he took from the god of the sea, Yamm. The Canaanites worshipped him as present in many local sanctuaries. As a result, some texts speak of Baals in the plural. The Canaanites also thought that Baal fought with the god of death, Mot. The outcome of this struggle determined whether successive periods of seven years would be fertile or barren.

Baal Shem Tov (*c.* 1700–1760) *the popular name of Israel ben Eliezer* He was a Ukrainian Jew whom many consider to have founded Hasidism. "Baal Shem Tov" means "Master of the Good Name." It refers to the miraculous powers that Israel ben Eliezer allegedly possessed. He is also known as the "Besht." This term is an acronym, made from the first letters of Baal Shem Tov.

Little is actually known about the Baal Shem Tov's life. He is said to have worked wonders such as healing through a special name of God. The Baal Shem Tov is important today because of the religious movement he is said to have started. In his day normative Judaism in eastern Europe stressed a detailed study of Torah and a strict observance of Jewish rituals and a Jewish way of life. For the Baal Shem Tov, this form of practice distracted people from their highest purpose, communion with God. God's light, he said, was all-pervasive. Therefore, communion with God could and should be had in all of life. The means to such communion included singing, dancing, and emotion-filled prayer. From these roots Hasidism grew.

Babel, Tower of The way the Bible explains the multitude of languages that human beings speak. According to Genesis 11, the inhabitants of the Earth decided to build a tower to reach to the heavens. The kind of tower that the writer seems to have had in mind is the ziggurat. Ziggurats were huge pyramids, built in several steps or parallel layers. On top of them Mesopotamians placed temples to their gods (*see* Mesopotamian religions). They were a typical form of religious architecture in ancient Mesopotamia.

As Genesis tells the story, the god YHWH ("the Lord") was worried about what great things human beings might be able to accomplish. So he created the various languages. Because the builders could no longer communicate, they could not complete the tower. This disruption can be seen as

GOD's punishment on people who want to overstep human limitations.

Genesis derives the name Babel from the confusion of languages that resulted: the Hebrew verb meaning "to confuse" is *balal* (Genesis 11.9). Modern scholars are more inclined to see the name as referring to a region or place. Many suggest that it refers to the city of Babylon. Some have suggested that it refers to a temple within Babylon known as Bab-ilu, the "gateway of God."

Babylonian religion   *See* MESOPOTAMIAN RELIGIONS.

Baha'i
A religion founded in Iran in the second half of the 19th century. The Baha'i faith sees itself called to unite spiritually all the peoples of the world.

HISTORY

During the 1840s a religious figure in Iran known as the Bab ("gateway") predicted the coming of "the one whom GOD shall reveal." In 1863, one of his followers, now known as Baha'ullah (1817–92), claimed to be that one.

The teachings of the Bab and of Baha'ullah threatened the authority of orthodox Islamic scholars. As a result, Baha'ullah spent much of his life in exile and in jail. From 1868 until his death he lived in what is now Israel. For that reason, the center of the Baha'i community is located in Israel.

When Baha'ullah died, control of the community passed to his son, known in the Baha'i community as Abd al-Baha (1844–1921), and his grandson, Shoghi Effendi (1899–1957). It then passed to a board known as the Council of the Hands of the Cause (1957–62) and finally to an elected assembly, the International House of Justice (1962–present).

The Baha'i faith first attracted widespread attention with the missionary travels of Abd al-Baha. By the end of the 20th century it had roughly two million adherents.

TEACHINGS, PRACTICES, AND ORGANIZATION

The Baha'i faith sees itself as continuing the revelation of God found in JUDAISM, CHRISTIANITY, and ISLAM. The prophets of each of these traditions, it teaches, were genuine messengers from God. Each of them fulfilled the task assigned by God. But Baha'is insist that the process of God's revelation will never end. Neither MOSES nor JESUS nor MUHAMMAD was the last of God's messengers. For the contemporary world there is a new messenger, Baha'ullah. He was made known a new task: to unite spiritually all people.

Baha'is are enjoined to pray in private every day. In addition, local communities gather together on the first day of every month. (Baha'i months are 19 days long). A major Baha'i festival is Noruz, New Year's. In accordance with Persian practice it is celebrated on March 21, the time of the spring equinox. During the month prior to Noruz, Baha'is observe a fast. They neither eat nor drink from sunup to sundown; they eat and drink at night. (Muslims observe a similar fast during the Islamic month of Ramadan. Moreover, Baha'is are never permitted to drink alcohol.

During the 20th century a leading initiative of the Baha'i community was the construction of major houses of WORSHIP, one on each continent. The design of each house of worship reflects significant elements of its location. For example, the house of worship in New Delhi, India, is in the form of a LOTUS, a sacred plant in India. The brick work of the house of worship in Panama reflects stone work in the ancient temples of middle America. At the same time, all Baha'i houses of worship share certain features. For example, they have nine doorways and nine-sided domes. Baha'is see the number nine as a sign of the highest unity. Therefore, the doors and domes emphasize the unity that Baha'is believe characterizes God, all people, and all religions.

Further reading: John Ferraby, *All Things Made New: A Comprehensive Outline of the Baha'i Faith* (London: Baha'i Publishing Trust, 1975); Peter Smith, *The Babi and Baha'i Religions* (New York: Cambridge University Press, 1987); ———, *A*

Concise Encyclopedia of the Baha'i Faith (Oxford: Oneworld, 1999); ———, *A Short History of the Baha'i Faith* (Oxford: Oneworld, 1997).

Banaras Also spelled Benares, officially Varanasi; for Hindus the most sacred city in India. Banaras sits on the banks of the sacred GANGES RIVER. It has been important since antiquity. For example, the BUDDHA (sixth-century B.C.E.) preached his first sermon in Sarnath, one of its outlying districts.

Banaras is renowned for its stepped bathing places. These are known as ghats. Tremendous numbers of people from all parts of India flock to Banaras to bathe. The city also boasts more than 1,500 Hindu temples. The largest number of these temples honor SIVA. In addition, the city contains representations of all of the most important sacred sites in India.

Banaras may have originally sat at a place to ford the Ganges, that is, a place to cross it without a boat. Today people come to the city to ford a metaphorical stream, the stream of SAMSARA, and attain release from rebirth. As a result, Banaras is an especially auspicious place at which to die.

baptism RITUAL bathing or washing. Baptism is best known as the ritual by which people become members of the Christian church.

Many religious groups have practiced baptism. For example, baptism is the central ritual of the Mandaeans, who live in southern Iraq and southeastern Iran. It is so important that others who live around them call them "baptizers." The Mandaeans baptize in "living water," which they call "Jordan." A priest immerses them completely three times in this water. Afterward they are anointed with oil. Ideally, Mandaeans are baptized every Sunday. They have claimed that they are practicing the religion taught by John the Baptist.

Baptism seems to have been particularly important to religions of the Near East around the time of JESUS. The people that we learn about in the DEAD SEA SCROLLS seem to have baptized every day. Jews baptize, too. According to tradition, converts

to JUDAISM take a ritual bath known as a *mikveh*. This bath was also traditionally used by women after their menstrual periods.

Today, baptism is best-known as the ritual by which people join the Christian church. For Catholic, Orthodox, and some Protestant Christians, this ritual is a SACRAMENT. That is, it is a special way or means of receiving GOD'S GRACE. To modern scholars Christian baptism is a RITE OF PASSAGE. It is a ritual for passing from one stage of life to another. In baptism people pass from being outside the Christian church to being members of it.

Unlike the Mandaeans, Christians baptize a person only one time. Once baptized, a person is always baptized. That is true even for a person who renounces Christianity and then wants to be Christian again. But Christians have disagreed about when to baptize, how to baptize, and how it works. These disagreements are part of the reason why there are so many different Christian churches and denominations.

The earliest Christians baptized people as they converted to CHRISTIANITY. Most of these people were adults. In ancient times, some people waited to be baptized on their deathbeds. In other words, they practiced baptism as a rite of passage connected with death. They thought that if they were baptized at death, they would enter the world beyond with all their sins forgiven. One person baptized on his deathbed was the Roman emperor Constantine (*c.* 280–337), famous for removing all laws against Christianity.

Christians continue to baptize adult converts today. But for the most part Christian baptism is either a birth or a puberty ritual. Catholic, Orthodox, and some Protestant Christians generally practice baptism as a birth ritual. That is, they baptize infants. Other Protestants, such as Baptists, generally practice baptism as a puberty ritual. That is, they baptize people only when they have reached an age of spiritual maturity. At that age, the thinking goes, people are able to choose for themselves whether or not they want to be Christian.

Some Christians baptize by sprinkling with water. This is the way those who baptize infants prefer to baptize. Others insist that baptism requires total immersion. They have argued over such details as the number of times a person has to be immersed and whether or not a person must go into the water face first. Christians also disagree about how baptism works. Christians who baptize infants generally insist that in baptism God is active: His Holy Spirit stirs within the heart of the baptized person. Other Christians insist that baptism simply recognizes publicly a change that has already taken place in a person's heart.

In any case, Christians generally see baptism as a rebirth. Those baptized die to an old life and rise to a new one. This symbolism is in fact common in rites of passage. The New Testament connects the dying and rising of baptism with the death and resurrection of Jesus.

Baptist churches A variety of Protestantism especially common in the United States. Baptists accept only "believer's baptism," that is, the baptism of those who have personally accepted Christ. Traditionally they have also been some of the strongest advocates of a separation of church and state.

HISTORY

The Baptist churches resemble the Anabaptists of the Protestant Reformation in one very important respect: Both groups have insisted that only those persons should be baptized who were old enough to decide that they wanted to be baptized. The Anabaptists, however, arose on the European continent in the 16th century. They were the ancestors of the Mennonites and the Amish. The Baptist churches arose in the British Isles in the 17th century. They developed in quite a different direction.

At the beginning of the 17th century, people living in England generally thought that Christianity should be a state church, that is, a religion that the government officially accepted and promoted. This was the view held by Roman Catholics and Puritans as much as by Anglicans (*see* Anglicanism and Puritanism). In the setting of a state church, people were baptized as a matter of routine at birth.

In the mid-17th century, church leaders like Thomas Helwys and John Smyth reacted against this situation. In their eyes, the institution of the state church meant that a person's commitment to Christianity was not very serious. They began to preach that only believers should be baptized. They also began to insist that the relationship between believers and God was a private one. Government should have nothing to do with it.

The Baptists had their greatest success in the North American colonies of Great Britain and, after the Revolutionary War, in the United States. Several distinct movements have shaped the American Baptist churches. These include evangelism, abolitionism, modernism, and fundamentalism.

In the 18th century the Baptist churches embraced the evangelistic movement (*see* Evangelical Christianity and Fundamentalism, Christian). This movement sought to instill in people a fervent, heartfelt faith in Jesus. It emphasized the need for conversion and a personal experience of salvation. In order to reach the people who most needed to hear this message, preachers left church buildings behind and held public meetings known as revivals. Baptists adopted these methods enthusiastically. As a result, they found many adherents, especially in the Old South and on the frontiers. In addition, they attracted a large number of African Americans, both free and slave.

In the mid-19th century, the Baptist churches split over the issue of slavery. They formed two major "Conventions," the Northern, which favored abolishing slavery, and the Southern, which favored keeping it. For a variety of reasons, the Southern Baptist Convention was more successful. Today Southern Baptists outnumber any other Baptist group.

Toward the end of the 19th century North Americans became aware of a movement called modernism. This movement applied critical methods to the study of the Bible. It also generally favored an active agenda of social reform. Several prominent Baptists, such as the preacher Harry Emerson Fosdick and the biblical scholar Shailer Matthews, assumed leadership roles in the modernist movement.

At the beginning of the 20th century a reaction to modernism set in. Several groups advocated what they called the "fundamentals" of Christianity, including the view that every word of the Bible is literally true. In the first half of the 20th century controversies between modernists and fundamentalists rocked the Northern Baptists. Toward the end of the 20th century similar controversies erupted in the Southern Baptist Convention.

TEACHINGS

Baptists recognize no CREEDS or statements of faith. For them, the Bible is the final and ultimate authority. As a result, the beliefs and teachings of different groups of Baptists differ widely. For example, some Baptists emphasize that people are predestined for salvation. Others are "free will Baptists."

Baptists agree, however, that the Bible is the ultimate authority in all matters of faith. They generally conceive of the religious life in terms that derive from the evangelistic movement: An individual must recognize her or his sinful condition, accept God's gift of salvation, and be born again in order to be saved. As a result, Baptists emphasize that the church is a voluntary association.

PRACTICES

Baptist churches are nonliturgical. That is, they do not use the LITURGY or mass, which centers on the EUCHARIST, that the Orthodox and Catholic churches developed. The centerpiece of Baptist worship is the sermon (see PREACHING). Besides the sermon, Baptist services include music performed by soloists and choirs, hymns sung by the congregations, and prayers. Baptists continue to use the revival meetings that developed during the 18th century. They have also made effective use of mass media, for example, radio and television.

Baptists take their name from the practice of baptizing only believers, that is, people old enough to choose Christianity. Early on in their history they adopted the practice of baptizing by total immersion. Baptists also celebrate the eucharist or communion. But while Catholic and Orthodox Christians celebrate communion every Sunday, Baptists may celebrate it once a month. Instead of approaching an altar to receive communion, members of Baptist churches receive it where they are sitting.

ORGANIZATION

Baptists accept the NEW TESTAMENT teaching of the priesthood of all believers. For them, this teaching means that any person is qualified to minister to any other. But individual congregations appoint persons to perform the functions of pastor and deacon.

Baptists also strongly emphasize the independence of individual congregations. Some Baptist churches have remained isolated, but most have joined with other Baptist churches in regional and national associations. Representatives of the individual congregations make decisions about joint activities at meetings of these larger associations. In principle, however, the larger bodies have no authority over the individual congregations.

SIGNIFICANCE

Baptists have been actively involved in foreign missions, but they are sparsely represented outside of the United States. Within the United States, however, Baptists comprise the largest group of Protestants. Historically they were important in helping to separate church and state in American law. Through public figures like Billy Graham, Jerry Falwell, and Pat Robertson, they continued to influence American public life in the latter part of the 20th century. Although some devout Baptists, like President Clinton, were moderate or liberal, many Baptists have been associated with conservative causes, such as opposition to abortion (see ABORTION AND RELIGION).

Further reading: Nancy Ammerman, *Baptist Battles: Social Change and Religious Conflict in the Southern Baptist Convention* (New Brunswick, N.J.: Rutgers University Press, 1990); Bill J. Leonard, *Baptist Ways: A History* (Valley Forge, Penn.: Judson Press, 2003); James E. Wood, Jr., *Baptists and the American Experience* (Valley Forge, Penn.: Judson Press, 1976); R. Wayne Stacy, *A Baptist's Theology* (Macon, Ga.: Smyth & Helwys Publishing, 2000).

bar/bat mitzvah Hebrew meaning "son/daughter of the commandment." The term refers to a person of adult status in the Jewish community. It also refers more commonly to the RITE OF PASSAGE that marks the beginning of adulthood.

A Jewish boy is considered to reach religious adulthood at age 13, a girl at age 12. All forms of JUDAISM hold bar mitzvahs for boys. In the 20th century Reform and then Conservative and Reconstructionist Judaism developed a corresponding ritual for girls called bat mitzvah.

The bar mitzvah is typically celebrated during a Sabbath SYNAGOGUE service. The heart of the celebration consists of reading in Hebrew the TORAH and Haftarah portions assigned for the day. These are portions selected from the first and second part of the Hebrew BIBLE, respectively. It is also common for the bar mitzvah to comment on the passages read.

Because it is newer, the ritual for the bat mitzvah varies. It tends, however, to be observed with the same procedures as a bar mitzvah.

A bar/bat mitzvah is a festive occasion. The celebration includes a meal with family and friends and generally the receiving of gifts. It is also a major step in one's religious life. During the service one wears a prayer shawl for the first time in a synagogue. Afterward, a male and, in more liberal congregations, a female can be counted in the *minyan* or quota needed to hold prayer services.

Bardo Thodol (Tibetan "Book of the Dead")

Properly, Bar do thos grol; a group of writings in Tibetan BUDDHISM that describe the passage between death and rebirth. Tibetan Buddhism envisions an intermediary period between death and rebirth known as *bardo,* the time "between (*bar*) the two (*do*)." Ideally the period lasts 49 days. (Forty-nine is the square of seven, which is considered a sacred number.) In actuality the length of the *bardo* may vary with the amount of KARMA a person has. The writings of the Bardo Thodol describe what happens during this period.

The Bardo Thodol identifies three stages between death and rebirth. First comes the state immediately after death, known as *Chikhai Bardo.* Then comes a transitional state known as *Chonyid Bardo.* The final state is the state of being reborn, known as *Sidpa Bardo.* In between each state a period of unconsciousness intervenes. People who are so enlightened that they have no karma do not experience these stages.

At the beginning of the first stage, deceased persons are unconscious and unaware that they have died. This condition lasts perhaps three and a half to four days. The first stage culminates in a vision of clear light. At first the light is pure. Eventually it becomes obscured by the reflexes of karma.

During the second stage the deceased see VISIONS. These visions result from the karma that was acquired during life on Earth and must now work itself out. During the first seven days the deceased see visions of peaceful deities, among them the BUDDHAS associated with the center and the four cardinal directions: Vairocana, Vajrasattva, Ratnasambhava, Amitabha, and Amoghasiddhi. They see these Buddhas in both their masculine and feminine aspects. During the second seven days the deceased see visions of wrathful deities, or rather, of the same Buddhas, but now under their wrathful aspects.

During the second stage people believe that they actually have physical bodies. The third stage begins when they realize that their bodies are only illusory. They begin to desire bodies, and this desire leads to rebirth. As desire arises, the deceased begin to see the world into which they will be reborn, whether it be the world of *devas, asuras,* human beings, animals, *pretas,* or hell. (Devas, asuras, and pretas are mythological beings.) Each of these worlds is associated with a particular colored light: dull white, green, yellow, blue, red, and smoke-colored, respectively. The third stage concludes when the deceased are actually reborn. Only those who are reborn in the world of human beings advance along the way to ultimate release (*see* NIRVANA).

Many Tibetans believe that one's final thoughts determine one's existence after death. As a result, they read the Bardo Thodol to a dying person or over an image of the corpse. These writings also form the basis of a ritual that seeks release for the living. Those who perform this ritual spend 49 days shut up in completely dark caves. During that time they attempt to experience while still alive the events that the Bardo Thodol describes. This experience is helpful, they say, in attaining ultimate release.

Benedictines One of the earliest and most influential orders of Roman Catholic MONKS AND NUNS. Benedictines follow the rule of St. Benedict (*c.* 480–*c.* 547). This rule divides the day into times for worship, work, and study. It is moderate rather than harsh. For example, it does not greatly emphasize fasting or lack of sleep. By following the rule Benedictines cultivate obedience, endurance, humility, and gentleness.

Benedictines were extremely important to European civilization in the medieval period. The most important monastery was at Cluny, France (founded 909/910). Benedictine MISSIONARIES were crucial in bringing CHRISTIANITY to Europe. The two best examples are probably Augustine of CANTERBURY (d. 604) and Boniface (*c.* 675–754), who brought Christianity to the Anglo-Saxons and the Germans, respectively. Benedictines were also intellectual leaders. They copied manuscripts and, like Rabanus Maurus (780–856), helped create cultural revivals. The poetry and music of a medieval Benedictine nun, Hildegard of Bingen (1098–1179), attracted considerable interest in the late 20th century.

The Benedictines experienced a worldwide revival from about 1800 to the second VATICAN COUNCIL (1962–65). As part of the revival, Benedictine houses were founded in North America. At the end of the 20th century North American Benedictines were active in promoting Christianity, teaching, and providing health care.

Bhagavad-Gita A Sanskrit title meaning "The Song of the Lord"; perhaps the most widely revered of the Hindu scriptures. The Bhagavad-Gita is a poem that makes up a small part of the mammoth Hindu epic, the *Mahabharata.* Its author is unknown. The epic is attributed to an ancient sage named Vyasa, "the compiler." He is said to have dictated the *Mahabharata* to GANESA, the elephant-headed god. Like much of Indian literature the Bhagavad-Gita is difficult to date. Scholars usually assign it to the period between 200 B.C.E. and 200 C.E.

The Bhagavad-Gita contains 18 chapters. They present a conversation between the warrior hero, Arjuna, and his charioteer, KRISHNA. The conversation occurs early in the morning before the beginning of a great battle. In the battle Arjuna and his brothers will fight against their cousins. The problem for Arjuna is that many other revered figures, such as Arjuna's teacher, are fighting for his cousins. Seeing in the ranks of the enemy those to whom he owes the utmost respect, Arjuna throws down his bow and refuses to fight.

During the conversation that follows, Krishna teaches many important truths of HINDUISM. The poem is very complex, and no brief summary can do it justice. But it is possible to identify some of the poem's main topics.

Krishna identifies three paths in Hinduism, which he calls YOGAS, "disciplines." These are the path of insight, the path of action, and the path of devotion to Krishna alone as GOD. In the path of insight Krishna teaches the true nature of the ATMAN or self. Eternal and unchanging, the self does not experience change. Therefore, it cannot truly be born, die, or be injured. In the path of action he teaches the proper attitude with which to act. According to Krishna one should perform one's DHARMA or duty without thinking about the "fruits" of one's action. As a warrior, Arjuna's duty requires him to fight.

One climax of the Bhagavad-Gita comes in chapter 11. The *Mahabharata* as a whole presents Krishna as a neighboring prince who has come to help Arjuna and his brothers win back their kingdom. During the Bhagavad-Gita, Arjuna asks Krishna to reveal his true nature. What follows is chapter 11, one of the masterpieces of the human attempt to describe the encounter with God. Another climax of the Bhagavad-Gita comes near the end of the poem. There Krishna summarizes the path of devotion this way: "Abandoning all thought of proper action [*dharma*], seek refuge in me alone. I will free you from all ills. Do not fear" (18.66).

Taken at face value, the Bhagavad-Gita encourages soldiers to fight. The great Indian thinker B. G. Tilak (1856–1920) saw the Bhagavad-Gita as a call to use armed violence and expel the British conquerors and rulers from India. But the Bhagavad-Gita was also a favorite scripture of Mohandas Gandhi (1869–1948). He read it allegorically and used it to champion his way of opposing the British with "soul-force" and nonviolence rather than "body-force" and violence.

bhakti   A Sanskrit word meaning "devotion"; one of the major "paths" or forms of Hinduism. When Hindus practice bhakti, they try to cultivate a personal relationship with a god or a Goddess. The general religious attitude is expressed well in the Bhagavad-Gita, where the divine Krishna invites worshippers: "Abandoning all thought of proper action [*dharma*], seek refuge in me alone. I will free you from all ills. Do not fear" (18.66).

The bhakti movement began in south India around the seventh century. At that time its advocates included poets known as Alvars, who were devotees of Vishnu, and Nayanars, who were devotees of Siva. This early bhakti became popular for many reasons. It utilized the language commonly spoken as well as the priestly and scholarly language, Sanskrit; it offered religious rewards to all despite their standing in the system of ritual classes (*varnas*, *see* Caste in Hinduism); and it appealed directly to worshippers without requiring a priest as an intermediary. As a result, bhakti was a major factor in the revival of Hinduism in India. It helped Hinduism replace ascetic movements like Buddhism and Jainism.

From the Tamil-speaking region of south India where it began, bhakti spread to the rest of south India. By the 14th century it had spread to north India as well. Especially in the north bhakti poets had close contacts with Muslim mystics known as Sufis (*see* Sufism). The Hindu devotees and Muslim mystics shared a common vocabulary, metaphors, ritual techniques, and aspirations. In the region of Bengal in northeastern India a saint named Caitanya began a movement of intense devotion to Krishna as the supreme Godhead. In the mid-1960s this form of bhakti came to the United States. There it became known as the Hare Krishna movement. In the Punjab in northwestern India a religious leader named Nanak (1469–1539) built a religious structure on the foundations of bhakti, one that transcended the divisions between Hindus and Muslims. Those who follow him and the other nine gurus in his tradition are known as Sikhs (*see* Sikhism).

Hinduism classifies devotees into three main groups: worshippers of Siva (Saivas), worshippers of Vishnu (Vaishnavas), and worshippers of the feminine divine power known as *sakti* (Saktas). Devotees often use images in worship, but some worship is aniconic or imageless. One common practice is to repeat one of the god's names for an extended period. This practice led to the popular designation "Hare Krishnas." Devotees also use poems and songs extensively. These poems and songs may be sung by groups of devotees in public as well as in private. The goal of bhakti is emotional enthusiasm and ecstasy, which devotees consider to be the experience of the very presence of God. In bhakti this experience is equivalent to ultimate release.

Devotees may develop a variety of relationships with God. For example, a devotee may be God's servant, God's child or, as in the case of the worship of the child Krishna, God's parent. But from the Alvars and Nayanars to the present, one relationship has been most common: that symbolized by sexual love. Usually the devotee claims to be married to the God, perhaps in repudiation of a human marriage. In Bengali Vaishnavism the more profound relationship is said to be the extramarital affair. In relation to God as Vishnu or Siva, male as well as female devotees always assume the female roles of wife and lover.

Bible, biblical literature   The sacred book of Jews and Christians, and similar writings by ancient Jews and Christians. The name *Bible* ultimately derives from Byblos, a center of the papyrus trade in the ancient world. The writings of the Bible and biblical literature were often preserved on papyrus in ancient times.

CONTENTS OF THE BIBLE AND OTHER BIBLICAL LITERATURE

Both Jews and Christians call their sacred writings the Bible. They differ, however, on what writings make up the Bible. The distinction between the Bible and biblical literature more broadly comes from the formulation of canons, that is, lists of authoritative books. Ancient Jews and Christians produced a wealth of religious literature. Canons allowed them to distinguish between books that they accepted as authoritative and those that they

did not. For both Jews and Christians, it took a number of centuries to agree upon the canon of the Bible. Some see that long process as guided by GOD.

The Bible for Jews

Jews use a Bible that contains 24 books. Because it is written in Hebrew, it is sometimes known as the Hebrew Bible or Hebrew scriptures (*see* SCRIPTURES, HEBREW). A better name for it may be *Tanakh*. This word is an acronym made from the first letter of each of the Bible's three parts: TORAH (teaching), *Nevi'im* (PROPHETS), and *Ketuvim* (writings). The formulation of the canon for these three parts took place over a period of more than 500 years, from the end of the Babylonian exile (538 B.C.E.) to a council of rabbis in 90 C.E.

TORAH	THE FIVE BOOKS OF MOSES	NEVI'IM	THE PROPHETS
בראשית	Genesis	יהושע	Joshua
שמות	Exodus	שופטים	Judges
ויקרא	Leviticus	שמואל א	1 Samuel
במדבר	Numbers	שמואל ב	2 Samuel
דברים	Deuteronomy	מלכים א	1 Kings
		מלכים ב	2 Kings
		ישעיה	Isaiah
KETUVIM	THE WRITINGS	ירמיה	Jeremiah
תהילים	Psalms	יחזקאל	Ezekiel
משלי	Proverbs		
איוב	Job		THE TWELVE MINOR PROPHETS
שיר השירים	The Song of Songs	הושע	Hosea
רות	Ruth	יואל	Joel
איכה	Lamentations	עמוס	Amos
קהלת	Ecclesiastes	עבדיה	Obadiah
אסתר	Esther	יונה	Jonah
דניאל	Daniel	מיכה	Micah
עזרא	Ezra	נחום	Nahum
נחמיה	Nehemiah	חבקוק	Habakkuk
דברי הימים א	1 Chronicles	צפניה	Zephaniah
דברי הימים ב	2 Chronicles	חגי	Haggai
		זכריה	Zechariah
		מלאכי	Malachi

The Jewish scriptures, consisting of the Torah, the Prophets and the Writings

Torah, sometimes translated "law" rather than "teaching," is for Jews the most important part of the Bible. It consists of the first five books, traditionally attributed to MOSES. Through stories of CREATION and the FLOOD; ABRAHAM, SARAH, and their descendants; and the EXODUS, Torah teaches how god wants his people to live (*see* TEN COMMANDMENTS).

Nevi'im contains two kinds of prophets. The "Former Prophets" detail how God was active in his people's past. They include the books of Joshua, Judges, Samuel, and Kings. The "Latter Prophets," describe how God was active at their time. They include the books of ISAIAH, JEREMIAH, EZEKIEL, and The Twelve. (Christians print The Twelve as 12 separate books and call them "Minor Prophets.")

Jews consider *Ketuvim* the least important part of the Bible. It contains a variety of books, such as PSALMS, Proverbs, Ezra-Nehemiah, Chronicles, JOB, and DANIEL (*see also* WISDOM LITERATURE).

The Bible for Christians

Christians call the Hebrew scriptures the Old Testament and recognize them as part of their Bible. To this Old Testament they add another 27 books that they call the NEW TESTAMENT. The formulation of the canon of the New Testament took place from the second to the fourth centuries.

The New Testament contains several types of material. It begins with four GOSPELS, Matthew, Mark, Luke, and John. They present the "good news" (or gospel) of CHRISTIANITY by recounting the life and sayings of JESUS. The ACTS OF THE APOSTLES tells how the followers of Jesus, known as APOSTLES, spread that good news out from Jerusalem through the eastern Mediterranean world (Turkey and Greece today) to Rome. The most prominent apostle in Acts is PAUL, and the next portion of the New Testament consists of several EPISTLES or letters that he allegedly wrote. Some of them are almost certainly not by Paul. The New Testament also contains letters by other followers of Jesus—JAMES, PETER, John, and Jude—and an anonymous letter known as Hebrews. The final book, the REVELATION to John, is an example of APOCALYPTIC LITERATURE.

It provides a symbolic account of how God will defeat those who are tormenting Christians and establish a new HEAVEN and earth.

For Protestants, the Bible consists simply of an Old Testament that is identical with Tanakh but is divided into 39 books and the New Testament. But for Roman Catholics and Eastern Orthodox Christians the Old Testament contains more books than the Hebrew Bible. That is because Christianity arose before the canon of the Hebrew Bible was set. The earliest Christians used a larger collection of writings as their Old Testament, and Catholics and Orthodox Christians continue to do so.

Catholics call the extra writings in their Old Testament "deuterocanonical." The term means that although these writings are not in the Hebrew scriptures, they are equally authoritative. Protestants call these books the APOCRYPHA. They include story literature (Tobit and Judith), wisdom literature (Wisdom of Solomon and the Wisdom of Jesus Son of Sirach, also known as Ecclesiasticus), history books (1 and 2 Maccabees), writings attributed to Jeremiah and his secretary Baruch, and parts of the books of Esther and Daniel that are not in the Hebrew Scriptures, such as the story of Susanna. Roman Catholics and Eastern Orthodox Christians differ somewhat on the deuterocanonical books. In addition to the books that Catholics accept, Eastern Orthodox churches also accept a book that has several names, depending upon the collection in which it is found: 2 Ezra, 1 Esdras, and 3 Esdras.

Other Biblical Literature

Jews and Christians have always known about writings that were omitted from the Bible. Such writings include books like the Shepherd of Hermas and the Didache (the Teaching) of the Twelve Apostles. Before the canon was set, some people thought of them as authoritative scripture.

In the early 19th century, European scholars began to comb through ancient manuscript collections in the Middle East. They also began to uncover ancient writings in archaeological excavations. In the process, they have found copies of many works of biblical literature, some of which had been lost and forgotten. Two discoveries from the 1940s have become particularly famous. The DEAD SEA SCROLLS, discovered in 1948 in jars hidden in caves, contained biblical texts from the second and first centuries B.C.E. They also contained writings specific to the community that produced the manuscripts. The Nag Hammadi Codices, discovered in Nag Hammadi, Egypt, in 1945, contain many writings in the Coptic language, especially in the tradition of GNOSTICISM. (*Codices* means books.) Among them was a complete copy of the ancient Gospel of THOMAS.

In modern times scholars have gathered 52 writings left out of the Bible into a collection that they call the Pseudepigrapha. It includes several apocalypses, books of wisdom literature, psalms and prayers, books that expand on biblical stories, and a set of books called testaments, such as the Testament of the Twelve Patriarchs. Unlike the Old and New Testaments, these testaments are actually individual books. Other modern collections, less standardized but no less interesting, gather all that remains of the various gospels outside the New Testament.

Jews and Christians do not recognize these texts as authoritative. Nevertheless, they are very important. They also help us understand much better the religion of Second Temple JUDAISM (from 538 B.C.E. to 70 C.E.) and early Christianity. They help us understand the processes that led the books of the Bible to be written, standardized, and accepted into the canon. Finally, they help us identify and appreciate the distinctive themes of biblical books.

INTERPRETING THE BIBLE

Many people use the Bible as a source of "proof texts." That is, they want to demonstrate a point, so they look for a sentence that makes the point and quote it. Members of other religious communities, such as BUDDHISM, often approach their religious texts in the same way. One problem with this method is that it takes quotations out of context. Another is that it usually depends uncritically upon a translation of the text. A third is that people can use it to prove contradictory positions.

Compare "a person is justified by faith apart from works prescribed by the law" (Romans 3.28) with "a person is justified by works and not by faith alone" (James 2.24).

From ancient times, Jews and Christians have developed other means of interpreting the Bible. They sometimes call this interpretation exegesis, which means "reading out of" the texts. Some distinguish exegesis from eisegesis. This very obscure word means "reading into" the texts.

Traditional Jewish Interpretations

In Jewish tradition God did not just reveal himself to his people through written words. He also did so orally, in the form of traditions handed down from generation to generation. Judaism has traditionally held that worshippers need this "oral Torah" to make sense of the written Torah. For example, the written Torah says to keep the Sabbath holy, but what does that mean? The oral Torah answers that question. For example, it tells what kinds of things one can and cannot do on the Sabbath. According to tradition, oral Torah began with Moses, the first rabbi, and continued through rabbinical discussions. Today the oral Torah is found in the TALMUD.

In antiquity and the Middle Ages, Jews interpreted the Bible in other ways, too. Many ancient interpreters favored a kind of interpretation known as allegory. They thought that biblical stories such as the Tower of Babel may not have been literally true but were told to make some point. Other interpreters favored the literal meaning. In the Middle Ages some of them wrote commentaries on parts of the Bible, explaining what the text actually said. An important example is the commentary on Torah by a writer known as Rashi (1040–1105). The approach of Moses Maimonides (d. 1204) was different. A philosopher, he believed that God was one and incorporeal, that is, had no body. His famous *Guide of the Perplexed* demonstrated that, although the Bible speaks of God as having body parts such as a face and arms, he actually has neither. Thinkers in the tradition of KABBALAH took yet a different approach. They found hidden, mystical teachings in the biblical books. The *Zohar,* a kabbalistic book, introduced the idea that the biblical text has four kinds of meaning. The four meanings are the literal (*peshat*), the allegorical (*remez*), the meaning related to HALAKHAH or living a Jewish life (*derash*), and the mystical (*sod*). Taking the first letter of each word, some called this system of interpretation *pardes* for short; the pronunciation of the word alludes to paradise.

Traditional Christian Interpretations

Allegorical interpretation attracted many ancient Christian interpreters, just as it attracted many ancient Jewish ones. Christian interpreters connected allegories with a saying from Paul: "the letter kills, but the Spirit gives life" (2 Cor. 3.6). Unlike Jews, however, ancient Christians tended to find in the Hebrew scriptures prefigurations of Jesus. This kind of interpretation is already found in writings of the New Testament. Paul sees ADAM as a "type" of CHRIST (Rom. 5.14), and 1 Peter sees the great flood as prefiguring Christian BAPTISM (1 Pet. 3.18–22). Some early Christians thought that the entire Old Testament foretold Jesus. They were willing to make liberal use of allegorical interpretation to prove it.

Similar to the Jewish notion of *pardes,* Christians in the Middle Ages formulated a fourfold method of interpretation. Each text was said to have four meanings: the literal, the allegorical (concerned with doctrine), the tropological (concerned with morality), and the anagogical (concerned with the believer's final destiny). But some in the Middle Ages emphasized just the literal meaning of the Bible.

During the Renaissance scholars made intense efforts to study the original languages of the Bible in order to determine its literal meaning as precisely as possible. They also began to use ancient manuscripts in an effort to reconstruct as accurately as possible the original text of the Bible. The Protestant Reformers benefited from these approaches (*see* REFORMATION, PROTESTANT). They rejected all meanings but the literal, which they determined by grammatical analysis and historical context. But the Reformers did not always accept all of the Bible as equally true. For example, Martin Luther said that the central message of the Bible was the teaching of God's love in Christ. One should accept everything else that the Bible had to say only to the extent that it helped communicate this message.

Modern Interpretations

In the 17th century, a Jewish philosopher, Baruch Spinoza (1632–37), anticipated modern biblical criticism. He did not assume that God had revealed truth in the Bible and then try to find that truth. He took the Bible as a human product and tried to determine the extent to which it and Jewish traditions about it were historically true. Even before these efforts Spinoza's ideas had gotten him expelled from the Jewish community. Eventually, however, this form of interpretation came to dominate among academic biblical scholars in Europe and North America—Jews, Protestants, and Catholics alike.

These scholars have tried to determine how the biblical texts came to be written. One famous example is the "documentary hypothesis" of the origin of Torah developed by the German scholar Julius Wellhausen (1844–1918). It sees Torah as combining four documents, denoted J, E, P, and D, written over several centuries. Another famous example concerns the "synoptic problem," that is, how to explain the similar words and structures of Matthew, Mark, and Luke. The common answer today makes Mark the source of Matthew and Luke, along with a collection of sayings of Jesus that Mark did not use (*see* Q SOURCE).

Modern scholars have also tried to read the books of the Bible not as timeless revelation but in terms of the contexts in which they were written. Some psalms, for example, seem designed to be used for the coronation ceremony of the kings of ancient Israel and Judah. This kind of criticism can have radical results. For example, German critics in the middle of the 19th century explored the difference between the Aramaic world of ideas, in which Jesus and his disciples lived, and the Greek world of ideas, in which Christian doctrine developed (*see* DOGMA AND DOCTRINE). They pointed out that in ancient Aramaic "son of God" simply meant a righteous person. In ancient Greek, however, it had special connotations. Greek-speaking Christians later developed these connotations into the doctrine of the INCARNATION. The scholars claimed, however, that Jesus and his followers would neither have understood nor accepted those later ideas.

In the last 200 years archaeologists have contributed much to our understanding of the Bible. Much of their work has confirmed claims in the Bible, but much of it has also called the Bible into question. For example, the book of Joshua famously records the collapse of the walls of Jericho during the Israelite invasion. According to archaeologists, however, Jericho had already been uninhabited for a long time by the time of that invasion. The story was probably invented later to explain ruins that people could see.

New Testament interpreters have been particularly interested in the life of Jesus. Many have tried to reconstruct "the historical Jesus." The controversial "Jesus seminar" has done this recently. Members of the seminar produced a book identifying the authentic and inauthentic sayings of Jesus by voting on each passage. Other scholars, however, doubt that it is possible accurately to reconstruct the historical Jesus. For one thing, the best attempts to do so have produced very different images of Jesus. For example, according to Albert Schweitzer (1875–1965), what was distinctive about Jesus was his "eschatological consciousness," his sense that the world was about to end. More recent scholars have begun to reject that view.

Modern interpreters of the Bible take an interest in many more methods and topics than those just mentioned. But it is also important to remember that not all Jews and Christians have embraced such views. For them the Bible is not a human product but contains ultimate truth. At the beginning of the 20th century, an extreme reaction against this biblical criticism emerged in FUNDA-MENTALISM. It insists that the Bible is the verbally inspired word of God. As such the Bible is literally true and without error.

Further reading: Adele Berlin and Marc Zvi Brettler, eds., *The Jewish Study Bible: Jewish Publication Society Tanakh Translation* (New York: Oxford University Press, 2004); Benson Bobrick, *Wide as the Waters: The Story of the English Bible and the Revolution It Inspired* (New York: Simon & Schuster, 2001); R. H. Charles, *Apocrypha and Pseudepigrapha of the Old Testament* (Oxford: Oxford University Press, 1998); Michael D. Coogan et al., eds., *The New Oxford Annotated NRSV Bible with the Apocrypha*, 3d ed., ed. (New York: Oxford University Press, 2001); Bart D. Ehrman, *Lost Scriptures: Books That Did Not Make It into the New Testament* (New York: Oxford University Press, 2003); William Yarchin, *History of Biblical Interpretation: A Reader* (Peabody, Mass.: Hendrickson Publishers, 2004).

birth rituals Religious rites performed in connection with a birth of a child. The mystery of birth is recognized by RITUALS and observances in virtually all religions. It is a joyous occasion for parents and the community, yet at the same time is recognized to be dangerous and perhaps also polluting, especially for the mother. During pregnancy, often special spiritual as well as physical precautions are taken on behalf of her well-being and that of the child. In HINDUISM, for example, she may be covered with flowers and amulets. At the time of birth, she may be moved to a separate lodge apart from family and community, as in ancient Japan. The secluded mother may be accompanied by selected women. But she is taboo to all others, including even her husband, because of the pollution and sacred awe associated with the event. After birth, the mother in many societies purifies herself, perhaps by a ritual bath. In the traditional usage of the Church of England, she went to church for a rite of thanks and blessing called the "Churching of Women," and was expected to do this before appearing socially.

Birth rites for the newborn child are also common. In Japan a child is presented to the local SHINTO shrine about a month after birth. In many Christian traditions infants are baptized as soon after birth as convenient (*see* CHRISTIANITY and BAPTISM), thus accompanying physical birth with a sign of spiritual birth. In Hinduism, many stages of a small child's life, such as the first eating of solid food and the first haircut, are marked by life-cycle rituals. In JUDAISM young males receive CIRCUMCISION eight days after birth in a rite giving the child a Hebrew name and establishing religious identity. A Muslim father whispers the call to PRAYER in a newborn infant's ear so that the first words he hears are sacred.

Birth is also fraught with larger symbolic significance for religion. Stages of the spiritual life, particularly major initiations and religious encounters, are often seen as spiritual equivalents of physical birth, and are full of symbols to that effect (*see* INITIATION, RELIGIOUS). In the initiations of young men in some primal societies, the boys are buried under leaves or left in small, round, womb-like huts, and when they first emerge are treated like newborn infants. The Christian rite of baptism is said by the apostle PAUL to represent spiritual death and rebirth. Persons who have undergone profound conversion experiences often speak of themselves as "born again," as though now doing spiritually what was once done physically. Birth is therefore a continuing presence in human life on all planes of being.

Bodhidharma (sixth century C.E.)   *known in Japan as Daruma; the first patriarch of the Ch'an or Zen school of* BUDDHISM   It is difficult to separate fact from legend in accounts of Bodhidharma's life. In any case, the details of his biography illustrate significant aspects of ZEN BUDDHISM. As the following shows, they sometimes resort to extreme events to do so.

Bodhidharma is said to have been a scholar of a Buddhist scripture known as the *Lankavatara Sutra.* He was brought from India to China by Emperor Wu of the Liang dynasty, a Chinese emperor concerned with fostering Buddhism. In disgust at the self-importance of the emperor, a violation of fundamental Buddhist teachings, Bodhidharma left the capital and took up residence in a cave on a moun-

tain. There he sat facing the cave wall and meditating for nine years. As often happens when meditating, Bodhidharma had difficulty staying awake. To alleviate this problem, he is said to have cut off his eyelids. Falling to the ground, they became the first tea plants. (Zen monks cultivated tea to help them stay awake while meditating.)

The distinctive approach that Zen takes to Buddhism emerges from another legendary event. Emperor Wu is said to have asked Bodhidharma what Zen was. Bodhidharma replied with four brief statements: It does not depend upon words; it points directly to the human mind or heart; it sees into one's true nature; it attains Buddhahood.

bodhisattva   A Sanskrit word that literally means "a being whose nature (*sattva*) is perfect wisdom (*bodhi*)"; an important figure in BUDDHISM. The term is used differently in the various Buddhist schools. It is especially important in the schools known as Mahayana.

In THERAVADA BUDDHISM, the Buddhism common in southeast Asia, a bodhisattva is a being who is on the way to becoming a BUDDHA. (A Buddha is a being who discovers the path to enlightenment and NIRVANA. In this school the most important bodhisattva was Siddharta Gautama (sixth century B.C.E.), the Buddha who appeared in this world, prior to his enlightenment. Theravada Buddhists often tell stories about this bodhisattva's previous lives. Known as *jatakas* or "birth stories," they frequently take the form of animal fables. Some, such as "The Monkey and the Crocodile," have even become children's stories in North America. Another important bodhisattva in Theravada is the present form of the Buddha Maitreya. Maitreya is the Buddha who will come and usher in a golden age. At the present he lives in a heaven known as Tushita.

MAHAYANA BUDDHISM, the form of Buddhism common in east Asia, developed a somewhat different idea of the bodhisattva. It urges all Buddhists to strive to become bodhisattvas.

According to Mahayana teachings the bodhisattva path begins when the thought of enlightenment arises in the mind. This thought involves a desire for wisdom; it also involves compassion for others. The thought of enlightenment leads persons to make a series of vows. These vows in turn determine their future efforts.

Some Mahayana texts describe the bodhisattva path in terms of six perfections. Other texts add four more. The ten perfections are: giving, morality, patience, valiant effort, concentration, wisdom, skill in means, the vows of the bodhisattva, power, and knowledge. To cultivate these perfections takes not years or centuries but lifetimes and eons. The more time spent as a bodhisattva, the more time there is in which to act out of compassion for the benefit of other beings. So the longer the time spent as a bodhisattva, the better.

Mahayana Buddhism tells many myths about bodhisattvas. It also has many cults dedicated to those bodhisattvas who have reached the highest levels of perfection. Such bodhisattvas are so great that they reside not on Earth but in HEAVEN. From heaven they act out of compassion for those who are suffering here on Earth and in other worlds.

In Mahayana Buddhism three celestial bodhisattvas are most important. One of them is Maitreya, whom Theravada Buddhists also recognize. Mahayana says that Maitreya is a figure of light who inspires Buddhist teachers and guides persons after death. Because he is coming to usher in a golden age, his worship has given rise to messianic societies that have fostered political unrest and revolution (*see* MESSIAH).

Another important bodhisattva in Mahayana Buddhism is Manjusri. He is said to be an eternal youth. Images show him wearing a five-pointed crown, holding a book and a sword, and accompanied by a lion. According to Mahayana teachings, Manjusri could become a Buddha immediately, but he refuses to enter the ultimate enlightenment so long as a single other being remains in SAMSARA.

The bodhisattva AVALOKITESVARA is renowned for compassion. Known in Chinese as Kuanyin and Japanese as Kannon, he has often been envisioned in female form in China and Japan. A helper in every need, he—or she—is a protector of women, especially women in labor.

Bon   A religion in Tibet. It dates to the period before the coming of BUDDHISM in the eighth century (*see* TIBETAN RELIGION). Practitioners of Bon are known as Bon-pos.

A bodhisattva is a follower of the Buddha who renounces the path to nirvana in order to help others seek enlightenment. This wooden image of a bodhisattva is from Japan's Heian period (794–1185). *(Art Resource, N.Y.)*

Before the coming of Buddhism, Bon-pos seem to have practiced elaborate rituals to ensure the fate of the soul, especially the souls of kings, after death. In the eighth and ninth centuries, however, Bon was suppressed in favor of Buddhism. It has been a minority religion ever since.

After the ninth century Bon developed forms very similar to Buddhism. Today it recognizes an enlightened being, similar to the BUDDHA, named Tonpa Shenrap; he is said to have revealed the truth of Bon teaching. It also has a monastic tradition, a large body of literature, and its own deities, whom Buddhists have adopted as lesser gods. Bon RITUALS are similar to Tibetan Buddhist rituals, but they differ in some details. For example, Bon-pos circumambulate or walk around sacred sites counterclockwise: Buddhists circumambulate clockwise. Bon priests also have a distinctive headcovering: They wear black hats instead of the yellow or red hats worn by members of some Buddhist schools. Only recently has Bon literature started to become accessible to North American and European scholars.

Brahma The creator god in texts of Hindu mythology known as the PURANAS. The Puranas identify three families of deities according to function. The heads of these families are Brahma the creator, VISHNU the preserver, and SIVA the destroyer. The name Brahma is related to BRAHMAN, the word for the ultimate reality that, according to the UPANISHADS and VEDANTA philosophy, underlies all appearances. Indeed, in some contexts the two words have the very same form. So it is possible that modern readers have sometimes mistaken the one for the other.

Several myths connect Brahma with the origin of the world at the beginning of each cycle of generation and decay. For example, one well-known image depicts Brahma as seated on a LOTUS, which grows from the navel of Vishnu while the latter sleeps on the coiled world-serpent Sesha. Myths also tell of Brahma granting the gift of eternal life. Despite such myths, Brahma is rarely worshipped.

brahman A crucial idea in HINDUISM, especially in the UPANISHADS and VEDANTA philosophy. Brahman refers to the reality that underlies and supports the world as it appears to the senses.

Originally, brahman referred to the ritual formulas spoken during the SACRIFICES described in the sacred books known as the VEDA. In this sense, brahman is related to two other words: BRAHMIN or "priest," the name of the RITUAL class in Hinduism whose members performed the sacrifice, and Brahmanas, the commentaries on the ritual texts of the Veda. The Brahmanas identified rich webs of connections between the world at large and the Vedic sacrifices. They refer to brahman as the energy that made the sacrifices work.

The Upanishads have a wider view of brahman. In them brahman is no longer limited to the sacrifice. Instead, it is considered to be the unseen, unseeable support for everything that is seen. The Upanishads teach many things about this brahman, and what they teach is not always consistent. For example, some verses of the Upanishads claim that everything is brahman. Others deny that brahman can be identified with anything. Many passages, however, assert that the brahman is identical with the reality that underlies the human person, which is often known as ATMAN.

It is difficult to grasp what is unseen and unseeable. The Upanishads try to understand brahman in many ways. One particularly important method that they use is known as regressive reasoning. A person takes up an object for consideration, say, the body. She or he asks what supports that object, then what supports the support, and so on. The hope is that the procedure will eventually work back to what supports or sustains all things. A famous example occurs in the text known as the *Brihadaranyaka Upanishad*. That Upanishad records a series of questions that Gargi Vacaknavi asks her husband, Yajnavalkya. Gargi first asks what sustains water. Then she goes through a series that includes such items as wind and the worlds of sun, moon, and stars. Her questioning eventually leads her to ask what supports the world of brahman. At that point Yajnavalkya warns Gargi that it is dangerous to ask too many questions: "Gargi, do not question too much, lest your head fall off" (3.6).

In the first centuries C.E. thinkers attempted to systematize the teachings of the Upanishads in short formulas of two or three words. These "aphorisms" are so short that they are almost meaningless without a commentary. The most important collection of these teachings was the *Vedanta-Sutra* of Badarayana, also known as the *Brahma-Sutra*. Later, from roughly 500 to 1500, thinkers wrote commentaries on these aphorisms and on the Upanishads themselves. In doing so, they founded several schools of philosophy known as Vedanta.

According to SANKARA, the best known of the thinkers, brahman has three characteristics: being, consciousness, and bliss. Sankara actually identifies two levels of brahman. In and of itself, brahman is impersonal. But on a lower level, brahman appears to human beings in the form of a person, that is, as a god. Sankara's Vedanta is known as Advaita, which means "non-dual." That is because Sankara teaches that the reality of the world—brahman—and the reality of the human being—atman—are "not two" different realities.

Other Vedanta teachers, such as Ramanuja and Madhva, reject Sankara's impersonal brahman. For them, brahman is simply the personal God, known by various names as VISHNU, SIVA, and Devi. For Ramanuja, the universe is the body of this God. For Madhva, however, brahman or God is completely different from the atman.

In the 20th century Vedanta was the most prominent school of traditional philosophy in India. Many of the most widely recognized philosophers, but not all, favored Sankara's views. So did many accounts of brahman written by European and North American scholars.

brahmin Also spelled brahman; in HINDUISM, a member of the highest of the four *varnas* or RITUAL classes. According to tradition, the ideal occupation for brahmins is that of the priest (*see* CASTE IN HINDUISM).

Brahmins descend from the priests who performed the sacrifices described in the sacred books known as the VEDA. Some scholars have identified their ancestors as priests among the Indo-Europeans. The Indo-Europeans were supposedly ancestors of the people who inhabit north India today, as well as of European peoples such as the English, the French, and the Germans.

About 2,000 years ago Hindu lawbooks known as *Dharmasastras* carefully listed the duties and privileges of brahmins. They also assigned brahmins the highest position in Hindu society, but not everyone has agreed. Many records from roughly 2,000 years ago tell about disputes between brahmins and *sramanas*. Sramanas were wandering ascetics who practiced religions such as BUDDHISM and JAINISM. (Ascetics are people who give up pleasures and sometimes even the necessities of life for religious purposes.) A thousand years later brahmins were often the butt of jokes in classical Indian drama.

The lawbooks focus specifically on the roles of boys and men. Brahmin men often have other occupations, but according to the lawbooks it is best for them to be priests and to teach the Veda. Public SACRIFICES described in the Veda still occur in India, but they are relatively rare. It is much more common for brahmins to serve as spiritual teachers for boys, a relationship that the boys are supposed to remember throughout their lives. Some brahmins serve as priests in temples. In addition, all brahmins are supposed to observe household rituals taught by the Veda. Good examples are the *sandhya* or twilight rituals addressed mornings and evenings to the god Surya, the sun. In theory the lives of women are limited: They are supposed to obey in turn their fathers, husbands, and sons. In practice some Hindu women have been strong and self-assertive.

Although all brahmins belong to the highest varna, it should be stressed that varnas are ritual classes, not economic ones. Brahmins may be the most ritually pure members of Indian society, but some brahmins are extremely poor. At the same time, brahmins have played an enormous role in the government of India. Only 3.5 percent of Indians are brahmins, but at the end of the 20th century brahmins held almost 70 percent of all government jobs.

Strict brahmins have traditionally observed a number of rules. These rules were designed to maintain the brahmins' purity. For example, if brahmins came into physical contact with persons considered impure in ritual terms, especially Dalits ("untouchables"), they had to perform a series of rituals to wash away what they saw as defilement. During the 20th century, however, traditional concerns with maintaining purity often gave way to the pressures of modern urban life.

brain, mind, and religion From the 1980s on, scientists have been thinking seriously about what their studies of the brain and the mind might have to say about religion. We often think of the brain and the mind as identical, but they are not. The brain is a physical object inside the head. It consists of cells and undergoes chemical reactions and electrical pulses. The mind is the collection of our thoughts and experiences. Many scientists think that these two are just one thing, a mind-brain, seen from two different angles. Nevertheless, it is still impossible to connect most ideas people have with specific chemical and physical events in their brains. As a result, scientists usually focus on either the brain or the mind. Those who focus on the brain are called neuropsychologists. Those who focus on the mind are called cognitive scientists.

THE BRAIN AND RELIGION

Neuropsychologists who study religion often explore peculiar experiences that some religious people call "mystical." Some are experiences that God is present. Others are experiences of being one with the universe. Neuropsychologists believe that these experiences result from events in the brain, but they do not agree on what those events are. One researcher might believe that people experience God as a result of electrical discharges in parts of the brain known as the temporal lobes. (These lobes are found near the temples on either side of the head.) Another might believe that a person will have an experience of "absolute unitary being" if two different systems in the brain are stimulated at the same time. These two systems are the system responsible for being aroused, as when running a tight race, and the system responsible for being calm, as in deep relaxation. A third researcher has examined Zen meditation in detail. He has tried to link the many different experiences people have during ZAZEN with a large number of events in the brain—too many to summarize here. Clearly, these ideas are complicated. Much more work needs to be done before neuropsychologists will be able to agree on which explanations work best.

STUDIES OF THE MIND

Cognitive scientists are not interested in "mystical" experiences. Most religious people, they say, do not have such experiences. What they want to explain are the ideas that religious people have. They especially want to explain why human beings, unlike other animals, believe in beings that cannot be perceived by the senses, beings like gods, spirits, and demons. They, too, have many different, complicated explanations. One researcher claims that the mind is programmed to see humanoid and animal-like beings even where no such beings exist. He points out that it is better for a person hiking in the woods to mistake a rock for a bear than a bear for a rock. A hiker who mistook a bear for a rock is in serious danger of being injured or killed. From such mistakes, he says, the belief in gods arose. Another thinker believes that religious ideas are precisely the kinds of ideas that the human mind most likes to think. They attract attention because they violate expectations. For example, spirits can move through solid objects, and human minds find that idea interesting. At the same time, religious ideas do not violate too many expectations. If they did, people would not be able to remember them. Some call these ideas "minimally counterintuitive."

IMPLICATIONS

At the beginning of the 21st century both neuropsychologists and cognitive scientists are trying to refine their ideas and test them through experiments. They, along with theologians, have also considered what their ideas mean for religious people. Some brain and mind researchers are adamantly atheistic. They think scientists have sufficiently explained that supernatural beings are based only on processes within the brain. Others see their research as making possible a new way for religious people to think about their religions. They call that way "neurotheology." Despite such great differences, many researchers seem to agree that religion is somehow programmed—"hardwired"—into the brain. As a result, human beings will always be religious.

Further reading: Justin L. Barrett, *Why Would Anyone Believe in God?* (Walnut Creek, Calif.: Altamira Press, 2004); Andrew Newberg, Eugene d'Aquili, and Vince Rause, *Why God Won't Go Away: Brain Science and the Biology of Belief* (New York: Ballantine Books, 2001); Harvey Whitehouse, *Modes of Religiosity: A Cognitive Theory of Religious Transmission* (Walnut Creek, Calif.: Altamira Press, 2004).

Brazil, new religious movements in Brazil has traditionally been a Catholic country because it was colonized by Portugal. In fact, Brazil has been ranked as the largest Catholic country in the world, but that is somewhat deceptive. Brazil is also home to thriving new religious movements.

For a century or more people in Brazil have developed new religions built on African roots called Afro-Brazilian religions. More recently, in the last 50 years, PENTECOSTALISM has grown extremely rapidly there. Since the 1990s, the Catholic Church has been responding especially to the growth of Pentecostalism through media-friendly "show masses."

Europeans were not the only people who came to Brazil after the discoveries of Columbus. People of African ancestry came, too, often, of course, against their will. Although slaveowners tried to make Africans Christian, Africans also maintained their earlier beliefs. In particular, the Yoruba people from Nigeria managed to preserve their traditional beliefs and practices. As a result, Afro-Brazilian religions often use Yoruba gods and names.

There are many different Afro-Brazilian religions. Candomble is the oldest. It is also the most African. It identifies Yoruba spirits, called *orisha,* with Catholic saints. Traditionally, its leaders have been women, called *maes de santo,* that is, mothers of the saint. They perform RITUALS such as animal SACRIFICE. They also supervise people who are "ridden" or possessed by various spirits.

Catimbo is another Afro-Brazilian religion. Unlike Candomble, it calls upon supernatural beings that the native peoples of Brazil worshipped. Like native religions, it also uses an intoxicant to induce visions.

Yet another new Afro-Brazilian religion is Umbanda. It has elements from Christianity, African religions, and native Brazilian religions. To them it adds ideas from a 19th-century French spiritualist, Allan Kardec (1804–69), who taught that people had many lives (*see* REINCARNATION).

Pentecostal churches are rather different from Afro-Brazilian religions. In fact, Pentecostal churches deliberately attack the beliefs and practices of Afro-Brazilian religions as "demon-worship." Those who practice Afro-Brazilian religions often complain that Pentecostals harass and discriminate against them.

Pentecostal churches attribute the violence and drug trafficking in Brazil's cities to demons. To address these problems, they perform public exorcisms. Like Pentecostals elsewhere, they emphasize a strict lifestyle and various gifts of the spirit.

The largest Pentecostal church in Brazil is the Igreja Universal do Reino de Deus, the Universal Church of God's Kingdom or IURD for short. A self-appointed bishop, Edir Macedo (b. 1945), founded the IURD in 1976. Within 10 years it had grown to 3 million members. It now runs television and radio stations and boasts churches in Portugal, South Africa, Great Britain, and the United States.

During the late 20th century, the future of the Roman Catholic Church in Brazil looked bleak. People who practiced the Afro-Brazilian religions had often practiced Catholicism, too, but members of the new Pentecostal churches insisted that their members belong only to them. Tens of millions of people left the Catholic Church.

In the 1990s young Catholic priests began to respond in the spirit of the Pentecostal churches. They sang with bands, danced, and put on stage shows, all in the service of their religion. The performances attracted many people. For example, in November 1997 one controversial priest, Marcelo Rossi (b. 1967), drew a crowd of more than 100,000 people to a rally in a soccer stadium in Sao Paulo. The theme was "I'm happy to be Catholic."

This new form of Catholicism probably does not count as a new religious movement. But together with Afro-Brazilian religions and new Pentecostal movements, it helps make for religious vitality and diversity in Brazil.

Further reading: José Oscar Beozzo and Luiz Carlos Susin, eds., *Brazil: People and Church(es),* trans. Paul Burns (London: SCM Press, 2002); André Corten, *Pentecostalism in Brazil: Emotion of the Poor and Theological Romanticism,* trans. Arianne Dorval (New York: St. Martin's Press, 1999); Toyin Falola and Matt D. Childs, eds. *The Yoruba Diaspora in the Atlantic World* (Bloomington: Indiana University Press, 2004).

Buddha, the A title meaning "awakened" or "enlightened." It is most commonly applied to Siddharta Gautama (c. 560–c. 480 B.C.E.), the person who founded the religion of BUDDHISM. Buddhist mythology actually identifies many different Buddhas. Siddhartha Gautama is the historical Buddha, that is, the Buddha who has appeared in our world's history. In some traditions he is known as Sakyamuni, "sage of the Sakyas," because he was born in northeast India among a people known as the Sakyas.

LIFE

Buddhists believe that when people die, they are reborn (*see* SAMSARA). In keeping with this belief, they believe that Siddhartha Gautama had many births prior to the birth in which he became the Buddha. Texts known as *jatakas,* "birth stories," recount events from some of these prior births.

Siddhartha's birth into our world was to be his last. It is said that he carefully chose the time and location of that birth, to a princely family in northeast India in the sixth century B.C.E. According to legend, his mother, Queen Maya, dreamed that four deities were carrying her bed to the Himalaya Mountains. They were followed by a white elephant. The white elephant circled the bed, then plunged his tusk into Maya's side. When she awoke, she discovered she was pregnant.

During the sixth month of her pregnancy, Maya went to visit her cousin. Along the way, she stopped in a grove at Lumbini (today in Nepal). There she gave birth to Siddhartha prematurely. Astrologers who read the body marks predicted a double destiny for the baby: He would either conquer the world or renounce it. Siddhartha's father wanted to ensure that his son chose to conquer the world, so they protected him from the EVILS of the world and saw that his every wish was fulfilled. As a result, Siddhartha lived the life of pleasure that many people only dream about, but in living that life, he found that it was insufficient.

Siddhartha married and had a son. Then, at the age of 29, he made the fateful decision to explore the world outside his palaces. On successive trips he encountered four new "sights": an older person, a sick person, a decaying corpse, and a wandering ascetic. Siddhartha had finally confronted the realities of *duhkha* or suffering: old age, sickness, and death. He resolved to renounce his life of pleasure and search for the solution to these problems.

First he tried various techniques of MEDITATION. He mastered the skills quickly but found that they did not provide the answers he was seeking. Then, for five years he practiced various ascetic exercises, denying his body until he was so thin it was said one could feel his backbone through his abdomen. Close to death from these exercises, Siddhartha resolved to find a middle way between indulgence and denial. After sitting for an extended period under the so-called bodhi-tree in Bodh Gaya (today in Bihar state, India), he spent an entire night in meditation. During that night he discovered the principles that govern the processes

Statue of Lord Buddha located in Colombo, Sri Lanka *(Getty Images)*

of rebirth (*see* KARMA) as well as the path to release from suffering (*see* NIRVANA). As morning dawned, he achieved enlightenment (*bodhi*) and became the Buddha.

Out of compassion for the sufferings of all sentient, or conscious, beings and at the urging of a Hindu god, the Buddha remained in his human body to teach others the path he had discovered. He gave his first sermons at the deer park in Sarnath (near BANARAS, India) to ascetics—persons who deprive themselves of luxuries for religious purposes—with whom he had been living. Hearing his teachings, they too quickly attained liberation (nirvana) and became the first Buddhist ARHATS.

During the remaining years of his life, the Buddha wandered widely over northeast India, teaching his path and ordaining followers—men at first, later women, too—into the SANGHA, the order of wandering mendicants. At the age of 79 he ate some spoiled food offered by a lay (unordained) follower and died or, as Buddhists say, entered the ultimate nirvana (*parinirvana*) in Kushinagara (today Kasia, India). His closest followers decided to treat his body the way they would a royal corpse: They cremated the Buddha's remains and gave portions of his ashes to several kings. Portions of these remains were later enshrined in STUPAS throughout the Buddhist world.

TEACHINGS

Unlike MOSES, JESUS, and MUHAMMAD, the Buddha did not advocate the worship of any particular god. He did not deny that gods existed, but he thought that because gods are living beings, they, too, ultimately need to escape from suffering. (In the Buddhist view nothing is eternal, not even gods.) Like a compassionate physician, the Buddha diagnosed and prescribed the cure for the suffering that plagues all sentient existence.

The Buddha's diagnosis and prescription are formulated most compactly in his FOUR NOBLE TRUTHS. The Buddha identified the symptoms of our illness as duhkha, suffering, but suffering in the sense that ultimate satisfaction is unavailable in this life. The cause of duhkha is craving, longing, or desire, brought about by ignorance of reality. The disease, however, can be cured. The Buddha taught that duhkha disappears once one eliminates craving. But that requires an entire transformation of one's thought, practice, and perceptions, a transformation that results from practicing the Buddha's eightfold path.

Several principles underlie the Buddha's teaching. One of them is "no-self" (Sanskrit, *anatman).* This principle denies that people have an eternal soul or an unchanging self or essence, such as one finds, for example, in the teachings of CHRISTIANITY and HINDUISM (*see* ATMAN). A related principle, "no-permanence" (Sanskrit, *anitya*), emphasizes that change characterizes all existence. A third principle, "co-dependent origination" (Sanskrit, *pratitya-samutpada*), highlights the interrelatedness of all things. According to this teaching, everything is tied together in a complex net of causes, so that there can be no "first cause" from which all beings derive.

Many religions have worried about the origin of the universe or the fate of human beings after death (*see* COSMOGONY and AFTERLIFE IN WORLD RELIGIONS). The Buddha urged his followers to ignore these questions, not unlike the teachings of JUDAISM. In the image of his famous "Fire Sermon," human beings have awakened to find themselves in a house on fire. They should not worry about how the fire started, nor should they be concerned with what they will do after the fire has been extinguished. They should direct all their efforts to putting the fire out.

SIGNIFICANCE

The Buddha is known as the Tathagata, Sanskrit for "the one who went that way." The historical Buddha, Siddhartha Gautama, is important not because he revealed the messages of a god but because he discovered and taught the path that human beings can follow to attain release from suffering. He is most revered in the tradition of Buddhism known as Theravada, predominant in southeast Asia. A formula that Theravada often invokes signals the Buddha's importance: "I take refuge in the Buddha. I take refuge in the teachings

[Sanskrit, DHARMA]. I take refuge in the monastic community [Sanskrit, *sangha*]."

The other major tradition of Buddhism, predominant in east Asia, is Mahayana; it assigns the historical Buddha a somewhat lesser place. It reveres the Buddha Sakyamuni principally for having revealed the teachings and deeds of other Buddhas and BODHISATTVAS, such as AMIDA and AVALOKITESVARA, known in Chinese as Kuan Yin. ZEN BUDDHISM goes so far as to caution people against becoming overly attached to the person of the Buddha. (Recall that attachment and craving produce suffering.) A well-known KOAN or Zen riddle states: "If you meet the Buddha on the road, kill him."

Further reading: Sherab Kohn, *The Awakened One* (Boston: Shambhala, 1994); Walpola Rahula, *What the Buddha Taught* (New York: Evergreen, 1962); H. Saddhatissa. *The Life of the Buddha* (New York: Harper & Row, 1976); Hans Wolfgang Schumann, *The Historical Buddha* (London, New York: Arkana, 1989).

Buddhism   A religion that traces its history back to the BUDDHA, Siddhartha Gautama (c. 560–c. 480 B.C.E.). Buddhism is widely practiced throughout southeast and east Asia. It also has strong traditional ties to Tibet (*see* TIBETAN RELIGION). In the 20th century small but vigorous Buddhist communities were established in North America and Europe.

HISTORY

Siddhartha Gautama is said to have discerned the path that leads to release from suffering and rebirth (SAMSARA) at the age of 35. He lived almost to the age of 80. During his last 45 years he traveled widely in India, teaching and organizing the community of wandering ascetics (*see* SANGHA). By the time of his death or, as Buddhists prefer to say, his *parinirvana* (*see* NIRVANA), Buddhism was firmly established.

During the next 1,200 years, Buddhism spread beyond India in three major waves. The first wave, associated with the famed emperor of India, ASOKA,

began in the third century B.C.E. The dominant form of Buddhism at that time was Theravada, "The Teachings of the Elders." This school adheres to the letter of Siddhartha's teaching. Carried along the oceanic trade routes southeast of India, Theravada became the dominant form of Buddhism in Sri Lanka, Myanmar (formerly known as Burma), Laos, Thailand, and Cambodia (also known as Kampuchea).

The second major wave of Buddhist expansion began roughly in the second century C.E. By this time Mahayana or "Great Vehicle" Buddhism had become dominant. Mahayana does not adhere strictly to the Buddha's words. It strives instead to recover the Buddha's experience of enlightenment. Carried along the land trade routes from northwest India, Mahayana became the dominant form of Buddhism in China, Japan, Korea, and Vietnam.

The third wave of expansion began in the seventh century and carried Buddhism to Tibet and surrounding areas. The form of Buddhism that became dominant in these regions is Vajrayana, "Diamond Vehicle." It emphasizes the special powers of RITUALS, diagrams, and objects.

In India itself Buddhism virtually died out. First it succumbed to a Hindu revival movement centered on devotion to various gods that began about the eighth century C.E. This movement, known as BHAKTI, took lay supporters away from Buddhism. Then, starting in the 12th century Muslim invaders pillaged monasteries and convents and forced MONKS AND NUNS to abandon the order. Indian Buddhism began to revive, however, toward the end of the 19th century. During the 20th century some North Americans and Europeans became very interested in Buddhism (*see* BUDDHISM IN AMERICA).

BELIEFS

Although one sometimes hears that Buddhists are atheists, this is not quite correct. Buddhism does not generally deny the truth of other religions; instead, it tries to supplement another truth with a truth of its own. As a result, Buddhists often WORSHIP the gods that their non-Buddhist neighbors worship. But in Buddhism it is ultimately more important to follow the Buddhist path than to worship gods.

One follows the Buddhist path to redress the root problem that all sentient or conscious beings face: suffering (*see* FOUR NOBLE TRUTHS). Buddhism blames suffering, along with bondage to the world of ordinary existence and rebirth (samsara), on ignorance. Two kinds of ignorance are most important. The first kind leads people to think and act as if they are eternal, unchanging selves or souls. The second leads people to think and act as if things persist, when in fact, Buddhism teaches, absolutely nothing at all is eternal and unchanging. Ignorance of the truths of "no self" and "impermanence" leads to attachment and craving, and they in turn lead to suffering. To obtain release from suffering (nirvana), a person must overcome ignorance. That requires an intellectual acknowledgment of Buddhist truths, but it also requires much more. It requires a total transformation of one's thought, action, and experience.

There are paradoxes hidden in these basic truths of Buddhism, and Mahayana thinkers explored them. If one practices Buddhism to achieve nirvana, is one not craving nirvana? Again, if one practices Buddhism to achieve nirvana, is one not acting as if one had a self that could achieve release? Moreover, if one accepts Buddhist teachings as true, are they not eternal and unchanging? Questions such as these led Mahayana thinkers to formulate views that are subtle and difficult to understand. One such teaching, the "three body doctrine," suggests that the buddha who appeared in our world, Siddhartha Gautama, was only a manifestation in a world defined by names and forms of what is beyond all names and forms. Another very important teaching holds that everything is empty, including the content of Buddhist teaching. However, in order to attain this ultimate, nirvanic realization, one may first follow the pains of "relative" truths, such as worshipping the manifested forms of the Buddha or seeing enlightenment as something to be gained. In the end, one will understand that nirvana is here and now yet beyond name and form. But MAHAYANA BUDDHISM did not limit itself

to such subtle thinking. It also developed elaborate mythologies of celestial Buddhas and BODHISATTVAS. These beings practiced Buddhism not to benefit themselves but to make it possible for all beings to achieve enlightenment.

PRACTICES

Just as Buddhism has not required its adherents to reject other religious beliefs, so it has not required them to refrain from other religious practices. As a result, Buddhist practice varies widely. Japanese Buddhists participate in SHINTO rituals. Buddhists in parts of southeast Asia engage in spirit-cults.

Some specifically Buddhist practices aim at achieving nirvana. THERAVADA BUDDHISM emphasizes following the Buddha's Eightfold Path: right views, right thought, right speech, right action, right livelihood, right effort, right mindfulness, and right concentration. Most forms of Buddhism have well developed traditions of MEDITATION. In Theravada, *samadhi* meditation focuses one's concentration in turn on a series of exercises in order to correct certain vices; *vipassana* or insight meditation aims at a complete awareness of one's surroundings. Practitioners of ZEN BUDDHISM sit and walk in meditation (ZAZEN and *kinhin*) and at times experience moments of *satori*, enlightenment. Such moments may come during ordinary activities, too, so that Zen has developed many arts, from swordsmanship to flower arranging. Other forms, such as PURE LAND BUDDHISM, teach their followers to rely on the assistance of a Buddha.

Not all specifically Buddhist practices aim at enlightenment. Lay supporters within Theravada give charity, visit STUPAS, and perform other activities in the hope of acquiring merit. This merit will result in a better rebirth in the next life and take them one step closer to release. Instead of acquiring merit for oneself, Mahayana emphasizes acts of compassion to benefit all beings.

ORGANIZATION

During the 45 years of his wandering as the Buddha, Siddhartha Gautama organized his community into two groups, the Sangha, that is, the community of monks and nuns, and the lay supporters. This organization has been typical of Theravada Buddhism. Monks and nuns beg for their food and devote their lives to following the Buddha's path. Political authorities such as kings and queens have always been important lay supporters.

In Mahayana the distinction between the Sangha and lay supporters tends to be much less rigid. The monastic life is not unknown, but Mahayana makes ultimate release available to those who are not religious professionals. Furthermore, in certain Mahayana traditions priests may marry, eat meat, and drink wine. Such behavior violates Theravada guidelines for monks and nuns.

Although the Buddha made provision for an order of nuns, the number of nuns has traditionally been small. As Buddhism has begun to grow in Europe and North America, women are starting to assume more active leadership roles.

SIGNIFICANCE

Buddhism is one of the world's most important religions. At the end of the 20th century it had more than 300,000,000 adherents. Buddhism has profoundly influenced philosophy, literature, and the arts in Asia for over 2,000 years. In recent decades it has also been extremely popular in some segments of American society.

Further reading: Kenneth Ch'en, *Buddhism: the Light of Asia* (New York: Barron's Educational Series, 1968); Thich Nhat Hanh, *The Heart of the Buddha's Teaching* (New York: Broadway Books, 1999); Richard H. Robinson, and Willard L. Johnson, *The Buddhist Religion* (Belmont, Calif.: Wadsworth, 1982); Huston Smith and Philip Novak, *Buddhism: A Concise Introduction* (HarperSan Francisco, 2003).

Buddhism in America　Interest in and practice of BUDDHISM in the Western Hemisphere. This entry concentrates on Buddhism in the United States.

Buddhism was already in the United States in the 19th century (1800s). On the East Coast some educated Americans of European descent showed an interest in it. They included the "New England transcendentalists," a group of writers who gathered around Ralph Waldo Emerson (1803–82) in the 1830s and 1840s. More serious were the interests of a Russian noblewoman, Helena P. Blavatsky (1831–91), and an American, Henry S. Olcott (1832–1907). In 1875 they founded the Theosophical Society in New York. Later they traveled to south Asia and took Buddhist vows.

During the late 19th century Buddhism also appeared on the West Coast. There it was not associated with an intellectual elite. Rather, immigrants from east Asia who came to the West Coast and the island of Hawaii brought Buddhism with them. The Chinese first came to California in the heady days of the Gold Rush (1848–49). Japanese began coming to the West Coast at the end of the 19th century. Among the Buddhist traditions that the Japanese brought was a school very popular in Japan: the True Pure Land school (*see* PURE LAND BUDDHISM). Its adherents rely solely upon the power of the Buddha AMIDA to be reborn in the Pure Land after death. True Pure Land Buddhists formed the Buddhist Church of America. It grew into a major institution.

During the 1960s two other schools of Buddhism took root in American soil. NICHIREN Buddhism attracted many non-Asian adherents. It honors the Japanese "prophet" Nichiren (1222–82) as the BUDDHA for the present age and teaches its followers to chant a phrase known as the Daimoku: *Nam Myoho Renge Kyo* (Hail to the LOTUS SUTRA). In 1991 the community split. The branch known as Nichiren Shoshu preserves the tradition of Buddhist monks and maintains temples in Chicago, Hawaii, Los Angeles, New York, San Francisco, and Washington, D.C. The other group, known as Soka Gakkai, has no monks. Its members, led by lay leaders, gather at community centers spread widely across the United States.

During the 1960s a different group of immigrants also brought Buddhism to the United States. In the previous decade, China had annexed Tibet and closed down its monasteries. Many monks fled into exile. Their leader, the DALAI LAMA, occasionally visited the United States. He became highly visible, especially after he won the Nobel Prize for peace in 1989. Among his better known followers was the movie actor, Richard Gere. Some Tibetan monks established monasteries and Buddhist schools in the United States. A good example is the Naropa Institute in Boulder, Colorado, founded by the Tibetan monk Chogyam Trungpa.

The Tibetan monks saw the United States as an opportunity to teach the Buddhist DHARMA in a foreign land. Other Buddhist groups did, too. One of the most important of these was the school known as Zen (see ZEN BUDDHISM). It has attracted a large number of non-Asian followers in the United States. Indeed, it has broadly influenced American culture.

American awareness of Zen dates from the World's Parliament of Religion held in Chicago in 1893. Among the religious figures who attended the parliament was a Japanese Zen master, Shaku Soen. Later, the books of a lay follower of Soen, D. T. Suzuki, helped popularize Zen in the United States and around the world. In the 1950s Zen attracted the attention of the Beat poets. By the 1970s Americans of non-Asian descent had been certified as Zen masters. By the end of the century Zen MEDITATION centers were common in many parts of the United States.

Zen has become a feature of the American consciousness. Good examples are Robert Pirsig's novel, *Zen and the Art of Motorcycle Maintenance* (1974) and a World-Wide-Web site hosted by America Online in 1996 called "Zen and the Internet." Such titles show the extent to which Zen has fascinated Americans. These uses of the word "Zen," however, have little or nothing to do with the practice of Buddhism.

Further reading: James Wilson Coleman, *The New Buddhism* (New York: Oxford University Press, 2001); Rick Fields, *How the Swans Came to the Lake* (Boulder, Colo: Shambhala, 1986); Lenore Friedman, *Meetings with Remarkable Women* (Boston: Shambhala, 1987); Richard Seager, *Buddhism in America* (New York: Columbia University Press, 1999).

Buddhist festivals   Festivals play a very important role in the life of Buddhists. It is difficult, however, to generalize about them. The different schools—Theravada, Mahayana, and Vajrayana—celebrate different festivals (see MAHAYANA BUDDHISM, THERAVADA BUDDHISM, and VAJRAYANA BUDDHISM). So do different regions, such as Sri Lanka, Burma, and Thailand, all countries where Theravada predominates. In most places Buddhists celebrate festivals according to a lunar calendar in which the months are defined by the phases of the moon. In Japan, however, Buddhists use the calendar commonly used in the United States.

Important festivals commemorate events in the life of the BUDDHA. Theravada Buddhists believe that the Buddha's birth, enlightenment, and *parinirvana* ("ultimate NIRVANA," what non-Buddhists think of as his death) all occurred on the same day, a full-moon day that usually occurs in the month of May. Some Buddhists refer to it as Buddha Day. In Theravada countries this is a very important festival. Theravada Buddhists commonly celebrate this festival the way they celebrate most festivals: They give food to the monks and the poor, they dedicate themselves to the Five Precepts (instructions on how to live, similar to the TEN COMMANDMENTS in JUDAISM and CHRISTIANITY), they listen to DHARMA talks (sermons on Buddhist topics), and they walk in a devotional manner around STUPAS, monuments where Buddha relics are kept.

Unlike Theravada Buddhists, other Buddhists celebrate the birth, enlightenment, and *parinirvana* of the Buddha Sakyamuni, as they call him, on different days. For example, Japanese Buddhists celebrate his birth on April 8, his enlightenment on December 8, and his *parinirvana* on the 15th of February or March (traditions vary). Particularly striking is the celebration of Sakyamuni's birth. It is known in Japanese as *Hanamatsuri*, "flower festival." Japanese Buddhists decorate altars profusely with flowers to recall the flowers in the grove where Sakyamuni was born. They also pour sweet tea on an image of the baby Buddha. Other Mahayana Buddhists pour tea on Buddha images, too. According to legend, the skies rained sweet tea at Sakyamuni's birth.

RELICS of the Buddha play a large role in Buddhist practice. In Sri Lanka, the most important relic is a tooth of the Buddha. It has traditionally been the sign of the rightful ruler of the island. It sits inside a richly decorated gold reliquary that is kept for most of the year in a temple in the city of Kandy. But once a year, in July or August, at the climax of several days of celebration, the decorated gold reliquary with the tooth inside is brought out of the temple, mounted on the back of an elephant, and taken through the city in a large procession.

In addition to festivals focusing on the Buddha, Buddhists celebrate festivals in honor of BODHISATTVAS and other prominent Buddhists. The Chinese celebrate a festival in honor of Kuan-yin, the bodhisattva AVALOKITESVARA in female form. Especially important for Tibetan Buddhists is the festival in honor of Padmasmbhava. For members of the Jodo Shin school in Japan the most important festival honors Shinran (1173–1262), the founder of the school.

The NEW YEAR FESTIVAL is a major celebration for almost all Buddhists. Because they use different calendars, they celebrate it at different times. The focus of New Year's celebrations is generally on achieving health and prosperity in the coming year, not on any specific Buddhist teaching or practice.

In China, Korea, and Japan, the most popular festival for Buddhists who are not monks or nuns is Ullambana. The Japanese call it Obon and celebrate it on July 13–16. Ullambana honors the ancestors: It is believed that at this time the spirits of the dead return to earth. This is a joyous occasion, not a macabre one. Buddhists celebrate Ullambana by decorating household altars and cleaning grave sites. They may also light bonfires and sponsor events such as dances to entertain the spirits. At festival's end, the Japanese make little boats, often out of leaves, attach candles to them, and float them down streams and out to sea.

Further reading: Don Farber, *Tibetan Buddhist Life* (New York: DK Publications, 2003); Ruth Gerson, *Traditional Festivals in Thailand* (New York: Oxford University Press, 1996); Herbert Plutschow, *Matsuri: The Festivals of Japan* (Richmond, U.K.: Japan Library, 1996); Frank E. Reynolds and Jason A. Carbine, eds. *The Life of Buddhism* (Berkeley: University of California Press, 2000).

C

cakras A Sanskrit word meaning "wheels" or "discuses." In Hindu Tantrism, cakras (chakras) are energy centers of what is known as the subtle or psychic body.

Tantrism usually identifies six cakras. They are arranged along the spinal column as follows: the base of the spine, the region of the navel, the heart, the throat, the area between or above the eyebrows, and the fontanelle on the top of the skull. Each cakra has its own deities, powers, abilities, diagrams, colors, and letters. One goal of Tantrism is to move the vital energy at the base of the spine through the various cakras one by one. When the energy reaches the highest cakra, the practitioner achieves enlightenment and liberation.

John Calvin *(Library of Congress)*

Calvin, John (1509–1564) *one of the most important leaders of the Protestant REFORMATION* Calvin was born and educated in France. His father, a lawyer, had the young Calvin prepare first for a career in the church, then for one in law. When his father died in 1531, Calvin turned from law to humanism, that is, to the study of the classics of ancient Greece and Rome. In 1533 one of Calvin's close friends gave an address, at the University of Paris, which supported some ideas of Martin LUTHER. The theologians of Paris had earlier condemned these ideas. The friend had to flee for his life. Calvin was implicated in his friend's views, and he had to flee, too. Around this time Calvin seems to have had a profound personal religious experience.

In 1536 Calvin settled in Geneva, Switzerland. With the exception of three years spent in Strasbourg (1538–41), he spent the rest of his life in Geneva. At first he assisted the Reformation there. Eventually he led it.

Calvin organized Geneva's government, church, and schools. In his eyes, the government and the church needed to cooperate to ensure that the ideals of the BIBLE were observed. As a result, Geneva became a place where Christian regulations were strictly enforced. The inflexibility of the views was not unusual at the time, but it did have unfortunate consequences. The most famous example is the case of Michael Servetus, who was burned at the stake in 1553 for teaching that GOD is one, not a TRINITY.

Calvin made his mark as a writer, a thinker, and an organizer. His many writings include a catechism, sermons, hymns, commentaries on the Bible, and letters. But his most important book is *Institutes of the Christian Religion,* first published in 1536. Throughout his life Calvin revised and expanded it. He published the last version in 1559.

As a humanist, Calvin insisted on returning to the original sources. In THEOLOGY, that meant the Bible. His reading of the Bible owes a great deal to the thought of the apostle PAUL and AUGUSTINE OF HIPPO. Calvin emphasizes that, as a result of original SIN, human beings cannot live in the state for which they were created: communion with God. Nevertheless, God redeems sinners, although they do not in any way deserve to be saved. But God chooses to save some sinners and to condemn others to hell. This is Calvin's famous teaching of predestination. God saves people through the activity of JESUS, the prophet, priest, and king. He also does so through the Holy Spirit, who instills faith in the human heart.

Calvin recognized four offices in the church: pastors, who preached and administered the SACRAMENTS of BAPTISM and EUCHARIST; teachers, who instructed in faith; elders, who administered and ensured discipline; and deacons, who assisted the poor. The congregation was governed by a "consistory," a body made up of pastors and elders.

On some points Calvin differed from Martin Luther. One of the most significant was the interpretation of the eucharist. Luther had insisted that Jesus's body and blood were actually present in the bread and wine of the eucharist. Calvin taught that they were present spiritually. As a result, the Reformation gave rise to several distinct traditions. Calvinism is one of the most important. Calvinist churches are known as "Reformed" (*see* PRESBYTERIAN AND REFORMED CHURCHES). They predominate in Switzerland, the Netherlands, and Scotland. In the United States Calvinism is represented above all by the Presbyterian Church, which derives from the Scottish Calvinist tradition.

Canaanite religion   The religion of Palestine and Syria during the third and second millennia (3000–1001) B.C.E. In the first millennium B.C.E. Canaanite religion came into conflict with the worship of YHWH ("the Lord"), especially in the northern kingdom of Israel.

Technically, the name "Canaanite" applies only to the ancient inhabitants of Palestine. But people also use it for all peoples and settlements that spoke languages known as "Northwest Semitic." These peoples inhabited the region between two major ancient powers, Egypt and Mesopotamia. Not much is known in detail of their history. But during the 20th century two major archaeological finds unearthed many Canaanite texts. Among other topics, they shed light on Canaanite religion. These finds were the ancient cities of Ugarit (discovered 1929) and Ebla (discovered 1968).

The Canaanites worshipped several deities. Two were the pair El (the Semitic word for "god") and Athirat, also known as Asherah. El was the "father of gods and men." He created the world. Athirat was the mother of the gods. Together, they were worshipped as king and queen.

Another pair of gods was BAAL, also known as Hadad, and Anat, his sister and wife. The name Baal means "lord." A god of the storms, Baal is called "rider of the clouds." Anat was a GODDESS renowned both for beauty and violence. Yet another goddess renowned for beauty and violence was Athtart. Mesopotamians called her Ishtar; the BIBLE calls her Ashtoreth.

A prominent Canaanite myth concerns the god Baal. It tells how he fought and defeated the sea, a son of El named Yamm. But when Baal faced another son of El, Mot, the god of death, he was defeated and killed. His sister, Anat, avenged his death. Baal was restored to life and in the end defeated death in battle. Earlier scholars thought this story reflected the yearly cycle of the seasons. Current opinion takes it as referring instead to an irregular drought.

Canaanite WORSHIP was much like worship in other parts of the ancient Near East. It centered on SACRIFICES and offerings. The Canaanites performed these on at least two social levels. One level was the city. The king oversaw its worship. The second level was the local community. Individuals seem to have performed in local cults for themselves. They sacrificed at high places throughout the year. They also held celebrations in conjunction with planting and harvesting in spring and autumn. Like many ancient peoples, the Canaanites had a complex system of RITUAL specialists. It is not clear what any of the specialists mentioned in the Canaanite texts actually did.

During the first millennium, Canaanite religion in Palestine gradually gave way to the worship of YHWH. But the worship of YHWH also adopted Canaanite elements. In some sense, YHWH combines the characteristics of El and Baal. He creates the world. He is also a god of the storms. Like Baal, he rides the clouds (Psalms 68.4) and defeats the sea (PSALMS 89.9–10; JOB 26.12–13). It is also possible that Canaanite agricultural festivals lie behind the JEWISH FESTIVALS OF PASSOVER, Shavuot, and Sukkot.

Canada, religion in   The complex religious heritage of the nation of Canada. For thousands of years before European contact, Native Americans dwelling in what is now Canada practiced various forms of Native American Religions. In the far north, in areas bordering the Arctic Ocean, this heritage has been Inuit (Eskimo). Inuit spiritual practice has particularly involved hunting religion (see PRIMAL RELIGION) and SHAMANISM. The Native American religious heritage, evidenced in such common symbols as the "totem pole," has been important to many Canadians of both indigenous and European or other descent.

The Roman Catholic Church came to Canada with French settlement in what is now Nova Scotia in 1603, spreading to the present Québec in 1608. With the settlements came Jesuit and Franciscan missionaries eager to spread Catholicism among the native population. During the 17th century,

European Canada, centered around the St. Lawrence River, was essentially French and Catholic. But rivalry with Britain, as it established colonies on the Atlantic seaboard of what would become the United States, was intense and resulted in a few Protestant settlements in the area. In 1763, as a result of the treaty ending the Seven Years' War (known in America as the French and Indian War), Canada passed from French to British rule. British settlers, soon abetted by Loyalists from the rebellious Thirteen Colonies south of Canada, quickly occupied the territories now known as the Maritime Provinces and Ontario.

Soon the fundamental religious and cultural alignment of Canada that has prevailed ever since was in place: Québec, the main area of original French settlement, French in language and culture and Roman Catholic in religion; the Maritime Provinces, Ontario, and, in time, provinces further west were mainly Protestant, with significant Catholic minorities. Protestants were originally largely Anglicans from England, Presbyterians from Scotland, and members of smaller British denominations. Roman Catholics from Ireland also came to Canada.

Canada is, however, like the United States (see UNITED STATES, RELIGION IN), a nation of immigrants and so a nation of religious pluralism. Over the years, German, Scandinavian, Dutch, and eastern European newcomers brought Lutheran, Reformed, and EASTERN ORTHODOX religious life to the northern nation. Russian MENNONITES, seeking religious freedom, arrived in 1874, and Chinese Buddhist railroad workers in the 1880s. A Jewish synagogue was established as early as 1760 near Montréal. In the 20th century, SIKHS, Muslims (see ISLAM), and HINDUS came to Canada in significant numbers.

By the turn of the 21st century, Canada's population of 31 million was 45 percent Roman Catholic and nearly 25 percent Protestant and other Christians, such as Mormon and Eastern Orthodox. The largest Protestant denomination was the United Church of Canada, formed in 1925 as a union of Methodists, Congregationalists, and some Presbyterians. Next largest was the Anglican Church of Canada. Most other wings of Christianity were represented, and Canadians also included some 600,000 Muslims, 400,000 Jews, 300,000 Hindus, 300,000 Sikhs, and 250,000 Buddhists. Many Canadians were nonreligious.

In the latter half of the 20th century, religious life in Canada seemed to be in decline. It appeared to be at a midpoint between most of Europe, where church attendance has fallen precipitously since the end of World War II, and the United States, where it has remained at a high level. All major denominations had decreased in membership except Pentecostalism, which has increased. The Roman Catholic Church, while growing in absolute numbers, has seen attendance decline significantly. Québec, once a stronghold of traditional French Catholicism, is now no more religious than anywhere else. It seems clear that Canada has a distinct religious culture that is finding a middle way between Europe and the United States.

Further reading: Reginald Bibby, *Fragmented Gods: The Poverty and Potency of Religion in Canada* (Toronto: Irwin, 1987); Stewart Crysdale and Les Wheatcroft, eds., *Religion in Canadian Society* (Toronto: Macmillan of Canada, 1976); W. E. Hewitt, ed., *The Sociology of Religion: A Canadian Focus* (Toronto: Butterworth, 1993).

cannibalism and religion   The eating of human flesh by other humans. It has been practiced in a variety of places throughout human history for many reasons, only some of which can be considered religious. In extreme circumstances it has been done just to survive. In some cultures parts of the bodies of defeated enemies have been eaten simply to degrade them and demonstrate the completeness of the victory. In other instances, though, elements of religious or at least spiritist belief have come in, through the association of cannibalism with war, sacrifice, and kinship or alliance between the living and the dead and between different tribes.

Among certain South American and African tribes, for example, the bodies of killed foes were reportedly cooked and eaten, or burned, reduced to powder, and put in drinks. This was said to protect the victors against attacks by the souls of the deceased, and also to be a way of acquiring their energy. Other tribesmen have disapproved of the practice but claimed it is done by witches and sorcerers in order to gain magical power. In still other societies, such as some in New Guinea, parts of the bodies of relatives, who had died naturally, were eaten as a benign way of expressing kinship and assuring their REINCARNATION within the tribe.

Cannibalism has also sometimes been a part of religious sacrifice. In Fiji the communal eating of cannibal victims who had been sacrificed to a major god was said to be a way of cementing an alliance between chiefs. Among the Aztecs of Mexico (*see* AZTEC RELIGION) reports have alleged that the bodies of the victims whose hearts and blood were regularly offered to nourish the sun were then eaten by priests and nobility. To eat offerings, human, animal, or plant, presented to the gods is widely considered a means of having communion with that god and with other worshippers.

Recently some scholars have argued that accounts of the practice of cannibalism, repellent to most people, are greatly sensationalized. Cannibalism has rarely if ever been reliably observed firsthand, it is said, and accusations of human-eating have come from informants whose real motive was to slander rival tribes, or from tellers of tall tales who enjoyed shocking their listeners. The stories were then still more exaggerated by Western colonialists to smear their "native" subjects as barbaric and depraved, and so justify white rule.

Doubtless there is much truth to this. The majority of anthropologists and religion scholars, however, still believe that cannibalism has sometimes been engaged in for religious reasons, though probably not as often as was once thought.

Canterbury   A town in England roughly 50 miles southeast of London. In 597 C.E. Pope Gregory I sent a missionary named Augustine (not AUGUSTINE OF HIPPO) to the Anglo-Saxons in England. Augustine was the first missionary to the English. He settled in Canterbury and became bishop there. The line

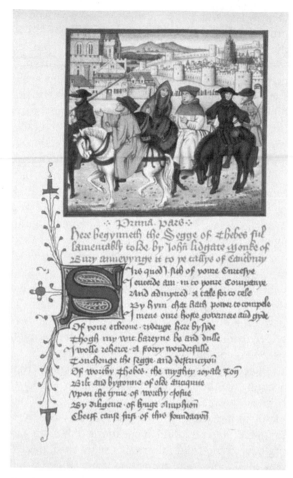

A 15th-century manuscript page of Geoffrey Chaucer's *Canterbury Tales* (Image Select/Art Resource, N.Y.)

of the archbishops of Canterbury stretches from Augustine to the present day without a break.

During the REFORMATION King Henry VIII declared the English church to be independent from the popes in Rome. Since that time (1534) the archbishop of Canterbury has been recognized as the most important leader of the Anglican Church (*see* ANGLICANISM).

Canterbury is famous for its cathedral. It is also famous as the place where in 1170 St. Thomas Becket, the archbishop of Canterbury at the time, was killed. In the 20th century this event was the subject of *Murder in the Cathedral*, a play by

T. S. Eliot, and *Becket,* a play by Jean Anouilh. Before the Reformation, many pilgrims traveled to Canterbury to visit Becket's shrine. The English writer Geoffrey Chaucer used that PILGRIMAGE in his famous *Canterbury Tales* (late 1300s). The book recounts many raucous and lively stories that pilgrims allegedly told on their way to Canterbury.

cardinals The chief administrative officers of the Roman Catholic Church. They can be distinguished by their red clothing. Cardinals are appointed by the pope (*see* PAPACY, THE). In turn they elect new popes. At one time the number of cardinals was capped at 70, but today they number more than 100.

Originally the cardinals were the bishops, priests, and deacons in the church at Rome and its immediate surroundings. These titles are preserved in the three ranks in the College of Cardinals: cardinal bishops, priests, and deacons. But today cardinals generally administer the Roman see itself, that is, the Catholic Church in Rome, act as bishops in major churches around the world, and serve as ambassadors of the pope.

cargo cults Groups believing that the gods will send wonderful cargoes to their followers, often native peoples in colonialized lands. Throughout parts of the world under colonial rulers, especially in the area of Indonesia and the South Pacific, religious movements have arisen based on the promise of a prophet that rich cargoes were on their way to the impoverished natives. Although comparable movements can be found as far back as prehistoric times, and some cargo cults are still active today, most flourished during the height of European colonialism, approximately from 1850 to 1950. They have much in common with millenarianism, or belief in the imminent and sudden oncoming of a world that was like paradise, and with movements like the 1890s GHOST DANCE of Native Americans by which oppressed indigenous peoples whose culture was being destroyed by white settlers sought to recover it through magical means.

In cargo cults as such, typically a teacher arises within a colonialized native community who says that although the white rulers seem to have all the wealth and advanced technology now, our ancient gods and ancestors have not forgotten us. Sometimes this prophetic teacher is himself thought to be an incarnation or emissary of one of the old gods. Soon, he says, the gods will send a ship or, more recently, airplanes, laden with cargo for the natives, and this will be the beginning of a millennial age of happiness in which they and their ways will be vindicated.

In order to prepare for the cargo, docks or airstrips must be built. At the same time, it is no longer necessary or appropriate to work for the old order or put stock in the old order's goods and money. At the height of cargo cult enthusiasm, natives have ceased working for their colonial overlords, and have stopped attending mission churches and mission or government schools. They have destroyed their property, killing their animals and throwing away money to make room, as it were, for the new cargo.

Needless to say, all this was very disruptive of the colonial economy and brought stern reprisals from the European rulers. Although based in an updating of traditional religious beliefs, including millenarian themes, cargo cults were sometimes also influenced by Christian missionary teaching about the Day of the Lord and the KINGDOM OF GOD. It is clear they had political overtones as well. While on the surface destructive and backward-looking, cargo cults sometimes in the long run clarified native issues and leadership in ways that helped prepare for independence.

Carnival In Latin countries, a festival held just before the beginning of the fasting season of LENT. During Carnival, joviality and rich foods, including meat, are enjoyed for the last time until EASTER. Mardi Gras in New Orleans is a good example. By extension, though, Carnival can be taken to refer to a type of festival found throughout the religious world, such as *holi* in HINDUISM and many of the *matsuri* of SHINTO, or in some ways PURIM in JUDA-ISM, when "letting go" through song and dance and ribald humor is the rule. Clowning, drunkenness, and the mocking even of sacred things may be in order at such times. Identities may also be changed as people wear masks and costumes (see MASKS AND RELIGION). Carnival shows that religion can sometimes be festive and fun.

caste in Hinduism Traditional social grouping in India into which persons are born. Each group ranks higher or lower than other groups in terms of its RITUAL purity. Thus, a caste is distinguished by limiting participation in rituals, including marriage and eating together, to members of the caste, as well as by specific occupations. The term "caste" usually refers to two distinct but related ways of organizing society; *varnas,* an ideal organization of human society into broad ritual classes, and *jatis,* specific, localized groups within the varnas.

VARNAS

In Sanskrit the word *varna* means "color." Applied to social groups it does not refer to skin color, and although it may be translated as "class," it does not refer to economic status, either. Varna refers instead to ritual status. It is quite possible to belong to the highest varna and be extremely poor. The varnas were systematized roughly 2,000 years ago in books of religious codes known as the *Smritis* or the *Dharmasastras.* Before then, many scholars maintain that distinctions of varna existed but were not so rigidly drawn or applied.

The four traditional varnas are, in order of descending ritual purity, BRAHMIN, kshatriya, vaisya, and sudra. According to the *Dharmasastras,* a brahmin should be a priest, a kshatriya a ruler or warrior, a vaisya a merchant or businessperson, while a sudra should meekly serve the other varnas. In addition, the varna system defines two groups of persons who are so impure that they fall outside the system altogether. The first group comprises the so-called untouchables, officially known today as Dalits. These were often people whose menial jobs were thought to be extremely polluting, for example, hunters and those who cleaned latrines. Pollution often comes from contact with body parts or with dead people or animals. The second group comprises foreigners. In traditional India "foreigners" were most often Muslims.

The focus of the varna system is on the purity of males, since they are the ones who perform household rituals. As a result, men may marry women from a higher varna, but a man who marries a woman from a lower varna loses caste. At the same time, men who cannot find work in an occupation appropriate to their varnas may do the jobs of lower varnas, but not higher ones. Thus, sudras cannot become Vedic priests, for that would pollute the ritual. Finally, the three upper varnas—brahmins, kshatriyas, and vaisyas—are called "twice-born," because the males born in these varnas undergo a "second birth," initiation into the study of the most sacred Hindu scriptures, the VEDA.

JATIS

The varnas represent the way certain thinkers thought society ought to be classified. In actual practice, Hindus have belonged to a more restricted jati, Sanskrit for "birth group." Jatis are relatively local groups that were ranked on the varna spectrum. There are literally thousands of jatis in Indian society.

The occupation that members of a jati perform is specified quite narrowly: Members of one jati may be barbers or shoemakers, those of another may be grocers. Traditional marriages also take place between members of jatis rather than between members of the broader varna classification.

In general it is not possible to change one's varna ranking because it is not possible to change one's jati. But even in traditional India a limited amount of mobility was possible. It is not unknown for the varna rank of a jati to alter when over several generations its fortunes changed. At the same time, individuals of ability or ambition have not always been limited to jobs within their jati. For example, several dynasties of India were begun by persons of low status.

CASTE TODAY

During the 20th century the caste system changed enormously. One of Mohandas GANDHI's most cherished goals was the elimination of untouchability, and the present constitution of India outlaws it. The Indian government has also established vigorous educational and employment quotas for underprivileged groups.

Today caste is much less visible and pervasive in India than it was a century ago, but its influence has not disappeared. Prejudices against low-caste people like the Dalits still remain strong among the higher castes, and marriages, an overwhelming majority of which are arranged, are still often performed within the boundaries of varna and jati.

Further reading: Louis Dumont, *Homo Hierarchicus* (Chicago: University of Chicago Press, 1980); J. H. Hutton, *Caste in India* (Bombay: Oxford University Press, 1963); Ursula Sharma, *Caste* (Buckingham, N.Y.: Open University Press, 1999).

cathedral A type of church building in Christianity. It gets its name because it contains the *cathedra* or "chair" of the bishop.

Bishops are religious leaders in Catholic, Orthodox, and some forms of Protestant CHRISTIANITY. They have charge of all the churches in a certain area. In the Roman Catholic and Anglican churches the area is known as a diocese. Other branches of Christianity use other names.

A cathedral is a bishop's home church. It is the most important church building in a region. That importance is generally reflected in the size of the building. Cathedrals have tended to be monumental structures.

Until the middle of the 18th century, the cathedral was one of the most important architectural structures in Europe. As a result, up to the mid-1700s the history of European architecture was largely a history of the changing styles of cathedrals. After the mid-1700s, cathedrals continued to be built. But developments like the Industrial, American, and French revolutions made them less important. Architects turned their creative energies to structures like government buildings—think of the Capitol Building and the White House in Washington, D.C.—train stations, theaters, museums, and eventually airports, office buildings, and shopping centers.

Many of the earliest Christians were Greeks and Romans who converted to Christianity. The earliest cathedrals, however, were not converted Greek and Roman temples. They were inspired by law courts known as basilicas and certain kinds of bath houses. These kinds of buildings allowed Christians to assemble in large groups for worship and BAPTISM. Unlike the law courts and bath houses, Greek and Roman temples were not very well-suited for such activities.

Later cathedrals in many different styles are extremely impressive. Hagia Sophia in Constantinople (sixth century)—now a mosque in Istanbul, Turkey—is a supreme example of a Byzantine cathedral. Its massive, central dome seems to float in the air above a lighted, unearthly space. St. Peter's in Rome contains the chair or throne of St. Peter himself, at least as designed by the Renaissance artist Giovanni Bernini (1598–1680). Built in an early baroque style, the richness of the

The Cathedral of Notre-Dame located in Paris, France, is an example of a Gothic cathedral. Note the flying buttresses (left) supporting the cathedral's ceiling and walls. *(Getty Images)*

church's decoration as well as the "arms' that surround the plaza in front of it were meant to draw people back into the Catholic Church after the Protestant REFORMATION.

Many people consider Gothic cathedrals to be the most sublime cathedrals of all. The Gothic style began in the area around Paris, France, in the mid-1100s. Gothic cathedrals are long, narrow, and tall. On the inside tall columns support the roof. On the outside a kind of support called a flying buttress supports the roof and the walls. Gothic cathedrals generally have arches that come to a point at their doorways, windows, and interior roofs. Earlier cathedrals had arches that were round. Gothic cathedrals also have large windows filled with stained glass. The cathedral at Chartres, France, is especially renowned for its stained glass.

Two extremely large church buildings in North America reflect the attitude that Gothic is the supreme form of the cathedral. One is St. John the Divine in New York City; the other is the National Cathedral in Washington, D.C.

cats and religion The symbolism and role of the cat in religion. The cat, an animal at once mysterious, independent, and familiar, has long been felt to have special spiritual power. In ancient Egypt, the GODDESS of pleasure, Bast, was symbolized by a cat, and her temple was full of sacred cats, which were mummified after death (*see* EGYPTIAN RELIGION). On the other hand, in medieval Europe, cats, especially black ones, were sometimes thought to be demonic, envoys or even personifications of the devil and familiars of witches, and sacrificed to ward off ill-fortune. The HALLOWEEN black cat is a carryover from those unhappy days for cats. In ISLAM, the prophet MUHAMMAD is said to have been especially fond of cats and so they are well regarded. In Japan it has been considered bad luck to kill a cat. For many people in the modern world, a pet dog or cat remains their closest contact with the wonder and mystery of the animal world.

See also ANIMALS AND RELIGION.

celibacy The state of remaining unmarried and abstaining from sex for religious reasons. In some religions living in a state of celibacy is considered the way of perfection and the state appropriate to its leaders or its most dedicated practitioners. Examples of religious celibates are priests and MONKS AND NUNS of ROMAN CATHOLICISM; bishops, monks, and nuns in EASTERN ORTHODOX CHRISTIANITY; Buddhist monks and nuns; Taoist monks; and Hindu sadhus or "holy men." Other religions, such as CONFUCIANISM, JUDAISM, ISLAM, and PROTESTANTISM in CHRISTIANITY have (with a few exceptions) taught marriage as a virtual obligation, or at least a state that in no way diminishes religious virtue and should be open to all regardless of religious role.

At the same time, what might be called "spontaneous" celibacy has occurred even in those faiths, in the case of persons so immersed in a religious life that marriage was quietly dismissed as a personal option. Examples have been (according to some scholars) Jews of the ancient Essene or Qumran communities, certain Muslim Sufi mystics (*see* SUFISM), and Protestants such as the Shakers or John Chapman ("Johnny Appleseed"), or many dedicated female Protestant missionaries and deaconesses. Sometimes deeply religious persons of homosexual tendency have found celibacy the best way of life for them. Sometimes celibacy is entered as a temporary state, as in the case of young men in some Theravada Buddhist countries, who become monks for a year or so before marrying and establishing themselves in the world. Sometimes celibacy is a kind of SACRIFICE or offering to GOD.

Advocates of the value of celibacy say that it allows one to channel sexual energy into spiritual advancement, that it frees one to practice spirituality and serve others selflessly without having to allow for family obligations, and that it is a way of attaining egolessness because it is a form of self-denial that can also support holy poverty and obedience. It sets an example of a way of life that is above the passions and obligations of the world and ordinary human nature. The celibate ideally can live as a completely free person, free from self and from entanglements, completely offered to

God or the spiritual quest, and can reach enlightenment or serve God without hindrance.

Yet celibacy is not easy and is not desirable for all. Controversies have arisen over the extent to which it should be required in such institutions as the Roman Catholic Church. Some forms of BUDDHISM, especially among the Japanese, now permit priests and monks to be married. The ideals of celibacy and modern attitudes toward sexuality and marriage find themselves deeply challenging to each other.

Celtic religion   The religion of the people who lived in France and Britain at the time of the Roman conquest. The Romans called the Celts *Galli,* in English, Gauls.

The Celts spoke a language related to German, Latin, Greek, Persian, and even Sanskrit, the classical language of India. Many people have noticed intriguing similarities between Celtic and ancient Indian culture. These include similarities in religion and mythology.

At first the Celts lived east of the Rhine River. About 1000 B.C.E. they crossed the Rhine into the area of modern France. By 300 B.C.E. they also lived across the English Channel. Their descendants include the Scots, Irish, and Welsh. In 279 B.C.E. some Celts sacked the Greek oracle at Delphi. Then they crossed into modern Turkey and founded a state called Galatia (cf. the NEW TESTAMENT book of Galatians).

Celtic religion is difficult to reconstruct. Ancient writers, especially Julius Caesar, described it, but they described it in terms of their own religions. They also emphasized Celtic brutality. That emphasis is often not reliable. Later Christians, especially in Ireland, preserved Celtic stories and other elements of Celtic culture. But it is often difficult to tell what is ancient Celtic and what is more recent and Christian. Archaeology and ancient inscriptions provide some help.

According to Julius Caesar the Celts worshipped several gods that the more savage Germanic peoples did not; these corresponded to the Roman Mercury (the most important Celtic god),

Associated with horses, Epona was an important Celtic goddess. She is shown here in a limestone relief from Gannat, France. *(Réunion des Musées Nationaux/Art Resource, N.Y.)*

APOLLO, MARS, JUPITER, and Minerva. It is not clear what were the Celtic names of the gods Caesar had in mind. The most important Celtic god seems to have been Lugh, also spelled Lugus, a god of technology and invention. The names of several European cities preserve his memory: Lyon and Laon in France and Leiden in the Netherlands. A fascinating image of the Celtic god Cernunnos resembles the Hindu god SIVA. It also resembles a seated figure from a seal of the Indus Valley Civilization (*see* INDUS VALLEY RELIGION). An important Celtic GODDESS was Epona. She was associated with horses. Other Celtic goddesses gave their names to rivers in Europe. One example is the Rhine.

Much Celtic religious activity centered on places in nature, such as groves of trees, high places, and bodies of water. Later folklore recalls these sacred places in stories of fairies. Archaeologists have recovered Celtic offerings from bodies of water.

Caesar stressed that the Celts practiced SAC-
RIFICE, especially human sacrifice. Indeed, he
described a RITUAL in which the Celts built a human
figure out of wicker, filled it with people, and set
it on fire, burning the occupants. Many scholars
have doubts about his account. It is worth noting
that some famous prehistoric monuments in Britain, such as the passage tomb at Newgrange, Ireland, and the megaliths at Stonehenge, England,
were not built and used by the Celts. They were
built and used by earlier peoples.

The Celts had priests called DRUIDS. The Druids
preserved the oral traditions of the people, served
as judges, conducted religious rituals, and divined.
According to Irish traditions, the Celts divided the
year into two equal parts. The most important festival, Samain, took place on October 31/Novem-
ber 1. (Like the Jewish day, the Celtic day began
at sundown.) The festival of Beltine occurred on
April 30/May 1. These festivals are the ancestors
of Halloween and May Day, respectively.

charismatic movement A Christian movement, emphasizing emotional, demonstrative religious practices that began in the 1960s. It is similar
to PENTECOSTALISM but is found in other Christian
communities.

"Charisma" is originally a Greek word; it refers
to a gift of grace. People in the charismatic movement see behavior such as speaking in tongues,
faith healing, vigorous weeping, or laughing as
gifts of the Holy Spirit. They differ from Pentecostals by remaining in their own communities rather
than founding Pentecostal churches.

In a narrow sense, the charismatic movement
refers to the appearance of charismatic practices
in Protestant and Roman Catholic churches in the
United States during the 1960s. For Protestants
the decisive year was 1960. That was when an
Episcopal priest in Van Nuys, California, Dennis
Bennett (1917–91), informed people that he had
experienced the gift of glossolalia, speaking in
tongues. For Roman Catholics the decisive year
was 1967, when students in several Catholic universities began to experience charismatic gifts.

Practices, such as speaking in tongues and faith
healing, spread among both Roman Catholics and
Protestants. Church leaders were sometimes suspicious, and noncharismatic members often looked
askance at charismatic practices. Nevertheless,
after the initial enthusiasm died down, charismatic
groups have managed to maintain small but dedicated followings.

In the 20th century, Pentecostalism grew more
rapidly than any other Christian movement, especially in the Southern hemisphere. Similarly, the
charismatic movement was not confined to North
America. Charismatic practices made their way to
Britain and the European continent. They have also
had a large impact on Christians in places as widely
separated as Nigeria in Africa, Korea in East Asia,
and far northern Canada among Inuit (Eskimo).

Today, scholars also identify charismatic movements in other religions, such as BUDDHISM. Clearly,
Buddhists do not attribute charismatic behavior to
the Holy Spirit, but some of them have the same
sort of practices. For example, in a Buddhist community in Taiwan known as Ciji, members, especially women, sometimes weep uncontrollably
when they recite Buddhist scriptures (*see* SCRIPTURE,
BUDDHIST) or the name of a BUDDHA or bodhisattva.
They also sometimes weep when viewing a statue
of the Buddha.

Charismatic movements sometimes appear odd
to outsiders. They have, however, made important
contributions to religious life in the past 50 years.

charms and amulets In popular religion,
devices to assure the everyday protection of GOD
or the gods. Charms are properly words or simple
practices of quasi-magical significance that are said
or done to this effect, such as the frequent chanting of a mantra or short PRAYER under one's breath
as one goes about daily work, or saying "Bless
you!" to a person who has sneezed (originally in
the hope that the soul would not escape through
the sneeze), or knocking on wood for good fortune. Amulets, or talismans, are small objects
worn for the same purpose, although the word
charm has sometimes come to be applied to these

objects as well. Amulets include religious medals worn around the neck, sacred stones or tiny divine images carried in purse or pocket, or nowadays religious pictures, small statues, or medals on the dashboard of a car. Sometimes, especially in HINDUISM and BUDDHISM, they may consist of a short sacred mantra or other text placed inside a small box. Many SHINTO shrines and other temples regularly present amulets to visitors. While the use of charms and amulets may be regarded by some as superstitious, it is important to remember that for many religious people they are seen not only as bearers of sacred power in themselves, but also as tokens of one's religious identity and reminders of one's spiritual commitment in the midst of the stresses of everyday life. Some people, of course, wear religious jewelry and other sacred objects as a general symbol of that identity, but without a belief in any special power in the object itself. Others hold that, in mysterious ways, special divine power can indeed by imparted in some degree to particular objects.

children, religion of   How children experience religion and spiritual realities. Religions seem to have two very different views of what children are like from a religious point of view. On one hand, there is the idea represented by the poet William Wordsworth's famous lines in "Intimations of Immortality":

> … *Trailing clouds of glory do we come*
> *From God, who is our home:*
> *Heaven lies about us in our infancy!*

And only after

> *Shades of the prison-house begin to close*
> *Upon the growing boy*

does that splendor "fade into the light of common day." This is the view that children have naturally a particularly acute religious sense, and indeed are particularly close to GOD and heavenly glory.

The other view, represented by AUGUSTINE OF HIPPO, John CALVIN, and other more conventional religious thinkers of several traditions is that children are naturally selfish, embodiments of "original SIN," and only through training, education, and religion can they learn to be good and to love God.

Perhaps children, like adults, are complicated and there are ways in which both perspectives are true. Certainly children can be selfish, demanding, and even very cruel, sometimes thoughtlessly, sometimes out of malice, to animals, other children, and adults. Sometimes these are things about which, as they grow older, they feel bad and confess to God, asking his forgiveness. Whether it is through disobedience, meanness of thought, word, and deed, or order things virtually all children, by the time they grow up, have enough experience to know personally what religions mean by sin and evil, and why they take it so seriously.

At the same time, children often have experiences that lay foundations for religion of a much more positive sort. They may, perhaps alone in nature or a garden or even their room, sense on occasion an overwhelming feeling of peace, wonder, and joy. They may have companions invisible to others that are like ANGELS or spirits. They may have a sense that something like their parents is supporting them even when they are alone.

All these experiences at first have no name, but if a child is raised in a religion, sooner or later she or he will probably think of them as experiences of God or buddhahood, of angels or of a heavenly Father or Mother. The religion within which one is raised serves to give names and ways of thinking that help the child to "place" religious-type experiences both of wonder and of sin. Some children may feel a conflict between their innermost spiritual experiences and having to interpret them according to a family religion; others may not. But dealing with that is part of growing up. Frequently children greatly enjoy the festivals and special celebrations of religions.

Religious experience and tension both are likely to be heightened by puberty and adolescence, when strong new emotions, a new sense of a need for a person's independent identity, and a yearning for idealistic beliefs, may be channeled in religious directions. This is often a time of intense religious experience, conversion experiences, and rebellion against family and conventional religion. Many religions try to help people find a new adult religious identity at this time through rites like confirmation or BAR/BAT MITZVAH. In all cases, though, we find roots of adult religiosity, whatever it is, reaching deep into childhood, but then conditioned one way or another by family and the religious institutions of the adult world.

China, religions of The various religions practiced in China. These religions include the native Chinese traditions of CONFUCIANISM and TAOISM, the imported tradition of BUDDHISM, and a loose set of practices known as "popular religion."

ANCIENT BELIEFS AND PRACTICES

The earliest known Chinese religions addressed two themes that have continued throughout Chinese history: respect for ancestors who have died and various practices known as divination. Divination attempts to determine the character of the forces of the universe at given moments, for example, whether these forces are favorable when undertaking a specific action.

Village life in China developed during the Neolithic or "new stone age," which began around 5000 B.C.E. Archaeology tells us only a little about religious activity in this period. Corpses were painted with red ochre and buried with grave goods, such as tools and drinking vessels. At Yuan-chin-miao corpses were laid out in a north-south direction. All of these features could indicate a belief in an afterlife. Beginning about 3500 B.C.E. evidence appears of scapulamancy, that is, divining by examining cracks in the dried shoulder blades of deer and sheep.

By the Shang dynasty (about 1800–1050 B.C.E.) the Chinese knew of an afterlife presided over by Shang-Ti, "Lord on High." The number of goods buried with important persons had grown to immense proportions. At Hsiao-T'un, for example, the deceased was buried with 15 horses, 10 oxen, 18 sheep, 35 dogs, five equipped chariots and their charioteers, and another 852 people. During this period the Chinese used vessels made of bronze,

such as bronze bowls, to present gifts to ancestors. A common way to divine was to stick hot rods into tortoise shells and examine the ways in which the shells cracked.

The Shang rulers fell to rival rulers known as the Chou. The Chou justified overthrowing the Shang by invoking the mandate of HEAVEN. According to this idea kings ruled on behalf of heaven; when they no longer maintained order, they lost heaven's mandate to rule and deserved to be overthrown. During the early Chou period Chinese believed ancestors resided in *T'ien,* "heaven," and worshipped them with grand feasts. Aristocrats performed elaborate festivals linked to the agricultural calendar. It also became common to divine by throwing down stalks of the yarrow plant and seeing whether they would break. This practice eventually led to the writing of the classic book, the I CHING.

CONFUCIANISM AND TAOISM

In the early eighth century B.C.E order began to break down, and a period of political, economic, and religious unrest set in. During the sixth century B.C.E., as this unrest continued, the two major native Chinese religious traditions arose, CONFUCIANISM and TAOISM. Over the next 600 years they received their classic forms from thinkers like Hsun Tzu, Mencius, and CHUANG TZU.

Confucius (551–479 B.C.E.) taught the way of heaven. In effect, he transferred to living human beings the respect and devotion traditionally given to ancestors. Confucius is said to have edited five ancient classics: the *I Ching* or *Book of Changes,* the *Book of History,* the *Book of Poetry,* the *Book of Rites,* and the *Spring and Autumn Annals.* His disciples preserved his own teachings in a book known as the *Analects* (*see* ANALECTS OF CONFUCIUS). Early in the second century B.C.E. the Han dynasty adopted Confucianism as its official ideology. Eventually all Chinese officials had to pass rigorous examinations in the Confucian classics. They also spent a good part of their time performing the Confucian RITUALS.

Taoism taught not the way of heaven but the way of nature. As encapsulated in the *TAO TE CHING* (the "Way Power Classic"), this way never acts deliberately, yet it accomplishes everything. Taoists saw action without deliberate intention—in Chinese, *wu wei*—as the model for human behavior. Applying this principle to government, they suggested that the government that meddles least in the lives of its subjects is the best government. Taoists eventually developed elaborate rituals and experimented with exercises, herbs, and minerals (*see* ALCHEMY) in their search for a long life and immortality. They also formed secret societies that occasionally attempted to overthrow the government.

In the centuries following Confucius, yet another set of views, the YIN/YANG THEORY, crystallized from very ancient roots. It analyzed the universe in terms of the complementary interaction of two opposites, yin and yang. Among other characteristics, it saw yin as dark, moist, female, and receptive, yang as bright, dry, male, and active. It also identified "five actions" at work in the world: metal, wood, water, fire, earth. The differences between Confucianism and Taoism parallel to those between yang and yin: Confucianism stresses activity and Taoism receptivity. Just as yang and yin are both necessary, so most Chinese have practiced elements of both religions.

BUDDHISM

Buddhism first arrived in China around the time of JESUS (first century C.E.). During the next 500 years it gradually became established, primarily as a tradition for MONKS AND NUNS. At first the Chinese resisted Buddhism. The monastic life went counter to the traditional Chinese emphasis on the family, and the Buddhist desire to achieve release from ordinary existence (*see* NIRVANA and SAMSARA) was opposed to the practical orientation dominant in China.

By the start of the Tang dynasty (618–906 C.E.), however, Buddhism had become not only the dominant intellectual tradition but a religion practiced by the people as well. Several different schools flourished. T'ien-t'ai Buddhism classified all the varieties of Buddhism in a graduated scale; it saw the *Lotus Sutra* as encapsulating supreme truth. PURE LAND BUDDHISM taught followers to rely upon the favor of the Buddha Amitabha (*see* AMIDA) and

AVALOKITESVARA, the BODHISATTVA known in China as Kuan-yin. Ch'an Buddhism—better known in North America by its Japanese name, ZEN BUDDHISM—rejected speech and reasoning as distorting truth; it advocated instead a direct, intuitive, ineffable awareness of things as they are.

In 845 C.E. the fortunes of Buddhism changed permanently—for the worse. In that year the "Great Persecution" of Buddhism took place, during which more than 40,000 monasteries were destroyed. Chinese Buddhism never recovered from this blow. It did not disappear, but it was never again the leading Chinese religion.

During the Buddhist period Confucianism had seemed unsophisticated, because it concentrated so heavily on proper behavior. Starting around 1000 C.E. Neo-Confucians made Confucianism respectable once again. They developed a Confucian metaphysics (theory of reality) comparable to that of Buddhism and Taoism. At the same time, broad segments of the Chinese population adopted a Confucian outlook. Confucianism again became the dominant Chinese religion. But Confucianism did not exclude China's other religious traditions. The most common view suggested that all three teachings—Confucianism, Taoism, and Buddhism—were essentially one.

By the late 19th century European colonialism had disrupted the self-confidence of traditional Chinese society. Confucian values seemed weak and outdated. The establishment of the People's Republic of China, as the Communist regime was called, in 1949 had even harsher consequences, especially at first. Numerous Buddhist and Taoist monks, along with some Christian missionaries, went into exile in Hong Kong and Taiwan, where traditional Chinese religion has been maintained.

RELIGION IN COMMUNIST CHINA

The relation between religion and Communism in China went through several stages. The first (1950–66) was a time of consolidation, when all foreign influences, including missionaries and many of their followers, were forced into exile. Remaining religious bodies had to form "patriotic" organizations aligning the faith with the new state and its ideology. Some churches and Buddhist temples became showplaces for outside visitors, although far more were confiscated and turned over to other uses. Uncooperative religionists were persecuted.

Then came the Great Cultural Revolution of 1966–69, when young Red Guards swept through the country destroying virtually everything "old," including religion. Whatever religious life survived went deep underground. But after the Cultural Revolution had run its course by around 1970, and especially after the death of Chinese Communism's leader, Mao Zedong, in 1976, more pragmatic counsels won out. China became more accessible to the world. Visitors reported that religion seemed generally able to flourish openly, though under tight supervision. But the situation in Tibet remained tense, and new religious movements outside official control, such as the Falun Gong (which received worldwide publicity in 2000 and after), were regarded as subversive and were dealt with harshly.

However, China is a vast country, often secretive, and reliable general information is not easy to come by. Some reports say that, of a population of 1.2 billion, perhaps 300 million (25 percent) are followers of various religious faiths, not counting those who only practice occasional forms of Chinese folk religion. The majority are Buddhist and Taoist, but some 18 million Chinese are Muslim, mostly in the far northwest. Protestants are said to number 25 million in several denominations, some officially recognized and some clandestine, and Roman Catholics 12 million, equally divided between two organizations, one aligned with the Vatican and another, descended from the days of "patriotic" religious groups, separated from it.

On the other hand, there are those who claim that the number of Christians in China may reach as high as 100 million, being largely unofficial followers who read the Bible privately and meet quietly in "house churches." They say that in this way Christianity is rapidly growing in the world's most populous nation. At the same time, the government and the majority of Chinese are perhaps more secular than in any other large nation on earth. The way China ultimately goes may say much about the future of religion on this planet.

See also FENG SHUI; TIBETAN RELIGION.

Further reading: Wolfgang Bauer, *China and the Search for Happiness* (New York: Seabury, 1976); Julia Ching, *Chinese Religions* (Maryknoll, N.Y.: Orbis, 1995); Daniel Overmyer, *Religion in China Today* (New York: Columbia University Press, 2003); Laurence Thompson, *Chinese Religion: An Introduction* (Belmont, Calif.: Wadsworth, 1988).

Christ   From the Greek word *christos*, meaning "anointed"; a title applied to JESUS, the founder of CHRISTIANITY. The earliest followers of Jesus most likely spoke Aramaic, which was the languages of Palestine in Jesus' day. As a result, they would not have applied the Greek word *christos*, "Christ," to Jesus. They would have used its Aramaic equivalent, which is usually rendered into English as MESSIAH.

Within 15 years of Jesus' death, however, MISSIONARIES such as PAUL were actively spreading the message about Jesus to people outside of Palestine. At the time Greek was the common language of the eastern Mediterranean, so they translated their message into Greek. Jesus the Messiah became Jesus the Christ, and the religion eventually came to be known as Christianity.

The word *christos*, "Christ," quickly assumed the status of a proper name—Jesus Christ rather than Jesus the Christ—and the name was limited to Jesus. Today the name Christ is rarely associated with its original Greek meaning, "the anointed."

Christianity   The religion centered on belief in JESUS as the Son of GOD. Although it has representatives throughout the globe, Christianity is especially prominent in Europe, the Americas, and Australia.

HISTORY

Jesus (*c.* 4 B.C.E./*c.* 30 C.E.) was a Jew who lived primarily in Galilee (today northern Israel). It is said that he wandered the countryside, teaching and working MIRACLES. Pontius Pilate, the Roman governor of Judea (today southern Israel), had him crucified on charges of sedition against the Roman government, but his followers soon became convinced that he had been raised from the dead. Some of these followers traveled as MISSIONARIES, mostly throughout the Roman Empire. They taught that Jesus was the promised MESSIAH or CHRIST and that he provided people with forgiveness for their SINS and eternal life.

Until the fourth century Christianity was illegal in the Roman Empire, because Christians refused to "venerate" or give a kind of worship to the emperor. But Emperor Constantine (c. 280–337) lifted the legal restrictions against Christianity, and Emperor Theodosius (347–395) made all other religions illegal. At this time Christians systematized their teachings. The most important teachings said that Jesus was both fully God and fully human (see INCARNATION) and that God was a trinity: Father (or Creator), Son, and Holy Spirit. At the same time they came to final agreement on which books should be included in the NEW TESTAMENT, that is, the specifically Christian part of the Bible.

The Roman Empire had two parts, an eastern, Greek-speaking part and a western, Latin-speaking one. Starting in the fifth century, the political ties that had held these two together snapped, and Christians in the two regions gradually grew apart. In 1054 the Great Schism severed relations between the Roman Catholic Church in the west (see ROMAN CATHOLICISM) and the Eastern Orthodox churches (see EASTERN ORTHODOX CHRISTIANITY). The official causes included differences in church teaching and the relative positions of the pope and the patriarch of Constantinople (see PAPACY, THE).

During the 16th century the western church split. This event, known as the REFORMATION, led to the creation of many Protestant churches (see PROTESTANTISM). The Protestants insisted that only the Bible, not the papacy or the traditions of the church, had authority in religious matters. They also used the common language in worship services instead of Latin.

The 17th to the early 20th centuries were the great age of European colonialism. Christian missionaries accompanied European conquerors and converted people all over the globe. Catholic missionaries had been active among the indigenous peoples of the Americas from as early as the 16th century. The 19th century was the era of large and influential Protestant missionary societies.

During the 20th century there were several important movements within Christianity. The ecumenical movement—named from the Greek word *oikoumene*, roughly meaning "the whole world"—tried to overcome the differences that divided Christianity into many separate churches and to unite Christians around the globe. A very different movement, fundamentalism (see FUNDAMENTALISM, CHRISTIAN), arose in response to challenges posed by historical and scientific investigation; it insisted that every word of the Bible was literally true. Still other movements addressed issues of equality and justice: Liberal Protestant churches began to admit women to leadership roles previously closed to them, while in poorer parts of the world some Christians worked for political and economic liberation.

BELIEFS

Christians have generally emphasized the role of belief in bringing about SALVATION. As a result, Christian churches have insisted on a uniformity of belief more than many religions have. Christians often recite statements of belief known as CREEDS in public worship.

Most but not all Christians endorse the beliefs established by the seven ancient ecumenical councils (325–787). (Councils are meetings of bishops, the heads of churches in various areas.) These beliefs include the belief that God is a trinity, Father (or Creator), Son, and Holy Spirit; that Jesus is the son of God and thus unites two natures, divine and human, in one person; that Jesus was conceived apart from human sexual activity (see VIRGIN BIRTH); that forgiveness of sins is available through Jesus' death and RESURRECTION; and that at the end of time the dead will be raised and judged (see JUDGMENT OF THE DEAD). Christians differ on which books make up the Old Testament, but virtually all

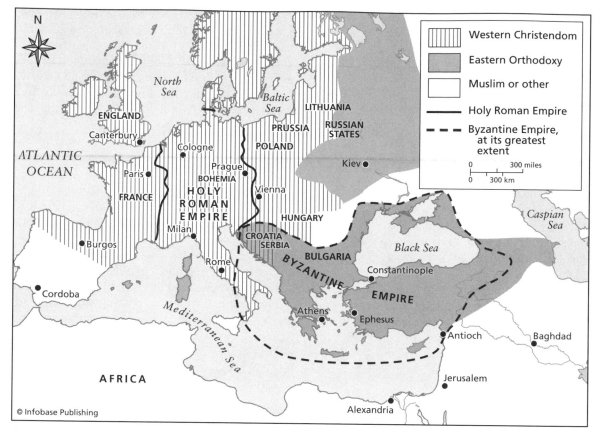

Christianity at the time of the Schism, 1054

Christians agree on the 27 books that make up the New Testament.

Christians have never been able to reach unanimity on all beliefs. One very significant difference concerns the process by which sins are forgiven. To what extent is salvation a gift from God, and to what extent do human beings need to perform certain actions in order to be saved? The Roman Catholic Church teaches that salvation requires both God's gift of GRACE and human actions. The most extreme Protestant view, "double predestination," suggests that God has determined whether a person will be saved or damned even before that person is born. Another point on which Christians differ concerns the significance of the bread and the wine in the RITUAL known as the EUCHARIST. Catholic and Orthodox Christians teach that the bread and wine actually become Jesus' body and blood. Most Protestants teach that they are only symbols of Jesus's body and blood.

PRACTICES

In recognition of Jesus' resurrection on a Sunday, most Christian churches have set aside Sunday as a day for communal worship. Orthodox and Catholic worship centers on the celebration of the eucharist in the Divine LITURGY or the Mass. Readings from the Bible, PRAYERS, and usually a homily (a short address or sermon) are also parts of the celebration. Specially ordained priests must perform the ritual of the eucharist itself, but in recent years steps have been taken to increase the participation of laypeople in other ways.

Protestant churches have tended to celebrate the eucharist less frequently, in some churches as infrequently as once or twice a year. Protestant worship has emphasized PREACHING the word of God. Worship consists of a sermon, generally by a specially appointed minister, along with readings from the Bible, prayers, and songs or hymns.

Most Christians follow a cycle of annual festivals linked to the life of Jesus: Advent prepares for the coming of Jesus; CHRISTMAS celebrates his birth; Epiphany celebrates his manifestation as God incarnate; LENT, which begins on Ash Wednesday, is a time for preparation and repentance; Palm Sunday recalls Jesus' entry into JERUSALEM just before his death, Maundy Thursday his last meal with his followers, and Good Friday his crucifixion; EASTER celebrates Jesus' resurrection from the dead.

One becomes a Christian through BAPTISM (sprinkling with or immersion in water). Catholic and Orthodox Christians generally practice baptism as a birth ritual. Some Protestants practice it as a ritual of maturation, like BAR/BAT MITZVAH in JUDAISM. In addition to baptism and the Eucharist, the Catholic and Orthodox churches recognize five other SACRAMENTS through which Christians receive God's grace: confirmation or chrismation, penance, marriage, holy orders, and anointing with oil for healing or as "extreme unction" for the dying. They also give special veneration to MARY, Jesus' mother, and SAINTS, exemplary Christians from the past. The Orthodox churches also emphasize the use of sacred pictures known as icons (*see* IMAGES, ICONS, IDOLS IN RELIGION).

ORGANIZATION

Christian churches are organized according to two models, the episcopal model and the congregational model.

On the episcopal model, authority resides with a bishop (Greek, *episkopos*) or archbishop. Bishops are persons in charge of an entire area, and they oversee the activities of a variety of subordinates, such as priests. The Roman Catholic Church concentrates ultimate authority in a single human being, the pope. The Orthodox churches are organized along national lines—Greek, Russian, Ukrainian, and so on. Each national church is headed by a patriarch or metropolitan.

The congregational model is found among many Protestants. On this model, authority resides with the local congregation, which selects a person to be its minister. Usually congregations are joined together into larger regional or national groups. However, fundamentalist and evangelical Protestants in the United States have founded a large number of independent "Bible churches."

CHRISTIANITY IN THE WORLD TODAY

At the beginning of the 21st century, Christianity was the world's largest religion. Some 2 billion people, about a third of the world's population, were at least nominally Christian or of Christian cultural background. However, the role and impact of the religion varied greatly from one place to another. Moreover, the Christian "center of gravity," that is, where its greatest number and dynamism are concentrated, was rapidly shifting from Europe and North America to what is called the Third World or Southern Hemisphere, the countries of Latin America, Africa, and southern Asia.

Traditionally, Christianity has been considered chiefly the religion of the white races of Europe and their immigrant descendents in the Americas. Since its origin within the Roman Empire, most significant Christian history appeared to take place in Europe or the Mediterranean basin. This is where the papacy ruled, dominant theologies were developed, theological wars were fought, the Protestant Reformation took place, and the major DENOMINATIONS were formed. Even Christianity in the Americas, including the United States (*see* UNITED STATES, RELIGION IN), although it soon displayed some distinctive features, has often been seen as little more than the transplanting of what was essentially a European faith.

Now, in Europe, although the great cathedrals still stand and traditional Christian festivals are observed, the religion seems to have lost considerable vigor. In a few places religious identity remains important and divisive, for example, whether one is

Roman Catholic or Protestant in Ireland or is Catholic, Eastern Orthodox, or Muslim (*see* ISLAM) in Bosnia-Herzegovina and surrounding areas. But in most parts of Europe not more than a small percentage of the population attends church regularly.

In the United States, church attendance by the professedly Christian 85 percent of the population is markedly higher than in Europe; the situation in Canada is between those of Europe and the United States (*see* CANADA, RELIGION IN). But the 225 million Christians in the United States in 2000 represented only a little over 10 percent of world Christianity, and that percentage will decline as the 21st century advances. Worldwide, according to projections, by 2025 half the world's Christians will live in Africa and Latin America; by 2050, only about one-fifth of the world's then 3 billion Christians will be non-Hispanic "whites," and some four-fifths of Christians will be Hispanic, African, or Asian. This is partly because of anticipated rapid population growth in those parts of the world and partly because Christianity is attracting converts there as it loses adherents in regions that were once its heartlands.

More significant are the changes this demographic (population) shift is making in the character of Christianity. In worldwide traditions such as ANGLICANISM, tensions between European/North American and Asian/African/Latin American wings of the denomination have already reached a critical point, as the former tend to be far more liberal than the latter on such issues as homosexuality and ordaining women.

Moreover, increasingly Christians in the Southern Hemisphere regions of rapid growth is moving away from traditional "mainline" denominations. PENTECOSTALISM, with its vibrancy, its strict moral standards, and its provisions for spiritual expression on the part of virtually everyone in its congregations, has flourished. It is now estimated that as many as one-fourth of active Christians in the world are Pentecostal. Many other new forms of Christianity (*see* CHRISTIANITY, INDEPENDENT) have appeared in Latin America, Africa (as many as 8,000 on that continent), and Asia, accommodating Christian expression to surrounding cultures

in ways traditional European and North American denominations perhaps never could. Many contain elements of SPIRITUALISM, Pentecostalism, or SANTERÍA as well as such indigenous features as ANCESTOR VENERATION and traditional music and dance. The face of Christianity in the 21st century and after will definitely look different from that of the past.

SIGNIFICANCE

Christianity is the largest single religion in the world today, practiced by roughly a third of the world's population. For centuries Christianity has made major contributions to European culture. During the 20th century, strong, independent Christian churches also developed among those who were not of European ancestry.

Further reading: David B. Barrett, George T. Kurian, and Todd M. Johnson, eds., *World Christian Encyclopedia,* 2d ed. (New York: Oxford University Press, 2001); Harvey Cox, *Fire from Heaven: The Rise of Pentecostal Spirituality and the Reshaping of Religion in the Twenty-first Century* (Reading, Mass.: Addison-Wesley, 1995); Robert S. Ellwood, and James B. Wiggins, *Christianity: A Cultural Perspective* (Englewood Cliffs, N.J.: Prentice Hall, 1988); Philip Jenkins, *The Next Christendom: The Coming of Global Christianity* (New York: Oxford University Press, 2002); Daniel L. Migloire, *Faith Seeking Understanding: An Introduction to Christian Theology.* (Grand Rapids, Mich.: W. B. Eerdmans, 2004); Ninian Smart, *The Phenomenon of Christianity* (London: Collins, 1979); Williston Walker, *A History of the Christian Church,* Rev. Ed. (New York: Scribner, 1984).

Christianity, independent Christian churches that do not belong to a broader Christian institutional organization. That definition would seem self-evident, but in fact it means different things, depending upon what broader institutional organizations prevail in a given place.

In the years immediately after JESUS, there seem to have been many communities that called themselves Christian. Some banded together to form larger associations; others, apparently, did not. With time, what we now know as normative Christianity developed out of a tradition that saw itself as in the line of Jesus' APOSTLES. When, during the 300s, Christianity became first legal and then mandatory in the Roman empire, the "apostolic-orthodox" tradition was established. Churches were organized by territories governed by bishops. In the Western half of the Roman empire the PAPACY assumed the role of overseeing all bishops.

Some Christian churches, such as the Coptic (*see* COPTIC CHURCH) and Nestorian churches, were independent of these structures, but it would be a misnomer to consider them independent Christianity. They had their own institutional structures. Christian movements also continued to arise that opposed some elements of ROMAN CATHOLICISM or EASTERN ORTHODOX CHRISTIANITY. They were, however, condemned as heresy and found it difficult to flourish.

Independent Christianity did not become viable until the Protestant REFORMATION. The term means something different, however, in different geographical settings, such as Europe, the United States, and Africa.

In Europe Protestants in the tradition of Martin LUTHER (1483–1546) and John CALVIN (1509–64) formed churches that received the support of the state. For example, their ministers had been trained in state universities and paid salaries from tax revenues. Other churches refused to ally with the state. In the early days of the Reformation, the leading churches that did not do so were the Anabaptist churches, such as the MENNONITES in the Netherlands. With time, other churches independent of the state developed too. In Germany, for example, these included the Methodist Church (imported from England) and in some areas the Independent Lutheran Church, which disagreed with the state-supported Lutheran church (*see* LUTHERANISM). These churches represent independent Christianity in that they are supported by voluntary contributions, not the government.

In the United States, all churches are independent churches in this sense. Even churches such as the Roman Catholic Church, the Lutheran Church, the Episcopal Church (*see* EPISCOPALIAN-ISM), and the Presbyterian Church (*see* PRESBYTERIAN AND REFORMED CHURCHES), which are traditionally state-supported churches in Europe, are supported by voluntary contributions in the United States. In this climate, independent Christianity refers to churches that refuse to ally themselves with any denomination. Independent BIBLE churches, founded by a person who feels called to preach, are good examples found fairly widely throughout the country. Sometimes these churches enter into loose association with other churches, as long as the association does not require the establishment of a broader administrative structure. An example of such churches is the Undenominational Fellowship of Christian Churches and Churches of Christ. These churches refused to remain in fellowship with the Christian Church (Disciples of Christ) when the Disciples established a denominational structure in 1968. PENTECOSTALISM, a powerful religious movement of the 20th century, also produced many independent churches in this sense.

In Africa, independent Christianity means yet something different (*see* AFRICA, NEW RELIGIOUS MOVEMENTS IN). In Africa, independent Christianity refers to two types of church. One is the church that was started by MISSIONARIES from North America or Europe but then broke away from the parent church. Churches often did this because the parent churches did not trust Africans to control their own institutions. The other type of independent Christianity includes churches founded by African prophets or even messiahs. As a result of what they see as a revelation from God, they begin to preach, heal, cast out evil spirits, and attract a following. Some of these independent African churches have become large institutions. Some have also affiliated with the World Council of Churches.

Christians have always cherished the idea of unity, in the words of PAUL in the Bible: "one Lord, one faith, one baptism" (Ephesians 4.5). That ideal has not prevented them, however, from developing many different kinds of Christianity. Independent Christianity is an important means by which forms of Christianity not allowed by dominating institutional structures can develop and flourish.

Further reading: Kwame Bediako, *Jesus and the Gospel in Africa: History and Experience* (New York: Orbis, 2004); Elizabeth Isichei, *A History of Christianity in Africa* (Grand Rapids, Mich.: W. B. Eerdmans, 1995); Donald B. Kraybill, *Who Are the Anabaptists?: Amish, Brethren, Hutterites, and Mennonites* (Scottdale, Pa.: Herald Press, 2003).

Christian Science A Christian movement that emphasizes healing. Christian Science began in Boston, Massachusetts. In 1866 Mary Baker Eddy (1821–1910) experienced a sudden healing that she attributed to GOD. In 1875 she published *Science and Health* to expound her teachings about divine healing. When the various churches showed little interest, she and several followers formed the first Church of Christ, Scientist, in 1879. Since that time the teachings of Christian Science have spread throughout the world.

Christian Science teaches that all genuine reality is spiritual. Sickness and distress result when people mistake the material for the real. Christian Science denies that JESUS was God, but it sees itself as thoroughly Christian. It uses Jesus's healings as the basis of its teaching that healing is possible for those who follow God's spiritual laws.

The Church of Christ, Scientist, maintains a register of "practitioners" or healers. These are not exactly ministers; they do not lead congregational WORSHIP. Services consist of readings from *Science and Health* and the BIBLE. On Wednesday evenings congregations hold services at which people present testimonies of being healed.

Many municipalities have Christian Science reading rooms. The church also publishes one of the leading American newspapers, the *Christian Science Monitor*. The *Monitor* does not, however, explicitly advocate the church's teachings.

Christmas The Christian celebration of the birth of JESUS on December 25. The English name derives from the phrase "Christ's Mass." Christmas is probably the most popular Christian celebration.

The earliest celebration of Christmas that we know about took place in Rome in the middle of the fourth century. This is the period during which CHRISTIANITY was in the process of becoming the official religion of the Roman Empire.

A century earlier the Roman emperor Aurelian (ruled 270–275) had made the WORSHIP of Sol Invictus, "The unconquered sun," the official religion of the empire. In 274 he had required all subjects of Rome to celebrate the birth of the sun on December 25. This is the date when days in the Northern Hemisphere begin to grow longer again. Many speculate that Aurelian's celebration of the birth of the sun was the origin of the celebration of Christmas on December 25.

During the fourth century the celebration of Jesus' birth on December 25 spread. Many churches in the eastern half of the Roman Empire—the ancestors of today's Orthodox churches (*see* EASTERN ORTHODOX CHRISTIANITY)—were already celebrating Jesus' birth and BAPTISM on January 6. They continued to celebrate Jesus' baptism on that day. On December 25 they remembered his birth and the visits of the shepherds and the magi. Churches in the western half of the Roman Empire—the ancestors of today's Catholic and Protestant churches (*see* ROMAN CATHOLICISM and PROTESTANISM)—thought of the day somewhat differently. On December 25 they celebrated Jesus' birth and the visit of the shepherds. On January 6, called Epiphany, they celebrated the visit of the magi.

A rich variety of popular customs has developed around the celebration of Christmas. In North America Christmas observances include sculpted scenes of Jesus' birth known as creches, special songs known as Christmas carols, an evergreen tree decorated with ornaments and lights, legends about a popular figure named Santa Claus who gives gifts (especially to children), the sending of greeting cards, and midnight worship services.

Each of these elements has a different origin. Francis of Assisi (*see* FRANCIS OF ASSISI AND

FRANCISCANS) began the tradition of building creches to celebrate Christmas in the late Middle Ages. Christmas carols began in the late Middle Ages, too. At that time it became customary on Christmas to replace the kinds of hymns used for ordinary festivals with songs of a more popular nature. The Christmas tree originated in Germany, although precisely when is unknown. In the 19th century, Queen Victoria's husband, who was German, brought the custom to English-speaking countries. Americans invented the legends of Santa Claus from a variety of sources, while the custom of sending greeting cards began in England in the 19th century. The oldest of the elements is the one from which Christmas takes its name: the celebration of an early morning mass, eventually at midnight.

Despite the popularity of the festival, not all Christians observe Christmas. When the festival was first introduced, the church in JERUSALEM refused to recognize it for 200 years. The ARMENIAN CHURCH still insists on celebrating the birth of Jesus on January 6. Some Protestants have also rejected Christmas. To them, it is a human invention that has no basis in the BIBLE. One such group was the Puritans (*see* PURITANISM). Because of Puritan influence, Christmas was not widely observed in the United States until the mid-1800s. The "plain people," such as the AMISH, still refuse to observe it.

Chuang-tzu (Zhuangzi) (*c.* 369–*c.* 286 B.C.E.) *a Chinese thinker important in the development of philosophical* TAOISM Chuang-tzu is known for a collection of essays that goes by the same name, *Chuang-tzu*. Only selected essays in the collection actually seem to come from Chuang-tzu.

Chuang-tzu's language is highly imagistic. As a result, it is often difficult to determine the precise meaning of the texts. The essays pose puzzles designed to teach that truth, goodness, happiness, and everything in life is relative—everything, that is, except the *Tao* or way of nature. The *Tao* cannot be encapsulated in language. Rather, it can only be grasped intuitively.

In perhaps the most famous portion of the book, Chuang-tzu dreams that he is a butterfly. Then he wakes up and wonders whether he is actually a man who is dreaming he was a butterfly, or a butterfly that is dreaming it is Chuang-tzu.

church and state The relationship of religion and government in predominantly Christian areas. Throughout most of history and in all parts of the globe, governments have been interested in religion. Indeed, for many peoples government was actually supposed to perform statewide religious observances. Where distinct religious and political institutions existed, questions generally concerned their relative power. Medieval Europe provides a good example. The church and the political rulers argued vehemently over who had the right to appoint priests.

During the REFORMATION and its aftermath, Protestants such as the Anabaptists (*see* MENNONITES and AMISH), Baptists (*see* BAPTIST CHURCHES), and QUAKERS insisted that religion should be a purely private matter. Philosophers influenced by the intellectual movement known as the Enlightenment tended to agree. For a variety of reasons, their ideas first took institutional form in North America.

Most British colonies in North America originally had official or "established" religions. But by the time of the Revolutionary War, a movement to "disestablish" religion was in progress. Massachusetts was the last state to disestablish religion. It did so in 1833. In the early 1800s the state of Massachusetts still tried and convicted some of its citizens for religious crimes such as HERESY.

In 1789 the United States adopted its present Constitution. It was a strikingly secular document. The Constitution did not invoke GOD's name. It prohibited using religion to determine whether someone could hold office in the federal government (Article 6, Section 3). But that was all it said about religion. It is likely that the framers of the Constitution simply decided to ignore religious questions and leave them up to the states.

In 1791 the Bill of Rights added 10 amendments to the Constitution. Two clauses of the First Amendment deal with religion. The first says that Congress cannot pass a law that tends to establish religion—not a religion, but religion in general. This clause is known as the Establishment Clause. The second clause says that Congress cannot prohibit people from practicing their religion freely. It is known as the Free Exercise Clause. The Fourteenth Amendment, passed later during the Civil War, prohibited state and local governments from taking away rights granted at the federal level. As a result, the First Amendment now applies at all levels of government, from the federal government to school boards.

During the second half of the 20th century, many disputes arose concerning the interpretation of two religion clauses. In applying the Establishment Clause, the Supreme Court ruled that governments could neither promote nor inhibit religion. As a result, it declared unconstitutional many practices common in some public schools. For example, in 1962 the court ruled that schools cannot write prayers and have students recite them (*Engel* v. *Vitale*). Later, in 1985, the court also held that states cannot require public school students to observe a moment of silent meditation (*Wallace* v. *Jaffree*). According to a 1992 ruling, a religious official, whether priest, minister, RABBI, or IMAM, cannot offer prayers at public school functions (*Lee* v. *Weisman*).

Controversies also arose over the Free Exercise Clause. That clause clearly has its limits. People cannot simply do anything they want in the name of religious freedom. For example, no one suggests that human SACRIFICE should be legal. But where should the lines be drawn?

In 1963 the court took a broad view of religious freedom. It said that if the government wanted to deprive someone of religious freedom, it had to do more than simply give a reason. It had to show that a "compelling interest" left it no choice but to violate religious freedom. The 1963 case involved a Seventh-Day Adventist (*see* SEVENTH-DAY ADVENTISM) who had lost her job because she could not work on Saturdays. She wanted unemployment compensation, and the court ruled in her favor (*Sherbert* v. *Verner*).

Twenty-seven years later, in 1990, the court took a much narrower view of religious freedom. It said that religious freedom did not allow people to violate laws that applied to everyone. It only prevented the government from outlawing specific religious practices. The case at issue involved two Native American drug counselors. They lost their jobs because they had eaten peyote, an hallucinogen, in ceremonies of the Native American Church. (Their jobs required them to remain drug-free.) They, too, wanted unemployment compensation, but the court denied their request (*Employment Division* v. *Smith*).

The narrow view of religious freedom does offer religious people some protection. For example, in 1993 the Supreme Court ruled that a Florida town could not pass a law against animal sacrifice (*Church of Lukumi Babalu Aye* v. *Hialeah*). But many people felt that the narrow view did not provide enough protection. For example, what would prevent a state from convicting priests of serving alcohol to minors when they gave the EUCHARIST to teenagers? A state that convicted priests could claim that it was simply enforcing a law everyone had to follow.

Concerns such as these led Congress to pass the Religious Freedom Restoration Act in 1993. In line with the broader view of religious freedom, it required governments to demonstrate a compelling interest before they violated religious freedom. But in July 1996 the court declared this act unconstitutional, because Congress cannot tell the courts how to interpret the Constitution. At the time of writing, amendments to the First Amendment have been proposed in Congress, but it seems unlikely that any new constitutional amendments on religion will be ratified.

Further reading: Sidney Z. Ehler, and John B. Morrall, *Church and State Through the Centuries* (London: Burns and Oates, 1954); Edwin S. Gaustad, *Church and State in America* (New York: Oxford University Press, 1999); William Lee Miller, *The First Liberty: Religion and the American Republic.* (New York: Knopf, 1986).

Church of God Name of several denominations in the HOLINESS and PENTECOSTAL tradition. Now worldwide, they originated in the United States. The two main Churches of God, designated by the location of their headquarters, are the Church of God (Anderson, Indiana) and the Church of God (Cleveland, Tennessee). The former is a leading expression of the 19th-century Holiness movement, which taught that Christians can, after conversion and believer's baptism, receive a second gift of the Holy Spirit called sanctification, the ability to live a holy life. This church was founded in 1880 and follows congregational organization.

The larger Cleveland, Tennessee, church traces its origins to 1886, though the name was not adopted until 1907. It has put more emphasis than the other Church of God on Pentecostal-type gifts of the Holy Spirit as evidence of sanctification. Speaking in tongues, divine healings, and ecstatic behavior show that the Spirit is at work in a person and a congregation. Its organization is comparable to that of METHODISM, with bishops and superintendents. The Church of God of Prophecy, another Holiness/Pentecostal body, is an offshoot from it.

The Church of God in Christ is a largely African-American denomination tracing its origin, as does Pentecostalism generally, to the famous Azusa Street revival of 1907 in Los Angeles. It also embraces a combination of Holiness and Pentecostal features, and it has spread around the world.

cinema and religion Ever since motion pictures were invented in the 1890s, filmmakers have been fascinated with religious themes. They have explored such themes in a variety of ways. Some films tell religious stories. Others use religious elements to tell different stories. Still others explore— or allow their audiences to explore—religious issues. Of course, filmmakers have made many instructional films about religions, too. Such films are usually viewed in classrooms rather than in the cinema. This entry does not discuss them.

FILMS THAT TELL RELIGIOUS STORIES

Most religions tell stories, and filmmakers the world over have found that religious stories can make good cinema. For example, the film *Atanarjuat* (2001) presents a traditional story of the Arctic peoples of North America. The film *Whale Rider* (2002) explores tradition and change among the Maori of New Zealand from the perspective of a girl who emerges as a leader of her people. *Kundun* (1997) portrays the early life of the DALAI LAMA, while the Hindi film *Asoka* (2001) dramatizes—and fictionalizes—the early life of emperor ASOKA, a major figure in the spread of BUDDHISM. In the late 1980s filmmakers in India created a national sensation when they televised very long, serialized versions of two profoundly religious EPICS, *Ramayan* and *Mahabharaat*. Sensational for its time, too, was Cecil B. DeMille's epic, *The Ten Commandments* (1956), as was the 1976 film *The Message* about MUHAMMAD and ISLAM. Filmmakers have also found inspiration in the lives of Christian SAINTS, such as Thomas à Becket (*Becket* [1964]), FRANCIS OF ASSISI (*Brother Sun, Sister Moon* [1972]), and Thomas More (*A Man for All Seasons* [1966]). The story of JOAN OF ARC was first filmed as long ago as 1895.

One story that has attracted North American and European filmmakers over and over again is the life of JESUS. Because Jesus is so special to many North Americans and Europeans, some filmmakers have been reluctant to portray him. They have filmed stories in which they show Jesus' shadow, hands, or feet or even just the reaction of onlookers to him but do not show Jesus' entire body or face. Two films from the 1950s provide good examples of this technique: *Ben-Hur* (1959) and *The Robe* (1953). The British comedy troupe Monty Python parodied such films, among others, in *Life of Brian* (1979).

Other filmmakers have portrayed Jesus directly in many different ways. *The Greatest Story Ever Told* (1965) shows a formal, stiff, proper Jesus in a film with little action. *The Jesus Film* (1979) presents a very different Jesus: a friendly Jesus who, before he is arrested, constantly smiles and always sports neat hair, trimmed beard, and immaculate clothes. Others find the brusque Jesus in *The Gospel According to Matthew* (1964) by the Italian director Pier Paolo Pasolini more realistic. In *The Last Temptation of Christ* (1988) Martin Scorsese portrayed a mentally fragile Jesus in order to explore the struggles of a human being trying to fulfill divine expectations. Two rock operas from 1973 provide a different, nontraditional take on Jesus: *Jesus Christ Superstar* and *Godspell*. Mel Gibson graphically portrayed the physical sufferings of Jesus in *The Passion of the Christ* (2004). Viewers may find, however, that none of these films, or the many other films about Jesus, quite fit their image of what Jesus was like. That is because stories that are heard or read, unlike cinema, allow their audiences to imagine characters and settings as they see fit. People seem to have imagined Jesus in various ways.

Cinema can explore and highlight many dimensions and nuances of religious stories. In this way, it continues to do in a new medium what religious art, music, and literature have been doing for centuries.

FILMS THAT USE ELEMENTS FROM RELIGIOUS STORIES

At times screenwriters invent entirely new stories. They also frequently use elements and motifs from stories that they and their audiences already know. Among other things, these familiar elements make it easier for the film to communicate.

Many films have used religious elements in this way. Japanese anime films are filled with mythic themes, including Christian ones. The Star Wars saga is filled with mythic themes, too. It draws them mainly from the ideas of Joseph Campbell (1904–87), an interpreter of the psychologist Carl Gustav JUNG. Islamic resistance to foreign occupation forms the subject of *Lion of the Desert* (1981), which details the resistance led by Omar Mukhtar in Libya against Mussolini's Italy. *Lagaan* (2001), a Hindi film available in many video shops in the United States, uses Hindu themes. It alludes to stories of KRISHNA, Radha, and the gopis and to Krishna's salvific LILA or play as it tells a story of Indians resisting British colo-

nialism. They do so by challenging the British to a cricket match.

Most North Americans and Europeans would probably miss the references to Krishna in *Lagaan*, but they may notice allusions to the Jesus story more easily. Perhaps for that reason North American and European filmmakers have used elements of the story of Jesus widely.

One series of Westerns—*Shane* (1953), *Pale Rider* (1985), *The Quick and the Dead* (1995), and perhaps other films as well—provides an alternative to a savior who suffers and dies. They celebrate a gun-slinging savior who comes to town, defeats the forces of evil in a shoot-out, and rescues the helpless townspeople. The films tell this story from different angles. *Pale Rider* develops its story with the help of motifs not only from the Jesus story but also from the Book of Revelation (*see* REVELATION, BOOK OF). The title of *The Quick and the Dead* comes from the traditional translation of Christian CREEDS. It tells the story of a female savior who openly rejects the teachings of Jesus.

An old tradition in EASTERN ORTHODOX CHRISTIANITY celebrates "holy fools." Starting with the writings of Fyodor Dostoyevsky and Friedrich Nietzsche in the 19th century, a motif in Western literature has also connected Jesus with madness or insanity. Such figures are sometimes called "Christomaniacs" and are found in films such as the Argentine film *Man Facing Southeast* (1986), *K-Pax* (2001), and perhaps less obviously *One Flew Over the Cuckoo's Nest* (1975) and *Being There* (1979).

Less frequently, films make use of the Jesus story told from a perspective of GNOSTICISM. Good examples are *Blade Runner* (1982) and the *The Matrix* (1999).

FILMS THAT EXPLORE RELIGIOUS ISSUES

Most films touch upon the problems and challenges that human beings face, even if they do not explore them with much depth. As a result, given enough ingenuity most films can lead to reflection on religious issues. There is little point in trying to survey such films comprehensively, but it might be helpful here to list a few films generally available in video shops that are not, perhaps, widely known to most Americans.

A once popular director who often treated religious themes is Ingmar Bergman (b. 1918). His films, such as *The Seventh Seal* (1957) and *The Virgin Spring* (1960), explore existentialist ideas, which deal with aspects of life that seem meaningless and absurd. *Schindler's List* (1993) is one of many films that deal with the Shoah or HOLOCAUST. The earlier film EXODUS (1960) recounts the founding of the state of Israel. Deepa Mehta (b. 1950) has explored interreligious violence in her powerful but graphic film *Earth* (1998). It portrays events in Lahore during the partition of India and Pakistan in 1947. *Himalaya* (1999) deals with an issue found in many societies—the conflict between age and youth, traditional religion and modern science—from the perspective of people living in Nepal. *The Burmese Harp* (1956) uses BUDDHISM in exploring the situation of Japanese soldiers faced with defeat in World War II. An Iranian film, *Children of Heaven* (1997), and a Kurdish film, *Time for Drunken Horses* (2000), may be more ethical than religious. Both deal in powerful ways with brothers and sisters who look out for one another in situations of poverty and war. The recent Spanish film *The Sea Inside* (2004) explores the controversial issue of suicide and euthanasia (*see* SUICIDE AND RELIGION) by telling the story of Ramon Sampedro, a paralyzed Spanish man who committed suicide with the help of friends. Two Danish films, *Babette's Feast* (1987) and *Italian for Beginners* (2000), find religious fulfillment in close human relationships. In doing so, they echo Christian emphases on the communion meal and the word of God.

Further reading: Albert J. Bergesen and Andrew M. Greeley, *God in the Movies,* preface by Roger Ebert (New Brunswick, N.J.: Transaction Publishers, 2000); John Lyden, *Film as Religion: Myths, Morals, and Rituals* (New York: New York University Press, 2003); S. Brent Plate, ed., *Representing Religion in World Cinema: Filmmaking, Mythmaking, Culture Making* (New York: Palgrave Macmillan, 2003); Adele Reinhartz, *Scripture on the Silver Screen* (Louisville, Ky.: Westminster John Knox Press, 2003); W. Barnes Tatum, *Jesus at the Movies: A Guide to the First Hundred Years* (Santa Rosa, Calif.: Polebridge, 1997).

circumcision   The cutting away of the male foreskin. The term is sometimes also applied to clitoridectomy, the cutting away of corresponding female organs.

Circumcision is widely practiced among indigenous peoples, especially in Australia and East Africa. It is obligatory among Jews, Muslims, and Coptic Christians. Catholic, Orthodox, and Protestant Christians do not require circumcision. Starting in the last half of the 19th century, however, circumcision also became common among Christians in Europe and especially in North America. It did so allegedly for reasons of hygiene. The actual medical benefits seem minimal.

Indigenous peoples have often practiced circumcision as part of the RITUALS that mark the male reaching adulthood (*see* INITIATION, RELIGIOUS). Practices vary widely, and so do the reasons given for the practice. For some, circumcision is a way to remove residual feminine characteristics from the maturing boy. In any case, it prepares the boy for future adult life, including sexual relations with women.

For Jews, Coptic Christians, and Muslims, circumcision is a sign of membership in the group. It is an old rite. It was practiced in ancient Egypt even before the time of ABRAHAM (*see* EGYPTIAN RELIGION). In Hebrew, circumcision is known as *brit milah,* "covenant of circumcision." Colloquially, Jews refer to it simply as *bris.* In Arabic, circumcision is called *tahur,* "purification."

Jews circumcise men as a sign of God's COVENANT with them. The command to circumcise was given to Abraham (Genesis 17.9–27). Under MOSES it was extended to non-Jews who wanted to eat the PASSOVER meal (Exodus (12.43–49). Jewish boys are to be circumcised on the eighth day after birth. Jews have traditionally required adult male converts to be circumcised, too. The Reform movement has not always insisted on this.

In JUDAISM a special religious functionary called a *mohel* performs the circumcision. Circumcision is also an occasion for a party.

Circumcision is not mentioned in the QUR'AN. It was, however, an Arabic practice before the rise of ISLAM, and the prophet MUHAMMAD was himself circumcised. Circumcision is thus considered mandatory. In some Islamic traditions, circumcision is required for males and recommended for females. Other traditions say it is required for both. The age at which Muslims circumcise varies. Some Muslims circumcise on the seventh day after birth (the eighth day counting birth). Others circumcise later. As in Judaism, circumcision is often a time for a party.

In the Mediterranean region and the Islamic world, the circumcision of girls has been seen as a way of keeping their later sexual desires in check. The amount of tissue removed, pain involved, and physiological change varies widely. In some but not all cases female circumcision results in significant disfiguration. At the end of the 20th century and today, feminists have severely criticized these practices.

clothing, religious The symbolism and significance of clothing worn for religious purposes. Clothes have always served not only the practical function of keeping people warm, and the universal function of making people attractive according to the canons of their society while preserving some degree of modesty, but have also shown through well-known indicators such things as comparative wealth, ethnic background, and social status. They have also had very widespread religious meaning, though the way they have done this has varied greatly. The conservative wings of most religions insist on modesty in dress, especially for women. In some cases all adherents of a religion, or all of one gender (most often women), have followed rules in dress, such as the AMISH use of "plain" clothes without buttons, or the Muslim prescription that women should be covered completely. In other cases, special clothes are worn only by religious specialists and leaders. The somber garb worn by MONKS AND NUNS is seen in some branches of CHRISTIANITY, especially Roman Catholic, Eastern Orthodox, and Anglican, and among Hindus, Buddhists, and Taoists. The color of the monastic "habit" or robe is often indicative of affiliation: in the West, Franciscans wear brown (*see* FRANCIS OF ASSISI AND FRANCISCANS), BENEDICTINES black, and TRAPPISTS and DOMINICANS white. Theravada Buddhist monks wear saffron (a yellow-orange), Mahayana Buddhist monks gray. Hindu monks or sadhus vary considerably (some have gone completely naked), but some modern orders use a reddish-orange gown.

Priests and other religious leaders frequently have special dress too. In the Catholic-type traditions of Christianity, they often are attired in black or dark-colored suit or cassock (a long black gown) and round white collar. It is while conducting services, though, that the full richness of religious garb may become apparent, though it ranges from the simple sacred cord of BRAHMIN priests and the black pulpit gown of some Protestants, to the rich and colorful vestments of some Buddhists, or of Catholic priests celebrating mass in colors appropriate to the season of the church year, or bishops in cope and mitre (a high pointed hat), or the temple priests of biblical Israel. In all cases, the dress is part of the religious symbolism; it properly does not glorify an individual but the office and the role in WORSHIP, and is a way by which that person identifies with it.

clowns, religious Persons who dress and act humorously in religious activities. In some Native American cultures a solemn RITUAL by the priests will be followed by a burlesque (or comic) repetition of the same by ritual clowns making fun of it. Their performance may be related to the folklore role of the TRICKSTER, such as Coyote, who is clever enough to break rules and fool the gods in all sorts of ways. In medieval Europe some festivals, especially those of CARNIVAL or the season just before the fast of LENT, would install a "boy bishop" selected from among the choirboys who would ridicule the functions of a church leader in parodies that went to the extent of fake masses that substituted obscene songs for litanies and burned old shoes instead of incense. At the Jewish PURIM, solemn rabbis may be mockingly imitated by comedians or children. In the Roman Saturnalia, held at the same time as modern CHRISTMAS and NEW YEAR FESTIVALS, roles would also be reversed as masters waited on slaves, for a major feature of religious clowns is the way they and their antics upset the usual social order and the expected way of doing things.

Religious and other clowns particularly appear in boundary times and situations, such as festivals that appear at the winter solstice, like Saturnalia or New Year's, or like Carnival around the beginning of spring, and among groups like choirboys or students or marginalized clans in some Native American tribes that are ambiguously situated between priests and laypeople. They often dress in costumes that combine stripes or dots of wildly contrasting color, and are baggy and ill-fitting.

All this gives clues to the meaning of clowns. They are meant to provide comic relief at solemn occasions, and simply to entertain. More than that, though, they also show something important about the sacred cosmos: It includes all opposites, high and low, funny and serious, that which fits and that which doesn't fit. It is bigger than the neat categories of the human mind, and so it has to bring in those things that show up the pretensions and limitations of the mind. Humor is very religious when it shows that we humans are not as great or as perfect as we like to think we are, and religious clowns make that clear.

computers and religion The development of electronic computers in the second half of the 20th century changed many aspects of life, including religion. In particular, changes in religion have been brought about by the development of the personal computer in the 1980s and of the Internet in the 1990s. These effects are still taking place, and people are still trying to determine exactly what they have been.

Computers and the Internet have benefited religious organizations in several ways. They have even benefited some ultraconservative communities that may otherwise appear old-fashioned, such as the Lubavitch community of Hasidic Judaism.

Computers allow organizations, including religious organizations, to keep more accurate records and analyze them more quickly. They can identify trends more easily—for example, when they are losing or gaining members—so that they can respond to those trends. Some religious organizations and individuals have also used computers for study purposes. It is possible to store entire volumes on a single CD and then to search those volumes quickly for information on a specific topic. For example, CDs allow people to compare quickly many different translations of the BIBLE or to find a HADITH on a specific subject. Some wealthy organizations have even made individual, computer-aided learning a part of their educational programs.

Through the Internet religious organizations can communicate with people over greater distances much more quickly. For example, a Hindu organization in India can now communicate virtually instantaneously by e-mail with one of its branches in South America, as can a community in Japan with one of its branches in Europe. Such organizations may use e-mail to spread news, distribute new instructional materials, raise money, or even, in a few unfortunate cases, coordinate violent activities. In addition, most religious organizations now have Web sites. These Web sites make it much easier for people to learn about the organizations. For example, people with access to the Internet can now find out quickly where the synagogue, church, temple, or mosque closest to their home happens to be. In fact, Web sites are a relatively inexpensive way for new and small religious organizations to establish themselves.

People have worried about what effects computers might have on religion. For example, some have worried that computers might harm religious communities. Because of computers people would encounter each other less. Many people now think, however, that computers have been more helpful than harmful. They have especially helped members of minority communities living away from their home base, such as Hindus and Muslims in North America, find others who share their hopes and beliefs. They also strengthen such people's sense of belonging to the religion by allowing them to participate in a virtual community. One problem with such communities, however, concerns authority. For example, the advice a person receives from a GURU, RABBI, or priest online may turn out to come from a well-meaning adult who does not have the education that is expected in a religious professional—or even from a 13-year-old having fun.

Because human beings find religion in so many places, it would not be surprising to discover that computers have taken on religious significance for some people. One might even say that computers have already given the world one millennial cult, a cult built around expectations of disaster at the end of an age. In 1999 many people worried about "Y2K": What disasters might strike if the world's computer networks all failed on January 1, 2000? The disasters people imagined and the steps they took to avoid them resembled what has happened in many earlier millennial movements.

Further reading: Brenda E. Brasher, *Give Me That Online Religion* (San Francisco: Jossey-Bass, 2001); Gary R. Bunt, *Virtually Islamic: Computer-Mediated Communication and Cyber Islamic Environments* (Cardiff: University of Wales Press, 2000); Heidi Campbell, *Exploring Religious Community Online: We Are One in the Network* (New York: P. Lang, 2005); Douglas E. Cowan, *Cyberhenge: Modern Pagans on the Internet* (New York: Routledge, 2005); Jeffrey K. Hadden and Douglas E. Cowan, eds., *Religion on the Internet: Research Prospects and Promises* (New York: JAI, 2000).

confession of sin   *See* SACRAMENT.

Confucianism   Influential East Asian spiritual and ethical tradition. It originated with CONFUCIUS at the end of the sixth century B.C.E. Since then, Confucianism has often been the official ideology of the Chinese state.

HISTORY

Confucius [Latin for K'ung-fu-tzu, "Master K'ung" (551–479 B.C.E.)] was a profoundly influential teacher who emphasized that, because human beings are social creatures, a good society is important to a good human life. But he also realized that a good society in turn depends on good, highly motivated people. The first goal, then, must be to cultivate humaneness within oneself. He believed this was something all people can do. He is said moreover to have edited five classic books of Chinese thought, and his disciples gathered his own teaching into a collection known as the Analects (*see* ANALECTS OF CONFUCIUS).

Later Confucians taught proper behavior in terms of five relationships: ruler–subject, father-son, elder brother–younger-brother, husband–wife, and friend–friend. They also developed specific views of humaneness. Mencius (Chinese, Meng-tzu) (*c.* 372–*c.* 289 B.C.E.) had an optimistic view of the human being. Humaneness, he said, is present in all human beings; it simply needs the right nurturing in order to blossom and flourish. Hsun Tzu (*c.* 300–238 B.C.E.) disagreed. In his view people are by nature evil and uncivil. To avoid the evils that result from greed and contention, people must be restrained by teaching and observances. At the time Hsun Tzu was more influential. As time passed, however, Mencius's positions came to dominate Confucian thinking.

In 195 B.C.E. the Han emperor offered a pig, a sheep, and an ox at the grave of Confucius. This act marked the beginning of the official link between Confucianism and the Chinese government. To become a government official, one had to pass grueling examinations in Confucianism and the Confucian classics. The cult of Confucius also became a major part of an official's duties.

When the Han dynasty ended in 220 C.E., Confucianism was temporarily eclipsed. Its place at court was taken by BUDDHISM and TAOISM. But around 1000 C.E. the fortunes of Confucianism began to rise again. Important neo-Confucian thinkers like Chu Hsi (1130–1200 C.E.) and Wang Yang-ming (1472–1528) provided Confucianism with what it had seemed so severely to lack: a metaphysics (thought about the nature of reality) as lofty as that of Buddhism and Taoism. Confucianism became the dominant ideology of China. It was also the senior partner in a religious union that included Taoism and Buddhism.

By the 19th century, Confucianism had become moribund. Many Chinese rejected it as old-fashioned and powerless, especially in contrast to the newly arrived European powers. The democratic revolution associated with Sun Yatsen (1866–1925) and then especially the communist regime established by Mao Tse-tung (1893–1976) cut the ties between Confucianism and the government. On the mainland, Confucianism suffered severely during the Cultural Revolution of 1966–69, but the Chinese state in Taiwan preserved Confusion rituals as part of its cultural heritage.

TEACHINGS

Confucianism focuses on how human beings behave in society. It strives to identify the ideal way to live.

In Confucianism the ideal person is the noble person. For Confucius, nobility did not derive from birth. It derived from cultivating true humaneness (*jen*). This was done, Confucius believed, through the practice of RITUALS (*li*). The rituals Confucius had in mind, however, were not religious rites. They were rituals of respect that one showed one's fellow human beings. One can begin to see how truly radical Confucius's teachings were. He redirected the focus of religious observance. The attention one used to give to the ancestors one now gave to life in this world.

The five relationships within which people cultivate virtue mentioned above are clearly not relationships between equals. They are also clearly male-centered. Indeed, some Confucians have suggested that since the relationship between a mother and her child is a natural one, the father–son relationship should be seen as the foundation of society. In any case, the relationships are not one-sided.

Each person has responsibilities. For example, a younger brother should respect an older brother. But if the older brother wants respect, he should act only in ways that are worthy of respect.

PRACTICES

To practice Confucianism individual persons cultivate virtue by carefully performing their responsibilities. These include responsibilities that North Americans would call religious as well as those they would call ethical. For example, the philosopher Wang Yang-ming recommended sitting quietly as a way to cultivate spirituality.

The primary ritual of Confucianism, as the Chinese state religion, was SACRIFICE. Confucians performed sacrifices for ancestors, especially the ancestors of the emperor, for those who first brought culture, and for Confucius himself. They also performed sacrifices for spirits associated with political institutions, for the powers of nature, and for the universe as a whole.

The elaborateness of a sacrifice depended upon how important the occasion was. On the most important occasions the sacrificial victims included a pig, a sheep, or an ox. In performing the sacrifice, either the emperor or a high official would bow, present the offerings, and pray. At the same time, INCENSE was burned and musicians would play.

ORGANIZATION

No professional priests conducted the cult of Confucianism. Scholars trained in Confucian teachings did. This was one of their duties as officials of the Chinese state. When the emperor was present, he took the leading role.

A special government ministry was in charge of the state cult. Among other things, it provided the materials used in the sacrifice, established the proper procedures to be followed, and set the calendar, so that the rituals would be performed at the proper time.

SIGNIFICANCE

Confucianism has defined the traditional values and ideas of proper behavior in China. Although it is out of favor in communist China, it lives on in Taiwan. Confucianism has also profoundly influenced traditional values and ways of life in Korea, Vietnam, and Japan.

Further reading: Ch'u Chai, and Winberg Chai, *Confucianism* (Woodbury, N.Y.: Barron's Educational Series, 1973); David S. Nivison, and Arthur Wright, *Confucianism in Action* (Stanford, Calif.: Stanford University Press, 1959); James R. Ware, *The Sayings of Confucius* [The Analects] (New York: Mentor, n.d.); Hsin-chung Yao, *An Introduction to Confucianism* (New York: Cambridge University Press, 2000).

Confucius (551–479 B.C.E.) *Latin for the Chinese name K'ung-fu-tzu, "Master K'ung"; a profoundly influential Chinese moral teacher whose thought gave rise to* CONFUCIANISM Confucius was born in China at a time of unrest in the middle of the Chou period. Little is known for certain about his life, and many details that follow are legendary.

It is said that Confucius's family had some status but little wealth. Despite the family's poverty, he received an education and hoped for a political career. He served the government in some minor posts, such as overseeing sheep and cattle. Perhaps around the age of 40, he also began to teach. With time Confucius rose to a position of some responsibility, but he became disillusioned because he was unable to influence the duke of Lu, his home state. He resigned around the age of 54, and for the next 13 years he traveled around China, looking for a ruler who would put his ideas into practice. He was unsuccessful, perhaps because his teachings emphasized virtue at a time when rulers were looking for action. About five years before his death he returned to Lu, where he taught and may have held another office. During his lifetime, then, Confucius's influence was minimal. After his death, his teachings came to exercise a profound influence on the Chinese state.

Some suggest that Confucius should be seen as a moral rather than a religious teacher. Indeed, Confucius's teachings redirected to the living the

Engraving of Confucius *(Image Select/Art Resource, N.Y.)*

respect and *li* (RITUALS) that Chinese had traditionally given to dead ancestors. Confucius also made revolutionary innovations in the institution of teaching. Before his time, education was available only to those with the means to buy it. Confucius taught that education should be open to all who had interest and intellectual ability, regardless of whether they could pay. Despite these radical innovations, Confucius saw himself not as an innovator but as a restorer of Chinese traditions. In keeping with this self-image, he is said to have edited five traditional Chinese classics (*see* I CHING).

As a teacher, Confucius did not aim to impart knowledge or foster intellectual ability but to nurture a quality of the inner person known in Chinese as *jen*. The term is difficult to translate but means something like "genuine humanity." Confucius taught that people could realize this internal quality by means of external observances: They could become genuinely humane by performing their duties without thought of reward (*yi*) and by observing the rules of propriety (*li*) that govern relations between human beings. When applied to specific roles, Confucius referred to the process of cultivating virtue as a "rectification of names," that is, making reality conform to the names. For example, Confucius taught that if one is called a parent or a child, one ought to behave like a parent or child.

In Confucius's teaching, family relationships are the cornerstone of society, and the respect of children for parents is a cardinal virtue. Within society, Confucius advocates the principle of reciprocity: "Do not impose on others what you yourself do not desire" (Analects 15.24). He also teaches that the best way to govern is not with rules and punishments but through propriety and the moral example of the rulers.

After Confucius died, followers gathered sayings attributed to him into a volume known as the Analects (*see* ANALECTS OF CONFUCIUS). It is the major source for Confucius's ideas. Beginning with the Han dynasty (206 B.C.E.), Confucianism became officially established in China. Civil servants were required to pass a grueling examination in the five Confucian classics. Imperial officials maintained the cult of Confucius as part of their official duties. Eventually every prefecture (a political unit something like a county) in China—over 2,000 in all—had its temple to Confucius. Although the specific fortunes of Confucianism varied, Confucius's teachings shaped official Chinese life until the Communist Revolution under Mao Tse-tung in 1949. It is likely that they continue to shape unofficial life today.

Further reading: Herrlee Creel, *Confucius and the Chinese Way* (New York: Harper, 1960); Raymond Dawson, *Confucius* (New York: Hill & Wang, 1982); D. Howard Smith, *Confucius* (New York: Scribner, 1973); Bryon W. Van Norden, ed., *Confucius and*

the Analects: New Essays (New York: Oxford University Press, 2002).

Congregationalism   A way of organizing Christian churches. It is especially associated with a group of churches that has played a major role in the history of religion in the United States.

At its most general, Congregationalism insists that local Christian congregations should be independent and govern themselves. This does not mean that these congregations should not join together for joint activity. Indeed, most Congregationalist churches have been eager to work with others who hold similar views. But it does mean that congregations call their own ministers and determine for themselves how they will WORSHIP. This "congregational polity" is quite different from the "episcopal polity" found in, for example, the Roman Catholic Church, the Orthodox churches, and the Church of England. In an episcopal arrangement, the church is governed by a bishop. The bishop appoints priests and, in conjunction with other bishops, determines what beliefs and practices the church requires.

As a name for a group of churches, Congregationalism is mostly a movement in the English-speaking world. It arose in England in the late 16th century as an alternative to the Church of England (*see* ANGLICANISM). Congregationalism has continued in England up to the present day. But the movement thrived in North America, especially in New England.

In 1609 a group of Congregationalists fled to Holland to escape persecution in England. In 1620 some of them traveled to the shores of North America. Their boat was the *Mayflower*, they landed at Plymouth, they founded Plymouth colony, and they entered American legend as the Pilgrims. These Congregationalists joined with the Puritans (*see* PURITANISM) who settled nine years later in the area of Boston. Congregationalism became the established or official religion of the colonies of Massachusetts, Connecticut, and New Hampshire.

In the 1730s a Congregationalist minister, Jonathan Edwards, started the first "Great

Awakening." This was a time of increased religious emotion. Around 1800 the Congregationalists in New England experienced a split. Many Congregational churches abandoned the teaching that GOD was a TRINITY—Father (or Creator), Son, and Holy Spirit—and became UNITARIAN. That is, they affirmed that God was a unity and thus denied that JESUS was divine. Later in the 19th century, Congregationalists moved to positions then considered liberal. In 1931 they merged with another group to form the Congregational Christian Church. In 1961 they merged with the Evangelical and Reformed Churches to form the UNITED CHURCH OF CHRIST.

In the 20th century Congregationalism modified some of its earlier emphases. The independence of local churches is no longer a burning issue, and most congregations accept some direction from larger associations. For example, the general church usually has a role in certifying persons as fit to be ministers. In addition, Congregationalists have begun to use set prayers and worship services, which they had traditionally avoided. Worship services center on the sermon (*see* PREACHING). Congregationalists also recognize two sacraments: BAPTISM and the EUCHARIST. They generally baptize infants. They have also tended to be among the most liberal of the Protestant denominations. For example, in 1917 Congregationalists in England ordained their first woman minister.

Congregationalism is by no means the largest Protestant denomination in the United States or the world. But its cultural contributions have been large. In England the poet John Milton and the hymn-writer Isaac Watts were committed Congregationalists. In the United States, Congregationalists have founded a number of colleges and universities, beginning with Harvard (1636) and Yale (1701).

Constantine, Emperor (*c.* 285–337 C.E.) *Roman emperor who supported Christianity* Constantine's father Constantius was emperor of the western half of the Roman empire. When he died in 306, his troops declared Constantine emperor in his place. Constantine was then about 20 years old. Through

battles and political maneuvers, Constantine managed to keep his position. In 324 he became sole emperor of the Roman empire. He ruled until his death in 337.

Constantine attributed his success to CHRISTIANITY, to which he converted around the year 310. In 312 he defeated a rival at the Milvian Bridge, which is near Rome. In the battle his troops fought with a sign of Christianity painted on their shields. The next year Constantine and his coruler issued the Edict of Milan, which removed all laws against the practice of Christianity, making Christianity fully legal in the Roman empire for the first time. Constantine also tried to mediate disputes between Christians. One concerned Donatism, or the idea that PRIESTS and bishops who abandon Christianity under persecution should not be allowed to resume their positions later. Even more important was the dispute about Arianism. It concerned whether JESUS, as Son of God, was uncreated or the first-born of all creation. To try to resolve this dispute, Constantine called bishops together at the Council of Nicaea in 325 (*see* COUNCILS, CHRISTIAN). The Council's decision became the basis for the later Nicene Creed (*see* CREEDS).

Constantine built a new capital for the empire and named it Constantinople after himself (now Istanbul, Turkey). He also sponsored the building of many churches. He was not baptized until he was on his deathbed. Because of all that he had done for Christianity, he thought of himself as the Thirteenth Apostle (*see* APOSTLES).

Coptic Church The predominant form of CHRISTIANITY in Egypt. Egypt was an important center of Christianity in the ancient world. Tradition says that Mark, who wrote one of the GOSPELS, first brought Christianity there. Leading early Christian thinkers such as Origen (*c.* 185–*c.* 254) lived and taught in Alexandria, the cultural center of Egypt. Bishops of Alexandria such as Athanasius (*c.* 295–373) guided the development of Christian doctrine. Other Egyptians became the first Christian MONKS AND NUNS.

In 451 the Christian bishops met in council at Chalcedon (near Istanbul, Turkey) to determine what Christians should teach about Jesus. They decided that in Jesus two natures, divine and human, were combined into one person. Most Egyptians disagreed. They taught that in Jesus divinity and humanity were united into one nature. These Egyptian "monophysites," as they were called, became the Coptic Church.

Until the middle of the seventh century the emperor of Byzantium severely persecuted the Coptic Church. He wanted to force it to adopt the teachings of Chalcedon. But in 642 Arab Muslims conquered Egypt, and the Coptic Church achieved peace.

The leader of the Coptic Church is the patriarch of Alexandria, known as the pope (not to be confused with the pope in ROMAN CATHOLICISM). In 1971 Shenouda III became the 117th Coptic pope. By 1992 there were roughly 85 Coptic churches in the United States with a total of 180,000 members. Coptic churches are also found today in many other countries outside Egypt, including Canada, Great Britain, France, Germany, Australia, and Brazil. One of the most prominent Coptic Christians in recent years has been Boutros Boutros-Ghali, secretary-general of the United Nations from 1992 to 1996.

cosmogony A story of how the world came to be. Not all religions talk about the origin of the world and of human life. For example, the BUDDHA adamantly refused to address questions about origins. He said these questions were unimportant. Instead, one should analyze the world as it stands and seek to gain release from SAMSARA, or rebirth.

Few religions, however, have been able to take such an agnostic attitude. When they talk about the origin of the world and human life, they usually tell stories or myths. These myths are known as cosmogonies. The American scholar, Charles H. Long, has identified five different kinds of cosmogony. For beginners his classification is ideal.

One kind of cosmogony, or story, attributes the origins of the world to the sexual activity of two parents. These parents may be the earth and the sky, as in the mythology of Rangi and Papa in certain Pacific Ocean societies (see PACIFIC OCEAN RELIGIONS). The *Enuma Elish*, a Mesopotamian myth, calls the first parents Tiamat and Apsu (see MESOPOTAMIAN RELIGIONS). They are the fresh and salt waters whose mixing produces silt. (Think of a river delta.) One Egyptian cosmogony says that the creator first produced the pair Air and Moisture (see EGYPTIAN RELIGION).

Another kind of cosmogony begins with a cosmic egg. One of the UPANISHADS in India describes the creation of the world from a primal egg. As the egg splits, the bottom part of the shell becomes the earth, the top part becomes the sky. The contents of the egg divide to become the various features of the universe.

A third kind of cosmogony is "creation from nothing." Religions that worship a high god or a single god favor this kind of cosmogony. The best known examples are JUDAISM, CHRISTIANITY, and ISLAM. Genesis 1 gives a "soft" version of creation from nothing. God does not actually create from nothing. He gives order to "the waters." A well-known Hindu hymn assumes creation from nothing, but it asks who can know how creation came about. "The one who looks down from the highest heaven, that one knows—or perhaps even he does not know" (Rig-veda 10.129).

Other religions say that the world as we know it emerged from the bowels of the earth. Indigenous Americans of the southwest often tell of the emergence of the ancestors from within the earth and their transformation into people (see NATIVE AMERICAN RELIGIONS). Yet another kind of cosmogony is the "earth-diver myth." The earth comes into existence when primal beings recover raw material from beneath the waters. The Yokuts, an Indian people in California, told how the primal animals sent a duck down to bring up earth from the bottom of the ocean.

Sometimes these types combine. For example, an Egyptian cosmogony begins with creation from nothing, but the first item created is the world-parent pair. There may also be other types of cosmogony. For example, a famous hymn in the sacred

Hindu books known as the VEDA attributes the world as we know it to the sacrifice of the primal person (Rig-veda 10.90).

The rise of scientific theories of the origin of the universe and of life has raised problems for traditional religious cosmogonies. Some have responded by rejecting science. For example, some Christian fundamentalists advocate what they call "creation science" (see EVOLUTION AND RELIGION). Others have rejected religious cosmogonies out of hand. Still others have taken a path in the middle. They accept the scientific accounts so far as they go, but they claim to see in the religious accounts deeper meanings that science lacks.

cosmologies The image or models of the universe found in various religions. Most if not all religions provide their followers with an image of what the world looks like. This image is known as a religion's cosmology. Scientists have cosmologies, too. For example, the ancient astronomer Ptolemy developed an image of the universe centered on the Earth. This was a geocentric or "Earth-centered" cosmology. Copernicus said the Earth traveled around the sun. His was a heliocentric or "sun-centered" cosmology.

Religious cosmologies relate to human life. They may be very abstract. They also may envision an infinite number of worlds. But they never lose their focus on people and the way people experience the world. Religious cosmologies, then, are more than geocentric. They are anthropocentric, or "human-centered."

Some cosmologies describe the paths along which people move and the resources that they use. Ideal examples are the cosmologies traditional among indigenous Australians (see AUSTRALIAN RELIGIONS). These cosmologies associate features of the landscape and patterns of traveling with mythical beings and events from the Dreaming, that is, the time of creation. Indeed, indigenous Australians traditionally believe that these beings are somehow still present in the landscape.

Other cosmologies describe the world in terms of overarching structures. Before air and space travel, all human beings experienced a world that had the same general shape: a surface of earth and water covered by the dome of the sky. This is the world that GOD creates in the first chapter of Genesis. It is also the image found in indigenous American SWEAT LODGES. Some speculate that the ancient Chinese saw this world in the turtle-shells that they used for divination (see CHINA, RELIGIONS OF).

To this model many religions add vertical layers above or below the earth or both. In HINDUISM the sacred books known as the VEDA speak of "three worlds": earth, atmosphere, and sky. Early Japanese collections of mythology speak of three different worlds: heaven, earth, and underworld. Religions may use a natural symbol to connect these three worlds, say, a cosmic tree or mountain. Some scholars call such a symbol an *axis mundi*. Cosmologies may also involve more than three layers. After the Vedic period Hindus generally began with a seven-layer universe. Then they subdivided it and supplemented it. The Maya knew seven (or 13) layers of heaven and five (or nine) layers of the underworld (see MAYA RELIGION). GNOSTICISM spoke of the planetary spheres. Religions may connect human life with celestial events through ASTROLOGY.

The preceding cosmologies emphasize the vertical. Other cosmologies emphasize the horizontal. Indigenous American cosmologies associate the four cardinal directions with various colors, for example, west with black, north with white, east with red, south with yellow. Hindu mythology identifies various "continents." They take the form of concentric rings around a central continent, known as Jambudvipa, and its central pillar, Mount Meru. Other religions imagine many worlds or universes. For example, certain forms of MAHAYANA BUDDHISM teach that there are an infinite number of heavens or, more precisely, "Buddha fields."

Yet another kind of religious cosmology is more abstract. It identifies the forces and principles that underlie the world. Chinese traditionally see the world as resulting from the complementary interaction of two opposed principles, yin and yang (*see* YIN/YANG THEORY). Dualists such as Zoroastrians see the world as a battleground between good and EVIL (*see* ZOROASTRIANISM). The Indian school of philosophy known as Sankhya divides the world between two principles: spirit and nature.

Modern science, of course, has developed a very different cosmology. It places the Earth in a solar system, which sits in an arm of the Milky Way galaxy, which is itself part of a galactic cluster. Some see this scientific cosmology as disproving religion. Many religious people, however, hold on to and cherish the religious meanings underlying their traditional cosmologies.

councils, Buddhist   Meetings of Buddhist monks to determine proper Buddhist teachings and ways of life. Buddhists call these councils *sangitis* or recitations. That is because they often involved the recitation of Buddhist scriptures (*see* SCRIPTURES, BUDDHIST). Some Buddhist councils were supposedly ecumenical; that is, they included representatives from all Buddhist communities. Actually, participation has often been more limited.

Buddhists held councils especially within the 500 years or so after the BUDDHA's *parinirvana* (*see* NIRVANA) in 483 B.C.E. (Non-Buddhists think of the Buddha's *parinirvana* as his death.) In reports about these ancient councils it is often difficult to separate legend from actual events.

According to tradition, the first Buddhist council took place during the rainy season (mid-June through early September) in the year of the Buddha's *parinirvana*. At this council followers of the Buddha sought to preserve his teaching. They recited together texts of monastic discipline (the *Vinaya*) and the Buddha's sermons (*Sutras* or *Suttas*). Other early councils recognized by Buddhist tradition include the Council at Vaishali in 383 B.C.E., which resolved a dispute about loose practices by some monks; the council at Pataliputra, convened by the famous Emperor ASOKA around 247 B.C.E., which may have resulted in sending missionaries to other parts of Asia; and the council at Anuradhapura in Sri Lanka in 25 B.C.E. At this council the scriptures of THERAVADA BUDDHISM, known as the *Tipitaka*, were put into final form.

Some Buddhists have looked on meetings held within the last 200 years as councils, too. An example is a council convened in Burma in 1954 to recite all of the scriptures recognized by Theravada Buddhism. It celebrated the 2,500th anniversary of the Buddha's *parinirvana*.

councils, Christian   Meetings of leaders of the Christian church to discuss matters of belief and practice. Ideally, but not always in practice, a council includes Christian leaders from around the world. Most Christian churches recognize seven early councils as ecumenical or universal. Since the eighth century, councils have been particularly important in ROMAN CATHOLICISM. Meetings of Protestant leaders usually have other names.

The first Christian council may have been the meeting between the apostle PAUL and the leaders of the JERUSALEM church described in the ACTS OF THE APOSTLES (Acts 15). The seven ecumenical councils, however, took place only after Christianity became legal. Indeed, the Roman emperors called many of them. The Council of Nicaea (325) declared that JESUS was God, "of the same substance with the Father." The Council of Constantinople (381) produced the document now usually called the Nicene Creed. The Council of Chalcedon (451) affirmed that Jesus was "two natures, divine and human, in one person." Other ecumenical councils dealt with more subtle matters.

The last ecumenical council, held in Nicaea in 787, is perhaps most important for EASTERN ORTHODOX CHRISTIANITY. It allowed the use of icons or images in worship. Later, in 1351, a council of Orthodox churches approved *hesychasm*, a kind of meditative prayer.

In 1075 Pope Gregory VII decreed that only the pope had the authority to call a general council. The Roman Catholic Church has since held several major councils. The Fourth Lateran Council (1215) accepted the term transubstantiation in describing the relationship between the bread and wine of the EUCHARIST and Jesus' body and blood.

The Council of Constance (1415) condemned the teachings of John Wycliffe (c. 1325–84) and Jan Hus (c. 1369–1415). The Council of Trent (1545–63; see TRENT, COUNCIL OF) formulated the Catholic Church's response to the Protestant REFORMATION. The First Vatican Council (1870–71) established that the pope was infallible. The Second Vatican Council (1961–65) changed many of the Church's practices. For example, it recommended singing the Mass in local languages rather than in Latin (see VATICAN COUNCILS).

covenant A legally binding agreement; especially the way in which the relationship between GOD and human beings has been conceived in JUDAISM. In origin, a covenant was a formal agreement, often between two unequal parties and political in nature. The people of Israel adopted the covenant form to express the nature of their relationship with God.

Jewish tradition recognizes several covenants, such as the covenant with NOAH that applies to all human beings and the covenant with ABRAHAM. But "the" covenant is that made with the people under MOSES at Mount Sinai—called Mount Horeb in the book of Deuteronomy. In that covenant, the god YHWH ("the Lord") enters into a special relationship with the Jewish people. The covenant obligations begin with the TEN COMMANDMENTS.

Later biblical writers continued to use the covenant idea. In reflecting on his nation's history, the prophet JEREMIAH looked forward to a new covenant, which will be written in people's hearts (Jeremiah 31.31–34). Christians claim that their religion is this new covenant. The QUR'AN also talks about the relationship of people and God as a covenant.

creation and world cycles Religious views on the origin and course of the universe. Many religions tell about the origins of the world, but not all do. For example, the BUDDHA refused to talk about the origin of the universe. Buddhists therefore usually envision the universe as a series of cycles, stretching infinitely into the past and the future. Other religions have cyclical views of the universe, too.

Religions explain the origin of the universe in different ways. One familiar way is creation by a GOD. This may be creation from nothing, as Jews, Christians, and Muslims usually think today, or it may also involve creation by a god who works on preexisting matter, which is one way to read the first verse of GENESIS. Other stories may not tell of creation in a strict sense, but they do tell about the origin of things.

One common story attributes the world to the sexual activity of two divine beings. For example, a Babylonian poem, the "Enuma Elish," attributes the world to the union of Apsu and Tiamat, sweet waters and salt waters. Navajo tradition tells what is sometimes called an "emergence myth." Originally, the ancestors lived in the center of the earth, but through a variety of means they arrived on the earth's surface and organized the world that is known today. Another type of Native American myth attributes the creation of the earth to an "earth-diver." For example, the Yokuts Indians of California believed that a duck dove down deep below the surface of the waters and brought up dirt, from which dry land was made. Somewhat similarly, ancient Japanese stories identified the islands of Japan with dirt that divine beings brought up from the bottom of the sea. A passage in the UPANISHADS, a sacred text in HINDUISM, envisions the origin of the universe as the splitting of a primal egg. Different parts of the egg became parts of the world; for example, the shells became the sky and the earth. Another Hindu text, a hymn in the Rig VEDA, attributes the origin of the world to the sacrifice of a primal person. A similar motif appears in NORDIC RELIGION and some stories from Oceania.

Jews, Christians, and Muslims generally think of time as beginning at creation and extending to the Day of Judgment, but other religions think in terms of world cycles. That is, they think that worlds come into and go out of existence repeatedly.

Human beings often measure time by referring to cycles such as months. Some people have used more than one cycle to keep track of time. For example, the Maya calendar used two cycles, one 260 days long (20 "months" of 13 days each), the other 365 days long (18 "months" of 20 days each). Every 18,980 days or 52 years, the first day of the 260-day cycle coincided with the first day of the 365-day cycle. When that happened, the Maya thought that a new world had begun.

Fifty-two years is a relatively short world cycle. The Maya knew another world cycle, too, one that they calculated using a calendar known as the Long Count. This cycle began in the year 3114 B.C.E. It will end on December 23, 2012. Some Buddhists thought of a world cycle that was roughly the same length, 5000 years. After that many years, they suggested, the Buddha's teachings will disappear, and another Buddha will arrive.

Hinduism has some of the longest world cycles. The basic unit is the *yuga* or age. There are four *yugas*: the *Satya* (or *Krita*) *yuga* (1,728,000 years), the *Dvapara yuga* (1,296,000 years), the *Treta yuga* (864,000 years), and the *Kali yuga* (432,000 years, not to be confused with the goddess KALI.) We are now about 5,000 years into the *Kali yuga*.

But for Hindu ideas of world cycles, that is only the beginning. According to one version, the four *yugas* make up an age of MANU. Fourteen ages of Manu make up a unit known as a *kalpa*, which is a day in the life of the god BRAHMA. When the day is over, the universe goes out of existence for the same amount of time (that is, 60,480,000 years). Then it returns for the next day in Brahma's life. This happens for a full life of 100 Brahma-years. At that point one needs to talk about another, even larger cycle.

Existence and its meaning are one of the most important issues with which religions deal. The length of the Hindu cycles (deliberately) boggles the mind. Nevertheless, many scholars believe that by talking about creation and world cycles religions make the world meaningful and intelligible.

Further reading: Mircea Eliade, *Cosmos and History: The Myth of the Eternal Return* (New York: Garland, 1985); Charles H. Long, *Alpha: The Myths of Creation* (Chico, Calif.: Scholars Press, 1983); Barbara C. Sproul, *Primal Myths: Creation Myths around the World* (San Francisco: HarperSanFrancisco, 1991); Barbara Tedlock, *Time and the Highland Maya* (Albuquerque: University of New Mexico Press, 1992); Keith Ward, *Religion and Creation* (New York: Oxford University Press, 1996).

creeds Brief, official statements of faith; from *credo*, Latin for "I believe." Some religions insist that their followers act in certain ways; others insist that their followers subscribe to certain beliefs. In the latter case, it is useful to have official statements of the required beliefs. Creeds developed in CHRISTIANITY as brief statements of FAITH, generally used in WORSHIP services.

The earliest and perhaps most widely used creed is the so-called Apostles' Creed. Its precise origin is unknown, although it seems related to professions of faith made by the earliest Christians at baptism. The Nicene Creed is a statement adopted by the Council of Nicaea (325 C.E.) and then modified by the Council of Constantinople (381 C.E.). Its major concern is to insist that the divinity of JESUS CHRIST is the same as that of GOD the Father. The Athanasian Creed, which tradition ascribes to Athanasius, bishop of Alexandria in the fourth century, further clarifies the nature and relationship of the three persons of the TRINITY: Father, Son, and Holy Spirit.

cross A Roman instrument of torture that became one of the main symbols of CHRISTIANITY. Pre-Christian religions used the form of the cross—two lines that intersect—in many ways. Two examples are the ankh, an ancient Egyptian symbol of life, and the swastika, a symbol of well-being in ancient India. But the cross takes on special meaning in Christianity because it was the instrument on and by which JESUS died.

For its first 300 years, Christianity was illegal, and Christians were reluctant to use the cross as a symbol. But in 313 Emperor Constantine won an important battle after seeing a cross in the sky and hearing the words, "In this sign you will conquer." He removed the restrictions against practicing Christianity, and Christians used the cross widely for decorative purposes. At first Christians depicted bare crosses. Eventually artists also portrayed Jesus suffering on the cross, sometimes in graphic detail.

The symbol of the cross has played an important role in Christian RITUAL. Cross-bearers have led processions, perhaps at first in imitation of processions put on for the rulers. Christians have marked out a cross as they prayed by touching their forehead, their heart, and their shoulders. In 326 Constantine's mother, Helena, claimed to have discovered remains of the actual cross on which Jesus was crucified. Christians have used these remains, and others, as relics to help them WORSHIP, especially in the Middle Ages.

The symbol of the cross has also been important socially and intellectually. The CRUSADES got their name from the red crosses that the crusaders wore emblazoned on their shirts. Many theologians have used the cross to guide their reflections. An ancient theologian, Justin Martyr (c. 100–c. 165), saw the cross in every tool necessary for human survival. Others have seen in the cross a symbol of GOD's domination over the entire universe. The sufferings and death of Jesus stand at the center of Martin LUTHER's thought. Therefore, many have called it a "THEOLOGY of the cross."

Not all Christians, however, have used visible representations of the cross. Churches influenced by the thought of John CALVIN have not traditionally displayed crosses or crucifixes. Crosses were thought to violate the restrictions against worshipping images. In the 20th century many, but not all, Calvinist churches abandoned this restriction. They now use crosses the way other Christians do.

Crusades A number of movements in Catholic Western Europe, especially during the 12th and 13th centuries, that aimed to free the "holy land" from Muslim rulers. The name derives from *crux,* the Latin word for CROSS. The Crusaders wore large red crosses sewn onto their shirts.

In the course of the 11th century, the territory of Palestine came under the control of the Seljuq Turks. The Seljuqs were less welcoming than the earlier Muslim rulers had been to Christians who wanted to visit holy sites such as Bethlehem and JERUSALEM. In addition, the advance of the Seljuqs posed political and economic threats to the Latin-speaking parts of Western Europe. In response, on November 27, 1095, Pope Urban II appealed to Christendom to liberate the Holy Land. To entice people to participate in the efforts, he offered Crusaders forgiveness of their financial debts as well as of their sins.

There were four major Crusades and a number of minor ones. The First Crusade lasted from 1096 to 1099. The major contingent, led by several noblemen, crossed the Mediterranean Sea, engaged the Turks in battle, and eventually managed to establish four Crusader states along the coast of Palestine. The most important was the Latin Kingdom of Jerusalem.

Surrounded by hostile forces, these states were not genuinely viable. After 200 years they disappeared entirely. The second and third major Crusades were attempts to recover territory that the Crusader states had lost to Muslim counterattacks. The Second Crusade (1147–49) was a response to the fall of the Crusader state of Edessa; the third (1188–92) to the capture of Jerusalem and other territories by the great Muslim leader Saladin. The Third Crusade, whose leaders included King Richard I, the Lion-Hearted, of England, was moderately successful.

The Fourth Crusade (1202–04) illustrates well the questions that loom over the entire crusading enterprise. The Crusaders had assembled in Venice, but they could not pay for their passage. So at the instigation of the Venetians, they sacked a mercantile competitor of Venice, Zara, a Christian city in Dalmatia across the Adriatic. They also took up with a claimant to the throne of the Byzantine Empire. He promised the Crusaders that if they restored him to power, he would provide them with the funds that they needed. The deal fell through, and the Crusaders sacked Constantinople, the capital of (Christian) Byzantium, in 1204. Constantinople became the center of a Latin state, which did not last out the century; the Crusaders also established small states known as Frankish kingdoms in the Greek Peninsula. They never engaged Muslims in combat.

The Crusades have provided European culture with much legend and literature. They were a particularly rich source of material during the Romantic movement in the early 19th century. They also led to the founding of several religious orders. One order was the Knights Templar, a short-lived military-religious order, originally based in Jerusalem, that turned to banking when the last of the crusader states fell. Another was the Knights Hospitalers, an order originally charged with caring for the needs of pilgrims. It continues today as the Knights of Malta.

On balance, however, the main outcome of the Crusades would seem to be senseless expenditure and misery. Although technically warring against Muslim armies, the Crusaders found excuses to attack others, many of whom had no adequate means of defense. In addition to Orthodox Christians, such as those who fell victim to the Fourth Crusade, a large number of European Jews were slaughtered by those infused with the crusading spirit. Equally senseless was the so-called Children's Crusade of 1212. In this venture, children from the area around the Rhine attempted to cross the Alps under the leadership of a 12-year-old boy. They wanted to go and fight for the Holy Land. Most died of hunger and exposure. Ten to 20 years later rumors spread that some of these children had been spotted, now grown up, working as slaves on galleys sailing the Mediterranean.

cults and sects, religious An act of religious WORSHIP, or a small intense religious group, often one considered controversial. In religion, the word "cult" can mean any kind of worship, especially that of a particular god or shrine, as in speaking of ancient Greece one might refer to the "cult of APOLLO." Likewise, "sect" can denote any faction or group, especially a small one strongly devoted to a certain belief. In the 20th century, however,

these words have come to have particular meanings in the sociology of religion, and "cult" especially has acquired a very negative meaning in the media and in the eyes of the general public.

In the traditional sociology of religion, cults and sects are religious "withdrawal groups," that is, groups of people who withdraw from the dominant religion of the society in order to practice what they believe to be a purer, truer, or better religion, even if that means being associated only with a small body of like-minded believers. They are likely to regard the predominant religion as lukewarm and hypocritical, if not plain wrong. These groups are bound to offer a strong, intensely-felt commitment or experience; this takes the place of looser but important community and family and traditional bonds supported by the conventional faith. Usually they have, or were founded by, a powerful leader of strong charisma or personal appeal.

Sociologists use the word "sect" to refer to such a withdrawal group *within* a predominant or major faith, which presents a "purer" and more intense version of the same. Examples would be the AMISH or JEHOVAH'S WITNESSES within CHRISTIANITY, certain strict Hasidic groups (*see* HASIDISM) in JUDAISM, and comparable movements within ISLAM or HINDUISM. Usually followers of sects live close-knit lives regulated in many important respects, from dress to diet to occupation, by the sect; this of course sets them apart from the rest of society.

Cult, on the other hand, means a withdrawal group based on an alternative or imported religion, like those in the United States grounded in Eastern religions or in an esoteric tradition like ROSICRUCIANISM. Often they offer subjective practices like MEDITATION or chanting. Some may enjoy a close-knit, regulated community, but may also have a more diffuse following of people who just attend their lectures or read their books and perhaps do the practice from time to time.

It is important to realize that this scheme does not apply too well to the fluid religious situation in the United States. It is based on Europe, where a society typically has one state church or dominant religion—ROMAN CATHOLICISM in Spain, LUTHERANISM in Scandinavia—against which withdrawal groups are tiny and clear-cut entities. In America, while doubtless some religions are more dominant and considered more respectable than others, the scene is far more pluralistic and is always changing. Groups once stigmatized as sectarian or cultish move up to become major faiths, as have the Mormons, Methodists, and Catholics. Others may lose influence they once had. People now move from one to another with far less social penalty than in the past. For this reason the terms "cult" and "sect" should be used cautiously. "Cult" should also be used with care because it has come to have a negative meaning. People use it to refer to religious groups that are believed to be excessively authoritarian, to destroy the freedom and values of members, to cut them off from their families and community, and even to incite them to criminal activity. Undoubtedly religions past and present have acted in such destructive ways. But no one calls their own religion a cult; that is always an outsider's label. The trouble is that the term imposed by an outsider may stereotype it before one has really looked at how it is different, and how different people within the group may have different experiences. Scholars increasingly just speak of "new religious movements" and study them on a case-by-case basis.

Further reading: Robert S. Ellwood, and Harry B. Partin, *Religious and Spiritual Groups in Modern America,* 2d ed. (Englewood Cliffs, N.J.: Prentice Hall, 1988); Timothy Miller, ed., *America's Alternative Religions* (Albany: State University of New York Press, 1995); Elizabeth Puttick, *Women in New Religions* (New York: St. Martin's Press, 1997); Stephen J. Stein, *Communities of Dissent* (New York: Oxford University Press, 2003).

D

Dalai Lama   The head of the Tibetan Buddhist community and traditionally the ruler of Tibet. The first Dalai Lama assumed office in 1438, although he was not given that title until 1578, when the Mongol king, Alta Khan, gave the name Dalai Lama to the head of the Tibetan religious community. Dalai means "ocean, all-encompassing"; lama means "supreme teacher."

The first Dalai Lama resided at the Tashilhunpo monastery in central Tibet, but his successors have ruled from Lhasa.

The Dalai Lama is seen as an INCARNATION of AVALOKITESVARA, a BODHISATTVA. Tibetan BUDDHISM teaches that rebirth occurs 49 days after death (*see* BARDO THODOL). Successive Dalai Lamas are found by identifying signs on a child born 49 days after the death of the previous Dalai Lama. The candidate also demonstrates knowledge of the previous Dalai Lama's possessions.

In 1959 the 14th Dalai Lama, Tenzin Gyatso (b. 1935), fled into exile to escape Chinese rule. In 1989 he received the Nobel Prize for peace for leading a peaceful resistance to the Chinese takeover.

dance and religion   The significance and role of religious dancing. Like the music that usually accompanies it, dance has had a very wide role in religion but has sometimes been regarded with suspicion for its intoxicating effect and its association with sensual feeling. In primal societies, dance frequently served the role of creating sacred times and places, dances being occasions of rich community activity when the gods were close and per-

haps even possessing people while they danced. Shamans especially danced to create and express their ecstasy as their patron god danced through them (*see* SHAMANISM).

Dance has been performed and interpreted in different ways. In HINDUISM, dance often expresses the nature and mythology of the gods. The great god SIVA is called "nataraja," king of the dance, and his repertoire of 108 dances enacts the stages of the world from creation to destruction. In SHINTO, sacred dance is more often seen as an offering to the gods for their entertainment. So is it also in China, though the solemn dance RITUALS of Confucian students and mandarins also powerfully express the traditions and cohesion of their class. In the more devotional wings of JUDAISM (HASIDISM) and ISLAM (SUFISM, the "whirling dervishes"), dance expresses religious ecstasy or at least uninhibited, loving PRAYER and fervor. In the Catholic traditions of CHRISTIANITY, folk dances have usually been tolerated as a part of the celebration of holidays like May Day or CHRISTMAS but have rarely had a part in formal WORSHIP itself. PROTESTANTISM has tended to reject dance altogether, or to regard it as purely secular.

In recent times, however, there has been a move in some quarters to revive sacred dance, even performing decorous and expressive modern dances as parts of church or temple services. In Pentecostal circles, on the other hand, free and ecstatic dancing has increasingly arisen spontaneously as a sign of the Holy Spirit. Some of the new religions of Japan, like TENRIKYO and Odori Shukyo (the "Dancing Religion"), have made dance their central act of worship. In one form or another, dance seems sure to be a part of religion for a long time to come.

Daniel The title character in the book of Daniel in the BIBLE. He is likely based on a figure in Canaanite and earlier Hebrew literature.

Ancient texts discovered at Ugarit in Syria during the 20th century reveal that, well before any of the Bible was written, the Canaanites knew a legendary hero named Dan'el. This figure appears in the biblical book of the prophet EZEKIEL (14.14; 28.3).

The book of Daniel records stories and VISIONS. They allegedly took place during the exile of the Judeans in Babylon (586–539 B.C.E.). The book's account of this period is, however, very confused. Much of the book is written in Aramaic, a later language, and it does make detailed and accurate allusions to some later events. Therefore, it is customary to ascribe the book to an anonymous author who lived during the Hasmonean revolt (167–164 B.C.E.).

Jews classify Daniel with the Ketuvim or "writings"; Christians consider it a prophetic book. It is unique in the Hebrew Bible in that it is an apocalypse (*see* APOCALYPTIC LITERATURE). It does not recount historical events. Instead, its purpose was to call the Jewish people to remain faithful to their religious heritage, despite oppression and persecution. In giving reassurance, the book looks forward to a RESURRECTION from the dead (12.2–3). This idea influenced later Christians, as did the figure of the "Son of Man" (Daniel 7.13; cp. Mark 13.26). The NEW TESTAMENT book of REVELATION borrowed much imagery from Daniel's visions.

David (ruled *c.* 1000–960 B.C.E.) *in the Hebrew Bible, king of Israel and founder of the ruling dynasty of Judah* After the death of King SAUL and his sons, David united the kingdoms of Israel (today in northern Israel) and Judah (today in southern Israel). He took JERUSALEM (previously the stronghold of a people known as the Jebusites), made it his capital, and brought the ark of the COVENANT to it.

The books of Samuel in the Hebrew Bible recount many stories about David. Among them are his anointing while yet a boy by the prophet Samuel to be king, his battle with Goliath—the giant champion of the Philistines—and his close relations with Saul's son Jonathan. Less positively, David is said to have engineered the death of Uriah the Hittite in battle so that he in turn could marry Uriah's wife Bathsheba. At the end of his life his sons fought to succeed him. These struggles included a failed coup attempt by Absalom.

David was famed as a musician. Tradition attributed the biblical book of Psalms to him. In the late Second Temple period (roughly 200 B.C.E.–70 C.E.), some Jews hoped for a MESSIAH descended from David. Christians assert that this messiah was JESUS.

Day of Atonement English for the Hebrew phrase *Yom Kippur;* the most sacred of the "days of awe" in JUDAISM. Jews observe the Day of Atonement on the tenth day of Tishri, the first month of the Jewish year. This date falls in September or October.

The Day of Atonement is a time for restoring one's relationship with GOD. The Jewish people collectively repent of their SINS and receive God's forgiveness. If one has offended human beings, one should also make amends to them.

The BIBLE calls the Day of Atonement the "Sabbath of Sabbaths" (Leviticus 16.31). It is the most solemn day of rest. Observant Jews do not eat or drink from one sundown to the next. (In the Jewish calendar, days begin at sundown.) They spend the day at a SYNAGOGUE in PRAYER.

The LITURGY for the Day of Atonement includes several well-known prayers. An example is the "Kol Nidre," which asks forgiveness for breaking vows made to God. It is as famous for its melody as it is for its words.

Dead Sea Scrolls Scrolls roughly 2,000 years old found in caves on the northwestern edge of the Dead Sea. In February or March 1947, a 15-year-old Arab boy named Muhammad adh-Dhib accidentally made one of the greatest discoveries in modern archaeology. Accounts of what happened vary. According to one account, he was taking shelter from a thunderstorm. According to another, he was looking for a lost goat. In any case, he entered a cave in the Wadi Qumran, northwest of the Dead Sea. There he found jars containing scrolls from about the time of JESUS.

During the next 20 years scholars and Bedouin found ancient manuscripts hidden in 11 different caves at Qumran. These manuscripts are what many scholars mean by the Dead Sea Scrolls. They were written between the third century B.C.E. and 68 C.E. Originally, they belonged to the library of a monastic-type community located below the caves. Some people take a more inclusive view of the Dead Sea Scrolls. They use the term to designate ancient manuscripts discovered not only at Qumran but also in the entire Dead Sea region. According to this view, the Dead Sea Scrolls were written over a longer period of time. The oldest scrolls in the entire region were hidden by SAMARITANS when Alexander the Great conquered the region around 331 B.C.E. The most recent manuscripts in the entire region date from the time of the revolt of Bar Kokhba against Roman rule (132–135 C.E.).

The Dead Sea Scrolls are extremely important. They provide at least fragments of almost every book of the Hebrew BIBLE (Old Testament). These fragments—sometimes complete books—are centuries older than any other surviving copies. They allow us to see what the books of the Bible were like 2,000 years ago and how they grew into their present forms. For example, some scholars have identified what they see as ancestors of three different versions of the Bible, all equally ancient. The three are the version used by the Samaritans; the Greek version, known as the Septuagint, that the earliest Christians used; and the "Masoretic text," that is, the Hebrew Bible that we know today.

The Dead Sea Scrolls are important for another reason, too. They provide new insight into the religious world of ancient Palestine between the Hasmonean revolt (167–164 B.C.E.) and the so-called Jewish Wars (66–74 C.E.). This was the time when

JUDAISM as we know it, rabbinical Judaism, was just beginning. It is also the time when Jesus lived.

The scrolls tell us much about the community at Qumran. Many scholars think it was a community of ESSENES. One scroll contains the rules for the community. Its members followed a rigid discipline designed to ensure purity. Another scroll, called "The War of the Sons of Light with the Sons of Darkness," describes a great battle at the end of time. Apparently, the community expected that the final battle between GOD and the forces of evil would take place in the very near future. It was also waiting for two messiahs: a son of DAVID to rule politically, and a son of AARON to take charge of religious RITUALS.

Neither rabbinical Judaism nor CHRISTIANITY came directly from the Qumran community. Nevertheless, the scrolls allow us to see some of the variety of religious beliefs and practices that were current when both of them began.

Further reading: James H. Charlesworth, *Jesus and the Dead Sea Scrolls* (New York: Doubleday Anchor, 1992); Robert Eisenman, *The Dead Sea Scrolls and the First Christians* (Boston: Element Books, 1996); Florintino Martinez and Julio Barrera, *The People of the Dead Sea Scrolls* (Leiden: Brill, 1995); Geza Vermes, *The Complete Dead Sea Scrolls in English* (New York: Penguin, 2004).

death and religion Religious concepts and practices in relation to death and dying. It would be hard to imagine a religion truly indifferent to death, the end of an individual human life as we knew it in this world. That is because religion tries to look at life from the largest possible perspective, in the light of that which is ultimate. It is death that forces people to look at their own lives in that way. Knowing that one has only so much time in this world means one must make choices and must choose the values on which to base those choices. Knowing that many religions say there is more to life than just the present short span on Earth, one wants to know what the rest of it is and how it relates to here and now.

In regard to the event of death, religion tends to provide two things. First, it usually teaches about what happens after death, often including in that teaching accounts of an after-death judgment or rebirth, which will reflect on the choices one has made in life (*see* AFTERLIFE IN WORLD RELIGIONS). Second, religions surround the experience of death itself with rites and attitudes designating it as a great experience of transition. The death-practices of various religions say much about their deepest values.

Devout Hindus, for example, want to die on the banks of the sacred river, the GANGES, particularly in the holy city of BANARAS. If that is not possible, they wish at least for their remains to be brought there to be cremated, and the ashes thrown into the sacred river. The funeral pyre should ideally be lit by the deceased's eldest son. These practices teach us several things: that death is a time for returning to one's spiritual roots and the main symbols of one's FAITH; that the physical body is not important after death and can be reverently returned to the elements from which it came: fire, water, earth, and air; that death is a time of transition in this world too, from father to son, when the social order rent by death must be symbolically restored.

The same themes of individual transition, significant dispersal of the remains, and family and community healing occur in most traditions, though the particulars may vary greatly. In TIBETAN RELIGION the words of the BARDO THODOL, or "Tibetan Book of the Dead," may be whispered in the ear of the dying person as a kind of guide telling what will be encountered—the Clear Light, the BUDDHAS of the MANDALA—and how to respond to them in order to gain liberation or a good rebirth. The physical remains may be just cut up and left in a field for carnivorous birds to consume to show their unimportance. But memorial services to help the deceased through the transition and bring the family together continue afterward.

In JUDAISM, the dominant theme is the importance of each individual to the community and the preciousness of each human life. When death approaches, the dying person might recite a PRAYER confessing SINS and asking GOD for forgiveness and a place in his realm after death—the individual transition. After death, a group of volunteers from the community might care for the body, watching over it, washing it, dressing it for burial. Immediate relatives observe deep mourning until seven days after the funeral, traditionally staying at one place such as the home of the deceased during this time. A meal is given them by others in the Jewish community after the return from the cemetery. All this clearly helps with working through grief and reestablishing family and society bonds after the loss.

In ISLAM, death is also often preceded by an affirmation of faith. After death, the body is washed, shrouded, and buried facing MECCA in imitation of the posture of prayer—the symbolic reaffirmation of religious roots. Funeral and memorial services follow, centering on recitations of parts of the QUR'AN while the family receives condolences—affirmation of faith and reaffirmation of family and community ties.

Christian practices vary among traditions but repeat the same themes. Prayer is properly said with the dying person. In Catholic traditions these include confession of sins, absolution or forgiveness of them pronounced by a priest, final holy communion, and holy unction or anointing with oil—the "last rites." These mark the individual transition and preparation for judgment after death. On this side the family gathers for the funeral, sometimes added to by a "wake" or friends sitting up with the body in the home, and a meal given the mourning family by relatives or the church community. The body is returned to the earth by burial, or nowadays often cremated. Death is dealt with in more intimate and personal ways in religious writings. Some speak of a "good death" as something to prepare for during all of one's life. Sometimes it is seen as a time to be particularly close to the holy figures of one's faith, the SAINTS and ANGELS and others. Popular religious art may show a deathbed surrounded by angels, and the "Hail Mary" of Catholic piety asks MARY, the Mother of God, as though she were our mother too, to "pray for us now and at the hour of our death." Death is a precarious time, and yet may be a welcome time, a time of judgment and of release, of the loss of loved ones here and the gaining of loved ones on the other side. Sometimes it is also presented as a great adventure, a time for growth and learning of things now hidden. Above all, religions present death as a time for meeting face to face with God or an ultimate reality, in love and fulfillment. The process of death, dying, and grieving has interested many writers and readers in the second half of the 20th century.

denomination   A fairly large, well-established branch of a major religious tradition, uniting many local churches under a common national organization. The individual churches in a denomination hold to roughly similar beliefs, ways of WORSHIP, and forms of local governance. Unlike the cult or sect, the denomination is seen as part of the religious mainstream. A religious pattern made up of a collection of denominations large and small, each more or less equal and in practice having responsibility mainly for ministry to their own members, has been called a "denominational society." The United States of America is undoubtedly the best example, though the pattern can also be found in certain British Commonwealth countries and in some respects in Japanese BUDDHISM; otherwise, it is really a religious anomaly in a world of mainly one-religion or "church and sect" countries.

In the United States, the major Protestant groups—Methodist, Baptist, Presbyterian, Lutheran—are called denominations. The Roman Catholic, Jewish, and Eastern Orthodox traditions in America also have had to act as denominations for all intents and purposes. Denominations have distinctive histories and usually a revered founder or principal theological teacher. Their reason for founding and historical background is generally ethnic or located in a past religious conflict. Ordinarily, formal organization is along national lines except for overseas missions. Denominational loyalty can be a factor in promoting the overall health of religion in a society.

devils and demons   Personalized sources of EVIL. The two words mean about the same thing, though demons may be subordinate to a principal devil, or to SATAN, the chief of the forces of evil in Western religion. Most traditional religions have given a place to individual powers that work wickedness in the world, and usually are related to a principle of cosmic evil. These entities may be called demons or devils. For simple believers they may help explain many unfortunate things: sickness, madness, war, disasters. They may even have a positive role as an agent of the divine to punish the wicked. The more sophisticated may see demons as symbolic of important truths of FAITH: that evil exists despite a good GOD or universe, that it afflicts and can even possess humans yet also comes from outside them, and finally that evil is a force of cosmic dimensions—perhaps part of a "war in HEAVEN" of God and his ANGELS against Satan and his demons—and so the defeat of evil requires divine action on a large scale. At the same time, the actual history and meaning of demons in various religions says much about them. Sometimes the gods of one era or religion are turned into the demons of another that supersedes it.

In ancient HINDUISM, for example, the asuras, demonic deities, were originally good gods but became malevolent beings to the next race of gods, gods like INDRA and VISHNU. The asuras are in constant conflict with those gods, but the latter always outwit them in the end. Another class of demons are the raksasas, like Ravana in the great EPIC, the *Ramayana* (see RAMA, *RAMAYANA*); they delight in causing misery to human beings.

Many of these Hindu entities were borrowed by BUDDHISM. The realm of the asuras is one of the six places of rebirth, for those overly dominated by anger, violence, and stupidity; those condemned to the worst of those six places, the HELLS, are tormented by raksasas-like demons. But the most important Buddhist demon is MARA, who tempted the BUDDHA on the night of his enlightenment. Significantly, Mara is not so much consumed by evil will as blinded by ignorance, unable to see that the Buddha's enlightenment could be of benefit to him too, though the Buddha is "teacher of gods and men" alike. For in Buddhism as in Hinduism the ultimate source of evil is not in the will but in ignorance of the true nature of reality.

The demons in Western religion, like the Western Satan, are beings in rebellion against God out of evil will, though even here ambiguities may occur. An early example is Satan in the Hebrew scriptures' book of JOB. Here Satan appears as an adversary to God in the sense of a prosecutor whose function is to present an opposing point of view to the Lord, in this case that Job should be unjustly afflicted to test him. Other demonic figures, probably influenced by Babylonian examples, like Leviathan and Rahab representing chaos, Lilith the demoness of night, and Azazel the wilderness, also appear but only on the margins of the divine story (see MESOPOTAMIAN RELIGIONS).

However, by the sixth century B.C.E. and probably under the influence of ZOROASTRIANISM from Persia, JUDAISM became much more prone to see the world in terms of an eternal cosmic war between two opposing forces of good and evil, led by two personal commanders, God and Satan.

Zoroastrianism believed the universe was a battleground between the high god Ahura Mazda and the hosts of darkness under Angra Manyu or Ahriman. Hellenistic Judaism likewise saw Satan as the adversary of God from the beginning and the world infested by demons under his rule. This is the world view carried over into the NEW TESTAMENT and CHRISTIANITY. In mainstream rabbinical Judaism after the Diaspora of the Jews throughout the world, belief in Satan and demons became less of a central force and today has relatively little importance, although it lives on in Jewish folklore about Lilith, about magicians who had dealings with demons, about dibbuks or evil spirits, and about golems or artificial humans created by sorcery.

Christianity in its traditional form perceived Satan as a fallen angel in age-long rebellion against God, who corrupted ADAM and EVE in the Garden of Eden and thus brought SIN to the world, and who continues to twist toward himself whom he can out of his hatred for the good. Cast down from heaven, Satan and his minions landed in hell at the center of the Earth. There they not only plot their war against God waged through tempting humans on the world's surface, but also receive the souls of those condemned to eternal torture and gleefully impose that punishment. This story is familiar to readers of Dante and Milton. In it evil in the world can be attributed both to perverse human will and human entanglement in the cosmic rebellion of Satan and his angels. The height of Christian demonism was the 15th to 17th centuries, the period of the notorious witch-persecutions and of related elaborate beliefs in the powers of demons, their pacts with humans, their signs and methods of operating (see WITCHCRAFT). But the horrible injustice and cruelty to which such beliefs could lead produced a reaction, and they went into decline with the 18th century and the "Age of Reason."

Since then, liberal theologians and psychologists have taken demons as allegorical personifications of the evil within the human consciousness. In conservative Christian circles belief in the Devil and his demons often remains strong; much that is bad is attributed to them, and there are RITUALS and services for exorcism or the driving of demons out of persons and places.

In ISLAM, the opponent of God is Iblis or Shaitan, who first disobeyed God by refusing to bow before his greatest creation, human beings. While not always totally evil, he and his jinns (genies; spirits) and shaitans (demons) are ill-disposed toward humans and keep trying to lead them astray. Demon-doctrine is not a central feature of Islamic thought, but acknowledgment of the reality of angels and demons is required of the orthodox, and there is a large store of popular belief and folklore about the jinns and shaitans.

Though not as strong as it once was, belief in devils and demons remains alive in the modern world. Some have contended that the horrors of the 20th century, such as the demonic Nazi regime, show that it is not outdated to speculate about the presence of such malevolent forces. It is as though some intelligent energy of more than merely human wickedness possessed a brief hold on an entire nation at that time, and has shown its hand in other places from Cambodia to Bosnia as well. However that may be, devils and demons live on as parts of many religious worldviews.

Further reading: Peter J. Awn, *Satan's Tragedy and Redemption* [On Iblis in Islam] (Leiden: Brill, 1983); James W. Boyd, *Satan and Mara* (Leiden: Brill, 1975); Wendy Doniger, *The Origin of Evil in Hindu Mythology* (Berkeley: University of California Press, 1976); Robert Muchembled, *Damned: An Illustrated History of the Devil* (San Francisco: Sevil/Chronicle, 2004); Jeffrey Burton Russell, *The Prince of Darkness* (Ithaca, N.Y.: Cornell University Press, 1988), and other works by this author.

devotion, devotionalism Religious acts and inward attitudes marked by deep emotional feelings of awe, love, and fervent commitment to GOD. Movements like BHAKTI in HINDUISM, HASIDISM in JUDAISM, or the spirit of St. FRANCIS OF ASSISI and Franciscanism pietism and much of Evangelicalism in CHRISTIANITY may be regarded as devotional. The devotionalist typically centers WORSHIP, in the mind and often on the ALTAR, on a vivid, precise representation of the divine in some form: the god KRISHNA, the Sacred Heart of JESUS, CHRIST on the cross, and god in one's own heart. Simple prayers, chants, and moving hymns, and even the dance of PENTECOSTALISM are among the varied expressions of devotion, though it may also be subjective and free-form. Devotional attitudes and movements have done much to keep religion alive throughout the ages.

dharma in Hinduism and Buddhism From the Sanskrit verb *dhri*, which means "to sustain." Dharma is the order that sustains the universe. Although it always retains this root meaning, it is used somewhat differently in HINDUISM and BUDDHISM.

HINDU DHARMA

In Hinduism, dharma refers to all forms of order. Thus, it can refer to the regular cycles of the sun.

But in religious terms dharma refers most specifically to the moral standard by which human actions are judged. The impact of this standard is very broad ranging. At its most universally human, dharma is sometimes said to be the Hindu equivalent of the English word "religion."

Starting perhaps in the second century B.C.E., dharma was systematized in books known as *Smritis* or *Dharmasastras,* the most famous is the *Laws of* MANU. These books recognize that different dharmas or ideals of behavior are appropriate to different groups of people. It is customary to identify these ideals in terms of the *varna* or RITUAL class into which one is born (*see* CASTE IN HINDUISM), the *asrama* or stage of life in which one finds oneself, and, although it is not often stated, one's gender.

Technically, the stages of life apply only to males of the highest three varnas: BRAHMINS, kshatriyas, and vaisyas. In youth boys should study the VEDA. In maturity they should marry, support a household, perform the household rituals, and have children, especially sons. In old age they should retire. Some choose yet a fourth stage, a life of total renunciation.

The traditional ideal for women stresses their subservience to men: in youth to their fathers, in maturity to their husbands, and as widows to their sons. This ideal has often made life very hard for Indian women. Nevertheless, powerful and independent women have emerged in every period of Indian history.

BUDDHIST DHARMA

Buddhism rejected the ritual classes of Hindu dharma. Indeed, it rejected Hindu rituals altogether.

In Buddhism, dharma was originally identified with the BUDDHA's teaching. Then it became the teachings of Buddhism in general. With this meaning it appears as one of Buddhism's three jewels. An example is the formula, "I take refuge in the Buddha; I take refuge in the SANGHA; I take refuge in the Dharma."

Buddhist dharma is summarized in the Buddha's FOUR NOBLE TRUTHS. For THERAVADA Buddhists the teachings of Buddhism make up a large collection of books in the Pali language known as the Tipitika or "Three Baskets." These "baskets" or collections are the basket of the Buddha's sermons (dharma, properly speaking), the basket of the monastic discipline, and the basket of philosophical speculation known as "abhi-dharma."

In MAHAYANA BUDDHISM, which is found especially in east Asia, the word dharma sometimes takes on an even broader sense. The "three-body doctrine" identifies three different bodies (Kaya) of the Buddha or three different manifestations of the Buddhist dharma. They are the earthly (nirmanakaya), heavenly or "enjoyment" body (sambhogakaya), and absolute (dharmakaya). The historical Buddha is the ideal form in which the dharma appears in our world. But it is not the highest form of dharma. The heavenly body refers to the most excellent manifestations of dharma possible in worlds of name and form. In other words, it refers to the Buddhas and BODHISATTVAS who live in the various HEAVENS. Beyond name and form is the dharma body itself. In this body the dharma underlies and sustains all that is.

dialogue   A method by which religious people in the second half of the 20th century tried to understand one another. Dialogue was especially popular among liberals of all three branches of CHRISTIANITY: EASTERN ORTHODOX CHRISTIANITY, ROMAN CATHOLICISM, and PROTESTANTISM.

Talking with people who practice a religion different from one's own is certainly not new. Akbar (1542–1605), a Muslim emperor of India, was noted for his religious tolerance. At his capital, Fatehpur Sikri, he built a structure that provided him an elevated seat in the center of a room. Different religious teachers—Muslim, Hindu, Buddhist, and Christian—occupied elevated "pulpits" in each of the room's four corners. In this way, Akbar entered into discussion with all four teachers simultaneously.

During the 20th century, Christian denominations and MISSIONARIES became increasingly interested in "interreligious dialogue." Different Christian churches, for example, Catholics and Lutherans, established official dialogues with one another. Some Christian groups established official dialogues with representatives of other religions, for example, Jews, Muslims, and Buddhists. Indeed, the Second VATICAN COUNCIL saw dialogue as the most appropriate means to use in missionary efforts.

In 1983 Leonard Swidler, a theologian, published 10 ground rules for interreligious dialogue. He called them the "Dialogue Decalogue." The following points drawn from his rules give a good idea of what interreligious dialogue is about.

◆ People participate in interreligious dialogue to learn what other people believe, not to teach them what is true (rule 1).

◆ Participants must accept one another as equals. For example, one cannot consider people of other religions savage, primitive, demonic, deluded, or evil (rule 7).

◆ Each participant has the right to define what her or his view actually are. For example, if a person insisted that a physical image was not GOD but simply a means to help one WORSHIP God, one should not insist that that person was worshipping the image or idol itself (rule 5).

◆ Participants must be willing to look at their own religions critically (rule 9).

◆ All participants must share their positions honestly. That means they must be willing to share their doubts and hesitations as well as their convictions (rule 3).

◆ In a dialogue people should compare the practices of others with their own practices, their own ideals with the ideals of others. In the past, people had often used their ideals to condemn the practices of others. They had conveniently ignored problems with their own practices (rule 4).

Swidler claimed that interreligious dialogue was "something new under the sun." Others claimed that only dialogue and the attitudes found in dialogue could save human beings from universal threats, such as nuclear holocaust or an ecological imbalance that would poison the Earth. These claims are probably too enthusiastic.

Some have rejected interreligious dialogue altogether. More traditional Christians have seen dialogue as abandoning the basic calling of a Christian: to proclaim the truth of Christianity. Some non-Christians have seen dialogue as a new and underhanded way for Christians to try to convert them. In their eyes, those who advocated dialogue were wolves in sheeps' clothing.

Diamond Sutra

Diamond Sutra A relatively brief MAHAYANA Buddhist writing. It became important for practicers of ZEN BUDDHISM as well as for other schools of BUDDHISM.

The *Diamond Sutra* is one of a group of writings known as *Prajna-paramita sutras,* that is, "discourses concerned with perfect wisdom." Originally an Indian book written in Sanskrit, it was translated into Chinese around 400 C.E.

The sutra records a conversation between the BUDDHA and Subhuti, one of his most advanced disciples. The two rapidly recount a series of bold paradoxes that encapsulate Buddhist wisdom. For example, the Buddha teaches Subhuti that if anyone suggests that the Buddha has taught anything, that person slanders the Buddha, because truth cannot be taught. The sutra also teaches that things that appear to us are transient, like objects in dreams.

Diana A Roman GODDESS. Diana seems to have been a goddess of the woods and perhaps of the moon and its light. She was early identified with the Greek goddess ARTEMIS. In this capacity the Romans thought of her as a hunter, a midwife, and a goddess of the crossroads.

The most important festival of Diana took place on the Ides of August (August 13). During this festival women would wash their hair and carry torches from Rome to Diana's most important shrine, a grove at Aricia. The festival was also especially important to slaves.

Diana had an ancient temple in Rome. Her grove at Aricia was on the shores of Lake Nemi. In ancient times this lake was known as "the mirror of Diana." Offerings at Aricia attest to Diana's connections with childbirth: They include models of human sexual organs. Stories about the priests of Diana at Nemi provided the title and structure to an influential study of religion published in the early 20th century, *The Golden Bough* by James George FRAZER.

diet and religion Religious regulations about what people may eat and drink. Most religions order and regulate what people eat and drink. Sometimes they make eating and drinking into RITUALS. Examples include the Japanese tea ceremony and the Christian EUCHARIST. Sometimes they teach their adherents to slaughter animals in special ways or dedicate food to religious beings or for religious purposes. That is, they SACRIFICE and make offerings. Sometimes they ask followers to give up eating, drinking, or both, either partially or entirely, for a limited period of time. This is FASTING, which Muslims, for example, do during the month of Ramadan. Religions also make rules about ordinary eating and drinking. That is, they have dietary laws. Dietary laws answer such questions as what foods people should and should not eat, who may prepare and serve food, and when and how much people may eat. There is probably no item on which all religions agree.

REGULATIONS CONCERNING MEAT

One of the most common topics for dietary laws concerns the eating of meat. Some religions do not allow the eating of meat at all. Traditionally, most Hindus of the highest religious status have not eaten meat. Other Hindus consider some meat and animal products, such as milk, more acceptable than others, such as beef. Many Buddhists have practiced vegetarianism. So have Jains, the Pythagoreans of ancient Greece, Manichaeans, and some Taoists. In the last decades of the 20th century a number of North Americans adopted vegetarianism. They often did so because they wanted a healthy diet, a diet that was responsible to the environment, or both.

Other religions allow the eating of meat but strictly regulate which meats may be eaten. The Jewish laws of *kashrut*—more colloquially, kosher foods—are a good example. Traditional Muslims observe many of the same restrictions on meat products as Jews. Christians do not.

Observant Jews eat water animals as long as they have scales and fins. Therefore, sole and trout are kosher or acceptable; lobster, shrimp, eels, and catfish are not. Observant Jews also eat birds that meet certain requirements. But the best known kosher law concerns land animals. These animals must chew the cud and have cloven hoofs. Pigs do not chew the cud; therefore, observant Jews do not eat pork—and many other meats as well.

Observant Jews also do not eat blood. This regulation requires special preparation of meat before cooking. The BIBLE forbids boiling a kid in its mother's milk. The RABBIS extended this rule: It is not proper to eat meat and dairy products in the same meal. Thus, cheeseburgers and pepperoni pizzas are not kosher. Observant households often have two sets of kitchen ware—one for meat meals, the other for dairy meals. After eating a meat or dairy dish, observant Jews also let an appropriate interval—say, six hours—pass before eating foods of the other variety.

REGULATIONS CONCERNING OTHER FOODS

Religions have had less to say about plant food and dairy products, but they have not ignored them. The followers of Pythagoras were forbidden to eat beans. Members of the Nation of Islam (*see* ISLAM, NATION OF) are supposed to avoid certain vegetables that recall the experiences of slavery. Technically, Jains may eat only living beings that have a single sense. This principle prohibits them from eating some plants as well as meat. (Most North Americans limit senses to animals, but Jains do not.) Traditional HINDUISM distinguishes between two types of food, *pakka* and *kacca*. Hindus who are most concerned about the purity of their diet eat only food that is pakka. They avoid onions and garlic as well as animal foods. They also eat food that is prepared with clarified butter, known as "ghee," rather than with oils from plants or animals.

Many religions also regulate the consumption of alcohol. One of the five precepts of BUDDHISM rejects alcohol altogether. Some Buddhists, however, ignore this precept, especially in Japan. JUDAISM permits alcohol in moderation, but ISLAM strictly forbids it. Christian attitudes vary. Some Christians drink to excess when they celebrate certain rituals, such as CARNIVAL. Some Protestants, however, avoid alcohol altogether. They even celebrate the EUCHARIST with unfermented grape juice. After World War I this Protestant attitude, represented by groups like the Women's Christian Temperance Union, helped to pass a constitutional amendment that made alcohol illegal in the United States. This started the era of Prohibition (1920–33).

OTHER DIETARY LAWS

Many dietary laws detail what foods may be eaten. But religions also tell their followers who may prepare, serve, and clean up food, as well as when and how much a person may eat.

In traditional Hinduism dietary rules help define ritual classes (*varnas*) and castes (*jatis*) (*see* CASTE IN HINDUISM). According to these rules, a person should eat only cooked food that is prepared by someone of equal or higher status. Similarly, people should clean up only food that has been eaten by someone of equal or higher status. Buddhism teaches that MONKS AND NUNS should not eat after noon. MANICHAEISM taught that its elite, called "the elect," must eat all the food that laypersons brought to them.

WHY REGULATE DIET?

People often wonder why others observe dietary laws that they do not. Some people attribute these laws to medical concerns. For example, some people think that observant Jews do not eat pork because pigs carry trichinosis. However, when the Jewish dietary laws of kashrut were established, no one knew that pigs carried trichinosis.

Many modern scholars trace dietary laws to a different cause. They say that these laws help create group identity. For example, the laws of kashrut help distinguish Jews from non-Jews. There is something to this claim. During the 20th century people all over the world moved into modern, pluralistic cities. When they left their traditional communities behind, many of them gave up their traditional dietary practices. But group identity explains only when people observe dietary laws. It does not explain the particular laws that they observe.

It is important to note what the religions themselves say about these laws. Buddhists say that it takes a clear, crisp mind to pursue enlightenment, or understanding. Someone who is intoxicated does not have such a mind. Therefore, they refrain from alcohol. Jains do not eat meat because of their devotion to the principle of AHIMSA. Many observant Jews say that there is only one good reason for practicing the dietary laws. GOD instructed them to do so. Who are human beings, that they should second-guess God?

Further reading: K. C. Chang, ed., *Food in Chinese Culture* (New Haven: Yale University Press, 1977); Isaac Klein, *A Guide to Jewish Religious Practice* (New York: Ktav, 1979); Frederick Simoons, *Eat Not This Flesh: Food Avoidances from Prehistory to the Present* 2d ed. (Madison: University of Wisconsin Press, 1994); Reay Tannahill, *Food in History* (New York: Stein & Day, 1973).

disciples   *See* APOSTLES.

disciples of Christ   *See* RESTORATION MOVEMENT.

Dogen (1200–1253) *a Buddhist monk who in the late 1220s founded the Soto school of ZEN BUDDHISM in Japan* In 1223 Dogen left Kyoto for China. He had already studied two schools of BUDDHISM: Tiendai Buddhism and Zen Buddhism. In China he attained enlightenment, or a deep understanding of nature and the causes of sorrow. In 1227 he returned to Japan to teach the path that he had followed.

Dogen emphasized the practice of sitting in MEDITATION (ZAZEN) without any purpose. From his point of view, one did not sit in meditation to attain enlightenment. Sitting in meditation was itself enlightenment.

Dogen's teachings disagreed with Buddhist tradition in important ways. He taught that all beings are Buddha-nature and that Buddha-nature is impermanence. Traditionally Buddhism had taught that all beings have, not are, Buddha-nature, and that Buddha-nature lies beyond impermanence.

Dogen's most important writing is the Shōbhōgenzō or "The Treasury of the True DHARMA eye." Today Soto Zen is one of the largest schools of Japanese Buddhism.

dogma and doctrine   A religion's official beliefs and teachings.

Religions create unity in many ways. Members of a given religion may see themselves united by shared behavior, which usually includes both participation in religious RITUAL and living according to prescribed ways of life. A good example is traditional orthodox JUDAISM. Other religions stress correctness of belief. Members are united by shared adherence to dogma (what the group officially believes) and doctrine (what it officially teaches). These terms appear often in discussions of CHRISTIANITY, since Christianity grew by attracting people to a set of new beliefs rather than as a shared way of life.

Christians have recognized several sources of dogma and doctrine. Protestants derive Christian truth from the BIBLE (*see* PROTESTANTISM.) Roman Catholics and Orthodox Christians derive Christian truth also from tradition (*see* ROMAN CATHOLICISM and EASTERN ORTHODOX CHRISTIANITY). Most, but not all, Christians recognize the ancient CREEDS and the decrees of the ancient church councils as defining their dogma and doctrines. Individual churches often have their own special statements as well. Examples include the Pope's pronouncements in the Catholic Church and the "confessions" of various Protestant churches.

Dominicans   An order of Roman Catholic MONKS AND NUNS properly known as the Order of Preachers.

The Dominican order was founded by Dominic in 1216. Like the Franciscans (*see* FRANCIS OF ASSISI AND FRANCISCANS), it is an order centered on mendicant friars. Its members take vows of poverty, and they are not under the control of a diocese and its bishop.

The Dominicans received as their special mission the tasks of preaching and study. Preaching had earlier been the privilege of bishops and those to whom they had delegated the task. The Dominicans, it was hoped, would effectively counter various heresies that were beginning to spread. Later the Dominicans played a major role in INQUISITIONS.

Other Dominican accomplishments are more likely to win admiration today. The order has included the great theologians Albertus Magnus (*c.* 1200–80) and Thomas AQUINAS; the mystics Meister Eckhardt (*c.* 1260–*c.* 1328), Johannes Tauler (*c.* 1300–61), and Catherine of Siena (1347–80); the reformer Savonarola (1452–98); the painter Fra Angelico (*c.* 1400–55); and the champion of Mesoamericans' rights, Bartolomé de las Casas (1474–1566). From the 16th through the 18th centuries, the Dominicans were in decline. Since the middle of the 19th century the order has experienced a revival.

Dominicans have been active in the United States continuously from the year 1786. In 1806 the first Dominican province, the Province of St. Joseph, was established at St. Rose, Kentucky. The first Dominican nuns arrived in the United States in 1853. Today Dominicans are active in North America teaching, promoting a life of contemplation, and supporting missions overseas.

drama, religious Religion has included drama or theatrical performances in a number of ways. Religions use drama in RITUALS and as acts of worship. Religions have also influenced dramas that are performed primarily for entertainment. Not to be overlooked is the opposition that some religious people have to drama.

DRAMA AS RITUAL AND WORSHIP

Drama is originally a Greek word that means an act or a deed, particularly deeds acted out on a stage. Some scholars suppose that people have been acting out stories of one sort or another for as long as there have been people. For example, a cave in France has footprints that some claim go back to early hunters. The footprints make a circle, and some scholars suggest that the hunters made them as they were acting out hunting scenes as part of their rituals.

It is quite common for religions to use drama as a form of worship. One way to do so is to act out stories about gods and other supernatural beings. A good example is the Ramlila celebration in HINDUISM, which takes place in the fall. Ramlila acts out the story of RAMA, an avatar of VISHNU, as told in the *RAMAYANA*. Some perform just the bare outline of the story; others perform it in great detail. The climax comes with the final battle, when Rama finally defeats the demon Ravana. It is common to build effigies of Ravana and other demons that are several times the size of a human being. These effigies are stuffed with fireworks and set alight when Rama shoots a lighted arrow into them. Other famous dramatizations of religious stories include the dance drama and puppet theater of Indonesia and depictions of the passion of JESUS among native peoples of Latin America as well as at places like Oberammergau, Germany, and Eureka Springs, Arkansas.

To the extent that acts of ritual or worship involve performance, they inevitably have a dramatic side. For example, some people speak of the Mass in ROMAN CATHOLICISM as a sacred drama. More clearly theatrical were dramas that some scholars believe characterized worship in the ancient Near East, for example, ancient Babylonia. Taking the part of a god, the king reenacted various stories. One concerned the humiliation of the god, during which the king was whipped and beaten. Another told of the sacred marriage between a god and goddess. On some views these acts were clearly linked to the forces of the cosmos, such as the growth and decay of plants. The king's reenacts of them were rituals that aimed to ensure the flourishing of his territory.

Traditional healers known as shamans (*see* SHAMANISM) have also performed a kind of ritual drama. Many shamans heal by traveling to the realm of the spirits, because spirits are thought to make people sick. In that realm they discover the cause of a patient's illness and, in some traditions, battle and defeat the evil spirits. Shamans may use dance, song, and drama as they act out their encounters with beings in the spirit realm, including their struggles with and victory over the illness-causing spirits.

Another form of religious drama takes place when a spirit overcomes a person, as happens when a spirit "rides" a person in the Caribbean religion known as VOODOO. This, too, is a kind of religious drama, but a spontaneous one which members of the religion take to be not a performance but the very actions of the spirit itself.

The presence of supernatural beings may bring about another kind of religious drama. People who believe that GOD is actually present in a temple may perform dramas to please her or him. This was the function of special women in Hindu temples known as *devadasis,* "servants of god." Their dancing acted out stories at the same time that it entertained the divinity present.

Religious dramas are not restricted to adult actors. In many religions children, too, perform religious dramas in the context of ritual and worship. In JUDAISM children act out the events surrounding ESTHER's saving of her people at PURIM. Many Christian children in North America dramatize the story of Jesus' birth around the time of CHRISTMAS. Children in schools in India may also put on plays about the life of Rama during Ramlila. These dramas provide ways for children to learn religious stories by participating in them rather than simply listening to them. Actors identify with the characters, and as a result the stories begin to define who they are.

RELIGION INFLUENCES DRAMA

The line between drama performed as ritual and drama performed as entertainment is often difficult to draw. For example, are Purim plays and plays about the birth of Jesus performed for religious purposes, for entertainment, or both? It has been suggested that drama for entertainment began as ritual. That statement may be an exaggeration.

Nevertheless, religions have played important roles in the development of kinds of drama that are usually associated with entertainment.

It is customary to locate the beginning of Western drama with Greek tragedy and comedy. Some of the religious influences on these plays are hard to miss. Tragedies use religious stories, such as the story of Oedipus, to explore the human situation. These tragedies were performed as part of a festival in Athens known as the Greater Dionysia, in celebration of Dionysos.

During the Middle Ages, too, drama had a strong religious character. Guilds performed mystery plays to dramatize stories from the Bible. Morality plays, such as *Everyman,* talked about the human condition. From such roots, European drama of the Renaissance and later periods grew.

Religious influence on theater is hardly limited to Europe. In Japan, a form of drama known as Noh combines elements of SHINTO and BUDDHISM. Actors sometimes perform Noh plays for religious purposes, but they also perform them today to entertain audiences. During the plays actors represent gods, spirits of the dead, and demons. These beings come on stage to relate their stories to the audience.

In the 20th and early 21st centuries some leading theater directors have paid close attention to the religious and ritual dimensions of drama. Important leaders of this movement include the British director Peter Brook (b. 1925), the American director Richard Schechner (b. 1934), and the African director Wole Soyinka (b. 1934).

RELIGION OPPOSED TO DRAMA

Not everyone has approved of drama, religious or secular. Perhaps the most famous person who opposed it was the Greek philosopher Plato (c. 427–c. 347 B.C.E.). He accused dramatists and poets of lying about the gods. When he envisioned his ideal state, he excluded drama and poetry from it.

Others have opposed drama, too. Many Muslim thinkers have opposed drama, just as they have opposed two-dimensional representations of human beings and animals. Nevertheless, there are dramatic traditions within ISLAM; for example, more Muslims live in Indonesia, with its traditions of dance drama and puppet theater, than in any other country in the world.

Despite very strong traditions of drama within Hinduism, even in Hindu worship, the Laws of MANU did not look favorably upon drama. In Buddhism, too, the ten precepts followed by MONKS AND NUNS, novices, and devout laypeople forbid attendance at worldly amusements such as the theater. Such amusements encourage attachment to sensory pleasure and, through the presentation of fictions, distract the mind from waking up to reality.

In North America, too, some religious people have opposed drama. One such group to do so were the Puritans (see PURITANISM). Today churches in some traditions of PROTESTANTISM, such as the HOLINESS MOVEMENT, either reject theatrical entertainment altogether or find it highly suspicious as a source of immorality and vice.

It might be suggested that religious people who oppose drama recognize the immense power of performance and theater. They simply view that power as evil, just as religious people who use drama see in it as a potential source of great benefit.

Further reading: Richard Schechner, *The Future of Ritual: Writings on Culture and Performance* (London: Routledge, 1993); Victor Witter Turner, *From Ritual to Theatre: The Human Seriousness of Play* (New York: PAJ Publications, 1982).

dreams and religion Dreams of religious significance. Dreams have been thought to have spiritual importance in many traditions. The 19th-century anthropologist Edward Tylor, in fact, thought that the origin of religion lay in the experience of dreams. It seemed natural to think that figures appearing in those mysterious nighttime adventures might be gods or spirits of ancestors, and that their words or stories might bear divine messages. The ability to interpret dreams rightly was also a divine gift. In the biblical book of Genesis, JOSEPH was able to win his freedom from prison by

rightly predicting the fate of two fellow-prisoners from their dreams, and then foretelling the seven good years and seven lean years on the basis of pharaoh's dream. In the NEW TESTAMENT another Joseph, the spouse of MARY the mother of JESUS, was told by an ANGEL in a dream that her child was conceived by the Holy Ghost, and later was warned in the same way to take the infant to Egypt and avoid the wrath of Herod. The Greeks and Romans also considered dreams to be messages from the gods, though they recognized they were not always reliable. Penelope, in a famous passage in *The Odyssey,* said that there are two gates through which dreams pass: the gate of ivory, whose dreams are deceitful, and the gate of horn, whose dreams are true. The ancients, like the Chinese more recently, would also practice incubation or sleeping in a temple in order to receive advice from a god through a dream. CHRISTIANITY has sometimes seen dreams as a means of divine revelation, but has also recognized that demons can tempt the unwary through dreams.

The hazy and fleeting nature of dreams has also had religious meaning. Buddhist literature such as the DIAMOND SUTRA has spoken of this world with its empty attractions as like a dream, a phantasm, a bubble, a shadow, a dew-drop, and a flash of lightning. Here dreams mean not revelations of truth, but illusion and unreality. Yet Eastern accounts have also presented positive experiences of dreams, and there are advanced yoga techniques for controlling and using them.

Twentieth-century analytic psychology in the tradition of Carl Gustav JUNG has given dreams a renewed spiritual importance as mirrors or indicators of what is going on in one's psychic and spiritual life. Jung pointed to the marked similarity of the symbolic language of dreams to the language of the world's mythologies and religions, showing that, rightly understood, one's dreams could be like a personal story telling what is needed to fulfill one's life. Other modern psychologists, however, have said there is very little of real importance in dreams, thus closing the door on a venerable religious tradition. In any case, dreams have always been important in the myths and religions of the world, whether as the voice of the divine or as warnings not to get lost in fantasy and that which is passing away.

See also VISIONS.

drugs and religion The religious use and meaning of mind-altering drugs. There are drugs both natural and synthetic that can produce experiences similar to religious experiences: VISIONS, ecstasy, cosmic journeys, what the poet Baudelaire called "artificial paradises." They can also produce inner HELLS as terrible as any that can be imagined. Nonetheless drugs have had a spiritual or sacramental use the world over. Shamans of PRIMAL RELIGION in Siberia and the Americas have taken hallucinogenic mushrooms, peyote, datura, and other plant substances to help induce visions of the divine realms and messages from gods. Some scholars believe that soma, the famous sacred drink spoken of in the VEDAS of ancient India, may have been made from the fly-agaric mushroom, and a few have speculated that the mysteries of Eleusis in ancient Greece may have employed the same hallucinogenic plant (*see* GREEK RELIGION). Today the Native American Church in the United States uses peyote, a hallucinogenic cactus, as a sacramental substance to be taken in a reverential setting as a means of communion with GOD. (*See* NATIVE AMERICAN RELIGIONS.)

However, religions such as JUDAISM, CHRISTIANITY, ISLAM, and the major eastern FAITHS have generally rejected the use of drugs in religion, believing that the visions and raptures they induce are spurious and not authentically from God. (Certain nonmainstream Hindu, Buddhist, and Taoist sources, chiefly related to TANTRISM, have seen some positive spiritual value in the materials, but for the most part as an initiation into realities that ought later to be realized by nondrug means.) They have recognized and condemned the dangers that can lie in drug use: lethargy, escapism, indifference to other issues of life, and finally addiction to the point that one will neglect responsibilities and commit crimes for the sake of the drug.

In the mid-20th century, a new interest in the spiritual meaning of drug experience arose. One important impetus for it was a book, *The Doors of Perception* (1954), by the famous mystic and novelist Aldous Huxley (1894–1963). Huxley vividly described the way the ordinary world became transfigured and splendid as though it were all divine, like the way it was seen by great artists and Zen masters, after he had taken mescaline, a substance made from peyote. However, Huxley also believed such stimulants should be restricted to those truly mature and ready for them. Another impetus was the invention of LSD (lysergic acid diethylamide), a highly visionary synthetic substance. The use of drugs, allegedly for spiritual purposes, was an important aspect of the counterculture of the 1960s. But the "drug culture" quickly filled with drug-induced crime, sickness, mental breakdown, and exploitation, and hallucinogenic drugs were outlawed everywhere in the United States by 1966, with exceptions allowed for the Native American Church, where drug use has continued to be a legal issue. Whatever role drugs may have had in the religious life of the remote past, they are generally not welcome in that of the modern world, and most faiths see combating drug use as an important part of their mission to help people live disciplined and productive lives.

druids Ancient Celtic priests. The word *druid* means "wise one." The druids formed a separate, elite class of Celtic society (*see* CELTIC RELIGION). They were close allies of the kings. According to Julius Caesar, the druids "watch over divine matters, administer public and private sacrifices, and rule all matters of religion" (*Gallic Wars* 6.13). Caesar goes on to describe the druids as preserving the sacred verses of the Celts in memory rather than in writing, educating the young, and teaching that at death souls are reborn.

In all of these characteristics the druids resemble the BRAHMINS of India. Unlike brahmins, however, druids did not have to inherit their status. They could choose to become druids. Other ancient authors identify different kinds of druids:

priests, poets, and soothsayers. Women could hold the position of soothsayer.

Druids ceased to exist when the British Isles were converted to CHRISTIANITY during the first millennium (1–1000) C.E. But during the 19th and especially the 20th centuries, people in Britain and the United States tried to revive the order of druids. They not only used ancient traditions but also relied on images of the druids that arose as late as the 18th century.

Druze, the

A small religious community in the Near East. The Druze are an offshoot of SHI'ITE ISLAM. In 1017 C.E., a Fatimid ruler of Egypt named al-Hakim became convinced that he was divine. Two MISSIONARIES, Hamza ibn Ali and Darazi, promoted his divinity. Shortly thereafter all three "disappeared." The Druze believe that they went into hiding. A follower named al-Muktana assumed leadership of the community. His letters, as well as those of Hamza and al-Hakim, form the community's sacred book.

The Druze observe seven "pillars" or practices. These include always speaking the truth within, but not outside, the community; helping members of the community by military means, if necessary; and confessing the oneness of GOD, who was incarnate in al-Hakim. The Druze expect al-Hakim and Hamza to return at the end of time to establish universal justice.

The Druze do not accept converts. Their community consists of two groups, the initiated and the ignorant. Only the initiated may read the Druze secret writings and attend the secret RITUALS. Druze also accept "dissimulation." That is, for survival they may pretend to practice the majority religion wherever they are. In the 19th and 20th centuries the Druze were intensely involved in the military conflicts of Lebanon and the surrounding regions.

Durga

A Hindu GODDESS, especially popular in eastern India. She is usually shown with eight arms that hold weapons and riding either a tiger or a lion.

According to legend, the goddess Durga was created when a powerful water buffalo demon, Mahisha, began to savage the Earth. Each of the gods tried to stop him, but they were unable to, so they decided to combine their powers into one being more powerful than any of them. Perhaps because the Sanskrit word *sakti*, divine power, is feminine, the being they created was female, Durga. Her images portray her defeating Mahisha.

Durga is one of several manifestations of the Goddess in HINDUISM. She is worshipped by followers known as Saktas. Her major festival is Navaratri, observed in Bengal in the cooler time of the year just after the monsoons (*see* HINDU FESTIVALS). It celebrates Durga's victory over Mahisha.

Durkheim, Émile

(1858–1917) *a French thinker who helped invent the study of sociology* He has had an immense impact on the study of religions.

Durkheim's early writings contributed some terms that scholars have used to study religions. An example is the term "anomie." It refers to the social and moral disorder that arises when traditional social forms break down. But Durkheim's most important book for the study of religions appeared later: *The Elementary Forms of the Religious Life* (1912).

The Elementary Forms starts with the idea that TOTEMISM and TABOO in Australia are the most basic forms of religion. Although this idea is no longer accepted, other ideas in Durkheim's system have proven very useful. Durkheim proposed that religion serves to bind individuals to society. It does so, he says, because religious symbols, such as totems and gods, along with religious rules objectify and represent society and its values. Therefore, religious RITUALS actually celebrate human society.

dynamism

Also called preanimism; a once-popular theory of the origin of religion. At the end of the 19th century, scholars tried to identify the earliest form of religion. Many followed E. B. Tylor, who suggested that the earliest religion was ANI-

MISM. R. R. Marett (1866–1943), an anthropologist, disagreed. He said there was an earlier form of religion. He called it preanimism. Later, others called it dynamism.

According to Marett, before people believed in spirits, they felt awe before the supernatural energy that pervaded the universe. Marett called this energy *mana,* a Polynesian word. Mana was life-giving, but like electricity, too much of it was dangerous. So people protected themselves by creating TABOOS. Animism resulted when people associated personal characteristics with mana.

Like all other theories of the origin of religion, Marett's theory was entirely speculative. His description of mana also distorted the Polynesian idea. Today dynamism is no longer accepted. But the ideas that it made popular, mana and taboo, have taken on a life of their own.

E

Easter The most important Christian festival, a time when Christians celebrate the RESURRECTION of JESUS from the dead. According to the NEW TESTAMENT, Jesus was crucified on a Friday. The following Sunday he rose from the dead. These events took place around the time of the Jewish festival of PASSOVER. As a result, Christians do not observe Easter on a set date. They observe it on a Sunday in spring around the time of Passover. That Sunday is the first Sunday after the first full moon after the spring equinox (roughly March 21).

For Catholic, Orthodox, and some Protestant Christians, the most "liturgically correct" way to observe Easter is with a vigil. This is a lengthy service late Saturday evening, which looks forward to the resurrection Sunday morning. Another common practice is to hold "sunrise services" early Easter morning. In North America and Europe, Christians also celebrate Easter with colored eggs. The eggs are said to symbolize the new life that the resurrection of Jesus made possible. They probably also preserve ways of celebrating the coming of spring that were common in Europe before CHRISTIANITY.

Not all Christians observe Easter. Some Protestants reject it as a human invention. Among those who do not observe Easter are the "plain people," such as the AMISH.

Eastern Orthodox Christianity One of the three major branches of CHRISTIANITY. The Eastern Orthodox churches are properly known as "the Orthodox Catholic Church."

The word "orthodox" means "having the proper opinions or beliefs." In the case of the Orthodox churches, it means adhering to the decrees of the seven ancient, ecumenical councils. (The Roman Catholic Church and some Protestant churches accept these decrees, too.) The councils were meetings of bishops to determine Christian teaching, especially with regard to Jesus. Some Eastern churches, such as the ARMENIAN CHURCH and COPTIC CHURCH, refused to accept the councils' decrees.

The Orthodox churches see themselves as continuing the traditions of the APOSTLES. Indeed, important centers of Orthodoxy were founded by apostles. Orthodox bishops also preserve "apostolic succession," as do the bishops in the Roman Catholic and some Protestant churches. They go back in an unbroken line of succession to Jesus's immediate followers.

The Orthodox churches arose in the Eastern, Greek-speaking Roman Empire. ROMAN CATHOLICISM arose in the Western, Latin-speaking Roman Empire. Political and cultural tensions between the two led to theological disputes in the 800s. In 1054 the Pope and the head of the Orthodox churches, the Patriarch of Constantinople, excommunicated one another. In 1204 the Fourth CRUSADE viciously attacked Constantinople. Not until 1965 did the Pope and the Patriarch reestablish friendly relations.

Orthodoxy comprises 15 independent territorial churches—for example, the churches of Constantinople, Russia, and Greece—and three other churches that are semi-independent in Crete, Finland, and Japan. The independent churches call their chief officials either patriarchs, archbishops, or metropolitans. The Patriarch of Constantinople is recognized as the first among equals. The leaders of the Orthodox churches have never claimed the political powers that the PAPACY claimed in the West. That is because in the Eastern Roman Empire political power did not disintegrate the way it did in the West. Until 1453 the Byzantine Empire patronized Orthodoxy. The Russian Empire took over that role until 1917.

Orthodox theologians have generally expressed the truth of Christianity differently than Catholic and Protestant theologians. Catholics and Protestants have tended to think in judicial terms. They have talked about original SIN, guilt, reparation, and atonement. Orthodox theologians talk instead about the divinization of humanity. In their eyes, human beings were made for communion with GOD. Indeed, human beings find their fulfillment in the divine. The INCARNATION and especially the RESURRECTION of Jesus testify to that fulfillment, despite the obstacles that life in the world presents. The church and its SACRAMENTS are the places where such communion and divinization take place today.

Like the Roman Catholic Church, the Orthodox churches recognize seven sacraments. Their central WORSHIP practice is the celebration of the EUCHARIST in the Divine LITURGY. Orthodox services are long but are noted for their beauty and mystical quality. Orthodox churches allow even infants to receive the bread and wine of communion, provided they are baptized (*see* BAPTISM). Orthodox churches also make rich use of sacred pictures known as icons (*see* IMAGES, ICONS, IDOLS IN RELIGION). They have well-developed traditions of monasticism. Although Orthodox priests may be married men, bishops must be celibate.

Orthodox churches have not won as many converts through foreign missions as have Catholic and Protestant churches. The rise of ISLAM in the seventh century restricted their opportunities. So did the relative weakness of the Christian territories in which they lived. But the Russian church spread across Asia and then established missions in Alaska. In the 19th and 20th centuries, immigrants also brought many other forms of Orthodox Christianity to the United States. In 1970 the patriarch of Moscow established the Orthodox Church of America, but not all Orthodox churches in America belong to it.

See also ROMAN CATHOLICISM AND EASTERN ORTHODOXY IN AMERICA.

Further reading: John Binns, *An Introduction to the Christian Orthodox Churches* (New York: Cambridge University Press, 2002); Emmanuel Clapsis, *The Orthodox Churches in a Pluralistic World: An Ecumenical Conversation* (Brookline, Mass.: Holy Cross Orthodox Press, 2004); Timothy Ware, *The Orthodox Church* (Baltimore, Md.: Penguin, 1963); Nicholas Zernov, *Eastern Christendom* (London: Weidenfeld and Nicolson, 1961).

ecumenical movement A movement among Christian churches that seeks to reunite them. Throughout its history, CHRISTIANITY has experienced divisions. The most important divisions occurred in the fourth and fifth centuries C.E., when Christians such as Arians and Nestorians were expelled as heretics; in 1054, when the Orthodox churches and the Roman Catholic Church split; and in the 16th century and later, during the Protestant REFORMATION. The ecumenical movement has attempted to overcome these divisions. It began in the early 20th century and continues today.

The impetus for the ecumenical movement developed in the 19th century. At that time, missionaries from Europe and North America were taking the message of Christianity to other parts of the world. They discovered that divisions at home were not so important overseas. In fact, they found that these divisions confused people and made mission work more difficult. In response, they started to look for ways to eliminate the divisions.

In 1910 several missionary societies held a conference in Edinburgh, Scotland. Their goal was to formulate a common plan of action. Eventually these societies organized three groups to work on three sets of issues. One group was the International Missionary Society, responsible for coordinating activities so that missionaries did not compete to convert the same people. A second was the Commission on Life and Work; it dealt with cooperation in serving other people. The third was the Commission on Faith and Order; it explored whether it was possible for churches to come together on teachings about which they had disagreed. In 1948 the two commissions combined to form the World Council of Churches (WCC). In 1961 the International Missionary Council joined them.

In the early years of the ecumenical movement, Protestants took the lead. By the time the WCC was founded, Orthodox churches were also actively involved. The Roman Catholic Church (see ROMAN CATHOLICISM) has never joined, in part because some in the church think that the only way for Christians to reunite is for all those who left the Catholic Church to rejoin it. Nevertheless, the Second VATICAN COUNCIL (1961–65) opened the Catholic Church up to the ecumenical movement. Since then it has cooperated with the WCC. At the beginning of 2005 the WCC had 347 member churches in more than 120 countries. It officially defined itself as "a fellowship of churches which confess the Lord Jesus Christ as God and Savior according to the scriptures, and therefore seek to fulfill together their common calling to the glory of the one God, Father, Son and Holy Spirit."

The World Council of Churches was not the only organization to grow out of the ecumenical movement. Churches around the world that shared the same heritage also formed global organizations. Two examples are the Lutheran World Federation and the World Alliance of Reformed Churches. In addition, churches in individual countries came together to form associations, such as the National Council of Churches in the United States. In some places churches with varying heritages merged. One such merger produced the Church of South India. Some churches, too, opened up official dialogues with other churches. One result was that some churches entered into full fellowship with one another, agreeing, for example, to accept each others' ministers.

The ecumenical movement was part of a larger trend in the 20th century. For example, Buddhists formed a World Buddhist Council and a World Buddhist Sangha Council. Even more encompassing is the Council for a Parliament of the World's Religions, organized in the 1990s. It brings representatives of all religions together, as it did, for example, in the summer of 2004 with its parliament "Pathways to Peace" in Barcelona, Spain.

Not all churches, however, have participated in the ecumenical movement. Many conservatives prefer to emphasize their particularity and view the ecumenical movement with suspicion. Some prominent churches in the United States do not participate in either the World or National Council of Churches. They include the Southern Baptist Convention, the Assemblies of God, and the Lutheran Church–Missouri Synod. In addition, at the beginning of the 21st century churches that did belong to these Councils were grappling with issues that threatened to divide them once again. The most controversial issue was whether churches should ordain sexually active homosexuals and perform marriage ceremonies for gay and lesbian couples.

Further reading: Thomas E. FitzGerald, *The Ecumenical Movement: An Introductory History* (Westport, Conn.: Praeger, 2004); Ruth Rouse and Stephen Charles Neill, eds., *A History of the Ecumenical Movement, 1517–1968,* 4th ed. (Geneva: World Council of Churches, 1993).

Egyptian religion The religion practiced in ancient Egypt.

Much of the evidence for Egyptian religion comes from burial practices. Clearly, Egyptians gave the afterlife a great deal of attention (see AFTERLIFE IN WORLD RELIGIONS). But their religion dealt with life in this world, too.

HISTORY

Ancient historians divided the history of Egypt into 30 dynasties or families of rulers. Modern scholars have divided Egyptian history into several periods. Some were more important for religion than others.

Egyptian history begins around 3100 B.C.E. At that time a king whom the Greeks called Menes unified Upper and Lower Egypt. Like virtually every king after him, he claimed to be the god HORUS on Earth. Menes established his capital at Memphis, where Upper and Lower Egypt meet. He built a temple for the nation there. The temple served the god PTAH.

During the first part of the Old Kingdom (Dynasties 3–6, 2650–2180 B.C.E.), the kings of Egypt built massive stone tombs. These include the great pyramids at Giza outside Cairo. During the second half of the Old Kingdom, a new god, Re, the sun god of Heliopolis, became dominant. Many texts about him have survived.

After the Old Kingdom, Egypt fragmented into local districts that competed with one another. The Middle Kingdom (Dynasty 12, 2050–1800 B.C.E.) interrupted this disorder briefly. At that time the god AMON first became associated with the southern city of Thebes. But Amon and Thebes achieved much greater glory during the New Kingdom (Dynasties 18–20, 1570–1080 B.C.E.). Amon-Re became the national god. His temple at Karnak near Thebes became a powerful institution.

During the New Kingdom, many people were buried with texts to help them in the next life. Today these texts are known as The Book of Going Forth by Day or, more popularly, The Egyptian Book of the Dead. During the 18th dynasty the king AKHENATON directed his religious attention to the disk of the sun, known as the Aton. Some have seen him as an early monotheist.

In 332 B.C.E. Alexander the Great conquered Egypt. One of his generals, Ptolemy, began a Greek dynasty there. It ruled Egypt until the Romans

Shown here are the sphinxes lining an avenue of the Temple of Amon at Karnak. *(Getty Images)*

annexed the region around the time of Jesus. The Ptolemies lavishly sponsored Egyptian religion. In particular, they built great temples. Their temples at Edfu, Dendera, and Philae are especially well-known. During this period the "mysteries" of the Egyptian GODDESS Isis spread throughout the region of the Mediterranean Sea (*see* MYSTERY RELIGIONS).

CHRISTIANITY came to Egypt as early as the first century C.E. It thrived there, but some Egyptians continued to practice the traditional religion. In the fourth century C.E. Christianity became first a legal religion, then the required religion. Some Egyptians persisted in traditional ways. In 415, Christians stoned an Egyptian woman philosopher and mathematician named Hypatia. By the end of the fifth century, the last functioning non-Christian temple in the Roman Empire, the temple of Isis at Philae, had shut down.

BELIEFS

Many writings tell us about Egyptian beliefs. They include writings from tombs: the Pyramid Texts (Old Kingdom), the Coffin Texts (Middle Kingdom), and the so-called Book of the Dead. These and other writings often portray Egyptian gods with the heads of animals. The heads helped distinguish one god from another. There is little evidence that Egyptians actually worshipped animals.

Most Egyptian gods began as the gods of particular places. When Egypt became unified, priests at different temples tried to fit all the gods together. Different temples developed different systems.

One influential system was the "ennead," or group of nine gods, which developed during the Old Kingdom at Heliopolis. According to this system, the first god, Atum, produced two others, the god Shu (air) and the goddess Tefnut (moisture). These two produced the god Geb (the earth) and the goddess Nut (the sky). Geb and Nut gave birth to two couples, Osiris and Isis, and Seth and Nephthys. The EVIL god Seth killed his brother Osiris. Osiris's son Horus avenged his father by killing Seth. Horus ruled as the living god of Egypt; Osiris was the god of the dead.

The Egyptian language did not sharply separate gods from human beings. The king was

a living god. The same word was also applied to important nobles. In general, the Egyptians thought human beings had three different parts that we might call "souls." The *ba* was a bird-like spirit that went up into the sky at death. The *ka* was a spirit that resided in an image of the person after death. The *akh* went to the realm of the dead and sometimes returned as a ghost. A famous illustration from the so-called Book of the Dead shows the heart of a dead person being weighed in a balance against a feather. The feather is the sign of Maat, goddess of truth and justice.

PRACTICES

Egyptian WORSHIP centered on temples. Temples were buildings that housed images of the gods. The RITUALS of the temples helped maintain the harmony of the universe and of human beings within it.

A series of reliefs from a temple in Abydos shows what happened in these temples every day. A privileged group of priests entered the chamber where the image lived. They bathed it, clothed it, fed it, and praised it. As they left the chamber, they were careful to remove every trace of their footsteps.

On special occasions called festivals the images would leave their temples and travel. During festivals the gods were visible to ordinary people. Many temples also had places at the backs of their sanctuaries where common people could consult the gods.

ORGANIZATION

The distinction between religion and politics that is common in North America was unknown in Egypt. In theory the king was the chief priest of all Egyptian temples. The reliefs at Abydos show the king worshipping the gods. In practice priests worshipped the gods on the king's behalf. Only the highest priests could enter the gods' chambers. Priests who were experts in writing produced the many texts that are found in Egyptian tombs. Temples also had many lower order priests that we might call servants.

SIGNIFICANCE

Although Jews, Christians, and Muslims may be reluctant to trace their beliefs and practices back to ancient Egyptian religion, some similarities are certainly suggestive. The name MOSES is Egyptian. Although Jewish MONOTHEISM almost certainly does not derive from the religion of AKHENATON, as some have suggested, JUDAISM probably preserves general cultural elements that spread from Egypt to ancient Phoenicia, Israel, and Judah. The influential Neo-Platonic philosopher Plotinus thought of the universe as emanating from a single principle. Triads of Egyptian gods may have influenced the Christian notion of the TRINITY. At Luxor near Thebes, Muslims hold processions of boats at the feast of the SAINT Abul Hagag. They look much like processions at ancient Egyptian festivals.

Further reading: Adolf Erman, *A Handbook of Egyptian Religion* (Boston: Longwood, 1977); Donald B. Redford, ed., *The Ancient Gods Speak: A Guide to Egyptian Religion* (New York: Oxford University Press, 2002); John H. Taylor, *Death and the Afterlife in Ancient Egypt* (Chicago: University of Chicago Press, 2001); Claude Traunecker, *The Gods of Egypt* (Ithaca, N.Y.: Cornell University Press, 2001).

Eleusis A town in ancient Greece near Athens that hosted the most famous mysteries in the ancient world (*see* MYSTERY RELIGIONS). The Eleusinian mysteries were celebrated in the fall during our months of September and October. Originally only Athenians could participate. Later, all Greeks were admitted to the mysteries, and later still people throughout the Roman empire.

At the beginning of the mysteries, participants gathered at Athens for an assembly. Then they bathed in the ocean and fasted for three days. After this they marched in a procession from Athens to Eleusis. At the front of the procession was an image of the god Iacchos. No one knows precisely what happened when the participants reached Eleusis, but participants had to give a password to enter the hall of the mysteries, and they spent all night in the hall. Toward the end of the night they received some sort of revelation. Taking part in the mysteries was supposed to give people a better afterlife.

The mysteries of Eleusis had some connection to the story of Demeter and her daughter Kore or Persephone. When the god of the underworld, Hades, abducted Persephone, her mother Demeter, the goddess of crops, went into mourning, and the plants on earth died. Eventually Demeter found her daughter in the underworld and negotiated her release. But because Persephone had eaten some seeds of a pomegranate, she could only spend six months of the year on the earth, when plant life flourished; during the other six months, when Kore was in the underworld, plants died. As a result, most scholars connect Kore with the seasonal growth of vegetation. In fact, ancient rumors suggest that the revelation in Eleusis had something to do with an ear of grain.

In any case, in the early 390s C.E. the Roman Emperor Theodosius, a Christian, outlawed the mysteries. In 395 invaders sacked Eleusis. The mysteries disappeared forever.

Eliade, Mircea (1907–1986) *in the second half of the 20th century, one of the most influential scholars of religion and myth* Eliade, born in Rumania, was interested as a child in biology. His most creative contributions to the study of religion resemble an area in biology known as "morphology," the study of underlying forms and patterns. It has also been important in the study of language.

Eliade's work explored the "morphology" of "hierophany." The idea is not as complicated as the words. Eliade believed that one aspect made all religions special: In religion, the Sacred revealed itself. He believed further that the Sacred revealed itself in certain forms or patterns that different religions shared. He called these patterns "ARCHETYPES."

According to Eliade, any aspect of the world could be and has been a means for revealing the Sacred. But some have been more prominent than others. These include natural phenomena like the sun, the moon, the earth, the oceans, and patterns of death and rebirth associated with initiations and RITES OF PASSAGE.

Although some scholars consider some of Eliade's interpretations forced or artificial, his ideas have been rich, exciting, and far-reaching.

Elijah (ninth century B.C.E.) *a prominent prophet of ancient Israel (the "northern kingdom")* The book of Kings in the BIBLE recounts Elijah's opposition to Canaanite WORSHIP and his advocacy of the worship of YHWH ("the Lord") at the time of kings Ahab (ruled *c.* 869–850 B.C.E.) and Ahaziah (ruled *c.* 850–849 B.C.E.). One of the best known events is his battle with the prophets of BAAL. He called down fire from HEAVEN to ignite an ALTAR soaked with water (1 Kings 18). According to the Bible, Elijah did not die but was taken to heaven in a chariot of fire (2 Kings 2).

Elijah later became an important figure in Jewish tradition and folklore, most notably as the precursor of the messianic age. At the celebration of the PASSOVER meal a place is set for Elijah in recognition that he might return.

Enoch *See* APOCALYPTIC LITERATURE.

epics, religious Long narrative stories, often poetic, dealing with gods and heroes, and regarded as foundational to the identity and world view of the people from which they come. They are not quite myths in the grandest sense, stories of creation and salvation that express in narrative form a culture's most basic religious vision, but they may contain mythic elements and do the same thing for the nation itself. Epics characteristically describe events at the beginning of a nation or civilization, perhaps leading up to its golden age; they were probably based on oral tradition but later put into literary, written form. They recall days when long stories were told to while away evenings before books or television, in the process imparting cultural perspectives important to anyone living in

that society, for many epics reveal in story form virtual libraries of information about attitudes, values, RITUALS, beliefs, and styles of behavior appropriate to their world. At the same time they tell listeners about the key historical events and figures that ought to be common knowledge: the major battles, kings, and achievements of the people's past. The religious world is inevitably part of these stories. Examples of ancient epics with religious overtones are the *Iliad* and *Odyssey* of Homer, the *Aeneid* of Virgil, the *Mahabharata* and *Ramayana* of ancient India (*see* RAMA, RAMAYANA), the *Kojiki* in Japan, and the great historical narrative running through much of the Hebrew Scriptures or Old Testament and describing events from the Creation in Genesis to the death of King David (1 Kings) and the exile in Babylon.

The great epics appeared as finished products at about the time that some people were trying to understand how one can live in a world in which so many bad things happen: wars, slaughters, plagues, suffering, and loss. Epics were one way of looking at this problem. As in all great stories, there are moments of defeat and despair in epics as well as of triumph. At these times only hope and faith sustain the heroes and their people. But in the end they prevail, or at least the very heroism of their suffering is shown to make it worthwhile. The pattern of epics suggests a guiding hand in the lives of great men and the events of history. Broadly speaking, the great age of epics, 1300 B.C.E.–700 C.E., was the time of the origin of the major religions and their founders, such as MOSES, BUDDHA, JESUS, and MUHAMMAD. Like these faiths, and often coming to work in tandem with them (as in the incorporation of the Hebrew epic into the BIBLE), epics assured people that however dark things may seem, GOD or the gods are in control and victory will come at the end.

Episcopalianism The Episcopal Church, formerly (before 1967) called the Protestant Episcopal Church, is the expression of ANGLICANISM, the form of CHRISTIANITY of the Church of England, in the United States of America. The words *Episcopal* and *Episcopalianism* mean "having bishops" and refer to the way church governance is centered on the role of bishops as leaders of dioceses, which include all churches in a geographical area. Bishops alone can ordain PRIESTS and other ministers. In this and other ways, this church follows traditional Catholic patterns of organization and worship, though it also has a Protestant side emphasizing the Bible, preaching, and freedom of individual interpretation.

The Anglican tradition that was to become the Episcopal church first came to America in 1607, with the establishment of an English colony and church at Jamestown, Virginia. By the time of the Revolutionary War, Anglican churches were found throughout the Thirteen Colonies. After the war they separated from the Church of England, forming the Episcopal Church. They were led by bishops consecrated to that office by bishops of the Episcopal Church of Scotland, the minority Anglican church there, since relations with the Church of England were still difficult. The Episcopal Church spread west with the new nation, although its greatest numbers have remained on the eastern seaboard. In 2004 it had nearly two and a half million members in some 7,400 churches.

In the late 20th and early 21st centuries the Episcopal Church was convulsed by divisive issues. One was whether women should be ordained to the priesthood. Another centered on a new, considerably changed edition of the *Book of Common Prayer*. Commonly called the Prayer Book, this book contains the forms of worship used in church. (Episcopal churches are supposed to follow a set LITURGY and RITUAL.) Both the ordination of women and the new Prayer Book were authorized by the church's General Convention in 1976. Then controversy arose over the ordination of homosexuals. Some dissenters left the Episcopal Church because of these issues, but the majority have adapted to change.

See also ANGLICANISM.

epistles   In the NEW TESTAMENT, letters attributed to one of the APOSTLES of JESUS, and included in the sacred scriptures of CHRISTIANITY. Of the 21 epistles in the New Testament, 13 are said to be by the apostle PAUL, one by JAMES, two by PETER, three by John, and one by Jude. The Epistle to the Hebrews was attributed to Paul by tradition but does not actually bear his name and is now believed to be by another hand.

Many scholars believe that some of the epistles were not written by the attributed apostolic author but by admirers or followers of the apostle writing in his name, a common practice in ancient times. However, the earliest of the epistles, probably including those generally recognized as having been written by Paul himself—those to the Thessalonians, the Corinthians, the Romans, the Galatians, the Philippians, and Philemon—represent the earliest Christian literature, that written closest to the time of Jesus. Only a little later are several other epistles, including Ephesians and those attributed to Peter, James, and John.

However, neither those nor any other of the epistles contain much about the actual life of Jesus, apart from his death on the CROSS and his RESURRECTION. Their emphasis is basically the meaning of those events and the way to lead a Christian life. Later epistles, such as I and II Timothy, Titus, II Peter, and Jude, deal more and more with sound doctrine and good order in the young churches.

Other early Christian epistles, such as those of Barnabas, Clement of Rome, and Ignatius of Antioch, were and still are read for inspiration but are not included in the New Testament.

See also APOCALYPTIC LITERATURE; APOCRYPHA; NEW TESTAMENT.

eschatology   Religious doctrines about the end of human life and the end of the world. The word basically means the "study of the last things." Religiously, the "last things" can be seen as either gloomy, the "twilight of the gods" or descent into an underworld like the Greek Hades or the Hebrew Sheol, or glorious, the RESURRECTION of the body and the new HEAVEN and earth (*see* AFTERLIFE IN WORLD RELIGIONS). Individual eschatology includes beliefs about death, judgment, heaven, HELL, or REINCARNATION. World eschatology involves the destiny of the world as a whole: the future coming of MESSIAHS or saviors, the last judgment, the divine destruction and perhaps recreation of Earth as a new paradise.

HISTORY

Idea of world eschatology as we know it probably did not begin until people started to think in terms of historical time, not the cyclical time in which the world just repeated itself year after year and age after age. This realization broadly coincides with the invention of writing and the emergence of world religions in which GOD or ultimate reality is seen as doing something of immense importance within historical time: giving the law to MOSES, saving the world in JESUS, showing supreme enlightenment in the BUDDHA, delivering the QUR'AN to MUHAMMAD. If God can act to save the world within history, can there not also be a supreme consummation of history in which its meaning is fulfilled and revealed, justice is done, and perhaps a new and better age begun? World eschatology comes from seeing the course of a world as a line, not a circle, commencing with creation and ending in a last judgment or supreme revelation that sums it all up and makes it meaningful. This would be the end of history.

WESTERN RELIGIONS

This style of world eschatology may well have begun with the ancient Iranian prophet ZARATHUSTRA and his religion ZOROASTRIANISM. He taught that the world is a battleground between Ahura Mazda, the Lord of Light, and the principle of EVIL, the Lord of the Lie, Ahriman. As Ahura Mazda would defeat Ahriman, the prophet Zarathustra would return, all those who had died would be raised in a general resurrection, and God would create for them a new and perfect earth. Ideas highly reminiscent of these, perhaps influenced by Zoroastrianism, are found in the three great Western monotheistic religions, JUDAISM, CHRISTIANITY, and ISLAM. In their traditional forms, they emphasize a divine judgment of the world on the Last Day; Christianity says the judgment will be by Jesus CHRIST, who will then come in glory to judge the living and the dead.

HINDUISM AND BUDDHISM

In the Eastern religions of HINDUISM and BUDDHISM, individual eschatology is seen more in terms of KARMA, though its popular scenarios may include personal judgment by the lord of the underworld, Yama or Yenlo, and possible perdition to the hells or the realm of GHOSTS, or reward in one of the heavens, as well as human or animal reincarnation—all for as long as it takes to expend one's bad or good karma. World eschatology may be ultimately within the context of cycles, but may more immediately include the coming of Kalki, the final avatar or divine appearance, or in Buddhism of Maitreya, the future Buddha. In popular lore Maitreya's coming realm is often seen as a paradisal age. New religious movements both East and West frequently have a highly eschatological cast.

Further reading: S. G. F. Brandon, *Man and His Destiny in the Great Religions* (Toronto: University of Toronto Press, 1962); Norman Cohn, *Cosmos, Chaos, and the World to Come* (New Haven: Yale University Press, 2001); Mircea Eliade, *Death, Afterlife, and Eschatology: A Thematic Source Book* (New York: Harper & Row, 1974); Wilson LaDue, *The Trinity Guide to Eschatology* (New York: Continuum, 2004).

Essenes Members of a group of ancient Jewish ascetic communities. These communities are called "ascetic" because their members practiced rigorous self-denial. They existed from the time of the Hasmonean revolt (167–164 B.C.E.) to the Jewish wars (66–74 C.E.).

For centuries the only information on the Essenes came from ancient writers, such as Philo, Josephus, and Pliny the Elder. In the mid-20th century a library of scrolls was unearthed at Qumran. These scrolls are known colloquially as the DEAD SEA SCROLLS. Despite some differences in teaching, most scholars believe that these scrolls represent the library of an ancient Essene community.

The Essenes formed ascetic communities to which only males could fully belong. On entering the community, an Essene gave up his private property and adopted a way of life that was strictly regulated. He gave much attention to maintaining purity. Sources differ on whether Essenes accepted a RESURRECTION of the body, but they clearly believed in the immortality of the soul (see SOUL, CONCEPTS OF). They were also famous for being able to predict the future.

Some have tried to connect the Essenes with John the Baptist and JESUS. This seems unlikely. If the Essenes influenced rabbinic JUDAISM and emergent CHRISTIANITY, they probably did so indirectly.

Esther A Jewish woman allegedly married to the Persian emperor Ahasuerus, and a book of the BIBLE that tells about her.

According to the book of Esther, Haman, the vizier of Ahasuerus (Xerxes I, who ruled 485–464 B.C.E.), plotted to destroy the Jews. Esther, whom the emperor did not know was Jewish, and her cousin Mordecai managed to thwart the plot. On the day appointed for the attack on the Jews, the Jews destroyed their enemies instead.

The book is not generally regarded as history. It probably derives from the time right before the Hasmonean revolt against the Seleucid Empire (167–164 B.C.E.). It is important today because it is the basis for the festival of PURIM. During Purim the book of Esther is read in the SYNAGOGUE with light-hearted revelry.

eternity Unending time and a state beyond time altogether. In popular usage the word often means days without end, the way the afterlife (see AFTERLIFE IN WORLD RELIGIONS) in HEAVEN or HELL is often popularly understood. But in the philosophy of religion, eternity is more likely to mean a state beyond time and space altogether, as the state of GOD, NIRVANA, or other ultimate, as infinite, unconditioned reality. The term is also used for the state of souls after death, as in entering "eternal life."

ethics and religion Right behavior in the light of religion. The word "ethics" means standards or norms of behavior expected by a society and justified by religion or philosophy in such matters as right and wrong, honesty, the legitimacy of certain practices (as in "medical ethics" or "business ethics"), and, in "social ethics," in respect to what a society as a whole should do about issues like poverty or whether war is ever justified. The line between ethics and a related term, morality, is fuzzy. But today "ethics" is usually taken to refer to the philosophical and religious study of right behavior, to the ideals of society, of certain professions, and of individuals in a public context, while "morals" refers more to a personal code of conduct.

Any thoughtful ethical system begins with a view of the universe as a whole within which the ethics make sense. One could hold that ethics begins with the will of GOD, with "natural law" or the way the universe works, or an assessment of what the results of an action would be, or even with purely individual choice. Ethical views are divided by philosophers into two types. Deontological ethics are "oughts," coming from something that is considered prior or given: the will of God, the laws of nature. Teleological or consequentialist ethics are determined on the basis of the consequences or results of an action and whether it is good or bad in the eyes of the person making the decision. A deontologist might say, for example, that killing is always wrong because God has forbidden it, and therefore capital punishment or any killing in war is always sinful. Another of the same camp might say it is right if it is a matter of meting out true justice, since establishing justice is always God's will too. A consequentialist might respond that it depends on how much good the capital punishment would do, or whether the war is a "just war" and how much benefit winning it would bring. Many religious people would also say that the real will of God is love or compassion, not simple "do's and don't's," and that different circumstances may call for different ways of exercising love or caring about the real good of others, and they may range from indulgence to firmness when people need firmness. Another issue is intention: Do we judge ethics by the good intentions of parties, or only by consequences?

Thinking about ethics is an important part of religion. Ethics are where the ideals of a religion intersect with the crucial problems of society and of everyone's everyday life. Many ethical issues today, such as abortion, war, public honesty, "mercy killing," and others, are not easy to debate. But religions must deal with them or risk being irrelevant.

Eucharist

Eucharist The central RITUAL of CHRISTIANITY; also known as the Lord's Supper or Holy Communion. The name "Eucharist" comes from the Greek verb "to give thanks," from the traditional PRAYER of the priest in performing the ritual.

JESUS established the Eucharist during his last meal with his disciples. He distributed bread and wine among them and asked them to do likewise in remembering him. Christians follow these instructions in different ways. In EASTERN ORTHODOX CHRISTIANITY and ROMAN CATHOLICISM, the Eucharist is the focal point of regular WORSHIP: the Holy LITURGY and the Mass, respectively. Anabaptist churches—the MENNONITE, AMISH, and Brethren—celebrate it only twice a year in the context of a communal meal. Not all churches use wine, and some use specially made wafers instead of bread. During the Middle Ages it became customary for Roman Catholic laypeople to eat only the bread; the wine was reserved for priests. In Orthodox churches, bread and wine are often taken together.

Christians have also differed on—indeed, fought over—what the Eucharist means. For example, Roman Catholics believe that the bread and wine actually become Jesus's body and blood. Many Protestants believe that they are only symbols.

Evangelical Christianity

Evangelical Christianity Kind of Protestant CHRISTIANITY. Evangelical Christianity has been especially prominent in the United States, while MISSIONARIES have also spread the movement throughout the world.

"Evangelical" comes from the Greek word for GOSPEL or "good news," *euangelion*. It means "based on the gospel."

During the REFORMATION Martin LUTHER and his followers preferred to call themselves Evangelical rather than Lutheran. Many Lutherans today still use the term, for example, the Evangelical Lutheran Church in America. Lutherans like this term because they emphasize the "gospel" or "good news" of SALVATION by GRACE through FAITH: that GOD saves people freely if they accept his gift.

But in the English language Evangelical Christianity generally does not refer to LUTHERANISM. It refers to a very different kind of Protestant Christianity. This form began in England and North America during the 18th century. It is associated with a personal experience of conversion, revival meetings, and intense missionary activity. Evangelical Christianity in this sense was the dominant religion in the United States after the Revolutionary War.

EVANGELICAL CHRISTIANITY

Most Christians believe that God acts in the world through the Holy Spirit. Evangelical Christianity began from a distinctive view of how the Spirit acts.

Orthodox, Catholic, and most Protestant churches have traditionally taught that the Spirit acts especially in SACRAMENTS and, for Protestants, in preaching "the Word." Evangelical Christians taught that the Spirit acts in the human heart. They emphasized a personal, emotionally powerful experience of conversion. As a result, they are popularly called "born again" Christians. They also taught that after Christians are saved, they should strive for "sanctification" and moral perfection. One moral demand was extremely important in the history of Evangelical Christianity: not drinking alcohol. It led eventually to the legal prohibition of alcohol in the United States from 1920 to 1933.

John WESLEY (1703–91), who founded the Methodists, played an important role in the rise of Evangelical Christianity in England. In the United States, Evangelical Christianity began during the First Great Awakening. This was a revival movement that swept through the British colonies in North America in the middle 1700s. Until the middle 1800s all major branches of PROTESTANTISM in the United States—Methodists, Baptists, Congregationalists, and Presbyterians—were evangelical. They often stressed patriotism and opposed Catholicism.

By the late 1800s Evangelical Christianity had gone from the dominant religion to a religion on the outside. Many members of churches that were once Evangelical became attracted to modern ways of looking at the world. In response, Evangelicals insisted that they could tolerate no compromise with the world. It was in this climate that fundamentalism was born.

Apart from fundamentalism, Evangelical Christianity remained relatively quiet until after World War Two. At that point evangelical thinkers like the American theologian, Carl F. H. Henry (1913–2003), tried to formulate a version of evangelicalism that was conservative but not fundamentalist. The popular American preacher, Billy Graham, is often seen as part of this movement. The strictest fundamentalists rejected him because he agreed to associate with more liberal Christians.

By the middle of the 1970s Evangelical Christianity was again a major force in American life. Liberal churches were losing members, but conservative churches were growing. "A born-again Christian," Jimmy Carter, was elected president. Other Protestant churches, such as the Lutheran Church-Missouri Synod and the Christian Reformed Church, were moving in an Evangelical direction.

At the end of the century Evangelical Christianity became a force in American politics. Its members often, but not always, supported conservative causes.

See also FUNDAMENTALISM, CHRISTIAN.

Further reading: Karen Armstrong, *The Battle for God* (New York: Knopf, 2000); Randall Balmer, *Mine Eyes Have Seen the Glory; A Journey into the Evangelical Subculture in America,* 3d ed. (New York: Oxford University Press, 2000); Joel A. Carpenter. *Revive Us Again: The Reawakening of American Evangelicalism* (New York: Oxford University Press, 1997); Amy Johnson Frykholm, *Rapture Culture* (New York: Oxford University Press, 2004); Mark A. Noll, *American Evangelical Christianity: An Introduction* (Oxford: Blackwell, 2001).

Eve From the Hebrew *Hawwah,* perhaps related to the word for "living"; the name of the mother of all human beings in JUDAISM and in religions it has inspired. In the BIBLE Eve appears in the second and third chapters of Genesis. There she is created from the rib of ADAM as a companion for him. It is she who first listens to the serpent and violates GOD's command not to eat from the tree of knowledge. In punishment, she must bear children in pain (*see* FALL, THE).

Ancient Christians sometimes looked on MARY, JESUS' mother, as a second Eve, just as they looked on Jesus as a second Adam. They also justified the subordinate position of women by recalling that Eve was created from Adam and led him into SIN (see 1 Timothy 2.11–15).

Another ancient religious complex, GNOSTICISM, used the figure of Eve differently. Gnostics often inverted relations in Jewish stories. That happens with Eve in, for example, an ancient book "On the Origin of the World." (*Nag Hammadi Codices* 2.5). In that book, Adam is the lifeless creation of EVIL, dark demigods. Eve is a representative from the world of light and life. She sees Adam, pities him, gives him life, instructs him, and lays the foundation for future SALVATION.

evil That which is bad, yet is. Perhaps the most difficult problem in religion is the problem of evil. If GOD or ultimate reality is good, why is there evil? Evil is serious suffering in mind or body, especially when the pain is seen as unjust and undeserved. It is that which is not as we believe it was meant to be and should be: the innocent child upon whom cruel tortures are imposed, the horrors of war and plague, any being unable to fulfill the life for which it was born. Evil seems to be deeply ingrained in our world, yet because religion wants to look at things from a perspective above the world and from which to interpret all that transpires in it, it must say something about the reasons for evil.

JUDAISM, CHRISTIANITY, and ISLAM basically see evil as the result of the disobedience to God of creatures having the free will to obey or not. In some traditional stories, it was first ANGELS, who on rebelling against God, then became DEVILS AND DEMONS, although the notion of a devil is foreign in Judaism. Then humans, as in the story of ADAM and EVE in the Garden of Eden, succumbed to evil of their own will though they were also tempted by a devil. By bringing in devils and demons as well as humans, these stories seem to be saying that not all evil is directly due to human agency. In Christianity, there is also evil embedded in nature—floods, droughts, the cruelty of animals. Perhaps it goes back to a cosmic rebellion and "fall" before humans came onto the scene. GNOSTICISM, a religion of the ancient world related to Judaism and Christianity, thought that our entire world was made by a "demiurge" or lower and incompetent god with little good will toward humans, who botched the job of fashioning this particular abode of life. SALVATION is out of this world altogether, back to the Halls of Light from which we ultimately came, before we were trapped in the demiurge's mess of an evil world.

ZOROASTRIANISM adopted a dualistic view, saying the world is a battleground between Ahura Mazda, the Lord of Light, and Ahriman, the source of evil; in one view, these two are eternal principles, though Ahura Mazda will eventually prevail in this world. That perspective has probably influenced the other Western religions, as when in Christianity the role of SATAN as Prince of Darkness and great adversary of God is emphasized, and this world is seen as provisionally his domain. In the East, evil is basically ascribed to KARMA, or cause and effect from our thoughts, words, and deeds, and from ignorance, not seeing things as they really are and so not rightly assessing the results of acts. There is not only individual karma, but also group karma, of communities, nations, the world as a whole, and one may be entangled in it as well.

Religions have also said that some apparent evil is not really such, but has a purpose in evolution, in educating persons, or in teaching non-attachment, and so is experienced only by those of imperfect spiritual development. Yet the problem of evil must undoubtedly be regarded as not completely solved. Many people who reject religion altogether do so on the grounds of its seeming inability to deal with the problem of evil in a world created by a good God.

evolution and religion The ways in which religion relates to evolution. Evolution is the idea that life, and sometimes human culture, has developed from simple to more complex forms.

Evolution is an old idea. Some ancient philosophers, such as the Roman poet Lucretius (c. 95–55 B.C.E.), had already written about it. But evolution came into its own in Europe and North America during the 19th century. Two kinds of evolution are especially important with regard to religion. One is the theory that life on Earth has evolved over a period of hundreds of millions of years. Today virtually all reputable scientists—and a good many religious people—accept this theory. The second is the question of whether religion itself has evolved.

The theory of the evolution of life is inseparable from the name Charles Darwin (1809–82). In 1859 Darwin published *On the Origin of Species*. It made the theory of evolution unavoidable. Darwin did not actually propose the idea that life had evolved. Others, such as Jean Baptiste Lamarck (1744–1829), had already done that. Nor did Darwin argue that life evolved from nonliving matter. That idea only came later. What Darwin did was show how evolution could work. He proposed a theory of "natural selection." In his view, forms of life change constantly, if only in minor ways. Only the best forms survive. The word "best" here means best able to compete for resources and reproduce.

By the end of the 19th century the theory of evolution had been widely accepted by theologians as well as by scientists.

But in the 20th century a backlash against evolution arose among some American Protestants. This was fundamentalism (*see* EVANGELICAL CHRISTIANITY, and FUNDAMENTALISM, CHRISTIAN). Besides rejecting evolution, fundamentalists opposed historical methods of studying the BIBLE and a movement in Christianity that emphasized social reform. In 1925 fundamentalists and scientists squared off in the famous "monkey trial" of John Scopes in Dayton, Tennessee. He was accused of violating the law by teaching evolution in a biology class. In the middle 1970s fundamentalists began demanding that public schools in the United States teach "creation science" in addition to evolution. Almost all reputable scientists reject "creation science" as bogus.

Unlike the fundamentalists, many have accepted evolution without rejecting traditional religion. Indeed, Darwin himself remained a committed Christian all his life. Some have asserted that science is about facts, while religion is concerned with values. This was the position of the German theologian Albrecht Ritschl (1822–89). Others have maintained that biological evolution explains material aspects of human life, but not its mental or spiritual side. This was the position of A. R. Wallace, an associate of Darwin's, and of Rudolf OTTO, a philosopher of religion. Still others, such as the Catholic priest Pierre Teilhard de Chardin (1881–1955), have taught that the human spirit evolves.

During the 19th and early 20th centuries, some anthropologists, especially in Great Britain, debated whether religion itself had evolved. Well before Darwin, the Scottish philosopher David Hume (1711–76) had suggested that all religion had grown out of POLYTHEISM, the WORSHIP of many gods. In the 19th and early 20th centuries some thinkers claimed that religion began with other forms: the belief in GHOSTS (Herbert Spencer), a "disease of language" (Friedrich Max Müller), the belief in spirits (E. B. Tylor), a powerful, nonpersonal, electric-like force called *mana* (R. R. Marett). The most widely known figure may have been James George FRAZER. He divided human history into three stages: magic, religion, and science.

Charles Darwin *(Library of Congress)*

After World War I anthropologists rejected all of these ideas. More important, they rejected the attempt to identify a single series of steps through which religion had evolved into the forms we know today. Most English-speaking thinkers have remained suspicious of the topic of religion's evolution.

Exodus The central story of the Hebrew BIBLE and a formative event in the history of JUDAISM. The root meaning of the word "exodus" is "a going out." During the Exodus, MOSES led the people of Israel out of slavery in Egypt. They wandered through the desert of Sinai for 40 years before entering the promised land of Canaan. During this time they entered into a COVENANT with the god who had freed them, YHWH ("the Lord"), at Mt. Sinai. There they received the TEN COMMANDMENTS and, according to Jewish tradition, the entire law (*see* TORAH).

The only information about the Exodus comes from the Bible; no outside sources confirm it. Most scholars think that some slaves did escape from Egypt, but they disagree on the details. For example, they disagree on how many slaves escaped and what route they took. They also disagree on the date. Many date the Exodus to around 1250 B.C.E. Some prefer to date it earlier, around 1425.

The three major JEWISH FESTIVALS—PASSOVER, Shavuot, and Sukkot—commemorate the major events of the Exodus.

exorcism The driving out of evil spirits by religious means. A particular place, or a person, believed to be "possessed" by DEVILS AND DEMONS, may be exorcised. In PRIMAL RELIGION, exorcism is frequently a part of WITCHCRAFT and MAGIC. It is practiced in Hindu, Buddhist, Taoist, and Islamic contexts, typically by specialist priests or lay shamans rather than by the regular clergy. In the NEW TESTAMENT, JESUS is described as casting out demons, and saying that his doing so was a sign of the coming of the kingdom of HEAVEN. Accordingly, the Christian church has generally had a place for the practice of exorcism, though it has not always been much emphasized. The Roman Catholic Church has an exorcism RITUAL, which may be performed by priests authorized to do so. In EVANGELI-CAL CHRISTIANITY, FUNDAMENTALIST CHRISTIANITY (*see* FUNDAMENTALISM, CHRISTIAN), and PENTECOSTALISM, exorcism is sometimes done with scripture reading, intense prayer, and the laying on of hands. The exorcism of a possessed person is reportedly a very difficult and grueling engagement, both for the exorcist and for the subject. Often, as in Jesus' own driving out of demons, exorcism is thought to be a prelude to spiritual HEALING.

Ezekiel (sixth century B.C.E.) *A priest who authored one of the prophetic books of the Hebrew* BIBLE, *also named Ezekiel* Ezekiel uttered both words of warning before the destruction of JERUSALEM (587 B.C.E.) and words of hope afterward. His prophecies are remarkable for their symbolic, visionary quality. Among them are the throne of YHWH ("the Lord") with its four living creatures (Ezekiel 1), the valley of dry bones (Ezekiel 37), and the vision of a new temple (Ezekiel 40–48).

The symbolism of Ezekiel's visions greatly influenced later APOCALYPTIC LITERATURE, for example, the New Testament book of REVELATION.

Ezra (586–539 B.C.E.) *a priest important in shaping* JUDAISM *in the period after the Babylonian exile and the name of one biblical and two apocryphal books* According to the BIBLE, Ezra the priest went from Babylon to Judah in the seventh year of King Artaxerxes. There were two kings with this name and opinions vary on which Artaxerxes is meant. Ezra's arrival would date either 458 or 398 B.C.E.

In Judah, Ezra opposed what struck him as the lax practices of the Jews, including intermarriage with non-Jews. He convinced Jewish men to divorce their non-Jewish wives; he organized Jewish life in accordance with the instructions given in the TORAH; and he conducted a ceremony of dedication in which the Torah was read. Some think that he was acting as an official of the Persian state. Nevertheless, his activity exercised a profound influence on the formation of Judaism. As a result, some call him the "father of Judaism." He is also seen as a second MOSES, who would have received the Torah if Moses had not already done so.

At least three different ancient books go by the name Ezra. The biblical book of Ezra-Nehemiah continues the history told in the books of Chronicles. It recounts in detail Ezra's reforms and NEHE-MIAH's building activities. The apocryphal book known as 1 Esdras (Latin for Ezra) in effect summarizes—with changes—most of Ezra-Nehemiah as well as the end of Chronicles. The Book of 2 Esdras is probably a Jewish apocalypse (*see* APOCA-LYPTIC LITERATURE) with a later Christian overlay.

F

fairies In traditional folklore, nonhuman, quasi-supernatural but not divine beings who dwell on this planet. Fairies, elves, gnomes, dwarfs, brownies, trolls, and pixies are familiar names. While not strictly religious, belief in fairies is interesting and important for showing that the sense of wonder that is one source of religion can have other manifestations than the reverence of GOD alone. In some religious mythologies, one finds not only HEAVENS above and HELLS beneath, but also "horizontal" wonderlands somewhere on our plane. For example, Avalon, the Isles of the Blessed, and the Eastern grottoes of immortals, are comparable to Fairyland.

faith The state of mind by which religious people are able inwardly to accept and act on the teachings of a religion. Faith is called for especially when there are few outward proofs that a religion is true. In the most famous definition of faith, that of the Epistle to the Hebrews in the Christian NEW TESTAMENT, it is "the assurance of things hoped for, the conviction of things not seen."

IS FAITH FOUND IN ALL RELIGIONS?

In the 1950s a professor at Harvard, Wilfred Cantwell Smith (1916–2000), made a suggestion that extended this usage of the word "faith." He said that instead of talking about religions scholars should talk about faith and cumulative traditions. Both common usage and Smith's suggestion imply that faith is found in many, if not all, religions.

Actually, scholars disagree about whether most religions involve faith. Some take a narrow view and make faith characteristic of JUDAISM, ISLAM, and especially CHRISTIANITY. They stress ways in which what appears to be faith in other religions differs from the faith that characterizes Judaism, Christianity, and Islam. Others acknowledge these differences but argue that the religious elements of other beliefs still count as faith. They think that the others have simply defined faith too narrowly.

The paragraphs that follow use illustrations from various religions, not just Judaism, Christianity, and Islam. Readers should realize that these illustrations offer rough approximations that not everyone would accept.

VARIETIES OF FAITH

Faith has different shades of meaning in religion. In some contexts it means chiefly fidelity, the ongoing loyalty of worshippers to GOD and of God to humanity even when all seems darkest. It is thus really a kind of inner stability of character and predictability of action. Muslims may express this attitude in part when they profess their faith in the words of the *shahadah:* "I profess that there is no God but God (ALLAH), and that MUHAMMAD is his Messenger." This is certainly the attitude displayed in the BIBLE by JOB.

In ROMAN CATHOLICISM faith first of all means acknowledging the truths of the religion, which are contained in the established DOGMAS AND DOCTRINES. The most basic expressions of these truths are the CREEDS. Such teachings may be arrived at in part by reason rather than simple acceptance. Protestants, too, especially Protestant laypeople, sometimes think of faith as believing in propositions, for example, that the Bible contains no errors.

Many Protestant theologians stress that faith is not so much saying one believes certain "propositions" but rather an attitude of dependence and trust in God, especially as revealed in CHRIST. It is therefore an inward attitude and perhaps emotional disposition as much as an intellectual framework, though it may include the latter. A similar kind of faith seems to be found in HINDUISM, for example, when KRISHNA tells Arjuna toward the end of the BHAGAVAD-GITA, "Abandon all DHARMA; trust only in me; I will free you from all evils; do not fear" (18.66). Consider, too, the trust that some adherents of PURE LAND BUDDHISM place in the "original vow" of the BUDDHA AMIDA and that followers of NICHIREN have in the *Lotus Sutra* or simply in the power of chanting the praise of the *Lotus Sutra* in the phrase "Nam Myoho Renge Kyo."

Some believe that faith excludes doubt, but not all agree. The theologian Paul Tillich (1886–1965) regarded faith as an openness toward an ultimate reality wholly beyond one's understanding. For him, even honest doubt was a form of faith. Some modern Buddhist teachers have presented faith as simply a willingness to take, say, the Buddha's FOUR NOBLE TRUTHS as a "working hypothesis," the final truth or falsity of which will be determined not in theory but in practice.

FAITH AND REASON

Philosophers, especially Western philosophers influenced by Christianity, have often pondered the relation of faith and reason. They have not come to any agreement.

One position suggests that faith completes reason. This view was popular with medieval thinkers such as Thomas AQUINAS. Some truths, these thinkers believe, can be established by reason, such as the existence of God, but that is not all the truth there is. Faith completes reason with the views that, for example, God is a TRINITY and JESUS was God.

Another position asserts just the opposite view, that faith comes not after but before reason. That is, all reasoning starts from assumptions, propositions that the reasoner assumes to be true. Without those assumptions, reasons can do noth-

ing. Therefore, even reason requires some kind of faith, namely, faith in the propositions from which it begins. A medieval Christian theologian, ANSELM of Canterbury (c. 1033–1109), summarized this view with the phrase *credo ut intelligam,* "I believe, in order that I may understand."

A third position is possible. This is the position that faith and reason belong to two different domains. In this view the question of faith and reason mistakenly adopts an "intellectualist" view of faith. It sees the content of faith as a series of propositions about which reason can pass judgment. In a different view of faith—for example, if faith is seen as an attitude of trust—the question may disappear.

Others, however, find this position too simple. Faith may be an attitude of trust in God, but that attitude entails holding to some claims, like the claim that God exists. Some who take this view find a tension between faith and reason. Indeed, they celebrate the tension and urge religious people to have faith despite the absurdity of what one believes or even, in extreme cases, because of the absurdity.

WHERE DOES FAITH COME FROM?

Faith may be derived in various ways. Inner psychological dynamics may push a person toward one or another religious system. It may come out of experience, whether of a mystical or conversion sort, or just an experience of life problems that point toward a certain religion as the answer. WORSHIP and living in a "community of faith" can incline a person to want to share in that faith and make it his or her own.

According to the QUR'AN, as well as many Christians, faith is a gift of God. For others, faith requires at some point making a "leap" and affirming things beyond reason and sight alone. A faith commitment thus becomes a choice freely and fully given. Some would say making such a choice about one's life is the whole point of faith, as it is of religion.

Further reading: James W. Fowler, *Stages of Faith: The Psychology of Human Development* (San

Francisco: Harper & Row, 1981); Paul Helm, ed., *Faith and Reason,* Oxford Readers (New York: Oxford University Press, 1999); Sharon Salzberg, *Faith: Trusting Your Own Deepest Experience* (New York: Riverhead Books, 2002); Paul Tillich, *Dynamics of Faith* (New York: HarperPerennial, 2001).

Fall, the   A story told by Jews, Muslims, and especially Christians. It explains why human beings no longer live in paradise close to GOD.

Religious people have told many different stories to explain why the world we live in is not everything we might wish for. According to several stories told in ancient Mesopotamia, the gods created human beings to do the work they themselves did not want do (*see* MESOPOTAMIAN RELIGIONS). Other peoples have told stories about successive ages in which the world gets progressively worse and we, unfortunately, are living in the last age. Examples of this kind of story are Hesiod's account of the five ages of the world, gold, silver, bronze, heroic, and iron; stories in India of the four *yugas;* and the Japanese Buddhist notion of MAPPO. According to Gnostics and Manichaeans, the universe and people came into being when light and goodness somehow became mixed with darkness and EVIL. In this view, it is not the fall but creation itself that disturbs the original ideal state (*see* GNOSTICISM and MANICHAEISM).

The Hebrew BIBLE records another story, the story of the Fall. According to Christian interpretation, it tells how the serpent tempted the mother of all people, EVE. The god YHWH ("the Lord") had forbidden ADAM and Eve to eat from two trees, the tree of life and the tree of the knowledge of good and evil. The serpent convinced Eve to eat from the tree of knowledge. She did, and then tempted Adam to do so, too. As a result, God expelled Adam and Eve from the garden. He cursed Eve to bear children in pain, and he cursed Adam to till the ground with difficulty. Death was also a result of the Fall.

Later folklore elaborated this story. Jews, Christians, and Muslims came to identify the ser-

pent with SATAN. They told different versions of a story in which Satan was a fallen ANGEL. Muslims also told how Adam and Eve quarreled after the Fall and how God reconciled them at the Mount of Mercy in the sacred area around MECCA.

The story of the Fall is especially significant in CHRISTIANITY. Traditional Christians see it as the event that made it necessary for JESUS to become incarnate and die on the cross. In the NEW TESTAMENT PAUL develops these ideas most fully. He makes Jesus into the second or new Adam, who undoes what the first or old Adam had done. Later, under the influence of Paul, AUGUSTINE OF HIPPO formulated the idea of original SIN. In this view sin is not an act done against God's will; it is a state of life that began with the Fall. Because of the Fall, all human beings live in sin from the moment they are conceived. Augustine's views later became the basis for John CALVIN's notion that after the Fall, human beings live in a state of utter depravity. That is, without GRACE they are unable to do what pleases God.

Not all of those who have told the story of the Fall of Adam and Eve have seen it as something negative. Many Gnostics believed that the god of the Jews who created the world as an evil, deluded being. For them the central religious problem was ignorance; knowledge was the means to SALVATION. Salvation began when Eve violated the commands of the evil creator and ate from the tree of knowledge. Thus, what Jews, Christians, and Muslims see as the first transgression was, for Gnostics, the beginning of salvation.

family and religion, the   Religiously, the fundamental and most sacred natural unit of society. "Family" is an elastic term that can be construed in at least two ways: as the "nuclear" family, consisting of a father, a mother, and their immediate children; and as the "extended" family, including grandparents, aunts, uncle, cousins, and all other relatives regularly involved with each other or, in some religious traditions, people sharing common ancestral shrines. There are also single-parent families and same-sex families. Father-mother-child may be seen as an analogy or model of creation: the sky-father, the earth-mother, the fruits of the earth and above all humanity as their children. The extended family, moreover, may be seen as an image of the ideal organization of society, with the sacred king as the father of all.

Family structures vary, of course. In traditional societies, they may be patriarchal, ruled by the father; matriarchal, ruled by the mother; patrilocal, with the bride dwelling in her husband's family home; matrilocal, when the husband moves into his wife's family home; polygamous (several wives for one man) or polyandrous (with several husbands for one woman). In each case, HEAVEN may be considered to be set up in something like the same way. The most common arrangement in traditional societies, however, is patriarchy. It may be a reflection of the belief that GOD above is also a supreme father. Patriarchy may also be evidenced in careful attention to the shrines of male ancestors, as in Confucian China, where it is seen as an extension beyond the grave of "filial piety," or the obligation of children to parents (see CONFUCIANISM and CHINA, RELIGIONS OF).

Religious mythology involving family images is not restricted to the highest deity, however. As we have seen, the earth is frequently portrayed as a mother. Siblings are also frequently important. Sometimes the primal parents of humanity are presented as twin brother and sister. On the other hand, two brothers may be rivals, like Cain and Abel in the Hebrew scriptures.

The family is important as a center for religious RITUALS, with a household ALTAR as an important place for DEVOTION. Among devout Hindus, the most important offerings are really those made in the home, where food offerings are prepared by the wife and the husband acts as chief priest. In JUDAISM, celebration of the Sabbath in the home, with Sabbath PRAYERS and meal, is a primary obligation. Most festivals of all religions, like CHRISTMAS for Christians, have important home components. And most religions emphasize the importance of good, loving, and devout family life for all who are set in families.

fasting Giving up eating or drinking or both. Eating and drinking are simple biological acts that human beings generally do every day. Most religions have found it useful to order and regulate them. They have told people what they may and may not eat or drink.

A religion's dietary laws do this. They make restrictions that are permanent (see DIET AND RELIGION). Fasting imposes restrictions, too, but it makes restrictions that are temporary. A fast may involve only specific items, or it may be total. In any case, fasting is a particularly pointed way to involve one's body in religious observance. It may also be used to evoke mental events that occur when someone is deprived of food and drink.

When people fast, how long they fast, who fasts, what they give up in fasting, and why they are fasting—these are questions that religions answer very differently.

Some fasts are short; others are long. On the DAY OF ATONEMENT, observant Jews fast from one sunset to the next (see JUDAISM). Catholic, Orthodox, and some Protestant Christians have traditionally fasted during the 40-day period before EASTER known as LENT. Muslims fast from sunrise to sunset for the entire month of RAMADAN (see ISLAM). BAHA'IS fast in the same way for an entire month, but the Baha'i month is only 19 days long. Fasts may take place before life-cycle RITUALS. For example, some Native Americans fast before seeking a VISION. Fasts may also take place before rituals performed for HEALING and renewal. Orthodox Christians fast before receiving the EUCHARIST.

Some fasts involve the entire community: the Day of Atonement, Lent, Ramadan. But even here there may be exceptions. For example, those for whom the Ramadan fast may present difficulties—the elderly, the sick, the very young, pregnant women, travelers—are not supposed to fast. Other fasts involve small groups, for example, those who will participate in an indigenous American sweat lodge or Orthodox Christians who will receive the eucharist at a particular service. Still others may be entirely private. Hindu women often take personal vows that may involve fasting.

At the maximum, fasting involves total abstention from food and drink. On the Day of Atonement observant Jews do not eat, drink, or smoke for 25 to 26 hours. Certain Jain SAINTS give up eating and drinking as a way to bring on death (*see* JAINISM). But many fasts are partial. For example, it was once common for Roman Catholics not to eat meat on Friday.

The reasons people fast are as numerous as the reasons people practice religion. In ancient Greece, people fasted to get ready to be initiated into secret cults known as "mysteries" (*see* MYSTERY RELIGIONS). Some people fast to purify their bodies or control their appetites and desires. The fast on the Day of Atonement is part of a ritual asking for GOD's forgiveness. Jains fast in order to stop the accumulation of bad KARMA. Some people fast to acquire spiritual merit and benefits; for example, a Hindu woman may fast to have the same husband in her next life. Christians fast at Lent as a reminder of their SINS. The Ramadan fast commemorates important events in early Islam. It also helps Muslims develop sympathy for the less fortunate, for whom fasting is a way of life.

In the 20th century, Mohandas GANDHI made special use of fasting. He said that he fasted to learn to control his senses and to atone for the sins of his followers. But his fasts were also very effective political tools. In the time since Gandhi, many others have gone on hunger strikes to bring issues of injustice to public attention.

feminism A way of thinking prominent in the second half of the 20th and beginning of the 21st centuries, concerned with overcoming the subordinate position that women have often occupied in societies. Feminism has been important in religions themselves as well as in the study of religions. In many respects, North American and European feminists have taken the lead, but feminists have been active in most parts of the globe.

In the 19th century, feminists addressed such issues as voting rights and access to education. At times they also addressed issues of religion, as when Elizabeth Cady Stanton (1815–1902) edited *The Woman's Bible* (1895). Beginning in the 1960s many feminists turned sustained attention to religion. Since then, they have studied women's contributions to religion. They have also sought to reformulate traditional religions or to develop religions of their own. In addition, feminists who have identified themselves with religious communities have played prominent roles in working for women's rights.

WOMEN'S CONTRIBUTIONS TO RELIGION

In the past scholars often overlooked the contributions that women made to religions. That still happens today, but as a result of feminism women's contributions have received more attention. Early feminist scholars who helped draw attention to women's contributions include Marija Gimbutas (1921–94), who specialized in the goddesses of Old Europe; Judith Plaskow (b. 1947), a scholar of JUDAISM, and Rosemary Radford-Ruether (b. 1936), a scholar of the NEW TESTAMENT.

As a result of feminism, scholars have begun to appreciate the important role of GODDESSES in religions, such as the village goddesses so prevalent in ordinary HINDUISM. They have come to recognize that male gods traditionally have feminine dimensions, too, such as the Presence and Wisdom of God personified as feminine in the Hebrew scriptures (e.g., Proverbs 1:20–33, 8:1–9:6) (*see* SCRIPTURES, HEBREW).

In addition, recent research has revealed that, even if JESUS, MUHAMMAD, and the BUDDHA were men, women played formative roles in the early years of CHRISTIANITY, ISLAM, and BUDDHISM. In some religious contexts, women are important leaders, such as the female SHAMANS of Japan and Korea. Women have made important contributions even to heavily patriarchal religions. For example, many women in medieval Europe produced inspiring reports of their powerful mystical experiences. A good example is Hildegard of Bingen (1098–1179), who is also prominent in the history of music.

Feminists not only have drawn attention to prominent women but also have shown how important it is to pay attention, too, to the religious lives of ordinary women, who make up a sizable proportion of almost every religion. Indeed, some practices, such as the observance of *vrats* or vows in Hinduism and the experience of God in PENTE-COSTALISM, have tended to be more characteristic of women than of men.

Feminists have also called attention to the ways in which religion contributes to women's subordination and oppression. Some myths, including stories from the BIBLE, subtly or blatantly consign women to subordinate positions. The same is true of many stories told by early Buddhists. Women have suffered from rituals as well, such as SATI (widow burning) in traditional Hinduism and clitoridectomy (female CIRCUMCISION, also called genital mutilation) in many initiation rites (*see* INITIATION, RELIGIOUS); many believe that these rituals violate the authentic teachings of their religions. Feminists disagree, however, about the oppressive nature of some practices, such as the wearing of head coverings by Muslim women.

Scholars of religion have not accepted all ideas associated with feminism. At the beginning of the 20th century, the British scholar Jane Ellen Harrison hypothesized that before the patriarchal society of classical Greece, matriarchy prevailed. Many have found this idea attractive, but no unambiguous case of matriarchy has ever been found. Feminists have also at times contrasted male with female approaches to knowledge, including knowledge about religions. Some feminists have suggested that while males speak with authority as experts, telling others what to think, females emphasize dialogue and sharing in a manner that avoids hierarchy and preserves a plurality of viewpoints. The second approach has much to recommend it, but identifying these two approaches as male and female is a case of gender essentialism. That is, it falsely presumes that all males or all females share certain essential characteristics in their approach to knowledge.

CHANGING RELIGIOUS COMMUNITIES

Over the last 50 years feminists have not only changed the way people study religion. They have also changed the way people practice religion. Prominent scholars at the forefront of such changes include Elizabeth Schüssler-Fiorenza (b. 1938), a Christian theologian, and Rita Gross (b. 1943), a well-known Buddhist feminist in North America.

Feminists find the issue of authority in religious communities extremely important. They have worked hard to open up leadership roles to women that had once been reserved for men. As a result, the Episcopalian church now ordains women as bishops and priests (*see* ANGLICANISM and EPISCO-PALIANISM), and so do most mainline Protestant churches. Reform Judaism became the first branch of Judaism to ordain women to the rabbinate (*see* RABBI, RABBINATE). In Buddhism monks seem always to have had the predominant role, and in many parts of the Buddhist world the order of nuns had disappeared. But as a result of the efforts of feminists, some Buddhists have sought to reestablish the order of nuns.

Some groups, however, have resisted efforts to open up leadership roles to women. At the beginning of the 21st century, only men can be priests in ROMAN CATHOLICISM and EASTERN ORTHODOX CHRISTIANITY. There was a similar preference for male leadership in most Evangelical, fundamentalist, and Pentecostal churches worldwide, as well as in Orthodox Judaism and Islam.

Many feminists find the teachings of traditional religions unsatisfactory because they are too "androcentric," that is, male-centered. Some have responded by trying to reformulate traditions. In one important move, feminists have inspired scholars to examine the text of the Bible more carefully. Older translations often use androcentric terminology even when it violates the sense of the original texts. As a result, some newer translations, such as the New Revised Standard Version, use inclusive language. Feminists have also reformulated standard doctrines and prayers, such as the LORD'S PRAYER, to eliminate their androcentric focus. In 1995 the UNITED CHURCH OF CHRIST became the first church in North America to produce a hymnal whose language was neutral with regard to gender.

Feminists have inspired reformulations of other traditions, too. Women have become much more important as teachers in North American Buddhism than they have ever been in Asia. This role has resulted in some changes. For example, some women trained in Zen have sought to eliminate male-oriented, martial elements that Zen practice acquired in Japan (*see* ZEN BUDDHISM). For their part, many Muslim feminists have grappled with the meaning of the QUR'AN. They have claimed that many of the traditional teachings that favor men result from faulty interpretations of the Qur'an.

Not all feminists are convinced that traditional religions can be saved from their patriarchal pasts. They have formulated their own rituals, beliefs, and communities. They often see themselves as recovering a primal tradition of goddess worship that had been lost or suppressed. In North America and Europe this desire has inspired the development of communities dedicated to Wicca. In Africa, too, some women have sought relief from male-dominated Christianity and Islam by recovering native traditions.

WORKING FOR WOMEN'S RIGHTS

Many feminists working for women's rights derive their primary inspiration from their religious identity. Their identities and goals vary widely. Here it is possible only to give examples.

Some people distinguish three kinds of Roman Catholic feminism in North America. Reconstructive feminism seeks to change official teachings of the Catholic Church; it has been particularly interested in the church's teachings on sexuality and birth control. Moderate feminism takes less notice of teachings on sexuality; it seeks to empower women within the Catholic Church, making them responsible, independent members of the church. Holistic feminism rejects what it sees as the tendencies of the more radical feminism of the 1970s to reject experiences that stand at the center of many women's lives. It emphasizes women's rights, but it also recognizes and respects the fulfillment many women find in the traditional roles of wife and mother. Unlike reconstructive and moderate feminism, holistic feminism has little to say against the male-dominated structures of the church.

Holistic feminism is not the only form of feminism that has arisen as a reaction to earlier feminist positions. Latina and African-American women have often felt that feminism was a movement of white, privileged women. Its goals, such as having more women become Chief Executive Officers of companies, had little to do with the lives that Latina and African-American women were living. As a result, Latina women developed a kind of thinking they call *mujerista*. From this perspective, they have, for example, criticized the male-centered aspirations of people working for the benefit of the Latino/Latina community. Similarly, African-American women have developed a variety of feminism known as "womanism."

Feminist movements are found around the world today. Their visions of women's empowerment often change from context to context. For example, many Protestant and Jewish feminists in North America see abortion as an important right; it is part of the struggle for women to gain control of their own bodies. In India, however, feminists generally oppose abortion, because there people generally use abortion to get rid of unwanted female children before they are born. Feminists in the non-Western world sometimes feel that North American and European feminists have little understanding of the situations in which women elsewhere live but nevertheless try to dictate what all women's concerns should be.

CRITICS OF FEMINISM

Traditionalists within the various religions have often dismissed and condemned feminism. Conservative religious leaders in North America, Protestants, Catholics, and Jews, have often viewed feminism as a threat to the divinely ordained orders of society. In many traditions, the aspirations of some feminists have conflicted radically with the values of conservative religious people over the issue of abortion.

There has been opposition to feminism on a global scale, too. For example, at the UN World Conference on Women held in Beijing in 1995, the Vatican, together with several Catholic countries (Bolivia, Ecuador, Guatemala, Honduras, Peru, and the Philippines) allied with several Muslim countries (Egypt, Iran, Kuwait, Libya, and Sudan) to oppose feminist initiatives that violated their religious convictions. Catholic and Muslim cooperation on these issues has continued into the early part of the 21st century.

CONCLUSION

In the 1990s and early 2000s the word "feminism" acquired a bad reputation among some women. Although they actually supported many of feminism's goals, they began to distance themselves from the label. Still, feminism has changed the lives of women around the globe, and it promises to continue to do so.

Further reading: Nancy Auer Falk and Rita M. Gross, eds., *Unspoken Worlds: Women's Religious Lives,* 3d ed. (Belmont, Calif.: Wadsworth/ Thomson Learning, 2001); Jane H. Bayes and Nayereh Tohidi, eds., *Globalization, Gender, and Religion: The Politics of Women's Rights in Catholic and Muslim Contexts* (New York: Palgrave, 2001). Elisabeth Schüssler Fiorenza, *In Memory of Her: A Feminist Theological Reconstruction of Christian Origins,* 2d ed. (London: SCM, 1995); Rita M. Gross, *Buddhism after Patriarchy: A Feminist History, Analysis, and Reconstruction of Buddhism* (Albany: State University of New York Press, 1993); Judith Plaskow, *Standing Again At Zion: Judaism from a Feminist Perspective* (San Francisco: Harper & Row, 1990).

feng shui Traditional Chinese art of situating and designing the exteriors and interiors of buildings. Feng shui has sometimes been called the Chinese art of geomancy, "earth measuring." The words literally mean "wind and water." The main goal is to order dwelling spaces in such a way that the inhabitants are exposed to beneficial energies but protected from harmful ones. The dwelling spaces can be either for human beings or for spirits. In other words, Chinese have used feng shui to situate and design tombs as well as houses and other structures.

The principles of feng shui are very complicated. The most basic aspect concerns how a structure relates to land and water features that surround it. A southern exposure is often considered best. A hill or other natural feature should protect the site from behind, while a source of water should flow toward, but not directly at, the front of the structure.

In addition, feng shui practitioners analyze both the outside and the inside of structures. To do so, they use a compass based on traditional Chinese ideas about the universe as well as sacred squares consisting of three rows and three columns of numbers. These instruments as well as other principles help determine ideal positions for parts of buildings such as doorways, hallways, living rooms, sleeping rooms, bathrooms, and kitchens. For example, according to feng shui it is best to avoid front and back doors that are connected by a single hallway. Such a configuration allows whatever beneficial energy that flows into the house through the front door to escape immediately out the back.

People may consult feng shui practitioners while they are designing and building a structure, but they may also consult them while the structure is being used. If practitioners find problems, they may propose remedies. One example is to place a mirror at a certain spot to counter ill effects.

fire and religion The religious use and symbolism of fire. Fire is one of the most important symbols in religion. Its light, purity, and energy suggest GOD, the soul, or newness of life, while on the other hand, its destructive power indicates the burning wrath of God against EVIL, and the way all that comes into being in this world will go out of being and be destroyed in the end.

In the ancient Hebrew religion, fire was used to burn whole offerings, suggesting the utter purity and dedication of the sacrifice. Perpetual fire was kept burning in the temple in JERUSALEM, as it is in Zoroastrian temples and was by the Vestal Virgins of Rome (*see* ZOROASTRIANISM and ROMAN RELIGION). A principal deity of Vedic India was AGNI, the fire god, for SACRIFICES were offered to him, and he in turn was the "messenger" to the gods who carried their essence to other realms (*see* VEDA). Corresponding to fire on Earth was the lightning in the sky and the sun in HEAVEN; Agni went between those levels, and the sacrificial fire on Earth was believed to correspond to the processes of eternal creation and destruction.

In HINDUISM, the bodies of the deceased are generally burned, returning them to the elements and making them part of that process. In its purely terrible and destructive aspect, flames are the substance of HELL—the "Lake of Fire"—eternally punishing the wicked, though in Roman Catholic tradition the fires of Purgatory have the more benign though also painful role of purging away the impurity of SIN from those who do not deserve hell but are not yet ready for heaven. Fire has also symbolized life and the immortal spark that is the soul. Buddhist literature has used the image of passing the torch, or lighting one flame from another flame, to indicate the process of REINCARNATION. Statues of the BUDDHA sometimes show him with a flame above his head, pointing to his enlightenment. The Hindu UPANISHADS use the metaphor of a single flame that takes many different shapes to suggest how BRAHMAN, the One, assumes the form of all the different entities in the universe. In the book of Acts in the NEW TESTAMENT it is said that the Holy Spirit descended on the APOSTLES as "tongues of flame," making fire an embodiment of spiritual wisdom and power at the same time, even as JESUS had said he would baptize with fire.

Fire has also been employed as an instrument of divine HEALING. The ancient Celts would herd cattle between two fires, in the belief that this would help preserve them from disease (*see* CELTIC RELIGION). It can be a guide, especially to the other world, as Agni guided the dead to heaven; and it can bring the dead back to life like the Phoenix reborn out of his ashes. Finally, fire, especially in the form of soft and quiet candlelight, is widely used to indicate and hallow sacred places. Candles are frequently burned before Christian and other shrines as offerings and to demarcate their holiness. Candles are found on the ALTARS of many churches, and lighting them is a preliminary marking the beginning of the sacred time of a service.

The Jewish Sabbath begins with the lighting of special candles, customarily by the women of the house. Fire in the world of religion takes as many forms, and has almost as many meanings, as does fire itself.

flood stories   Also called the deluge; in mythology, a flood that covered the entire Earth and destroyed almost all human beings. Although extensive, localized floods have occurred, there is no evidence for any worldwide flood.

The flood story best known to most North Americans and Europeans is the one told in the BIBLE (Genesis 6–9). In this story, GOD wishes to destroy human beings because of their SINS. He decides, however, to save NOAH and his family. On God's instructions, Noah builds an ark in which he, his family, and representative animals ride out the flood.

The biblical story appears to be part of a large, older tradition of flood stories that derive from Mesopotamian mythology (*see* MESOPOTAMIAN RELIGIONS). The story of GILGAMESH was put into final form around 2000 B.C.E. In it, King Gilgamesh visits the two human beings who survived the flood, Utnapishtim and his wife. They have become immortal, and Gilgamesh wants to learn how he can become immortal, too. Another Mesopotamian story, the story of Atrahasis (1600 B.C.E. or earlier), tells a different account of the flood. Indeed, it parallels Genesis closely. Human beings were making too much noise. After trying several other remedies, the gods, led by Enlil, decided to destroy them with a universal flood. But the crafty god Enki told his faithful worshipper, Atrahasis, to build an ark. In it, Atrahasis, his family, and representative animals were saved.

Greek mythology knew a similar flood story. Because of human wickedness, ZEUS sent a flood to destroy the Earth. Deucalion and Pyrrha were saved in an ark; to repopulate the Earth they cast stones, which turned into people. The mythology of India knows a similar story, too. There the god VISHNU takes the form of a great fish that pulls MANU, the ancestor of humankind, to safety on

Animals loading two-by-two into Noah's ark   (Library of Congress)

a raft. Unlike the versions already recounted, in the Indian version no woman is saved. As a result, Manu must first create a daughter, Ila. With her he repopulates the Earth.

It seems likely that the Greek story derives from Mesopotamian roots. It is more doubtful that the Indian story does. Indian mythology tells of several successive universes that are each overwhelmed by primal waters. But flood stories are certainly not limited to the region stretching from Greece to India and through the Near East. Indeed, they are found on almost every continent.

For example, the Maya people of Mesoamerica (*see* MAYA RELIGION) tell an EPIC story known as the Popol Vuh. It begins with successive attempts to create human beings. In one attempt the creators fashion manikins. These prove unsatisfactory and are destroyed by a flood. The Aztec Legend of the Suns (*see* AZTEC RELIGION) talks not about successive attempts to create human beings but about successive suns or universes. During the fourth sun, called 4 Water, people lived 676 years. Then a sudden flood rushed upon them, destroying their world and changing them into fish.

Some people take flood stories as history. Others take the view that the stories were written to convey religious messages. Their concern is to identify what those messages are. For some, such as the scholar Mircea ELIADE, flood stories fit a universal mythological model. Water is both chaotic and creative. The flood represents a reversion to the primal chaos, but also the possibility that a new, fresh, pure creation will emerge. Rather than fit every myth into a single stereotype, it seems better to take each myth on its own terms and use more general interpretations only to the extent that the specific cultural context supports them.

folk religion The religious life of ordinary people who are not primarily oriented toward their religion as it is presented by its formal history, but who know and practice it as it is communicated and performed on family, village, or popular levels. In traditional societies, folk religion is generally associated with peasant societies, but in the modern world many of its characteristics can be found among working-class and other ordinary people in urban societies. Here it is often called popular religion.

Two fundamental features of folk religion are, first, that it is primarily "cosmic" rather than historical in perspective, and second, that it is chiefly passed on orally, through the words and examples of family, community members, and local-level spiritual leaders, whether shamans, evangelists, priests, or others.

Cosmic orientation means that folk religionists generally have little sense of history beyond living memory save as it is encoded in myth, but think more of how religion fits into their seasonal cycles and local geography. If they are agriculturists, festivals of planting and harvest are important. For all people in temperate climates spring and midwinter celebrations are very common. Even if the people officially belong to a religion with a historical orientation, like JUDAISM or CHRISTIANITY, the seasonal aspects of festivals with a theoretically historical origin, like PASSOVER, CHRISTMAS, Mardi Gras, and CARNIVAL, or EASTER, and the timeless aspects of the occasion, are likely to become central in practice. (This is why the snow and Santa Claus features of Christmas, and the rabbit and spring elements of Easter—a Christian holiday named after an Anglo-Saxon GODDESS of spring—are so prominent in folk or popular Christianity.) The geographical bearing of folk religion is perhaps more pronounced in some traditions than others; it means a tendency toward venerated holy places, like sacred mountains, trees, waterfalls, shrines, and PILGRIMAGE places that are accessible to ordinary people—like Mount Fuji in Japan or the famous grotto at the shrine of the Blessed Virgin MARY at Lourdes in France.

A related characteristic of folk and popular religion is emphasis on religious marking of the individual's life cycle. BAPTISMS, confirmations, BAR/BAT MITZVAHS, weddings, childbirths, personal SAINTS' days, and funerals, or the equivalents in various traditions, are likely to be extremely significant family or even community events, entailing perhaps great preparation and expense. The key occurrences of personal life thus blend into occasions that keep community identity alive. RITES OF PASSAGE into adulthood are ways for a community to perpetuate its own life; burial rites for the deceased become ways for the family and community to rebond and reaffirm their continuity after the loss.

Oral transmission, another fundamental feature of folk religion, means that folk religion is learned first of all through the words of people one knows locally and face to face, rather than through much study or in the way the religion is known by its literary sources or elites, its BRAHMINS or bishops. Folk FAITH is acquired in many ways—from parents, other family, peers, community example, festivals, services, lodges, INITIATIONS, local clergy and wise-women—but mainly in bits and pieces, rather than as a logically coherent whole. As popular religion becomes modern and urban, media like radio, television, and massmarket books or magazines may be added to the means of transmission, so that shamans become television evangelists. Very important, because of folk religion's living out of the present rather than out of history and institutionalization, is a leader's capacity to manifest direct and visible spiritual power, or immediate impressive credentials. Like a shaman, she or he should exhibit special charisma and preternatural-seeming states of consciousness; or like a priest, the ability to mount imposing and mystic-seeming services or ceremonies. Some very important religious leaders like the Japanese Buddhist prophet NICHIREN and the founder of METHODISM, John WESLEY, have managed successfully to bridge the gap between folk and institutional religion, and on a lesser scale so have many local priests and pastors.

Folk religion generally is quite open to belief in MIRACLES and immediate demonstrations of supernatural power, both good and bad. Miracles of HEALING and divine protections are commonly acknowledged, as is belief in negative WITCHCRAFT or comparable uncanny EVIL. Omens, amulets, divination, VISIONS, voices, signs, and MAGIC may be taken seriously.

Oral transmission does not mean that people who maintain a folk religion are necessarily illiterate. But reading is done in a different way. In folk-religion versions of scripture-oriented faiths like Christianity or ISLAM, the BIBLE or the QUR'AN may play an important role, to be read, believed, chanted, venerated. Yet they are not read or understood as they would be by a scholar of the faith's great institutions of learning, but in a direct way, without historical perspective. The scripture is really another sign, amulet, miracle or source of miracles—the greatest of all.

While often passive so far as social or political change is concerned, folk religion can rouse itself to become the voice of the common people and so to produce movements that intend major social change or even revolution, whether moral, social, or political. From out of the very nature of folk religion, such movements are likely to be cosmic, present-oriented, under visionary charismatic leadership, full of belief in miracles and expecting to be confirmed by miraculous signs and victories, up to and including direct divine intervention. But even if frustrated, folk religion movements like that of JOAN OF ARC can change the course of history.

Folk religion and its modern popular religion version, with all their color and festivity, remain important in the contemporary world.

Further reading: Charles Leslie, ed., *Anthropology of Folk Religion* (New York: Vintage, 1960); Robert A. Segal, ed., *Anthropology, Folklore, and Myth* (New York: Garland, 1996); Peter Williams, *Popular Religion in America* (Chicago: University of Chicago Press, 1989).

founders, religious   The six or eight persons who have been accounted the founders of the world's great religions have exercised far more influence in history than countless kings or presidents. These include ABRAHAM and MOSES for JUDAISM, ZARATHUSTRA (or Zoroaster) for ZOROASTRIANISM, CONFUCIUS for CONFUCIANISM, LAO-TZU for TAOISM, the BUDDHA for BUDDHISM, JESUS for CHRISTIANITY, and MUHAMMAD for ISLAM. (The traditional life stories, and even the historical existence, of some of these may be legendary, but that does not negate the tremendous importance their name and story have had for the hundreds of millions of people over many centuries for whom they have embodied the supreme human ideal and to whom they have been the central conveyers of the divine, or the divine word, to humanity.)

First we may note that all of these men lived during a relatively short period in terms of human history as a whole: from about 2000 B.C.E. (Abraham) to 632 C.E. (death of Muhammad). The Buddha, the Chinese founders, Jesus, and Muhammad all lived within only a little more than a millennium, 560 B.C.E. (birth of the Buddha) to 632 C.E. (There have been other founders of smaller religions, some later, but none have had the world-historical importance of these.)

This was a period of tremendous change for religion. In it, the foundation was laid for the replacement or absorption of archaic religion, based on traditional myths, RITUALS, and local gods, by religions based on the life and teaching of a founder who lived as a human being in historical time. This meant that the focus of the new religions was not the animal or plant of hunting and agricultural religion or the tribal loyalty or loyalty to a sacred king as in ancient Egypt or Babylon, but in a real sense was an individual human being. By example and teaching, the founders asked in a new and direct way, "What must I, as an individual, do to be saved or enlightened, or accounted a moral being?" and "What is the meaning behind the often-terrible events of human history to me as an individual and to humanity as whole?" (The latter question lies behind, for example, the Confucian keeping of historical records from which morals were drawn and the Jewish, and later Christian, emphasis on the histories in the Hebrew scriptures and the believers' attempts to understand how God's plan was working through them.)

The central core of this period, around the fifth century B.C.E., was called the Axial Age, or time of turning, by the philosopher Karl Jaspers (1883–1969). It was indeed a time of epochal change in human thinking, the time not only of some of the founders but also of the greatest Hebrew prophets, Greek philosophers, and Hindu sages like those of the earlier UPANISHADS, who all asked the same questions in their own ways.

What brought about this new kind of thinking? One factor was the prior invention of writing, which meant that historical records could be kept and studied and the teachings of the wise recorded. Another was the emergence of ancient empires like the Greek, Roman, and Chinese, which embraced different cultures and meant, for some, increased opportunity for travel and reflection. It all amounted to a time when a new awareness of change and diversity in human life was in the air, and there was yearning for new ways of looking at life.

How did the founders respond to this yearning? For one thing, they did not completely condemn the prior religion but built on it. His followers heard the founder saying, in effect, "Here is a new way of looking at what you already know," or "Here in my life and teaching is a model that sums up what went before and adds something significant to it." In his teachings, Jesus began with the prior spiritual teachings of Judaism, as he emphasized. Muhammad did not deny the holy city of Mecca; he instead gave it a new meaning.

Moreover, the founders gave the new outlook a central symbol: themselves. Their religion—drawing on the invention of writing—was inevitably centered on a sacred canon of scripture, usually based on their own teaching. More than the earlier religions, their faiths taught a definite process of salvation. Specific things were to be believed and done in response to the question, "What must I do to be saved, enlightened, or moral?" In this way, they offered a definite model of human life, showing what it is now and what it can be at its best.

By these means the founders changed the inner lives of millions and, through them and the religious institutions that followed in their wake, the course of history.

Further reading: Robert Ellwood, *Cycles of Faith* (Walnut Creek, Calif.: Altamira, 2003); Karl Jaspers, *The Origin and Goal of History* (New Haven: Yale University Press, 1953); Barbara McFarlane, *Sacred Myths: Stories of World Religions* (Portland, Ore.:

Sibyl, 1996); Huston Smith, *The World's Religions* (San Francisco: HarperSanFrancisco, 1999); Joachim Wach, *The Comparative Study of Religion* (New York: Columbia University Press, 1958).

four noble truths   Four compact statements that express the basic teachings of BUDDHISM. According to tradition, the BUDDHA Siddhartha Gautama discovered these truths during the night of his enlightenment. He then taught them in his first sermon, which he preached in the Deer Park near BANARAS.

In the four noble truths, the Buddha thinks like a doctor. He sets out to cure the disease that plagues all sentient beings (beings who have consciousness). The first noble truth tells what the symptoms of the disease are. The next noble truth identifies what causes them. The third noble truth sets out what can be done about the disease. The fourth provides a detailed prescription.

According to the Buddha, we can describe the symptoms of our disease with a single word: *duhkha*. Unfortunately, this word is difficult to translate. It means "suffering," but suffering in a very profound sense. According to the Buddha, ultimate satisfaction cannot be found in conditioned existence, that is, in this world or in any other. Even moments of profound happiness are characterized to some extent by duhkha.

The second noble truth tells us what the cause of duhkha is: craving. Many later thinkers say that craving itself derives from ignorance. We ignore the fact that we are temporary collections of elements produced by outside causes and mistakenly think that we have selves. We also ignore the fact that everything around us is unstable and impermanent. Therefore, we do not accept things as they are. Instead, we crave, and our craving produces suffering.

The third noble truth holds out hope. The disease from which sentient beings like us suffer is not an incurable cancer; in that case the only option is to make the patient as comfortable as possible. Instead, our disease can be cured. If one eliminates craving, duhkha ceases. But how can anyone do that?

The fourth noble truth tells us how. It spells out the Buddha's "Middle Way" between starving our senses and indulging them. The Buddha invites his followers to pay attention to, indeed, to change eight areas of life. As a result, the Buddha's way is known as the eightfold path.

The first two steps in the eightfold path help us acquire wisdom. We need to convince ourselves of the truths of Buddhism. This is known as right thought. But one can think the same thought with many different attitudes. According to the Buddha, one should try to think without craving and leave greed, hatred, and delusion behind. This is right understanding.

The next three steps in the eightfold path focus on morality. We should avoid killing, stealing, and sexual misconduct. This is right action. We should also always speak the truth—right speech. Furthermore, a great deal of every person's life consists of working for a living. We should not do jobs that harm other beings, such as hunting or selling liquor. This is right livelihood.

The last three steps involve concentration with the help of MEDITATION. We should be diligent in our practice. That is right effort. We should also work for right mindfulness and right concentration. THERAVADA BUDDHISM is the form of Buddhism that adheres to the eightfold path most closely. In Theravada, right mindfulness and concentration usually mean practicing two different forms of meditation, *samadhi* meditation and *vipassana* meditation.

Buddhism teaches that those who practice the eightfold path are transformed. They experience, think of, and act in the world differently. Eventually they lose ignorance and craving, escape from duhkha, and enter NIRVANA.

four unlimited virtues   In BUDDHISM, four attitudes accessible to all, which can be cultivated by meditation. They are Unlimited Friendliness, Unlimited Compassion, Unlimited Sympathetic Joy, and Unlimited Equanimity of Mind. They are said to be unlimited or immeasurable because there is no end to the extent to which they can be taken. Friendliness means giving encouragement and happiness to others. Compassion and Sympathetic Joy go together, since Compassion means the ability to share another's suffering, while Sympathetic Joy refers to the equally important ability to share in another's joy. Equanimity or evenness of mind means freedom from self-centered worries, and so enables one to express friendliness, compassion, and sympathetic joy without constraint or limit. In this sense, and guided by wisdom and the understanding of the true needs of others, which are also central Buddhist virtues, one could hardly be too friendly, compassionate, sympathetic, or even-minded.

Francis of Assisi and Franciscans (1181/1182–1226) *an Italian SAINT of the Middle Ages, and the orders of MONKS AND NUNS that he founded* Francis was the son of an Italian cloth merchant. As a young man, he was a soldier, but he was taken prisoner and spent the good part of a year as a prisoner of war. Soon after his release he had a number of religious experiences. In one famous experience he heard a command to repair a chapel near Assisi. He went to his father's store, took the cloth, sold it and the horse he was riding, and tried to give the money to the priest to repair the chapel. The result was a break with his father.

An even more fateful experience came in February of 1208 or 1209. Francis heard words from the NEW TESTAMENT in which JESUS commanded his followers to travel and preach without any possessions whatsoever (Matthew 10.9–11). Although he was not a priest, Francis began to preach. Several followers joined him, and in 1209 or 1210 the pope blessed his "order." In 1212 Francis received a noblewoman named Clare into the monastic life. She became the head of an order of nuns. In the early 1220s Francis established a third "order" for men and women who did not wish to leave their ordinary lives behind but were nevertheless inspired by Francis's vision and lifestyle.

Francis and his followers originally gave up all their possessions. They also had no permanent homes. This lifestyle was part of Francis's attempt

Painting from the 1400s of Saint Francis of Assisi
(Réunion des Musées Nationaux/Art Resource, N.Y.)

to imitate Jesus as much as possible. Francis's own religious attitude is perhaps summed up best by the words "brotherhood" and "sisterhood." Francis felt that all of GOD's creatures were members of the same family. That meant that all human beings, of whatever class or nationality, were brothers and sisters. So were natural phenomena: brother sun, sister moon, even sister death. As a result, Francis is often associated in the popular mind with wild animals and gardens.

In the centuries after Francis's death, his first order, the order of monks, fragmented. The basic problem was the extent to which brothers should be expected to live a life of poverty. In the 1300s the Pope recognized a group known as the Conventuals as the official Franciscan group. Its lifestyle is less strict, and it emphasizes preaching and study. But today it is the smallest of the major Franciscan groups. The largest group, the Observants, emerged in the 1400s. It stands for a strict observance of Francis's discipline. A third group, the Capuchins, arose in the 1500s. Its members adopted an even more austere life-style that inclined to the isolated life of the hermit.

The Franciscans do not often receive much publicity. That is partly because of their interests in the poor, and partly because of their manner of working. But there are more Franciscan monks and nuns in the Roman Catholic Church than monks and nuns of any other order. Throughout history women have been particularly active not only as nuns but also as members of the "third order," the order for those who do not renounce their ordinary lives.

Some Franciscans have, however, become prominent. When Dominican theologians such as Thomas AQUINAS began to use the writings of Aristotle in developing their theologies, the Franciscans strenuously opposed them. Those who did so included the theologian Bonaventure (1221–74) and the philosophers Duns Scotus (c. 1265–1308) and William of Ockham (c. 1280–1349). John of Capistrano (1386–1456), best known in North America for a mission in California to which swallows return regularly, was a Franciscan. The most famous member of the "third order," the order still in the world, must surely be Christopher Columbus. In addition to moving people to join one of his orders, Francis's vision of poverty and of the unity of all of creation has inspired countless persons. The Roman Catholic Church remembers him as a saint annually on October 4.

Further reading: T. W. Arnold, trans., *The Little Flowers of St. Francis* (New York: Dutton, 1940); John R. H. Moorman, *A History of the Franciscan Order* (Oxford: Clarendon Press, 1968); Michael Robson, *St. Francis of Assisi: The Legend and the Life* (London: Chapman, 1997); Donald Spoto, *Reluctant Saint: The Life of Francis of Assisi* (New York: Viking, 2002).

Frazer, James George (1854–1941) *pioneering British anthropologist and author of the influential book* The Golden Bough   Frazer was an "armchair ethnologist." He wrote about peoples all around the globe, but he never visited them. Instead, he based his ideas on printed materials, letters, reports, and conversations with travelers. His most famous work is *The Golden Bough*. It was first published in two volumes in 1890; by 1915 it had grown to 12 enormous tomes.

Frazer called his volumes "A Study in Magic and Religion." For him, MAGIC was misguided science. When people used magic, they were trying to apply the laws of nature. They just applied the wrong laws. They thought that there was a natural connection between objects that either looked alike or had been in contact.

When magic failed, people adopted a different attitude: religion. They concluded that personal beings controlled the world. They pleaded with those beings for personal favors. Actually, Frazer said, religion and magic are often found together. RITUALS connected with springtime and harvest—dying and rising gods—were especially prominent.

Frazer's successor, Bronislaw MALINOWSKI, started an entirely different way of thinking about cultures and religions. As a result, Frazer's ideas are discredited today. But they have been very influential. For example, the American-British poet, T. S. Eliot, gave Frazer the credit for inspiring some of his greatest poems.

free will and determinism The idea that human beings are able to choose their own actions. People act, and when we act, we make decisions. Most of us feel that we have the option of choosing between two or more alternatives. We may choose one of them, but we could have chosen another, if we wanted to.

This sense provides a basis for the idea that our wills are free. Another important basis for that idea has to do with morality. It seems unfair to condemn a person who had no real choice. In order to hold people responsible for their actions, we need to be able to say that they could have acted differently.

There is, however, an idea opposed to free will. It is the idea of determinism, sometimes conceived of as fate. According to this idea, what human beings do is already decided for them. A special form of determinism is predestination. It teaches that GOD has predestined or predetermined what will happen in the future. For some Christians, God predestines one item in particular: who will and will not be saved.

The tension between free will and determinism is a classic topic in European philosophy and in Christian, Islamic, and, to a much lesser degree, Jewish THEOLOGY. The issue arises in other religions, too.

Many religious people feel that fate determines certain events, such as the time of a person's death. In HINDUISM, BUDDHISM, JAINISM, and SIKHISM one's previous actions (KARMA) determine the circumstances in which one will be reborn and under which one will act. Note that karma does not determine what one will actually do.

Determinism is particularly attractive to religions that teach MONOTHEISM. It can help emphasize God's greatness: "God is in control of everything." If so, God must control our actions. For some, determinism is a consequence of saying that God knows everything. If God knows ahead of time what a person will do, how can the person really have a choice? For others, determinism means that human beings must rely upon God's grace for SALVATION. They cannot earn God's favor on their own. But determinism raises problems, too. If God is in control of everything, where does EVIL come from (see THEODICY)?

Many Christian, Islamic, and Jewish thinkers have discussed these topics (see CHRISTIANITY, ISLAM, JUDAISM). In the NEW TESTAMENT PAUL taught that God chooses whom he will save. AUGUSTINE OF HIPPO argued that without God's GRACE, human beings could not will to do what was good. During the REFORMATION Erasmus strongly defended free will; Martin LUTHER strongly attacked it in his book *On the Bondage of the Will*. Luther and his followers later modified these views. But John CALVIN and Calvinism emphasized a "double predestination"—predestination to salvation and to damnation.

Some Muslim thinkers have rejected the teaching of free will. "Determination," they argued, belongs to God alone. Beginning in the 10th century C.E. Jewish thinkers living in the Islamic world reacted to such claims. They argued that, according to Genesis, God created human beings in God's image and likeness, God's will is free; the human will must be free, too.

During the 20th century, Christian and Muslim thinkers tended to favor free will over determinism. But the old fatalistic cliché remains popular: "When it's your time to go, it's your time to go." The tension between free will and determinism also appears today in a nonreligious context: debates on public policy informed by contemporary psychology. Some stress that heredity and environment cause human behavior. Others insist that human beings are accountable for their actions regardless of conditions.

Freud, Sigmund (1856–1939) *the doctor who founded psychoanalysis* Freud grew up in the Jewish community of Vienna, Austria. Trained as a doctor, he became interested in people who behaved unusually. In the course of working with his patients, he developed influential ideas about human beings' subconscious and unconscious drives and desires. He applied these ideas to many areas of human life, including religion.

Freud suggested that religion began from group feelings of guilt. In prehistory the father was the head of a horde. He kept all the women for himself. One day in frustration his sons banded together and killed him. Their guilt was responsible for the creation of religion.

No one believes this story any more. Nevertheless, many people agree with Freud when he sees myths as expressing psychological realities.

Freud also wrote about RITUALS. He called them "collective neuroses." Just as neurotic people perform senseless, repetitive acts, religious people perform rituals. Clearly, Freud himself had little interest in religion. He was convinced that when human beings left the childhood of their race behind, the illusion of religion would disappear like a mirage.

Freud's ideas had a major impact on 20th-century thought. But toward the end of the century many criticized psychoanalysis as "pseudoscience."

Friends, Society of *See* QUAKERS.

functionalism
One of the most popular theories of religion in the 20th century. Functionalism has been especially important to social scientists.

The anthropologist Bronislaw MALINOWSKI coined the word "functionalism." He used it to describe what he thought scholars should do when they study cultures, including religions. Until his time anthropologists had tried to identify the stages through which culture and religion had evolved (*see* EVOLUTION AND RELIGION). A good example is James George FRAZER's famous book, *The Golden Bough*. Malinowski suggested that scholars do something else instead. He suggested that they limit themselves to a single culture and study that culture as a functioning whole. This starting point determined the goal of studying religious beliefs or RITUALS. According to Malinowski, scholars should explain these beliefs and rituals in terms of what functions they fulfill, that is, in terms of what they do for the culture as a whole. Almost every sociologist and anthropologist who studied religions followed Malinowski's advice until the 1960s.

For functionalists, function does not mean purpose. People do perform religious actions for particular purposes. For example, in the middle of a drought people living in a farming community may pray for rain. But functionalists would not consider the function of the PRAYER to be obtaining rain. That is because praying for rain does not actually produce it. Malinowski liked to say that the function of religious rituals was to fulfill biological and psychological needs. Thus, a prayer for rain in the middle of a drought may function to relieve anxiety.

A scholar who influenced Malinowski tremendously was Émile DURKHEIM. Unlike Malinowski, Durkheim emphasized social, not psychological, functions. For him, one important function of religion was that it integrated people into a society. A later sociologist, Peter Berger, suggested that religion functioned to legitimate cultural creations. For example, in North America children have traditionally taken their father's last name. But they could just as easily take their mother's. Religion, Berger said, helped make current practices seem legitimate. In the NEW TESTAMENT the apostle PAUL writes that the father is the head of the family, just as JESUS is the head of the church.

Functionalism has had its critics. Some accuse it of justifying the way things are. According to them, functionalism assumes that society works. It overlooks aspects of society that may need to be changed.

This criticism may apply to some functionalists. It does not apply to all. For example, Karl MARX made claims about religion that are similar to functionalism. He called religion the opiate of the masses. He meant that religion helped people tolerate miserable social circumstances. But for Marx that was not a good thing. Like opium, religion robbed the masses of energy. As a result, they failed to do what was needed to eliminate their misery.

Other critics of functionalism question just how much it actually explains. Consider the example of the farming community praying for rain. Psychological tests can show whether a particular prayer actually alleviates anxiety. But does that explain why the community prays? Perhaps not. Other acts may alleviate anxiety, too. The community could SACRIFICE to the rain god, or it could simply hold a meeting at which community members shared their concerns.

fundamentalism Movements that vigorously assert traditional religion in the face of modern developments. Fundamentalism arose within CHRISTIANITY in the United States at the end of the 19th and beginning of the 20th century. Some scholars insist that it is best to use the term only for Christianity. It is now common, however, to talk about fundamentalism in other religions, too, such as ISLAM and HINDUISM.

Modernism—industrialization; the development of the natural sciences, including the theory of biological evolution; the rise of states whose populations practice a number of religions and that are officially secular or neutral with regard to religion; research in history and archaeology that has called traditional religious claims into question—all of these developments and more have presented challenges to traditional religions. Many religious people have attempted to adjust their religious convictions to these developments. Fundamentalists have responded differently. They often think of themselves as preserving their religious traditions unchanged or as returning to the way things were. In many cases, however, they are producing something new. Nevertheless, they address modernism by opposing it.

Modernism has had different effects on different religious traditions. For Christians in the United States at the beginning of the 20th century, it called into question the accuracy of the BIBLE and teachings like the divinity, the VIRGIN BIRTH, MIRACLES, and the RESURRECTION of JESUS. Fundamentalist Christians responded by making a list of "fundamentals" that Christians had to believe (see FUNDAMENTALISM, CHRISTIAN).

Unlike Christianity, Hinduism does not have basic beliefs. Instead, Hindu fundamentalism has reacted to centuries of rule by Muslim and Christian rulers. Hindu fundamentalists see *Hin-dutva*—Hindu culture rather than Hinduism as a religion—under attack from two sources: secularism and Islam. They want to make India a Hindu state (see FUNDAMENTALISM, HINDU).

Islamic fundamentalism sees Islam, too, as under attack (see FUNDAMENTALISM, ISLAMIC). Muslim fundamentalists often consider Europe and especially the United States as their ultimate enemy. They urge stricter observance of SHARIAH, GOD's law for human beings. Fundamentalists living under Islamic governments often see those governments as being too lax in their support for Islam. Those born in Europe and, to a lesser extent, the United States favor strictly following Islam as a way to establish their identity as Muslims. Muslim fundamentalists also see the state of Israel as an attempt by European powers to take territory from Muslims, as happened during the CRUSADES.

Separate entries provide further details on Christian, Hindu, and Islamic fundamentalism. But it is also important to keep several more general points in mind.

First, fundamentalism is often a pejorative term, that is, a term that people use for something they condemn. Perhaps for that reason, people do not often speak of Jewish or Buddhist fundamentalism, even though JUDAISM and BUDDHISM, too, have movements that reject modernism. For example, instead of Jewish fundamentalism we tend to speak of HASIDISM and, a very different movement, ZIONISM.

Second, it is common to link especially Hindu and Muslim fundamentalism with violence and terrorism. We should be cautious. On the one hand, some Christian fundamentalists have committed violent and terrorist acts, too. Examples include antiabortion activists and, more loosely, Timothy McVeigh, the Oklahoma City bomber. McVeigh had connections with a movement known as Christian Identity, which recommended bombing federal buildings. On the other hand, just as most Christian fundamentalists do not engage in violence, the same is true of most Muslim and Hindu fundamentalists.

Third, fundamentalists may oppose some features of modernism, but they still live in the modern world. They are not old-fashioned and out of date. For example, they have been very willing to use modern inventions, such as television and the Internet, to promote their causes.

fundamentalism, Christian Historically, a movement in American PROTESTANTISM that insisted that true Christians must hold certain fundamental beliefs. One of them is the belief that every word of the BIBLE is verbally inspired by GOD and literally true. Christian fundamentalists still hold to the fundamental beliefs. In the last part of the 20th and early part of the 21st centuries, they also came to be associated with a broader range of moral and political positions, such as opposition to abortion and unions between homosexuals and support for the Republican Party in the United States.

THE CHALLENGE OF MODERNISM

Developments in Europe during the 19th century presented many challenges to traditional Christian belief. Perhaps the most famous challenge came in 1859. In that year Charles Darwin published his views on natural selection and evolution. His theory explained the origin of the forms of plant, animal, and human life without referring to any divine purpose or guiding hand. Many thought that science had overthrown the traditional Christian account of the creation of the world.

The 19th century presented many other challenges to traditional belief. With the advance of the natural sciences, people began to doubt claims about MIRACLES. Indeed, the Scottish philosopher David Hume (1711–76), had already argued persuasively in the 18th century for a position that made it almost impossible to accept any claims that miracles had occurred. That included claims that someone had risen from the dead.

Scholars who studied the Bible added other challenges. They treated the books of the Bible like any other human writing and in doing so explained many of their odd characteristics. A good example is the theory that TORAH, the first five books of the Bible, was not written by MOSES but emerged from combining four sources, known as J, E, P, and D

(see SCRIPTURES, HEBREW). In addition, historians seemed to show that the Bible was in error about crucial points. For example, Matthew and Luke seem to differ by at least ten years on the date of JESUS' birth. Both cannot be right. Furthermore, in showing how various doctrines (see DOGMA AND DOCTRINE) developed over time, critical scholars raised questions about fundamental Christian beliefs, such as the VIRGIN BIRTH, divinity, and RESURRECTION of Jesus.

Some theologians, who eventually became known as liberals, tried to develop a kind of CHRISTIANITY that was compatible with these developments. Their inspiration came from a German theologian named Friedrich Schleiermacher (1768–1834). Schleiermacher rejected the literal truth of many traditional Christian teachings. At the same time, he taught that religion was not about beliefs or about morals but about a feeling, which he described at different times as a feeling of being a part of the universe or as a consciousness of God. For him what made Jesus special was not that Jesus was God but that Jesus had the strongest consciousness of God possible.

THE FUNDAMENTALIST RESPONSE

Developments such as those given above, including the development of liberal theology, alarmed many people. In European Protestantism church leaders tried to keep liberals from spreading their views in churches. In ROMAN CATHOLICISM the Vatican directly and forcefully rejected modernism. Among a large number of American Protestants the response took the form of FUNDAMENTALISM.

The name *fundamentalism* came from a Bible conference held in 1895 in Niagara, New York. Participants adopted what they called five fundamental beliefs that they thought all Christians should hold. These are that the Bible is verbally inspired by God and without error, that Jesus is divine, that Jesus' mother MARY was a virgin when he was born, that Jesus rose from the dead physically and will return at the end of time, and that his death brought about what is known as a "substitutionary atonement." This view, first expressed by ANSELM (c. 1033–1109), bishop of CANTERBURY, in the Middle Ages, teaches that Christians receive SALVATION because Jesus, who had no SIN, died as a substitute for ordinary human beings, who are sinners.

Christian fundamentalists have generally held other views besides these five points. For example, many favor a view called "dispensationalism." This position uses the Bible and its prophecies to interpret history. It identifies seven "dispensations" or ages, the last of which will be the rule of Jesus for 1000 years (the "millennium"). Fundamentalists who adopt this position believe that Jesus will return, that Christians will be taken up into the atmosphere to meet him (an event known as the "rapture"), that all Jews will convert to Christianity, and that Jesus will rule the earth from Jerusalem. After these events will come the final judgment.

Christian fundamentalists were quite adamant about their views, and they did not hesitate to spread them vigorously. Perhaps the most famous early confrontation between early fundamentalists and the advocates of science was the trial of John Scopes (1900–70), a biology teacher in Dayton, Tennessee, in 1925. Under fundamentalist influence, Tennessee had passed a law making the teaching of evolution illegal in public schools. Scopes admittedly violated the law. Some evidence indicates that the whole affair was a publicity stunt to draw attention to the town. In any case, the trial became a national event. Two famous lawyers squared off against each other, William Jennings Bryan (1860–1925) for the prosecution and Clarence Darrow (1857–1938) for the defense. Radio stations carried live broadcasts of the trial. There was never any real question that Scopes had violated the law, but the trial brought much ridicule on Christian fundamentalism. Bryan, the advocate of fundamentalism, died immediately after it was over. His death seemed to be a symbol of the fate of fundamentalism among the American public.

RECENT DEVELOPMENTS

After World War II fundamentalism was not very visible in American life. Fundamentalists remained in their own churches, but they had little broader influence.

That changed in the late 1970s with the backlash against the liberalism of the 1960s. The efforts of some popular fundamentalist preachers, such as Jack Hyles (1926–2001) in Hammond, Indiana, and Jerry Falwell (b. 1933) in Lynchburg, Virginia, had created mega-churches, with membership numbering in the thousands and even the tens of thousands. Fundamentalists also began to spread their message effectively through the media of radio and especially television (*see* TELEVANGELISM). Indeed, leading fundamentalists, such as Falwell, Pat Robertson (b. 1930), Jimmy Swaggart (b. 1935), and Jim (b. 1939) and Tammy Faye (b. 1942) Bakker, became public figures. Fundamentalists organized their own groups for public action, such as Falwell's Moral Majority, founded in 1979. In addition, they began to oppose liberals in various church bodies. Perhaps the most successful example is the Southern Baptist Convention. Starting about 1980, fundamentalists have dominated the formulation of Southern Baptist teachings and policies and have managed to take control of its educational institutions.

Christian fundamentalists have also made the teaching of evolution in public schools an issue once again (*see* EVOLUTION AND RELIGION). Instead of seeking to outlaw evolution, they have generally preferred to insist on equal time for views of the origin and development of life that they claim are equally scientific. At first they focused on "creation science," a set of views developed by Henry M. Morris (b. 1918) and advocated by his Institute for Creation Research, founded in 1970. More recently, some have concentrated on views known as "intelligent design," developed by Phillip Johnson (b. 1940), Michael Behe (b. 1952), and William Dembski (b. 1960), among others. According to this view, the order of nature is too complex to have arisen by chance.

As the name of the Moral Majority indicates, fundamentalists also became widely critical of what they saw as the moral degeneracy of American society. Many of their concerns centered around sexuality, an area in which conventional morality had been abandoned in the 1960s. Legalized ABORTION became a contentious issue; some extreme fundamentalists went so far as to bomb abortion clinics and kill doctors who performed legal abortions. Fundamentalists have also tended to see HOMOSEXUALITY as voluntary behavior and have condemned it as sinful. They strongly opposed the sanctioning of unions between homosexuals, whether they be marriages or "civil unions." More broadly, fundamentalists saw the American family as threatened by a variety of movements, including FEMINISM. They sought to protect it by emphasizing what they saw as the biblically mandated roles for men and women. They also produced literature espousing their views, such as Hal Lindsey's (b. 1929) *The Late Great Planet Earth* (1970) and, more recently, Tim LaHaye's (b. 1928) "left behind" series. Such books were extremely popular in fundamentalist circles.

Finally, at the end of the 20th and the beginning of the 21st centuries Christian fundamentalists were also active in American politics. Like evangelicals more broadly, they tended to believe that the state should be subservient to God. These political views show strong parallels to similar interests in Islamic and Hindu fundamentalism (*see* FUNDAMENTALISM, HINDU; FUNDAMENTALISM, ISLAMIC). Some fundamentalists sought to have the United States recognized as a Christian nation. Many became active in the Republican Party.

By the beginning of the 21st century the center of gravity in the Christian world had shifted away from North America and Europe to the southern hemisphere, that is, to churches in Africa, Latin America, and some parts of Asia. Christians in these areas tend to be doctrinally and morally conservative. In many respects, their views resemble Christian fundamentalism.

See also EVANGELICAL CHRISTIANITY.

Further reading: Richard T. Antoun, *Understanding Fundamentalism: Christian, Islamic, and Jewish Movements* (Walnut Creek, Calif.: Altamira Press, 2001); Karen Armstrong, *The Battle for God* (New York: Alfred A. Knopf, 2000); Martin E. Marty and R. Scott Appleby, eds., *Fundamentalisms Comprehended* (Chicago: University of Chicago Press, 1995); Ralph W. Hood, Peter C. Hill, and W. Paul Williamson, *The Psychology of Religious Fundamentalism* (New York: Guilford Press, 2005).

fundamentalism, Hindu Movements that aim to make Hinduism culturally and politically dominant in South Asia. HINDUISM has had fundamentalist movements in a religious sense, too, such as the Arya Samaj, a "return-to-the-VEDA" movement that arose in the 19th century. The term *Hindu fundamentalism* usually refers, however, to movements that pursue the cultural and political ideal of *Hindutva*, literally, "Hinduness."

Hindutva derives from the writings of V. D. Savarkar (1883–1966). Unlike Mohandas GANDHI, Savarkar advocated armed resistance to British rule in India. In a book published in 1915 he defined Hindutva as the common culture of India, a culture shared by people who practiced all of the many religions there (*see* INDIA, RELIGIONS IN). An object of patriotic pride, Hindutva marked out the natural political boundaries of India "from sea to sea."

Today, three main organizations promote Hindutva. They are often known by their initials: RSS, VHP, and BJP.

Keshav Baliram Hedgewar (1889–1940) founded the Rastriya Svayamsevak Sangh (National Volunteer Association), or RSS, in 1925. It emphasized national pride and personal training through physical exercise. The government of India banned the RSS in 1948 because Gandhi's assassin had some connections with it. The ban was removed in 1962, but other bans have come and gone, so that the organization is sometimes legal, sometimes not. After India achieved independence in 1947 the RSS became active in opposing the secular Indian state.

A second Hindutva organization is the Vishwa Hindu Parishad (All-Hindu Congress), or VHP. Founded in 1964 to promote Hindu unity and further Hindu culture, the VHP has branches around the globe, including in the United States (founded in 1970). It defines Hinduism broadly to include all religions that have arisen in India, including

BUDDHISM, JAINISM, and SIKHISM. It also takes an active interest in projects for social benefit, such as medical relief and education. The VHP sees mainstream, secular society as antagonistic to Hinduism and Hindu causes. It also sees Hinduism as under attack by Islam; some VHP members feel threatened by the fact that Muslims are reproducing at a greater rate than Hindus.

The third Hindutva group is a political party, the Bharatiya Janata Party (Indian People's Party) or BJP. A successor to an earlier party known as the Jana Sangh, the BJP was formed in 1980 through the efforts of RSS members. It rose to prominence in the late 1980s as a result of Hindutva agitation, and it ruled India several times during the 1990s and early 2000s. When it fell from power in June 2004, some partisans of the Hindutva movement criticized its policies as having been too moderate or even anti-Hindu.

Hindu fundamentalists reject the example of Mohandas Gandhi and the ideal of a secular state enshrined in India's constitution. They see Pakistan and Bangladesh as rightfully parts of India and hold Gandhi responsible for their loss. They also see secularism as violating India's traditional culture and pandering to its enemies. These fundamentalists have attacked Indian Christians, as they did in tribal areas of Gujarat in western India in 1999. But the main object of Hindutva antagonism has been Muslims.

A single symbol has served to focus Hindutva anti-Muslim sentiment: the supposed birthplace of RAMA, an AVATAR of VISHNU, at Ayodhya. Since the 1500s the place had been the site of a mosque known as the Babri Masjid. Hindutva supporters claim that the mosque was built on top of a destroyed temple, and they consider the mosque a symbol of what Muslims want to do to all of Hindu culture. In the late 1980s the leader of the BJP, L. K. Advani, toured India lobbying for the demolition of the mosque and the building of a temple. The VHP gathered bricks donated from Hindus throughout the world to use in building the new temple. Although the government promised to protect the mosque, on December 6, 1992, mobs broke through the barriers and demolished it. In the aftermath, anti-Muslim fervor led to massacres in other parts of India.

The envisioned temple to Rama has yet to be built. The latest outbreak of violence occurred in 2002. On February 27 a train carrying volunteer workers returning from Ayodhya was attacked at the train station in Godhra, Gujarat. Over 50 volunteers were trapped in a train car and burned to death, presumably by Muslims opposed to Hindutva programs. In the ensuing riots, more than 500 people were killed throughout Gujarat, most of them Muslims.

Hindu fundamentalists have seen the September 11, 2001, attacks on the United States in terms of their own struggles. For example, one official spokesperson for the VHP in the United States has equated the Hindu fundamentalist struggle against Islam and the U.S. "war on terror" as two parts of the same struggle of civilization versus barbarity and democracy versus tyranny.

Further reading: Ainslie T. Embree, *Utopias in Conflict: Religion and Nationalism in Modern India* (Berkeley: University of California Press, 1990); Gerald James Larson, *India's Agony over Religion* (Albany: State University of New York Press, 1995); David Ludden, ed., *Making India Hindu: Religion, Community, and the Politics of Democracy in India,* 2d ed. (New York: Oxford University Press, 2005); Khushwant Singh, *The End of India* (New Delhi, India: Penguin Books, 2003).

fundamentalism, Islamic A common term for movements today that seek to revitalize ISLAM and return to stricter observance of Islamic practices. Especially because of the attacks of September 11, 2001, and suicide bombings directed against Israelis in the Middle East, many outsiders associate Islamic fundamentalism with terrorism and violence. That is not only true of people in the United States and Israel. Many Hindus, too, see themselves as engaged in a struggle against Muslim attempts to destroy their heritage (*see* FUNDAMENTALISM, HINDU). Only some Islamic fundamentalist groups, however, have engaged in terrorism and violence.

To understand violent as well as nonviolent forms of Islamic fundamentalism, one needs to know the background out of which they emerged.

MODERN CHALLENGES TO TRADITIONAL ISLAM

Islam first arose in Arabia in the seventh century C.E., and it spread quickly. By the end of the century Muslims ruled territory from Spain in the west through North Africa and the Middle East to Persia (Iran today) and beyond in the east. Muslims saw this tremendous expansion as a sign of GOD's pleasure (*see* ALLAH). Then, in the next several centuries, Islamic civilizations led the world in science, mathematics, and technology and produced wonders of architecture, such as the Alhambra in Spain and the Taj Mahal in India. To be sure, there were challenges. As a result of the CRUSADES Christians managed to carve out Christian states in the region of Israel and Palestine for a century or two. But for the most part, the Islamic Middle East remained dominant. It is also relevant, given the antagonism between Jews and Muslims today, that many Jews fleeing persecution in Europe during the Middle Ages and the INQUISITION found safety in the Islamic world (*see* ANTI-SEMITISM).

Today, of course, the status of Islamic countries is much different. In time Europe surpassed Muslim powers in scientific development and military technology. From the 18th to the middle of the 20th centuries Muslims found themselves ruled by European colonial powers. In the late 19th and early 20th centuries the most gifted Muslims went to Europe—and later the United States—for education. Many of these people brought Western ideals back home. Colonial rule also encouraged many Muslims to abandon their traditions and adopt Western customs. By the middle of the 20th century influential Muslims had come to believe that traditional Islam was outmoded, and they blamed what they viewed as this backwardness for their inability to resist colonial conquest.

Many hoped that modernization would make Islamic areas of the world strong and prosperous again. That did not happen. Prosperity did come, but it was largely limited to small groups. In addi-tion, newly independent Islamic governments failed to live up to expectations. In 1948 the United Nations, largely through the efforts of North Americans and Europeans, created the state of Israel. Many Muslims saw it as a new Crusader state. When Israeli forces quickly defeated Arab armies in the Six-Day War in 1967, Muslim self-esteem reached a profound low.

It was in this context that Islamic fundamentalism emerged and grew. Some Islamic leaders attributed the weakness of Islamic states not to the backwardness of Islamic traditions but to the states' having abandoned God and his law. One Iranian thinker, Jalal Ali Ahmad (1923–69), called the problem "Westoxification." Especially since 1967 many have heeded the calls to return to a stricter or more faithful practice of Islam. The result has been a tremendous growth in what people in North America often called Islamic fundamentalism.

REVITALIZING ISLAM

It is important to stress that not all Muslims today are fundamentalists and not all Muslim fundamentalists are terrorists. Two features above all characterize Islamic fundamentalism. Muslim fundamentalists reject the values and forms of American and European society. At the same time, they make a self-conscious effort to live their lives according to what they see as God's dictates.

Islam has traditionally presented itself as a total way of life. To Muslims, this makes sense, because God is not confined to a box. As creator, he has ordained the proper way for his creatures to live in all spheres of life. Muslims call God's law SHARIAH.

One consequence of this view is that Western secularism—among other things the separation of church and state, religion and government—presents problems for many Muslims. (Many Christians in the United States think in a similar way; they insist that the United States should be a Christian nation.) For fundamentalist Muslims, a just state is one that obeys God's law. That is, it rules in accordance with Shariah. When they see the modern, secular West as threatening this rule, they react by struggling to protect it. That struggle is known in Arabic as JIHAD.

Despite the notion common in North America that *jihad* means "holy war," most fundamentalist Muslims do not see themselves as called upon to take up arms. Instead, they see themselves as called to observe the traditions of Islam and to encourage others to do so. They also feel called upon to improve society through charitable organizations. (Such compassion for others is a major feature of Islamic teachings.) They deplore governmental corruption and seek governments that are responsible in their use of money and treatment of people. Further, they oppose changes in values and lifestyles that they see as going against God's will. One area where they—and others as well—see these changes occurring is in sexuality and gender roles. Fundamentalist Muslims stress modesty for women, often symbolized by wearing a *hijab* or head-covering. In the late 1990s they worked together with the Roman Catholic Church in opposing some of the changes to traditional society favored by feminists (*see* FEMINISM).

ISLAMIC FUNDAMENTALISM IN ISLAMIC STATES

Since the 1970s Islamic fundamentalism has been growing at a tremendous rate in states where Muslims constitute the majority of the population. Two early events in particular provided inspiration. The first was the performance of the Egyptian military in the 1973 war with Israel. Anwar Sadat (1918–1981), the President of Egypt, had presented the war as a challenge for Islam; the results seemed to confirm that the future lay in returning to Islam. Then, in 1979, the people of Iran overthrew the Shah, whose Westernizing government had been increasingly corrupt. In actuality, Iranians with many different political and religious convictions, liberals as well as conservatives, brought about the revolution. The establishment of Iran as an Islamic republic, however, and the rise to dominance of the Ayatollah KHOMEINI left liberals frustrated and gave hope to Muslim fundamentalists worldwide.

By the end of the 20th century, many Islamic states had experienced the effects of Islamic fundamentalism. Since the 1920s Turkey had been the most secular state in the Islamic world, but by the end of the century a powerful political party, the Refah party, advocated a return to Islamic practices. In Egypt the Muslim Brotherhood found many supporters, as did the Jamaat-i-Islami in Pakistan. Islamic fundamentalism has been particularly strong among Western-educated professionals such as doctors and engineers, so in addition to stressing the observance of Islamic practices, these organizations have often been active in furthering health, education, and welfare. In addition, political leaders like Mu'ammar Gadhafi (b. 1942) of Libya (technically a socialist), Anwar Sadat of Egypt, Zia ul-Haq (1924–88) of Pakistan, and Jafar al-Numayri (b. 1930) of the Sudan attempted to attract support by appealing to Islam. Perhaps the most ruthless governmental attempt to implement Islamic policies was that of the Taliban in Afghanistan.

Some Muslim fundamentalists, the ones most familiar in the United States, have gone further. They have embraced violence, just as some Christian fundamentalists have. They see themselves as engaged in a war with Western powers, ZIONISM, and the governments of what they see as nominally Islamic states. Because these governments fail to observe Shariah in all spheres of life, they have lost legitimacy in the eyes of the extreme fundamentalists, who feel that such governments should be overthrown. An early example was the assassination of Anwar Sadat in 1981. He had become unpopular not only for backing the separation of religion and politics in 1979 but also for the dictatorial character of his rule.

It is important not to overlook the violence in which such groups engage. Well-known examples include the suicide bombings sponsored by HAMAS in Palestine, which is anti-Israeli but not anti-Western, and the attacks against the U.S. and its allies by AL-QAEDA. These groups derive part of their appeal by acting on deep frustrations that many Muslims feel. But groups like Hamas also derive their support from efforts that they share with more moderate Muslim fundamentalists: charitable work for the betterment of society and a stress, unlike some other Islamic governments and groups, on honesty and responsibility to the people they represent.

REDISCOVERING ISLAM OUTSIDE THE "HOUSE OF ISLAM"

A number of Muslims now live as sizable minorities in countries like France, Great Britain, and the United States. Islamic fundamentalism appeals to some of them, too.

Many Muslims living outside the "house of Islam" wrestle with questions of identity. What does it mean to be a Muslim for someone born in the United States, for example, where CHRISTIANITY and more specifically PROTESTANTISM has shaped so much of the public culture? For example, how can Muslims observe noon prayers on Friday, when Friday is a workday and they do not get enough time off? This question is particularly difficult when Muslims experience discrimination either from government policy, as in France, or from elements of the society at large, as in Great Britain.

Islamic fundamentalism provides an answer to questions of identity that is particularly satisfying because it is clear and addresses feelings of social inferiority: Muslims must hold themselves apart from the broader society, which has abandoned God, and follow God's ways. Some who teach Islamic fundamentalism in the West advocate returning to Islamic lands. Others wrestle with just how to implement that insight in lands where Muslims are in the minority.

WHAT WILL THE FUTURE BRING?

In matters of religion predictions of the future are notoriously unreliable. It is impossible to say with certainty what the ultimate fate of Islamic fundamentalism will be. At present, however, Islamic fundamentalism is a powerful force that affects not just Muslims but the entire world.

Further reading: Lawrence Davidson, *Islamic Fundamentalism: An Introduction,* rev. and updated ed. (Westport, Conn.: Greenwood Press, 2003); John L. Esposito, *Unholy War: Terror in the Name of Islam* (New York: Oxford University Press, 2002); Bruce B. Lawrence, *Shattering the Myth: Islam beyond Violence* (Princeton, N.J.: Princeton University Press, 1998); Bernard Lewis, *The Crisis of Islam: Holy War and Unholy Terror* (New York: Modern Library, 2003); Joseph E. B. Lumbard, ed., *Islam, Fundamentalism, and the Betrayal of Tradition: Essays by Western Muslim Scholars* (Bloomington, Ind.: World Wisdom, 2004).

G

games, play, and religion Kinds of human activity alternative to work. Often the serious tone assumed by much contemporary religion seems to be at odds with games and play. But religious rite and games come ultimately from similar sources in human culture: the need to "take a break" and express through symbol and experience the full panoply of what it means to be human. Religion may do this by showing that people are more than just working drones, but also have a divine or eternal meaning. So does play, when it shows that people are not meant just to work and contend with serious matters, but also to run, dance, throw balls or dice, find the excitement of competing and pretending, even get into altered states of consciousness by spinning and falling.

It would be natural for these two then to begin together, and so they probably did, in ancient religious rites that were also times for dancing, playing, feasting, even loving. There are still reminders of that origin. The Olympic games of ancient Greece began with religious SACRIFICES and had a quasi-religious character (*see* GREEK RELIGION). In Japan, sumo wrestling, tugs-of-war, horse-racing, and other competitions can be traced back to SHINTO rituals reflecting in NEW YEAR FESTIVALS competition between the old year and the new, or different factions of a community. Medieval tournaments began with a celebration of mass and were supposed to teach the values of chivalry.

Let us look in more detail at parallels of religious rite and a game, like a modern American football or baseball game. Both have definite boundaries and a time-frame—sacred space and time—within which certain rules are followed, and people wear certain costumes indicating their role. Each gives observers a chance to participate vicariously in the excitement, and to feel refreshed afterward.

Here are some further ways in which games and play parallel the way religion interprets the world, within that sacred space and time framework. These in part follow Roger Caillois's book, *Man, Play, and Games*. Competition in games is like an analogy of the battle of good and EVIL, GOD and SATAN, in the world. The combination of skill and chance, or divine GRACE or favor, required to be successful in many games is like the need for the same combination in real life, and so gives instruction in dealing with it. Games often entail simulation, or "acting out," as when children "dress up" or otherwise play games that mimic adult life; religion also tells us to identify with its SAINTS and heroes. Many athletes find that meditation or a state of clear awareness like that taught by ZEN BUDDHISM or the martial arts, living in the moment and acting spontaneously, gives them an edge. Finally, some kinds of play—spinning around, riding roller-coasters—induce a vertigo that psychologically can approach ecstasy or trance. Play and religion can learn much from each other.

Gandhi, Mohandas K. (1869–1948) *known as the Mahatma (Sanskrit, "great-souled"); leader of nonviolent resistance to British rule in colonial India and father of Indian independence*

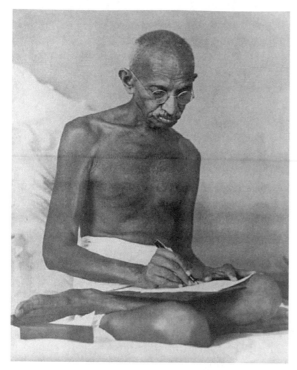

Mohandas Gandhi, seated and writing with a fountain
pen *(Library of Congress)*

LIFE

Gandhi was born on October 2, 1869, in the region
of Gujarat in western India into a family whose
members had held high-ranking government posts.
He also claimed to have been heavily influenced
by the profound piety of his mother.

In order to study law, Gandhi went to England
in 1888, after vowing to his mother to avoid eating meat, drinking alcohol, and engaging in sexual
relations with English women. He kept these three
vows, but in other respects he tried very hard to
assimilate to British ways. The most visible sign
was his European dress.

In 1893, Gandhi was sent by his law firm in
India to South Africa on a case. There he experienced the severity of restrictions imposed on Indians as on other non-European peoples. In one well-
known incident, he was thrown off a train when he
insisted on traveling in a first-class compartment

because he had bought a first-class ticket. Gandhi
remained in South Africa until 1914. During his
stay he developed his fundamental notions of nonviolent resistance, experimented with communal
living and diet, and took a vow of *brahmacarya*
(sexual celibacy).

After he returned to India, Gandhi eventually
joined the Indian National Congress, a group agitating for India's liberation from British rule. He
became the acknowledged spiritual leader of the
movement, revered as the "Mahatma" and loved as
"Bapu" (father). Because Gandhi's tactics involved
the public violation of laws, he spent much time
in jail.

India finally gained its independence in 1947
but at a severe price: British India was divided
into two countries, India and Pakistan, despite
Gandhi's vigorous opposition, and much violence
erupted between Hindu and Muslim communities.
On January 30, 1948, Gandhi was assassinated by
a member of a Hindu group that felt he had been
too accommodating to Muslims.

TEACHINGS

Gandhi's campaign against the British took many
forms, such as the insistence on buying Indian
goods and the spinning of one's own cloth by hand.
Gandhi also advocated Hindu-Muslim amity and
the elimination of religiously rooted distinctions
of caste, especially restrictions on the so-called
untouchables, whom Gandhi called Harijans, or
"children of GOD."

Underlying all of Gandhi's actions, however,
was a profound religious vision. Gandhi thought
of his goal not in the narrow terms of political
independence but in the broader terms of self-
rule. Because self-rule was necessary before one
deserved political independence, Gandhi urged his
followers to train their senses and desires through
fasting and *brahmacarya* or sexual abstinence.

In keeping with this emphasis, Gandhi rejected
"body force" (violence) in favor of *satyagraha* (the
force of truth). His basic tactics were to identify
the injustice in a law, publicly refuse to obey it,
and suffer the consequences. Gandhi felt that in
this manner the injustice of the law would eventu-

ally be apparent to everyone, including those who promulgated it.

Gandhi's method of nonviolence ultimately rested on his confidence in God not as a person but as a force, which he especially liked to call not Love but Truth. In 1925 he wrote of this force "I do dimly perceive that whilst everything around me is ever-changing, ever-dying, there is underlying all that change a Living Power that is changeless, that holds all together, that creates, dissolves, and re-creates. . . . I see it as purely benevolent. For I can see that in the midst of death life persists, in the midst of untruth truth persists, in the midst of darkness light persists. Hence I gather that God is Life, Truth, Light. He is Love. He is the Supreme God."

SIGNIFICANCE

In addition to profoundly shaping 20th-century India, Gandhi's vision of nonviolence influenced leaders outside India, too. The best-known example may be the American civil rights leader, Martin Luther KING, Jr.

Further reading: Louis Fischer, ed., *The Essential Gandhi* 2d ed. (New York: Vintage, 2002); Mohandas K. Gandhi, *An Autobiography: The Story of My Experiments with the Truth* (Boston: Beacon, 1966); Raghavan Iyer, *The Moral and Political Thought of Mahatma Gandhi* (New York: Oxford University Press, 1973); Stanley Wolpert, *Gandhi's Passion: The Life and Legacy of Mahatma Gandhi* (New York: Oxford University Press, 2001).

Ganesa Also called Ganapati; a popular Hindu (*see* HINDUISM) god easily recognizable from his elephant's head, broken tusk, and pot belly. He is also associated with the mouse.

Ganesa is said to be the son of the god SIVA or, rather, of Siva's consort PARVATI. One story about how Ganesa got his head tells that one day Siva came home after a long period of meditation alone. His way was barred by a son born in his absence, whom he did not recognize. In frustration, Siva decapitated the child. The mother was naturally

A statue of the elephant-headed Hindu god Ganesa *(Getty Images)*

upset, and Siva promised to make amends by giving the child the first head he saw. That happened to be the head of an elephant.

Ganesa is revered as the remover of obstacles and lord of beginnings. Accordingly, he is invoked at the beginning of most ceremonial and important occasions. Hindus who do not engage in the sectarian WORSHIP of a single god often worship five gods as a manifestation of the supreme. Ganesa is one of them.

Ganges River The most sacred river in India. It flows through the plains of north India from the Himalaya Mountains in the west to the Bay of

Bengal in the east. Hindus WORSHIP it as the GODDESS Ganga (*see* HINDUISM).

According to well-known myths, the Earth was polluted and needed Ganga's waters to be made pure. But Ganga was reluctant to drop from HEAVEN. So the god SIVA agreed to break her fall. In the mountains, where Siva meditates, Ganga drops onto his head, flows down his body, and spills onto the Earth.

The Ganges is a powerful religious force. Worshippers make offerings to it. Typical offerings include milk and flowers. Worshippers also bathe in its purifying waters. Because the Ganges purifies, Indians cremate corpses on its banks and dispose of the ashes in the river.

Today several sites along the Ganges are particularly auspicious as places of PILGRIMAGE: Hardwar where the river meets the plain; Allahabad or Prayag where the Ganges, the Yamuna, and the mythical river Saraswati flow together; and above all the holy city of BANARAS (Varanasi).

Genesis The first book of the BIBLE. Genesis, meaning "origin" or "birth," is the Greek name for the book. The Hebrew name is *Bereshith,* "in [the] beginning," which is the book's first word. Genesis contains some of the best-known stories in the entire Bible.

CONTENT

Genesis has two parts. The first part, chapters 1 through 11, deals with universal prehistory or mythology. It contains stories and genealogies that purport to relate to all people. The second part, chapters 12 through 50, contains prehistory or mythology that relates specifically to the children of Israel.

The first part opens with a famous story of creation: a hymn celebrating the creation of the world by GOD in seven days. A second story tells of the creation of ADAM, the animals, and EVE, all of whom lived in the Garden of Eden. This story leads directly into the story of the first SIN. Eve and Adam violated God's command by eating fruit from the tree of the knowledge of good and evil. As

a result, God expelled them from the garden and cursed them (*see* FALL, THE). Other famous stories in this part of Genesis include the FLOOD, which only NOAH and his family survived, and the Tower of BABEL. At Babel God created confusion among people by creating different languages.

The second part of Genesis tells the story of four generations of the same family: ABRAHAM and SARAH, ISAAC and REBEKAH, and JACOB (also known as Israel) and his wives and sons. Abraham's family originally lived in the city of Ur, now in southern Iraq. He migrated to Canaan, now Israel and Palestine. There he had two sons: Ishmael, who is the ancestor of the Arabs, and Isaac, the ancestor of the Jews. The Bible emphasizes Abraham's trust in God's promise that he would have a son by his wife Sarah, even though both were very old. It also tells of a sign of the special relationship between Abraham and God: CIRCUMCISION. Other well-known stories from this part of Genesis include God's command to Abraham to sacrifice Isaac, the destruction of Sodom and Gomorrah, Jacob's dream at Bethel ("Jacob's ladder"), and the saga of JOSEPH. Joseph's brothers were jealous of the special attention that Jacob gave Joseph, so they sold him into slavery. But Joseph became a high official in Egypt and saved his family from starvation.

COMPOSITION

Tradition says that MOSES wrote the first five books of the Bible, including Genesis. Modern scholars tend to disagree. In the last 200 years they have discovered and learned to read ancient writings from Egypt and the Middle East. Some of these writings resemble Genesis, but they are older. For example, the story of Atrahasis from Iraq tells about the flood, which Atrahasis survived with the help of the god Enki. The Egyptian Tale of Two Brothers is much like the story of Joseph and Potiphar's wife. At times, then, the writers of Genesis seem to have used well-known traditional stories in their book.

Furthermore, Genesis seems to have been assembled from several writings. Scholars have tentatively identified three sets of these writings. They call one account J, because it always refers to God as YHWH ("the Lord"; sometimes written

JHVH). Another account they call E, because it refers to God as Elohim ("God"). A third account, P for Priestly, seems to contain material that would interest priests, like the hymn of creation in Genesis 1. Scholars have suggested that J comes from the southern kingdom of Judah after SOLOMON, E from the northern kingdom of Israel after Solomon, and P from the exile in Babylon. Genesis itself, they suggest, was written either during that exile (587–538 B.C.E.) or shortly afterward. These are only suggestions based on the evidence that is currently available.

GENESIS AND HISTORY

Traditionally Jews, Christians, and Muslims have taken the stories in Genesis to be literally true. Most people know that there are disputes about the stories of creation and the Flood. But in fact, there is no evidence that any of the events recorded in Genesis actually occurred. The most that can be said is that the second part of the book mentions real places. It also presents Abraham, Sarah and their descendants as living the kind of life people lived in Canaan in the period 1800–1600 B.C.E.

Ghost Dance Religious movements among indigenous Americans in the last third of the 19th century (see NATIVE AMERICAN RELIGION). There were two ghost dance movements. The first occurred around 1870, the second around 1890. Wodziwob, an indigenous American who lived on Walker Lake Reservation, Nevada, led the first movement. Wovoka, a farmhand in Mason Valley, Nevada, led the second. His father had been a follower of Wodziwob.

Both movements shared the same basic ideas and practices. Each man had a VISION. He foresaw the RESURRECTION of the dead, the return of the animals, and the restoration of the traditional way of life. Wodziwob expected whites to disappear; Wovoka expected indigenous peoples and white settlers to live in peace. To bring about this new era, men and women were to perform a certain dance on several successive nights (see DANCE AND RELIGION). The dance was said to be the dance of the ancestors—or GHOSTS—in HEAVEN.

Lakota (or Sioux) people changed the Ghost Dance. They expected victory over whites. They also expected special shirts to make them invincible. The Lakota dance made the American government nervous. The Wounded Knee massacre (1890) was the result. AIM (the American Indian Movement) revived the ghost dance in the 1970s.

ghosts Shades or remnants of the departed, which take visible form and appear to living human beings. Sometimes ghosts come to bear messages, sometimes to haunt the grave or places familiar to the deceased. Usually though not always they are regarded with fear and apprehension; benign visitors from the world of the dead are more often referred to as spirits. Belief in ghosts is perhaps not a major focus of most religions, but it is related to beliefs about the AFTERLIFE, telling us that the dead can live on in another form and can still have relationships with the living and life on Earth.

Gilgamesh A legendary king of Uruk in ancient Mesopotamia. Gilgamesh may have lived in the mid-2600s B.C.E. Later the ancient Mesopotamians worshipped him as a god of the dead (see MESOPOTAMIAN RELIGIONS). But he is best known as the subject of an ancient EPIC. The best version of the epic is from tablets that date from the 600s B.C.E. By that time the story had been in circulation for a thousand years.

As we know it, the epic explores the inevitability of death. Gilgamesh is building the walls of Uruk when Enkidu, a powerful but wild creature appears. At first he sees Enkidu as a rival, but they become fast friends. Together they kill Humbaba, who guards a cedar forest. Then Enkidu is sentenced to die. Distraught, Gilgamesh tries to escape death himself. He journeys to see Utnapishtim, the immortal who survived the FLOOD. Utnapishtim shows Gilgamesh that he cannot even escape sleep. He does, however, teach him about a plant of immortality. Through valiant effort Gilgamesh obtains the plant, only to lose it to a serpent in a moment of carelessness. Resigned to his ultimate fate, Gilgamesh returns to building the city walls.

Gnosticism A religious trend in the ancient Mediterranean world that emphasized knowledge as the means by which people are saved. The name comes from the Greek word for knowledge, *gnosis*. The people who follow this trend are called "Gnostics."

Gnosticism has been viewed as a uniquely Christian heresy. But the movement actually extends beyond CHRISTIANITY. It is also often independent of Christianity. Therefore many in the 20th century considered Gnosticism a religion in itself. In important ways, however, Gnosticism is not a single religion but a trend in thought. In that way it resembles FEMINISM in the late 20th century. There have been feminist movements within many religions. Some feminists have also cultivated an independent GODDESS worship because they have found traditional religions unsatisfying. Similarly, there have been Jewish, Christian, and Islamic Gnostics as well as independent gnostic religions, for example, MANICHAEISM and Mandaeism.

HISTORY

Scholars do not agree on where or how Gnosticism began. Some have argued that it was inspired by Persian myths, for example, the myth of the savior who must first save himself. Others have suggested that Gnosticism grew from Jewish and Greek roots.

Some of the earliest Christians found Gnosticism attractive. According to many scholars, the people against whom PAUL argued in his NEW TESTAMENT letters included Gnostics. In the second century C.E. important teachers of Gnosticism emerged within the context of Christianity: Marcion, Basilides, and Valentinus. The ancestors of the Orthodox and Catholic churches rejected them.

In the late third century Christians began to settle in the desert of Egypt as MONKS AND NUNS. Gnostics found that environment attractive, too, perhaps because there they could avoid attacks from Christians. In the fourth century monks living near Nag Hammadi, Egypt, made copies of important Gnostic writings. These writings, called the Nag Hammadi Codices, were discovered in 1945. They are the most important source for the knowledge of Gnosticism today.

Also in the third century the Persian prophet Mani claimed to make perfect the revelations that had been given to ZARATHUSTRA, the BUDDHA, and JESUS. His preaching began the religion of Manichaeism. Many consider Manichaeism to be the Gnostic world religion. At one time it stretched from the Atlantic coast of Spain and Morocco to the Pacific coast of China.

In the late fourth century C.E. Christianity became the official religion of the Roman Empire. Gnosticism became illegal, and the government and the church sought to eradicate it. Nevertheless, throughout European history various movements seem to have revived Gnosticism. Examples are the Cathari and the Bogomils in the Middle Ages. In Asia Gnosticism survived much longer.

Some Gnostic groups still exist today. The best known are the Mandaeans. They live in southeastern Iraq and southwestern Iran. Mandaean priests baptize their followers weekly (*see* BAPTISM). They claim this practice derives from their founder, John the Baptist. The Mandaeans have also preserved sacred scriptures and teachings that have Gnostic characteristics.

IDEAS

The name Gnosticism presupposes a teaching in which people are saved by knowledge. But the knowledge that saves is not the knowledge one can get from studying, say, physics or chemistry. The saving knowledge is knowledge of the hidden truths about the universe and human beings and their relations to the highest GOD. This knowledge, like God itself, is inaccessible to ordinary human experience. In most Gnostic systems it is revealed by an emissary from the otherwise unknown God. For Christian Gnostics that emissary is Jesus.

Gnostic knowledge tends to be esoteric knowledge. That is, it is secret knowledge revealed only to the initiated (*see* INITIATION, RELIGIOUS). There was never any centralized authority in Gnosticism, and unlike Christians Gnostics did not meet in council to determine which teachings were acceptable and which were not. As a result, Gnostic teachings vary considerably. Two general topics, however, recur: the origins of the world and human beings, and the progress of SALVATION.

Most Gnostic teachings on the origins of the world and human beings were dualistic. Such teachings say that the world and its inhabitants arose from the mixing of two opposed principles: light-goodness and darkness-EVIL. The *Apocryphon of John,* found in the Nag Hammadi Codices, provides a good example. According to it, the unknown God and his spouse gave rise to the spiritual world. One of his creations, Sophia ("wisdom"), produced a monstrous demiurge who created the material world. Identified with the god of the Jews, this demiurge claimed that he alone was god. Human beings result from a mingling of the spirit of the unknown God with material reality.

Gnostics tend to conceive of human beings, then, as composite beings who combine elements of light and goodness with elements of darkness and evil. They generally conceive of salvation as the separation of the elements of light and goodness and their return to their original home, the realm of the unknown God. Some Gnostic writings detail the ascent of the soul through the various planetary spheres back to its original home. Indeed, some writings provide elaborate spells that the adepts should use as they make their way from one sphere to the next.

SIGNIFICANCE

Gnosticism is responsible for many features of Christianity. These features developed as the ancestors of the Orthodox and Catholic churches tried to refute Gnosticism. For example, many Gnostics favored a view of Jesus as a divine messenger who only appeared to be human. Orthodox and Catholic Christians insisted that Jesus was in fact human. The Gnostic Marcion rejected the Hebrew BIBLE and accepted a new scripture made up of Luke's gospel and Paul's letters. In response other Christians insisted that the Hebrew Bible—the "Old Testament"—was still valid; they also began to form their own "New Testament."

On a more positive note, Gnosticism influenced important elements of European culture during the 19th and 20th centuries. The Gnostic view of the world appears, for example, in the poetry of the greatest German writer, Johann Wolfgang von Goethe (1749–1832). The movement known as THEOSOPHY sees itself as continuing the ancient Gnostic teachings. Gnosticism also fascinated Carl Gustav JUNG, one of the founders of modern psychology.

Further reading: Stephan Hoeller, *Gnosticism* (Wheaton, Ill.: Quest Books, 2002); Hans Jonas, *The Gnostic Religion,* 2nd ed. (Boston: Beacon Press, 1963); Elaine Pagels, *The Gnostic Gospels* (New York: Random House, 1979); James M. Robinson, ed., *The Nag Hammadi Library* (San Francisco: Harper & Row, 1977).

Gobind Singh (1666–1708) *the tenth and last of the Sikh gurus (religious teachers)* In 1675 the Mughal ruler of India, Aurangzeb, a staunch Muslim, executed the ninth guru of the Sikhs, Tegh Bahadur (*see* SIKHISM). That guru's son, Gobind Singh, became the tenth guru.

Gobind Singh was particularly adept as a warrior. On April 13, 1699, he institutionalized the warrior ideal by founding the Sikh community known as the Khalsa. He called all Sikhs to assemble, then asked for five men to volunteer to be sacrificed. One at a time he took them behind his tent. Each time he came back with a bloody sword. Then he revealed that the blood was from sacrificed goats. Gobind Singh initiated the men by having them drink a sweet liquid stirred with a double-edged sword. Then he gave them the surname Singh and enjoined them to observe several regulations. These included the "five k's," five objects that all Khalsa Sikhs are to wear: uncut hair (*kes*), a comb kept under a turban (*kangha*), a sword or dagger (*kirpan*), a steel bangle on the right wrist (*kara*), and shorts (*kacch*).

Two of Gobind Singh's sons were killed in battle; the other two were executed. Before Gobind

Singh died, he gave instructions that he would be the last human guru. From that time on, the Sikhs have recognized a collection of the writings of earlier gurus and other poets as guru. It is called ADI GRANTH or, more reverently, *Guru Granth Sahib.*

God The supreme object of WORSHIP. Out of respect, some Jews write "G-d" instead of "God." They see this spelling as a way to avoid using God's name.

Monotheists believe that there is only a single God (*see* MONOTHEISM). Polytheists worship many gods (*see* POLYTHEISM). But many polytheists also speak of God. They may think of God as the highest god, or they may see all particular gods as manifestations of the supreme God.

WHAT DOES "GOD" MEAN?

Probably no definition of the word "God" is completely satisfactory. Some people characterize God as supernatural. But others, such as Baruch Spinoza, have identified God with nature. Some people characterize God as superhuman. But others see a human being as God; for example, some Christians see JESUS as the only God. The medieval philosopher ANSELM defined God as "that than which nothing greater can be conceived." But if one is examining a variety of beliefs in God, as we are here, Anselm's definition will not work. The definition given above—God is the supreme object of worship—has its limitations, too. Some people, such as the ancient Epicureans, have believed in a supreme God but have considered that God too remote to be concerned about human beings or interested in their worship.

HOW DO PEOPLE TALK ABOUT GOD?

Religious people talk about God in several ways. Most people talk about God mythologically. That is, they tell stories that treat God as a human-like being. Hindus have many stories about God in the forms of SIVA, VISHNU, KRISHNA, RAMA, and the GODDESS. Jews, Christians, and Muslims share stories about how God created the world, almost destroyed it with a universal FLOOD, and redeemed the people

of Israel from slavery in Egypt (*see* EXODUS). Many people envision God as well as talk about God. They worship God in the form of sacred images. For example, Hindus have many elaborate images through which they approach God.

Some people talk about God philosophically. Among other topics, they try to determine just what can be said about God. Some insist that one can talk about God only using negative terms. For example, the statement "God is infinite" says that God is not subject to ordinary limitations. Others speak of God positively, for example, "God is love." Most qualify that statement: God's love is very much more profound than human love. In the 20th century, some philosophers and theologians were interested in symbols as ways of talking about God.

Yet another group of religious people insist that it is not possible to talk about God at all. These are mystics (*see* MYSTICISM). Some mystics claim that God is so unlike anything in ordinary existence that God is beyond all speech and thought. All human beings can do is experience God in silence.

WHAT IS GOD LIKE?

Just as many religious people find meaning in stories about God, so many religious people tend to think of God in personal terms. Indeed, some insist that people can worship only a personal God. During the 20th century, many North Americans questioned the traditional Jewish and Christian images of a personal God. In their eyes, these ideas were too European and too male to be attractive to all human beings (*see* FEMINISM).

Philosophers and theologians have tended to describe God in terms of more abstract "attributes" or characteristics. Many Jews, Christians, and Muslims have said that God is one, eternal, unchanging, all-powerful, all-knowing, present throughout the universe, and beneficent. During the 20th century philosophers and theologians questioned many of these attributes: "Process theologians" suggested that God was always changing and developing. Dietrich Bonhoeffer, a Christian victim of the HOLOCAUST, taught that God suffers, too.

In addition to identifying the attributes of God, philosophers and theologians have tried to identify how God relates to the universe. On one extreme is God's transcendence: God is totally other. On the other is God's immanence: God is in the world (panentheism) or identical with it (pantheism).

Finally, some religions have adopted specific doctrines about God. Examples include the Christian ideas of the TRINITY and INCARNATION.

WHAT DOES GOD DO?

Some Hindus say that God creates the world, preserves it, and destroys it. God does these things in the form of three gods: BRAHMA, Vishnu, and Siva. Traditional Christians say that God both creates the universe and redeems fallen humanity. Gnostics deny that God created the world. For them, God simply redeems the particles of light that creation dispersed among particles of darkness. In the 20th century, some philosophers and theologians suggested that God was not active at the beginning but will be at the end of the world. That is, God is the supreme good to which all the universe is tending.

HOW COULD GOD . . .?

Jews, Christians, and Muslims have puzzled over two questions about God for centuries. The first question sets God's omniscience—his knowledge of everything—against the ability of human beings to act freely (see FREE WILL AND DETERMINISM). The question runs: If God knows everything, then God knows what I am going to do in the future; in that case, how can I act of my own free will? Many thinkers have proposed subtle answers to this question. Others simply assert that God knows everything, and that human beings act freely. They do not try to resolve the paradox.

A second question sets God's omnipotence—his ability to do everything—against God's goodness (see THEODICY). If God is both omnipotent and good, why do evil and bad things happen, especially to the good? Why does God allow some babies to be born without brains? Why does God allow people to torture and execute each other by the millions? To answer the second question, some appeal to "free will." In order for human beings to be fully human, God had to create people who could freely choose both good and evil. Others simply admit that there is no good answer to these questions.

DOES GOD EXIST?

In ancient Greece the philosopher Xenophanes noted that people made the gods in their own image. He noted: "if oxen and horses . . . had hands, . . . horses would paint the forms of the gods like horses, and oxen like oxen" (fragment 15). In the time since Xenophanes, many philosophers and theologians have tried to prove that God exists (see GOD, THE EXISTENCE OF).

In the 19th and 20th centuries, some prominent thinkers disagreed. The philosopher Ludwig Feuerbach said that God was simply a projection of what humans valued most. Karl MARX, Émile DURKHEIM, and Sigmund FREUD expressed similar ideas. Charles Darwin's theory of evolution caused many to doubt God's creative activity (see EVOLUTION AND RELIGION). The philosopher Friedrich Nietzsche celebrated "the death of God."

Nevertheless, at the end of the 20th century an overwhelming majority of North Americans still believed in God.

Further reading: Karen Armstrong, *A History of God* (New York: Knopf, 1993); John Bowker, *God: A Brief History* (New York: DK Publishing, 2002); Jean Daniélou, *God and the Ways of Knowing* (Cleveland: World, 1960); Richard H. Niebuhr, *Radical Monotheism and Western Culture* (New York: Harper, 1960).

God, the existence of A standard topic in the philosophy of religion. Because God does not appear to our human senses the way a chair or a desk or even these words do, how do we know God exists?

CLASSICAL ARGUMENTS FOR THE EXISTENCE OF GOD

Philosophers and theologians have proposed many arguments to prove that God exists. Perhaps the four most important are known in technical terms as the ontological, the cosmological, the teleological, and the moral arguments. The names may seem obscure, but the ideas are often more familiar.

If God Is God, God Must Exist

A medieval philosopher named ANSELM (*c.* 1033–1109) proposed the ontological argument. He argued that only a person who does not really understand what the word God means can ask whether God exists.

According to Anselm, the word *God* means "the greatest being that we can conceive of." If we conceived of something greater than God, that something would in fact be God. Our original idea of what was God would have been a mistake.

But, Anselm asked, what is greater, a God that we only imagine, or a God who actually exists? His answer was, clearly, a God who actually exists. As a result, it would be wrong to say that God only exists in people's imaginations. We can easily conceive of a being who is greater than that God, namely, a God who actually exists. Therefore, Anselm said, God must exist.

It All Had to Start Somewhere

Anselm's argument appeals to some people. But many people, even those who believe in God, suspect that it involves a verbal trick.

A second argument for the existence of God is the cosmological argument. In effect, this argument insists, "it all had to start somewhere." This argument reminds us that things in the world are caused and have limits. But, the argument goes, for something to be caused and have limits, there must be something uncaused and unlimited, in other words, God.

In technical terms, this argument depends on the idea that an "infinite regress" is impossible. Consider yourself as a person. Your parents caused you to come into existence. Your grandparents caused them to come into existence. The line extends far back. But can it extend back—regress—forever? On one line of thinking, such an infinite regress is impossible. Without a first set of parents,

the entire series of generations would never have begun in the first place.

That is certainly true when applied to human life, or better, to life on earth. According to the cosmological argument, the same principle applies to the whole universe. For the universe to exist there must at some point have been a first, uncaused cause, in other words, God.

How Can a Watch Exist without a Watchmaker?

A third argument, the teleological argument, points out that nature is not a chaos. It has its own rules, orders, patterns, and designs. But, this argument goes, order and design exist only as the result of planning and intelligence. Could a watch exist if there were no watchmaker? Indeed, the more complex an order is, the greater the intelligence that is required to create it. It requires more mental effort to make a digital-display watch that also keeps track of the date, times laps, and sounds alarms at selected times than it does to make a sundial.

But if order requires intelligence and complex order requires higher intelligence, what about the order and design of the entire universe? Everyone admits that they are larger and more complex than any order and design produced by human beings. The teleological argument says that such magnificent order shows that the highest intelligence was at work. In other words, the order of nature proves the existence of God.

In the late 1990s and early 2000s, some people developed a version of this argument called "Intelligent Design." They argued that evolutionary theory could not explain the origins of complex organic structures like the eye. Therefore, they reasoned, modern biology itself pointed to the existence of God.

God Must Exist for People to Be Moral

The German philosopher Immanuel Kant (1724–1804) tried a different approach to proving that God existed. He did not start by reflecting on the nature of the universe at large. Instead, he said that God had to exist if people were to be moral. The argument is subtle, but many people have followed his lead.

Consider, for example, the requirement "Do not murder." What authority stands behind such a requirement? Certainly it is not simply consensus among human beings. Even if every other human being in our community agreed that murder was acceptable, we would want to say that murder is wrong. Indeed, the Reverend Martin Luther King Jr. made just such a claim when he appealed to a higher law and disobeyed discriminatory laws.

According to the moral argument, this common moral experience shows that God exists. That is because God alone is capable of making moral requirements valid, despite what individual human beings think and say. If God did not exist, what is right would simply be a matter of individual opinion and whim. This chaotic situation is envisioned in Fyodor Dostoyevsky's novel *The Brothers Karamazov* (1879–80). In that novel, one character commits suicide to prove that God does not exist.

OTHER APPROACHES TO THE EXISTENCE OF GOD

The classical arguments try to use logical reasoning to show that God exists. Thinkers have taken other approaches in considering God's existence, too. Like the classical theologians, they conclude that God exists, but they arrive at the conclusion in different ways.

God's Existence Is a Good Bet

The European philosopher Blaise Pascal (1623–62) adopted a practical attitude to the question of God's existence. In effect, he asked, What are the costs and benefits of believing or not believing in God?

Pascal reasoned that if we believe that God exists and are wrong, it costs us relatively little. By contrast, if we do not believe that God exists and are wrong, we might suffer a great deal. Therefore, Pascal said, the best bet is to believe that God exists.

Others, like the Danish philosopher Soren Kierkegaard (1813–55), go a bit further. Kierkegaard says that faith in God is something that religious people have despite all rational proof. To have genuine faith, people need to take a "leap of faith." Belief in God that results from arguments or balancing costs and benefits is not the kind of faith God wants.

The Experience of God

A different approach appeals to experience. People believe things in the world exist because they experience them. According to one approach, people believe God exists because they experience God, too.

One person who developed this argument was the Christian philosopher Rudolf OTTO (1869–1937). He described the experience of God as the experience of a *mysterium tremendum et fascinans*—a profound mystery that was terrifying and overwhelming but also comforting and appealing.

Otto agreed that our experiential knowledge was not quite like our knowledge of a chair or a desk. It was, he said, not certain knowledge but a hunch. (The German word that he used can also be translated as "feeling.") But, Otto pointed out, hunches play a larger role in our thinking than many people are willing to admit.

What God Really Is

Others suggest that the classical arguments misunderstand God and so try to prove the existence of what God really is not. A good example of this position is process theology.

Process theology sees reality as made up not of things or substances but of processes and relations. When process theologians apply these views to God, they may call into question such views as that God is eternal and unchanging and that he is the first source of all that is. For example, an early process theologian, Henry Nelson Weiman (1884–1975), suggested that God is not an eternal, unchanging, omnipotent person but "the source of human good."

Process theology has been particularly important for people interested in questions of THEODICY. But process theology may also be helpful in dealing with the existence of God. Most people, for example, think that there is some source of human good, even if they cannot describe it very well.

Possible Worlds and Modal Logic

In the 20th century philosophers began to use a kind of logic known as "modal logic." This kind of logic talks not about what is but about what might be. For example, talking about possible worlds helps clarify some philosophical issues. These worlds may not be the world we live in, but they are worlds that we can imagine consistently, worlds that make sense.

The American Protestant philosopher Alvin Plantinga (b. 1932) has used this kind of logic to develop a version of the ontological argument. Like many arguments in philosophy, his argument is subtle, and it requires more knowledge of modal logic than most readers will possess, but roughly it goes like this. It is possible for a world to exist in which there is a being who is maximally great. But what does it mean to be maximally great? A maximally great being would be one that existed in all possible worlds, including our own. For such a being to exist in a possible world, it must exist in all possible worlds, including our own.

Many philosophers doubt that this argument actually demonstrates that God exists, and Plantinga himself is willing to grant that. But what he does claim is that the argument shows that it is rational to hold that God exists. Many philosophers also disagree that this conclusion follows from Plantinga's argument.

OBJECTIONS TO THE ARGUMENTS

European Christians have not been the only people to use these arguments that God exists. For example, a school of Indian philosophy that specializes in logic, known as the Nyaya school, developed all of the classical arguments except the ontological one. But not everyone has found these arguments satisfactory. Some have argued against one argument in making a case for another. For example, the Catholic thinker Thomas AQUINAS (1224–74) argued against the ontological argument in proposing the cosmological one.

Most people make the same objection to the ontological argument. They say that we cannot deduce that something exists simply from the definition of a word. We can only demonstrate that something exists by arguing from what we perceive with our senses. People who object to the cosmological and teleological arguments generally use one of two counterarguments. One counterargument claims that there are other, better ways to explain the characteristics of the universe, such as the theory of biological evolution. These people may view intelligent design the way they view a chemist who attributes the result of an experiment she or he cannot explain to an act of God; it is better simply to say that we do not yet know the cause. The other counterargument says that the cosmological and teleological arguments do not go far enough. They prove that the foundations of the universe exist, or perhaps that what Hindus call BRAHMAN exists, but they beg the question about whether we should call those foundations God. One problem with the moral argument is that it requires a view of morality that was not popular with North American thinkers in the last half of the 20th century.

People may also object to the other approaches mentioned above. For some, the probability of God's existence may be so small that they see little real benefit in believing in God. Some may equate Otto's hunch with hunches about spirits and spooks, making it much less compelling. For some, the God of process theology may not be what they mean by God at all; others may object that process theologians should stop talking about God and just talk about the world instead. Some people who accept the notion that knowledge has foundations take a narrower view of those foundations. Their view denies that God's existence is really a foundational proposition. Other people, known as "antifoundationalists," reject the notion that there are foundational propositions altogether.

SUMMARY

Philosophers and theologians have not come to any agreement about whether it is possible to prove that God exists. Many reject the attempt as misguided. Others continue to develop and revise arguments for the existence of God.

Further reading: John H. Hick, *Philosophy of Religion,* Foundations of Philosophy series (Englewood Cliffs, N.J.: Prentice Hall, 1990); Gary E. Kessler, *Philosophy of Religion: Toward a Global Perspective* (Belmont, Calif.: Wadsworth, 1999); Thomas Woodward, *Doubts about Darwin: A History of Intelligent Design* (Grand Rapids, Mich.: Baker Books, 2003); Matt Young and Taner Edis, eds., *Why Intelligent Design Fails: A Scientific Critique of the New Creationism* (New Brunswick, N.J.: Rutgers University Press, 2004).

goddesses Female deities. The Goddess, capitalized and singular, refers to the supreme deity envisioned in feminine form. Goddesses have played major roles in most religions.

ONE GODDESS OR MANY?

At the end of the 20th century some North Americans spoke of a single Goddess. For them, the names and myths associated with specific goddesses were simply manifestations of this Goddess.

The image of the Goddess often includes other ideas. One is the notion of a "primitive matriarchy." In 1861 a Swiss lawyer, J. J. Bachofen, speculated that at the beginning of history women rather than men had ruled. This matriarchy was a time of peace and justice. Religion centered on the WORSHIP of a goddess. Others have suggested that Goddess worship began at a specific time: when human beings shifted from hunting, gathering, and herding to a way of life based on agriculture.

Other ideas concern the Goddess's character. In the first half of the 20th century a Swiss psychologist, Carl Gustav JUNG, developed influential ideas about religious symbols. Jung suggested that religious symbols expressed ARCHETYPES, unconscious patterns that all human beings shared. Inspired by Jung, several writers developed an image of the Goddess. They connected her with the fertility of the Earth. They also connected her with the moon. Its phases were said to parallel a woman's menstrual periods. Influential popular writers, such as Joseph Campbell and Starhawk, advocated these ideas. Many serious scholars, including feminists, rejected them. Scholars often prefer to talk about individual goddesses rather than the Goddess.

Some goddesses are associated with the Earth and fertility, but not all. In Egypt the Earth was a god, Geb, the sky was a goddess, Nut. The Greek goddess ATHENA was a warrior and perpetual virgin. Similarly, some goddesses are connected with the moon and its phases. But others are connected with the sun. A prime example is the SHINTO *kami*, AMATERASU. Her brother, Tsukiyomi, is the moon. In the ancient Near East, too, the moon was often male, for example, Khonsu in Egypt, Nanna or Sin in Mesopotamia (*see* MESOPOTAMIAN RELIGIONS). The most important Near Eastern goddess was the planet Venus. She went by many names: INANNA, Ishtar, Astarte. The goddess ISIS was extremely important during the Roman Empire. She was Sirius, the brightest star in the sky.

Goddesses have also had many personalities. Some have been nurturing and maternal. A good example is the Virgin MARY. Christians do not worship her as a goddess, but Roman Catholic and Orthodox Christians venerate her (*see* ROMAN CATHOLICISM; EASTERN ORTHODOX CHRISTIANITY). Other goddesses have been horrific. For example, the Hindu goddess Kali sits on corpses, wears parts of human bodies, and always demands blood sacrifice. Until the middle 1800s some Kali cults demanded human sacrifice. But the same goddess may combine the nurturing and the horrific. Thus, Kali is also venerated as a mother who provides release from grasping and SAMSARA (*see* HINDUISM).

Finally, goddesses have related to gods in a variety of ways. They have often occupied subordinate positions, sometimes as wives and consorts. That does not necessarily deprive them of independence. In Greek mythology, ZEUS may be the most powerful, but Hera's will is often done. Independent goddesses, too, may be important without being supreme. Influential goddesses in India today include the river GANGES, whose waters purify, and Bharat Mata, "Mother India" herself.

GODDESSES IN HISTORY

Most scholars trace the worship of goddesses back to the Paleolithic period. This is the oldest period of human life. It ends around 10,000 B.P. (before the present). Paleolithic remains include large numbers of female statues. The oldest date to 30,000 or even 40,000 B.P. The statues come in many shapes, fat and thin, realistic and stylized. Scholars still debate what the images meant and how they were used.

Around 10,000 B.P. agriculture began, and the Paleolithic gave way to the Neolithic. A Neolithic community lived at Catal Huyuk in Turkey from about 6500 to 5500 B.C.E. It seems to have worshipped a mother goddess who is connected with plant life and served by male attendants. Since there are no written documents from this period (writing was not yet invented), it is difficult to know what to make of Neolithic remains. One scholar, Marija Gimbutas, tried to identify the different Neolithic goddesses of southeastern Europe by classifying the different types of statues these people made.

Writing begins by 3000 B.C.E. Then there is plentiful evidence for the worship of goddesses. Goddesses played major roles in the religions of ancient Egypt, Mesopotamia, Canaan, Greece, and Rome (see EGYPTIAN RELIGION, MESOPOTAMIAN RELIGIONS, CANAANITE RELIGION, GREEK RELIGION, and ROMAN RELIGION). As noted above, their symbols, personalities, and spheres of activity varied considerably. JUDAISM tended to conceive of its god, YHWH ("the Lord"), in masculine terms. But some have pointed out that YHWH has feminine sides, too: his Wisdom and his Presence (Shekhinah). The traditional symbols of CHRISTIANITY—God as Father and Son—are masculine. But the Roman Catholic and Orthodox churches both venerate Mary as theotokos, "mother of God." In many places the veneration of Mary seems to continue ancient traditions of goddess worship. One example is the Virgin of Guadalupe in Mexico. ISLAM, like Protestant Christianity, has had little use for goddesses or feminine images of the divine.

Goddesses have been extremely important in east and south Asia. In China, Japan, and Tibet, a "goddess of mercy" known as Kuan-yin, Kannon, and Tara, respectively, has been very important. She is AVALOKITESVARA, a BODHISATTVA in feminine form. Hinduism knows a tremendous variety of goddesses as well as gods. Hindu villages have local goddesses that look after their needs. Written mythologies tell about different goddesses who are consorts to gods. They include SARASWATI, LAKSHMI, Sita, and PARVATI. Hindus often say that the sakti or power of a god is a goddess. Two especially powerful goddesses in east India are DURGA and Kali. Some Hindu traditions teach that all goddesses are manifestations of a single, supreme being. She is simply called Devi, "the Goddess."

Ancient Americans such as the Incas, Mayas, and Aztecs worshipped goddesses (see INCA RELIGION, MAYA RELIGION, and AZTEC RELIGION). So do indigenous North Americans (see NATIVE AMERICAN RELIGIONS). Recently some scholars suggested that indigenous North Americans began to worship mother earth only after contact with Europeans. Others strongly disagree. In any case, respect for the sacredness of the Earth is an important part of indigenous American religion today.

THE GODDESS TODAY

Traditional goddesses remain important religious figures. In addition, some women and a few men in North America and Europe have begun to worship the Goddess anew. They found in the worship of the Goddess religious strength, power, and support that they had not found in the traditional European religions.

Further reading: Martha Ann, *Goddess in World Mythology* (Santa Barbara, Calif.: ABC-CLIO, 1993); Elizabeth Bernard and Beverly Moon, *Goddess Who Rule* (New York: Oxford University Press, 2003); Adele Getty, *Goddess: Mother of Living Nature* (New York: Thames and Hudson, 1990); David Kinsley, *The Goddesses' Mirror: Visions of the Divine from East and West* (Albany: State University of New York Press, 1989); Starhawk, *The Spiral Dance: A Rebirth of the Ancient Religion of the Great Goddess.* 20th anniversary ed. (San Francisco: HarperSanFrancisco, 1999).

gospels   Writings about the teachings and deeds of JESUS. Gospels are a special kind of biography.

Their primary concern is not to relate the life of Jesus as accurately as possible, the way a modern biography might do. Instead, they want to present the message of CHRISTIANITY, and they tell the life of Jesus to do so. As a result of this, most modern scholars have come to realize that it is not possible to write a modern biography of Jesus on the basis of the gospels. They do not provide the right kind of evidence.

The NEW TESTAMENT contains four gospels: Matthew, Mark, Luke, and John. Many other gospels circulated in the first few centuries C.E. Several of them have survived. Recently scholars have given one of these other gospels a great deal of attention: the gospel of Thomas as preserved in the Coptic language. It consists entirely of sayings attributed to Jesus. A few scholars have argued that Thomas preserves some sayings more accurately than the gospels in the New Testament do. More traditional Christians find this assertion implausible.

Matthew, Mark, and Luke follow the same basic scenario in presenting the life of Jesus. For that reason they are known as "synoptic" gospels. The synoptics tell the same basic story from Jesus' BAPTISM to his crucifixion and burial. They diverge when they tell about Jesus' birth and his RESURRECTION. Mark says nothing about Jesus' birth. Matthew tells about the visit of the wise men and the massacre of infants under Herod. Luke tells of a journey to Bethlehem and a visit of shepherds; he associates these events with a census that took place when the Romans replaced Herod's son as ruler of Judea and appointed a proconsul to rule the area. As concerns the resurrection, Mark only tells about a group of women discovering an empty tomb. Matthew adds appearances of the risen Jesus to his disciples in Galilee. According to Luke, the disciples stayed in JERUSALEM and surrounding areas, and the risen Jesus appeared to them there.

Scholars have long debated how to explain these characteristics. Most now adopt the view that Mark was the first gospel of the three. Matthew and Luke, they suggest, wrote their gospels by following Mark, sometimes word for word. Matthew and Luke also report some sayings of Jesus that are not found in Mark, so they seem to have followed another common source. This source would have been similar in form to Thomas but certainly not identical with it. For the birth and resurrection of Jesus, Matthew and Luke used very different sources.

Each of the synoptic gospels has its own distinctive concerns. For example, Mark emphasizes what scholars call the "Messianic secret." That is, in Mark Jesus continually tries to hide that he is the MESSIAH; this fact is revealed publicly only after Jesus' resurrection. The synoptics also tell the story of Jesus in distinctive ways. For example, Luke is part of a two-volume presentation that continues in the book of Acts.

The gospel of John is in a class by itself. It does not follow the general order of events that the synoptic gospels use. It also does not report the same sayings. John presents Jesus as reflecting a great deal on his special identity. Many sayings begin with the phrase, "I am," for example, "I am the light of the world" (John 8.12). These sayings include some that Christians cherish the most.

Tradition attributes John's gospel to a disciple who was the closest to Jesus, a disciple whom Jesus loved. For centuries many Christians preferred it to the synoptics. The tendency today is to see John as the latest of the gospels in the New Testament. In this view, it does not present Jesus' most intimate words. It presents the way a certain group of early Christians liked to think about him.

grace In CHRISTIANITY, the gift from GOD of power that makes SALVATION possible. According to orthodox Christian theology, because of human SIN and sinful nature, all people deserve eternal punishment, but through the sacrifice of CHRIST on the cross, God has given Christians the gift or grace of salvation even though believers may not have earned it. While good deeds are considered important as a part of a life lived in the power of divine grace, it is not the deeds themselves that win salvation but God's grace received through FAITH.

ROMAN CATHOLICISM emphasizes the SACRAMENTS, such as BAPTISM and holy communion, as means of grace; PROTESTANTISM emphasizes that God gives grace where he will, that the scriptures can awaken the faith that enables one freely to receive it, and that the sacraments are simply "signs" of grace. But both acknowledge that God is not bound to any particular means or institution in his giving of grace to the world. PURE LAND BUDDHISM has a concept of salvation by means of the grace of AMIDA Buddha received through a faith that is comparable to the Christian.

Grail A chalice sometimes said to be that used by JESUS in the Last Supper. Around the 12th century, legends arose of knights who set out on a quest for the Holy Grail, reportedly kept in a mysterious Grail Castle under the guardianship of the Fisher King, an invalid. His wound and the wasteland surrounding the castle were presented as symbols of human sin. If the Grail was found and its meaning rightly understood, the wound would be healed and the wasteland made to bloom. Of the many variants of the legend, the best known associate the Grail quest with the stories of King Arthur, the renowned ancient British ruler. In them, the quest was undertaken by the greatest knights of his Round Table.

A knight who succeeded in finding and entering the Grail Castle saw a strange procession, in which an attendant bore a lance from which a drop of blood fell (this is the spear that pierced Jesus' side on the CROSS), and a maiden carried the Grail, set with gems and radiating an unearthly light. Sir Percival, a well-meaning but foolish knight, was first to see the procession but failed to ask the right question, "Whom does the Grail serve?" The second to find his way into the castle, Sir Lancelot, was the noblest knight of his time but failed the test because of his adultery with Guinevere, Arthur's queen. Finally, Sir Galahad, the son of Lancelot and the Grail maiden, a youth of impeccable purity born for this task, succeeded and, in some sources, then died in mystic rapture as he gazed into the sacred vessel. But the Fisher King was healed and the wasteland restored to bloom.

The Grail legend has been attributed to many sources, both pagan and Christian, and has been given many allegorical interpretations. It remains a symbol of the supreme human quest.

Greek religion The religion practiced in the ancient Greek states. The term refers especially to the period from the rise of the city-state in the eighth century B.C.E. to the conquest of Greece by Alexander the Great in the 330s B.C.E.

HISTORY

Greek religion had several precursors. From roughly 3000 to 1450 B.C.E. the Minoan civilization thrived on the island of Crete. It seems to have worshipped, among other beings, an important GODDESS. From 1450 to roughly 1100 B.C.E. the Mycenaean civilization dominated mainland Greece as well as Crete. The Mycenaeans worshipped many gods of the later Greeks, such as ZEUS, Hera, and Dionysos.

After about 1100 Mycenaean civilization collapsed; scholars dispute why. In any case, a widespread "Greek Renaissance" occurred during the eighth century B.C.E. Population grew; the *polis*—usually translated as "city-state"—came together; overseas trade and colonization flourished; writing was developed; and poets composed works now attributed to Homer and Hesiod. During this period, too, Greek religion assumed its standard forms. With Homer and Hesiod the Greeks acquired common images of the gods. The new city-states built temples. Offerings at Mycenaean tombs led to the WORSHIP of legendary heroes. Sanctuaries for all Greeks, such as the sanctuary of Zeus at Olympia, began to host major festivals.

Subsequent centuries were periods of elaboration and refinement. During the seventh and sixth centuries, Greeks began to build temples in stone rather than wood and mud-brick. Great leaders, like Draco and Solon at Athens, tried to write workable law codes. Philosophers began to talk about the world not in terms of human-like divine beings but in terms of basic principles. One of the earliest, Thales, suggested that water underlay all things. At the same time, individuals known as tyrants took over governments. They often modified inherited religions to suit their own personal ends.

The fifth century was a time of glory, especially in Athens. Athenian playwrights like Aeschylus, Sophocles, and Euripides explored some of the deepest questions that human beings face. Pericles oversaw the construction of monuments on the Acropolis at Athens. These included the most famous of all Greek temples, the Parthenon, dedicated to that city-state's patron goddess, ATHENA.

During the fourth century Greek philosophy reached its pinnacle with Plato and Aristotle. But before century's end, Alexander the Great had redrawn the map of the eastern Mediterranean and the ancient Near East. Large Greek-speaking empires replaced the relatively isolated city-states. Traditional religious practices did not disappear, but they were often overshadowed by religions that were no longer tied to particular places. Among these religions CHRISTIANITY and ISLAM eventually came to dominate the old Greek territories.

BELIEFS

The Greeks did not have a common set of mandatory beliefs, as Christians and Muslims do. The real focus was on common practices. Nevertheless, the Greeks shared many stories about the gods and some ideas about the universe. They tolerated only a limited amount of deviation from these beliefs. For example, an Athenian court sentenced the famous teacher Socrates to death. The charges included rejecting the traditional gods, teaching of new ones, and corrupting the youth.

A procession of believers sacrifices to Demeter, goddess of the Earth, in this fourth-century B.C.E. Greek votive relief. (*Erich Lessing/Art Resource N.Y.*)

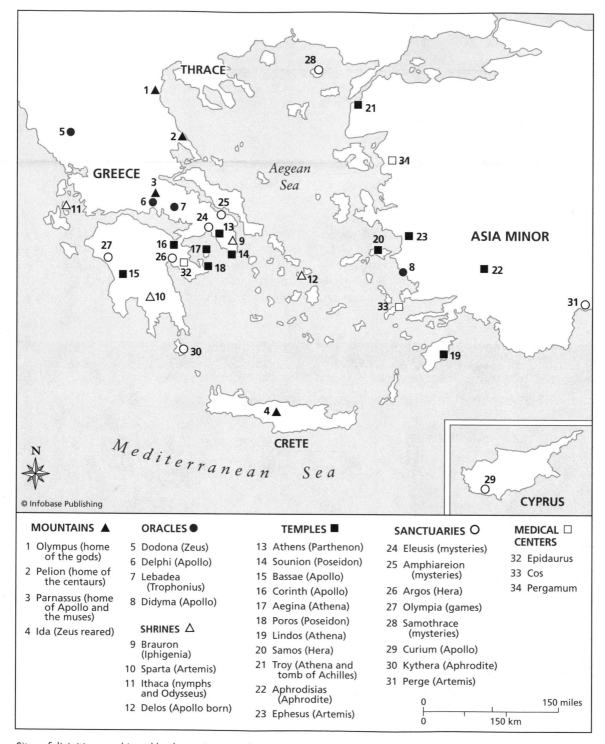

THRACE

28 ○

1 ▲

5 ●

GREECE

Aegean Sea

21 ■

34 ■

3 ▲

6 ● 7 ● 25 ○

24 ○ 13 ■

9 △

20 ■ 23 ■

ASIA MINOR

11 △

27 ○

16 ■ 17 ■ 14 ■

26 ○ 18 ■

32 ■

15 ■

10 △

12 △

8 ●

22 ■

33 ■

31 ○

30 ○

19 ■

4 ▲

CRETE

Mediterranean   Sea

N

© Infobase Publishing

29 ○

CYPRUS

MOUNTAINS ▲	ORACLES ●	TEMPLES ■	SANCTUARIES ○	MEDICAL ☐ CENTERS
1 Olympus (home of the gods)	5 Dodona (Zeus)	13 Athens (Parthenon)	24 Eleusis (mysteries)	32 Epidaurus
2 Pelion (home of the centaurs)	6 Delphi (Apollo)	14 Sounion (Poseidon)	25 Amphiareion (mysteries)	33 Cos
3 Parnassus (home of Apollo and the muses)	7 Lebadea (Trophonius)	15 Bassae (Apollo)	26 Argos (Hera)	34 Pergamum
4 Ida (Zeus reared)	8 Didyma (Apollo)	16 Corinth (Apollo)	27 Olympia (games)	
		17 Aegina (Athena)	28 Samothrace (mysteries)	
	SHRINES △	18 Poros (Poseidon)	29 Curium (Apollo)	
	9 Brauron (Iphigenia)	19 Lindos (Athena)	30 Kythera (Aphrodite)	
	10 Sparta (Artemis)	20 Samos (Hera)	31 Perge (Artemis)	
	11 Ithaca (nymphs and Odysseus)	21 Troy (Athena and tomb of Achilles)		
	12 Delos (Apollo born)	22 Aphrodisias (Aphrodite)		
		23 Ephesus (Artemis)		

0   150 miles
0   150 km

Sites of divinities worshipped by the ancient Greeks

A statement by the philosopher Thales gives a good idea of the Greek religious attitude: "all things are full of gods." Homer conceived of the gods in human form. But his gods differed from human beings in several important ways. They did not die. They had their own food and drink. Instead of blood, a special liquid known as *ichor* flowed through their veins. They were also more powerful and deserved more honor than the strongest of human beings.

The most important gods were celestial divinities known as Olympians. Myths treated these gods as an extended family, headed by Zeus, "father of gods and men." Other prominent Olympians included Hera, APOLLO, ARTEMIS, APHRODITE, and HERMES. The Greeks venerated other gods, too. Some of them, like ADONIS, were considered foreign imports. They also worshipped *daimones* and heroes. Although the English word "demon" comes from the Greek word *daimon,* daimones (plural of *daimon*) were not demons in our sense. They were vague spiritual forces. Heroes were great human beings from the past, like Theseus and Herakles.

The Greeks believed that certain important events in life were "portioned out." They did not often say by whom. It was clearly the responsibility of Zeus to ensure that "fate" was accomplished. The most important event that fate determined was death. In general, the Greeks were not optimistic about life after death. In the *Odyssey* the shade of the hero Achilles tells Odysseus that he would rather live as a slave on Earth than rule over the realm of the dead.

PRACTICES

The most important Greek RITUAL act was SACRIFICE. At home Greeks generally offered plant products to the gods. Larger communities sacrificed animals—usually domesticated animals but not always. The sacrifices offered to the Olympians were feasts that the Greeks and the gods shared. The gods received the blood, thighbones, fat, and smoke; the Greeks received the internal organs and the muscles. Heroes generally received a different kind of sacrifice, known as the holocaust. In this sacrifice, the victim was completely burned up. Another common Greek ritual act was libation. It consisted of pouring liquid out for the gods.

Households made offerings and libations to the gods daily. Larger communities generally did so on special occasions known as festivals. Most festivals were held every year according to a calendar that varied from community to community. Some festivals were observed by all Greek speakers. A well-known example of these "pan-Hellenic" festivals was the festival of Zeus at Olympia. It was the precursor of the modern Olympic games. In addition to sacrifices, festivals often involved processions, games, and in some cases theatrical performances or other special ritual acts.

Although the Greeks are famous for building resplendent temples, they did not worship inside them. Greek temples were basically storage facilities. The Greeks performed sacrifices at an outdoor ALTAR. Altars for sacrifices to the Olympians were mounded high; those for holocausts were low, sometimes even holes dug in the ground. The altar and temple were the central features of a sacred area known as the *temenos.*

ORGANIZATION

The Greeks did not require special intermediaries or priests to worship the gods. All individuals could worship the gods themselves. But larger communities generally delegated religious tasks to specific persons. Many of these communities—villages and poleis or city-states—were political as well as religious. In that case religious functionaries were basically officers of the state. But the Greeks also knew other religious communities that were not political units. These included groups banded together to maintain certain sanctuaries, to worship a particular god, such as Dionysos, or to ensure each other's mutual welfare.

SIGNIFICANCE

Greek religion is a relatively loose collection of practices rather than a carefully defined set of beliefs. It includes all practices by which the Greeks tried to make a better life for themselves through pleasing and placating a number of divine and spiritual beings. It is no longer practiced, but the art, literature, drama, and philosophy that it inspired have greatly enriched the cultures of Europe and North America.

Further reading: Francis M. Cornford, *Greek Religious Thought* (London: Dent, 1950); William Guthrie, *The Greeks and Their Gods* (Boston: Beacon, 1955); Jan D. Mikalson, *Ancient Greek Religion* (Malden, Mass.: Blackwell, 2005); Gilbert Murray, *Four Stages of Greek Religion* (New York: Columbia University Press, 1912).

gunas A Sanskrit word meaning "qualities" or "attributes." Indian thinkers have made lists of gunas that vary in length and content. The gunas most important from the point of view of religion are those associated with the Sankhya and YOGA philosophies. According to these schools, the world of nature derives from a primal material potency known as Prakriti. Prakriti has three gunas or qualities: the pure and transparent (*sattva*), the active (*rajas*), and the dark and static (*tamas*). By some unknown process the equilibrium between these three has been disrupted. Now they conflict, and their conflict produces the world.

Like yin and yang in China (*see* YIN/YANG THEORY), the three gunas have been used to classify a wide variety of objects. For example, the purest vegetarian diet has the guna or quality of sattva.

guru A religious teacher in HINDUISM and in some forms of BUDDHISM. In Sanskrit, the ancient language of India, *guru* means "heavy" or "weighty." In the context of education it refers to a teacher; in a religious context, to a "spiritual preceptor" or religious teacher. Gurus are important in Hinduism and in the forms of Buddhism known as Tantric Buddhism or Vajrayana. VAJRAYANA BUDDHISM is the major religion of Tibet, and Tibetans call gurus *lamas*.

Gurus and their disciples have special relationships. These relationships differ somewhat from the relationships between teachers and students in North American schools. Like teachers, gurus guide their disciples through the subject matter. But disciples are also supposed to take their gurus as models of the religious goals that they are trying to reach and to imitate them. As a result, students revere their gurus. They serve them and may even live with them. They may also meditate upon them and reverence them on their birthdays, for example, by washing their feet. If for some reason the guru is not present, they may wash foot-shaped prints that stand for the guru's feet. These are common practices in south Asia, and converts to Hinduism or Buddhism in North America sometimes perform them, too.

Guru Granth *See* ADI GRANTH.

H

Hadith The Arabic word for "story" or "news"; in ISLAM, reliable reports about the prophet MUHAMMAD. All Muslims profess, "There is no god but GOD [*see* ALLAH], and MUHAMMAD is God's messenger." The second part of this statement means first of all that Muhammad received God's revelation in the QUR'AN. It also means that, as God's messenger, Muhammad exemplifies the ideal response to God's revelation. As a result, his life takes on religious significance.

Hadith are for the most part records of what the prophet Muhammad said, did, and allowed. They are second in importance only to the Qur'an. Together with the Qur'an, Hadith are the traditional sources from which Muslims determine what is religiously true and proper. They define what Muslims call *sunnah,* "tradition."

Many reports about Muhammad circulated in the decades after his death. Because the prophet's example was valuable, some Muslims invented Hadith to support their views or practices. They may not have done so with the deliberate intention of deceiving others. They may have honestly felt that they were reporting what the prophet had said or done. In time, the number of Hadith proliferated. It became necessary to distinguish authentic from inauthentic reports.

To do this, ancient scholars examined the way in which a Hadith had been handed down. To be acceptable, a Hadith had to originate from a reputable person who was in a position to have reliable knowledge about what the Hadith claimed. It also had to have a known chain of transmission: For example, A learned from B, who learned from C, who learned from D, the companion of the prophet who was an eyewitness. Finally, the chain of transmission had to be able to withstand the strictest scrutiny. Scholars of Hadith studied each individual mentioned in the chain of transmission to determine whether that person was reliable. They also studied the process of transmission from one person to the next. For example, if A and B were both reliable witnesses, but A had never left Spain and B was never farther west than Egypt, the report was clearly false.

In the late ninth and early 10th centuries C.E., scholars of SUNNI ISLAM made six authoritative collections of Hadith. Their collections represent considerable effort: Scholars traveled widely to gather as many Hadith as possible. The collections also represent considerable sifting. For example, al-Bukhari, who made the most important collection, is said to have examined hundreds of thousands of Hadith from all over the Islamic world. His finished collection contains a little over 7,000. SHI'ITE ISLAM has its own collections of Hadith. They were made 400 to 500 years after the prophet lived, and derive especially from the prophet's cousin Ali and his supporters.

Each Hadith has two parts: the chain of transmission and the report itself. Many Hadith deal with Muhammad's pronouncements on central Islamic practices. For example, a large number tell in detail how to observe the five pillars of Islam: profession of faith, formal daily prayer (SALAT), almsgiving, FASTING during the month of RAMADAN, and PILGRIMAGE to MECCA. Others deal with matters that seem less important, for example, what kind of dates one can sell, how not to react when someone breaks wind, and the relative merits of sneezing and yawning (cf. *Sahih Bukhari* 3.34.400; 8.73.68; 8.73.245).

In the 20th century Muslims had varying attitudes to Hadith. Some Muslims with an interest in "modernizing" Islam questioned the authenticity of Hadith. In doing so, they also questioned their authority. Other Muslims defended the Hadith staunchly.

halakhah   Hebrew word meaning "the way"; Jewish law in its most comprehensive form. JUDAISM is a way of life more than a set of beliefs. Halakhah defines every aspect of this way of life, private as well as public. Thus, it is extremely important in Judaism. Indeed, it defines Judaism.

The basis of halakhah is TORAH, that is, the first five books of the BIBLE. RABBIS teach that Torah contains 613 instructions on life. These instructions are not, however, all sufficient. Questions arise when one tries to put them into practice, when one faces situations not discussed in Torah, and when the circumstances of life change. Other sources of halakhah include the rest of the Bible, oral Torah, that is, the TALMUD, and custom. The oral Torah consists of interpretations that MOSES supposedly received orally on Mount Sinai and passed on to authoritative successors.

The first important compilation of halakhah was the Mishna, made around 200 C.E. The compilation with the most authority is the Shulhan Arukh of Joseph Caro (1488–1575). Today, besides defining religious practice, halakhah is the official legal code in the state of Israel for some civil, but not criminal, matters. For example, halakhah governs procedures for marriage and divorce.

Halloween   All Hallow's Eve, October 31, a popular holiday emphasizing supernatural beings. This American festival, with its orange and black colors and witches, ghosts, and trick-or-treaters, is really a continuation of Samhain, the ancient Celtic New Year's Day (*see* CELTIC RELIGION and NEW YEAR FESTIVALS). Like all such times of beginnings, Samhain was seen as a day and night breaking the continu-

ity of things, when supernatural forces, such as spirits of nature and of the dead, could come into this world as on no other occasion. In Christian times Samhain was separated from New Year's and made the eve of All SAINTS (All Hallows, hence Halloween) Day. The old characteristics were remembered and brought to the United States especially by Irish immigrants. It is now a time for masks and changing roles and, at least in fun, believing in supernatural entities, good and bad.

Hamas   The Arabic word for "zeal;" an acronym for "Islamic Resistance Movement." Hamas is a Palestinian organization that seeks to recover all traditional Palestinian land from the Jordan River to the Mediterranean Sea. That includes land currently occupied by the state of Israel.

Sheikh Ahmed Yassin (1936–2004) founded Hamas in December 1987, shortly after the first Palestinian intifada, or uprising, began. Earlier Palestinian movements, such as Yasser Arafat's (1929–2004) Fatah, had taken seriously that not all Palestinians are Muslims; a sizable minority are Christians. They had taken as their goal the creation of a secular Palestinian state. Hamas adopted an Islamist position. It wanted to create an Islamic state, and it saw its struggles in specifically Islamic terms as JIHAD.

Outside Palestinian territory Hamas has become notorious and widely condemned for the activities of its militant wing, the Izzedine al-Qassam Brigade. The best known of all are the attacks of Hamas suicide bombers on Israeli civilians. These are barbaric acts, but many Palestinians see them as justified given the wretchedness of their living conditions and the hopelessness of their situation. In the Gaza strip, for example, 1.3 million Palestinians live on very little land; 80 percent of them live in poverty.

Hamas has done more than violence, however; it has also established effective social services in Palestinian territories. It has constructed public buildings such as libraries, clinics, and mosques. It has provided food for the needy. It has also supported education and sports. In addition, Hamas members have a reputation for being honest in their financial dealings rather than corrupt, as the Palestinian Authority is thought to be.

Israel sees Hamas as a major threat and has adopted a policy of assassinating Hamas leaders. That includes the founder, Sheikh Yassin, whom it assassinated on March 22, 2004. In addition, the United States has tried to eliminate funding to Hamas from overseas. Nevertheless, in January 2006, Hamas won a majority of the seats in elections for the Palestinian parliament. Some observers attributed its victory not to its anti-Israel stance but to its activities within the Palestinian territories. Still, the victory raised troubling questions about the future of the peace process and the relations of other countries to the Palestinian governing body.

Further reading: Khaled Hroub, *Hamas: Political Thought and Practice* (Washington, D.C.: Institute for Palestine Studies, 2000); Walter Laqueur, ed., *Voices of Terror: Manifestos, Writings, and Manuals of Al Qaeda, Hamas, and Other Terrorists from around the World and throughout the Ages,* (New York: Reed Press, 2004).

A German Hanukkah lamp (menorah) in silver with an eight-headed mythical animal resembling a peacock, from the 18th century *(Erich Lessing/Art Resource, N.Y.)*

Hanukkah   The Jewish festival of lights. It is celebrated for eight days every year, beginning on the 25th day of the Jewish month of Kislev.

Hanukkah is one of the Jewish festivals that non-Jewish North Americans know best. That is because it falls around the time of CHRISTMAS and now involves the giving of gifts.

Hanukkah celebrates the victory of the Maccabees over the former Greek rulers of Israel and Judah in 164 B.C.E. According to the book of 2 Maccabees, the festival began with the rededication of the Temple in that very year. Its eight days of celebration made up for the failure to celebrate the festival of Sukkot a few months earlier because of the war.

The TALMUD preserves a later story that is now invariably connected with Hanukkah. On rededicating the temple, the Maccabees found only enough oil to burn for one day. Miraculously, it burned for eight. This story supports what has become the central feature of Hanukkah: lighting an eight-branched candelabrum known as a menorah. The most traditional menorahs burn oil, but today many Jews use candles. Some RABBIS have even sanctioned the use of electric lights.

A popular game is played in celebration of Hanukkah. It uses a dreidel, that is, a small top that one spins with one's hand. A dreidel has four flat sides onto which Hebrew letters are inscribed. In Israel these letters are "n," "g," "h," and "p," the beginning letters of a four-word Hebrew sentence that recalls the reason for Hanukkah: "A great miracle happened here." Outside Israel the last letter is "sh," not "p," because the sentence reads "A great miracle happened there."

Hanuman   A hero in the Indian epic the *RAMAYANA*.

Many Hindus worship Hanuman as the ideal devotee or worshipper of the gods.

The Ramayana tells how a demon in the forest kidnapped king RAMA's wife, Sita. To rescue her, Rama made an alliance with the forest monkeys. Hanuman, the general of the monkey armies, discovered that Sita was being held in the city of Lanka. While spying in Lanka, he was caught, and his tail was set on fire as a form of torture. Hanuman escaped and set all of Lanka ablaze. Later, Rama's brother, Laksmana, was wounded in battle by a poisoned arrow. When it looked as if he would die, Hanuman flew to the far north. (As the son of the wind god Vayu, Hanuman can fly.) He brought back the top of a mountain where a medicinal herb grew. As a result, Laksmana was saved. After Rama rescued Sita and killed the demon, Hanuman returned to Rama's capital with Rama and Sita. From there he oversaw the affairs of state for 16,000 years.

Images of Hanuman show him with a human body but a monkey's face and tail. He also holds a large mace. One common image shows him flying through the air holding the mountain with the medicinal herb. Another shows him standing and holding open his chest to reveal Rama and Sita in his heart. This symbolizes his utter devotion to Rama, whom many Hindus worship as GOD.

Hindus have built many temples to Hanuman in northern India. In Ayodhya, Rama's city, worshippers visit structures in which they believe Hanuman actually lived.

Hasidism   From the Hebrew word *hasid*, meaning "pious"; a movement within JUDAISM. Hasidism began in the 18th century as a rejection of a rigid legalism and intellectualism in favor of an emotional, heartfelt religion. Today it is most often thought of as an ultraconservative form of Judaism that clings tightly to the ways of the past.

Hasidism began with a wandering healer and teacher in eastern Europe known as the BAAL SHEM TOV, the "Master of the Good Name" (*c.* 1700–60). Like most wandering healers and teachers at the time, he addressed not the elite of the community

but the poor and the uneducated. His teachings emphasized a kind of mystical communion with GOD that could and should be found in any sphere of life.

When the Baal Shem Tov died, his mantle was taken up by his followers, especially Dov Ber (d. 1772). Dov Ber turned his house into a court, similar to those of the minor nobility. People would flock to hear him hold court, that is, to preach and teach. His disciples formed courts or "houses" of their own. Each of them became the center of a community. The leadership of the communities soon became hereditary. Fathers would pass it down to their sons or occasionally their sons-in-law. Thus, a distinctive feature of Hasidism was born: the special relationship of the community to its leader.

The Hasidic leader is known as a *tzaddik*, a "righteous one." As Hasidic Jews see it, a tzaddik has no SIN of his own. Instead, he takes upon himself the EVIL done by his community and transforms it into good. Thus, the tzaddik stands between the community and God. He is the sole authority in the community over private as well as public matters. It is inspiring just to be in his presence.

Hasidic teachings and practices vary from one community to another. Hasidism arose, however, as a movement that played down the form of Judaism customary in eastern Europe at the time. This form emphasized studying TORAH and TALMUD and meticulously acting on what one had studied, God's instructions. In Hasidism, by contrast, one strove to experience an intimate communion with God. This attitude still characterizes most Hasidic groups.

During the 20th century, many Hasidic communities moved from eastern Europe to either America or Israel. In 1941 the most influential Hasidic community set up its headquarters in Brooklyn, New York. It is often called the Lubavitch community, after the town in Belarus (an independent nation formerly in the Soviet Union) where it was first located. Its technical name is Habad Hasidism. The Lubavitch community emphasizes study more than most Hasidic communities do. It has also taken a leading role in promoting Jewish traditionalism. But in doing so, it has not hesitated to make use of the most modern technology. From 1950 until his death in 1994 Rabbi Menachem Mendel Schneersohn led the Lubavitch community. At the time of his death his followers were speculating that he might be the promised MESSIAH.

Hasidism has consistently opposed changing the Jewish way of life to fit Gentile ways. In particular, Hasidic Jews have been very critical of Reform Judaism. They have also opposed ZIONISM. They have seen this latter movement, which led to the founding of the state of Israel, as an attempt to force God to usher in the Messianic age. Some Hasidic Jews have gone so far as to claim that the HOLOCAUST was God's punishment for the sins of Reform Judaism and Zionism.

Hathor   A GODDESS of ancient Egypt. The name Hathor means "house of HORUS." It links her with the sky. Hathor was given form as a cow or as a human figure with a cow's head. In the latter case, the disk of the sun rests between her two horns.

In mythology from the Old Kingdom of Egypt (2650–2180 B.C.E.) Hathor is the wife of Re, the sun god, and the mother of Horus. Because the king is the living Horus, Hathor is also the mother of the king. Later, Isis was said to be the king's mother. Nevertheless, illustrations from the New Kingdom (1570–1080 B.C.E.) often show Hathor as a cow giving the king milk.

In addition to this role, Hathor was a goddess of lovers and childbirth. Her main temple was at Dendera. In the area around Thebes she took on a somewhat different character. She was called "the lady of the west" and was associated with the dead.

Hawaiian religion   *See* PACIFIC OCEAN RELIGIONS.

healing, religious   Religious techniques for overcoming physical and mental illness. Whatever else it may be, religion is a means used by individuals and communities to help promote a better life.

Many Christians have sought SALVATION as eternal life in the midst of their current reality, sometimes seen as a vale of tears. Theravada Buddhists, very numerous in southeast Asia, distinguish NIRVANA, the goal of religious practice, from life in this world, SAMSARA. But most Christians and Buddhists think that religious practice benefits them here and now, too. And many other religious people expect religion to help promote a better life or a thriving and flourishing life primarily in this world. Among other things, they expect religion to heal them when they are sick. In many cultures, as evidence of the importance of religious healing, the first physician is said to have been a god.

The influential scholar Mircea ELIADE developed a model of how religions heal. He suggested that for religious people disease is not just a malfunction. It is a disruption in the being of the entire cosmos. In order to heal, one must restore, or better, recreate the entire cosmos. Not only the sick person but the cosmos itself must return to the moment of creation and be renewed. This can happen in a number of ways. A healer may recite the COSMOGONY—the myth of creation—and include in it the mythology that tells of the creation of the medicine that she or he is about to give (*see* MYTH AND MYTHOLOGY). Or a RITUAL may place the sick person in a fetal position. This position signals a return to the womb and a rebirth.

Eliade's model can be helpful. At the same time, one must be careful in using it. The model may tempt us to distort what religious people say and do so that their words and actions fit the model. It may also tempt us to read into words and actions symbolic meanings that might not be there or ignore other meanings that are there.

WHAT CAUSES ILLNESS?

Religions attribute illness to many causes. Sometimes they attribute them to personal beings.

Traditional AFRICAN RELIGIONS often attribute sickness to the acts of other human beings. That is, they talk about WITCHCRAFT and sorcery. According to a well-known study of the Azande, witchcraft was a substance in a person's abdomen. It harmed other people. Sometimes those who possessed witchcraft did not even know what they were doing.

Indigenous peoples have also attributed sickness to possession by spirits. They are hardly alone. According to the NEW TESTAMENT, JESUS cast out demons. Folk traditions in ISLAM have known local spirits that could harm as well as help people. Some scholars suggest that indigenous North Americans tended to talk about two different causes of disease. They tended to attribute physical illness to possession by a spirit; they attributed mental illness to the departure of a person's soul.

Yet another personal source of sickness and disease are the gods or GOD. At the beginning of the *Iliad*, APOLLO shoots his arrows into the Greek camp and causes a plague. The book of Deuteronomy promises that YHWH ("the Lord") will afflict those who do not observe the TORAH. The afflictions include "consumption, fever, inflammation . . . boils . . . ulcers, scurvy, and itch" (Deuteronomy 28.22, 27).

Many religions, especially in Asia, attribute disease to nonpersonal causes. Indigenous North Americans often thought that a foreign substance—say, a feather—had entered the body and needed to be extracted. The ancient Chinese traced illness to a disruption of the harmony of nature. Ayurveda, a Hindu body of medicine, teaches that, in addition to personal causes, diseases result from an imbalance in the body's three "humors," wind, bile, and phlegm. Hindus, Buddhists, and Jains also attribute disease to actions (KARMA) in this or a previous life.

Few religions have limited themselves to a single cause for disease. Most of them give a variety of explanations, personal and nonpersonal.

METHODS OF HEALING

At one time or another religious people have used virtually every element of religion in search of healing. Many indigenous religions rely on specially initiated healers called shamans (*see* SHAMANISM). Shamans generally fight the spirits that are making people sick. They often travel to the spirit world to do battle. If they win, the people recover; if they lose, the shamans may die. Many shamans

in North America also extract foreign objects from the body of the sick person.

A healer with special powers has also been important in CHRISTIANITY. Of all the founders of major religions, Jesus fits the image of charismatic healer most closely. He passed on the gift of healing to his APOSTLES. In time most Christians turned to other means for healing. But in the 19th and 20th centuries the idea that some Christians had the gift of healing reappeared in North America. One of the most famous healers was Oral Roberts (b. 1918), who built his own medical center in Tulsa, Oklahoma (*see* PENTECOSTALISM).

In addition to special healers, religions have found healing in rituals and changes in life-style. When indigenous people attribute illnesses to offended ancestors, they may acknowledge their offenses and make an offering to restore good relations. Among the Japanese, water—for example, bathing in a hot spring—has been an important way to seek health. Catholic and Orthodox Christians have a SACRAMENT of healing; a priest anoints a sick person with oil. In the ancient Mediterranean world sick people often slept in the sanctuary of the god Asklepios; they left behind many testimonials to show that the god had visited them at night, often in dreams, and healed them (*see* GREEK RELIGION). Taoists have stressed that one should live in harmony with natural processes. They have also experimented with medicines that produce health, long life, and immortality (*see* TAOISM).

Some religious people have also seen the source of healing in ideas and attitudes. From New Thought and CHRISTIAN SCIENCE to "the power of positive thinking," such movements have had much influence in North America.

HEALING IN 20TH-CENTURY AMERICA

During the 19th and 20th centuries, nonreligious, scientific medicine made tremendous advances. But people in North America have not abandoned religious healing. Some continue to reject medical techniques on religious grounds. For example, JEHOVAH'S WITNESSES refuse blood transfusions. Some continue to turn to FAITH and mind based healing. Alternative medicines, such as Ayurveda, have become very popular in some circles. Twelve-step recovery programs are effective in countering alcoholism and other conditions; they have a significant religious component. Those who practice scientific medicine have also often recognized the important role that spiritual well being plays in healing physical and mental illness.

Further reading: Mircea Eliade, *Shamanism* (New York: Pantheon, 1964); David Harrell, *All Things Are Possible: The Healing and Charismatic Revivals in Modern America* (Bloomington: Indiana University Press, 1975); Morton Kelsey, *Healing and Christianity* (New York: Harper & Row, 1973); Thomas G. Plante and Allen C. Sherman, eds., *Faith and Health: Psychological Perspectives* (New York: Guilford, 2001).

heaven A realm above the earth. Traditional CHRISTIANITY conceives of heaven as a realm where the redeemed go after either death or the final judgment. This image is the dominant one in North America.

Sometimes heaven simply refers to the region above the atmosphere. Most religions have something to say about this region. What they have to say differs tremendously. The beginning of the book of Genesis talks about the sky as the firmament that holds back the "waters above." Religions in the Mediterranean region around the time of JESUS often talked about several different layers of heaven, one atop the other. These were the spheres of the planets, of the sun and the moon, and of the fixed stars. Ancient Mesoamericans seem to have conceived of the layers of heaven as the different levels through which the sun ascends and descends during the day (*see* MAYA RELIGION). HINDUISM and BUDDHISM have described any number of heavenly worlds. These often have little, if anything, to do with what can be seen in the sky.

However religions conceive of heaven, they usually associate special beings with it. In ancient Egypt the sky was itself a GODDESS, the goddess Nut (*see* EGYPTIAN RELIGION). Jews of the Second Temple period occasionally used "heaven" as a substi-tute for the word GOD. This usage is also found in the gospel of Matthew. In Hinduism various gods dwell in heavens; in Mahayana Buddhism BUDDHAS and BODHISATTVAS dwell there, too. GNOSTICISM taught that EVIL archons ruled the seven planetary spheres. Far above them at a virtually inaccessible distance was the realm of the unknown God, a realm of goodness and light.

In some religions heaven directs human actions. CONFUCIANISM did not say much about what heaven was, but it did teach that people were to follow the "way of heaven." More broadly, Chinese rulers claimed to rule by the "mandate of heaven." Heaven can also be a source of justice. In the sacred books known as the VEDA, the sky-god Varuna looks down from heaven with his thousand eyes and notes whether people do good or evil.

According to the image dominant in North America, heaven is a place to which people go after they die. This kind of heaven is not limited to Christianity. Hindus, Buddhists, and Jains see the various heavens as places where people whose actions in life have been especially good—who have very good KARMA—are reborn after death (*see* JAINISM). PURE LAND BUDDHISM gets its name from the heaven that the Buddha AMIDA has created in the distant west. Those who rely upon him are reborn into the Pure Land and enjoy its delights until one day all sentient or conscious beings will enter enlightenment together.

In ZOROASTRIANISM, Christianity, and ISLAM heaven is the abode of those who are found worthy at the final judgment. The three religions have used different metaphors to describe this wondrous place. The book of REVELATION refers to it as a new JERUSALEM and describes it as a wondrously jeweled city. The QUR'AN often refers to it as a garden, which contrasts starkly with the desert climate in which Islam arose. Rivers supply the garden with abundant water, plants grow luxuriantly, and celestial beings cater to the whims of those who are found worthy of heaven. The particular vision of heaven seems to fulfill a given people's aspirations after utopia.

At the same time, heaven is not limited to some far off place. It also provides ideals on which to model life here on Earth. Jesus taught that the KINGDOM OF GOD or of heaven was at hand. This preaching has inspired some Protestants in North America to try to reform society. Heaven has also inspired artists such as architects. In places as far apart as Spain, Iran, and India Muslim landscape architects have taken the Qur'an's descriptions of heaven as the basis for the gardens they have designed. An inscription set up in Shalamar Bagh, Kashmir (India), gives evidence of their success: "If there be a Paradise on the face of the earth, it is here, it is here, it is here."

The development of modern astronomy has made it difficult for people to ascribe literally to traditional views of heaven as a realm immediately above the sky. Nevertheless, religions that have traditionally talked about heaven have not abandoned the teaching. Their followers think of it as a spiritual ideal rather than an astronomical place.

hell   A realm or realms, usually thought of as below the Earth, to which evildoers go after death. Hell figures prominently in the teachings of traditional CHRISTIANITY, but many other religions have analogous concepts.

Many religions associate the dead with a realm below the surface of the Earth. They often seem to do so because they bury the dead. For them the underworld is not necessarily a place of punishment, but it is not a place that one would choose to be, either. Such a view appears, for example, in the ancient Mesopotamian story of INANNA's descent to the underworld; in ancient Greek notions of Hades; in the realm to which Izanami, one of the world's parents in early SHINTO mythology (see IZANAGI AND IZANAMI), goes after she dies; and in the realm of Xibalba in the Maya EPIC, Popol Vuh. In several of these examples the underworld is associated with testing and trials.

The Hebrew BIBLE presents a view of life after death that is very much like the preceding views. Indeed, the Hebrew Bible does not focus on the realm of the dead, and that attitude has carried over into JUDAISM. Although Jews generally believe in a retribution after death for EVIL acts that remain unpunished in this life, they do not emphasize this belief.

Hell properly speaking appears in ZOROASTRIANISM, Christianity, and ISLAM. The ancient Israelites had close contact with Persians during and after the Babylonian exile (587–539 B.C.E.). Many scholars have suggested that the Persian religion, Zoroastrianism, gave its teachings about hell to Christianity and Islam. In any case, all three religions conceive of hell as a place where the unredeemed wicked go, generally for eternal torment. Fire has been the most popular torment in hell, but not the only one. Occasionally hell has been thought of as absolutely cold. Both Zoroastrianism and Islam also tell of a narrow bridge over an abyss. After death persons must walk across the bridge. The wicked lose their balance and fall to their eternal torment.

Some sayings in Islam indicate that the punishment suffered in hell might not actually be eternal. Christians, too, have at times been reluctant to make hell an eternal abode. The ancient Christian teacher Origen (c. 185–c. 254) pointed to a reference to universal restoration in the NEW TESTAMENT. According to him all creatures would eventually be restored to GOD. Hell was more like a penitentiary, where those unredeemed on Earth reestablished a proper relationship with God. Many liberal Christians in the last two centuries have also reinterpreted hell or rejected the idea altogether.

Religions of south and east Asia have generally handled the idea of hell differently. HINDUISM, BUDDHISM, and JAINISM believe in a lengthy series of rebirths known as SAMSARA. Hell is one place where those whose actions have been particularly bad may be reborn. Indeed, in all three religions hell is more than a single place. Hell is a whole series of worlds or universes. There is no single description of these various worlds that any one of the religions accepts. Instead, the worlds of hell have become a fertile ground for the mythological imagination.

Writers and artists have found hell to be a powerful subject. Indeed, some have observed that artists often produce much better works when their subjects involve sin, death, and hell, than when they involve virtue and HEAVEN. Well known European depictions of hell include Dante's *Inferno,* which describes in delightful detail a descent through the various levels of hell; the English poet John Milton's *Paradise Lost;* and the almost surrealistic paintings of Hieronymus Bosch (*c.* 1450–*c.* 1516).

heresy Beliefs considered dangerously wrong by religious authority or by popular opinion. The word "heresy" comes from a Greek word meaning "choosing," in the sense of choosing for oneself rather than in accordance with the consensus of a larger group. In religion, particularly CHRISTIANITY, this term is used to describe a belief considered by the religion's teaching authorities or mainstream opinion to be false, and dangerous to the SALVATION of those who hold it. Christianity has always had its heretics, from the GNOSTICISM of the early centuries down to medieval groups like the Albigensians. At the time of the Protestant REFORMATION, Protestants and Catholics regarded each other as heretics. Persons regarded as heretics have frequently been subjected to brutal persecution and horrible punishments, including burning at the stake. Because of this tragic history, the use of the term has fallen out of favor in many Christian circles today.

Hermes An ancient Greek god. In character, Hermes is a TRICKSTER. He both marks boundaries and crosses them.

The name Hermes is related to "herm." A herm is a pile of stones used to mark boundaries. In ancient Greek, herms were taken to be images of the god Hermes. Communities practiced local RITUALS at them.

As the god of the boundaries, Hermes is ideally suited to be a messenger. Art often shows him as a messenger, wearing a cap with wings and holding a herald's staff. He also escorts the souls of the dead to the underworld. Thus, in the last book of the *Odyssey* he escorts the souls of the suitors whom Odysseus has killed. In addition, Hermes is a god of thieves, merchants, and shepherds and a patron of literature.

Perhaps the most important myth about Hermes is the story of his birth. On the day he was born, Hermes invented the lyre, then stole the cattle of APOLLO. Although angered by the theft, Apollo was very fond of the lyre. In exchange for it, he allowed Hermes to keep the stolen cattle.

heroes and hero myths Extraordinary human beings and stories about them. The word "hero" comes from the Greek. In ancient Greece heroes were great people from the past. That does not mean they were particularly admirable. For example, Cleomedes of Astypalaea was a champion boxer. One day he went on a rampage and killed 60 schoolchildren. The ancient Greeks found this action as reprehensible as people of today would. But because Cleomedes's action was so extraordinary, the Greeks worshipped him as a hero.

Heroes were worshipped at what was claimed to be their tombs. The Greeks generally gave heroes the same kinds of SACRIFICES as they gave to gods of the earth. The blood of the animal was drained into a trench. Then the animal was burned up completely. Some of the heroes became central figures in EPIC tales and other legends. Examples include Achilles, Odysseus, Theseus, Oedipus, and Herakles. It is not always clear how these stories related to the WORSHIP of heroes.

In the 19th and 20th centuries, scholars of religion and folklore came to use the term "hero" in a somewhat different way. For them a hero was a man or woman prominent in mythology but not divine. One of the best known writers about heroes in the 20th century, Joseph Campbell, defined the ARCHETYPE or fundamental image of the hero as follows: "The hero . . . is the man or woman who has been able to battle past his personal and local historical limitations to the generally valid, normal human forms." Despite the partial inclusiveness of this definition, Campbell—and many others—tended to conceive of the hero in masculine terms. He most often saw preeminent women in the form of the "great mother." Some say that this male-centeredness derives from the people who tell hero-stories; it may just as likely derive from the scholars who study them.

Heroes stand out from the crowd because of their remarkable abilities and achievements. Homer's heroes routinely lift boulders that "two men of today" could not begin to budge. Beowulf defeats the dragon Grendel, who previously wreaked destruction far and wide. The military exploits of Lakshmi Bai (d. 1858), the rani (queen) of Jhansi, a town of central India, have become legendary there. Some heroes embody superior qualities that are as much moral or spiritual as physical. In the *Ramayana,* a Hindu epic, Rama and his wife Sita exceed all other human beings in virtue (*see* RAMA, *RAMAYANA*).

Some scholars have identified typical features of a hero's career. These features are helpful, provided they do not obscure the distinctive characteristics of a particular story. The writer F. R. S. Raglan noted several characteristics of a hero. They include birth through supernatural means, a battle with a supernatural enemy, such as a demon or a dragon, and a special destination after death. Campbell said that a hero's career followed the structure of RITES OF PASSAGE: separation, triumph over trials, and return. Each stage presented many possibilities for variation. For example, triumph could take the form of marriage to a GODDESS, reconciliation with the creator-father, becoming divine, or stealing the drink of immortality.

Founders of religions sometimes take on the characteristics of heroes. Examples include MOSES, JESUS, and the BUDDHA. Indeed, the Buddha's biography contains a tension between two different ideals of world-conquest: the military conquest that the Buddha's father wanted for his son, and the spiritual conquest that the Buddha achieved.

During the 20th century the ideal of the hero or heroine was applied to nonreligious figures: politicians (Abraham Lincoln), military leaders (George Patton), sports figures (Muhammad Ali), and leaders of social causes (Susan B. Anthony). Comic books and films celebrated a number of fictional heroes and "superheroes," such as Superman, Batman, and Wonderwoman. Joseph Campbell's ideas

deeply influenced the filmmaker George Lucas. He used them as the basis for his well-known movie trilogy, *Star Wars.*

Hindu festivals Religious celebrations in Hindu communities (*see* HINDUISM). Hindus celebrate most festivals once each year. But the Indian year is quite different from the Gregorian year observed in North America and Europe (January 1 through December 31). It is based on cycles of the moon, and the number of days in both months and years are different from what is found in the Gregorian calendar. Hindus regularly adjust the year so that the months occur during roughly the same season, but it is not possible to say that a Hindu festival, such as Holi, occurs on a specific Gregorian date, the way CHRISTMAS, for example, falls on December 25. In this way, Hindu festivals are like the Jewish holiday PASSOVER and the Christian holiday EASTER.

The Hindu year generally begins around either the spring or the fall equinox (when the day and night are the same length). Each month is divided into a bright half or fortnight, which is the time between the new and the full moon, and a dark fortnight, between the full and the new moon.

The renowned expert on Hindu religious practice, P. V. Kane, identified more than 1,000 different Hindu festivals. Some are observed only in certain regions; others are observed throughout India. The observance of all-Indian festivals may, however, vary from place to place. Festivals generally combine elements of a fair or carnival with religious RITUALS, narrowly speaking. Many are colorful, and Hindus decorate their temples with strings of colored flags and lights that North Americans may associate with store openings and Christmas, respectively.

Some festivals celebrate major events in the life of a god. Dussehra, celebrated during the bright fortnight of October–November, begins with Navaratri. The name means "nine nights," and the nights are generally associated with the battle of DURGA and the buffalo demon. The 10th day marks Durga's victory; in some places it also marks

Indian dancers practice in traditional dress as they prepare for the upcoming Hindu festival of Navratri, or Nine Nights, in Ahmadabad, India. *(AP Photo/Siddharth Darshan Kumar)*

October–November, is the festival of lights. Worshippers observe it by placing a multitude of lamps outdoors in the evening. Holi (the full moon of March–April) is a north Indian ritual that allows for excessive play. Worshippers spatter one another with colored powders or, if they are mischievous, dirt and muck. South Indians honor sacred cobras on Naga-pancami (the fifth day of the bright fortnight of August–September). In Rakshabandhana (the full moon of August–September) sisters symbolically protect their brothers by tying colored threads around their wrists. In western India Makarasamkranti (in mid-January according to the position of the sun) is a day for competitive kite-flying. Competitors coat the strings of their kites with sharp materials such as powdered glass. Then they try to fly their own kites in such a way as to cut the strings of the other kites.

Not all Hindu festivals are observed every year. Four times in the course of a 12-year cycle Hindus observe Kumbh Mela. This is a PILGRIMAGE festival held in succession at spots where, it is said, drops of the elixir of immortality once dripped on the Earth: Prayaga (Allahabad), Hard-war, Ujjain, and Nasik. Recent celebrations have drawn literally millions of worshippers. Those who celebrate acquire merit and are cleansed of defilements through a ritual bath.

RAMA's victory over Ravana. Sivaratri occurs on the 14th day of the dark fortnight of February–March. It is particularly sacred to worshippers of SIVA. They observe it by ritually anointing a consecrated *lingam*, a symbol of the god. Krishnajayanti, on the eighth day of the dark fortnight of August–September, celebrates KRISHNA's birth at the hour of midnight. Ramanavami, on the ninth day of the bright fortnight of April–May, honors the birth of Rama.

There are many other popular festivals. Divali or Dipavali, on the 14th of the dark fortnight of

Hinduism

Hinduism A set of religions that arose and are especially practiced in India. Hinduism is something of an umbrella term. It includes any Indian religious practice that does not claim to belong to another religion. Nevertheless, most of these religions share certain characteristics, such as acknowledging the authority of the sacred texts known as the VEDA.

HISTORY

The first religious practices on the Indian subcontinent that we have any distinct knowledge of are those of the Indus Valley civilization (fl. 3500–1500 B.C.E.) (*see* INDUS VALLEY RELIGION). Our knowledge of these practices is, however, limited to physical artifacts that are difficult to interpret. These artifacts include seals that seem to show a person in costume meditating and a pool that seems designed for RITUAL bathing.

According to traditional European scholarship, the religion of the Veda was brought to India about 1500 B.C.E. Traditional Indian scholarship sees it as having originated in India much earlier. The practices that we know the most about were elaborate public SACRIFICES sponsored by wealthy patrons and performed by priests. Some parts of the Veda give evidence of what may have been more popular practices: spells and incantations used for medical purposes.

Starting perhaps around 600 B.C.E. speculation on the Veda gave rise to philosophical texts known as the UPANISHADS. Somewhat later more practically oriented scholars systematized the Hindu way of life in *Smritis* or *Dharmasastras,* the most important of which was the *Laws of MANU.* Over many centuries mythological material developed into a body of literature known as *itihasa*-PURANA. It includes the mammoth epic poem the *Mahabharata* and an especially revered portion of it, the BHAGAVAD-GITA.

From 500 to 1500 C.E. Hinduism as we know it today took shape. Beginning in south India, a movement of devotion to deities (BHAKTI) drew people who had supported BUDDHISM back to Hinduism. Hindus started to build temples to house their gods and goddesses. The orthodox schools of philosophy, especially the various forms of VEDANTA, were formulated. TANTRISM, a tradition of esoteric rituals, provided alternative means to release. Eventually an elaborate and sophisticated religious literature grew up in the languages of everyday life.

BELIEFS

Virtually all forms of Hinduism acknowledge the authority of the Veda, but that does not mean that they derive any specific content from it. There is no Hindu creed, and Hinduism encompasses many different beliefs.

For example, some Hindus are polytheists (worshipping more than one god), some are henotheists (acknowledging many gods but devoting themselves to one), some are monotheists (acknowledging and worshipping GOD as one), and some are atheists (denying that God exists). Instead of worshipping a personal God, Hindu atheists may postulate that a single, nonpersonal reality underlies the world of appearances (*see* BRAHMAN). Hindus who are monotheists generally see the many Hindu gods as different manifestations of the one same God.

The Veda celebrates gods like INDRA, AGNI, Surya, Varuna, and, a little later, Prajapati. The gods of the *Puranas* are generally grouped together under the triad of BRAHMA the creator, VISHNU the preserver, and SIVA the destroyer, together with their consorts SARASWATI, LAKSHMI, and PARVATI. Actual Hindu worship tends to focus on a somewhat different triad: Vishnu with his avatars KRISHNA and RAMA (sometimes the BUDDHA and JESUS, too) and his consort Lakshmi; Siva with his consort Parvati and his son GANESA; and Devi, the goddess, especially in the form of DURGA and KALI. Much worship focuses, too, on the deities of the local village, often female, who may or may not be identified with the pan-Indian deities just named.

Despite this plurality, most Hindus share a set of beliefs about the structure of life and the universe. They believe that upon death, living beings are reborn. The conditions of their rebirth are determined by whether their action (KARMA) has been morally good or bad. The universe, too, alternates between creation and destruction, although the number of years in each cycle is immense. Most Hindus also acknowledge that the ultimate religious goal is to attain release (*moksha*) from the cycle of rebirth (SAMSARA).

PRACTICES

Hindu practices are just as diverse as Hindu beliefs.

The codes of DHARMA, religiously sanctioned order, discuss practice in terms of a *sanatana dharma,* an order that applies universally. According to this order, what one is supposed to do is determined by the *varna* (ritual class; see CASTE IN HINDUISM) into which one is born and the *asrama* (stage of life) in which one happens to be. In youth, males of the top three *varnas* are to study the Veda; in maturity they are to marry, support a household, and produce children, especially sons; in old age they relinquish their duties. Some even take a fourth step, known as *sannyasa,* in which they totally renounce their possessions and identity and search for ultimate release from repeated rebirth.

Hindu law codes give much less freedom to women. According to the *Laws of Manu,* "Her father guards her in childhood, her husband guards her in her youth, and her sons guard her in old age. A woman is not fit for independence." This hardly does justice, however, to the many Hindu women through the centuries renowned for their accomplishments in intellectual, political, military, and religious realms. For example, many of the doctors in India today are women.

Accompanying this life cycle is a series of RITES OF PASSAGE known as *samskaras.* The most important is probably the initiation of the boy into Vedic study. Those who study the Veda ideally perform Vedic rituals throughout their working years and retirement. Vedic twilight rituals, known as *sandhya* and performed morning and evening, punctuate the rhythms of daily life.

By far the most common worship practice in Hinduism is PUJA, worship of a god in image form either at home or at a temple. A number of festivals punctuate the Hindu year (*see* HINDU FESTIVALS). Pilgrimage to sacred sites sometimes involves millions of devotees at a time. A number of spiritual disciplines (YOGAS) attempt to produce ultimate release from repeated rebirth. Not to be overlooked, too, are the many vows that Hindu women make. Although Hinduism often highlights the religious role of men, women are important teachers of their children. For example, Mohandas Gandhi attributed his religious seriousness to the profound religious devotion of his mother.

ORGANIZATION

Hinduism is above all a religion of the family. It is possible to be a devout Hindu and never set foot in a temple. Families do, however, participate in broader religious institutions. All Hindu families are classified in terms of caste (*jati*) and ritual class (*varna*). For those families who participate in Vedic ceremonies, the GURU or spiritual preceptor is an important authority.

Astrologers are seen as important spiritual advisers. Many Hindus consult them on all important occasions, especially birth and marriage. Hindus also consult renunciants (SADHUS). In the past century or so these have included such prominent figures as RAMAKRISHNA Paramahamsa, Sri Aurobindo, and Ramana Maharshi. Renunciants are usually members of institutions, for example, the monasteries founded by the great Indian philosopher SANKARA.

HINDUISM TODAY

Since the 19th century, Hinduism has faced many challenges. One was how to react to British rulers, who considered Hindu traditions backward. The Brahmo Samaj, founded by Raja Ram Mohan Roy (1772–1833) sought to modernize Hinduism. The Arya Samaj, founded by Dayananda Saraswati (1824–83), sought instead to purify Hinduism by returning to its Vedic roots.

A second challenge was how to deal with living in non-Hindu territories. Starting in the 19th century Hindus emigrated to eastern and southern Africa, the West Indies, Australia, Great Britain, Canada, and eventually the United States. Those who did so have been formulating what it means to be Hindu in these lands (*see* HINDUISM IN AMERICA). Especially since the 1960s some Hindus have been traveling outside of India as missionaries.

Yet another challenge was how to respond to British rule in India. What was the appropriate way for Hindus to fight the British? In the 19th century B. G. Tilak read the BHAGAVAD-GITA as calling Hindus to armed struggle. In the early 20th century, however, Mohandas GANDHI used it to advocate nonviolence.

India won its independence in 1947. Since then, Hindus have argued vigorously about whether India should be a secular or a Hindu state. The heirs of Gandhi, the Congress Party, have favored a secular state. Others have advocated the ideal of *Hindutva,* "Hindu-ness." According to this ideal, Hindutva is not a religion but the traditional culture of India.

All Indian citizens should embrace it, even if they are Muslims, Christians, Parsis, Sikhs, or Jains or have some other religious identity.

A number of organizations advocate the Hindutva ideal (*see* FUNDAMENTALISM, HINDU). They include the RSS (National Service Society), the VHP (World Hindu Congress), and the BJP (Bharatiya Janata Party), a political party that has ruled India off and on in the 1990s and early 2000s.

In agitating for Hindutva, these groups have taken as their symbol the alleged birthplace of Rama. A MOSQUE had stood on the site, but on December 6, 1992, crowds favoring Hindutva tore it down. Their actions sparked riots in which thousands of people, mostly Muslims, were killed. In 2001 violence against Muslims once again broke out, especially in the western Indian state of Gujarat, that resulted in hundreds of deaths. In the summer of 2004, the BJP lost the national elections. It is, however, too early to tell what the ultimate outcome of the push for Hindutva will be.

SIGNIFICANCE

Hinduism is the religion of roughly one-seventh of the world's population. In addition, it has given the rest of the world a rich tradition of religious thought, literature, and art as well as examples of profound religious devotion.

Further reading: Kim Knott, *Hinduism: A Very Short Introduction* (New York: Oxford University Press, 2000); R. K. Narayan, *Gods, Demons, and Others* (New York: Bantam Books, 1986); Patrick Olivelle, trans., *Upanishads* (New York: Oxford University Press, 1998); Satguru Sivaya Subramuniyaswami, *Dancing with Siva: Hinduism's Contemporary Catechism*, 5th ed. (Kapaa, Hawaii: Himalayan Academy, 1999).

Hinduism, new movements in   There is no centralized authority for HINDUISM that is analogous to the PAPACY within ROMAN CATHOLICISM. In a sense, then, new movements appear within Hinduism whenever a new teacher or holy person attracts followers. During the 20th century some move-

ments within Hinduism began to appeal to people of non-Indian as well as Indian ancestry. They even began to seek converts and establish centers outside of India. This entry will concentrate on such movements. For a discussion of recent movements within Hinduism that have a political orientation, *see* FUNDAMENTALISM, HINDU.

According to one common scheme, Hindus follow one of three *margas* or paths, the paths of insight, moral action, and devotion to the gods. This is a convenient scheme for talking about new religious movements in Hinduism, too. In general, movements in the paths of devotion and moral action have had only limited appeal to non-Indians. Non-Indians, especially in North America and Europe, have preferred movements that promise insight, wisdom, and inner peace.

The path of action traditionally defines DHARMA according to the family into which one is born. It has not had much concern for people who are not born within Hindu families. It is difficult, therefore, for movements in the path of action to appeal to non-Indians. It is true that the nonviolent teachings of Mohandas GANDHI have inspired many people around the world. This inspiration has never, however, led to the development of a unified and independent religious community.

There is much popular interest in Hindu gods in North America and Europe. Feminists often find the goddess KALI attractive. Many people use images of Hindu gods to decorate homes, offices, or other buildings, but they often do not actually worship these gods. The best example of a movement that fosters devotion to a god is probably the International Society for KRISHNA Consciousness (ISKCON), whose members are sometimes called Hare Krishnas. Other devotional movements tend just to serve the needs of Hindus living outside of India. An example with some connection to devotion is the Himalayan Academy of Satguru Sivaya Subramaniyaswami. It publishes *Hinduism Today* in the United States and promotes the worship of SIVA.

Movements within the path of insight tend to be of much greater interest to people who were not born into Hindu families. The oldest such organization in the United States may be the Vedanta

Society. It is a branch of a movement founded by Vivekananda (1863–1903), a disciple of the Bengali saint RAMAKRISHNA Paramahamsa (1836–86). At regular meetings members of the Society listen to talks about such themes as BRAHMAN being the ultimate reality of the universe and of all beings within it. Two movements devoted to simplified versions of Hindu MEDITATION are Transcendental Meditation (TM), founded by Maharishi Mahesh Yogi (b. 1917), and the Rajneesh Foundation, founded in 1974. Both groups are no longer as popular in the United States as they once were. Another group that stresses meditation, the Brahma Kumari or "princess of BRAHMA" movement, founded in 1937, is notable for the leadership roles that women assume.

One feature of Hindu new religious movements that often troubles outsiders is the manner in which participants are often expected to treat the teacher or GURU. Followers of Rajneesh, also known as Osho, were expected to consider him as a god incarnate. Similarly, followers of Sri Sathya Sai Baba, who teaches the unity of the world's religions, worship him as an AVATAR of god and a loving deity. Both have been accused of sexual misconduct by former followers.

There is certainly room for caution in assessing anyone's claims to special status. At the same time, claims to divine status do have precedents in Hinduism. For example, the Swaminarayan movement, founded in 1801, is prominent among Hindus from Gujarat and very active in social relief activities. Its members consider themselves devotees of God, but they also revere their founder, Swaminarayan, as Lord.

Hinduism in America   Interest in and practice of the traditional religions of India in the Western Hemisphere, especially North America. Interest in HINDUISM among European North Americans began in the 1830s and 1840s. At that time New England Transcendentalists such as Ralph Waldo Emerson (1803–82) and Henry David Thoreau (1817–62) studied selected writings of Asian religions, including Hindu scriptures such as the UPANISHADS and the BHAGAVAD-GITA. Although their writings used Hindu-sounding concepts, such as the "oversoul," their understanding of Hinduism was not profound.

At the end of the 19th century, Hinduism gained considerable visibility in North America as a result of the World's Parliament of Religion, held in Chicago in 1893. Most of the participants in the Parliament were Christian. But a representative of Hinduism named VIVEKANANDA, a follower of the Bengali SAINT RAMAKRISHNA, made a strong impression on participants and observers. Soon after the Parliament he founded the VEDANTA Society, which taught Hindu philosophy in many American cities and attracted some high-profile adherents, including the writers Aldous Huxley and Christopher Isherwood.

Until the 1960s, Hinduism in the United States was mostly limited to an interest in certain aspects of Hindu philosophy. That was not true of other places in the Western Hemisphere. For example, during the 19th century indentured servants were brought from India to the West Indies. They brought their religions along with them. An early novel of V. S. Naipaul, *A House for Mr. Biswas* (1961), gives a portrait of their community.

In the mid-1960s, the United States changed its immigration laws. The number of people of Indian descent living in the United States began to grow. As a result, the practice of Hinduism as a religion supplemented the earlier interest in Hindu philosophy.

Public attention often focused on missionary efforts directed at North Americans of non-Indian descent. Many young Americans tried meditation techniques purveyed by traveling gurus. The International Society of KRISHNA Consciousness, an offshoot of Krishna worship in the Bengal region of eastern India, became highly visible. Founded in 1965 by A. C. Bhaktivedanta Swami Prabhupada, ISKCON instructed its followers to adopt traditional Indian dress, distributed literature, conducted devotional singing in public places, and founded communes and restaurants.

The practice of Hinduism by Indian immigrants received much less public attention than did the Hinduism of American converts, but it involved a significantly large number of people. Indeed, by the end of the 20th century even ISK-CON was primarily serving the needs of immigrants from India. Much of Hinduism is practiced household by household. Many Indian Americans regularly performed daily household RITUALS and the special rituals associated with different stages of human life, from birth to death. In addition, Indian American communities began to build temples. The first Hindu temple in the United States, the Venkateshvara temple outside Pittsburgh, was dedicated in 1976. Immigrant Hindus also formed various associations. The Visva Hindu Parishad or "World Hindu Congress" is a good example. One pressing need for Hindu families was how to teach Hinduism to children born in America. To meet this need, Hindu communities developed educational institutions such as Sunday schools. In general, the resources and clientele available for Hindu institutions in North America were considerably more limited than in India. As a result, American Hindu temples and organizations often combined gods and loyalties that had been kept separate in India.

By the end of the 20th century Hindus, especially Hindus of Indian descent, constituted a thriving community in North America. American Hinduism was thriving along with them.

Holiness movement

Holiness movement A movement within PROTESTANTISM that emphasizes the possibility of perfection, that is, of living without SIN. The Holiness movement began in the United States during the 19th century. Efforts of missionaries have spread it throughout the world.

The Holiness movement grew out of the teachings of John WESLEY (1703–91) and METHODISM. Indeed, Holiness churches see themselves as maintaining true Methodism. Wesley taught that, after Christians were justified (forgiven of their sins and put right with GOD) through God's grace at baptism, they could receive a second gift of grace that provided sanctification, that is, that helped them live a life without sin. The goal of all Christians, he taught, should be to seek perfection.

In the early 1800s many American Methodists did not have much use for Wesley's teachings about sanctification. Others, however, did, such as the revivalist preacher Charles G. Finney (1792–1875), president of Oberlin College in Ohio. In striving for perfection, the founders of the Holiness movement actively sought to improve American society. Among other issues, they promoted the abolition of slavery, peace, social work in city slums, and women's rights.

The early Holiness movement differed from most Protestant churches at the time in insisting that women could hold any church office. In fact, in the Holiness churches, many women did hold high offices. Examples include Antoinette Brown (1825–1921), ordained in 1853 as the first female minister in an American church, and Alma White (1862–1946), who was, she herself said, the first woman in the history of Christianity to hold the office of bishop (consecrated in 1918). In addition, many Holiness preachers worked among the urban poor. An example, first organized in Great Britain, is the SALVATION ARMY.

In the early days, the Holiness movement took two forms. Some churches left larger Methodist bodies to form their own independent churches. One example is the Wesleyan Methodist Church, founded in 1843. Another is the Free Methodist Church, founded in 1860. Other people who favored Holiness teachings stayed within the larger churches and tried to influence them. The organization that brought them together was called the National Campmeeting Association for the Promotion of Holiness, founded in 1867. The word *campmeeting* in the name referred to a form of meeting common since the Second Great Awakening (*see* REVIVALISM). Through campmeetings Methodism had spread widely among settlers on the frontier; in the 1830s, that had meant the area west of the Appalachians but east of the Mississippi.

Toward the end of the 19th century, Methodist bishops began to be especially strict in trying to control the activities of members who preached entire sanctification. As a result, most of these groups left the Methodist church to found churches of their own. The most important of these churches are the Church of the NAZARENE and the CHURCH OF GOD (Anderson, Indiana):

In the 20th century Holiness churches tended to align themselves with the fundamentalist movement (*see* FUNDAMENTALISM, CHRISTIAN); that is, they tended to emphasize the entire BIBLE as the verbally inspired word of God. At the beginning of the century, some Holiness churches called themselves Pentecostal. They meant by this the second gift of the Spirit that brought about sanctification. But they rejected speaking in tongues and became sharply critical of PENTECOSTALISM. Some Holiness churches did, however, allow faith healing practiced together with scientific medicine.

The social activism of the earliest Holiness believers waned in the 20th century. Holiness churches became widely known instead for stressing a Puritanical lifestyle: no tobacco, liquor, gambling, or attendance at theatrical performances. The old National Campmeeting Association served as an umbrella group for many of these churches under various names: the National Holiness Association, the Christian Holiness Association, and then the Christian Holiness Partnership.

Already in the 19th century members of the Holiness movement took foreign missions seriously. Today, many members of the movement, perhaps the majority, live outside the United States.

Holocaust, the (Hebrew, Shoah)

Holocaust, the (Hebrew, Shoah) The imprisonment and systematic killing of millions of people, especially Jews, by the Nazis in Germany and German-occupied Europe from 1933 to 1945. The word *holocaust* is derived from Greek for a sacrifice wholly consumed by fire. Sometimes the equivalent Hebrew word, Shoah, is used.

HISTORY

Anti-Semitic violence has occurred in Europe from the Middle Ages on (*see* ANTI-SEMITISM), but in the Holocaust it grew to monstrous proportions. The Nazis came to power in Germany as part of a coalition government in January 1933. Their virulently anti-Semitic chancellor, Adolf Hitler, assumed dictatorial powers under emergency rule, as permitted by the German constitution. Government action against Jews began almost immediately.

During the period from 1933 to the outbreak of World War II, the German government systematically deprived Jews of their property and of all civil rights. For example, in 1933 Jews lost civic equality and were prevented from practicing many professions. The Nürnberg laws of 1935 outlawed sexual relations between "Aryans" (persons who were supposedly of pure German ancestry) and Jews. During this same period, there were outbreaks of violence against Jews. The most notorious was Kristallnacht (German for "the night of broken glass," November 9–10, 1938), when the Nazi paramilitary severely vandalized German-Jewish businesses and synagogues. Despite the violence, many Jews were reluctant to leave German territories. They had lived in Germany for generations and had survived successive waves of sporadic persecution. Many others wanted to leave but were unable.

The outbreak of war in 1939 brought a drastic change. As Germany conquered territories, especially to the east, the number of Jews living under German rule swelled. Jews were required to wear yellow badges in the shape of the star of David; others whom the Nazis considered undesirable had to wear different badges. The Nazis contemplated an "ethnic cleansing" of Europe by exporting Jewish residents to a colony in, for example, Madagascar. Eventually, however, they determined on a "final solution" to the "Jewish problem": They deported Jews to concentration camps where they were exploited for labor and then killed when no longer useful. In addition, Nazis conducted hideous medical experiments on those incarcerated. By January 1942 the "final solution" was in full operation. Auschwitz, Buchenwald, Belsen, Dachau, and Treblinka may be the best-known camps, but there were, in all, more than 300 death camps.

Resistance to the deportations did occur. One example is the Warsaw ghetto uprising of April 1943. But knowledge of the camps was extremely limited, and in many Jewish communities it seemed better to cooperate in the deportations than to face immediate, violent reprisals from the Nazis. Although the Allies fighting Germany had reliable reports of the mass exterminations, they did nothing to disrupt railway access to the camps. Doing so would have been relatively easy and effective.

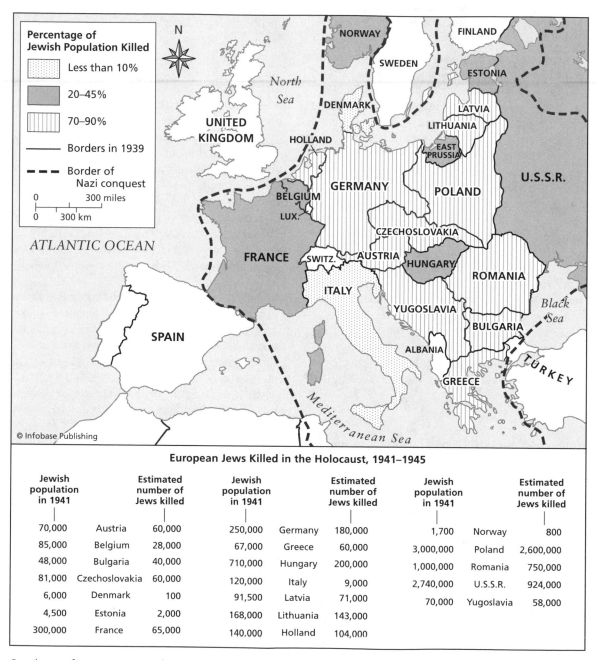

European Jews Killed in the Holocaust, 1941–1945

Jewish population in 1941		Estimated number of Jews killed	Jewish population in 1941		Estimated number of Jews killed	Jewish population in 1941		Estimated number of Jews killed
70,000	Austria	60,000	250,000	Germany	180,000	1,700	Norway	800
85,000	Belgium	28,000	67,000	Greece	60,000	3,000,000	Poland	2,600,000
48,000	Bulgaria	40,000	710,000	Hungary	200,000	1,000,000	Romania	750,000
81,000	Czechoslovakia	60,000	120,000	Italy	9,000	2,740,000	U.S.S.R.	924,000
6,000	Denmark	100	91,500	Latvia	71,000	70,000	Yugoslavia	58,000
4,500	Estonia	2,000	168,000	Lithuania	143,000			
300,000	France	65,000	140,000	Holland	104,000			

Population of Jews in Europe before and after the Holocaust

All told, almost 12,000,000 people lost their lives during the Holocaust. Roughly half of these were Jews, a third of the Jewish population in the world. Other victims included communists, gypsies, homosexuals, and the mentally ill.

REACTIONS

One reaction to the Holocaust has been the attempt to bring the perpetrators to justice. In trials held in Nürnberg, Germany, from November 1945 to October 1946, the Allies tried and convicted several Nazi leaders. Since then, other Nazi leaders have also been brought to justice. The most notorious was Adolf Eichmann, the overseer of the concentration camps, who was executed in 1962.

A second reaction to the Holocaust has been the attempt to memorialize the victims. Structures at former camps, such as Auschwitz, remind the world of the atrocities committed there. So do monuments and museums like the Holocaust Museum in Washington, D.C. Works of literature, such as the powerful novel, *Night,* by the Nobel Prize-winning author Elie Wiesel, convey a sense of the horrors of the camps. In addition, a new day has been added to the Jewish calendar, Yom ha-Shoah, Hebrew for Holocaust Day.

A third reaction to the Holocaust was increased support for establishing a Jewish state in the territory of Palestine (*see* ZIONISM). Before the Holocaust many Jews opposed this goal or were lukewarm in supporting it. After the Holocaust only Hasidic Jews continued to oppose the idea (*see* HASIDISM). On May 14, 1948, Israel was officially declared a state. A Jewish state, Israel is seen as a haven for all Jews in times of persecution.

Finally, many Jews and Christians have seen the Holocaust as a challenge to FAITH. It seems to call into question many of their cherished beliefs about GOD. Some have found resources in their traditions to deal with these atrocities. Others have felt it necessary to modify or abandon traditional assertions. For example, some have concluded that God cannot be omnipotent. Others have concluded that after the Holocaust it is no longer possible to believe in God.

Further reading: Lucy S. Dawidowicz, *The War against the Jews, 1933–1945* (New York: Holt, Rinehart and Winston, 1975); Ann Frank, *The Diary of a Young Girl* (New York: Pocket Books, 1953); Martin Gilbert, *The Holocaust* (New York: H. Holt, 1987); Richard Rubenstein, *After Auschwitz* (Indianapolis: Bobbs-Merrill, 1966).

holy, idea of the Concepts of that which is set apart because of its divine power. Religion presupposes a split-level universe. To the traditionally religious person, the world is not homogeneous. Religious people are likely to have a definite awareness of spiritual places, whether churches or temples or PILGRIMAGE sites, as different from ordinary places, such as homes or offices. There one speaks in a hushed voice and makes special gestures in a reverent way.

Two words are used in English to describe these kinds of places and experiences: holy and sacred. They have been the subjects of two important books on religion, *The Idea of the Holy* by Rudolf OTTO and *The Sacred and the Profane* by Mircea ELIADE. Reflecting the way the two words have somewhat different nuances, Otto emphasized the powerful, mysterious, "numinous," shuddery if not terrifying yet also fascinating and attracting quality of holy times and places and the divine being within them. These ranged from the burning bush and the summit of Mount Sinai as MOSES knew them to divine encounters of today. Eliade discussed more human sacred places and times, such as those of temples and festivals. But he recognized that they depend ultimately on "theophanies" or divine manifestations that marked them out and set them apart.

Either way, religion in anything like its traditional form needs to have at its core awareness of the holy and the sacred. It must recognize that GOD or ultimate reality is wholly other than the human world, confronting it with awesome power and presence.

Religion adds something else. It says that between the holy and the ordinary world are "doors and windows." God can reveal himself to people, and people can rise up to glimpse the divine. These "doors and windows" are the province of religion, for they are the words, scriptures, mystical or visionary experiences; the shrines, temples, RITUALS, sacred dances, holy days and sacred sites, which communicate what is holy to the world.

homosexuality and religion Religious attitudes toward sexual relations between persons of the same sex, and the ways in which religions have used those relations. In the United States during the late 20th century, homosexuality was a controversial issue in both politics and religion. In the 1990s the state of Colorado passed a referendum against granting "special rights" to homosexual men and women (gays and lesbians). The Supreme Court overturned it. In the same decade a committee of the Evangelical Lutheran Church in America presented a draft of a statement on sexuality that urged love and respect for homosexuals. Controversy forced the draft to be withdrawn.

The Christian church has generally opposed homosexuality. Indeed, CHRISTIANITY has at times seen all sexual behavior as tainted by SIN. Many Christians see homosexuality as a disruption of the order that GOD created. They also point to passages that condemn homosexuality in the BIBLE: Leviticus 18.22 and 20.13 or Romans 1:26–27. Traditional Christians certainly reject any suggestion of homoeroticism—love between two persons of the same sex—in the relationship between, for example, DAVID and Jonathan in the Hebrew Bible or JESUS and the disciple "whom he loved" in the GOSPEL of John.

There have, however, been other voices within the Christian community. Some point out that Christians blithely ignore other injunctions in Leviticus, such as the dietary laws. Some suggest that the proper Christian attitude should be governed by God's love, which extends to all people. By the end of the century some academic theologians were actively writing gay and lesbian THEOLOGY.

Other religions besides Christianity have traditionally condemned homosexuality. In JUDAISM and TALMUD and later law books (*see* HALAKHAH) have

The hero Achilles, at right, bandages his wounded friend Patroclus in a red-figure scene on an Athenian cup, *c.* 500 B.C.E. The painting conveys Patroclus's distress and Achilles' sympathetic concentration. Although the *Iliad* never portrays Achilles and Patroclus as lovers, the Greeks after Homer came to view the pair as models of aristocratic military male homosexuality. *(Margaret Bunson)*

repeated and even strengthened the Bible's injunctions against homosexuality. In ISLAM the QUR'AN rejects the sexual practices of Sodom and Gomorrah (26.165–173); this has generally led Muslims to dismiss male homosexuality. (Muslim tradition does not say much about female homosexuality.) During the 20th century, more liberal Jews and Muslims, like their Christian counterparts, began to rethink traditional attitudes.

Not all cultures and religions have had negative attitudes toward homosexuality. Some cultures and religions have made positive use of it. In many cases, the meaning that the word "homosexual" often has in the United States is too narrow. Homosexual may not refer to a person but to behavior. The same person may be expected to engage in both homosexual and heterosexual behavior.

Many cultures have expected men to form homosexual relationships with boys. There is less evidence of women forming homosexual relationships with girls, but that has occurred, too. The ancient Greeks provide good examples of such relationships among both men and women. They provided the education boys and girls needed to become mature men and women. In some cultures these kinds of relationships are integral parts of INITIATION rituals. Homosexual RITUAL activity was seen as necessary for the boys to become heterosexual men.

Many Hindus reject homosexuality as unthinkable. BUDDHISM celebrates the life-style of MONKS AND NUNS and tends to urge sexual restraint. Nevertheless, a Hindu and Buddhist tradition known as TANTRISM sometimes makes use of sexual rituals. These rituals usually strive to unite opposites (male and female), but homosexual rituals have not been unknown. In addition, Buddhism has sometimes seen homosexual relationships as less harmful to a monk's spiritual progress than heterosexual ones.

Among indigenous peoples, shamans may practice homosexual behavior (see SHAMANISM). In traveling to the spirit world, they routinely cross boundaries that limit ordinary human beings. They may reflect this crossing of the boundaries in features of their ordinary life. Thus, shamans may wear clothing of the opposite sex; they may also enter into homosexual relationships. For example, the Chukchi, who live in northeastern Siberia, permitted shamans to engage in only homosexual activity.

Honen   *See* PURE LAND BUDDHISM.

Horus   A GOD in ancient Egypt, depicted either as a falcon or with a human body and a falcon's head. His eyes were the sun and the moon.

Some myths made Horus the son of the god Re and the goddess HATHOR. But he was especially known as the son of the god Osiris and the goddess ISIS. According to a well-known myth, Osiris was killed by his brother and enemy, Seth. Osiris's wife, Isis, gave birth to Horus and hid him in papyrus marshes to keep him safe. Eventually, Horus grew up and avenged his father's death by defeating his uncle.

Between them, Osiris and Horus, father and son, shared the task of ruling. Osiris was king of the dead, Horus king of the living. The Egyptian king was said to be Horus incarnate. After the Persian conquest of Egypt in 525 B.C.E. and the end of Egyptian independence, the mythology of Horus killing Seth to avenge Osiris was sometimes given a "nationalistic" twist. It held out hope that an independent Egyptian kingdom would be reestablished.

Horus had two chief sanctuaries, at Bekhdet in Lower (northern) Egypt and Edfu in Upper (southern) Egypt. He also had several different cult names. For example, Harpokrates referred to Horus the child and his secret upbringing. Harakhte was Horus of the horizon, the god as associated with the sunrise.

Hosea   A book in the BIBLE, and the name of the prophet whose words it supposedly contains. The book of Hosea belongs to the collection of prophets known as "The Twelve."

Hosea was a native of the northern kingdom of Israel. This kingdom consisted of the 10 tribes who had rejected SOLOMON's son Rehoboam and formed their own kingdom under Jeroboam around 922 B.C.E. Hosea began to prophesy during the reign of Jeroboam II (786–746 B.C.E.).

In international affairs the kingdom of Israel was larger and more important than the southern kingdom of Judah. But in terms of religion many thought that it was too lax in its WORSHIP of the traditional god YHWH ("the Lord") and too tolerant of other deities.

The prophet Hosea is best known for dramatizing this laxness and YHWH's continuing concern for Israel. On GOD's instructions he married a prostitute. She bore three children, although Hosea might not have been the father. Then she left him. Nevertheless, Hosea bought her back. The message was this: Although Israel has acted like a prostitute in worshipping other gods, YHWH will not forsake her.

humanism, religious

As used today, a religious philosophy of life that emphasizes attention to human needs and values in this world, rather than to GOD, the AFTERLIFE, and otherworldly concerns. Those who believe that putting the good of human life and society in this world first, while living perhaps with a sense of wonder and awe toward human life and nature, can be seen as taking a religious path, though one without God in the traditional sense, and may be called religious humanists. Characteristically humanists hold that only that which can be learned through science or direct observation can be regarded as known for sure, and that a good, useful, and happy life can be lived based only on this kind of knowledge. Many would add that religion in the traditional sense is outmoded, unneeded, and causes more trouble than good. There are a number of religious humanists in Unitarian-Universalist churches, and in the American Humanist Association.

humor and religion

Fun, satire, and laughter that have a role in religion. Humor has often been disdained by the more solemn sort of religionists, such as the Protestant Puritans (*see* PURITANISM). Yet humor can have a positive religious role. People laughing together create a community. Humor can deflate the pride and pomposity that is usually a religious SIN, and show the importance of the meek who not seldom outsmart the mighty. Humor provides a way of dealing with the irrationality of the universe, which seems to be there despite the best efforts of theologians, and it can tap off the tension built up by serious religious rites.

Thus in some Native American cultures "RITUAL CLOWNS" would follow the serious priests about and do humorous burlesque versions of their solemn rites. In medieval Europe it was customary on certain festivals to name a child as "boy bishop" for the occasion, dress him in appropriate robes, and encourage him to make fun of the real rulers of the church. In many mythologies the figures known as TRICKSTERS appear, like Coyote in Native American lore or LOKI in Germanic legend. He plays cruel tricks on people, outwits the gods, has a prodigious appetite, but like Prometheus stealing the fire will sometimes use his cleverness for human good. In some cultures like old Russia, there was a place for the "holy fool," a devout half-wit whose remarks and mocking laughter sometimes struck home. Some societies even have humor-based festivals, like Holi in India, whose main features include raucous pageants and good fun based on the mythologies of gods. One of the "new religions" of Japan, Seicho no Ie, has a quasi-religious rite called "laughing practice" that consists simply of laughing (*see* JAPAN, NEW RELIGIONS IN). Laughing as a token of the presence of the Holy Spirit has also appeared in Christian PENTECOSTALISM.

Attitudes may vary, but basic to all religions is the belief that there is a difference between what the world seems to be, and claims to be on its own terms, and what it really is. It may claim to be real, to be perfect or capable of getting there, and that its important people are really important. Religion knows otherwise: The world, it says, is illusion and only GOD is truly real; it is sinful and in ignorance rather than perfect; and the important people may not really be as important as simple, humble, and obscure SAINTS who see things as they really are. Humor can be a most useful means of puncturing the illusions that keep us from religious truth.

I Ching "Classic of Changes"; an ancient Chinese book used to divine the forces at work in the universe (*see* CHINA, RELIGIONS OF). The *I Ching* is the most important of the five classics that CONFUCIUS (551–479 B.C.E.) supposedly edited. The other four are the *Book of History,* the *Book of Poetry,* the *Book of Rites,* and the *Spring and Autumn Annals.* The *I Ching* dates at least to the fourth century B.C.E., perhaps even earlier. It had become an important book in CONFUCIANISM by the second century B.C.E.

The Ancient Chinese used several methods to divine or discern the cosmic forces that were in operation at any given time. One method was to cast stalks of the yarrow plant. The object was to see whether the stalks would break or remain whole. Those that broke were said to be yin; those that did not were said to be yang (*see* YIN/YANG THEORY). As a result, the ancient Chinese represented yin with a broken line (--). They represented yang with an unbroken line (—).

A single stalk, whether yin or yang, does not give much information about the universe. Cosmic forces are too complex to be described by a simple "yes" or "no" answer. So the ancient Chinese grouped lines together. The basic grouping contained three lines drawn horizontally, one on top of the other. The figure that resulted was known as a trigram. One can see four trigrams around the central yin-yang diagram on the South Korean flag.

Mathematics tells us that it is possible to draw eight different trigrams. But the system used in the *I Ching* is more complex still. It groups two trigrams together. The resulting figure is known as a hexagram, because it contains six lines. The *I Ching* starts with a hexagram of six unbroken or yang lines. Next comes the hexagram in which all six lines are broken or yin. The book continues until it exhausts all 64 possible combinations of six broken and unbroken lines.

In and of themselves, the hexagrams are meaningless. The *I Ching* provides their meanings. It provides a name and brief description for each hexagram. Then it provides two more sets of meanings, known as "judgments" and "images." All three—name, judgment, and image—are rather vague. That makes it possible for the person consulting the book to adapt the meanings to suit her or his own situation.

To use the *I Ching,* one must be in the proper state of mind. One reflects on one's question, then tosses either yarrow stalks or coins. By examining the tossed stalks or coins one identifies two different hexagrams. The first hexagram provides information on the current state of affairs. The second hexagram identifies the changes that are coming. Turning to the *I Ching* one looks up the names, judgments, and images associated with the two hexagrams. Each person must decide individually how the names, judgments, and images apply to her or his life.

images, icons, idols in religion The religious use of pictures and statues. The religions of the world run a gamut in terms of the object of WORSHIP on ALTARS and in shrines, from those who venerate three-dimensional statues of gods, buddhas, or SAINTS with candles, incense, and food-offerings, accompanied by prostrations or kneeling, to those who totally reject all such worship. In the former camp would be much of HINDUISM, BUDDHISM, and ROMAN CATHOLICISM, together with much of PRIMAL RELIGION and ancient EGYPTIAN RELIGION, GREEK RELIGION, and ROMAN RELIGION. On the latter side would be ISLAM, JUDAISM, and Protestant Christianity. However, mediating positions can be found between extremes. EASTERN ORTHODOX CHRISTIANITY venerates sacred pictures of saints, called icons, but not three-dimensional statues. Many Protestants will accept pictures of biblical and other religious scenes, often in the form of stained-glass windows, together with crosses on altars and occasionally even statues, so long as they are not actually worshipped. Jews will usually accept pictures and symbols so long as they do not attempt to depict the divine and are not worshipped in the place of the divine.

Those who reject the worship of images call such images "idols" and their veneration "idolatry," holding that they are honored in the place of the true GOD, and that such worship is highly offensive to God. Those who do use images in worship usually respond that this is not the case, though ways of interpreting the use of images may vary. Sometimes it is said that, though the statue is not exactly a god or saint in itself, it does have a definite and permanent relationship to the holy entity, who chooses to dwell in or, as it were, behind or above the image, so that worship of the form is definitely received by the divine being. Others would say the image is only a symbol or reminder of the divine, though one that it is quite appropriate to use.

Nonetheless, the question of using images or not has been the stuff of bitter religious conflict and even bloody persecution. It was an issue in the Protestant REFORMATION in Europe, and in the confrontation of Hinduism and Islam in India. Two different views of religion, and of the relation to religion of works of art and of the visual sense, lie behind the conflict. Do we use that which is seen, and is made by human hands usually in human form, to lift us to the sacred, because the sacred can in fact live in human

form as gods, buddhas, and saints? Or do we find God best by taking away all that is not God, all that is man-made, worshipping him only as spirit and with the help only of words, not of things seen? These are questions that still divide the religious world.

imam   Arabic word meaning "leader." The word is used in very different ways in ISLAM. In SUNNI ISLAM an imam is a leader of a MOSQUE. He is recognized for his understanding of the FAITH and his upright life. His duties include preaching the sermon at the Friday noon PRAYER service (*see* SALAT).

In SHI'ITE ISLAM the word takes on quite a different sense. Shi'ites are distinguished by their conviction that the leadership of the Islamic community should have passed through the prophet MUHAMMAD's cousin Ali, husband of the prophet's daughter Fatimah, to his grandchildren and their male descendants. These leaders, who were denied their rightful rule over the entire Islamic community, are called imams.

Shi'ites hold that these imams should exercise both political and religious authority. However, even when they were not in political power, they continued to exercise religious authority by interpreting Islam to their communities and preserving its values.

Different Shi'ite factions recognize different lines of imams. The largest and most conservative group, known as the Twelvers, believe that their 12th imam went into hiding in 873 C.E. and will reappear at the end of time. Another major group, the Ismailis, believe that the line of imams continues today. For example, a branch or subgroup, the Nizari Ismailis, recognize the AGA KHAN as their 49th imam.

Inanna   The most important Sumerian GODDESS. Inanna's name means "Lady of the Sky." She herself was associated with the planet Venus. She was identified with the Akkadian and Babylonian goddess Ishtar, was related to the Canaanite goddess Astarte (*see* CANAANITE RELIGION), and is in some respects similar to Aphrodite and VENUS among the Greeks and the Romans.

Inanna was a goddess of sexuality and fertility. Accordingly, her most sacred city, Uruk, was reputed to be a city of prostitutes. At times Inanna was also associated with the battlefield.

Perhaps the best known story about her tells of her descent to the underworld, ruled by her sister Ereshkigal. As Inanna proceeds toward Ereshkigal, she loses articles of clothing one by one. In her sister's presence, she becomes like a dead slab of meat. Revived by a servant, she returns to the Earth to find her alleged lover, Dumuzi, not mourning her absence at all. She has him hunted down and killed.

Inca religion   The religion of the people who ruled much of the Andes region in South America just before the Spanish conquest. In 1527 Francisco Pizarro first arrived in Peru. He found a single power in control of the west coast of South America and the Andes Mountains, from what is now Ecuador to central Chile. This power, the Inca Empire, was called Tawantinsuyu, "region of the four quarters." It ruled from its capital at Cuzco.

The Incas were relative newcomers to power. They had ruled for only about a hundred years. In asserting their rule, they had conquered many different peoples, each of whom had their own cultures, languages, and religions. Inca religion, then, represents only a fraction of pre-Columbian Andean religions. Unfortunately, none of these peoples used writing. We know about Inca religion from two basic sources: archaeology (*see* ARCHAEOLOGY AND RELIGION) and accounts written after the Spanish conquest. The authors of these accounts were often people of mixed indigenous and Spanish ancestry. New discoveries continue to add fresh insights. For example, in 1995 climbers discovered the preserved body of a young Inca woman, 13 or 14 years old, on Mount Ampato in southern Peru. She appears to have been offered there as a SACRIFICE.

Religion was an important part of the way the Incas governed their empire. The emperor, who was known as the Inca, patronized temples of the various peoples whom he controlled. These peoples, in turn, sent objects to be offered in the temples at Cuzco. Sometimes they even sent their own children. The "four regions" in the Inca name for their empire were four quadrants—northeast, southeast, northwest, and southwest—that extended from Cuzco and its central temple, the Temple of the Sun.

The Inca—that is, the emperor—claimed to be the son of the Sun, the Inca god Inti. Inti was particularly associated with gold. His temple at Cuzco was the most important Inca shrine. It stood where two rivers met. The Inca may have thought that these two rivers resembled the Milky Way. Other Inca deities included: Mama-Kilya, the moon and the wife of the sun, to whom silver was sacred; Viracocha, who created much of the world and human culture; Pacacamac, who ruled over the lowlands and the sea; Pacamama, his wife, mother earth; and Illapa, who was responsible for the weather.

To these and other gods the Inca presented sacrifices. Sacrifices to the sun took place every day. One of them was the clothing that the emperor wore. The emperor wore a new cloak each day, and each day it was burned in offering to the sun. The Inca also sacrificed at festivals. The two most important took place around the solstices in December and June. The Inca presented to the gods animals, plants, beer, cloth, statues—and, at times of extreme importance, human beings.

Another important Inca practice was divination. The kind of sacrifice, the cause of a disease, the time for battle—all were determined by divination. Means of divination included taking oracles from sacred objects, observing spiders, "reading" coca leaves, drinking narcotics, and examining the lungs of a sacrificed llama. Special priests performed RITUALS of sacrifice and divination and tended the temples. Specially chosen women also served the temples.

The Spanish vigorously tried to eliminate the religion of the Andean peoples. As a result Inca religion, that is, the religion of the empire, disappeared when the empire fell. Local religious practices survived even as the people converted to ROMAN CATHOLICISM.

incarnation   A divine being becoming human. The term "incarnation" is usually used in the context of CHRISTIANITY. It refers to the process through which GOD the Son (*see* TRINITY) became human in the person of JESUS. This notion is similar to, although not identical with, the Hindu idea of the AVATARS of Lord VISHNU.

Scholars are divided on the question of whether Jesus himself claimed to be divine. In any case, writings in the NEW TESTAMENT make that claim. For 500 years Christians argued and struggled to formulate precisely what that claim meant.

In the end two meetings of bishops, known as councils, decided what Christians were supposed to believe. The Council of Nicaea (325) tried to clarify how Jesus related to God as revealed, for example, in the Hebrew BIBLE. It asserted that Jesus, God the Son, was not a creature that God had made; instead, he had the same being as God the Father. The Council of Chalcedon (451) tried to end arguments about how Jesus could be both human and divine. It adopted the formula that he was "two natures in one person," fully God and fully human at the same time.

incense   Fragrant substances made from spices and gums that are sometimes burned for religious purposes. Religions use incense for many purposes. Some religions, like that of the ancient Greeks, use incense to purify an area from pollution and protect it from EVIL. Some religions use incense as an offering. The presentation of *dhupa* (incense) is a standard feature of Hindu PUJA. It is also used as an offering and sign of devotion in Roman Catholic and Eastern Orthodox Christian WORSHIP. Some Buddhists use incense as a sort of initiatory ordeal for monks (*see* MONKS AND NUNS). Incense cones are placed on the skin and lighted. They leave a permanent scar. Some religions use incense to accompany PRAYERS. The incense rises into the air the way prayers rise to gods or ancestors. Chinese religions use incense in this way. Religions may also use incense simply to create a pleasant atmosphere, as is done in ISLAM as well as in the Japanese tea ceremony.

India, religions of   Until 1947 the name India referred to the Indian subcontinent, that is, the territory of the modern states of India, Pakistan, and Bangladesh. For religions, this has been one of the richest regions in the world.

Evidence for religious activity on the Indian subcontinent goes back into prehistory. The earliest major civilization, the Harappan or Indus Valley civilization, flourished in what is now Pakistan between 2500 and 2000 B.C.E. All we know about the INDUS VALLEY RELIGION comes from tantalizing hints associated with material remains, such as pictures on clay seals and a large pool for bathing.

Only traces of the Indus Valley religion have survived, but two religions that arose in India in the sixth century B.C.E. are much better known: JAINISM and BUDDHISM. Both of these religions began from movements of wandering monks. Both also rejected animal sacrifice and sought release from the defilements of KARMA or action.

Jainism has remained confined to India. There it is practiced today by two sects. The Svetambara, or white-clad, are common in western India. The Digambara, whose monks are sky-clad (that is, go naked), are common in southern India. According to the 2001 census there are about four and a quarter million Jains in India, making up .4 percent of the population.

Buddhism has spread far beyond India and developed several distinct regional forms. In south and southeast Asia THERAVADA BUDDHISM predominates; in East Asia MAHAYANA BUDDHISM predominates, while VAJRAYANA BUDDHISM is the religion of Tibet. Oddly, Buddhism disappeared from the land of its founding until 1956, when Dr. B. R. Ambedkar, the main author of the Constitution of India, led a mass conversion of untouchables to Buddhism. Since 1959 Buddhist exiles from Tibet, including the DALAI LAMA, have also lived in India. The 2001 Census counted almost 8 million Buddhists in India, about .75 percent of the population.

In the 1500s SIKHISM arose in India. Originally a peaceful tradition, its adherents were forced to develop a martial tradition in order to defend themselves. Sikhs are quite visible in North America and Europe today, because Sikh men wear turbans and sport long beards. In 2001 over 19,200,000 Sikhs lived in India, almost 1.9 percent of the total population.

Not all religions of India arose there. Several have come from elsewhere. Until recently, a small but vigorous community on the southwestern coast practiced JUDAISM, but most Indian Jews have emigrated to Israel.

According to tradition, CHRISTIANITY in India goes back to the APOSTLE Thomas. Many Indians have also converted to Christianity to escape the CASTE system (*see* CASTE IN HINDUISM). About a fourth of all Christians in India, especially Thomas Christians, live in the southwestern state of Kerala, where they make up about 19 percent of the population. Indian Christians, including adherents of ROMAN CATHOLICISM and PROTESTANTISM, live elsewhere in India, too. In 2001 Christians made up a little over 2.3 percent of the total population, numbering more than 24,000,000.

More Muslims live in Pakistan, Bangladesh, and India than anywhere else in the world. (Indonesia has more Muslims than any of these countries individually.) ISLAM first came to India around the year 1000 C.E. For centuries Muslims ruled much of India. They made immense contributions to Indian arts and culture. Besides living in Pakistan and Bangladesh, Islamic states, Muslims made up slightly more than 13.4 percent of the population of India in 2001, numbering just under 138,200,000.

Less known are the Parsis, who practice a form of ZOROASTRIANISM. They came to India from Persia, now Iran, to escape Muslim rule. They are a small but prosperous community in western India, numbering perhaps 200,000.

By far the largest number of Indians—about 80 percent of the population of the country of India

in the 2001 census, or more than 827,000,000 people—practice HINDUISM. Hinduism is, however, difficult to define. It basically consists of all Indian religious practices that do not belong to some other religion. Especially since the late 1980s India has witnessed violent clashes between Hindus on one side and Christians and especially Muslims on the other (*see* FUNDAMENTALISM, HINDU).

People known as "tribals"—people who have lived in jungle regions and until recently outside the money economy—often count as Hindus. Some tribals insist, however, that they have their own religions. Indeed, tribal people often do not worship the major Hindu deities. Instead, they perform animal SACRIFICES—largely absent from Hinduism—to their own local deities.

The Indian subcontinent is one of the most religiously varied places on earth. That diversity has caused strains, but it has also resulted in much religious creativity.

Further reading: Paul Dundas, *The Jains,* 2d ed. (New York: Routledge, 2002); Klaus K. Klostermaier, *Hinduism: A Short History* (Oxford: Oneworld, 2000); Khushwant Singh, *A History of the Sikhs,* 2d ed. (Oxford: Oxford University Press, 2004); Sooni Taraporevala, *Parsis: The Zoroastrians of India: A Photographic Journey* (London: Overlook Duckworth, 2004).

Indra   The most prominent of the Vedic gods. In the sacred writings of India known as the VEDA Indra is the chief of the gods. His abode is the sky, his weapon the thunderbolt. He is called *sahasraksha,* "thousand-eyed," and he leads a band of warriors known as the Maruts.

In many ways Indra resembles the gods of Greek mythology. Prone to violence, he eats and drinks to excess. He is especially fond of *soma,* an intoxicating plant extract whose precise identity is unknown. When intoxicated he boasts. Indra is also renowned for fertility. He is said to have gotten several human women pregnant.

One of the most important stories about Indra concerns his killing of the demon Vritra, releasing the life-giving waters (*see Rig-Veda* 1.32). Some see in this story a reference to the release of the eagerly awaited monsoon rains.

By the time of the Brahmanas (perhaps 1000–600 B.C.E.), Indra was beginning to lose his importance. The mythology of the PURANAS even makes fun of him, telling lewd stories about occasions when he was humiliated.

Indus Valley religion   Religion as practiced in the Indus Valley civilization, also called the Harappan civilization. Around 3500 B.C.E. a city-based way of life began to emerge in the plains of the Indus River Valley (Pakistan today). By about 2500 B.C.E. settlements at sites like Mohenjo-Daro and Harappa were at their peak, with populations between 25,000 and 50,000. A thousand years later, the Indus Valley civilization had disappeared. At its greatest extent, it reached down into Gujarat in western India and also spread to the northeast above the Thar Desert, covering an area more than three times that of the state of California.

Indus Valley sites are characterized by carefully constructed brick buildings, straight streets laid out on a grid pattern, advanced engineering of water, and careful burial of the dead. More recent scholars have tried to connect its people with the Elamites, an ancient people of the Persian Gulf, and the Dravidian-speaking peoples of south India today.

Because the Indus Valley script has not been deciphered, it is difficult to say much about the religion with certainty. A famous seal depicts what appears to be a horned human-like being in MEDITATION, surrounded by massive animals—a figure reminiscent of the later Hindu god SIVA in his aspect as Pasupati, lord of animals. Another famous figure, with beard, slanted eyes, trefoil garment, and headband, appears to show a religious and political functionary. Other apparently religious artifacts may emphasize the powers of sexual fertility. That emphasis would be in keeping with the civilization's agricultural base. The Great Bath at the center of Mohenjo-Daro—39 feet by 23 feet by 8 feet deep—could have been the site of RITU-ALS of purification by the society's leaders. Finally, more recent scholars have also claimed to detect evidence of Vedic rituals (*see* VEDA) at Indus Valley sites, for example, remnants of fires constructed for Vedic SACRIFICES.

Most scholars agree that elements of Indus Valley religion continued in later HINDUISM, but disagree about exactly what elements continued.

initiation, religious   A RITUAL used to make someone a member of a religious group. In some places, but not in the United States, the religious community is identical to society as a whole. In these places, initiation rituals make people full adult members of the society.

Writings on religious initiation often make two questionable assumptions. The first assumption limits "real" initiation—initiation in its fullest and truest form—to indigenous societies, sometimes called "archaic" or "primitive." The second questionable assumption views male rituals as somehow typical. For example, the well-known scholar Mircea ELIADE made the following claims about initiation: (a) male initiation rituals are more prevalent than female; (b) male initiations are group affairs whereas female initiations are done for individuals; and (c) the reason for the difference is that male initiations deal more with culture (society's forms and values), while female initiations deal more with nature (bearing children).

Other scholars question these claims. They suggest that female initiations may be more common than male. They point out that it is not clear that female initiations are mostly individual affairs, because female initiations have been less studied. They also suggest that if female initiations are individual affairs, this may not result from biology. It is just as likely that female initiation rituals simply reflect the systematic exclusion of women from dominant social structures.

Many initiations take place at the time of religious maturity. In indigenous communities, this often correlates with sexual maturity. "Major" religions usually stress nonsexual elements, but they still initiate people in their early teens. JUDAISM has bar and, in liberal congregations, bat mitzvah (*see* BAR/BAT MITZVAH). CHRISTIANITY has confirmation or, for some Protestants, BAPTISM. Upper caste Hindu boys undergo several rituals, especially the *upanayana*. In this ceremony they receive a sacred thread and begin to study the sacred texts known as the VEDA. The traditional initiation ritual for Hindu girls was marriage (*see* MARRIAGE AND RELIGION). That is because according to Hindu tradition a girl should be married before she begins to have menstrual periods. This practice is much less common today.

Religions initiate people on other occasions, too. MONKS AND NUNS undergo an initiation to join their orders. In some Buddhist countries, young people traditionally become adults when they take monastic vows for a limited period of time. In the ancient Mediterranean world, people were initiated into special "mystery societies." The most famous example is the mysteries of Eleusis in Greece (*see* MYSTERY RELIGIONS). People sometimes receive religious office through initiation. The best example is probably the traditional healer known as the shaman (*see* SHAMANISM). Communities are usually said to "ordain" rather than initiate priests (*see* ORDINATION). The distinction is somewhat artificial.

Initiations often follow the structure of RITES OF PASSAGE. They usually involve instruction to enable persons to fulfill their new roles. Boys who underwent labi initiation among the Gbaya in the Cameroons learned by doing. They lived on their own in the forest for several years. Other religions impart "book learning." Hebrew instruction precedes bar and bat mitzvah; religion classes precede confirmation. Some initiations, such as CIRCUMCISION or the removal of hair, alter the body as well as the mind.

inquisition, the   A religious court established by the Roman Catholic Church in the early 1200s to try and convict heretics. Heretics are people who are members of the church by BAPTISM but who do not believe and practice CHRISTIANITY according to the church's teachings. Until the early 1200s local princes and bishops were responsible for discovering and punishing heretics. In the early 1200s, however, the Pope established his own inquisition. Those in charge were often DOMINICAN friars who reported directly to the Pope. This inquisition was active especially in northern Italy and southern France. It was directed especially against heretics known as Cathari and WALDENSIANS. By the 1400s it was also investigating charges of WITCHCRAFT.

During the 1400s Christians managed to conquer all of Spain. (Spain had been largely Muslim since the late 600s.) In order to Christianize the territory, the conquerors required all Jews and Muslims to leave, even though many families had lived in Spain for centuries. To ensure that everyone living in Spain was Christian, the rulers, in cooperation with the Pope, established the Spanish inquisition. This inquisition was particularly interested in persecuting *maranos* and *moriscos*—Jews and Muslims, respectively, who pretended to practice Christianity in order to avoid being forced to leave.

The inquisitors were notorious for their brutality. A prime example is the first grand inquisitor of Spain, Tomas de Torquemada (1420–98). There were, however, some restraints. A few overly zealous inquisitors lost their positions and even wound up in prison. The inquisitions required those who repented of heresy to attend masses, make PILGRIMAGE, wear yellow crosses, or spend time in prison—sometimes for the rest of their lives. They turned over to the secular government those who refused to repent or who lapsed after repenting. The government burned these offenders at the stake.

JOAN OF ARC, John Hus, Giordano Bruno, and Savonarola are among those who lost their lives in the inquisitions. The scientist Galileo received a lesser sentence. Even Ignatius Loyola, the founder of the JESUITS, had to appear twice before the inquisition.

Isaac   In the BIBLE, the son of ABRAHAM and SARAH and the father of JACOB. With his father Abraham and his son Jacob, Isaac is one of the three traditional male ancestors of the people of Israel. But unlike Abraham and Jacob, he is not the main character in many stories.

The name Isaac means "he laughs." The Bible connects the name with the behavior of Abraham and Sarah when they were told they would bear a son in old age: They laughed (Genesis 17.17–19, 18.12–15, 21.6–7).

The Bible tells how Abraham was willing to SAC-RIFICE Isaac at GOD's command (Genesis 22). It also tells how Abraham arranged for Isaac's marriage to REBEKAH (Genesis 24), and how Rebekah helped her son Jacob deceive Isaac and steal the blessing that should have been Esau's (Genesis 27).

Among Arabs, Isaac's counterpart is Ishmael, the son of Abraham and Hagar. For example, Muslims believe that Abraham was commanded to sacrifice Ishmael, not Isaac.

Isaiah   *A prophetic book in the Hebrew* BIBLE   It preserves some of the most beautiful prophetic statements from ancient Israel.

Christians have traditionally read the prophets of the Hebrew Bible (Old Testament) as predicting the coming of JESUS as the MESSIAH. They found it particularly fruitful to read Isaiah this way. The GOSPEL of Matthew quotes a Greek translation of Isaiah 7.14 that predicts the birth of a child from a virgin. This passage provided the precedent for the important idea that MARY, Jesus's mother, was a virgin (*see* VIRGIN BIRTH). The latter part of Isaiah contains several sections known as the songs of YHWH's ("the Lord's") servant. Christians saw these songs as predicting the sufferings and death of Jesus.

Recent biblical scholars have tended to adopt a view of prophecy much closer to the traditional Jewish attitude. In this view, prophets spoke on GOD's behalf to his chosen people. They addressed issues of their own day. Thus, the Hebrew original of Isaiah 7.14 does not mention a virgin; it speaks only of a young woman. This woman may have been the queen; the prophet may have seen the child she was carrying, the future king, as a sign of God's promise. Similarly, in talking about YHWH's

servant who suffers, the prophet was probably talking about the people of Israel itself.

The book of Isaiah addresses three different historical situations facing the southern kingdom of Judah and its descendants. Given the date of these situations, scholars conclude that the book contains the words of at least two and perhaps three different prophets. For convenience, they call them First, Second, and Third Isaiah.

First Isaiah is Isaiah, the son of Amoz, after whom the whole book is named. He prophesied in the time of kings Uzziah, Jotham, Ahaz, and Hezekiah (roughly 742–701 B.C.E.; Isaiah 1–39). At this time Judah's political existence was threatened. First, its neighbors to the north, Syria and Israel, formed an alliance to try to place a puppet ruler on the throne of Judah. Then Assyria, a growing superpower, annexed Syria and Israel and threatened to do the same to Judah. Isaiah responded by identifying the ultimate cause of the military threat: The rulers of Judah had acted improperly. Isaiah also issued a series of oracles against other nations. At the same time, he insisted that God would keep his promise. Despite the threats, a descendant of DAVID would remain on the throne of Judah.

The setting and tone of Second Isaiah (Isaiah 40–55) are completely different. In 587 B.C.E. Judah fell not to Assyria but to Babylon. The conquerors destroyed the Temple built by SOLOMON in JERUSALEM and deported the leadership of Judah to Babylon. Second Isaiah addresses these exiles with moving words of comfort, hope, and encouragement. He also develops a very profound view of Israel's God as the creator of the entire universe. Second Isaiah was probably prophesying just before the conquest of Babylon by Cyrus, the emperor of Persia, in 539 B.C.E. He celebrates the rise of Cyrus. He even calls him God's messiah, which means anointed one (Isaiah 45.1).

With Third Isaiah (Isaiah 56–66) the scene abruptly changes once more. The exiles have returned to Judah, and the Temple has been rebuilt. (The Temple was rededicated in 515 B.C.E.) This portion of Isaiah addresses the returnees with words of both comfort and warning.

Ise Site of one of the most important SHINTO shrines. Ise is located in southern Honshu, Japan's largest island. It is home to several shrines. The inner shrine is sacred to AMATERASU, the KAMI of the sun and the ancestress of the Japanese emperors. The most important building contains one of the symbols of the Japanese imperial family: the sacred mirror.

The shrine buildings are constructed in a very old style. They sit on stilts. They also have massive wooden pillars at each end and thatched straw roofs. On each end, the crossbeams of the roof form something of a giant X. The buildings are reconstructed every 20 years, perhaps because they are made of natural wood.

According to a RITUAL centuries old, offerings of food—including rice, vegetables, and fruit grown on the shrine grounds—are made to the kami twice a day. New clothing is presented twice a year, in spring and autumn. Several million pilgrims visit Ise each year. The shrine also hosts a large number of festivals. Of these the most important is the Shikinensengu, the reconstruction every 20 years.

The buildings of Ise shrine were reconstructed for the 61st time in 1993. The shrine itself celebrated its bimillennium (2,000th anniversary) in 1996.

Isis, Isaic religion A GODDESS of ancient Egypt and her worship in the Greco-Roman world. In Egypt, Isis was the daughter of Geb and Nut (Earth and Sky), wife of Osiris, and mother of Horus. Osiris was a god of fertility who was also identified with the deceased pharaoh. After his funerary rites, the divine ruler came back to life in the Underworld as Osiris, reigning there as king of the dead. A myth tells us that when Osiris was slain by his brother, Seth, Isis gathered together the parts of his dismembered body and, with the help of Thoth, the god of funeral rites, was able to revive him. Isis was seen as the ideal wife and support for her husband, as model for the queen of Egypt, and as queen of the dead. In popular worship, she was invoked as protector of woman, especially in childbirth; as giver of life and rebirth, as for Osiris;

The goddess Isis nursing the child Horus. This Hellenistic version of the Egyptian goddess Isis wears a fringed cape around her shoulders and vine branches in her hair. *(Erich Lessing/Art Resource, N.Y.)*

and as a goddess of fertility, controller of the Nile's life-giving floods. Her symbols included the cow, the serpent, and the *sistrum,* a jangling musical instrument used in her worship.

In Greco-Roman times, especially in the days of the Roman Empire, the WORSHIP of Isis became popular throughout the Mediterranean world. Isaic temples and RITUALS were noted for the beauty and dramatic quality of their music, dances, processions, and festivals. The cult was one of the most famous of the MYSTERY RELIGIONS. Candidates underwent an impressive initiation that simulated participation in the death of Osiris and his resuscitation by Isis. In general, Isis was seen as the Great Mother, identified with all other great goddesses, and addressed as "O Thou of countless Names." Some have suggested that her worship influenced Christian devotion to MARY, the mother of JESUS.

Islam Arabic for "submission," specifically, submission to the will of God; a religion that took final form in Arabia after revelations to the prophet MUHAMMAD (570–632 C.E.). People who practice the religion are called Muslims (earlier spelled Moslems).

HISTORY

Muslims call the time before the prophet Muhammad *al-Jahiliya*, "the times of ignorance." At that time seminomadic herders, caravaners, and towns-people lived in Arabia. Their primary loyalty was to their clans, and their religions were polytheistic and local. The revelations to Muhammad proclaimed that human beings owed primary loyalty to the one true God, whom alone they should obey (*see* ALLAH). As a result a new community, the Ummah of Islam, was created, based not on blood relationship but on shared FAITH. Muslims date its existence from the *hijra* (also spelled *hegira*), the flight of Muhammad and his followers from Mecca to Medina in 622.

After the prophet's death, the revelations he had received were collected and compiled into a book known as the QUR'AN. Over the next 300 years, scholars collected stories of the prophet's deeds and sayings, the HADITH. At the same time, several schools of thought arose. The most important disagreement divided a minority of Muslims, known as Shi'ites, from most other Muslims, known as Sunnis (*see* SHI'ITE ISLAM and SUNNI ISLAM). Sunnis accepted the Umayyad dynasty, which ruled in Damascus, while Shi'ites claimed that the prophet's male descendants should lead the community of Islam.

Islam expanded rapidly. Within a century of the prophet's death, it extended from Spain and Morocco in the west through the Near East and Iran to central Asia in the east. In 750 the Abbasid dynasty succeeded the Umayyads and, ruling from Baghdad, presided over a magnificent civilization. During this period Islam developed sophisticated traditions of philosophy and profound schools of MYSTICISM, known as SUFISM.

After the fall of the Abbasids in 1258, the Islamic world was divided among regional powers. The powerful Turks overthrew Constantinople in 1453 and lay siege to Vienna, Austria, in the 1520s and again in 1683. The Mughals produced great monuments of South Asian civilization, including the famed Taj Mahal, a mausoleum in Agra, India. From South Asia, Islam spread east to Indonesia, the most populous Islamic country today. In Africa south of the Sahara, Muslims also developed several long-lasting societies.

In the 18th and 19th centuries, European colonizers overran much of the Islamic world and ruled it until after World War II (1939–45). Some Muslims, including Turkish reformers, reacted by rejecting Islamic traditions as outmoded. They adopted a secular worldview informed by modern science. Others, like the South Asian poet Muhammad Iqbal (1877–1938), maintained that Islam provided a spiritual grounding for science. From the 1930s on in North America some African Americans found meaning in the teachings of Elijah Muhammad, who led an organization known as the Nation of Islam (*see* ISLAM, NATION OF); many Muslims in other parts of the world question whether Elijah Muhammad was actually teaching Islam.

Islam in the World Today

At the beginning of the 21st century, Islam finds itself second only to CHRISTIANITY in its number of active adherents among the religions of the world. The sharp decline in the practice of BUDDHISM and the other traditional religions of China after the communist triumph in 1949 contributed to Islam's status as the world's second-largest religion.

Moreover, seldom in the history of the religions of the world has the outer status of a religion changed as dramatically as has Islam since the beginning of the 20th century. In 1900, most Muslims lived under the humiliating colonial rule of professedly Christian overlords—British, French, Dutch, or Russian—or in weak and backward Muslim empires, the Ottoman and Persian. Most of the Muslim world was sunk in poverty and underdeveloped. Many, among both Muslims and non-Muslims, had a sense that Islamic culture was stagnant, its day perhaps past.

In 2000, the situation was radically different. Virtually all Muslim societies were independent nations by then, and some had become wealthy and technologically advanced, mostly from oil revenue. Vibrant new Islamic cultural and political movements insisted that, far from dead, Islam was a contemporary way of life that had much to offer the world in the various moral and economic crises it now faced. But Islam's new confidence and assertiveness sometimes led to harsh confrontations with the non-Muslim world around it.

Many of these conflicts stemmed from Muslim unease. Islamic economic and political gains were far from evenly distributed. Some nations, like Saudi Arabia and Kuwait, were rich, while others, like Bangladesh and some of the Muslim African states, remained among the poorest on earth. Some Muslim governments, while independent, were corrupt and undemocratic. Some Muslims felt that, despite independence, the West still exercised far too much influence, both economic and cultural, in their societies. They saw Muslim officials as too easily swayed by Western alliances and money. Some devout Muslims believed that their young people were being seduced by false Western fashions, values, and loose sexual mores.

Recent Islamic history has been largely shaped by the underlying problem of what an authentic Muslim society in the modern world would be like and how it could be actualized. The first responses tended to say that to be relevant, Islamic societies must modernize, westernize, and to a great extent secularize. By the 1970s, however, a powerful reaction against such policies had set in.

Many modernized Muslims did not find the fruits of such progress as gratifying as they had been promised, and instead they only felt spiritually lost and alienated from their own culture. Some had studied in Western countries and came back feeling that the West was itself far from ideal. Indeed, much about it offended them. Their idea instead was to create a society that, in a way they contended Islam itself had not been for many centuries, was thoroughly and consistently Islamic. It should follow the SHARIAH, or code of Islamic law; give Islamic teachers and scholars an important role in government; distribute wealth fairly in accordance with Islamic ideals of justice and brotherhood; and resist all non-Muslim influence in such matters as dress, family life, education, and the role of women.

This was the program of the revolution in Iran in 1979, which overthrew the monarchy of the pro-Western Shah to create such an Islamic state. Similar movements, though not as successful politically except for a while in Afghanistan and Libya, have become important and influential elsewhere. Some have resorted to violence (*see* AL-QAEDA and HAMAS). Others, in relatively stable nations such as Turkey, Malaysia, and Indonesia, have been content to function as normal political parties. In still other lands, such as Algeria, Egypt, and Iraq, the situation remained complex, volatile, and uncertain.

Early in the 21st century, there were scattered signs of growing moderation on both sides, as "Islamic revolution" countries like Iran began to liberalize somewhat and secularists recognized the stature of Islam as a civilization. But the future shape and role of the Islamic one-fifth of the world remains open.

A further important factor has been the large-scale immigration of Muslims to other places, especially Europe, North America, and Australia. Despite some tensions in the host countries, these immigrants are discovering basic Islamic values in settings where they have to be clearly defined over against what is merely cultural, and in the process they are exploring new ways to be Muslim. Many others are also meeting Muslims as neighbors and

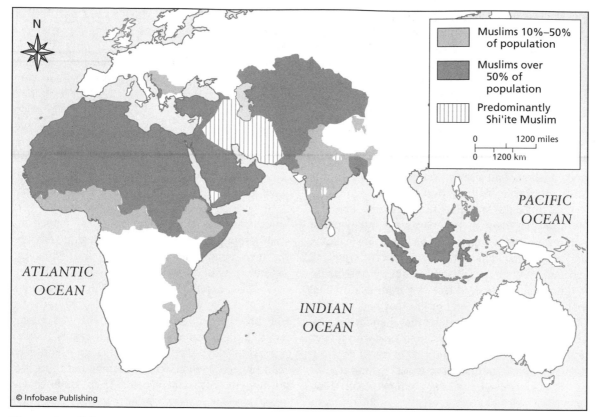

The peoples of Islam

friends for the first time, rather than a people talked about in the news. But tensions remain high, especially in the wake of the Iraq War and acts of terrorism attributed to Islamic extremists.

BELIEFS

The basic beliefs of Islam are expressed in a statement that all Muslims profess: "There is no God but God, and Muhammad is his Messenger (*Rasul*)."

Islam maintains that God is absolutely one, without a second, neither begetting nor begotten. Thus, it strongly rejects the Christian notion of the TRINITY. Islam also maintains an absolute distinction between the creator and creation. To confuse creation and creator is to commit the fundamental SIN of idolatry, that is, the association of other things with God (*see* IMAGES, ICONS, IDOLS IN RELI-GION). Muslims believe that Christians commit this sin when they claim that JESUS was God incarnate (*see* INCARNATION). So do people who place any goal above following the will of God, such as the pursuit of wealth.

Muslims believe that God has everywhere revealed himself to his creation in some form. They also believe that prophets in a line beginning with ADAM and including such figures as ABRAHAM, MOSES, and Jesus have disclosed special revelations from God. Muslims call the communities that follow these revelations "People of the Book." But through the activity of Shaytan (more commonly known in North America as SATAN), these revelations were misunderstood. With Muhammad, the line of God's prophets comes to a climax, and God's revelation to human beings is complete. This implies that the Qur'an is the complete and final manner in which God addresses human beings. And because God would not give his most sacred truth to just anyone, it also implies that Muhammad provides the model of how human beings should respond to God's revelation and implement justice in the world.

In addition, Muslims believe in ANGELS, one of whom, Shaytan or Iblis, rebelled against God. They also believe that there will be a final judgment at the end of time (*see* JUDGMENT OF THE DEAD and RESURRECTION) and that the faithful will enjoy an eternal existence in Paradise (*see* HEAVEN).

PRACTICES

In discussing how Muslims practice their religion, it is customary to identify five "pillars" of Islam. All Muslims practice these pillars, although they differ over details.

The first pillar is profession of the faith (*shahadah*). A Muslim cannot truly submit oneself to God's will without professing the divinity of God and the special place of the prophet Muhammad.

The second pillar is obligatory PRAYER (SALAT). Muslims may pray at any time, but they are also enjoined to pray more formally five times a day. (Many Shi'ites incorporate these prayers into three daily prayers.) They face the town of Mecca (the compass direction varies depending on where in the world they happen to be), adopt several postures, and recite a series of prayers. Noon prayer on Fridays is, when possible, done as part of a congregation at a MOSQUE. There an imam also preaches a SERMON to the assembled congregation.

The third pillar of Islam is almsgiving (*zakat*), for the Prophet urged his followers to care for the poor and the needy. In Islamic countries almsgiving has generally been administered by the government. Private charity is also widely practiced.

The fourth pillar is fasting during the ninth month of the Islamic calendar, the month of RAMADAN (*sawm*). From sunup to sundown during that month Muslims refrain from eating, drinking, and sexual activity. The fast recognizes significant events in the early history of Islam, such as the first revelations to the prophet Muhammad.

It also teaches compassion for those for whom fasting must be a way of life. Those who are pregnant, sick, old, or traveling are not expected to fast. The month of fasting ends with a feast, the *Id al-fitr.*

The last pillar of Islam is PILGRIMAGE to Mecca (*hajj*) (*see* MECCA, PILGRIMAGE TO). This is a formal ritual that takes place during the final month of the Islamic year. Ideally, all Muslims should make pilgrimage once in their lives, but they may not do so if they are too sick to travel, if their absence would mean hardship at home, or if they incur economic hardship to do so. On the tenth day of the month, Muslims throughout the entire world SACRIFICE a goat, sheep, or cow. Known as *Id al-Adha,* this feast commemorates the story of God commanding Abraham to sacrifice Ishmael (for Jews and Christians, ISAAC).

The Islamic calendar is based on the cycles of the moon rather than on the solar year. As a result, over an extended period the Ramadan fast and pilgrimage to Mecca will have occurred in every season of the year. This also applies to Ashura, which Shi'ites observe on the tenth day of the first month, Muharram. It commemorates the death of Husayn, son of Ali and grandson of Muhammad, the third Shi'ite imam, who lost his life in battle at Karbala (in Iraq) in 680 C.E.

The five pillars do not appear as such in the Qur'an. They come from the Hadith. Some Muslims occasionally speak about six pillars, adding JIHAD to the five above. Although *jihad* has come to be associated in North America with "holy war," it technically refers to the struggle against temptation. This struggle can involve warfare if one is called on to defend the faith in response to military aggression.

ORGANIZATION

Sunni and Shi'ite Muslims differ over how the community should be organized. For Sunnis, political and religious leadership may be exercised by different persons. Traditionally, caliphs and sultans oversaw matters of internal order and external defense. Today different officers, namely, presidents and prime ministers, fulfill these functions.

Religious authority resides with the ulema, scholars of Islam.

For Shi'ites, political and religious leadership are ideally exercised by the same person, the male descendant of Muhammad known as the imam. A Shi'ite community known as the twelvers believes that the imam, last seen in 873 C.E., is exercising authority while in hiding. Their religious leaders, headed by the AYATOLLAHS ("reflections of God"), are considerably more independent than their Sunni counterparts. Another Shi'ite community, known as the Nizari Ismailis, believe that the imam is still present in the world. Known as the AGA KHAN, he exercises authority over a worldwide community.

Like some schools of Christianity, Islam has not traditionally recognized the ideals of separation of religion and government and of religious pluralism that have now become common in Europe, North America, and other parts of the world. Like other societies, contemporary Muslim societies are addressing the issues posed by the modern ideal of the secular state.

ISLAM TODAY

The most frequent images of Islam that readers in the United States are likely to encounter today connect it with FUNDAMENTALISM and terrorism (see FUNDAMENTALISM, ISLAMIC). It is important to keep these images in perspective. Europeans and North Americans have a tradition of "demonizing" Muslims—of unfairly thinking of them as less than fully civilized or even fully human—that goes back all the way to the Middle Ages.

In the late 20th century some Muslim communities, like some Christian and Hindu communities, became more religiously conservative. Examples include Islamic states such as Turkey, which for much of the 20th century had been adamantly secular, and immigrant Muslim communities, such as Muslims born to immigrant parents in Great Britain. Some Muslims, especially in the Middle East, have taken up arms against what they perceive as threats to their religion and freedom (see AL-QAEDA and HAMAS). Many non-Muslim groups have performed similar acts of violence, but their targets have not always been the United States. After the terrorist attacks of September 11, 2001, U.S. President George Bush rightly stated that these acts were not representative of Islam. It is sometimes hard for people to remember that.

At the end of the 20th and beginning of the 21st centuries, Muslims, like people of other religions, have been wrestling with the impact of globalization and technological change on their lives. In many respects Muslims have embraced these developments. Computers and the Internet provide good examples (see COMPUTERS AND RELIGION). Resources for learning about and practicing Islam are widely available on the Internet. Moreover, e-mail allows Muslims in Alberta, Canada, for example, to remain in much closer contact with people in areas where Islam is more prevalent.

At the same time, contemporary changes present challenges. Many Christians in the United States worry about the morals their children encounter in movies and on television. Muslims do, too. Muslims are also particularly sensitive, as other previously colonized people are, to ideas and practices imposed on them from the outside. As a result they sometimes favor alternatives to ideals that Westerners cherish. For example, the United Nations Declaration of Human Rights recognizes as a basic human right the right to proselytize (to try to convince other people of the truth of one's own beliefs). This right is particularly important for traditions of CHRISTIANITY with strong missionary traditions. Many Muslims, however, prefer not to encounter people trying to convert them, especially when they are living in Muslim states. For that reason, the Islamic Declaration of Universal Human Rights does not recognize the right to proselytize.

One movement that deserves more attention than it has received in North America is Islamic FEMINISM. Muslim feminists are sometimes puzzled by the issues that interest Westerners. For example, many Muslim feminists do no think issues of dress are that important. At times, some have even chosen to wear the veil, as Iranian feminists did before the 1979 Revolution. They wanted to show their solidarity with other Muslims. Muslim feminists have tended to focus more on other issues, such as education for girls and women, equal access to health care, adequate nutrition, and equal treatment before the law.

SIGNIFICANCE

Since the time of the prophet Muhammad Islam has been one of the world's major religions. At the beginning of the 21st century roughly one-fifth of the world's population practiced it, including more than four and a half million North Americans. In addition, Islam has given the world rich cultural traditions, including art and architecture, literature, and philosophy.

Further reading: Ahmed Ali, trans., *Al-Qur'an: A Contemporary Translation,* (Princeton, N.J.: Princeton University Press, 1988); Karen Armstrong, *Islam: A Short History* (New York: Modern Library, 2002); Lawrence Davidson, *Islamic Fundamentalism* (Westport, Conn.: Greenwood, 1998); John L. Esposito, *The Islamic Threat: Myth or Reality?* (New York: Oxford University Press, 1992); John Esposito, ed., *The Iranian Revolution* (Miami: Florida International University Press, 1990); John L. Esposito, *Unholy War: Terror in the Name of Islam* (New York: Oxford University Press, 2003); Seyyed Hossein Nasr, *The Heart of Islam: Enduring Values for Humanity* (San Francisco: HarperSanFrancisco, 2002).

Islam, Nation of An important African-American religion that derives from the teachings and activities of Elijah Muhammad. Members of the Nation of ISLAM are known as Black Muslims.

The Nation of Islam was founded in the 1930s. It was not the first manifestation of Islam among African Americans. Muslims were among the Africans brought to North America as slaves. But the Nation of Islam inherited two other, more recent traditions of African-American thought. The first advocated Islam as the appropriate religion for African Americans. It rejected CHRISTIANITY, the religion of the slave-owners, as an instrument of oppression. The second tradition rejected the ideal of integration advocated by W. E. B. DuBois and

later by Martin Luther KING Jr. It stressed black separatism as the only viable means to a thriving African-American community.

The Nation of Islam began in Detroit in the early 1930s. A man named Wallace D. Fard, also known as Wali Farrad Muhammad, began preaching. He claimed to bring a message to African Americans from Mecca, the town in Saudi Arabia associated with the life and activities of the prophet MUHAMMAD. Fard disappeared in 1934. His chosen successor, Elijah Muhammad (born Elijah Poole), proclaimed him the promised MESSIAH and Mahdi, or bringer of divine justice. Until his death in 1975, Elijah Muhammad directed the community from Chicago. In the 1950s, a convert to the Nation, MALCOLM X, became its best known spokesperson. However, Malcolm left the Nation to found his own organization in 1964. Among other things, he had made a PILGRIMAGE to Mecca (*see* MECCA, PILGRIMAGE TO) that year, and he had been impressed by the universalism of SUNNI ISLAM. After Elijah Muhammad's death, his followers split. Elijah Muhammad's son, Warithuddin Muhammad, changed the name of the organization to the American Muslim Mission. He established it as a branch of Sunni Islam. Others, led by Louis Farrakhan, rejected this move and reorganized the Nation once again.

The Nation of Islam has its own distinctive mythology (*see* MYTH AND MYTHOLOGY). Elijah Muhammad taught that originally all human beings were black and practiced Islam. The white race was created by an evil scientist named Mr. Yacub. Whites were inferior to blacks; they were also devils, and they taught Christianity. To test blacks, GOD had allowed whites to rule the Earth for a period of 6,000 years, but their rule was about to end. At that point blacks would once again assume their rightful place. This mythology helps Black Muslims understand the African-American experience and gives them hope for the future.

In keeping with such views, the Nation of Islam rejected any attempts at integration with whites. It advocated black separatism and urged African Americans to establish their own businesses. Indeed, it demanded that the United States government establish a separate state for blacks. It also provided African Americans with a lifestyle that emphasizes personal responsibility. Thus, Black Muslims observe strict rules regarding diet and dress (*see* DIET AND RELIGION). They are forbidden to use alcohol, tobacco, or illegal drugs, and women are taught to dress modestly. They also refuse to fight in the armed forces. On these grounds the champion heavyweight boxer, Muhammad Ali, refused to be drafted during the Vietnam War.

Many complain about the anti-white teachings of the Nation of Islam. Both Malcolm X and Warithuddin Muhammad eventually rejected these views. In the 1990s, many also accused Louis Farrakhan of blatant anti-Semitism. Nevertheless, some believe that the Nation's message of self-reliance, pride, and personal integrity made a strong, positive contribution within the African-American community.

Islam in America The practice of ISLAM in the Western Hemisphere. Muslim seafarers from Spain and northwest Africa may have come to the Americas before Columbus. In any case, Muslims were expelled from Spain in 1492, and some seem to have gone to the new world, because in 1543 Charles V ordered Muslims to be expelled from Spanish lands overseas. That order makes sense only if Muslims were in fact living in Spanish lands overseas. By the end of the 20th century almost every nation in the Americas was a home to Muslim communities.

Before the 20th century, most North American Muslims were of African descent. They were slaves on southern plantations. Scholars estimate that as many as 20 percent of the slaves may have been Muslims. Some were clearly educated and literate. Accounts written by slaves in Arabic survive from the period before the American Civil War. Slave-owners as well as some other Christians pressured all non-Christian slaves to convert to CHRISTIANITY. As a result, Muslim slaves practiced their religion in secret, but by the start of the 20th century, their descendants had lost most of the Islam that had been brought to the new world.

During the 19th century, Muslims from other parts of the world settled in the Caribbean region. They came from places as diverse as British India, Java, and China. Some came as indentured servants. They generally maintained their national identities. For example, while Indian Muslims retained their Islamic identity, they shared a common culture with Indian Hindus.

During the 20th century, immigration to the Americas from the Muslim world increased tremendously. Especially during the second half of the century many Muslims came to North America for higher education, in pursuit of economic opportunities, and as refugees. The immigrant Muslims quickly established Islamic institutions. During the 1910s, 1920s, and 1930s they built MOSQUES in such places as Maine, Connecticut, South Dakota, Iowa, New York City, and Edmonton, Alberta. They formed chapters of Islamic associations, such as the Red Crescent (the Islamic equivalent of the Red Cross). They established Islamic educational institutions to pass on Islamic teachings and traditions to their children. One important problem was hardly unique to Muslims: how to negotiate the tension between a traditional Islamic way of life and the way of life prevalent in North America. As in JUDAISM and Christianity, the solutions define a wide spectrum of responses to these tensions.

Also during the 20th century, some African Americans rediscovered Islam. In 1913 Noble Drew Ali established the Moorish Science Temple in New Jersey. It eventually died out. But another community was much more successful: the Nation of Islam (*see* ISLAM, NATION OF), founded in the 1930s by Wallace D. Fard and his successor, Elijah Muhammad. As originally founded, the Nation of Islam had little in common with SUNNI ISLAM or SHI'ITE ISLAM. But after his visit to Mecca in 1964, a former spokesperson for the Nation, MALCOLM X, adopted Sunni Islam. In 1976 Elijah Muhammad's son, Warithuddin Muhammad, transformed a portion of his father's community into a Sunni group, the American Muslim Mission. Many African-American Muslims (as distinct from the Black Muslims of the Nation of Islam) cherish the memory of Bilal, an African slave whom the prophet

MUHAMMAD freed. According to tradition, he was the first MUEZZIN.

Izanagi and Izanami In SHINTO mythology, the primal parents. They are the father and mother respectively of the KAMI (gods), islands, and people of Japan. They descended from the high plain of HEAVEN on a floating bridge, the rainbow, from whence they churned the ocean with a spear to make the first land. On it they mated and produced their numerous progeny, until Izanami died giving birth to the fire god and went to the underworld. Izanagi followed after her but was unable to rescue his consort since she had already eaten of the food of the underworld. So he returned to the surface and bathed in the ocean to cleanse himself of the impurities he had acquired in the land of the dead. Out of his washings he produced AMATERASU, the sun GODDESS, as well as the moon and storm deities.

J

Jacob Hebrew patriarch; also known as Israel. According to the BIBLE, Jacob was the son of Isaac and the grandson of ABRAHAM. There is no way to verify whether he actually lived. Many scholars feel that he, like Isaac and Abraham, may simply be a legendary ancestor.

The Bible tells several well-known stories about Jacob. A younger brother, he deceived his blind father and cheated his older brother, Esau, out of his father's blessings. Fleeing, he slept with his head on a rock, saw ANGELS ascending to and descending from HEAVEN (the well-known "Jacob's ladder"), and consecrated the place as Bethel. He worked 14 years for his Uncle Laban in order to marry his cousins, Leah and Rachel. With them and two concubines he fathered the ancestors of the 12 tribes of ancient Israel.

On his way to meet his brother Esau, Jacob wrestled all night long with what most readers take to be an angel or divine being. In the process, he received the name Israel. It may mean "GOD rules."

Jainism A religion in India. Jains get their name because they follow the teachings and example of the *jina,* which means victor. For them, the victor is MAHAVIRA (sixth century B.C.E.). He discovered the way to conquer the forces that keep people bound to continuous rebirth, known in Sanskrit as SAMSARA.

Jains claim that their religion is millions of years old. For them, Mahavira is the 24th in a line of *tirthankaras* or ford-makers. These are people who have made fords across the stream of sam-

sara. At least in its present form Jainism grew from a broad movement in northeast India in the sixth century B.C.E. At that time *sramanas*—men and to a lesser extent women—gave up ordinary family life. They also rejected the SACRIFICES described in the sacred books known as the VEDA. Instead, they wandered, begged for food, and devoted themselves to teachings and practices that promised spiritual liberation. The most famous religion to grow out of this movement is BUDDHISM. Jainism is another.

Buddhism is practiced all over the world, but Jainism remains confined to India. In the centu-

© Infobase Publishing

Jainism symbol

ries after Mahavira, it spread along trade routes to southern and western India. These are its two strongholds today. In the first century C.E. the community split. The cause was a dispute over what those who wander must give up. One group insisted that they must give up clothes entirely. Their community is called Digambara, "sky-clad." Another group insisted that it is enough if the wanderers wear only a simple white cloth. Their community is called Svetambara, "white-clad." Digambara Jains are particularly strong in the south Indian state of Karnataka. Svetambara Jains tend to live in the west Indian state of Gujarat.

Digambaras and Svetambaras have different sacred books, but they share the same basic beliefs. Like Hindus and Buddhists, Jains believe that people are continually reborn. This rebirth results from action (Sanskrit, KARMA). Unlike Hindus and Buddhists, however, Jains say that a particularly fine kind of matter is involved in this process. Whenever the human life-force, the *jiva*, acts, this fine matter sticks to it and weighs it down. The goal of Jain practice is to cleanse the jiva of karmic matter. When the jiva is clean, it rises to the highest point in the universe. There it remains undisturbed forever.

The Jain community has two unequal levels. MONKS AND NUNS adopt a lifestyle based on wandering and begging. Laymen and laywomen maintain households and work. On both levels women are generally in an inferior position.

MONKS AND NUNS are said to be closer to ultimate liberation. A cardinal rule that governs their behavior is noninjury (Sanskrit, AHIMSA). Svetambara monks and nuns wear cloths over their mouths, sweep the paths where they walk, and strain their water to avoid harming little living beings. The most advanced Jains go even further: In old age they enter liberation by refraining from eating and drinking until they die.

Laymen and laywomen follow ahimsa, but to a lesser extent. As a result, all Jains are strict vegetarians. Jains have also established several animal sanctuaries. In addition, laymen and laywomen give food and drink to monks and nuns—gifts that help them make spiritual progress. They also visit temples. There they WORSHIP before images of the tirthankaras. Jain temples include some of the most famous religious monuments in India: the lush marble temples at Mount Abu and some of the richly decorated temples at Khajuraho.

At the end of the 20th century there were only about four million Jains in the world. But in championing ahimsa and vegetarianism, Jainism has had a profound impact on Indian society. For example, it strongly influenced the leader of the Indian independence movement, Mohandas GANDHI.

Further reading: John E. Cort, *Jains in the World* (New York: Oxford University Press, 2001); Paul Dundas, *The Jains* (New York: Routledge, 1992); P. S. Jaini, *The Jaina Path of Purification* (Berkeley: University of California Press, 1979); Michael Tobias, *Life Force: The World of Jainism* (Fremont, Calif.: Jain Publishing, 1991).

James   The name of three APOSTLES in CHRISTIANITY, as well as the name of a book in the NEW TESTAMENT. In Greek the name is *Iakobos,* a variant of the Hebrew name *Yakob,* Jacob. Scholars debate whether the James who wrote the New Testament book is one of the apostles or yet a different person with the same name.

THE APOSTLES NAMED JAMES

Three Christian Apostles had the name James. Two of them were also disciples of JESUS; that is, they followed him during his lifetime. The third is generally referred to as Jesus' brother.

Of the two disciples, James the son of Zebedee is much better known. In the synoptic GOSPELS (Matthew, Mark, and Luke), he, together with his brother, John, and Simon, later renamed PETER, belonged to the innermost circle of Jesus' disciples. Among other things, these three witnessed the transfiguration of Jesus. James and his brother once angered the other disciples by asking to sit at Jesus' right and left hand when he returned in glory. The ACTS OF THE APOSTLES records that Herod (not the Herod in the stories of Jesus' birth) had James killed by the sword. It gives no further details. According to Spanish legend, James' bones were taken to Spain. There, in 813 C.E., his tomb was discovered. This place, Santiago (Saint James) de Compostela, served as an inspiration to Christian forces seeking to reconquer Spain. It has also been a major destination for Christian pilgrims. Indeed, during the Middle Ages pilgrimage to Compostela stood in rank only behind pilgrimages to JERUSALEM and Rome. The Christian church remembers this James on July 25.

A second disciple of Jesus was named James, James the son of Alphaeus. Although his name appears in the list of Jesus' disciples, no stories are told about him. The Catholic Church remembers him on May 1, the Orthodox churches on October 9.

Much more important for the establishment of Christianity was a third James, referred to as the brother of Jesus. Many scholars consider him actually to have been Jesus' brother. According to some traditions, however, MARY, Jesus' mother, always remained a virgin. Indeed, some ancient Christian teachers suggested that this James was either Jesus' stepbrother or his cousin. James was the leader of the early Christians in Jerusalem. He came to be considered an Apostle. The BIBLE gives him a key role in discussions with the apostle PAUL about converted Gentiles. James agreed that although Jewish Christians should continue to observe TORAH, Gentile converts did not need to. Later, this James became known as James the Just because of his devotion to Torah. The Jewish historian Josephus (37 c.–100 C.E.) records that he was stoned to death. The Christian church remembers him on May 1.

THE BOOK OF JAMES

Besides being the name of three apostles, James is also the name of an EPISTLE, or letter, in the New Testament. It presents itself as written by James to the "Twelve Tribes in the Dispersion." Christians usually interpret this phrase as meaning the whole Christian church. Much of what James teaches, however, is compatible with Judaism. Many modern scholars doubt that an apostle wrote James.

The book contains much moral advice. It particularly encourages people to be careful about what they say. It gives even more attention to questions of wealth and poverty. It warns Christians not to favor the rich over the poor. It also tells the wealthy to act properly in their business dealings and to use their wealth to take care of those in need.

James is probably best known for its observations about faith and works. The Apostle Paul wrote that Christians are saved by faith apart from works of Torah. James urges Christians not to abandon what he calls the "royal Torah": "You shall love your neighbor as yourself." Unlike Paul this book teaches that "a person is justified by works and not by faith alone." Many of its teachings echo the teachings of Jesus in the synoptic gospels, for example, the Sermon on the Mount (Matthew 5–7).

Further reading: Bruce Chilton and Jacob Neusner, eds., *The Brother of Jesus: James the Just and His Mission* (Louisville, Ky.: Westminster John Knox Press, 2001); Robert Eisenman, *James, the Brother of Jesus* (London: Faber and Faber, 1997); John Painter, *Just James: The Brother of Jesus in History and Tradition*, 2d ed. (Columbia: University of South Carolina Press, 2004).

Japan, new religions in New religious movements that have emerged in Japan since the early 19th century. These are among the most interesting and most studied of new religions worldwide. They have obviously grown up in tandem with Japan's phenomenal modernization and the traumas of Japan's modern history, but they have features that compare with those of new religions everywhere. These are a few characteristics:

1. Founding by a charismatic prophet. Generally the founder, often a woman, like the majority of the shamans of ancient Japan, has had a powerful VISION or religious experience communicating a new revelation, and has the personality to draw other people into it.

2. MONOTHEISM or monism. The new religion may select one god or Buddhist reality out of the SHINTO or Buddhist pantheon and make it central, so that in effect religious reality centers on one principle or divine will.

3. Syncretism, or drawing from several traditions. Many of the new religions combine Shinto ways of WORSHIP, perhaps including dance, with Buddhist teachings like REINCARNATION, Confucian morality, and perhaps Christian ideas about GOD.

4. This-worldly eschatology and SALVATION. Most of the new religions do not talk about going to HEAVEN after death or salvation in another world. Instead they say that God is bringing about a radically new paradisal order here in this world; the present troubles are but the birth-pangs of a new age. If not in this life, then through reincarnation we will be born into it soon.

5. Emphasis on healing. Most of them began essentially as spiritual healing movements.

6. A sacred center. Most of them have a sacred center, even a holy cry, to which people go on PILGRIMAGE.

7. A simple but definite process of entry. Joining one of the new religions means making a definite decision, yet it is easy enough that the simplest persons enter; they are for ordinary people, not just an elite. People have to take responsibility for their own spiritual life by joining, but anyone can do so.

8. A single, simple, sure technique that is the key practice. This would be like chanting the Daimoku ("Nam myiho renge kyo") in SOKA GAKKAI, doing jorei or channeling light in World Messianity, and so forth. Like all new religions worldwide, they tend to isolate as their "trademark" one powerful practice that anyone can do and that brings quite powerful results for many people.

The well-established new religions of Japan fall into three main groups. First are the "old" new religions, like TENRIKYO (1838) and KONKOKYO (1859), founded by peasant prophets, which have Shinto-type worship but are monotheistic. Then, there are

the Omoto (1892) group of new religions, including not only Omoto itself but also World Messianity (1935), Seicho-no-Ie (1930), and Perfect Liberty (1946), started as a peasant religion stressing the imminent coming of a new age. The original foundress of Omoto was a peasant woman, Nao Deguchi, but her son-in-law, Onisaburo Deguchi, expanded Omoto in several directions: healing, art, radical politics, and spiritualism. Partly as a result of government persecution in the 1920s and 1930s, it spun off several other movements. World Messianity continued the eschatological emphasis. The more conservative Seicho-no-Ie has a science of mind kind of teaching, a positive thinking emphasis. Perfect Liberty, whose motto is "life is art," stresses the spiritual meaning of art.

Finally, there is a group of new religions based on NICHIREN Buddhism: Reiyukai (1925), Rissho Kosei Kai (1938), and the largest of all, Soka Gakkai (1952). They emphasize the power of the Nichiren chant, the Daimoku, to change life for the better here and now. Changing life for the better in this present world, but through contact with spiritual reality, is really the theme of all the new religions of Japan.

In the last decades of the twentieth century a fresh set of religious movements, sometimes called "new new religions," arose in Japan. Some of them could be identified with the world-wide NEW AGE MOVEMENT, which has had a large following among the Japanese. Some were, at the same time, new forms of BUDDHISM or Shinto.

One with Buddhist roots was Agonshu, founded in 1978. It teaches a form of Shingon or esoteric Buddhism (see JAPANESE RELIGION). Its worship centers on a spectacular fire RITUAL called, as in Shingon, goma, believed able to burn away evil KARMA in those who participate in it with faith.

Another movement of Buddhist background is Shinnyo-en, "Garden of Absolute Reality," which was established in 1936 under a different name but only more recently has become prominent. The two founders, husband and wife, were deep students of Shingon. They lost two sons to incurable childhood diseases; seeing spiritual significance in this, they believed the death of the "holy brothers" meant that the spiritual path between this and the invisible world is now fully opened and its power of salvation unleashed for the world. To receive that power, they taught a special form of guided meditation.

A new religion that has been aggressively promoted is Kofuku no Kagaku (Science of Happiness), based on the teachings of Ryuhu Okawa, who founded it in 1986. Believing himself to be a special revealer of God's truth, Okawa taught that happiness stems from love, knowledge, development, and self-reflection. He also taught that a world catastrophe is imminent, after which a utopia will arise.

Mahikari (Divine True Light) began in 1959. Its founder had been a member of the Church of World Messianity. Like the latter, it teaches a practice of radiating the divine light through the palm of one's hand.

The most notorious of the recent new religions is Aum Shinrikyo (Teaching of OM, the Divine Principle), which was responsible for a deadly nerve-gas attack on the Tokyo subway in 1995 under the direction of its leader, Shoko Asahara. He had founded the religion in 1984 to teach methods of Buddhist yoga and meditation. However, the followers became a withdrawn, tightly knit communal group who anticipated a coming purifying event (see APOCALYPTIC LITERATURE), which they apparently thought the attack would precipitate. The instigators of the crime, including Asahara, were tried and convicted, but a remnant has kept the group alive, changing its name to Aleph. The tragedy led to much debate in Japan about new religions, even though no other new religion has perpetrated an offence of this magnitude.

Some of the new religions of Japan have successfully expanded overseas, especially among Japanese immigrants in Brazil and the United States. They have often served as envoys of Japanese culture as well as religion.

Further reading: Helen Hardacre, *Lay Buddhism in Contemporary Japan* (Princeton, N.J.: Princeton University Press, 1984); Robert Jay Lifton, *Destroying the World to Save It: Aum Shinrikyo,* *Apocalyptic Violence, and the New Global Terrorism* (New York: Henry Holt, 2000); Harry Thomsen, *The New Religions of Japan.* (Tokyo and Rutland, Vt.: Tuttle, 1963).

Japanese religion A religious complex comprised of SHINTO, various forms of BUDDHISM, and new religions plus elements of TAOISM, CONFUCIANISM, and CHRISTIANITY. the religions of Japan are like a series of layers. New forms are added on top of older strata, but the old seem never to die out. Thus Japanese religion is a very complex mixture. Many Japanese have a relation to at least two religions, Shinto and Buddhism, and affirm the basic ethical principles of Confucianism without practicing it as a religion. Taoism and Christianity in nearly all its forms have also had influence in Japan, and in addition, a number of new religions have arisen in the 19th and 20th centuries.

SHINTO

The oldest layer or stratum is Shinto, which may be translated as the "Way of the Gods." This religion represents a perpetuation of the religion of ancient and prehistoric Japan, when the society was divided into many clans, each of which had its own patronal deity. Some of these, together with other gods, are now the KAMI, or gods of Shinto, a polytheistic religion. This FAITH is now recognizable by its distinctive torii or gateway, representing entry to its lovely shrines, and by its colorful matsuri, or festivals.

BUDDHISM

Buddhism came to Japan around the sixth century C.E., imported from Korea. It represented a more advanced level of culture than Japan had at the time, and with it came new arts and skills, including writing and even the Confucian classics, from the continent. Buddhism soon also became a faith by which the rulers of Japan tried to unify the nation, since it was not identified with any of the local clans. But though there was tension, Shinto did not disappear, as did the old religions of Europe around the same time as Christianity

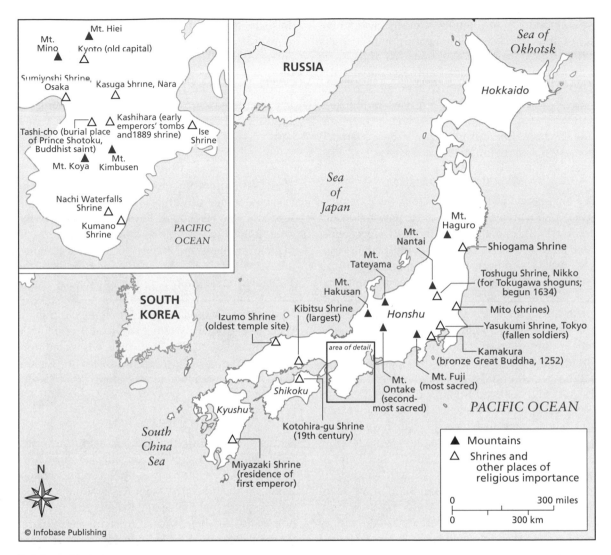

Religious sites in Japan

became dominant. Rather, in the case of Japan, the old religion continued alongside the new as theories arose saying that the Shinto kami were guardians of the BUDDHA's temples, or students of the Buddha, or even the same spiritual forces under local Japanese names rather than the universal Buddhist forms.

However, in the Middle Ages, Buddhism was the most active and visible religion. It took several denominational forms. During the Heian period (794–1185), the two most important forms were Shingon and Tendai. Shingon was a type of esoteric Buddhism that emphasized the presence of the Buddha-nature here and now, in each person in their present body, which can be realized with the help of hand gestures, chants, and visualization meditations. It used many mandalas or mystic paintings and statues of cosmic buddhas, giving great impetus to art. Tendai stressed the supremacy of the *Lotus Sutra* but tolerantly allowed many forms of practice to develop under its aegis, since it thought there were many paths for people in different stages of spirituality. In the end, it became almost as given to esoteric practices as Shingon. Both Shingon and Tendai were complex, sophisticated styles of Buddhism; each was headquartered in its own vast mountaintop monastery.

KAMAKURA BUDDHISM

The next period in Japanese history, the Kamakura (1185–1333), brought a new class to power, the samurai warlords, and also new Buddhist movements: PURE LAND BUDDHISM, NICHIREN, and ZEN BUDDHISM. Each was a reaction against the complexity of Heian Buddhism, in favor of radical simplification and popularization. The new people, warriors preparing to die on the field of battle, as well as peasants and shopkeepers, wanted to learn of some single, simple, sure key to SALVATION, which was accessible not just to monks, but also to those facing death in battle, or in the midst of everyday life. Faith was the answer. Pure Land Buddhism, taught by Honen (1133–1212) and his disciple Shinran (1173–1262), said that all one really needs is to have faith in the vow or promise of the Buddha AMIDA to bring all who call upon his name into the Pure Land or Western Paradise after death. Honen founded the Jodo-shu sect of Pure Land and Shinran the Jodo-shinshu sect, both major DENOMINATIONS of Japanese Buddhism today. Nichiren (1222–82), a fiery prophet, taught faith in the *Lotus Sutra,* expressed through a chant; his message also spawned major denominations and the largest religious movement in 20th-century Japan.

ZEN

Zen came to Japan from China as a separate institutional presence, and two major denominations, in the Kamakura period. It appealed especially to the samurai class because of its emphasis on self-discipline and an austere way of life, and also because of the artistic creativity it fostered. Traditional Japanese arts, like rock gardens, flower arrangement, No plays, and the tea ceremony, have Zen roots, as do such "martial arts" as Zen archery and swordsmanship. They are seen as ways of expressing the universal Buddha-nature in spontaneity of expression. Zen and its arts flourished especially in the Muromachi period (1336–1573); during this time, Japan suffered like Europe in its Middle Ages from feudal wars, and as in Europe it was monasteries, particularly Zen, that kept culture alive.

CHRISTIANITY

The short Momoyama period, 1573–1600, was the first golden age of Catholic Christianity in Japan. Jesuits under St. Francis Xavier and later Franciscans, following Portuguese lines of trade, brought the faith to the island empire and, amidst troubled times, at first had remarkable success. But the Tokugawa house came to power as shoguns or military dictators in 1600 and persecuted Christianity, fearing that it would lead to more foreign influence if not foreign rule. Where it survived it was forced deep underground. The Tokugawa, who ruled from 1600 to 1868, tried to keep out nearly all foreign ideas and to organize society along strict Confucian lines.

MODERN JAPAN

By the 19th century, there was growing social ferment within and growing outside pressure from Europe and America to open up the country. Eventually, in the so-called Meiji Restoration of 1868, the shoguns were retired and the emperor restored, nominally, to direct rule. Christian missionaries returned. Part of the Meiji ideology was to bring back ancient Shinto as a national religion of patriotism and loyalty to the throne. At the same time, Japan was being built up as a modern industrial and military power. This was the situation that led to the extreme nationalism and militarism of the 1930s and 1940s and Japan's World War II surrender in 1945. Shinto and the "imperial will" were used, often cynically, by the militarists as supports for their policy; religion was under tight government control during this period.

After 1945 Japan enjoyed religious freedom. Shinto reorganized itself independent of the state. Buddhism, though shorn by land reform of estates that had supported temples and monasteries, found its place as Japan's prosperity increased. The greatest growth, however, was in the so-called new religions, like Tenrikyo, Konkokyo, and above all the Nichiren-related Soka Gakkai movement (*see* JAPAN, NEW RELIGIONS OF). These religions had deep roots in Japanese cultural attitudes, yet were not tainted by association with the prewar regime as were mainline Shinto and Buddhism. They also found ways to relate to the needs of ordinary individuals.

So it is that new things, from Buddhism to the latest new religion, have piled up on top of the still-living Shinto substratum of Japanese religion. But virtually all have in common basic Japanese religious attitudes: acceptance of pluralism or many faiths, traditionalism, and a support of Confucian moral values centering on family and community loyalty.

Further reading: H. Byron Earhart, *Japanese Religion: Unity and Diversity,* 4th ed. (Belmont, Calif.: Thomson/Wadsworth, 2004); Robert S. Ellwood and Richard Pilgrim, *Japanese Religion: A Cultural Perspective* (Englewood Cliffs, N.J.: Prentice Hall, 1985); Ian Reader, *Religion in Contemporary Japan.* (Honolulu: University of Hawaii Press, 1991); Michiko Yusa, *Japanese Religious Traditions* (Upper Saddle River, N.J.: Prentice Hall, 2002).

Jehovah's Witnesses A Christian movement that began in the United States in the 1870s. *Witnesses* is the name that members believe God wants them to use for themselves. Jehovah is an old rendering of YHWH, the name of God used in the Hebrew Scriptures (*see* SCRIPTURES, HEBREW). (Written Hebrew originally had no vowels, so God's name was written YHWH. But in antiquity Jews stopped speaking God's name and used a different word instead: Adonai, "The Lord." When vowels were added to the text of the BIBLE, the writers used the vowels for Adonai, because no one actually said YHWH. *Jehovah* resulted when early English translators, whose knowledge of Hebrew was limited, tried to combine the consonants of YHWH and the vowels of Adonai,

which had never previously been combined into a single word.)

Jehovah's Witnesses consider themselves Christians. Some of their teachings differ, however, from the beliefs of other Christians. On the basis of their reading of the Bible, Witnesses believe that God is Jehovah, not a TRINITY. They also believe that JESUS was not divine but the first of God's creatures, that he was killed on a stake, not a cross, and that he rose from the dead as a spirit, not a person. Because of these and other beliefs, some Christians refuse to recognize the Witnesses as a form of CHRISTIANITY.

The movement began with a Bible study group organized by Charles Taze Russell in Allegheny, Pennsylvania, now a part of Pittsburgh, in 1872. That group adopted a millenarian view; that is, it believed that the end of times was at hand. It quickly grew, and in 1909 it moved its headquarters to Brooklyn, New York. Originally organized as the Zion's Watch Tower Tract Society in 1881, it adopted the name Jehovah's Witnesses in 1931.

The Witnesses believe that the "Gentile Times" ended in 1914. They further believe that when Christ returns, those who have been faithful will be raised from the dead to live on Earth forever. Specially anointed persons, numbering 144,000, will be transformed and taken to heaven to rule there with CHRIST forever. The Witnesses have predicted that the second coming of Christ would occur on several dates, but these predictions have not come true.

Witnesses meet three times a week for WORSHIP and study. One meeting is usually on Sunday. They meet in special structures known as Kingdom Halls, but some meetings also take place in homes. Elders or officially recognized assistants lead the meetings, which include PRAYER, singing, and discussions of the Bible, guided by official publications. Witnesses also practice how to teach the Bible and their beliefs in public. Indeed, witnesses are probably best known for their door-to-door proselytizing and their publications, *The Watchtower* and *Awake!* All Witnesses are expected to proselytize, and their activities are carefully organized and recorded.

Several other practices have also made the Witnesses stand out: They refuse blood transfusions, they refuse to celebrate CHRISTMAS, EASTER, and birthdays (they celebrate the "Memorial of Christ's Death"), and they are neutral regarding governments and wars. Their faith forbids them to pledge allegiance to any government or to salute any flag. Especially the last characteristics have provoked governments around the world, resulting in persecution and even death. As a result, the Witnesses have been at the forefront of legal efforts to guarantee religious freedom. As of August 2004, the organization claimed to have about 6,500,000 members in over 230 countries.

Further reading: Andrew Holden, *Jehovah's Witnesses: Portrait of a Contemporary Religious Movement* (New York: Routledge, 2002); M. James Penton, *Apocalypse Delayed: The Story of Jehovah's Witnesses,* rev. ed. (Toronto: University of Toronto Press, 1997).

Jeremiah *a prophet in Judah during the late seventh and early sixth centuries B.C.E. and a book in the Hebrew BIBLE that contains his prophecies* Jeremiah began to prophesize around 627. He was last heard from after the fall of JERUSALEM 40 years later, in 587. He dictated his prophecies to a man named Baruch. In fact, part of the book of Jeremiah contains records about Jeremiah written by Baruch (fl. early sixth century B.C.E.). These prophecies and records are closely related to the complicated history of the times.

CONTEXT

Jeremiah lived at a time when momentous events were taking place in the Middle East. A century earlier the empire of Assyria had destroyed Israel, the "northern kingdom." The "southern kingdom," Judah, had become a subject state. But in 622 ministers presented the king of Judah, Josiah, with a book they had found in the temple in Jerusalem. This was probably an early form of the book of Deuteronomy. In response, Josiah began a massive redesign of his kingdom. He tried to eliminate the worship of all gods besides YHWH ("the Lord"). He also tried to make the temple in Jerusalem the only place where the people worshipped YHWH. Although these changes were religious, they also meant that Josiah was declaring independence from Assyria and trying to unify his kingdom. Indeed, according to some scholars, the TEN COMMANDMENTS have the same form as Assyrian treaties, but they make the people subjects of YHWH, not the king of Assyria.

In 609, Josiah died fighting Egypt, an ally of Assyria, and Egypt made one of his sons king. But in 605 Babylon defeated Assyria and Egypt, and Judah became a Babylonian possession—until it rebelled. In 597, the Babylonians conquered Jerusalem and gave Judah a new king, another son of Josiah. When that king rebelled, the Babylonians destroyed Jerusalem in 587 and simply took Judah over. It was during these stormy days that Jeremiah prophesied.

CONTENT

Jeremiah's prophecies mostly predict the destruction of Judah. He started making those prophecies about the time Josiah, already king, turned 21. He said Judah would be destroyed because it had abandoned YHWH, worshipped other gods, and had submitted to Assyria and Egypt. These were precisely the abuses that Josiah sought to correct five years later. But Josiah's sons did not continue his religious policies, so Jeremiah continued to prophesy destruction. He said that YHWH would use a "power from the north" to destroy Judah. That power turned out to be Babylon. Eventually Jeremiah urged the people to surrender to Babylon and accept the consequences. Judah would be free again, he said, but only after 70 years. At that time GOD would establish a new covenant. Christians later identified the new covenant with CHRISTIANITY.

Like other prophets, Jeremiah gave his messages in deeds as well as words. For example, to symbolize that Judah would lose its independence, he wore a yoke. To symbolize that it would be restored, he bought a field.

Many government officials did not like Jeremiah's prophecies. Many prophets opposed him, too.

When Jeremiah urged surrender to Babylon, his opponents considered him to be a traitor in time of war. They imprisoned him and even tried to kill him by abandoning him in a dry well.

When the Babylonians did conquer Judah, they gave Jeremiah complete freedom (Jeremiah 40.4–5). But that was not to last. After a series of political assassinations, a group of Judeans were afraid that Babylon would punish them. Jeremiah advised them to stay in Judah, but they fled to Egypt instead. They took Jeremiah along with them. There he ended his days prophesying much as he had begun: The Jews in Egypt would be destroyed because they had abandoned YHWH and were worshipping other gods.

Jerusalem   A city sacred to Jews, Christians, and Muslims. Its sacredness is intertwined with its history.

Around the year 1000 B.C.E. Jerusalem was a stronghold of people known as Jebusites. King DAVID (ruled roughly 1000–961 B.C.E.) captured the city. He made it the capital of a united monarchy of Israel and Judah. His son SOLOMON (ruled roughly 961–922 B.C.E.) built a temple there for the dynasty's god, YHWH ("the Lord"). This is the structure Jews know as the First Temple.

When Solomon died, the united monarchy split into two kingdoms, Israel and Judah. Jerusalem became the capital of Judah, and David's descendants continued to rule there. Israel built alternative sanctuaries at Dan and Bethel, but some, including some very vocal prophets, still favored Jerusalem. King Josiah of Judah (ruled 640–609 B.C.E.) instituted a religious reform. Earlier the people of Judah seem to have offered SACRIFICES at local sanctuaries. Josiah made the Jerusalem Temple the only acceptable place of sacrifice. This meant that Jews would travel to Jerusalem to celebrate the major festivals of PASSOVER, Shavuot, and Sukkot (*see* JEWISH FESTIVALS).

In 587 B.C.E. the Babylonians sacked Jerusalem, destroyed Solomon's Temple, and deported the Judean elite to Babylon. In 539 B.C.E. Cyrus, king of Persia, conquered Babylon. He allowed the Jews to return home, but many decided to stay in Babylon instead. The resettling of Jerusalem and the rebuilding of the Temple under such leaders as NEHEMIAH and EZRA went slowly. Later, in 164 B.C.E., after a revolt led by Judas Maccabeus, Jerusalem became the capital of a thriving Jewish kingdom, known as the Hasmonean kingdom.

In 63 B.C.E. the Romans defeated the Hasmoneans. They eventually made Herod king to rule the territory for them. Although he was unpopular, Herod did expand the Temple to its most glorious form. After Herod's death in 4 B.C.E., the political situation became increasingly unstable. From C.E. 66 to 74 Roman armies fought with Jewish freedom-fighters. They destroyed the Temple for good in C.E. 70. The western retaining wall of the temple mount became an important place where Jews mourned this loss. After a revolt in 132–135, the Romans renamed Jerusalem and expelled all the Jews. Jerusalem became for most Jews a mythical, ancient city, essential to their identity but of no direct, practical significance. RABBIS preserved the regulations concerning the Temple in the Mishnah. Prophecies concerning the restoration of Jerusalem also seemed to point to future glory.

In the first century, JESUS, the founder of CHRISTIANITY, was active in the region. He was tried, executed, and, Christians believe, rose from the dead at Jerusalem. In Jerusalem, too, his closest followers created the first church. In this way Jerusalem became an important site in the Christian Holy Land. The places that tradition associates with Jesus, especially the Via Dolorosa—the path he took on his way to being executed—have become important destinations for pilgrims. Christians have also called the world to be established when Jesus returns "the new Jerusalem."

In 635 Jerusalem fell to Muslim rule. Because Muslims revere figures like ABRAHAM, David, and Solomon as prophets, they, too, consider Jerusalem a sacred place. In 691 they built a shrine, the Dome of the Rock, on the temple mount. Islamic tradition has identified a rock outcropping in this shrine as the place from which MUHAMMAD was taken up one night into HEAVEN.

From 635 to 1948, Jerusalem remained under Muslim rulers, with one exception. In 1099 Crusaders from Catholic western Europe captured Jerusalem and established a Christian kingdom there (*see* CRUSADES). It lasted until 1247. In 1948, Jerusalem was divided. The Jewish section became the capital of the new state of Israel. During the 1967 war the Israeli army took the entire city. It remained under Israeli control for the rest of the century. In the second half of the 20th century Palestinians also claimed Jerusalem as the capital for the state they wished to establish.

Jesuits Members of the Society of JESUS of ROMAN CATHOLICISM. The society of Jesus is a religious order made up of both priests and brothers. Priests are men ordained to the office of priesthood and thus able to celebrate the EUCHARIST. Brothers are members of the society who are not ordained.

The founder of the society was Ignatius Loyola (1491–1556). Ignatius was a soldier. While he was recovering from a cannonball injury, he experienced a religious conversion. As a result, he wrote a book entitled *Spiritual Exercises* (1523–35; approved, 1548), entered school, and attracted several followers. From this seed his order grew. In 1540 Pope Paul IV gave his approval to the order, which was extremely active in the Counter-Reformation, the movement within the Roman Catholic Church that responded to the Protestant REFORMATION.

Unlike previous orders, Ignatius's order relied upon a strong, central authority known as the superior general. Also unlike previous orders, members of the Society of Jesus were not required to wear a special habit nor to spend a considerable part of their days chanting WORSHIP services. Members take vows of poverty, chastity, and obedience. Their aim is to work wherever instructed "for the greater glory of GOD"—the society's motto.

Jesuits have engaged in primarily two kinds of activity: education and mission work. From the beginning, their schools provided a rigorous education in the humanities, philosophy, and THEOLOGY. They came to dominate education in Catholic Europe. They also evoked resentment, especially in the 18th century from spokespersons of the Enlightenment, such as Voltaire.

Jesuits started mission work in connection with European overseas colonization. Francis Xavier established a church in south India in 1541; he entered Japan in 1549. In 1582 Matteo Ricci brought Roman Catholic Christianity to China. Like their educational work, Jesuit missionary practices evoked controversy. The Jesuits adapted CHRISTIANITY to the culture of the people to whom they were preaching. Others saw this as a distortion of true Christian teaching and practice.

By the mid-18th century, opposition to the order was at a high point. Portugal, Spain, and France expelled the Jesuits from their territories and colonies. Finally in 1773, Pope Clement XIV dissolved the order. But within 40 years the climate had changed. In 1814 Pope Pius VII restored the order. Although opposition did not cease, since 1814 the Jesuits have once again devoted themselves to education and missionary work.

Jesuits have long been active in North America. In 1566 Jesuit MISSIONARIES preached to indigenous Americans in what would later become Florida; in 1570 other Jesuits preached in what would later become Virginia. The first Catholic bishop in the United States, John Carroll (1735–1815) of Baltimore, was a Jesuit until the order was dissolved. Today, Jesuit schools include such prominent universities as Georgetown University and Loyola University.

Jesus (*c.* 4 B.C.E.–*c.* 30 C.E.) *the founder of CHRISTIANITY* According to Christian tradition, Jesus was born from a virgin named MARY (*see* VIRGIN BIRTH) who was engaged to a man named Joseph. Jesus' importance for Christians is emphasized by a portion of the Nicene Creed (*see* CREEDS), which many Christians use regularly in WORSHIP: "We believe in one Lord, Jesus CHRIST, the only Son of GOD."

LIFE

The BIBLE presents two different stories about the birth of Jesus. The GOSPEL of Matthew tells that

Jesus was born in Bethlehem to Joseph and Mary during the reign of King Herod the Great (d. 4 B.C.E.). MAGI—the Bible does not say how many—came from the east to present to the child gifts of gold, frankincense, and myrrh. Then Joseph, warned by an angel in a dream, took Mary and Jesus to Egypt to protect the baby from the jealous rage of Herod, who ordered all baby boys to be killed.

The gospel of Luke tells a different story. It connects Jesus' birth with a census that occurred when Quirinius was governor of Syria. On the least strained interpretation, this event occurred when the territory of Judea (now southern Israel) was transferred from Herod's son and successor to Roman rule in 6 C.E., 10 years after Herod's death. According to Luke, the ANGEL Gabriel announced to Mary that she was pregnant. Because of the census, Mary and Joseph journeyed to Bethlehem. All the rooms were taken, so Jesus was born in a stable. Angels announced Jesus' birth to shepherds, who came and worshipped him. When he was eight days old, Jesus was circumcised; then he was presented at the Temple in JERUSALEM, where two pious older people, Simeon and Anna, praised him.

According to the gospels, Jesus began a special mission when he was baptized by John the Baptist in the Jordan River. With a band of close followers, he wandered the countryside from Galilee (now northern Israel) to Judea and sometimes farther afield, teaching and working MIRACLES, especially HEALING. As preserved in both the Bible and books outside the Bible, Jesus' teachings took several basic forms. The most well-known teachings include parables, stories told to teach a religious lesson, and beatitudes, statements beginning "Blessed are . . ."

Scholars have tried to place Jesus in several historical contexts. He has some affinities to early rabbinical JUDAISM (see PHARISEES). For example, Jesus taught in SYNAGOGUES, his followers called him RABBI, and his teachings about love, the commandments, and PRAYER (for example, the LORD'S PRAYER) are all reminiscent of rabbinical teachings, especially the teachings of the school of the Jewish sage Hillel. At the same time, Jesus' empha-sis on the KINGDOM OF GOD and the coming of the Son of Man may link him to other, more obscure movements that seem to have expected some sort of social and political upheaval. Some late 20th-century scholars emphasized Jesus' connections to the peasant classes in Galilee. They also saw both Jesus's moral teachings and his way of living—his wandering—as a Jewish Galilean version of the moral advice and way of life of Greek-speaking philosophers known as Cynics (not to be confused with "cynic" in its ordinary English sense.)

Jesus was executed by crucifixion under the Roman governor Pontius Pilate, whom sources outside the Bible depict as particularly cruel. The Bible records that on the night before his trial and execution, Jesus celebrated a final meal with his disciples (see APOSTLES). During the meal, Jesus distributed bread, which he had broken, and wine to his disciples. This act became the model for one of Christianity's most important acts of worship, the EUCHARIST. Jesus' crucifixion began early on a Friday morning. He is said to have died around 3:00 P.M. The gospels record how Jesus' body was removed from the CROSS that afternoon and placed in a sealed, guarded tomb. The next Sunday morning several followers found the tomb unsealed, unguarded, and empty. On that basis, and on the basis of appearances of Jesus to them, these followers proclaimed that Jesus was the MESSIAH whom God had raised from the dead (see RESURRECTION). He is said shortly thereafter to have ascended into HEAVEN, and he is expected to return again at the final day of judgment (see JUDGMENT OF THE DEAD).

TEACHINGS

According to one account, Jesus identified two preeminent commandments: Love God and love your fellow human beings (Matthew 22.34–40, Mark 12.28–34, Luke 10.25–28). In the famous Sermon on the Mount (Matthew 5–7), Jesus shows how far these commandments extend. For example, he teaches that if someone strikes a person on one cheek, that person should turn the other cheek and allow it to be struck, too, and that if someone takes a person's coat, that person should give away her or his cloak, too.

At the same time, Jesus is said to have proclaimed that the kingdom of God was at hand. He connected this with the return of a figure known as the Son of Man. He urged his followers to watch for the coming of the kingdom, for it would come as a thief in the night. He is also said to have given his followers signs that would indicate the coming of the day of the Lord, beginning with the destruction of Jerusalem (Matthew 24, Mark 13, Luke 21).

Finally, several sayings found in the gospel of John pertain directly to Jesus' own identity. In these passages Jesus connects himself very closely with God, whom he calls "Father," for example, "The Father and I are one" (John 10:30). He also characterizes his relationship with his followers in metaphors: "I am the bread of life"; "I am the light of the world"; "I am the vine, you are the branches" (John 6.35; 8.12; 15.5). One of the best loved of these passages reads: "I am the good shepherd. The good shepherd lays down his life for the sheep" (John 10.11). Some scholars question whether the words about the coming day of the Lord and the teachings in John actually come from Jesus.

SIGNIFICANCE

The earliest Christians became convinced that Jesus was God's anointed one—the Messiah or the Christ—prophesied in the texts of the Hebrew Bible. They also identified him with the preexistent principle—the Logos or Word—through which God had created the world (e.g., John 1.1–14; Colossians 1.16–17).

Within the first few centuries of Christianity, thinkers developed the idea that God is a TRINITY, one God in three persons. They did so partly on the basis of baptism "in the name of the Father, and of the Son, and of the Holy Spirit." On this view Jesus was God incarnate, that is, God who has become a human being (see INCARNATION).

The Christian church began to establish an authoritative teaching about who Jesus was at the Council of Nicaea (325 C.E.). The council condemned the ideas of a teacher named Arius, who taught that the Son of God was the first being whom God created. The council preferred

the metaphor of begetting—fathering a child—to the idea of creation; it declared that God the Son was "begotten not made, of one Being with the Father." Roughly 125 years later, at the Council of Chalcedon, the Christian church settled upon a common set of formulas to express who Jesus was. These formulas emphasized that "the one and only Son [of God], our Lord Jesus Christ" was actually, fully, and perfectly divine and human at the same time, two "natures" perfectly united in one "person."

Later Christians developed many different images of Jesus, for example, Jesus as the ruler of the universe, Jesus as a sacrifice and ransom, and Jesus as the model of how to live a perfect life. Throughout all of these variations, the teachings of Chalcedon have continued to define Christian orthodoxy. In the last 200 years, however, some thinkers have seen a great gulf between the "Jesus of history" and the "Christ of FAITH." Christians influenced by this manner of thinking have often preferred to talk about Jesus not as God but as a great moral teacher and example.

Further reading: Marcus Borg, *Jesus in Contemporary Scholarship* (Valley Forge, Penn.: Trinity Press International, 1994); John Dominic Crossan, *Jesus: A Revolutionary Biography* (San Francisco: HarperSanFrancisco, 1994); Howard Clark Kee, *What Can We Know about Jesus?* (New York: Cambridge University Press, 1990); Jaroslav Pelikan, *Jesus through the Centuries,* rev. ed. (New Haven: Yale University Press, 1997).

Jewish festivals RITUALS that are celebrated once a year in JUDAISM. The most important Jewish festivals are the Days of Awe and the PILGRIMAGE festivals. The Days of Awe, more commonly called High Holy Days, are Rosh ha-Shanah ("Head of the Year," New Year's) and Yom Kippur (DAY OF ATONEMENT). The pilgrimage festivals are Pesach (PASSOVER), Shavuot (Weeks or Pentecost), and Sukkot (Huts or Booths). The pilgrimage festivals are often simply called "the festivals." However, they are also called pilgrimage festivals because in ancient times people observed them by making pilgrimage to the Temple in JERUSALEM.

Rosh ha-Shanah occurs on the first and, for traditional Jews, the second day of the Jewish month of Tishri. Yom Kippur occurs on the tenth of Tishri. In the Gregorian calendar, these dates fall in September or October.

Rosh ha-Shanah services emphasize that GOD is the supreme ruler of the universe. They also emphasize God's activities in revealing himself and redeeming his people. At morning services the reading and discussion of passages from the TORAH, such as ABRAHAM's expulsion of Hagar and binding of ISAAC, provide central dimensions of morality and faith. During the course of the services a shofar, an ancient musical instrument made from a ram's horn, is blown. At home, Jews often eat apples dipped in honey in the hope that the new year will be sweet.

Repentance is an important theme of Rosh ha-Shanah. It culminates in Yom Kippur. On Yom Kippur Jews are supposed to fast from before dusk to an hour after dark the next day, a period of roughly 25 to 26 hours. During this period they do not eat, drink, or wash. Yom Kippur services include a PRAYER known as the "Al Chet." This prayer lists, in order, SINS whose names begin in turn with every letter of the Hebrew alphabet. A public and collective confession, this prayer symbolically confesses every possible sin. Yom Kippur restores one's relationship to God, but not one's relationship to other human beings. If one has sinned against another human being, one should ask that person's forgiveness before the start of the festival.

A few days later, on the 15th of Tishri, the atmosphere changes from solemn to celebratory. This is the beginning of the festival of Sukkot. Originally Sukkot was a harvest festival. It also recalls the 40 years that the Israelites wandered in the wilderness, and it served as a model for the American celebration of Thanksgiving. Sukkot gets its name from *sukkah,* a makeshift temporary dwelling built for the festival. A sukkah must have three sides and an entrance way, it must be made entirely of natural materials, and one must be able to see at least three stars through its roof. Jewish families hang fruit and other natural objects as decorations within the sukkah. They often eat their meals there. Some even sleep there.

Immediately after Sukkot, on the 23rd of Tishri, is a minor festival called Simhat Torah ("Joy of the Torah"). During the synagogue service on this day, the last verses of Torah (the first five books of the BIBLE) are read from the book of Deuteronomy. They are immediately followed by the first verses in the Bible, the creation account in Genesis. Thus, in the course of a year, all of the Torah—or at least representative portions from every part of the Torah—is read aloud in Sabbath services.

The two remaining pilgrimage festivals take place during the spring. Like Sukkot, they were originally agricultural, but they also celebrate important events in Israel's prehistory. Pesach (Passover), from the 15th to the 22nd or 23rd of Nisan, recalls the freeing of the Israelites enslaved in Egypt. Fifty days (a week of weeks) later, on the sixth and, outside Israel, the seventh of Sivan, Shavuot (weeks) celebrates the giving of the Torah on Mount Sinai. These festivals occur from late March to early June.

Other Jewish festivals are more minor but certainly not unimportant. They include PURIM, Yom ha-Shoah (HOLOCAUST Day), Yom ha-Atzmaut (Israel's Independence Day), Tishah Be'Av (Ninth of Av, which recalls the destruction of both SOLOMON's and Herod's Temples in Jerusalem), and a festival especially popular with Jewish children in North America, HANUKKAH.

jihad   Islamic notion of the struggle against SIN and EVIL. *Jihad* is often translated as "holy war," but its meaning is actually broader.

For Muslims the goal of life is to submit oneself to the will of GOD. But forces opposed to God tempt human beings to abandon God and pursue other goals. In every arena of life, then, people should struggle to resist temptations and evil. This struggle is called jihad.

Jihad includes a personal, internal struggle against temptation (jihad of the heart). It also

The execution of Joan of Arc, from *Les Vigils de Charles VII*, by Martial de Paris, 15th-century manuscript illumination *(Ms. Fr. 5054, fol. 7, Bibliotèque Nationale, Paris; Giraudon/Art Resource, N.Y.)*

includes attempts to combat error and spread the truth of ISLAM orally and in writing (jihad of the tongue and the pen). In addition, because Islam does not dichotomize or split religious and secular spheres, Muslims believe that it may also be necessary to fight for God's truth with military means (jihad of the sword).

Muslims have disagreed about what jihad of the sword entails. Muslim scholars traditionally taught that rulers should engage in jihad to extend Muslim rule over the entire world. (This ideal applied to political control; it did not advocate forced conversion.) In the late 19th and the 20th centuries, modern Muslims tended to limit military jihad solely to wars of self-defense. In the second half of the 20th century, some Muslims who embraced religious NATIONALISM advocated aggressive military jihad even against fellow Muslims.

jivanmukti   A Sanskrit word meaning "liberation while living." Hindus believe that the self (ATMAN, *jiva*) is bound in a series of rebirths (SAMSARA) as a result of its actions (KARMA). By practicing various psycho-physical disciplines, a person may become free of these bonds and achieve the state of release or liberation. When that happens, the self cannot simply abandon the body immediately. The effects of past actions still need to work themselves out.

Jivanmukti refers to the state of being liberated while still living in the body. Some schools, such as the Saiva Siddhanta, recognize several stages of jivanmukti. Persons who achieve jivanmukti are called jivanmuktas.

Joan of Arc   (*c.* 1412–31)   *a French woman who, inspired by voices, spurred on the French against the English in the Hundred Years' War*   When

Joan was 13, she began to hear voices. She later said these were the voices of Saints Catherine and Margaret and of the archangel Michael. The voices told Joan that it was her responsibility to help Charles, son of King Charles VI, acquire the throne of France. As a result of Joan's activities, Charles did become Charles VII.

Following the instruction of the voices, Joan wore men's clothing and joined the French army as a commander. Her presence reinvigorated the French troops. Her first success came in May 1429, when she broke the siege that English troops had made by completely surrounding the city of Orleans. That July Charles VII was consecrated king in Reims.

In 1430 Joan was captured by the English. The INQUISITION tried her for HERESY. Its verdict required her to repudiate the voices and wear women's clothing. For several days she did so. But when she returned to her former ways, she was burnt at the stake.

In the mid-1400s, Charles VII managed to have the verdict against Joan overturned. After all, he had became king largely because of her activities. In 1920 the Catholic Church recognized Joan as a SAINT. She is remembered annually on May 30, the day of her death.

Job One of the best known books of the Hebrew BIBLE, and the central figure in that book. Job belongs to the part of the Hebrew Bible known as the *Ketuvim*, Writings. It deals with questions of THEODICY: "Why do good people suffer?" Some people may believe that it reports actual events. Many scholars, however, think that it was a work of literature and that Job himself was a hero in folk tales. No one knows when the book was written.

One of the peculiarities of Job, at least from the point of view of later Jews, Christians, and Muslims, is the figure of SATAN: He is not the devil. The Hebrew word from which "Satan" comes really means "accuser." In Job, Satan may be one of the "sons of GOD," as they are called in the book. For example, he comes along with these sons when they meet with God. Satan patrols the earth and enters into conversations with God. Sometimes he raises sticky questions, as he does about Job.

CONTENT

Job combines poetry with prose. Most of the book is poetry, but the beginning (Job 1–2) and the end (Job 42.7–17) are prose. So is a brief part in the middle when a new speaker arrives (Job 32.1–5).

The beginning sets up the story. Job is both rich and righteous. God notices Job's faithfulness, and he boasts about it to Satan. Satan replies that Job is faithful only because he is rich; if he lost his family, possessions, and health, he would curse God instead. God wants to prove Satan wrong, so he gives Satan permission to destroy Job's riches, to kill off his children and grandchildren along with his servants, and to destroy his health. Once this has occurred, three friends come to comfort Job. The poetic part of the book begins with their conversations.

The friends mostly take the position that God rewards the virtuous and punishes the wicked. Therefore, if Job is suffering, it must be his own fault. He should repent, and then God will reward him. In response, Job protests that he has done nothing to deserve his suffering. He says he wishes he had never been born; he also says that he wants to talk with God face to face. In chapter 32, a younger man begins to speak. He is angry that the friends have not criticized Job more effectively. He says Job is wrong to question God. He also says that if people learn from their afflictions, they come out better in the end.

At the climax of the book, God himself appears. In chapters 38 to 41, he speaks to Job out of a whirlwind. God does not explain or justify what has happened to Job. Instead, he overwhelms him, presenting himself as the Lord of the Universe. In response, Job admits he was wrong to question God. God then scolds Job's friends for thinking he had done something to deserve his suffering. He also restores Job's fortunes, and Job lives to a ripe old age.

MESSAGE

The book of Job does not display any concern that God would allow Job's family, servants, and animals to be killed off simply to win an argument. Some find that disturbing. But the focus of the book is Job himself, and its strength lies in the way it treats his suffering. It does not settle for easy answers to the question "Why do the good suffer?" In fact, God does not give Job an answer to that question. Instead, the book rejects the simplistic point of view that good people prosper while bad people suffer. It also explores the emotional pangs of undeserved suffering. At the same time, it suggests that, in the presence of God, even those who suffer unjustly must acknowledge God's greatness. Not everyone agrees with this solution or even sees it as a solution. But many religious people have found in it the strength to endure suffering.

Further reading: Ralph E. Hone, ed., *The Voice out of the Whirlwind: The Book of Job* (San Francisco, Calif.: Chandler, 1960); Bill Thomason, *God on Trial: The Book of Job and Human Suffering* (Collegeville, Minn.: Liturgical Press, 1997); Bruce Zuckerman, *Job the Silent: A Study in Historical Counterpoint* (New York: Oxford University Press, 1991).

Jodo Shinshu   *See* Pure Land Buddhism.

Jodoshu   *See* Pure Land Buddhism.

John, Saint   *See* Gospels.

John XXIII   *See* Papacy, The.

Jonah   A book in the Bible. It tells the story of a prophet by the same name. The book of Jonah belongs to the collection of prophets known as "The Twelve."

Jonah was a prophet who lived in the eighth century B.C.E. (*see* 2 Kings 14:25). According to the book with his name, God commanded Jonah to go to Nineveh and preach repentance. But Nineveh was the capital of the Assyrian Empire, mortal enemies of Israel and Judah. Jonah had no desire to preach there, so he booked passage to Spain.

When a storm came up, Jonah was judged responsible. He was thrown overboard and was swallowed by a great fish. In the fish's belly he repented. Spit out on dry land, Jonah went to Nineveh and preached. His preaching had such success that the whole empire repented. But Jonah was disgusted by this turn of events. So God sent a sign to teach him that he should be concerned for all people.

The story of Jonah is a fictional account. Some people question whether Jonah could have lived in the belly of the fish, but the real difficulty is the supposed conversion of Nineveh. It never happened. The book probably dates from the fifth or fourth century B.C.E. It addressed the Jews who had returned from exile in Babylon. Many of them wanted to form a strictly exclusive community. The book of Jonah urged them not to overlook God's concern for their neighbors.

Joseph   A son of Jacob and great-grandson of Abraham in the Bible. Joseph is the subject of many stories in the book of Genesis (37–50). A favorite son, he receives from his father a multicolored coat. In jealousy his brothers waylay him, sell him into slavery in Egypt, and tell his father that he has died.

In Egypt Joseph works for Potiphar, a military officer. When he is falsely accused of sexual harassment by Potiphar's wife, he is thrown in jail. There he languishes until pharaoh (the king) summons him to interpret a dream about seven fat and seven thin cows. Joseph predicts good harvests for seven years, followed by seven years of famine.

The king appoints Joseph to supervise the stockpiling of food for the famine years. When his family comes to Egypt from Canaan in search of food, Joseph is reunited with them. In time the descendants of Jacob become enslaved in Egypt.

Many detailed records from Egypt have survived, but none of them mentions Joseph. Some elements of his story are clearly legendary. For example, the story of Potiphar's wife essentially repeats the Egyptian "Tale of Two Brothers." That tale was told even before the time of Abraham.

Judaism The religion centered on the covenant revealed to MOSES at Mount Sinai and preserved in the TORAH, the first five books of the Hebrew BIBLE. Judaism is a major religion. In addition, both CHRISTIANITY and ISLAM see themselves as continuing the ancient traditions of Judaism.

HISTORY

The Hebrew Bible (Old Testament) preserves the sacred stories of Judaism. It tells the history of the people of Israel from their first ancestors, ABRAHAM and SARAH (perhaps 18th century B.C.E.) to the attempts to rebuild the kingdom of Judah (now southern Israel) after the Babylonian Exile (ended 539 B.C.E.).

From roughly 600 to 1789, Jews developed this way of life in several different directions. Jewish thinkers like Maimonides (1135–1204) and Judah Halevy (before 1075–1141) thought intensely about the relationship between GOD's revelation and human reasoning. Other Jews sought to grasp intuitively the ultimate truth beyond all words and language; they developed Jewish mysticism, known as KABBALAH. Beginning in the 18th century, Jews in eastern Europe began to emphasize a religion of the heart as opposed to external observances. They began the movement known as HASIDISM.

Judaism as we know it began when the Romans destroyed the Second Temple in JERUSALEM in 70 C.E. After that event, a group of religious scholars known as RABBIS formulated the Jewish way of life on the basis of the Torah, the first five books of the Bible attributed to Moses. The rabbis compiled rules of behavior into a collection known as the Mishnah, then recorded the meanings of those rules in the TALMUD.

Until 1789, Jews, especially those living in Europe, were denied civil rights. But in the 17th and 18th centuries, an intellectual movement known as the Enlightenment taught that all people had certain inalienable rights. As a result, Jews began to be integrated into European society. The first significant "emancipation" of Jews came with the French Revolution in 1789.

Emancipation posed two challenges. The first was the issue of what it meant to be Jewish in a secular state. Different responses gave rise to the Orthodox, Conservative, and Reform movements (see JUDAISM IN AMERICA). At the same time, Jews had to confront the backlash of conservative Europeans (see ANTI-SEMITISM), seen most gruesomely in the HOLOCAUST. One significant response to anti-Semitism and the Holocaust was ZIONISM and the creation of the state of Israel in 1948.

BELIEFS

As a religion, Judaism is much more a way of life than a set of beliefs. The Talmud, for example, concentrates on what one needs to do in order to follow God's commandments, not on what one ought to believe.

Nevertheless, Jews have generally held several beliefs. These include the conviction that there is one, eternal, omniscient, incorporeal God who created the universe, that he alone deserves WORSHIP, and that he revealed the unchanging Torah to Moses as a guide to life. Jews have generally spoken of God in male terms, but feminine images of the divine are not unknown. Primary examples include God's creative Wisdom in Proverbs (see WISDOM LITERATURE) and God's *Shekinah* or manifestation in the mystical writings.

PRACTICES

The goal of Judaism is to make life holy, to grace the temporal with the eternal and the material with the spiritual. Jews do this by following God's commandments (*mitzvot*), so far as they can. These commandments are taken as a sign of God's love and concern. Furthermore, in Judaism God is like a compassionate parent. God forgives people when they sincerely repent of their wrongdoings. The notion common among some Christians that the "God of the Old Testament" is a stern "God of the law" presents a totally misleading picture of Judaism.

The central Jewish observance is keeping the Sabbath, the time from sundown Friday to sundown Saturday. Jews rest on the Sabbath in imitation of God's resting on the seventh day of creation. Sabbath observance varies in strictness in the different Jewish movements, but the ideal is always one of a Sabbath rest. At the Sabbath meal on Friday evening, the mother of an observant family will light the Sabbath candles and welcome Queen Sabbath. Observant Jews also generally attend a service at the SYNAGOGUE or temple on Saturday morning or, among the more liberal, on Friday evening. This service consists of readings from the Bible, PRAYERS, and songs.

During the course of the year, there are several major and many minor festivals (*see* JEWISH FESTIVALS). The most holy days are Rosh ha-Shanah (the New Year) and Yom Kippur (DAY OF ATONEMENT), which occur in the fall. On Yom Kippur, Jews fast, collectively confess their SINS to God, and receive God's forgiveness. The other major festivals are Pesach (PASSOVER), Shavuot (Pentecost or Weeks), and Sukkot (Tabernacles). Originally celebrations of the harvest, these festivals were later connected with the liberation of the people of Israel from slavery in Egypt (*see* EXODUS), the giving of the Torah to Moses on Mount Sinai, and the wanderings in the wilderness. The minor festivals include HANUKKAH, PURIM, Simhat Torah, and Holocaust Day.

Like most other religions, Judaism sanctifies the rhythms of life. During RITUALS performed soon after birth, Jews enter into the covenant with God and receive their names. The ritual for boys is CIRCUMCISION, known as *brit milah*, "covenant of circumcision," or more colloquially as *bris* and performed on the eighth day of life. Rituals for girls vary; the traditional ritual is for fathers to introduce baby girls to the community at the synagogue service. When boys and, in the more liberal traditions, girls reach the age of 12 or 13, they become BAR or BAT MITZVAH, "son or daughter of the commandment" respectively, that is, members of the adult Jewish community. The ceremony involves reading a portion of the Torah in Hebrew and then commenting upon it. Distinctive features of a Jewish wedding include the *huppah*, the canopy under which the bride and groom

stand, and the glass that the groom breaks with his foot at the end of the ceremony. Judaism also has distinctive funeral practices. When Jews learn that a close relative has died, they are supposed to tear their clothes. They also observe various periods of mourning; the most intense lasts from the moment of death until burial is over. Judaism does not as a rule allow cremation. Embalming is forbidden, and ideally the corpse should be buried within 24 hours.

ORGANIZATION

Judaism is organized according to local congregations that join together to form national organizations. A congregation maintains a synagogue, which is a place for prayer, study, and fellowship. It also supports a rabbi, a person who, after intensive study, is ordained to serve a congregation's spiritual needs (*see* ORDINATION). In Reform, Reconstructionist, and more recently Conservative Judaism, women have been ordained to the rabbinate. Orthodox and Hasidic Jews ordain only men.

Rabbis are generally respected for their learning and their service to the community, but within Hasidism, the rabbi, or rather the *rebbe*, assumes an extraordinary position. The leader of a community that may span the globe, the Hasidic rebbe is thought to be blessed with special insight into God's revelation and will. His person is especially revered, his word is taken as close to divine revelation, his advice is sought on all matters, and even his presence is spiritually uplifting.

The state of Israel, established after the Holocaust, has a special place in the Jewish world. Its political leaders have no religious authority, but by its constitution every Jew in the world may become an Israeli citizen. Most Jews outside Israel strongly support the state. A few Hasidic Jews have rejected Israel as a human attempt to do what only God should do, restore the glories of ancient Israel.

JUDAISM IN THE WORLD TODAY

One important topic for modern Jews is what it means to follow HALAKHAH, the Jewish "path." Many followers still consider *halakhah* to embody the commands of God, but others see it as a code of customs that people are free to adopt or adapt according to their own consciences. In keeping with this distinction, some Orthodox Jews maintain that women cannot be rabbis, are not permitted to read Torah in services, cannot count toward a *minyan* (traditionally, the number of men required for a prayer service), and cannot hold their own prayer services. Other Jews, however, believe that women hold an equal place in society and religious practices.

Jews from various religious backgrounds also differ on other controversial topics, such as homosexuality (*see* HOMOSEXUALITY AND RELIGION). Furthermore, because Judaism is a small community that does not proselytize, particularly important are issues relating to interfaith marriage and how to regard children of such marriages. (Traditionally, a child's mother must be Jewish for the child to be considered Jewish.)

Relationship with non-Jews also continue to demand attention (*see* ANTISEMITISM). For example, the last of the survivors of the Holocaust are now very old or dying, and, in an effort to avoid new surges of antisemitism, many Jews are actively trying to document their experiences before they can no longer do so. Also, in North America, Jews are sometimes the targets of vigorous attempts to convert them to other religions, especially by Evangelical and fundamentalist Christians (*see* EVANGELICAL CHRISTIANITY; FUNDAMENTALISM, CHRISTIAN). Most Jews regard those attempts as annoying and disrespectful. Particularly troubling at the beginning of the 21st century is the degree of antisemitism and violence against Jews in the Middle East, especially the terrorist attacks on Jews in the state of Israel. As seen in the world media, the devastation caused by such acts as terrorists' suicide bombings tends to drown out the voices, on both sides, of those working for peace.

SIGNIFICANCE

At the end of the 20th century roughly 15 million people practiced Judaism. Although this is only a small percentage of the Earth's population, Judaism remains a major religion. In addition, Judaism has enriched other religions of the world, such as Christianity and Islam, and individual Jews have made major contributions to the world's culture.

Further reading: Nicholas de Lange and Miri Freud-Kandel, *Modern Judaism: An Oxford Guide* (New York: Oxford University Press, 2005); Abraham Heschel, *Between God and Man: An Interpretation of Judaism* (New York: Free Press, 1965); Jacob Neusner, *The Way of Torah; An Introduction to Judaism*, 2d ed. (Encino, Calif.: Dickenson, 1974); Herman Wouk, *This Is My God* (Garden City, N.Y.: Doubleday, 1959).

Judaism in America   The practice of Judaism in the Western Hemisphere. This entry focuses specifically on JUDAISM in the United States. By the end of the 20th century, that Jewish community was second in importance only to the Jewish community in Israel.

As a result of the European intellectual movement known as the Enlightenment (18th century), Jews received full civil rights. That first happened on American soil. With American independence and the adoption of the U.S. Constitution, Jews could participate in the federal government, hold federal office, and seek legal recourse in the federal courts. The status of Jews in the various states was somewhat different. For example, at that time some states still required legislators to profess their belief in GOD "the Father, Son, and Holy Ghost." This requirement excluded from the government not only Jews but also everyone who was not a trinitarian Christian (*see* TRINITY).

The first Jewish community in what would later be the United States was established in New Amsterdam (later New York City) in September 1654. At the end of the 18th century (1800), roughly 2,000 Jews lived in the United States. Most of them had assimilated to a large extent into American society. Assimilation—for example, the use of English in WORSHIP, the adoption of a Gentile diet—was destined to be the issue on which the American Jewish community would divide.

During the 19th century, two waves of Jewish immigrants approached this issue in two different ways. Until roughly 1880, most Jewish immigrants were of German background. They developed far-reaching ideas about how to adapt Judaism to the American situation. After several attempts throughout the century, Reform Judaism finally coalesced in the 1870s. In that decade, the Union of American Hebrew Congregations was formed in Cincinnati. It established Hebrew Union College to train rabbis.

Then from 1881 to 1914, a second wave of Jewish immigration arrived at American shores. The new immigrants came from eastern Europe. They vastly outnumbered the Jews already living in America. They also rejected Reform Judaism in favor of maintaining their traditions, and some formed the Jewish Theological Seminary of America. In 1913 they also established the United Synagogue of America. These became the central institutions of Conservative Judaism. Although this new form of Judaism accepted change as inevitable, it also insisted on making changes that still respected Jewish traditions.

After World War I, Orthodox Judaism coalesced. Its premier institution was Yeshiva College, later Yeshiva University, founded in 1928. A Conservative thinker, Mordecai Kaplan, added yet another variety of Judaism to the American mix: Reconstructionism. Reconstructionism emphasizes Judaism not as a religion but as an everchanging civilization. With the rise of Hitler, Reform Jews began a move to recover traditions that they had abandoned. After World War II, ultraconservative Hasidic communities settled in the United States (*see* HASIDISM). A prime example is the Lubavitch community in New York City.

In the second half of the 20th century, American Judaism was still negotiating the conflict between preserving traditions and adapting to the American environment. One very important issue concerned the place of women in the community. Reform and Reconstructionist Judaism ordained women to the RABBINATE. The Orthodox refused to do so. The Conservative movement eventually decided to ordain women, but some within the community continued to resist this move.

judgment of the dead   The idea that after people die, their lives are assessed. It is especially important in CHRISTIANITY and ISLAM.

Religions have many different teachings about what happens after death (*see* AFTERLIFE IN WORLD RELIGIONS). Some teach that all people lead the same kind of existence, an existence that is not particularly desirable. Examples include the religions of ancient Mesopotamia and Israel. Other religions teach that reward for a good life and punishment for a bad one occur according to "natural" laws. Examples are notions of KARMA in HINDUISM, JAINISM, and BUDDHISM, and the "bridge of the requiter" that Zoroastrians say the dead must cross (*see* ZOROASTRIANISM). Still other religions teach that after people die, they must answer to a judge or panel of judges for what they have done. Strictly speaking, judgment of the dead refers to this last teaching.

Some religions of the ancient Mediterranean world contain hints of a judgment of the dead. The Egyptian Book of Going Forth by Day contains a well-known image of a person's heart being weighed in a balance after death. In one pan stands the heart; in the other rests a feather. The feather symbolizes Maat, the Egyptian GODDESS of truth and justice (*see* EGYPTIAN RELIGION). Some Greeks also taught that the dead appeared before a panel of judges. According to Plato, in his *Apology,* the philosopher Socrates identified these judges as Minos, Rhadamanthus, Aeacus, Triptolemus, and other demigods. The Jewish New Year, Rosh ha-Shanah (*see* JEWISH FESTIVALS), is sometimes called the Day of Judgment. But JUDAISM has tended to be less specific about what happens after death than its younger cousins, Christianity and Islam. The opening verses of the QUR'AN emphasize the importance of the judgment of the dead in Islam: "In the name of ALLAH, the Beneficent, the Merciful. All praise is due to Allah, the Lord of the Worlds, the Beneficent, the Merciful, Master of the Day of Judgment" (Qur'an 1.1–3).

Christians and Muslims share many ideas about the judgment of the dead. They generally think that the souls of the dead are already with GOD. At the same time, they expect a final judgment at the end of time. In this final judgment, God, or an agent acting on God's behalf, will separate "the sheep from the goats" (Matthew 25.32). In both religions, written records of a person's life form the basis of the judgment. Those destined for paradise go to the right; those destined for HELL go to the left. According to the Qur'an, JESUS himself will return at the last day and testify against the Christians, who blasphemed by making him divine (Qur'an 4.159).

The judgment of the dead is a prominent theme in Christian art. (Islam does not allow artists to portray people.) In the time known as the Romanesque period (roughly 1000–1150), artists such as Gislibertus delighted in portraying terrifying images of the last judgment. Later, the last judgment figured in the macabre paintings of Hieronymus Bosch (c. 1450–1516). Of the many works on the theme, Michaelangelo's *Last Judgment*, on the ceiling of the Sistine Chapel in Rome (1536–41), is perhaps the most notable.

The theme of the judgment of the dead, or rather, judgment day, has also fascinated North Americans in the 19th and 20th centuries. Countless religious groups, mostly Protestant, have proclaimed that the day of judgment was at hand. Popular culture has also picked up on the phrase. For example, in 1991, a movie featuring bodybuilding champion Arnold Schwarzenegger was entitled *Terminator 2: Judgment Day*.

Jung, Carl Gustav (1875–1961) *a Swiss psychologist famous for his ideas about the collective unconscious* As a young man Jung was impressed with the ideas of Sigmund FREUD, the founder of psychoanalysis. Eventually, however, he broke with Freud.

Freud sees religion as a symptom of immaturity and even mental illness. Jung sees religion as helping to make a well-integrated person. That is, religion helps the different parts of a person's psyche fit together.

According to Jung, symbols make this integration possible. Religious symbols are especially important. Jung talks about them in terms of what

Portrait of the Swiss psychiatrist Carl Gustav Jung *(Snark/ Art Resource, N.Y.)*

he calls ARCHETYPES. Archetypes are symbols that all people share. They exist in the "collective unconscious," and they function like language. They provide the psychological "words" that people use to make sense of their worlds. One example is the archetype of the mother as found in various myths.

Perhaps the most famous follower of Jung in the second half of the 20th century was Joseph Campbell. A student of mythology, Campbell is well known for his ideas on the archetype of the hero (*see* HEROES AND HERO MYTHS).

Juno One of the most important GODDESSES of the ancient Romans. Juno was enshrined, together with JUPITER and Minerva, in the ancient temple on the Capitoline Hill in Rome. She was one of the major goddesses of the city.

Juno's special sphere was the life of women, particularly childbirth. As a protector in childbirth she was worshipped as Juno Lucina, "Juno who brings to light." She was also worshipped in other forms, such as Juno Sospita, "Juno the Deliverer or Preserver," Juno Moneta, "Juno who warns," and Juno Regina, "Queen Juno."

Juno was most often represented as a mature but young woman. As Juno the Deliverer she was shown bearing arms. An important festival was the Matronalia, held in honor of Juno Lucina on March 1. The story of how she protected the Capitol in 390 B.C.E. may have given her the name Juno Moneta. The Gauls were trying a sneak attack under cover of night. The honking of Juno's geese gave them away.

Eventually the Romans identified Juno with the Greek goddess Hera. The English month of June takes its name from her.

Jupiter The supreme god of the Romans. The name Jupiter is related to the Greek name ZEUS and the Sanskrit name Dyaus Piter. This relationship connects Jupiter with an ancient sky god worshipped as father. When the Romans encountered Greek culture, they identified Jupiter with Zeus.

From the founding of the Roman Republic in 509 B.C.E., Jupiter shared a temple on the Capitoline Hill with JUNO and Minerva. The Romans called this Jupiter "Optimus Maximus"—"Best and Greatest." He was their supreme god.

The Romans worshipped Jupiter under many other names, too. They include Jupiter Lucetius ("Bringer of Light"), Tonans ("Thunderer"), Fulgur ("Lightning Hurler"), Elicius ("Giver of Heavenly Signs"), and Latiaris ("God of the Latins"). Like other sky gods, Jupiter watched over treaties and oaths. His priests presided over the most solemn form of Roman marriage.

The days in the middle of the month known as "Ides" were especially sacred to Jupiter; they may once have been full moon days. The festival of the dedication of the Capitoline temple took place on the Ides of September. It became the occasion for major Roman games.

justification An important idea in Roman Catholic and Protestant theology. Justification is one of the topics that Christians debated the most during the REFORMATION.

"Justification" is a term that Christians borrowed from law courts. In the courts it meant "being declared not guilty." The apostle PAUL used the word to talk about the forgiveness of SINS. He said that, although people are guilty of sin, GOD justifies them freely. Therefore, Christians did not have to observe the TORAH ("the law"). They simply needed to have FAITH in JESUS' death and RESURRECTION.

Orthodox Christians have not talked much about justification, but Roman Catholics and Protestants have. AUGUSTINE OF HIPPO used the idea. Then, during the Reformation, it became an issue on which the church split. Martin LUTHER insisted that people are justified by faith alone, apart from works. Justification is a gift received in faith. By contrast, Roman Catholics have thought of justification as a process. Persons prepare for God's justification. Then they receive it through faith, hope, love, and SACRAMENTS such as BAPTISM and penance.

K

Kaaba Arabic for "cube"; the central shrine of Islam, located in Mecca, toward which devout Muslims pray. The Kaaba is one focus of the annual PILGRIMAGE to Mecca in ISLAM (*see* MECCA, PILGRIMAGE TO).

The Kaaba is a cubical structure made of black granite, roughly 42 feet by 36 feet by 55 feet high. It has only a single door and no windows. Inside it are only gold and silver lamps. The Kaaba is generally covered by a black cloth embroidered with gold thread known as the *kiswah*. During pilgrimage time, the "skirts" of this cloth are raised, so that pilgrims can see the actual structure.

The Kaaba is said to occupy the spot on Earth directly under God's heavenly throne. According to legend, ABRAHAM and his son Ishmael built the Kaaba. At that time the ANGEL Gabriel brought a black rock down from HEAVEN and gave it to them. The rock is now encased in silver in one of the corners of the Kaaba.

At the time of the prophet MUHAMMAD (570–632 C.E.), the Kaaba was filled with idols. But in the year 630, Muhammad returned to Mecca after having fled for his life. He emptied the Kaaba of all images and established pilgrimage to Mecca as a major RITUAL of Islam. During pilgrimage Muslims circle the Kaaba seven times in imitation of the angels, who continually circle GOD's heavenly throne.

kabbalah From the Hebrew word for "tradition"; from the 12th century C.E. on, the main form of Jewish mysticism. Kabbalah arose in northern Spain and southern France in the 12th century.

No one knows quite where it came from. It shares some characteristics with earlier forms of Jewish mysticism, but the way it talks about GOD is distinctive. Kabbalah began as an esoteric tradition. That is, it was a private, even secret subject that a student explored under the guidance of an experienced master. The most important writing to come from Spanish kabbalah was a book named the *Zohar*, the "Book of Splendor." When Jews were expelled from Spain in 1492, kabbalistic activity shifted locations. No place became more important than Safed in Palestine. It was there that the great kabbalist Isaac Luria (1534–72) lived and taught.

In talking about God, kabbalists identified a polarity between what they called the *Ein Sof* and the *sefirot*. Literally, Ein Sof means "endless, infinite." This is God at the greatest distance from human beings: unnameable, unknowable. Sefirot literally means "numbers." It refers to God's various powers or characteristics, usually 10 in number: kingdom, foundation, eternity, splendor, grandeur, mercy, stern judgment, wisdom, understanding, and thought. Kabbalists teach that these sefirot somehow proceed or emanate from God. Explanations of how they do so vary. In any case, kabbalah usually represents the sefirot as different parts of a cosmic man or tree.

Isaac Luria added to kabbalah his own very distinctive and influential ideas. He taught that creation occurred when God withdrew or contracted into himself (*tsimtsum*). When that happened, the universe arose in the space that was left. Light emanated from God and entered vessels that were finite in size, but it shattered them. That shattering created darkness and evil and resulted in the mixing of sparks of the divine light with dark, material substance. As Luria saw it, the goal of religious practice is to restore the divine sparks to the light of God (*tikkun*). Doing so prepares the way for the MESSIAH to come.

Besides developing these ideas, kabbalah gave new significance to following the Jewish way of life. It teaches that human actions actually alter God. Observing the instructions of TORAH strengthens God; violating them weakens God. Kabbalists also recommend more specific practices. Generally they urge the aspirant to contemplate God in prayer. By that means his or her intellect will enjoy communion with God. One kabbalist, Abraham Abulafia (*c.* 1240–*c.* 1291), formulated techniques that remind one of certain practices in yoga: breathing exercises, recitation of God's names (cf. MANTRA), and bodily motions to accompany the recitation (cf. MUDRAS). As a result of these practices, the limits of the self were supposed to disappear and the person was united with God.

Kabbalah is still pursued today. It has also had a wider influence. Especially the kabbalah of Isaac Luria played a significant role in the rise of HASIDISM. In addition, kabbalistic ideas influenced important European thinkers and poets, for example, Pico della Mirandola, Gottfried Leibniz, and William Blake.

Further reading: Arthur Green, *A Guide to the Zohar* (Stanford, Calif.: Stanford University Press, 2004); *Kabbalah Simply Stated: A Conversation with the Rabbi* (St. Paul, Minn.: Paragon House, 2004); Lawrence Kushner, *Kabbalah: The Way of Light* (White Plains, N.Y.: Peter Pauper Press, 1999); Daniel C. Matt, trans., *The Zohar* (Stanford, Calif.: Stanford University Press, 2004).

Kabir (1440–1518) *an Indian saint* Saint Kabir is best known for his poetry, which combined Islamic and Hindu elements into a single religious path.

Kabir belonged to a religious movement in medieval India known as the "sants." This movement appealed to people of the lowest CASTES from all religious backgrounds. The sants rejected human religious authority and took the GOD who dwelled within their hearts as their guru.

Kabir was born into a Muslim family of weavers. At some point he was heavily influenced by Hindu traditions. In the end he rejected all sacred scriptures and much religious RITUAL, Hindu and Islamic alike. He sought instead the true God within, the one Reality. His ideas resemble ISLAM in emphasizing that there is only one God and in rejecting caste. His ideas also resemble HINDUISM in that they include notions of KARMA and rebirth.

Kabir composed his poems not in the language of the educated but in the language of the ordinary people. The poems quickly became popular throughout north India. Kabir exercised a great influence on NANAK, the first guru of the Sikhs. Indeed, Kabir's poems appear in the sacred book of the Sikhs, the ADI GRANTH. He did not himself establish the group known as the Kabirpanth, "Kabir's path," but the group continues today to try to put his insights into practice.

Kali A Hindu goddess, worshipped especially in the eastern Indian state of West Bengal. In Sanskrit, the classical language of ancient India, the word *kali* means "black." Images depict the goddess Kali with black skin. A goddess associated with the blood of the battlefield, her appearance is striking. Her face grimaces as she sticks her tongue from her mouth, dripping blood. She wears only a skirt of severed human forearms and a necklace of human heads. In her hands she holds a man's severed head and a sword. She often stands on the motionless body of the god Siva, who is lying on his back.

Despite these features, Hindus worship Kali as a beneficent mother. She stands on Siva because, according to one school of Indian philosophy, the male principle is inactive, while the female principle is active. The severed body parts symbolize release from SAMSARA, continual rebirth. Devotees worship Kali by sacrificing animals such as goats. This is one of the few instances of animal SACRIFICE in mainstream Hinduism. (Indians known as *adivasis*, the "original inhabitants" or commonly "tribals," also sacrifice animals.) The most famous temple to Kali is the Kalighat temple in Kolkata (Calcutta). In fact, it is from this temple that the city of Kolkata took its name.

Further reading: June McDaniel, *Offering Flowers, Feeding Skulls: Popular Goddess Worship in West Bengal* (New York: Oxford University Press, 2004); Rachel Fell McDermott, *Singing to the Goddess: Poems to Kālī and Umā from Bengal* (New York: Oxford University Press, 2001); Rachel Fell McDermott and Jeffrey J. Kripal, eds., *Encountering Kālī: In the Margins, at the Center, in the West* (Berkeley: University of California Press, 2003).

kami The gods of SHINTO. Some kami are nature spirits, dwelling in great trees, waterfalls, rocks, or mountains. Some are the spirits of famous persons regarded as kami after their deaths. Most originally functioned as protectors of particular communities, clans, families, or occupations, though some are worshipped by the nation as a whole. Although they are limited rather than all-powerful gods, in the eyes of believers, the Shinto kami add a sense of life and divine presence to the beautiful Japanese landscape. The Shinto shrines seen almost everywhere in Japan, with their distinctive *torii* crossbeamed gateway, are all home to one or more kami. Some shrines honor families of kami: father, mother, and child. One of the most distinctive sets of shrines, which are found throughout the Japanese islands, are those to Inari, a god of fertility and prosperity. They have bright red or orange torii with images of foxes, messengers of this god, on either side of them. The ancient Shinto mythologies, found primarily in the books called *Kojiki* and *Nihonshoki* (or *Nihongi*), tell the story of how kami made the Japanese islands and became ancestors of its imperial house.

karma Sanskrit word meaning action and the consequences of action. The word karma is used in HINDUISM, BUDDHISM, and JAINISM. Karma-YOGA, taught in the BHAGAVAD-GITA, is the discipline or yoga of uniting oneself with GOD through righteous action in the world. The term also commonly refers to the consequences of actions, even actions of the mind, reminding us that every thought, word, and deed will have consequences for the doer, good or bad, depending on the nature of the action. The consequence may come out in one's future life, though karma is not limited to reincarnation.

King, Martin Luther, Jr. (1929–1968) *the most important leader of the civil rights movement in the United States* Martin Luther King Jr. was born and raised in Atlanta, Georgia. His father and grandfather were Baptist ministers, and King followed in their footsteps. He took degrees from Morehouse College in Atlanta, Crozer Theological Seminary in Chester, Pennsylvania, and the School of Theology at Boston University. During these years he was profoundly influenced by the writings of Henry David Thoreau, especially his essay on "Civil Disobedience," the social gospel of Walter Rauschenbusch, the nonviolent resistance movement of Mohandas GANDHI, and a school of theology in Boston known as "personalism." A visit to India later in life reinforced the impact of Gandhi's teachings on King.

King's first pastorate was in Montgomery, Alabama. At that time the Montgomery public transportation system required blacks to sit in the back of buses. King was chosen to lead a boycott in protest of this practice. It made him into a national figure. Soon he founded the Southern Christian Leadership Conference to organize otherwise fragmented civil rights efforts.

King's goal was to overcome the barriers that separated whites and blacks. King expressed this goal perhaps most eloquently in the famous "I Have a Dream" speech that he gave during the March on Washington in August 1963: "I have a dream that my four children will one day live in a nation where they will not be judged by the color of their skin but by the content of their character. . . . I have a dream that one day the state of Alabama . . . will be transformed into a situation where little black boys and black girls will be able to join hands with little white boys and white girls and walk together as sisters and brothers. . . . When we let freedom ring . . . we will be able to speed up that day when all of GoD's children, black men and white men, Jews and Gentiles, Protestants and Catholics, will be able to join hands and sing in the words of the old Negro spiritual, 'Free at last! free at last! thank God Almighty, we are free at last!'"

King also advocated distinctive tactics for pursuing integration: active but nonviolent resistance. These tactics owed a great deal to Gandhi's nonviolent campaigns. In his famous "Letter from Birmingham Jail" (Spring 1963), King expressed the idea behind these tactics. "Nonviolent direct action seeks to create such a crisis and foster such a tension that a community which has constantly refused to negotiate is forced to confront the issue. It seeks so to dramatize the issue that it can no longer be ignored."

King remained the dominant influence on the civil rights movement until 1965. Some of his actions failed, but many achieved results. The widest success came when the United States Congress passed the Civil Rights Act of 1964 and the Voting Rights Act of 1965. The widest recognition came when King received the Nobel Prize for peace in 1964.

Beginning in 1965, younger members of the movement became impatient with King's nonviolent methods. They began to advocate a more active black power. In 1966 King tried to overcome segregation in northern American cities. He targeted Chicago, but his efforts there failed. In 1967 King spoke out strongly against the Vietnam War.

Martin Luther King Jr. delivering his memorable "I Have a Dream" speech at the Lincoln Memorial during the March on Washington, D.C., 1963 *(Archive Photos)*

At the end of his life he was reaching out to the disadvantaged of all races. In April 1968 he traveled to Memphis, Tennessee, in support of a strike by sanitation workers. There, on April 4, he was assassinated by James Earl Ray while standing on a hotel balcony.

King's contribution to contemporary American culture is immense. In recognition of his leadership and achievements, every state in the United States observes Martin Luther King day on the third Monday in January.

Further reading: Lewis V. Baldwin, *There Is a Balm in Gilead: The Cultural Roots of Martin Luther King, Jr.* (Minneapolis: Fortress Press, 1991); ———, *To Make the Wounded Whole: The Cultural Legacy of Martin Luther King, Jr.* (Minneapolis: Fortress Press, 1992); Clayborne Carson and Kris Shepard, eds., *A Call to Conscience: The Landmark Speeches of Dr. Martin Luther King, Jr.* (New York: Warner Books, 2001); Richard Deats, *Martin Luther King, Jr., Spirit-Led Prophet: A Biography,* foreword by Coretta Scott King (New York: New City Press, 2000).

kingdom of God   A Christian term for the ideal society and world. As presented in the BIBLE, the kingdom of GOD is a central element of JESUS' teaching. According to the GOSPEL of Mark (1.15), Jesus taught, "The kingdom of God has come near." (The gospel of Matthew speaks of the kingdom of HEAVEN.) Many of Jesus' parables tell about the kingdom. His sayings talk about entering the kingdom. The LORD'S PRAYER teaches Christians to pray, "Your kingdom come."

For most Christians, the kingdom of God is coming in the future. CHRISTIANITY teaches that Jesus will return. When he does so, he will judge human beings. He will also usher in the kingdom of God. The book of REVELATION in the NEW TESTAMENT presents a highly picturesque account of what will happen.

At the same time, Christians look upon the kingdom of God as a present reality—in imperfect form. According to Luke, Jesus taught, "The kingdom of God is among you" (Luke 17.22). Many

Christians have identified this kingdom with the church. Protestants in the United States, like Christians everywhere, have been inspired by the ideal of the kingdom to work for many social reforms.

kingship and religion   The religious role and significance of traditional sacred rulers. In many traditional societies the king is more than just the ruler of the state. He also has qualities of a priest and even a god. History tells us of such figures as the pharaoh of Egypt (*see* EGYPTIAN RELIGION), the emperors of China and Japan (*see* CHINA, RELIGIONS OF and JAPANESE RELIGION), and the maimed king in the Holy GRAIL stories of King Arthur, whose land withered as the monarch fell wounded.

The basic idea is that the king and the land are bound up together, and the king faces heaven on behalf of the land. He is the mediator between HEAVEN and Earth. Sometimes the sacred king has this function because he himself is believed to be virtually divine. The pharaoh in ancient Egypt was thought to be identical with the god HORUS, and would become OSIRIS, lord of life and death, after his own death. The Chinese emperor was called son of heaven, and the Japanese ruler was said to be descended from AMATERASU, the sun GODDESS.

Beliefs like these gave the king legitimacy in the eyes of heaven as well as of his subjects, and made his laws, ideally, enactments of the will of heaven. Western MONOTHEISM, in JUDAISM, CHRISTIANITY, and ISLAM, could not exactly identify the king with God, since for monotheism there was only one God and that God was in heaven, but kings were sometimes given titles that evidenced a close relationship. The caliphs in Islam were called "Shadow of God," and for many centuries, Christians talked seriously about the "divine right of kings."

Of course, such an exalted position also had its disadvantages, as the maimed king learned, for heaven could hold the king responsible for what happened in the lands entrusted to him and judge how well he executed his charge. The kings of ancient Babylon had to confess their SINS with tears before the gods on New Year's Day if they hoped to continue as heaven's viceroy on Earth (*see*

MESOPOTAMIAN RELIGIONS). The Chinese spoke of the sovereign's "mandate of heaven" to rule the "middle kingdom," and if a dynasty became unworthy, the mandate might pass to another. When the ruling dynasty had lost the mandate, natural disasters—earthquakes, floods, droughts—as well as social upheavals would indicate that heaven was displeased, the house in power had lost its mandate, and it was time for a better emperor to take power.

Many RITUALS of kingship make clear the religious character of the office. The coronation of European kings, like the rite installing the king or queen of England, takes place in a church or cathedral in the midst of a religious service. The new Japanese emperor communes with his divine ancestors in a mysterious SHINTO midnight ceremony called the Daijosai. Annual kingship rituals also make the same point. The emperors of China and Japan ritually planted the first rice each spring and offered the first fruits of the harvest in the fall. At a dramatic winter solstice ceremony at the ALTAR of Heaven in Beijing, the Chinese emperor would pray directly to heaven on behalf of the people.

Sacred kingship is in serious decline in the modern world, but remnants of it remain, and sometimes have been transferred to the secular state. In the United States, people often talk of the country as established under God's guidance, but say that to keep his blessing it is important for both leaders and ordinary citizens to follow God's commandments. Now as ever, humanity wants its political institutions to have sacred meaning and divine sanction.

Further reading: Julia Ching, *Mysticism and Kingship in China: The Heart of Chinese Wisdom* (New York: Cambridge University Press, 1997); Dale Launderville, *Piety and Politics: The Dynamics of Royal Authority in Homeric Greece, Biblical Israel, and Old Babylonian Mesopotamia* (Grand Rapids, Mich.: W. B. Eerdmans, 2003); John Pemberton III and Funso S. Afolayan, *Yoruba Sacred Kingship: "A Power like That of the Gods"* (Washington, D.C.: Smithsonian Institution Press, 1996); Michael E. Smith and Marilyn A. Masson, ed., *The Ancient Civilizations of Mesoamerica: A Reader* (Malden, Mass.: Blackwell Publishers, 2000).

koan A riddle or puzzling saying used to provoke enlightenment, especially in the Rinzai school of ZEN BUDDHISM. One koan is very well known in North America: "Show me the sound of one hand clapping."

Koan were first systematized by the great Zen master Hakuin (1686–1769). Because they present the mind with an insoluble problem, MEDITATION on koan should frustrate the meditator and ultimately force him or her to surrender reliance on language and reason. In Zen Buddhism, language and reason are thought inevitably to distort reality. Therefore, they must be overcome.

A student receives a koan from a Zen master and is expected to return with an answer. Serious students work on a single koan for a year or more. Nevertheless, the answer must be spontaneous rather than premeditated. Although students reflect on their koan during meditation, many stories relate how Zen practitioners unexpectedly discovered answers to their koan while engaged in quite menial activities.

Konkokyo One of the "new religions" of Japan (*see* JAPAN, NEW RELIGIONS IN), based on revelations in 1859 to its founder, Kawate Bunjiro (1814–83), called Konko Daijin. The revelations were from a deity called Tenchi Kane no Kami, officially translated as "Parent God of the Universe." They called Kawate to a ministry of mediation between humans and the divine. The religion has WORSHIP in a SHINTO style but is monotheistic (*see* MONOTHEISM). A distinctive feature is a practice called *toritsugi*, mediation, whereby believers can formally receive personal spiritual guidance from a priest; it has sometimes been compared to confession in the Roman Catholic Church. The religion also puts great emphasis on the presence of *mitama* or ancestral spirits guiding us today. It has spread throughout Japan and to Japanese communities around the world.

Koran *See* QUR'AN.

Korean religion Religious traditions of Korea. Lying between China and Japan the Korean Peninsula has a distinctive religious heritage. It was strongly influenced by Chinese culture, from whence it received CONFUCIANISM and BUDDHISM, and was a major channel of communication of the same to Japan. Yet Korea has also maintained its own identity.

The ancient religion of Korea centered on SHAMANISM. Going into trance states, shamans would transmit the words and power of heavenly gods or gods of the locality. Shamanism persists today as an important feature of popular spirituality, especially in the form of shamanesses called *mudang*, who perform colorful rites known as *kut* for healing, expelling EVIL spirits, or delivering divine messages. Shamanism has been especially important as a religious venue for women in a highly patriarchal culture.

Buddhism entered Korea from China in the fourth century C.E. and quickly established itself. The golden age of Buddhism was the period of the Koryo dynasty, 935–1392. The dominant form of Buddhism in Korea has been Mahayana, with monks meditating in the Zen (sun in Korean) manner, and popular devotion centering on PURE LAND BUDDHISM, the BODHISATTVA known as AVALOKITESVARA (Korean, Kwan-um), and the coming BUDDHA Maitreya (Korean, Mi-ruk).

The next dynasty was the Yi, 1392–1910. It emphasized Confucianism instead. Indeed, in some ways the old Korea of those centuries was virtually an ideal Confucian state, with emphasis on literature, the traditional examinations for entry into public service, and vast national temples. But this society was very restrictive of women and was too conservative to meet the challenges of modern times. Korea was called the "Hermit Kingdom" because of its unwillingness to receive visitors or ideas from outside, but by the mid-19th century, the outside was forcing its way in.

Roman Catholic and Protestant MISSIONARIES were active, bringing with them Western learning.

In opposition, a movement called Tonghak (Eastern Learning), or Ch'ondo-kyo (Way of Heaven Teaching), arose to resist foreigners; its activities led to the Sino-Japanese War on 1894, after which Japanese influence and subsequent rule controlled Korea until 1945.

CHRISTIANITY grew in Korea, especially after the end of World War II. After the Philippines, Korea is the most Christian country in east Asia. Korea has also produced new religious movements, the best known worldwide being the quasi-Christian Unification Church of the Rev. Sun Myung Moon. Korea remains a mix of religious traditions and movements.

Further reading: Kim Chongsuh, ed., *Reader in Korean Religion* (Kyonggi-Do Songnam-Si: Academy of Korean Studies, 1993); James Huntley Grayson, *Korea: A Religious History*, rev. ed. (New York: Routledge, 2002); Lewis R. Lancaster and Richard K. Payne, ed., *Religion and Society in Contemporary Korea* (Berkeley: Institute of East Asian Studies, University of California, 1997).

Krishna A Sanskrit word meaning "black"; the name of one of the most beloved of Hindu gods. According to Hindu mythology, Krishna is an AVATAR of the god VISHNU. For many worshippers, however, Krishna is himself the supreme GOD. Indeed, many scholars believe that Krishna was at first an independent deity. Only later was he incorporated into the myths of Vishnu. Stories of Krishna are numerous and have given rise to some of the masterpieces of Indian literature.

Ancient traditions know Krishna as a prince, a hero, and a sage. In this form Krishna is called Vasudeva. Vasudeva Krishna appears in the great Sanskrit EPIC, the *Mahabharata*. That epic pits five brothers, the Pandavas, against their cousins, the Kauravas. Krishna has ties to both groups. In the final battle of cousins against cousins, his troops fight on behalf of the Kauravas, while Krishna himself advises, but does not fight for, the Pandavas. The famous Hindu scripture, the BHAGAVAD-GITA, records a conversation between

An 1825 Indian miniature of Krishna and Radha on a canopy *(Réunion des Musées Nationaux/Art Resource, N.Y.)*

Krishna as adviser and Arjuna, one of the five Pandava brothers.

Krishna may be Vishnu on earth, but he still dies. After the Mahabharata war, he moved to western India and the city of Dwarka. There an arrow shot into his foot by mistake killed him.

Other stories tell of the birth and youth of Krishna. This Krishna is known as Gopala, "cowherd," because he grows up among a cowherding people. Krishna's parents are not cowherds. He is born into the ruling lineage of Mathura, a district in north central India. But Mathura is in the hands of the wicked ruler Kamsa. In order to keep him safe, the gods secretly entrust the infant Krishna to a cowherding couple. After Krishna grows up, he returns to Mathura, kills the wicked Kamsa, and assumes the throne.

Krishna Gopala is a mischievous child and an enchanting lover. The very young Krishna is fond of stealing freshly churned butter. On one occasion, too, it is said that a witch came to poison him with her milk. But the baby Krishna was unaffected by the poison. He drank so hard and long that he sucked the very force of life out of the witch. A somewhat older Krishna is said to have convinced the people of the region not to worship the Vedic god Indra. In his anger Indra sent a torrential rain. But Krishna lifted up Mount Govardhana and held it over the people as a gigantic umbrella.

Krishna's relations with the *gopis*, the cowherding girls, provide favorite stories, for they express in graphic terms the relations of God and the human soul. On one occasion, the *gopis* were bathing in a river. Krishna stole their clothes, which were sitting on the riverbank. Then he climbed a nearby tree, taking the clothes with him. He refused to give them back until each *gopi* had come naked to the foot of the tree to retrieve them herself. The idea behind this story is that we cannot hide anything from God. Before God, our souls are as good as naked.

On another occasion, Krishna danced with the *gopis* at a village celebration. Each *gopi* left convinced that Krishna had spent the night dancing with her alone. This dance, called *ras-LILA*, also expresses a religious truth. God is actually available to everyone, but each person experiences God as being totally engaged with him or herself.

Krishna also has a favorite lover, named Radha. Hindus who worship Krishna often see themselves as friends of Radha or Krishna, assisting them in their love-play. Indeed, play underlies many of the stories of Krishna. These stories show Krishna devotees that God relates to the world through *lila*, play.

An important source for the stories about Krishna, both Krishna as a baby and child and Krishna as an adult, is the *Bhagavata* PURANA, sometimes called the *Srimad-Bhagavatam*. Jayadeva's rather explicit poem, the *Gita-Govinda*, celebrates the love between Radha and Krishna. Krishna and his tales provide the subject of many other works of literature, too.

In art Krishna is shown with dark blue skin. He is also often shown playing the flute, with which he enchants the *gopis*. Statues in temples often show him standing with Radha. The lovemaking of Radha and Krishna and *ras-lila* have provided painters with favorite subjects. Artists in Rajasthan who have used these subjects for their miniature paintings have made a particularly important contribution to Indian art.

Several important Hindu festivals celebrate Krishna. Holi occurs in spring and is known for the colored powders with which worshippers decorate one another, sometimes raucously. Janmastami, the celebration of Krishna's birth, takes place in late summer.

The community of Krishna worshippers best known in North America today is ISKCON, the International Society for Krishna Consciousness. Its members are often called "Hare Krishnas" because they frequently chant the "Hare Krishna" mantra. A. C. Bhaktivedanta Swami Prabhupada (1896–1977), an immigrant to the United States, founded ISKCON in 1966. The community stands, however, in a tradition of Krishna worship that began in the 16th century with the eastern Indian saint Caitanya. By the beginning of the 21st century ISKCON claimed to have roughly 260,000 members as well as temples, rural communities, and restaurants in 71 countries.

Some practices once made ISKCON notorious. One was *sankirtan,* the public chanting of praises to Krishna. Since ISKCON members wear Indian clothing and adopt Indian styles, such as shaved heads for men except for a particular lock of hair, they made a striking appearance chanting in public places in the United States. Another controversial practice was the distribution of free literature about Krishna in public places such as airports. Although laws now limit the public distribution of literature, the movement still publishes a great deal, especially writings by its founder, Prabhupada.

Members of ISKCON observe a strict diet: They eat no meat and also avoid onions, garlic, and mushrooms. In some parts of the world it has not been easy for them to do so. Perhaps for that reason ISKCON manages restaurants that serve appropriate food. In addition, ISKCON temples generally provide free meals to the public on a daily basis.

Other ISKCON activities include programs to ensure the welfare of members' children (once a topic of public critique), prison ministries, and the maintenance of cow sanctuaries. Although the movement began as a missionary endeavor, its temples have become important spiritual centers for Hindus who have emigrated from India.

ISKCON has constructed a major complex in Mayapur, the town in the Indian state of West Bengal where Caitanya was born. It includes a large temple centered on its founder, Prabhupada. Two other sites in India are also important to ISKCON members: Puri, where Caitanya lived, and places in Mathura associated with Krishna. These places are also sacred to Krishna devotees unaffiliated with ISKCON. They draw millions of visitors every year.

Further reading: Edwin F. Bryant, ed., *Krishna: The Beautiful of God (Srimad Bhagavata Purana, Book X)* (New York: Penguin, 2003); J. A. Van Buitenen, ed., *Bhagavadgita in the Mahabharata: A Bilingual Edition* (Chicago: University of Chicago Press, 1981); Edward C. Dimock and Denise Levertov, *In Praise of Krishna: Songs from the Bengali* (Chicago: University of Chicago Press, 1981); John Stratton Hawley, *Krishna, the Butter Thief* (Princeton, N.J.: Princeton University Press, 1983); Barbara Stoler Miller, ed., *Love Song of the Dark Lord: Jayadeva's Gitagovinda* (New York: Columbia University Press, 1997); E. Burke Rochford Jr., *Hare Krishna in America* (New Brunswick, N.J.: Rutgers University Press, 1985).

Krishnaism in the West   The WORSHIP of the Hindu god KRISHNA by the International Society for Krishna Consciousness. Popularly known as the Hare Krishnas, this form of BHAKTI or DEVOTIONAL-ISM was brought to the United States from India in 1965 by A. C. Bhaktivedanta Swami (1896–1977). Since then its chanting, dancing devotees in saffron robes and shaven heads have been a colorful presence on American streets. Although its numbers have never been large, the movement has been controversial because of its attraction to young people. By the 1980s, however, many of the worshippers in its temples in the United States were ethnic Hindus.

kundalini   A Sanskrit word for "serpent"; in TANTRISM, the energy of life. People who practice Tantrism envision the energy of life as a coiled serpent that sleeps at the base of the spine. Through Tantric practices this energy is awakened. It gradually proceeds up the spine through the various CAKRAS or energy centers. As it does, it appropriates the characteristics of these cakras, for example, the deities who reside in them. Each appropriation gives the practitioner ever new experiences, insight, and powers. When kundalini reaches the highest of these centers, it unites with the god whose power it is. The result is illumination and blissful release for the worshipper.

Kwanzaa   A Swahili word that means "first fruits of the harvest." Kwanzaa is an African-American holiday. African Americans celebrate it for seven days beginning December 26. In 1966 Maulana Ron Karenga, an African-American activist, founded

Kwanzaa. He wanted a holiday in the time around CHRISTMAS and HANUKKAH that was specifically African American. He also wanted to celebrate the values, especially family unity, that had sustained African Americans throughout the centuries.

At the heart of Kwanzaa are seven principles (in Swahili, *Nguzo Saba*): unity, self-determination, responsibility, cooperation in economic endeavors, purpose, creativity, and FAITH. Celebrants recall these principles on seven successive days. They use them to greet each other. They also light seven different candles, one for each principle.

The candleholder is placed on a straw mat along with ears of corn (one for every child in the family, but always at least one), first fruits, gifts, and a unity cup used to pour offerings to ancestors. Children may receive gifts every night. They may also simply receive gifts on December 31. On that night the most festive celebration takes place.

L

Lakshmi   Also known as Sri; the Hindu GODDESS of wealth and prosperity. She is also worshipped by Jains (*see* JAINISM). Lakshmi is the consort of the god VISHNU. When he descends to Earth in his various AVATARS, Lakshmi often accompanies him. For example, when Vishnu took form as a dwarf, Lakshmi appeared as Padma or Kamala; when he took form as RAMA, she appeared as Sita.

People worship Lakshmi in order to prosper, whether that prosperity is conceived of in agricultural or monetary terms. She is often shown with LOTUS blossoms, for the lotus symbolizes flourishing. A common image shows her standing atop a lotus flower and holding lotuses in her two upraised hands. At times she is shown with two white elephants.

The festival of lights, known as Divali or Dipavali, is particularly sacred to Lakshmi (*see* HINDU FESTIVALS). It takes place in October or November. On this occasion Hindus offer the goddess food, money, clothing, and jewels. Men also gamble, for Lakshmi is the goddess of good luck.

lama, lamaism   *See* TIBETAN RELIGION.

Lao-tzu (Laozi) (sixth century B.C.E.)   *Chinese for "old master" or "old man"; the alleged founder of the Chinese religion TAOISM* Lao-tzu is also the name of a book attributed to Lao-tzu, more commonly known as the *TAO TE CHING*.

Lao-tzu has long been identified with Lao Tan, an older contemporary of CONFUCIUS (551–479 B.C.E.). If that identification is correct, he would have lived during the sixth century B.C.E. Not much is known about his life, however, and what little is reported reads like legendary material developed to illustrate Taoist teachings.

The central event recorded about Lao-tzu concerns his retirement. A worker in the Chinese archives, he is said to have resigned his position at an advanced age due either to discontent or political unrest. Having resolved to leave China, he mounted a water buffalo and headed off to the west. At the border he was stopped by a gatekeeper, Yin Hsi. Unable to pay the toll with currency, he gave the gatekeeper his wisdom instead: He dictated the 5,000 characters that make up the central Taoist classic, the *Tao Te Ching*, the "Classic of the Way and Its Power." Allowed to pass, Lao-tzu rode off into the west. Among other things, this story illustrates the Taoist principle of *wu-wei*, the abandonment of deliberate, acquisitive action.

Other stories about Lao-tzu also illustrate Taoist teachings. For example, Taoists believe that people who act entirely in harmony with nature do not dissipate any vital energy. The most modest claims suggest that Lao-tzu lived to an advanced age of, say, 160 or 200 years. Taoists were also intensely interested in ALCHEMY, a "science" that tries to mature substances that have been born prematurely. One legend relates that Lao-tzu spent a considerable amount of time inside his mother's womb. When he was born, he was already an old man.

Still other stories reflect tension between Taoism and its religious neighbors in China. For example, some say that when Lao-tzu left China, he went to India. There he became the BUDDHA and taught Buddhist DHARMA. There are indeed some similarities between Taoism and BUDDHISM; for example, the Sanskrit word for the Buddha's teachings, "dharma," was first translated into Chinese as "Tao." But the story also bears witness to the antagonistic relations of the two religions. Similarly, Taoist accounts like the CHUANG-TZU dispute the *ANALECTS OF CONFUCIUS,* which show Lao Tan to be Confucius's respected teacher. In the Taoist writings, Confucius comes off as a fool who is too dull to understand Lao Tan's teachings.

In time, notions of Lao-tzu's longevity gave way to the idea that he was immortal. Beginning in the second century C.E., the Chinese state established sacrifices to Lao-tzu. Some Chinese treated him as a savior to whom they could pray for help. Others made him into the physical embodiment of an eternal principle that continually incarnated itself to advise the Chinese kings. Religious leaders known as the Celestial Masters saw themselves as Lao-tzu's representatives on Earth. The faithful have dedicated a large number of shrines to Lao-tzu in these forms.

Further reading: Stephen R. Bokenkamp, *Early Daoist Scriptures* (Berkeley: University of California Press, 1997); Livia Kohn, *God of the Dao: Lord Lao in History and Myth* (Ann Arbor: Center for the Chinese Studies, University of Michigan, 1998); Livia Kohn and Michael LaFargue, eds., *Lao-tzu and the Tao-te-ching* (Albany: State University of New York Press, 1998).

Latter-day Saints   People who practice an American offshoot of CHRISTIANITY. They are popularly called Mormons.

HISTORY

The Latter-day Saints trace their history back to a prophet named Joseph Smith Jr. (1805–44). Smith lived in upstate New York along the banks of the Erie Canal. This was at the time of the Second Great Awakening in American religious life. People in the area enthusiastically supported many differ-

ent Christian denominations. That left the young Smith confused. At the age of 14 he received a revelation from GOD the Father and JESUS that cleared up his confusion. He learned that all varieties of Christianity then being practiced were wrong.

In 1827 Smith claimed that he had discovered, with the help of an ANGEL named Moroni, gold plates near his father's farm. The gold plates disappeared, but several witnesses claimed to have seen them before they disappeared. With the help of special instruments, Smith translated the writings on the plates into English. The result was the *Book of Mormon.* Smith published the book in 1830. In the same year he officially organized what would become the Church of Jesus Christ of Latter-day Saints.

Smith and his followers moved from New York to Ohio and later to Missouri. Eventually they founded the town of Nauvoo, Illinois, on the banks of the Mississippi River. In Nauvoo Smith taught things that disturbed more conservative Mormons. He taught that a man could have more than one wife, that human beings who practiced Mormon teachings would become divine, and that those who had died without knowing the truth could be saved if family members were baptized on their behalf.

Smith's teachings aroused opposition among non-Mormons. Indeed, persecution had driven the community from Ohio and Missouri. In 1844 Smith was killed by a mob after being imprisoned in Carthage, Illinois. He is buried in Nauvoo.

After Smith's death, the community split. Most Latter-day Saints followed Brigham Young, leader of the governing body of the church at the time Smith died. He and his followers continued to accept the teachings and practices that Smith had begun in Nauvoo. In 1846 they moved to Utah. They became the Church of Jesus Christ of Latter-day Saints.

Other community members rejected the Nauvoo teachings. The largest group of dissenters insisted that Smith's descendants should lead the community. (In this they somewhat resemble Shi'ite Muslims [see SHI'ITE ISLAM], who insist that descendants of the prophet MUHAMMAD should lead the Islamic community.) As a result, they followed Smith's son, Joseph Smith III. They made their headquarters at Independence, Missouri, because during his lifetime, the prophet had identified Independence as Zion. This group became the Reorganized Church of Jesus Christ of Latter Day Saints.

In Utah the Latter-day Saints openly proclaimed the practice of polygamy. They also talked of establishing a Mormon kingdom. This led to difficulties with the United States government. After President James Buchanan sent in the army in 1857, Young lost his position as governor of the territory. It was not until 1890, however, that the church abandoned its teaching on polygamy.

From the very founding of the church, Latter-day Saints were active in mission work. That activity continues up to the present. They have been especially successful in Europe and the Western Hemisphere.

BELIEFS

Mormons accept the BIBLE as the word of God. They maintain, however, that it has been translated improperly. The proper translation, they believe, predicts the coming of Joseph Smith. Mormons also accept the *Book of Mormon*. It tells of Hebrews who allegedly immigrated to North America around the year 600 B.C.E. Their story involves themes familiar from the Hebrew Bible: SIN, punishment, and repentance. The *Book of Mormon* also teaches that Jesus appeared in the Western Hemisphere as well as in Palestine.

The Latter-day Saints who belong to the church based in Utah have many distinctive beliefs. They teach that human beings can become divine, and that this has already happened in the case of God. They teach that what orthodox Christians consider three persons of the TRINITY are actually three distinct gods. They teach a detailed scenario for the RESURRECTION of the dead and the end of the world. They teach that God's revelations continue today. In particular, their prophet-president receives revelations from God that apply to the whole church.

PRACTICES

Latter-day Saints worship in both temples and meeting-houses. Only practicing Mormons can enter a temple.

Distinctive Mormon RITUALS include BAPTISM and endowment. Mormons generally baptize around the age of eight. They also baptize by proxy those who have previously died. This has led them to be intensely concerned with genealogy. The ritual of endowment provides a Latter-day Saint with special temple clothes that are worn under regular clothing. Saints also learn secret passwords and handshakes.

In personal life Latter-day Saints observe rules and cherish values that others sometimes find very strict. They are encouraged not to use alcohol, tobacco, coffee, and tea. They must observe a dress code. In addition, good members of the church tithe, that is, they give 10 percent of their income to the church.

ORGANIZATION

Traditionally only males hold office in the church. They become deacons, teachers, and priests when they turn 12, 14, and 16 years old, respectively. At the age of 18 they may become elders and enter into missionary work for 18 months (A smaller number of women undertake missionary work in their early twenties.) Until 1978 only white men could be priests in the Utah-based church. In 1978 men of color were admitted to the priesthood. The Reorganized Church has always recognized black priests; it has also opened the priesthood to women.

Several executive bodies govern the church. The most important are a three-member Presidency, the Council of the Twelve APOSTLES, and the Quorum of the First Seventy. A General Conference, which all Mormons may attend, approves actions by these bodies. On the local level Mormons are organized into congregations.

SIGNIFICANCE

In many ways Mormonism is typical of religions that have arisen in the United States. Its characteristic concerns have been with the possibility of progress, the end of the world, and acceptable behavior. Today Mormons are known for emphasizing the traditional family. They are also known for valuing hard work. An important example is the large number of young people in their late teens and early twenties who devote 18 months of their lives to the work of the church.

Further reading. *The Book of Mormon* (Salt Lake City, Utah: Church of Jesus Christ of Latter-day Saints, 1982); Claudia Lauper Bushman and Richard Lyman Bushman, *Mormons in America* (New York: Oxford University Press, 1999); Terryl L. Givens, *The Latter-day Saint Experience in America* (Westport, Conn.: Greenwood Press, 2004).

Lent In CHRISTIANITY, the period of 40 days before EASTER, beginning with the day known as Ash Wednesday. Lent has traditionally been a time of fasting and penitence, though the discipline may range from an almost complete fast to abstaining from meat on certain days to a personal practice of giving up luxuries. Lent is observed in the Roman Catholic, Eastern Orthodox, Anglican, and some Protestant churches.

Lévi-Strauss, Claude (1908–1994) *French anthropologist and a leading figure in a kind of analysis called structuralism* Lévi-Strauss was concerned with exploring the way people think. In doing so, he created an approach called structuralism. It was inspired by work in linguistics, that is, the scientific study of language. (Linguistics is different from learning to read or speak a language.)

Lévi-Strauss tried to identify the codes that enabled human beings to think. He was especially interested in human beings that earlier anthropologists had called "primitive" or "savage." According to Lévi-Strauss, mental codes were made up of "binary oppositions," such as nature and culture, or raw and cooked.

Lévi-Strauss focused most of his attention on mythology. He argued for a striking position. In his view, one did not find the meaning of a myth in the story itself or its symbolism. A myth's meaning was the code that underlay the myth. Structural analysis was the way to uncover that code.

See also RELIGION, STUDY OF.

lila A Sanskrit word for "sport" or "play." Hindus explain the relation of GOD to the world in several ways. One way uses the term lila. God creates and sustains the world by playing, that is, through action that lacks any purpose or self-interest. The term lila is not limited to any particular Hindu sect. For example, those who worship SIVA see the dance by which Siva creates the world as lila. But lila has been especially important for worshippers of VISHNU. It is most especially important for those who WORSHIP the young KRISHNA.

The mythology of the youthful Krishna emphasizes his mischievous, playful exploits. His worshippers see their ultimate goal as participating forever in Krishna's play.

Lilith A female demon in Jewish folklore. Lilith seems to be historically related to the Babylonian spirits known as Lilu and Lilitu. She appears only once in the BIBLE, in ISAIAH 34.14. In later folklore she is said to snatch children, especially babies, to threaten women in childbirth, and to seduce men, especially in the middle of the night. According to some traditions she was ADAM's first wife, renowned—and rejected—for her independence. She also came to figure prominently in KABBALAH.

Traditionally, Jews used amulets, or charms, to ward off Lilith. Today, they generally dismiss her as outdated superstition. In the late 20th century, however, some Jewish feminists saw in Lilith's independence from Adam a positive mythic image of womanhood, which they have sought to recover.

liturgy An ordered form of WORSHIP, especially in CHRISTIANITY. The word liturgy comes from a Greek word meaning "public work." Before Christianity, a liturgy was any public work that people with money had to sponsor. These public works included religious festivals.

In Christianity liturgy refers to a fixed order for worship. It applies especially to the order for worship used to celebrate the EUCHARIST in Orthodox and Catholic Christianity (*see* EASTERN ORTHODOX CHRISTIANITY and ROMAN CATHOLICISM). In the

Orthodox churches this worship service is actually called the Divine Liturgy. In Catholic churches it is called the Mass.

During the REFORMATION some Protestants, such as Anglicans and Lutherans, retained the traditional liturgy (*see* ANGLICANISM and LUTHERANISM). Other Protestants rejected it. They adopted freer forms of worship in an attempt to return to the practice of the earliest Christians.

During the 19th and 20th centuries there was a liturgical revival. Catholics tried to make the Mass more accessible to ordinary people. Protestants tried to recover traditional forms of worship that had been abandoned.

Loki A god in Norse mythology. Loki is an ambiguous figure. Renowned for his cleverness, he helps the gods. For example, he gives birth to the god Odin's horse, who has eight legs. (Among other abilities, Loki can change sex.) He also helps the god Thor get his hammer back. At the same time, Loki opposes the gods. He fathers Fenriswolf, the enemy of the gods. He also kills the god Balder with a mistletoe arrow.

Loki's fate is like that of Prometheus in Greek mythology: He is tied to a rock. In Loki's case, the ties that bind him are his own sons' intestines. A poisonous snake hangs above him. His wife sits by his side to catch the poison that drips from its mouth. Legend says that Loki will return at the end of time. He will lead the armies of his daughter Hel, "death."

Sakyamuni preaching the *Lotus Sutra* on the Vulture Peak, accompanied by two disciples and the bodhisattvas Avalokiteshvara and Mahasthampapta. Silk embroidery on hemp cloth from Cave 17, Dunhaung. This is one of the largest examples of Chinese embroidery known. *(Erich Lessing/Art Resource, N.Y.)*

lord of the animals *See* PREHISTORIC RELIGION.

Lord's Prayer Also known as the "Our Father"; the most sacred PRAYER in CHRISTIANITY. JESUS teaches his followers the Lord's Prayer as part of the famous Sermon on the Mount (Matthew 6.9–13). The prayer is made up of seven petitions, each of which resembles prayers that RABBIS at the time taught. According to Jesus, the prayer embodies the ideal of simplicity. A simi-

lar, even simpler prayer appears in the GOSPEL of Luke (11.2–4).

It has been customary in some churches to conclude the Lord's Prayer with a doxology or statement of praise: "For the kingdom and the power and the glory are yours forever. Amen." This practice appears to be very old, because the *Didache*, a book of Christian instruction written in the middle of the second century, ends the Lord's Prayer with a doxology. Later the doxology found its way into some manuscripts of the gospel of Matthew.

lotus An aquatic flowering plant of special religious significance in HINDUISM and BUDDHISM. The range of meanings connected with the lotus and its bloom are extensive.

In connection with LAKSHMI, the Hindu GODDESS, the lotus symbolizes wealth, beauty, and fertility. One common image shows Lakshmi standing on an open lotus and holding two lotus blooms in her upraised hands.

In TANTRISM the outline of an open lotus appears in many YANTRAS and MANDALAS, which are symbols for the forces of the universe. Lotus forms also define the various CAKRAS, which are energy centers of the human person.

Because the lotus grows from mud but remains clean, it sometimes symbolizes a going beyond or transcendence of the world. Examples include lotuses in association with the Buddha Amitabha (AMIDA) and the BODHISATTVA known as AVALOKITESVARA. Amitabha and Avalokitesvara shower gifts of compassion on human beings but remain untouched by the world. The lotus is also associated with YOGA. The cross-legged sitting posture that yoga practitioners frequently adopt is the well-known lotus position.

Lotus Sutra A Mahayana Buddhist scripture. The Tendai and NICHIREN schools of Japanese BUDDHISM consider the *Lotus Sutra* absolute truth.

The *Lotus Sutra* was written in Sanskrit around the first century C.E. and translated into Chinese in the third century. It develops a very high view of the BUDDHA. It teaches that the Buddha is an eternal being that appeared in history in the form of the Buddha Sakyamuni (Siddhartha Gautama). It also invites people to attain enlightenment not by following the path of THERAVADA BUDDHISM but by relying on the grace and favor of various BODHISATTVAS. Chapter 25 is particularly important; it celebrates the bodhisattva AVALOKITESVARA.

The Japanese nationalist Buddhist leader Nichiren (1222–82) established a school of Buddhism centered on chanting the phrase "Namu Myoho-Renge-Kyo," roughly, "Hail to the marvelous teaching of the *Lotus Sutra.*"

Luther, Martin (1483–1546) *German priest whose disagreements with the Roman Catholic Church began the REFORMATION.*

LIFE

Luther was born on November 10, 1483, in Eisleben, Germany. His father, a businessman in the mining industry, sent Martin to school, with the intention of having him become a lawyer. But one day in July 1505 Luther was walking through a severe thunderstorm. According to tradition, he called out to the patron saint of miners, "Saint Ann, save me, and I shall become a monk!" Having survived the storm, he entered the Augustinian monastery in Erfurt. Ordained to the priesthood, he was sent in 1508 to the recently founded University of Wittenberg, where he soon became professor of the BIBLE.

During this period, Luther was wracked with worries about the certainty of his SALVATION. How could he do enough to make satisfaction to GOD for his SINS? Reading a passage from the apostle PAUL's letter to the Romans helped alleviate his anxieties: "The one who is righteous will live by faith" (Romans 1.17). Reflection on this passage and others led Luther to his characteristic insistence that human beings are saved by God's GRACE received through FAITH.

In Luther's day the Roman Catholic Church had a virtual monopoly on religion in Europe (*see* ROMAN CATHOLICISM). Luther unintentionally ended this monopoly and started the Protestant Reformation. In 1517 a preacher named Johannes Tetzel had begun to sell what were known as plenary indulgences in a nearby town. They were called plenary indulgences because Tetzel promised that if people bought his indulgences, they would receive forgiveness for all their sins. Disturbed by this practice, Luther posted 95 theses or statements for debate on the door of the Castle Church at Wittenberg on October 31. The theses were published elsewhere, and the debates quickly grew to include fundamentals of church teaching and authority. Luther's differences with the Catholic Church of his day proved to be profound and irreconcilable. He was excommunicated on January 3, 1521.

Technically an outlaw, Luther received support from several German princes. From May 1521

Portrait of Martin Luther *(Scala/Art Resource, N.Y.)*

through March 1522 he lived in hiding at the Wartburg Castle overlooking Eisenach. After returning to Wittenberg, he devoted the rest of his life to organizing the breakaway church. He translated the Bible as well as the Mass (*see* LITURGY) into German. To encourage congregational participation in WORSHIP, he wrote a number of hymns, such as the well-known "A Mighty Fortress Is Our God." And he wrote two catechisms, a smaller and a larger one, for use in teaching laypeople the fundamentals of the Christian faith. In 1525 Luther married a former nun, Katherina von Bora. Together they had six children. He died in Eisleben, the town of his birth, on February 18, 1546.

TEACHINGS

At the center of Luther's thought stands the notion of justification. Following the apostle Paul, Luther insisted that people attain a right relationship with God only as a result of God's grace, not of anything that they do. They learn about God's gift through the Bible, the ultimate religious authority, and they accept it through faith.

Luther called these ideas the GOSPEL, as distinct from the law, which human beings cannot fulfill and which therefore leads to condemnation. But Luther was not one to resolve oppositions quickly. God's Word, he said, always comes to human beings as both law and gospel. Christians are at one and the same time justified and sinful. And God himself, as human beings experience him, has two aspects: the hidden God who insists on justice and the revealed God of grace and mercy. Luther teaches in his *Small Catechism* that people should respond to this God with fear, love and trust.

SIGNIFICANCE

By the 1520s Luther's dispute with the leaders of the Catholic Church had incited people with somewhat different perspectives to rebel as well. The result was a split of Western European Christianity into two branches, the Roman Catholic Church and the Protestant churches (*see* PROTESTANTISM). In response, the Catholic Church reformulated its teachings at the Council of TRENT (1545–63) and eliminated abuses about which the devout had complained for years.

But Luther's significance was more than religious. Even though the Reformation resulted in religious fragmentation and wars, it helped to crystallize a feeling of political and cultural independence among German peoples. And because Luther insisted that God comes to human beings not through human actions but through God's Word, his interest in and impact on the German language was immense. His writings, especially his translation of the Bible, helped to establish a common German idiom and made him a pioneer in the development of modern German literature.

Further reading: Susan C. Karant-Nunn and Merry E. Wiesner-Hanks, eds., *Luther on Women: A Sourcebook* (New York: Cambridge University

Press, 2003); Martin E. Marty, *Martin Luther* (New York: Penguin, 2004); James A. Nestingen, *Martin Luther: A Life* (Minneapolis, Minn.: Fortress Press, 2003); Jaroslav Pelikan and Helmut T. Lehmann, eds., *Luther's Works* (CD-ROM; Philadelphia and St. Louis: Fortress Press and Concordia Publishing House, 2002).

Lutheranism The branch of CHRISTIANITY that marks its rise directly from Martin LUTHER. Lutheran churches sometimes call themselves "evangelical." This term goes back to German usage. It means something quite different from "Evangelical Christianity" in the British context (*see* EVANGELICAL CHRISTIANITY and FUNDAMENTALISM, CHRISTIAN).

HISTORY

Martin Luther began the Protestant REFORMATION in October 1517, when he nailed 95 "theses" or propositions to be debated to a church door in Wittenberg, Germany. The Reformation eventually produced many forms of PROTESTANTISM. Those who followed Luther's teachings became known as Lutherans. In Europe they are found especially in Germany and Scandinavia.

Lutheranism spread in the 1500s to Scandinavia, where it became the established or official religion of various states. In Germany Lutherans lived in a state of war—literally—with Catholics until 1648. Then Lutheranism became the established religion of various German principalities. In both settings, in a war for survival and as state church, Lutheran leaders emphasized the need to maintain "pure doctrine," which meant the truth of Christianity as Luther had taught it. Lutheranism became a detailed set of beliefs to which people had to subscribe.

A reaction to this kind of religion began in the late 1600s. It was called Pietism. Pietism emphasized what it saw as a genuine religion of the heart, as opposed to a sterile religion of the head. When Pietists put this emphasis into practice, they founded charitable institutions such as orphanages. They also engaged in missionary work.

In the 1700s another intellectual and cultural movement, the Enlightenment, influenced some Lutheran theologians. Thinkers and philosophers of the Enlightenment rejected MIRACLES and supernaturalism. Theologians whom this movement influenced advocated a religion strictly consistent with the laws of nature.

In the early 1800s the king of Prussia tried to join Lutheran and Calvinist churches (*see* PRESBYTERIAN AND REFORMED CHURCHES) into a single Protestant church. Some Lutherans reacted strongly both to the Enlightenment and to the "church union." They insisted on preserving the traditional teachings of Lutheranism as found in written summaries known as the "confessions."

At the same time, large numbers of Lutherans began immigrating to the United States. Lutherans had lived especially in the mid-Atlantic region even earlier. But American Lutheranism grew tremendously from the immigrations of the 19th century. The Lutheranism that resulted was extremely fragmented. People of various nationalities—Germans, Swedes, Danes, Norwegians, Finns—preferred to WORSHIP in their own languages in their own national churches. At the time of the Civil War, the oldest American Lutherans even split into Northern and Southern churches. In addition, Lutherans influenced by the confessional movement in Germany did not consider other Lutherans genuinely Lutheran.

The watchword of the 20th century was unification. But Lutheran unification was not total unification. At the end of the century there were two major American Lutheran bodies. The larger body, the Evangelical Lutheran Church in America, included the Lutheran churches founded in colonial days as well as many of the 19th-century national churches. The other body, the Lutheran Church-Missouri Synod, preserved the heritage of the German confessional movement of the 19th century. On a global scale, 20th-century Lutherans began to work together in the Lutheran World Federation.

BELIEFS

Lutherans acknowledge the BIBLE as the Word of GOD. They differ on what that means. Some insist that every word of the Bible is literally true. Others say that, while the Bible may contain historical and scientific errors, what is important is the message underlying the biblical account.

Lutherans also accept a distinct set of writings known as "confessions." After the ancient CREEDS, two writings from the Reformation are the most important confessions: the *Small Catechism* and the *Augsburg Confession*. The *Small Catechism* is a book Luther wrote to teach the basics of Christianity to children. The *Augsburg Confession* is an account of Lutheran beliefs that Lutherans presented to the Holy Roman Emperor at Augsburg in 1530.

Lutherans insist on one basic principle: SALVATION by GRACE through FAITH. They teach that people are sinners and cannot earn a proper relationship with God. Therefore, God sent his son JESUS to establish that proper relationship. This proper relationship is given freely as a gift. Human beings do not need to do any "good works" in order to receive it. They simply have to accept God's gift. This acceptance is known as faith.

To express these ideas, Lutherans often distinguish between "law" and "gospel." The law is what a person must do. It is useful, for example, in governing people. But following the law cannot save people. The gospel is the message of God's gift of salvation.

PRACTICES

Traditionally, Lutherans talk about two "means" or ways by which human beings receive God's grace. They call them "Word" and SACRAMENT.

"Word" refers to communicating the gospel. In Lutheran worship services this takes place in two main ways: through readings from the Bible and through the PREACHING of a sermon.

"Sacrament" refers to two acts that Lutherans say were established by Jesus himself: BAPTISM and the EUCHARIST. Lutherans insist that both sacraments are effective not because they are human acts but because in them God gives his grace to human beings. In keeping with this view, Lutherans continued the Catholic practice of baptizing infants. They have also insisted that in the Eucha-

rist Jesus' body and blood are really present, regardless of the faith of the person who eats the bread and drinks the wine.

Lutheran worship services generally preserve the form of the Catholic Mass, but they have always been in the ordinary language of the people. Lutheran worship also has a distinctive tradition of hymn writing and singing that stretches back to Luther himself.

ORGANIZATION

Lutheran congregations belong to state and national churches. No official, council, or organization has authority over all Lutheran churches. Lutherans often call those in charge of the churches in a specific region "bishops." The power of bishops is balanced by elections both within individual congregations and in regional and national assemblies.

Each Lutheran congregation has one or more ordained ministers, who may be married. At the beginning of the 21st century, Lutherans were split over whether women could be ministers. The Evangelical Lutheran Church in America accepted women ministers. The Lutheran Church-Missouri Synod did not.

SIGNIFICANCE

Lutheranism has been most important in Germany, Scandinavia, and places where emigrants from those countries settled in sizable numbers. It has not, however, had great influence on the broader currents of American religious history. In the United States the most influential form of Protestantism has tended instead to be Calvinism.

Further reading: Richard Cimino, ed., *Lutherans Today: American Lutheran Identity in the Twenty-first Century* (Grand Rapids, Mich.: W. B. Eerdmans, 2003); Eric W. Gritsch, *Fortress Introduction to Lutheranism* (Minneapolis, Minn.: Fortress Press, 1994); Martin E. Marty, *Lutheranism: A Restatement in Question and Answer Form* (Minneapolis, Minn.: Fortress Press, 1995).

M

magi The priests of Persia (Iran) before ISLAM. In the time of classical Greece and Rome, the magi were the traditional Persian priests. They practiced ZOROASTRIANISM and were very important in preserving its writings. The Greeks respected their wisdom a great deal. They also felt that these priests had special, secret knowledge. This attitude gave us the English words "magic" and "magician," which come from magi.

According to the GOSPEL of Matthew (2.1–15), magi came to visit JESUS soon after his birth. The BIBLE does not say anything specific about them. Early legend suggested that they were kings. In the Middle Ages these kings were said to be three in number. They were given names and kingdoms: Balthasar, king of Arabia; Melchior, king of Persia; and Caspar, king of India.

The Orthodox churches celebrate the visit of the magi on CHRISTMAS Day. The Catholic Church and some Protestant churches celebrate it on Epiphany (January 6).

magic The use of means outside ordinary cause and effect to achieve desired objectives. In modern times, it implies means outside the laws of conventional science and technology. It would mean the employment of seemingly irrelevant gestures or chants (abracadabra or magic spells), or even just concentrated thought, to reach a goal, rather than ordinary labor or engineering.

There are several types of traditional magical means, as defined by Sir James George FRAZER. "Sympathetic magic" indicates doing to an object what you want done to something else, like the pro-verbial sticking of pins into a doll in Caribbean culture; perhaps a hair or some other item belonging to the intended victim can be used to put the doll in harmony with that person. "Correspondence" is the idea, found in ancient Greek magical texts, that there are magical relationships between apparently disparate things, as between gemstones, parts of the human body, certain chants and spells, and astrological signs. These correspondences can be used to work magic both good and bad.

Finally, there is the magic of evoking supernatural aid. The traditions of RITUAL magic or high magic, going back to the Middle Ages and before, are meant to call up gods, ANGELS, demons, and other spirits to help the magician and to do his will. The vivid performances of this school, involving the ceremonialist standing for his own protection in a magic circle, and evoking an entity into a triangle with the help of sword, wand, and vehement words of command, are the height of magical drama.

Many practitioners of magic teach that the ultimate meaning of the art lies in the power of will. The mind can change things on its own if thought is powerful and concentrated enough; the instruments of magic, like a doll or gems, or the evocations of ritual magic, are really simply devices for helping the magician concentrate his or her will.

Although it is sometimes said that magic and religion are two completely different things, there is clearly some overlap. Religious PRAYER and rites can be used like magical charms, while magic can call forth feelings of awe toward the mysteries of the universe, which approach the religious. Both involve ideas of supernatural forces and powers, by whatever name they are called. Religion, however, sorts them out rigorously between good and bad, and ideally is concerned with a highly giving, loving, and moral way of life. Magic can be more ambiguous.

Further reading: Alice B. Child and Irvin L. Child, *Religion and Magic in the Life of Traditional Peoples* (Englewood Cliffs, N.J.: Prentice Hall, 1993); Claire Fanger, ed., *Conjuring Spirits: Texts and Traditions of Medieval Ritual Magic* (University Park, Penn.: Pennsylvania State University Press, 1998); Kathryn Rountree, *Embracing the Witch and the Goddess: Feminist Ritual-Makers in New Zealand* (New York: Routledge, 2004); Randall Styers, *Making Magic: Religion, Magic, and Science in the Modern World* (New York: Oxford University Press, 2004).

Mahavira (sixth century B.C.E.) *a Sanskrit word meaning "great hero"; a title applied to Vardhamana, the founder of* JAINISM. Jains consider him the 24th *tirthankara* or "ford-maker." A tirthankara is one who makes it possible to ford or cross the stream of SAMSARA (rebirth) and achieve liberation.

The birth of Mahavira, the founder of Jainism, is shown here in this *Kalpa Sutra* manuscript page. *(Borromeo/Art Resource, N.Y.)*

Mahavira lived in roughly the same place and time as the BUDDHA—northeast India in the sixth century B.C.E. Like the Buddha, he was part of a movement that rejected the RITUALS of SACRIFICE described in the sacred books known as the VEDA. At the age of 30, he asked his brother—his parents had died—for permission to renounce ordinary life. Receiving it, he adopted the lifestyle of a wandering beggar. Instead of shaving his head, he pulled out his hair. Either immediately or after 13 months—traditions vary—he gave up every last possession, including the wearing of clothes.

As a beggar Mahavira strictly observed AHIMSA, that is, noninjury. He practiced severe austerities and suffered vile abuse from others. Roughly 12 years after his renunciation he achieved complete insight. He is said to have then reformed the teachings of an earlier tirthankara, Parsva. He also reorganized the institutions that Parsva had established. In doing so he created Jainism as we know it.

At the age of 72 Mahavira entered the ultimate NIRVANA.

Prajnaparamita, the virtue of wisdom or insight, is expressed in the Prajnaparamita Sutras, important philosophical texts in Mahayana, or "Great Vehicle" Buddhism. Wood, sheet copper, and silk cloth. *(Erich Lessing/Art Resource N.Y.)*

Mahayana Buddhism The form of BUDDHISM prevalent in China, Korea, Japan, and Vietnam. It differs from THERAVADA BUDDHISM in significant ways. *Mahayana* means the "Great Vehicle," that is, a large and commodious vessel for carrying aspirants from ordinary life to enlightenment. It arose gradually in the early centuries of Buddhism over the issue of whether laypersons as well as monks could follow Buddhist practices fully and become enlightened.

The party that in time became Mahayanists took the more liberal view. Soon they also advocated the reconciling of popular religious rites with Buddhism and taught that the BUDDHA was really a transcendent being who came into our world as a teacher. As a liberal and innovative movement, Mahayana accepted new doctrines and revelations attributed to the Buddha. Its canon of scripture contains numerous books outside the Theravada Tripitaka. These are often said to be teachings of the Enlightened One that were hidden until the world was ready for them. They include such famous Buddhist texts as the *LOTUS SUTRA,* the *Heart Sutra,* the *Diamond Sutra,* and the *Garland Sutra.*

By the first century C.E. Mahayana had consolidated into a distinctive Buddhist party with its own scriptures, teachers, and practices. The greatest Mahayana philosopher, Nagarjuna (*c.* 150–*c.* 250 C.E.) taught two basic principles: that SAMSARA (the "wheel of existence"—our ordinary life) and NIRVANA (its opposite, and the ultimate goal of Buddhist realization) are really one and the same, and that the best metaphor to describe this kind of universe is to call it Emptiness or Void. In other words, Nirvana is not some place to which we "go" in the AFTERLIFE. It is here and now, a state of mind rather than a place, and the universe as perceived by that state of mind can be called Void, not because there is nothing in it but because it offers nothing to grasp hold of by mind or hand, any more than one could grasp a flowing river. The world is fluid, continually changing, and continually blissful to those who know how to swim with its flow. These insights lead to or interpret several distinctive features of religious Mahayana:

1. We are, Mahayana believes, really in nirvana and enlightened Buddhas right now. We just do not realize it. But we "have" or dwell in a universal Buddha nature.

2. Any means to enable us to realize that nature is all right. Therefore Mahayana has many paths to enlightenment: Zen MEDITATION (see ZEN BUDDHISM), the elaborate RITUALS of TIBETAN RELIGION, faith in AMIDA in PURE LAND BUDDHISM, chanting from the *Lotus Sutra* in NICHIREN Buddhism, or the simple awesome experience of being in a Mahayana TEMPLE.

3. Mahayana says there are innumerable buddhas throughout the universe, not just the one historical Buddha, and they can all be of help to us. Mahayana temples may contain images of several of these "cosmic" buddhas, such as AMIDA. According to Pure Land Buddhism, Amida vowed countless ages ago to bring all who call on his name in faith into his "Pure Land" or Heaven, from which entry into nirvana is easy. Sometimes he and other transcendent buddhas are arranged into a MANDALA, or pattern, for devotional purposes.

4. Mahayana also emphasizes the role of the BODHISATTVA, one who fully realizes the truth of samsara and nirvana, lives in the Void, and works actively in the world out of wisdom and compassion to help all beings along the path to enlightenment. A favorite is AVALOKITESVARA, who as Kuan-yin in China and Kannon in Japan is worshipped as a goddess of mercy. Sometimes bodhisattvas are seen as active expressions of a buddha, as Avalokitesvara is of Amida. In a deeper sense, we can all realize we are bodhisattvas, just as we are all Buddhas.

5. In time Mahayana developed a teaching that there are three forms of expression of the universal buddha nature: the Absolute, or nirvana, or what we may think of today as the dance of the atoms and galaxies, the universe as a whole conscious and unconscious; the Heavenly expression, thinking of the cosmic buddhas and bodhisattvas as like heavenly beings because this is the way our minds work; and the Earthly, when universal buddhahood appears to us as a teacher in this world, like the historical Buddha, or within ourselves. This perspective can help us understand Mahayana temples and practices.

It was in this Mahayana form that Buddhism spread into the northern tier of Buddhist countries, forming schools and denominations emphasizing various aspects of the complex Mahayana worldview, but commonly also embracing its broad and tolerant nature.

Further reading: Edward Conze, *Buddhism: Its Essence and Development* (New York: Harper Torchbooks, 1959); Holmes Welch, *The Practice of Chinese Buddhism 1900–1950* (Cambridge, Mass.: Harvard University Press, 1967); Paul Williams, *Mahayana Buddhism: The Doctrinal Foundations* (New York: Routledge, 1989).

Maitreya The BUDDHA who is to come. BUDDHISM has taught about many buddhas besides Siddhartha Gautama (563–483 B.C.E.), the Buddha of our world. One such teaching concerns the Buddha Maitreya. His name comes from *maitri,* a word in Sanskrit, the ancient language of India, which means "friendship" or "benevolence."

Buddhists believe that all things change. Change characterizes the Buddha's teachings, too. Eventually these teachings will lose their appeal and be forgotten—according to some stories, after 5000 years. But the Buddhist DHARMA or teaching will not be lost forever. When the time is right, another buddha will appear who will once again teach the truth. That buddha is Maitreya, who now resides as a BODHISATTVA in a HEAVEN called Tushita.

Unlike many bodhisattvas, Maitreya is revered by Buddhists of all schools—Theravada, Mahayana, and Vajrayana (see MAHAYANA BUDDHISM, THERAVADA BUDDHISM, and VAJRAYANA BUDDHISM). He is not always, however, given the same respect. From about 300 to about 600 C.E. the rulers of China especially favored Maitreya. Then they seem to have become interested instead in PURE LAND BUDDHISM and its Buddha, Amitabha (Japanese, AMIDA). Starting around 1000 C.E., however, the

Chinese began to portray Maitreya as a laughing holy man with a big belly. In this form he remains popular today.

Throughout the centuries Maitreya has inspired much Buddhist MILLENARIANISM in various parts of Asia, that is, enthusiastic movements built on the belief that Maitreya was about to appear. Some rulers claimed to be Maitreya. Sometimes believers, inspired by the teachings about Maitreya, banded together to overthrow the government. Many today still look for Maitreya to come.

Malcolm X (1925–1965) *The best-known preacher of the Nation of Islam, popularly known as the Black Muslims* He advocated black nationalism and black pride.

Suffering, disruption, and criminal behavior characterized Malcolm's childhood and young adulthood. He was born Malcolm Little in Omaha, Nebraska. His father, Earl Little, was a Baptist minister and follower of Marcus Garvey, who preached black separatism. The Little family lived under threats from white racist groups. When Malcolm was six, his father died—allegedly murdered by whites.

Malcolm's mother found the strain of raising the family alone too much to bear. She was hospitalized. Malcolm lived for a while with a foster family in Michigan. Then he dropped out of school and moved to Boston to live with his sister. In Boston and later New York he ran drugs and engaged in burglary. Eventually he was caught and imprisoned.

It was in prison (1946–52) that Malcolm discovered the Nation of Islam (*see* ISLAM, NATION OF). It changed his life. The Nation's teaching that "the white man is the devil" made intuitive sense to Malcolm. Even more important, in the Nation of Islam Malcolm found pride and self-respect as a person of African descent. On release from prison, Malcolm proved to be especially good at public speaking and in using radio and television. He became the most effective Black Muslim spokesperson.

Malcolm's goal was quite different from that envisioned by Dr. Martin Luther KING Jr. King and his associates promoted integration. Malcolm advocated separation. In his eyes, African Americans could develop a sense of dignity only if they had their own nation and their own businesses. Integration would simply continue to make blacks dependent upon whites. Malcolm expressed this in typical fashion when he reacted to King's famous "I Have a Dream" speech. Malcolm said that while Dr. King was having a dream, most African Americans were living a nightmare.

Malcolm also differed from King on what tactics were acceptable for their followers. King emphasized nonviolence and civil disobedience. In Malcolm's eyes, that was the wrong approach. It did not invite African Americans to discover their own dignity and self-worth. It simply invited them to suffer more public degradation and humiliation. Malcolm said that African Americans should pursue their goals "by any means necessary"—a statement that disturbed many white Americans.

Malcolm eventually became leader of the second most important temple in the Nation of Islam, Temple No. 7 in Harlem. But in 1963 he compared the assassination of President Kennedy to "chickens com[ing] home to roost." This incensed the leader of the Nation of Islam, Elijah Muhammad, and Malcolm left. In 1964 he made PILGRIMAGE to MECCA. There he encountered traditional ISLAM. He experienced firsthand its teaching that all people, regardless of color, are brothers and sisters. It was his second eye-opening experience.

When Malcolm had become a Black Muslim, he had adopted the name Malcolm X. After visiting Mecca he changed his name again, to El-Hajj Malik el-Shabazz. He renounced the teaching that white people are devils and adopted SUNNI ISLAM. He also began to talk about human rights rather than civil rights. But Malcolm did not have the chance to develop these ideas. He was killed in a ballroom in Harlem in 1965. Official reports attribute his death to gunmen operating under orders from the Nation of Islam.

In the 1990s there was a "Malcolm revival" among African Americans. His message of pride, self-sufficiency, and personal responsibility seemed to many to be just what the community needed.

Further reading: *The Autobiography of Malcolm X*, with the assistance of Alex Haley (New York: Ballantine Books, 1999); David Gallen, ed., *A Malcolm X Reader* (New York: Carroll & Graf, 1994); Bruce Perry, *Malcolm: The Life of a Man Who Changed Black America* (Barrytown, N.Y.: Station Hill, 1991).

Malinowski, Bronislaw (1884–1942) *anthropologist who was born in Poland and worked in England* Malinowski was one of the founders of the movement known as FUNCTIONALISM. He is important for several reasons.

Before Malinowski's time, those who studied the religions of indigenous peoples simply relied on reports of travelers, missionaries, and colonial officials. Malinowski actually lived among the Pacific islanders about whom he wrote. He established the practice of "fieldwork," which is now expected of all anthropologists.

Malinowski also developed important ideas about religion, MAGIC, and myth. As he developed these views, he criticized the ideas of thinkers like Émile DURKHEIM and Sigmund FREUD.

In Malinowski's view, religion functioned to comfort people when they experienced anxiety or tragedy. Magic was an activity to which people resorted when they could not be sure that practical, goal-oriented activity was going to work. Myth provided a society with its "charter." It made society legitimate by tracing its parts back to the activity of religious beings.

Malinowski's ideas dominated the study of religion by anthropologists until the 1960s. Since that time many anthropologists have been more interested in religious symbols and meanings.

See also RELIGION, STUDY OF.

mandala Sanskrit for "circle"; a sacred diagram used in HINDUISM and BUDDHISM, especially in secret RITUALS known as Tantric rituals. The same basic shape underlies most mandalas: a point at the intersection of two perpendicular axes, located at the center of a square or circle. The area of the circle or square is further subdivided in conformity with the axes, often by means of concentric circles or other designs.

A mandala is a schematic representation of the cosmos. Its various areas are often seen as the abode of various deities, BUDDHAS, and BODHISATTVAS. By using mandalas in rituals and as objects of MEDITATION, practitioners aim at realizing within themselves the central force that sustains the universe.

Mandalas have been rendered in a variety of media. They have provided the grids upon which architects have built Hindu temples. Similarly, the mountain-like STUPA at Borobudur in Indonesia is a massive Buddhist mandala. Mandalas have also been executed in less permanent media, such as paint or ink on paper or cloth, and with colored powders or sands. Tibetan *thang-kas* or scroll paintings are particularly well-known examples of these sorts of mandala.

Manichaeism Religion founded by the prophet Mani (c. 216–c. 276 C.E.). At one time or another Manichaeism was practiced in Europe and Asia, from Spain to China. It died out for good around 1500. The name comes from "Manichaeos." This term transcribes the title, *Mani Hayya*, "Mani the Living," into Greek.

Mani was born around 216 C.E. in what is today southeastern Iraq. In the year 240 an angelic messenger, "The Twin," appeared to him. It told him to leave his religious community and begin teaching. He did.

Mani saw himself as the Seal of the Prophets. He combined into one supreme truth the partial truths that the BUDDHA, ZARATHUSTRA, and JESUS had taught. Mani carefully recorded his teachings in writing so that his own views would not be distorted. These writings, however, have largely disappeared. In addition to writing, Mani traveled widely. His first missionary journey took him to the area near present-day Pakistan. Mani's teaching aroused the opposition of the Zoroastrian priests. Under their influence, Bahram I, king of Persia, interrogated Mani for four days, imprisoned him for 26, and executed him. These events, known as "the Passion," took place around 276 C.E.

MISSIONARIES must always translate their visions of truth into terms that other people can understand. The same was true of Mani and his followers. In some places Manichaean beliefs appeared more Christian. In others, they appeared more Zoroastrian or Buddhist. In general, Mani taught that the world was made of two principles, light and darkness. These principles were not created. They have existed from eternity. Mani also divided the history of the universe into three stages. in the past, light and darkness were separate. Now, light and darkness are mixed together and battle one another. In the future, they will again be separated. Manichaeans help free light from darkness.

Like the Buddhist SANGHA, the Manichaean community consisted of two classes. Manichaeans called them the elect and the hearers. The elect had several levels of leaders: a maximum of 360 stewards under the direction of a maximum of 72 deacons under a maximum of 12 APOSTLES led by a figure some call the Manichaean pope. Women could be members of the elect, but they could not hold any higher offices.

Manichaean hearers performed several RITUALS. They prayed four times a day. They fasted on Sundays and for a month prior to the major festival (celebrated at the spring equinox). They confessed their SINS. They tithed; that is, they gave a tenth of their earnings to the elect. They also renounced violence.

The Manichaean elect abstained from violence, sex, and impure food, including all meat. They were always to tell the truth; they also had no possessions. The ideal life for the elect was one of wandering. With time, however, Manichaeism, like BUDDHISM, developed monastic institutions at specific places. Manichaeans believed that when the elect ate the food that the hearers gave them, they purified it, releasing particles of light.

Christian, Muslim, and Zoroastrian rulers all vigorously persecuted Manichaeism. For example, in 527 the Roman Empire, which was Christian, made it a crime punishable by death to be a Man-

ichaean. As a result of this opposition the head of the Manichaean hierarchy shifted his residence to Samarkand, now in southern Uzbekistan. Manichaeism also suffered in east Asia. The Chinese government banned Manichaeism in 843. Nevertheless, Manichaeism seems to have survived for several centuries in China as a secret society. It finally died out around 1500. Manichaeism was also the basis of medieval Christian "heresies" in Europe, like that of the Albigensians or Cathars (12th–13th centuries).

mantra Sacred words or phrases in HINDUISM and BUDDHISM. Originally mantras were statements made during the SACRIFICES described in the sacred books known as the VEDA. As RITUAL words they had power over the universe. Over time the meaning of the word mantra expanded. It came to include any powerful word or phrase.

Mantras may produce benefits in this world. They may also lead to liberation. In traditions of YOGA it is common to meditate on mantras. In the devotional traditions of BHAKTI mantras often combine various names of GOD. A good example is the mantra that gives "Hare Krishnas" their nickname: "Hare KRISHNA Hare Krishna . . ."

Buddhists use mantras in much the same way. Some Japanese followers of the Buddha AMIDA repeatedly say the *nembutsu,* a phrase that means "Praise the Buddha Amida," to be reborn in Amida's Pure Land at death. A common mantra among Tibetan Buddhists reads *Om mani padme hum,* literally, "Om, the jewel in the lotus, hum."

Manu The first man in Hindu mythology. Most North Americans are familiar with the story of NOAH and the universal FLOOD. Manu figures in a similar story. Hindu mythology relates that, thanks to the help of VISHNU in one of his AVATARS or appearances on Earth, Manu survived the flood. He was the only human being who did so. When Manu set foot on dry land, he performed various RITUALS that produced a "daughter," named Ida or Ila. With her he populated the Earth.

As the first man, Manu is also the ultimate ancestor of all royal dynasties. He gave rise to the solar dynasty through his son Iksvaku and to the lunar dynasty through his grandson Pururavas. An ancient sage, Manu is also alleged to have authored the most influential of the Hindu law books, the *Laws of Manu*.

Maori religion   *See* PACIFIC OCEAN RELIGIONS.

mappo   Japanese for "latter law." It is the notion that we are living in a degenerate age in which no one can achieve enlightenment through one's own efforts.

Mappo is the last of three stages of history. In the first, people practiced the BUDDHA's teachings and attained enlightenment. In the second, it became rare for those who practiced the Buddha's way to attain enlightenment. Today people are unable even to practice the Buddha's way.

Japanese Buddhists believed the age of mappo began in 1052. The idea became very significant for medieval Japanese BUDDHISM, especially the PURE LAND BUDDHISM schools founded by Honen (1133–1212) and Shinran (1175–1262). These two preached that in the age of mappo our own power is inadequate. Therefore, we must rely on the "other-power" of the Buddha AMIDA.

Mara   A Sanskrit word for "death"; the embodiment of EVIL in Buddhist legend. Mara constantly strives to frustrate the efforts of the BUDDHA and his followers.

Mara's most famous appearance in Buddhist traditions occurs just prior to Siddhartha Gautama's enlightenment as the Buddha. Mara is disturbed that Siddhartha will escape from the realm of desire and rebirth (*see* NIRVANA). Therefore, he appears before Siddhartha and tempts him. The temptation culminates when Mara offers Siddhartha his three daughters, Discontent, Delight, and Desire. Siddhartha refuses. When the sun goes down, Mara departs. During the night that follows, Siddhartha attains enlightenment.

Later Buddhist tradition talks of literally millions of Maras or demons. Their overseer is the Mara who tempted Siddhartha.

marriage and religion   The religious background and meaning of the institution of marriage. Marriage, the socially recognized union of a particular man and woman for the purpose of living together and (if of the right age and capable) procreating and raising children, is found in every culture of the world. It is basic to the establishment of the family, the foundational institution of all societies. It is therefore acknowledged by the religions of all cultures to be sanctioned by the divine powers that made the world and regulate the social order. In many societies and religions, marriage is also seen as a religious state in its own right, not just a civil circumstance, and the wedding or marriage ceremony that establishes it as a religious rite. The pair may be brought together by family, or community arrangement, sometimes without ever having met, or of their own will on the basis of love. In many societies, marriages seal important family alliances as well as individual preferences and may include major expense, usually on the part of the bride's family, in the form of dowries and the wedding celebrations.

Some religions in their traditional form, such as traditional CONFUCIANISM, ISLAM, and JUDAISM, have regarded marriage as virtually obligatory, or at least essential for one's full completeness as a human being fulfilling one's adult role in the community. Others, like HINDUISM, BUDDHISM, and CHRISTIANITY, have recognized CELIBACY, as MONKS AND NUNS, priests, or even laypersons, as a valid alternative to marriage. In some cases, it is considered to be spiritually superior to the married state.

However, the great majority of human beings throughout history have been married, frequently in RITUALS demonstrating the religious character of the occasion. These rites characteristically emphasize both the community and family nature of the event and its obviously special meaning for the couple. The act of joining in marriage may be symbolized in various interesting ways: by tying a sacred string between the two in Hinduism, dipping hands together in a bowl of water in Burmese Buddhism, exchanging rings in Christianity, and in Judaism eating together in a place of seclusion.

The regulation of mating and procreation for the good of society as a whole is probably among the oldest functions of human religion. Issues such as appropriate conditions for divorce or annulment of a marriage, interracial marriages, interreligious marriages, and same-sex marriages, although not new, have been the subject of much religious debate in the 20th and 21st centuries. Marriage, family, and the moral issues surrounding them remain a central concern of all religion.

See also FAMILY AND RELIGION, THE.

Mars The second most important Roman god. Mars was the second god in a very ancient triad of Italian gods: JUPITER, Mars, and Quirinus (a god of the common people). He was a god of war. He was also a god of agriculture, at least in the sense that he protected fields. The Romans worshipped Mars especially in March and October. These months began and ended the seasons for fighting and planting. When the Romans encountered the Greeks, they identified Mars with Ares.

Mars had his own high priest (*flamen*). At some of his festivals ancient priests known as the Salii danced in antique armor. Mars also enjoyed a particular kind of SACRIFICE. It was a sacrifice of a pig, a sheep, and a bull. When the Romans declared war, one of the two consuls (highest political leaders) shook his sacred spears and cried out, "Mars, stay awake." According to Roman mythology, Mars was the father of Romulus, the founder of Rome. The month March gets its name from him.

martial arts and religion Fighting techniques viewed as spiritual practices. In many societies the way of the warrior has been seen as having a religious significance. Sometimes warriors are members of a fighting caste with its own code of conduct, like the chivalry of Europe's medieval knights or the bushido of Japan's samurai. Sometimes particular skills of combat, called martial arts, are perceived to have value as spiritual training or as a means of exercising spiritual insight as well. This has especially been the case with certain arts of swordsmanship, archery, or hand-to-hand engagement developed in India and east Asia. Among the martial arts best known in the West are Chinese kung-fu, Okinawan karate, Korean taekwando, and Japanese judo (wrestling), kendo (swordsmanship), kyudo (archery), and the modern general method called Aikido. These terms, ending in do (in Chinese, *tao*), meaning "way," suggest that these arts, like budo or bushido, the way of the warrior, are seen as indicating an entire way of life as well as a particular skill.

According to tradition, the spiritual source of the east Asian martial arts was the Shaolin monastery in China, where the monk BODHIDHARMA, who also had brought the Chan (Zen) school from India to China, devised fighting skills to afford his monks exercise and defense. Combining both Taoist and Buddhist (chiefly Zen) themes, they emphasize the activation of chi (in Japanese, *ki*), the life force or spiritual energy that with training can be projected and directed through spontaneous action. The warrior is then one who has realized the full potential of his inner life, who acts in accordance with nature, and who has the ability to live in the present moment with total awareness. Thus, he is able to act immediately and spontaneously with precision to achieve the goal, whether hitting the target with an arrow or felling a foe with a single blow of the sword.

martyrdom Giving up one's life instead of renouncing one's religion. The word "martyr" comes from a Greek word meaning "witness." A martyr's death "witnesses" to her or his religion. Martyrs inspire those who remain behind. They also provide them with examples to imitate. Religions may teach that martyrs receive special rewards in the next life. The NEW TESTAMENT book of REVELATION imagines the martyrs ruling with JESUS for a thousand years (20.4). Islamic tradition teaches that martyrs stand closest to GOD's throne. In ISLAM, martyrdom is closely connected with giving one's life for God or in defense of the FAITH (*see* JIHAD).

Martyrs have been especially important in JUDAISM, CHRISTIANITY, and ISLAM. Judaism has a long history of martyrdom. One important ancient example is Rabbi Akiba ben Joseph. Some traditions say he was burned to death in a TORAH scroll, others that he was flayed alive for teaching Judaism in public. The first Christian martyr was Stephen, who was stoned to death for blasphemy (ACTS OF

THE APOSTLES 7). Those who died in ancient persecutions include the apostles PETER and PAUL. The *Martyr's Mirror*, by Thieleman J. van Braght, preserves the memory of Anabaptist martyrs who were killed for their beliefs at the time of the Protestant REFORMATION. The most famous Muslim martyr is probably Husayn, the son of Ali, who is especially revered in SHI'ITE ISLAM. He was killed in 680 C.E. when he tried to assume the political and religious position that his grandfather, MUHAMMAD, had held.

An engraving of Karl Marx *(Image Select/Art Resource, N.Y.)*

Marx, Karl (1818–1883) *German social thinker*

Marx is important as the founder of a socialist movement, Marxism, that many people in the 20th century saw as a religion in itself. He is also important for his ideas on religion.

Marx accepted what earlier critics had written about religion. Therefore, he did not write much about religion himself. What he did write draws attention to the relationship between religion and economics, especially the struggle between the rich and the poor.

Marx's most famous sentence on religion calls it the "opiate of the people." Just as the wealthy turn to opium to relieve their pain, Marx said, poor working people—the proletariat—turn to religion. But this move only saps the proletariat of strength. Instead, they should eliminate the class structure that keeps them in poverty. Then they will no longer need religion.

During the 20th and early 21st centuries, many theologians accepted much of Marx's criticism of religion. They saw it as a call not to reject religion but to reform it.

Mary

Often called the Blessed Virgin Mary or Our Lady; the mother of JESUS. In the BIBLE Mary appears especially in the GOSPEL of Luke. There she is prominent in stories about Jesus' birth and one story about his childhood. Indeed, Luke claims that Mary is his source for these stories (Luke 2.51). In the gospel of Matthew, Mary appears in stories about Jesus' birth and early years that are not found in Luke. In Mark, Jesus' mother (unnamed) tries to convince him to quit making a spectacle of himself (3.31–35). In John, she stands at the foot of the cross (19.25–27). Mary last appears in an assembly of the first Christians (ACTS OF THE APOSTLES 1.14).

Christians have many teachings about Mary. These teachings sometimes have very old sources outside the Bible. An especially important example is a writing called the *Protoevangelium of James.*

The most important teaching about Mary is the VIRGIN BIRTH. This teaching says that Mary became pregnant with Jesus before she had sexual relations. Almost all Christians maintain this position. Roman Catholic Christians add that Mary remained a virgin for the rest of her life. Protestants object to this. They point out that the NEW TESTAMENT talks about Jesus' brothers. Catholics hold that these brothers were not children of Mary.

In the ancient church, the idea that Jesus had a mother was especially important in arguments with Gnostics (*see* GNOSTICISM). Gnostics denied that Jesus was a real human being. In the fourth century Christians also argued over whether Jesus was the creator or a created being. They decided on the first option. As the Nicene CREED puts it, Jesus is "begotten, not made, of one being with the Father." But that led to another question: If Jesus is GOD, should Christians call Mary "Mother of God?" In the fifth century two councils of bishops decided that they could use this phrase.

The Roman Catholic Church also adopted other teachings about Mary. From ancient times many Catholics had believed that Mary never committed an actual SIN. The medieval philosopher Duns Scotus taught that she was free from original sin, too. The second idea, known as the "immaculate conception," became official Catholic teaching in 1854. In 1950, the Catholic Church officially adopted another teaching about Mary: She did not die but was taken physically into HEAVEN. This teaching is known as the assumption.

No Christians WORSHIP Mary, but Roman Catholic and Orthodox Christians "venerate" her. Devotion to Mary was particularly important to Pope John Paul II (1920–2005). Holy days celebrate her birth, immaculate conception, the ANGEL's announcement of Jesus' conception, and Mary's purification in the Temple after Jesus' birth. Many Christians call upon Mary to intercede for them with Jesus and God. One way to do this is with the PRAYER *Ave Maria,* "Hail, Mary . . ." Many great works of European art depict Mary. She is often shown with the baby Jesus or standing at the foot of the cross. In the last 500 years, Mary has also appeared to various people (*see* MARY, APPARITIONS OF).

Not everyone accepts these teachings, claims, and practices. Orthodox Christians reject the idea that Mary never sinned. Most Protestants reject all veneration of Mary. Traditional Muslims accept the virgin birth of Jesus, but Jews and many modern scholars, including more liberal Christians, reject it. Many feminists also criticize the image of Mary as continuing male-centered stereotypes. Others, however, find her an inspiration. She was an unwed mother who belonged to a politically oppressed group. She also saw her son grow up to lead a group considered radical and dangerous and as a result be executed—an experience with which mothers in the developing world can identify.

Further reading: Sarah Jane Boss, *Mary* (New York: Continuum, 2004); Carl E. Braaten and Robert W. Jenson, eds., *Mary, Mother of God* (Grand Rapids, Mich.: W. B. Eerdmans, 2004); Jaroslav Pelikan, *Mary through the Centuries: Her Place in the History of Culture* (New Haven, Conn.: Yale University Press, 1996); Jenny Robertson, *Mary of Nazareth* (New York: Continuum, 2001).

Mary, apparitions of Reported appearances of MARY, the Mother of JESUS. Through the centuries Christians, above all those in ROMAN CATHOLICISM, have told of seeing visions, miraculous pictures, and other manifestations of Mary, who is often referred to as Our Lady. When she has spoken in these appearances, she has offered both words of encouragement and stern admonitions to the faithful, generally in very simple language.

Numerous such apparitions of Mary, as of other SAINTS, were recounted in the Middle Ages.

Most were of chiefly local interest. The sites of a few became centers of national or even international pilgrimages, such as Our Lady of Walsingham in England (based on a vision of 1061) or of Loreto in Italy (1291).

But it has been only in modern times that apparitions of Mary began to take on unique importance in Catholic Christianity. The first in the modern series must be the appearance of Our Lady at Guadalupe, Mexico, in 1531 to Juan Diego, an Indian whose account was initially rejected by the white conquerors of his country. This apparition had far more than local significance, for in it Mary took Indian features, and the recipient of the vision was Indian. Our Lady of Guadalupe has become a major symbol of identity for Mexicans, particularly Indians, and has been recognized as patroness of all the Americas.

The "Great Century" of modern apparitions of Mary, however, was approximately the years 1830 to 1930, when a series of visions in France and Portugal profoundly affected the inner life of modern Roman Catholicism. In 1830 Our Lady appeared to a nun, Catherine Labouré, at her convent in Paris. From this event stemmed the popular devotion of the Miraculous Medal, a talisman worn around the neck that depicts beams of light streaming from each of Mary's palms, as in Catherine's vision. In 1846 the Virgin Mary appeared to two shepherd children at La Salette, high in the French Alps. Both were very poor and neglected children, and it was a time of great hardship for peasants because of blight. Our Lady said that was because of human sin. She urged repentance and the recitation of simple prayers.

In 1858 Our Lady appeared to Bernadette Soubirous, another child of poor background, at Lourdes, in the far south of France. Here also the visitor conveyed messages urging repentance, and she revealed to Bernadette a grotto whose waters would be effective for healing. Lourdes has since become a place of pilgrimage for millions, especially the sick, who have sometimes reported miraculous healings.

From 1915 to 1917 three peasant children herding sheep near Fatima, Portugal, reported a series of extraordinary experiences of seeing the Lady radiant as the sun. They received from her messages again urging prayer and repentance, as well as prophecies concerning future world developments (some of them revealed only much later), including war, persecution, and the fate of Russia. During the tumultuous years of Word War II and the cold war, many Catholics found these prophecies of great interest.

Many other modern apparitions have been proclaimed at sites ranging from the United States to Egypt to Japan. The most famous undoubtedly is a series of visions seen at Medjugorje, Bosnia-Herzegovina, beginning in 1981. As with many of the others, the chief visionaries were children, and the messages urged repentance. It and many other recent apparitions have been controversial within the church. But the four greatest modern appearances—Paris, La Sallette, Lourdes, and Fatima—have the full approbation of the Roman Catholic Church and have been very influential.

These apparitions have important common characteristics. Most have occurred in out-of-the-way places, far from centers of power or population. All have come to humble persons, often children, who are poor and poorly educated. They thus serve as counterweights to religion of authority and sophistication and affirm the importance to heaven of those oppressed on earth. The fact that it is a woman who appears affirms the feminine side of the divine. Psychologists such as Carl Gustav JUNG have discussed this important feature of devotion to Mary. Often, in the apparitions, Mary says that out of her motherly compassion she is restraining the righteous anger of GOD and his Son against human sin, but she cannot do so much longer; therefore humanity must repent and turn to God.

Apparitions of Mary and their communications have often appeared naive on the surface, but the plain-spoken message and their coming to simple and impoverished people is part of their meaning. They have unquestionably enriched the spiritual lives of many.

Further reading: Ruth Harris, *Lourdes: Body and Spirit in the Secular Age* (New York: Viking, 1999);

Thomas A. Kselman, *Miracles and Prophecies in Nineteenth-Century France* (New Brunswick, N.J.: Rutgers University Press, 1983); Jaroslav Pelikan, *Mary through the Centuries* (New Haven, Conn.: Yale University Press, 1996); Sandra L. Zimdars-Swartz, *Encountering Mary: From La Salette to Medjugorje* (Princeton, N.J.: Princeton University Press, 1991).

Mary Magdalene More properly Mary of Magdala; a follower of JESUS. The GOSPELS in the NEW TESTAMENT say more about Mary of Magdala than about any other woman besides MARY, Jesus' mother. She has also been the subject of much speculation.

According to the gospels Jesus cast seven demons out of Mary Magdalene (Luke 8.2). She is also said to have stood at the foot of the CROSS during Jesus' crucifixion.

Mary is best known, however, for being the first person to learn of Jesus' RESURRECTION. In Mark and Luke, Mary and women with her discover that Jesus' tomb is empty. They learn of his resurrection from a man or two men dressed in white. In Matthew, Jesus actually appears to Mary and the others after they find the empty tomb. John recounts a more detailed encounter between Mary and the risen Jesus. Jesus appears only to Mary, but Mary mistakes him at first for a gardener.

Ancient writings not included in the BIBLE (*see* NEW TESTAMENT, APOCRYPHAL) hint that Mary was an important authority among early Christians. One such writing is the Gospel of Mary, parts of which have been lost. What remains tells that Mary had a secret vision of the risen Jesus, in which he taught that "the true seed of humanity exists within you. ... Those who search for it will find it." According to this gospel, Andrew and Peter improperly rejected Mary's vision, but Levi rebuked them for doing so.

The early Christian teacher Hippolytus identified Mary as an APOSTLE. Tradition eventually came to consider her the "apostle of the apostles" because she told the apostles the news of Jesus' resurrection.

In Western Christianity—ROMAN CATHOLICISM and PROTESTANTISM—much of the speculation about Mary has focused on sexuality. In a sermon delivered on September 14, 591, Pope Gregory I identified Mary with a prostitute whom Jesus had healed. Ever since, tradition has regarded her as a prostitute who repented and received forgiveness. That vision of Mary is portrayed in the rock musical *Jesus Christ Superstar* (1970; film, 1973) and in the controversial film by Martin Scorsese *The Last Temptation of Christ* (1988), based on a novel with the same title by Nikos Kazantzakis (English translation 1960). In 1969, however, the Catholic Church declared that the identification of Mary with a prostitute was a mistake. EASTERN ORTHODOX CHRISTIANITY never did accept the tradition that Mary was a prostitute.

Many artists have painted Mary as a repentant sinner, perhaps because that was an acceptable way in which they could paint female nudes. Another common subject has been Mary meeting the risen Jesus in the garden, as recorded in the Gospel of John. Artists and art historians often refer to this scene with the words that Jesus spoke to Mary: *Noli me tangere,* "Do not touch me"—a command given because Jesus was not yet purified. Artists influenced by Eastern Orthodoxy have also painted another scene: It shows Mary before the Roman emperor Tiberius, holding a red egg. The story is that Mary traveled to Rome to tell Tiberius about the resurrection of Jesus. Tiberius replied that a person could no more rise from the dead than that an egg could turn red. Mary picked up the egg, and it turned red.

At the end of the 20th and the beginning of the 21st centuries many people took a great deal of interest in Mary. A popular book, *The Da Vinci Code* (2003), claimed that she was the wife of Jesus. Feminist scholars saw in Mary an early Christian authority—indeed, the person on whose testimony all of Christianity was based—whose importance a male-centered church structure had overlooked.

Further reading: Holly E. Hearon, *The Mary Magdalene Tradition: Witness and Counter-witness in Early Christian Communities* (Collegeville,

Minn.: Liturgical Press, 2004); Karen L. King, *The Gospel of Mary of Magdala: Jesus and the First Woman Apostle* (Santa Rosa, Calif.: Polebridge Press, 2003); Marvin Meyer and Esther A. de Boer, *The Gospels of Mary: The Secret Tradition of Mary Magdalene, the Companion of Jesus* (San Francisco: HarperSanFrancisco, 2004); Jane Schaberg, *The Resurrection of Mary Magdalene: Legends, Apocrypha, and the Christian Testament* (New York: Continuum, 2002).

masks and religion   Disguises put on for religious reasons. The wearing of masks as a part of a religious occasion is a common feature of PRIMAL RELIGION, and though not a central aspect of most contemporary religion, is still seen at HALLOWEEN, in various traditional European quasi-religious festivals (St. Nicholas Day, Mardi Gras), and in some sacred dances of such traditions as SHINTO, TIBETAN RELIGION, and HINDUISM.

Masks are frequently employed in Native American religions. The fundamental purpose of RITUAL masks is to enable the wearer to identify with or represent a god or spirit, including demonic and ancestral spirits. This can be done for dramatic purposes, as when mask-wearing is part of a sacred play, dance, or rite in which supernatural entities must be portrayed in order to instruct an audience, or as an offering to the deities themselves. They can also, as in the case of shamans going into trance, be a part of the performer's own subjective identification with a god or spirit. Many religious masks are of remarkable artistic power and afford deep insights into the culture's spiritual consciousness.

maya   A Sanskrit word for "appearance," sometimes translated "illusion." Maya is especially important in the Indian philosophical school known as Advaita VEDANTA.

According to Advaita Vedanta, there is no ultimate difference between the reality that underlies the universe (BRAHMAN) and the reality that underlies the human person (ATMAN). The question naturally arises: If multiplicity and difference do not characterize reality, what is the source of the multiplicity and difference that everyone perceives? The Advaita answer is maya. Multiplicity and difference are merely appearances. They arise from ignorance of the true nature of reality. Because of maya, our perceptions are mistaken, in the way that a person may step on a rope at night and mistake it for a snake.

Maya religion   The religion of the people living in the Yucatan Peninsula and northern Central America before Europeans discovered the Americas. The Maya may be considered the classic civilization of pre-Columbian America. Their culture established patterns that all other Mesoamericans adopted. The Maya civilization began as early as 300 B.C.E. The classic period, associated with sites such as Tikal in Guatemala, ran from roughly 300 to 800 C.E. At the end of the classic period Maya civilization did not disappear; the postclassic Maya built wonders such as those at Chichén Itzá in Mexico.

Maya culture fully deserves the name "civilization," a term that denotes a way of life based on cities. Maya culture concentrated at ceremonial centers. The most outstanding religious features of these centers remain: tall, stepped pyramids. They provided a base for Maya temples and a platform for the performance of RITUALS. The well-known Maya ballcourts, shaped like a capital "I," were the sites of ritual ballgames.

Maya rituals were primarily sacrificial. The Maya sacrificed animals and, especially in the postclassic period, human beings. They also presented offerings of their own blood. They collected blood from a variety of body parts: tongues, arms, legs, earlobes, and genital organs. For example, in one ritual the queen pulled a thorned rope through her tongue. This use of blood may shock some North Americans today, who tend to overlook the extensive use of blood imagery in CHRISTIANITY. Some scholars suggest helpfully that in giving blood, the Maya entered into a relationship of exchange with the forces of life in the universe. These forces gave the Maya life; the Maya gave them life in return.

The most remarkable feature of Maya civilization was its elaborate conception of space and time. The Maya divided space into four quadrants surrounding a center point. The four quadrants represented the four cardinal directions. Each direction, as well as the center point, was associated with a tree. Each was also associated with a color: blue-green for the center, red for the east, black for the west, white for the north (perhaps better, the zenith), yellow for the south (perhaps better, the nadir). During the day the sun was said to traverse seven (or 13) layers of sky; during the night it traversed five (or nine) layers of the underworld.

The Maya calendar was extremely elaborate. It was based on patterns or "rounds" of recurring series, similar to the days of the week and the months of the year in North America today. One pattern combined a series of 20 names and 13 numbers, for a round of 260 days. A second pattern contained 18 "months" of 20 days, followed by five extra days, for a round of 365 days. The two patterns ran simultaneously. Once every 52 years the first dates in each of the two rounds would coincide. Scholars call each 52-year period a "calendar round." The longest running Maya dating system was the Long Count. It began in 3114 B.C.E. It will be completed on December 23, 2012 C.E.

In the 16th century, Spain conquered the Maya, as it did the rest of Mesoamerica. But Maya religion did not disappear. It gave a distinctive character to the rituals, festivals, and saints in the religion of the conquerors, ROMAN CATHOLICISM.

Further reading: Davíd Carrasco, *Religions of Mesoamerica: Cosmovision and Ceremonial Centers* (Prospect Heights, Ill.: Waveland Press, 1998); Lynn V. Foster, *Handbook to Life in the Ancient Maya World* (New York: Facts On File, 2002); *Popol Vuh: The Mayan Book of the Dawn of Life,* trans. Dennis Tedlock, rev. ed. (New York: Simon & Schuster, 1996).

May Day The first day of May, traditionally a day of celebrating fertility and the coming of spring. In

A Mayan pyramid, the Temple of Inscriptions, in Palenque, Mexico *(Getty Images)*

the British Isles, May Day was a continuation of Beltane, the pre-Christian Celtic spring festival. Its celebration remained important in rural England into the 19th century. Remnants of the old May Day can still be found in special dances, processions, the erecting of maypoles, and the gathering of spring flowers for may-baskets in various places in Britain and North America.

Mecca, pilgrimage to One of the "five pillars" of ISLAM. In Arabic, the PILGRIMAGE to Mecca is known as the *Hajj.* Mecca is the site of the holiest shrine in Islam, the KAABA. The Kaaba is said to have been built by ABRAHAM and his son Ishmael. Before the rise of Islam, people in the region used to make pilgrimage to the Kaaba. In the year 630 C.E., the prophet MUHAMMAD purified it of the 360 images it contained. He also established pilgrimage to Mecca as an important Islamic RITUAL. All Muslims should try to make pilgrimage to Mecca at least once. But this requirement should not pose any hardship. Muslims are not allowed to make the pilgrimage if they have debts or must incur debts to do so, if they are too ill to travel, or if their participation would mean difficulties for those left behind.

Pilgrimage takes place during the first half of the last month of the Islamic year. (Muslims use a lunar calendar, so as the years go by, the date of the pilgrimage slowly progresses through all the seasons.) Pilgrims traditionally arrive at Jidda on the coast of the Red Sea. They put on a simple, white garment worn specifically for the pilgrimage. They also vow not to cut their hair or their fingernails or to engage in sexual activity during the course of the pilgrimage. To enter the sacred area, which includes the other sites to be visited as well as Mecca, a person must be able to demonstrate that she or he is Muslim. The Saudi government does not recognize separation of religion and government, so the government controls entrance to the sacred area. Since 630 C.E. very few non-Muslims have entered the sacred area. One who did was the English explorer Richard Burton (1821–90) in 1853.

The first act most pilgrims perform is a ritual circling of the Kaaba. They circle the Kaaba seven

A bird's-eye view of the Kaaba crowded with pilgrims *(Library of Congress)*

times, in imitation of the ANGELS, who are continually circling GOD's heavenly throne. During the circling, pilgrims also kiss or at least gesture in the direction of a black stone built into the corner of the Kaaba. It is said that the angel Gabriel brought this stone down from heaven as a sign of God's favor to Abraham when he built the Kaaba.

The next act consists of running back and forth seven times between two hills, then drinking water from the well of Zamzam. This action recalls the plight of Abraham's wife Hagar and her son Ishmael. Abandoned by Abraham at this spot in the desert, Hagar frantically ran to what she thought were pools of water at the foot of the hills. When in desperation she returned to her son, she found that in playing he had kicked open an artesian well. Pilgrims recall that all human beings, like Hagar and Ishmael, depend upon God's gracious gifts to sustain life.

The most important ritual of the pilgrimage takes place from noon to sundown on the ninth day of the month. Pilgrims stand at the Mount of Mercy and the Plain of Arafat in front of it. Here they beseech God for forgiveness. Islam teaches that at this spot God reconciled ADAM and EVE when they quarreled. It also teaches that at this spot all of us will appear for the final judgment at the end of time.

On the tenth day pilgrims hurl stones at three pillars. Then, if finances permit, they sacrifice a goat. In doing this, they recall the faithfulness of Abraham and Ishmael. When God commanded Abraham to sacrifice Ishmael, the devil appeared to Ishmael and urged him not to cooperate. In response, Ishmael threw stones at the devil. At the last minute, God rewarded Abraham and Ishmael by substituting the sacrifice of a goat. At Mina, too, pilgrims leave the special state of pilgrimage by having at least three of their hairs cut. They may also visit Mecca and circle the Kaaba again. Many pilgrims take the opportunity of their journey to visit other sacred sites, such as the town of Medina where the prophet Muhammad is buried.

Over a million Muslims make pilgrimage to Mecca every year. It is a powerful, visual demonstration of the universality of Islam and the sisterhood and brotherhood of all human beings. After making pilgrimage to Mecca in 1964, the Black Muslim leader, MALCOLM X, began to teach that not all white people were devils, as he had previously thought.

Further reading: Ann Parker and Avon Neal, *Hajj Paintings: Folk Art of the Great Pilgrimage* (Washington, D.C.: Smithsonian Institution Press, 1995); F. E. Peters, *The Hajj: The Muslim Pilgrimage to Mecca and the Holy Places* (Princeton, N.J.: Princeton University Press, 1994); Michael Wolfe, ed., *One Thousand Roads to Mecca: Ten Centuries of Travelers Writing about the Muslim Pilgrimage* (New York: Grove Press, 1997).

meditation   Quieting the mind in order to focus deeply on religious experience and religious reality. For some people, meditation just means to think deeply and seriously about something. In a religious context, however, it is more likely to indicate either visualization of a religious topic, such as a symbol or a scene from the scriptures, with appropriate feelings and thoughts, or a stopping of the activity of mind altogether in order to experience religious reality directly.

The former method, visualization, is particularly associated with ROMAN CATHOLICISM in the Counter-Reformation period (16th–17th centuries) and in the writings of such SAINTS as Ignatius Loyola and Francis de Sales. Devotees were asked to picture in their minds scenes from the life of CHRIST or church teaching. Visualization is also found in BHAKTI (devotional) HINDUISM in relation to its gods, and in BUDDHISM, especially TIBETAN RELIGION, wherein one's patronal BUDDHA or BODHISATTVA is evoked before one's inner eyes through a combination of MANTRA (chant), MUDRA (hand gesture), and mental concentration. In JUDAISM, meditation has particularly been associated with KABBALAH and concentration on Hebrew letters and words.

Quieting the mind in order to go beyond all forms and concepts in the mind, sometimes called contemplation or contemplative prayer rather than meditation in the West, is found in older versions of Christian MYSTICISM, which were under the influence of Neoplatonic philosophy with its teaching that fully to experience the One the contemplative person should rise above all thought to absorption in oneness. This form of meditation can be found in Roman Catholic and Eastern Orthodox mysticism in all periods.

In the East, ways of stopping the stream of consciousness (or the "monkey mind" as it is sometimes called) are widely taught. The idea behind these "one-pointed concentrations" is that if the mind can be brought to rest on one object, the stream of consciousness will cease; eventually perhaps even that one point can be taken away. Such point of focus may be visual: a simple symbol, a candle flame; auditory, as a mantra chanted inwardly; or mental, a point of light, a picture, a word held still in the mind. The idea of this kind of meditation is to let the mind take a vacation, ceasing its activity in order to find out what it is when it is not thinking about anything in particular. According to the religious philosophies behind such practices, that will enable it to get in touch with its true nature: BRAHMAN, Buddhahood, GOD.

Melanesian religion   *See* PACIFIC OCEAN RELIGIONS.

Mennonites
A Christian group named after Menno Simons (1496–1561), a Dutch priest. During the Protestant REFORMATION, groups in Switzerland and the Netherlands came to reject the practice of infant BAPTISM. They believed that only persons who were able to attest to their FAITH should be baptized and that people who had been baptized as infants should be baptized again. As a result, they were known as Anabaptists, "re-baptizers." Some of the earliest Anabaptists used force in trying to order society in accordance with GOD's commands. But by 1535 their attempts had failed. Ever since then Anabaptists have followed Menno Simons in advocating a strict separation of church and state. They are now known as Mennonites.

From the 17th to the 19th centuries, many Mennonite groups immigrated to the United States and Canada. The earliest immigrants were important in the settlement of Pennsylvania. Perhaps the best known group is an offshoot called the AMISH. They separated from other Mennonites in the 1690s. At issue was how to enforce the community's discipline or way of life. The Amish believe that those who violate the discipline should be shunned, in other words, totally avoided. Other Mennonites find this penalty too harsh. Today, other subtle differences also separate the Old Order Amish from the "plain" or most traditional Mennonites. For example, even plain Mennonites allow buttons on clothing; the Old Order Amish allow only hook-and-eye fasteners.

Although Mennonites have drawn up statements of belief, they recognize the BIBLE as the only authority. Mennonite WORSHIP services tend to be simple, emphasizing reading from the Bible, preaching, and congregational singing. Mennonites sometimes celebrate the EUCHARIST or communion in the context of a "love feast." This involves not only eating and drinking but also washing one another's feet in imitation of JESUS at his last supper.

In accordance with a teaching in the NEW TESTAMENT, Mennonites have deliberately tried not to conform to the ways of the world. For some, but only for some, that has meant a rejection of modern dress and conveniences. For example, "black bumper Mennonites" have black cars with no chrome. Most Mennonites, however, nurture a life-style of simplicity and discipleship while wearing contemporary clothing and using modern conveniences.

From the 1530s on, Mennonites have refused to carry arms, hold public office, and take oaths. That behavior has caused various governments to question their loyalty. But the tradition of pacifism and, more broadly, the desire to put the teachings of Jesus into practice have given Mennonites a well-developed social conscience. Unlike some liberal branches of North American PROTESTANTISM, Mennonites have not generally tried to reform society. Instead, they have been extremely active in disaster relief, in promoting world peace, and in fostering economic development, especially among indigenous Americans and people living in the Third World. The Mennonite Central Committee (MCC), founded in 1920, coordinates these efforts for the Mennonite and Brethren churches in North America. (The Brethren are similar to the Mennonites but have a different history.) At the beginning of the 21st century the MCC was active in more than 50 countries worldwide as well as in the United States and Canada.

Mesopotamian religions   The ancient religions of the area that is now Iraq. Mesopotamian religions existed from the beginnings of city-based culture down to 539 B.C.E., when Mesopotamia was conquered by the Persian Empire.

HISTORY

Mesopotamia means "the land between the rivers." It refers to the land between the Tigris and the Euphrates rivers. In ancient times the northern and western half of this region was known as Assyria. The southern and eastern half was known as Babylonia. Both regions figure prominently in the BIBLE. The Assyrians destroyed the northern kingdom of Israel; the Babylonians destroyed the southern kingdom of Judah, and with it SOLOMON's temple in JERUSALEM. In the earliest days, Babylonia was itself divided into two parts. Its northwestern half was known as Akkadia; its southeastern half was known as Sumer.

Around 3500 B.C.E. civilization, that is, city-based culture, emerged in Sumer. Earlier there had been small cities in other parts of the Near East. But Sumer appears to have been the earliest civilization. The historian Samuel Noah Kramer once claimed that "history begins at Sumer." He had in mind the many "firsts" that the Sumerians could boast. They devised the first system of writing; they were the first to have mass production (they had mass-produced dishes); and they built the first monumental temples.

The Sumerians lived in independent city-states, each with its own special god. The Sume-

rians imagined that the gods of their city-states met in assembly. At any given time, the most influential god in the assembly was the one whose city had the most power on Earth. Each city's gods resided in image form in temples. Servants—that is, priests—tended to their needs. They were supported in part by the land that the god owned.

For several centuries various city-states competed for power. One city would take control of an area. But its rule never lasted very long. In about 2350 B.C.E., that pattern began to change. Rulers arose who sought to dominate all of Mesopotamia. In the end two regional powers, Babylon and Assyria, competed with each other to be supreme. When Assyria was in charge, its god Assur was thought to be the greatest; when Babylon ruled, its god Marduk was supreme.

But neither the Assyrians nor the Babylonians could maintain their rule indefinitely. They could not resist the rising power of Persia to the east, in the area known today as Iran. In 539 Cyrus the Persian conquered Babylon and thus became the ruler of the entire region. If Cyrus's victory is remembered today, that is because he allowed the Jews who were living in exile in Babylon to return home to JERUSALEM.

BELIEFS

The names of some Mesopotamian gods clearly connect them with forces in nature. Inanna's name means "mistress of the sky," Enki's means "lord of the earth." But the Mesopotamians thought that their gods looked like human beings. They also thought that the gods of the different cities were relatives of one another, and that they met in assembly to discuss their differences.

By the third millennium B.C.E. (3000–2001 B.C.E.), Mesopotamians had ranked their gods in order of importance. The highest god was An, god of the sky and father of the gods. Enlil, the god of wind and storms, was the leader of the assembly of gods. Other important gods included Ninhursaga (GODDESS of the foothills), Inanna and her lover Dumuzi, Ereshkigal (queen of the dead), and Enki. These gods were eventually eclipsed in importance by Assur, god of Assyria, and Marduk, god of Babylon.

The Mesopotamians developed a rich literature. It explored some topics that are still profound today. The story of GILGAMESH tells of a powerful king who is disturbed by the fact that all people, himself included, must die. A poem known as

The hero Gilgamesh, holding a serpent in one hand, with a lion cub tucked under his arm *(Bonomi, Nineveh and Its Palaces, 1875 [after Bottal])*

"Enuma Elish" tells how the world came to be. One story attributes human sickness and disease to a drunken argument between the god Enki and the goddess Ninhursaga.

The story of Atrahasis is equally pessimistic about the place of human beings in the world. The gods did not wish to work, it says, so they killed a god, mixed its blood with dirt, and made human beings. But human beings were too noisy for Enlil, so he tried to kill them off with a great FLOOD. He failed, but only because Ea—Akkadian for Enki—told Atrahasis to build an ark. When the flood came, Atrahasis, his family, and representative animals entered the ark and were saved.

PRACTICES AND ORGANIZATION

The Mesopotamians thought that their gods lived in heaven, but they also felt that the gods dwelled on Earth in image form. These images were kept in special buildings known as temples. It was there that much of Mesopotamian RITUAL took place.

Two kinds of rituals were performed at the temples. In daily rituals the needs of the gods were met. Priests would change the image's clothes according to a regular schedule. They also placed food in front of the image at meal times for it to eat. When the god was finished, the food would be distributed among the priests themselves and perhaps the king.

A second kind of ritual comprised the festivals that occurred throughout the year, such as the New Year's ritual. On these occasions the sacred image was brought outside the temple, and people besides priests would take part in the celebration. Some influential scholars have called the festivals sacred dramas. They have identified several different dramas: the sacred marriage, death, the journey, ritual plowing, and ritual combat.

Not all Mesopotamian worship centered on images in city temples. Individuals had their personal gods, whom they thought of as parents. They worshipped these gods daily on altars at home. In addition, Mesopotamians were particularly interested in learning the will of the gods. They believed that at times gods appeared to them in dreams.

They also believed that they could determine the character of the universe at a given moment by examining the entrails of sheep and, in the later period, by watching the stars and planets.

SIGNIFICANCE

Although Mesopotamian religions are no longer practiced, they have left behind a rich legacy in the world's oldest literature. As the story of Atrahasis shows, Mesopotamian religions also had an impact on the religion of ancient Israel, and through it on JUDAISM, CHRISTIANITY, and ISLAM.

Further reading: Jeremy Black and Anthony Green, *Gods, Demons, and Symbols of Ancient Mesopotamia: An Illustrated Dictionary* (London: University of Texas Press, 1992); Jean Bottero, *Religion in Ancient Mesopotamia* (Chicago: University of Chicago Press, 2001); Diane Wolkstein and Samuel Noah Kramer, *Inanna, Queen of Heaven and Earth: Her Stories and Hymns from Sumer* (New York: Harper & Row, 1983).

messiah An English adaptation of the Hebrew word *mashiah*, which means "anointed with oil." Technically, the messiah is a figure in Jewish tradition. He will come in the future to restore the glories of Israel at the end of time and establish peace among the nations. Christians claim that the messiah has already come in the person of JESUS. In fact, the word CHRIST—and thus the name for the religion—derives from the Greek word for "anointed with oil."

More loosely, messiah refers to any religious figure who will come and rescue a group of people from situations of suffering and usher in a golden age. The Mahdi of ISLAM fits this description. He will come at the end of time to reestablish order and faith in GOD when all around has become chaos. Similar figures, more or less messianic, include the future incarnation of the Hindu god VISHNU known as Kalki; the BUDDHA who is to come known as Maitreya; and many religious leaders among colonized peoples in the 19th and early 20th centuries.

The word "messiah" is not used in the Hebrew BIBLE (Old Testament) in any of these ways. Instead, the word refers to people who have received a special office through a RITUAL of anointing. It refers especially to priests and kings. The Hebrew Bible does contain passages that envision a future golden age. But none of the visionary passages connect this restoration with a figure called the messiah. ISAIAH comes closest to doing so. He calls Cyrus, the king of Persia, YHWH's ("the Lord's") messiah (Isaiah 45.1). That is because, acting on YHWH's behalf, Cyrus had conquered Babylon and allowed the Jews to return home.

A little before the time of Jesus, the idea of a messiah was joined to expectations of a future bliss coming at the end of time. Jews began to look for many messiahs. Some of them were priestly in nature; some were kingly. A community connected with the DEAD SEA SCROLLS seems to have expected two messiahs, one of each kind.

In this climate the early followers of Jesus proclaimed that he was the messiah. They combined the idea that the messiah will come at the end of time with a notion that the messiah had already come. They also separated the ideal of the messiah from the nationalist aspirations of the Jewish people. Very early on CHRISTIANITY became a movement among non-Jews rather than Jews.

With the destruction of the Second Temple (70 C.E.) and the failure of Bar Kokhba's revolt (135 C.E.) expectations of a messiah grew within JUDAISM. These expectations addressed the life of an excluded and persecuted minority. Not only did Moses Maimonides (1135–1204) list belief in a coming messiah as one of the 13 beliefs that all Jews shared; messiahs often actually came. The most famous was Shabbatai Zvi (1626–76). He proclaimed himself the messiah and gained a large following among Jews in Turkey. Some of his followers refused to abandon their belief in him even when, under pressure, he committed the unpardonable sin of converting to ISLAM.

The experience of such false messiahs had its effect. Today many Jews downplay any expectations that a messiah will come. But some, such as Abraham Kook (1865–1935), have connected

ZIONISM with messianism. And shortly before RABBI Moses Menachem Schneersohn, the leader of the Lubavitch Hasidic community, died in New York in 1994, many of his followers expected that he was the messiah.

Further reading: Wim Beuken, Seán Freyne, and Anton Weiler, ed., *Messianism through History* (Maryknoll, N.Y.: Orbis Books, 1993); Richard S. Hess and M. Daniel Carroll R., ed., *Israel's Messiah in the Bible and the Dead Sea Scrolls* (Grand Rapids, Mich.: Baker Academic, 2003); Jerry Rabow, *Fifty Jewish Messiahs: The Untold Life Stories of Fifty Jewish Messiahs since Jesus and How They Changed the Jewish, Christian, and Muslim Worlds* (New York: Gefen Pub. House, 2002).

Methodism   A variety of CHRISTIANITY begun by John WESLEY (1703–91). Wesley was a priest in the Church of England (see ANGLICANISM). In 1738 he experienced a "strange warming" of his heart. It led him to undertake a distinctive form of ministry. Instead of preaching in a particular parish, he traveled and preached throughout the country. His preaching emphasized the power of GOD's GRACE to save sinners, a personal relationship with God, and the possibility of developing Christian perfection. Wesley preached especially to the poor. He also authorized laypersons to preach.

Wesley formed his followers into a society within the Church of England, but that relationship to the church did not last. One reason it did not was the North American experience. Methodists had brought Wesley's form of Christianity to the British colonies of North America. Francis Asbury, a blacksmith by trade, was the most successful early preacher. After the Revolution American Methodists did not want to remain in the Church of England. In 1784 they organized an independent church. That same year Wesley established a General Conference in England to govern his society when he died. In 1795, four years after Wesley's death, the Methodists in Britain also broke with the Church of England.

Methodism was particularly successful in the United States. Because its ministers traveled, they could meet the needs of settlers pushing the frontiers west. But Methodism paid for its success with division. African Americans found themselves second-class members of the white-dominated churches. They formed the African Methodist Episcopal Church (1816) and the African Methodist Episcopal Zion Church (1820), which still flourish today. During the Civil War, the Methodists split into Northern and Southern churches. During the 19th century other Methodist churches were organized as well. The Holiness movements emphasized ecstatic religious experiences; they caused some people to leave Methodism altogether (see PENTECOSTALISM).

During the 20th century fragmented Methodist groups reunited in both Britain and the United States. In Britain the largest Methodist body is the Methodist Church, formed in 1932; in the United States it is the United Methodist Church, formed in 1968. Methodist MISSIONARIES have also met with considerable success overseas.

Methodism respects the traditional teachings of Christianity, but unlike some other churches it does not insist on doctrinal unity. It prefers instead to emphasize that God's spirit has the power to change lives and to encourage Christians to cultivate a personal relationship with God. Thus, Methodism has a profound personal dimension. At the same time, Methodists have actively embraced social concerns.

Methodist WORSHIP sometimes takes the form of a LITURGY; sometimes it is freer. Services generally include the PREACHING of a sermon, readings from the BIBLE, PRAYERS, and singing. Hymn-singing has been a particularly important part of Methodist worship life. John Wesley promoted the use of hymns. His brother Charles wrote some of the best loved hymns in the English language, for example, the well-known CHRISTMAS carol, "Hark, the Herald Angels Sing."

Methodist churches have different institutional structures in different parts of the world. The Methodist churches in the United States are episcopal; that is, they are governed by bishops.

Traditionally Methodism employed itinerant ministers, sometimes called "circuit riders." These ministers would travel from group to group, preach, and supervise spiritual progress. Today Methodist ministers in the United States are more tied to specific localities.

Further reading: Riley B. Case, *Evangelical and Methodist: A Popular History* (Nashville: Abingdon Press, 2004); Stephen Tomkins, *John Wesley: A Biography* (Grand Rapids, Mich.: W. B. Eerdmans, 2003); John H. Wigger, *Taking Heaven by Storm: Methodism and the Rise of Popular Christianity in America* (Urbana: University of Illinois Press, 2001).

Micah A book in the BIBLE, and the name of the prophet whose words it supposedly contains. Micah is one of the prophetic books that make up the collection known as "The Twelve."

Micah is the least well-known of a group of eighth-century prophets in ancient Israel and Judah. Other prophets in this group included ISAIAH, Amos, and HOSEA. They emphasized worshipping YHWH ("the Lord") alone and furthering social justice.

Like Isaiah, Micah was a prophet in the southern kingdom of Judah. He witnessed the fall of Samaria, the capital of the northern kingdom, to Assyria around 721 B.C.E. and the Assyrian siege of JERUSALEM 20 years later. Unlike Isaiah, Micah came from the countryside, not the capital city.

Micah prophesied that Jerusalem would actually be destroyed—a prophecy that was relatively rare. Among Christians he is best known for associating the Messianic ruler with Bethlehem. Micah also envisioned a time of universal peace in stirring and influential images: "they shall beat their swords into ploughshares, and their spears into pruning hooks; nation shall not lift up sword against nation, neither shall they learn war any more" (Micah 4.3).

Micronesian religion *See* PACIFIC OCEAN RELIGIONS.

millenarianism Religious movements that expect SALVATION to come very soon in this world. (The word comes from the Christian belief, taken from the book of REVELATION, that speaks of a coming millennium, or golden age of a thousand years.) Millenarianism expects salvation to come to believers as a group, to come in this world through a miraculous total transformation of it into a paradise. Usually these beliefs have an apocalyptic character (*see* APOCALYPTIC LITERATURE) as well, that is, they say that though things may seem to be very bad, and getting worse and worse in this world, that is really just preparation for the new world. Suddenly, when least expected by all except those in on the secret, GOD will act, perhaps a savior will appear, a surprising and radical changes will take place. Then the FAITH of those who believed in the coming change, even during the darkest hours, will be vindicated.

A good example would be CARGO CULTS, those movements in colonialized areas, especially in the South Pacific, which said that ships or planes would come from the old gods to bring to native peoples goods like the white man's, and that this would start a golden age. In the Buddhist world, a succession of movements has been based on the expectation that Maitreya, the coming BUDDHA of the future, would arrive soon.

In JUDAISM and CHRISTIANITY, a succession of millenarian movements has predicted the imminent coming of the MESSIAH. In Judaism, perhaps the best known is that centered on Shabbatai Zvi (1626–76), whose claim to be the messiah caused great excitement within that tradition. In Christianity, SEVENTH-DAY ADVENTISM was originally based on the teachings of William Miller (1782–1849), who predicted the second coming of CHRIST in 1844. The JEHOVAH'S WITNESSES have also kept alive millenarian faith. Some more liberal Christians have interpreted millennial belief to mean a gradual, progressive coming of the kingdom of God.

Millenarianism usually implies a discouraged view of the world, a strong sense of the difference between the way things are and the way one would wish them to be. It may sometimes seem to be merely "wishful thinking," more wanting to escape from the world than wanting to change it. Yet millenarian movements have often had a profound historical impact. They have vigorously expressed the discontent of mistreated people, and mobilized them for eventual action on political as well as religious levels. Their visions of a better future have inspired both utopians and reformers. They have started religious movements that, sometimes with changes, have survived as important denominations. And they have repeatedly demonstrated the richness and power of religious VISIONS of the ideal world.

miracles   Extraordinary events that people claim point to religious truth. It is not quite correct to say that miracles are "supernatural" events. Some religions says that miracles happen by perfectly natural but unusual processes.

Many people throughout history have used miracles to argue that their particular religions are true. Those who practice Hindu YOGA claim that *siddhis,* miraculous powers, show that they have reached certain stages of realization. Celsus, an ancient opponent of CHRISTIANITY, thought that Christian claims were nothing special compared with pagan miracles. In fact, people in virtually every religion have experienced miracles.

Some miracles are events that affect our natural surroundings. The anthropologist Clifford Geertz once noted how some residents on the island of Bali saw spiritual force at work in a large, rapidly growing mushroom. In the fall of 1995 images of the Hindu god GANESA created a stir in India and around the world when they seemed to drink milk. Miracles of nature may be connected with SALVATION and deliverance. When YHWH ("the Lord") freed the people of Israel from Egypt, he did so with many miracles. In the 1960s lava from Mount Agung on Bali miraculously missed a temple of SIVA that it should have destroyed.

Miracles do not happen just in nature; they happen to human beings, too. Miraculous healings are ideal examples (*see* HEALING, RELIGIOUS). Shamans (*see* SHAMANISM) heal by means that we might consider miraculous. In the ancient Medi-

terranean world sick people often slept in the temple of Asklepios; some experienced dreams and were miraculously healed. Mountain ascetics in Japan known as *yamabushi* healed the sick and cast out demons. In the United States today some people offer miraculous healings over television sets.

Christianity claims miraculous powers for JESUS. The NEW TESTAMENT presents him as healing, casting out demons, and performing other miracles. BUDDHISM says the BUDDHA could perform miracles but was skeptical of them. He once met a person who, after years of spiritual discipline, could walk on water. He lamented that this person had wasted so much time; it is relatively cheap to hire a boat. According to the QUR'AN the prophet MUHAMMAD's miracle was having received God's revelation of the Qur'an.

In the Muslim tradition of SUFISM those close to God are believed to have performed miracles. Christian SAINTS are believed to have done so, too. Indeed, the Roman Catholic Church declares people to be saints only if they have performed authenticated miracles. The Virgin MARY has miraculously appeared to Roman Catholics on many occasions. RELICS often perform miracles, too.

Not everyone accepts miracles. The ancient Roman philosopher Cicero rejected them. The two most important leaders of the Protestant REFORMATION, Martin LUTHER and John CALVIN, encouraged their followers not to look for miracles. In his *Enquiry Concerning Human Understanding* (1748), the Scottish philosopher David Hume laid down a principle upon which many have rejected miracles. According to Hume, we can accept evidence that a miracle has occurred on only one condition: If it would be an even bigger miracle for the evidence of the miracle to prove unreliable.

Many still find miracles meaningful today. According to the Protestant theologian Paul Tillich, any event that reveals God is a miracle, regardless of whether it violates the laws of nature. The psychologist Carl Gustav JUNG explored miracles in his notion of "synchronicity." Philosophers of science such as Paul Feyerabend have argued that "worldviews" that reject miracles are no more valid than those that accept them. Just as significant, many religious people still retain their traditional views. For them, miracles are part of what happens when human beings encounter religious power.

missionaries People who attempt to convert other people to their religion. Not all religions proselytize, which is the attempt to convert others. In many religions, people practice their own religions, and they expect other people, usually living in other places, to practice theirs. Good examples are JUDAISM, some of whose branches also do not accept converts, and the Japanese religion SHINTO. Other religions have not proselytized for practical reasons. The PARSEES—modern Zoroastrians—are a good example. They do not even accept converts. According to tradition, when the Parsees migrated to India, they were allowed to live there on one condition: that they promise not to proselytize.

Other religions, however, have seen it as a religious duty to spread their truth throughout the world. If success is measured by the number of people converted, the most successful proselytizing religions have been BUDDHISM, CHRISTIANITY, and ISLAM. At best, missionaries present their religions and allow other people to accept or reject them in complete freedom. They adapt their messages to fit the cultures of the peoples whom they are proselytizing. They also exhibit a genuine concern for other people, for example, by sharing medical advances. Albert Schweitzer is a good example of a medical missionary.

Not all missionaries have observed these principles. Some missionaries have achieved conversion through physical coercion. For example, after defeating the Saxons (an early German people) in battle, Emperor Charlemagne gave them two choices: Be baptized or die. Many missionaries have declared local cultures depraved and sinful. For example, in the 20th century some African Christians still refused to use traditional African music in worship because European and North American missionaries had earlier condemned it. Some missionaries have also resorted to deception. At the end of the 20th century some fundamental-ist Christians were passing themselves off as "messianic" Jews. In this way they hoped to convert unsuspecting Jews to Christianity. Such excesses are not limited to Christianity, but North American readers are likely to understand these examples more readily.

BUDDHIST MISSIONS

According to tradition, the BUDDHA himself sent out the first Buddhist missionaries. He instructed monks to carry the DHARMA of Buddhism in every direction. The places where Buddhism is practiced today are a witness to their success. Only a small number of Buddhists live in India, the land where Buddhism arose. But Buddhist missionaries from India had a profound influence on southeast, east, and central Asia. Buddhist missionaries from China established large Buddhist communities in Korea, Japan, and Vietnam.

Buddhism has generally spread in two ways. Buddhist monks often traveled with merchants. They walked the ancient routes to southern India; they traveled by ship to southeast Asia; and they followed the Silk Road to China. Rulers who favored Buddhism have also spread it. Examples include ASOKA, an emperor in India in the third century B.C.E., and rulers in China and Japan.

After roughly 1000 C.E. there was relatively little missionary effort in Buddhism. But starting in the late 19th century, Buddhists began to proselytize once again. They did so largely in response to European colonization and Christian missionary efforts. Buddhist missionaries created a small Buddhist revival in India. Starting in the 1960s, they also attracted many North Americans and Europeans to Buddhism.

CHRISTIAN MISSIONS

Tradition says that JESUS, like the Buddha, sent his followers out into the world to spread his message. The most famous early missionary was the apostle PAUL. He carried the message of Christianity to non-Jews living in the northeastern Mediterranean region (modern Greece and Turkey). Tradition says that other apostles were missionaries, too.

The COPTIC CHURCH claims to have been started by Mark, who wrote one of the gospels. Christians in the southwestern Indian state of Kerala claim that the apostle Thomas started their church.

In its first few centuries, Christianity spread especially in the Roman Empire, which controlled the area around the Mediterranean Sea. Beginning in 600 C.E. Christian missionary efforts focused on Europe. The Roman Catholic Church converted western, northern, and central Europe. The Orthodox churches were active in eastern Europe and especially Russia. Monks were extremely important to this process. They often established their communities in lands that were not previously Christian.

With the discovery of the Americas and the beginning of European overseas colonization, Christian missionaries turned to areas outside of Europe. Indeed, Christian missions often played a very important role in spreading European domination over the rest of the world. In the 16th and 17th centuries, Roman Catholic missionaries converted Mexico, Central America, and South America to Christianity. They were also active in India, China, and Japan. In the 19th century Protestants caught the missionary fervor and formed many missionary societies. Missionaries from most Protestant churches were extremely active in European colonies overseas. That is especially true of missionaries from Great Britain, the United States, and Canada.

MUSLIM MISSIONS

The QUR'AN teaches that no one should be forced to accept Islam by physical coercion. People should become Muslims because they are persuaded that Islam is true. But Europeans and their descendants have tended to emphasize the role of military power in the spread of Islam. That is due, at least in part, to past European history. Islamic armies threatened Europe on several occasions, from the battle of Tours, France (732 or 733), to the conquest of Constantinople (1453) and the sieges of Vienna, Austria (1529, 1683).

Islam spread rapidly at first. One hundred years after the prophet MUHAMMAD began receiving messages from GOD, Islam stretched from Spain through all of North Africa to present-day Iran. In later centuries it spread in much of central Asia, Africa south of the Sahara, and in south and southeast Asia. Indeed, Indonesia is today the most populous Islamic country.

The main networks for the spread of Islam were trade, education, and expansion led by military rulers. This was true of the early expansion in North Africa and the Near East. It was also true of the expansion of Islam into south Asia. In south Asia people adopted Islam because they found its teachings and civilization attractive. Many also found that Islam allowed them to escape from the limitations of their caste (see CASTE IN HINDUISM).

MODERN DEVELOPMENTS

During the 20th century many Christian missionaries became embarrassed by some of the activities of their predecessors. They no longer told others that Christianity was right and other religions were wrong. Instead, they practiced interreligious DIALOGUE. In such dialogue people tried to understand each other's version of the truth.

At the same time, missionaries associated with Pentacostal Christianity were very active in Latin America and Africa. In Latin America, they often converted people who were Roman Catholics. In addition, North America itself became a fertile mission field for other religions. Hindu, Buddhist, Muslim, Sikh (see SIKHISM), BAHA'I, and other missionaries were all active in North America. Their success was generally limited, but they did help make North America more religiously plural.

Further reading: Meg Greene, *Mother Teresa: A Biography* (Westport, Conn.: Greenwood Press, 2004); Stephen Neill, *A History of Christian Missions* (New York: Penguin, 1986); Ruth A. Tucker, *From Jerusalem to Irian Jaya: A Biographical History of Christian Missions*, 2d ed. (Grand Rapids, Mich.: Zondervan, 2004).

Mithra A deity originally from Persia, where he became a leading subordinate of Ahura Mazda in ZOROASTRIANISM. In the days of the Roman Empire, Mithra moved west to become the central figure in a religion called Mithraism. He was identified with light and was closely associated with the sun. In Mithraism the god is usually portrayed killing a bull, the animal representing darkness and chaos; this sacrifice made possible the creation of the world. Mithraism, which offered several stages of initiation, a ceremonial meal and a sort of BAPTISM, was popular among soldiers in the Roman army and was an early rival of CHRISTIANITY.

monks and nuns   Men and women who adopt a special, religious way of life. This life usually means that they do not marry, have families, or work at secular jobs.

Not all religions have monks and nuns. JUDAISM has taught that marriage and family life are religious duties. Protestants have generally rejected monasticism, too. But monasticism has been important in many religions, including BUDDHISM, JAINISM, ROMAN CATHOLICISM, and EASTERN ORTHODOX CHRISTIANITY.

A GENERAL DESCRIPTION

Monks and nuns always belong in some way to a wider religious community. That is true even if they have no permanent homes or live off by themselves (hermits). If a group of people adopts a special life-style but has no connection to a wider religious community, its members are not monks and nuns. They belong to a sect, for example, the ESSENES in the late Second Temple period of Judaism (the time of JESUS).

Monks and nuns typically relate to the more general community in one of two ways. In some religions they constitute the core of that community. For example, in THERAVADA BUDDHISM monks and nuns devote themselves full-time to practicing the Buddha's teachings. They make up the SANGHA. Lay Buddhists hope someday to adopt the monastic lifestyle, perhaps in a future life. In the meantime, they provide monks and nuns with the necessities of life. They also make a beginning

in religious practice by observing the basic "precepts" or instructions. This relationship between monks and nuns on the one hand and lay sympathizers or supporters on the other also characterizes JAINISM and the now-defunct religion known as MANICHAEISM.

In other religions, monks and nuns are more peripheral. For example, Christianity did not grow up around, nor is it centered around, monks and nuns. Instead, monks and nuns arose later as specialists within some Christian traditions. Christians respect monks and nuns for their special religious devotion, but they do not consider monasticism a lifestyle that they will need to follow someday in order to achieve salvation. HINDUISM, TAOISM, and ISLAM also have monasticism of this kind.

In both kinds of monasticism, people go through a special initiation ritual to become monks and nuns (*see* INITIATION, RELIGIOUS). They may also spend several years as "novices" to see whether this life is right for them. As novices and then as monks and nuns they follow a discipline. Disciplines generally regulate diet (*see* DIET AND RELIGION). They may also require monks and nuns to wear special clothes. But above all, disciplines organize daily activities. They make time for religious practice—in Christianity, perhaps the daily services known as hours, in ZEN BUDDHISM ZAZEN or seated MEDITATION. They may also require monks and nuns to spend time in study and labor.

Most religions that have monks also have nuns. But religions have often been more willing to allow men to adopt this lifestyle than to allow women to do so. For example, it is said that although the BUDDHA established an order for nuns, he did so reluctantly. Indeed, within Theravada Buddhism the order of nuns has died out. Attempts are now under way to revive it.

MONKS AND NUNS IN ASIAN RELIGIONS

The oldest monastic traditions in the world are found in Buddhism and Jainism. These two religions arose during the sixth century B.C.E. in India. They did so among groups of ascetics known as *sramanas.* No one know precisely when the *sramana* movement began. In the time of the Buddha and

MAHAVIRA followers of this tradition rejected the life of the householder and wandered the countryside begging. They also rejected the religion of householders, that is, the SACRIFICES described in sacred texts known as the VEDA.

Both the Buddha and Mahavira formed their religions around groups of monks and nuns that are sometimes called SANGHAS. In time these communities split over issues of teaching and practice.

Today there are two major groups of Jain monastics: Digambara and Svetambara. The names refer to the clothing that these monastics do—or do not—wear. Digambara monks are "sky-clad"; they wear no clothes. Svetambara monks and nuns wear white clothes.

In theory, all Buddhist monks and nuns observe a discipline whose Sanskrit name is *pratimoksha*. The *pratimoksha* is recorded in different languages, and each version has a different number of regulations. All versions place more restrictions on nuns than on monks. A few Buddhist schools, such as the True Pure Land school in Japan, have abandoned many of these regulations (*see* PURE LAND BUDDHISM). For example, their priests marry and live in society. In China, however, Taoism created monasteries and convents in imitation of Buddhism.

Hinduism also has a place for those who want to reject the ways of the world. Such people become SADHUS and SADHVIS. Ideally, a Hindu man adopts a monastic lifestyle at the end of his life. But many do not wait that long. Even more never adopt it at all.

In the eighth century C.E. the great Hindu philosopher, Sankaracarya (*see* SANKARA), established several important monasteries. Today some *sadhus* and *sadhvis* are important leaders of conservative Hindu movements (*see* FUNDAMENTALISM, HINDU).

CHRISTIAN MONKS AND NUNS

Christian monasticism began in Egypt. The first Christian monks and nuns were hermits; each lived by himself or herself. They were inspired by the example of St. Anthony (*c.* 251–355), who lived in the Egyptian desert for 20 years. A little later a retired soldier named Pachomius (*c.* 290–346) formed the first Christian community of monks. He also founded a community of nuns for his sister.

Different rules organize monastic life in Christianity. Of these, the most important are the rules of Basil of Caesarea for the Orthodox churches and Benedict of Nursia for the Roman Catholic Church (*see* BENEDICTINES). In both the Orthodox and Catholic worlds, the monastic ideal influenced the way churches were organized. For example, all Orthodox bishops are usually monks, and all celibate priests ordained in the Roman Catholic Church can also become bishops. Roman Catholicism also developed several different monastic "orders." Of these, the Benedictines have historically been the most important. (Technically, DOMINICANS, Franciscans, and JESUITS are "religious" but not monks.) Roman Catholic monks and nuns have made tremendous contributions to European culture, especially during the Middle Ages.

MONKS AND NUNS IN THE TWENTIETH CENTURY

The 20th century saw important developments in the practice of monasticism. The Buddhist monastic community in China and Tibet suffered tremendously as a result of the communist revolution in 1949. Elsewhere in Asia, monks and nuns took part in efforts to expel former colonial rulers. Many Americans will never forget the images of Vietnamese monks burning themselves during the Vietnam War. In postcolonial Asian countries some monks have supported violent nationalist movements, for example, Buddhist monks in the Sri Lankan civil war. Some Buddhist monks and nuns also moved to North America. By the end of the 20th century a number of North American Buddhists had taken monastic vows (*see* BUDDHISM IN AMERICA).

During the 20th century Christian monks and nuns continued their traditional activities, such as teaching and social work. In North America monasteries also began to hold retreats of limited duration for those who had not taken religious vows, especially college students. Some Christian monks and nuns also began conversations with those who practiced other forms of monasticism. For example, the Trappist monk, Thomas Merton, was very interested in Buddhist techniques of meditation. By the beginning of the twenty-first century several Catholic monks and nuns had also taken initiation as Zen teachers.

A few Protestants became interested in monasticism during the 19th century; that interest continued into the 20th century. A good example of Protestant monasticism is the community of Taize, France, founded in 1940.

Further reading: Karl Suso Frank, *With Greater Liberty: A Short History of Christian Monasticism and Religious Orders* (Kalamazoo, Mich.: Cistercian Publications, 1993); Kim Gutschow, *Being a Buddhist Nun: The Struggle for Enlightenment in the Himalayas* (Cambridge, Mass.: Harvard University Press, 2004); Tim Vivian, trans., *Journeying into God: Seven Early Monastic Lives* (Minneapolis, Minn.: Fortress Press, 1996).

monotheism   Belief in one personal GOD. It may be contrasted with POLYTHEISM, or belief in many gods, and with monism, usually taken to mean that everything is really part of one impersonal absolute, like the BRAHMAN of Advaita VEDANTA Hinduism.

The three great Western religions, JUDAISM, CHRISTIANITY, and ISLAM, see themselves as traditionally monotheistic. They all stem ultimately from the faith of ABRAHAM and from the religion of ancient Israel. Another very important monotheist religion is ZOROASTRIANISM, the FAITH of ancient Iran, which may have influenced the Western monotheisms. It should also be pointed out that Hindu devotion to one of the great gods or GODDESSES, such as VISHNU, SIVA, or DEVI, is generally actually monotheism of that deity, for though the worshipper may grant that the god may be worshipped under other names, it is honored as the one supreme sustainer of the universe. Another religion of India, SIKHISM, is definitely monotheistic.

Monotheistic religion has a different character from polytheism or monism. By emphasizing one God, monotheism says that, despite appearances, the whole universe has one origin, one rule, and one center of meaning. Things do not work just by impersonal fate or laws of science, but ultimately by the personal will of a supreme intelligence. To many people this thought is very reassuring. Personal monotheism also says that people can have a close relationship with this personal God, as one would with another person, through loving PRAYER and service. Monotheisms tend to see God as male, or to use masculine language for God.

Monotheism also most often says that the personal God is the Creator of the universe. If God is in control of the cosmos through his personal will, at some point he must have started the process through a personal act of creation. Further, if the universe began at some definite point, it presumably will end at some point in time, or rather at the end of time. This means that monotheistic religions usually take history seriously. They say it began through God's creation and will end when his plan is completed, at a last judgment, and with the beginning of a paradisal world.

Personal monotheism also has God working in the world, in history, toward the accomplishment of his purpose. If God is personal, and can act freely in accordance with his will, it would be surprising if, having made the world, he did nothing to help it keep on track as it moves to the fulfillment of the divine plan. Thus monotheistic religions generally say that God has indeed revealed himself within human history, through sending prophets and saviors, through sacred scriptures, through MIRACLES and the divine guidance of his SAINTS and the true religion. But because God respects the men and women he has made, these signs are not such as to override human freedom.

Monotheistic religions have then tended to emphasize God's sovereignty, God's will, and God's action in history, and also human response through individual faith.

Moon and religion, the   The religious significance and symbolism of the moon. The Moon and the Sun have both had an important role in religion as astronomical bodies with mythological significance and an identification with divine beings. But the significance of the two has been different. The Sun has tended to be steady, jovial, life-giving, but the moon is more mysterious in tone. The moon deity can be either a god or GODDESS, usually the opposite gender from whatever the sun is in that mythology, the Greek and Roman, it is female, the Greek Artemis and Roman Diana (*see* MYTH AND MYTHOLOGY). She is a strong, independent woman, a hunter and wanderer in wild places, but the protector of all her sex. Male or female, the moon is divine ruler of women and the female cycle, and is associated with water and the sea. The Moon is often thought to be the divine giver of rain, and on a deeper, more symbolic level to be an emblem of rebirth and immortality, for in its monthly cycle it seems to die and then return to life. All this, together with its complex path in the sky and its association with the night and its mysteries, make the moon seem mystical and strange.

Yet the Moon can also be a steady and reliable governor of the social order and RITUAL patterns, for its phases can be calculated precisely. Indeed, the phases of the Moon were probably the origin of the calendar. Our word *month* is related to *moon*. So is an old word for "meetings," *moot*, for before artificial lighting tribal meetings and religious festivals would often be held at night, at the time of the full moon. Sometimes the waxing moon was considered benign, pouring out increased blessing, and the waning moon dangerous. The full moon was often a symbol of full divine inpouring. In BUDDHISM it is a sign of NIRVANA and full enlightenment, and the BUDDHA was said to have attained enlightenment on the night of the full moon. (But too much full moon can also be unsettling, making one a "lunatic" or "moon person."

Many religious celebrations are still set by the moon. ISLAM follows a lunar calendar, and the Jewish PASSOVER and Christian EASTER are set by the moon; they come after the paschal full moon, which is the first full moon after the spring equinox on the 21st of March. Traditional HINDUISM, Buddhism, and SHINTO have major services set by the new and full moon. Though human beings have now set foot on the physical moon and know it to be a dead, rocky sphere, the spiritual moon continues to exercise its enigmatic influence on the religious world.

See also SUN AND RELIGION, THE.

This is an abbreviated example of artistically re-created tablets that Moses brought down from Mount Sinai. *(Getty Images)*

Mormon, Mormonism   *See* LATTER-DAY SAINTS.

Moses (*c.* 1300 B.C.E.) *a central figure in the Hebrew BIBLE (Old Testament)* He led the children of Israel out of slavery in Egypt and received GOD's instructions on Mount Sinai, also called Mount Horeb.

People sometimes speak of Moses as the "founder" of JUDAISM. Moses is a central figure in the history of Judaism, but his role is somewhat different from those of JESUS, MUHAMMAD, and the BUDDHA, who founded CHRISTIANITY, ISLAM, and BUDDHISM. These other figures gave the religions they founded a distinctly new and definitive shape. But in important respects the religion of Moses is said to go back to ABRAHAM. At the same time, the religion of ancient Israel took shape around the Temple in JERUSALEM, well after Moses' time. Judaism as we know it today, rabbinical Judaism, came into existence only with the destruction of the Temple in 70 C.E.

Nevertheless, Jewish tradition considers Moses to be the author of the written TORAH, that is, the first five books of the Bible (despite the story of his death in Deuteronomy). He is also said to have received the oral Torah on Mount Sinai. Because the oral Torah forms the basis of the TALMUD, it is customary to refer to "our RABBI Moses."

The only information about Moses is found in the Bible and related writings. At birth, Moses is said to have been placed in a basket, floated down the river, discovered by the daughter of the Egyptian king, and raised in the royal court. Very similar stories are told about other, earlier great figures in the ancient Near East, such as Sargon of Akkad (c. 2350 B.C.E.).

After killing an Egyptian who was abusing a Hebrew slave, Moses fled to the wilderness of Sinai. There he married Zipporah, daughter of Jethro, and received instructions from God to liberate the slaves in Egypt. God also appointed Moses' brother AARON to be his spokesperson.

In an attempt to convince the Egyptian king to allow the Hebrew slaves to leave, Moses called down 10 plagues upon Egypt. These seem loosely related to phenomena that occur in Egypt naturally. For example, Moses turned the Nile into blood. A certain microorganism, which grows in the river, actually at times turns the Nile red.

The king of Egypt reluctantly agreed to let the children of Israel go free. When he changed his mind, the escape took place with some drama. In the wilderness, Moses received the Torah on Mount Sinai. When the people proved unfaithful, God condemned them to wander in the wilderness without entering the promised land of Canaan. Moses himself lost the privilege of entering the promised land when in anger he lashed out at God's instruction to draw water from a rock. At the end of Deuteronomy, Moses dies after looking upon the promised land from a distance.

Deuteronomy says quite clearly that no one knew where Moses was buried. This statement gave rise to stories that Moses was taken up into HEAVEN, as the nonbiblical books *The Assumption of Moses* and *Jubilees* assert. The NEW TESTAMENT book of Jude (9–10) alludes to a Jewish story in which the archangel Michael and the devil fought over Moses' body.

Outside sources do not even confirm his existence. The name Moses is Egyptian. And most scholars think that some kind of EXODUS from Egypt did occur, although the number of escaped slaves that is recorded in the Bible may be quite exaggerated. Many date the exodus, and thus Moses, to the time around 1250 B.C.E. Some like an earlier date around 1425.

mosque A place for congregational PRAYER and assembly in ISLAM. Muslims pray formally five times a day. They may do so in an area set aside for prayer known as a mosque. This is especially true of the noon prayer on Friday, which ought to be done communally.

A mosque is a walled enclosure that may or may not have a roof. All who enter the enclosed area must take off their shoes. Those who are entering to pray also wash themselves in preparation for prayer.

The requirements of communal WORSHIP determine the furnishings of the mosque. Because Muslims face MECCA when they pray, all mosques are oriented toward Mecca. They also have a niche in the front wall known as a *mihrab;* it identifies the *qiblah,* the direction toward Mecca.

In communal prayer, the prayer leader, known as the IMAM, stands directly in front of the niche. The gathered congregation of men forms long parallel rows directly behind him. Together they go through the various postures of prayer, from standing to prostration. As a result, the central area of a mosque consists of a large flat surface without any furnishings. The area may be carpeted. It may also contain lines perpendicular to the qiblah to indicate to worshippers the best places to stand in rows. Traditionally women are not allowed to pray in the same area as men. That is because the prayer RITUALS require postures that might be distracting in mixed company. A mosque may have a separate area for women with separate entrances for them.

It is customary for the imam to deliver a sermon at the Friday noon service. Another feature on the inside of the mosque, then, is a place from which he may speak. Traditionally, this has been a stepped platform known as a *minbar*.

Other structural elements are often found in conjunction with a mosque. It has been very common for a tower to be affixed to the outside of a mosque. This tower is known as a minaret. Traditionally a man known as a MUEZZIN climbed the tower and issued the call to prayer five times a day. Today loudspeakers and tape recorders have replaced the muezzins in areas where that sort of technology is widespread.

It has also been very common for mosques to have pools or fountains. These make it possible for worshippers to perform the ablutions or washings that are required before prayer. Structural features commonly associated with mosques include pointed domes and vaulted portals known as *iwans*. Islamic teachings strictly forbid the representation of human beings and animals. The observance of this prohibition varies in other spheres of life, but

Dome of the Rock, Jerusalem, or al-Quds, 1860–80 *(Library of Congress)*

it is strictly followed in mosques. Mosques are not, however, without decoration. Preferred forms of decoration include geometrical figures and verses from the QUR'AN written in calligraphy.

Muslims consider some mosques to be especially sacred. These include the great mosque at Mecca, in the center of which stands the KAABA; the mosque at Medina, the town to which the Prophet MUHAMMAD immigrated and where he and many of his early followers are buried; and the Dome of the Rock mosque built on the platform of the ancient Temple in JERUSALEM.

mountains and religion The religious significance and role of mountains. Mountains have generally exercised a powerful hold on the religious consciousness. Representing places lifted up from the level of ordinary human life, they are the abode of gods, like the Greek Mount Olympus (*see* GREEK RELIGION); the place of divine revelation to humanity, like Mount Sinai where MOSES received the Law from GOD; or locations where holy men go to practice austerities and gain spiritual power, like several of the sacred mountains of TIBETAN RELIGION and JAPANESE RELIGION. They have also been places of WORSHIP and SACRIFICE. The environs of the holy city of JERUSALEM contain two sacred mountains, Mount Zion where the ancient temple was built and Mount Calvary where JESUS was crucified. Muslims, as part of the PILGRIMAGE to MECCA, stand for an afternoon on Mount Arafat, where the Prophet MUHAMMAD delivered his final sermon. In HINDUISM, BUDDHISM, and JAINISM, the world is said to be founded spiritually on Mount Meru, a mythical mountain with its roots in the underworld and reaching up through all the levels of reality to the HEAVENS. It is reproduced in many of the temples and pagodas of these religions.

Because of their sacred importance and role as sites of spiritual training and realization, mountains have always been places of pilgrimage, from Mount Fuji in Japan to the sacred mountains of Arabia and Palestine. Occasionally, mountains have also been viewed negatively in religion, as the abode of demons and EVIL sorcerers, or as disruptions in the world that signal its fallen nature. For the most part, though, mountains are looked at with religious awe as godlike or as "cathedrals of nature" that inspire VISIONS and a sense of wonder.

mudras A Sanskrit word meaning "rings, signs, tokens." In HINDUISM and BUDDHISM, mudras are postures of the hands and fingers that communicate religious meaning.

According to tradition, Hinduism knows more than 88 million mudras. The number of well-known mudras is much more limited.

Mudras are used in RITUALS, classical dance, and sculpture. Two examples are seen in the depiction of the god SIVA known as Nataraja, "King of the Dance." Siva holds the palm of his right hand toward the viewer, fingers and thumb up, signalling "do not fear." His left hand hangs down in a pose reminiscent of an elephant's trunk. That image recalls Siva's son, the elephant-headed god GANESA.

Buddhist rituals and sculpture use mudras, too. One common mudra in images of the BUDDHA is similar to the "do not fear" mudra described above. Another mudra shows the Buddha touching the ground. Through that action the Buddha demonstrated his resolve when he was tempted by MARA.

muezzin From the Arabic word *mu'addhin;* the person who issues the call to PRAYER in ISLAM. Muslims make formal prayer to GOD facing MECCA five times a day (*see* SALAT). Traditionally, the time for prayer is announced by a muezzin. He may stand on top of a pillar known as a minaret. Turning to the four directions, he intones the call to prayer in Arabic: "God is most great [four times]. I testify that there is no god but God [twice]. I testify that MUHAMMAD is God's Messenger [twice]. Come to prayer [twice]. Come to SALVATION [twice]. God is most great [twice]. There is no god but God [once]." For the call to early morning prayer, the muezzin twice adds the statement, "Prayer is better than sleep," after the call "Come to salvation."

In the 20th century many modern communities replaced their muezzins with amplified recordings.

Muhammad (570–632) *the prophet who, according to Muslims, received GOD's revelation in the QUR'AN and established ISLAM* His importance for Muslims is emphasized by the central Islamic profession of FAITH: "There is no god but God [Arabic, ALLAH], and Muhammad is his Messenger [Arabic, Rasul]."

LIFE

Muhammad was born in the year 570 in a clan of the Quraysh tribe in MECCA (today in western Saudi Arabia). His father died before he was born and his mother soon afterward, so he was raised first by his grandfather and then his uncle, Abu Talib. Tradition reports that as a young man he developed a reputation for honesty and virtue. He earned his living managing caravans, and at the age of 25 he married his employer, a wealthy widow named Khadija. Only one of their children, a daughter, Fatima, survived to adulthood.

Muhammad was in the habit of retiring to the desert for reflection and MEDITATION. On one such occasion in the year 611, the ANGEL Gabriel appeared to him with a message from God. This event is venerated within Islam as the Night of Power. According to a widespread tradition, the first words that God spoke to the prophet were these: "Recite: And thy Lord is the Most Generous, who taught by the pen, taught man that he knew not" (A. J. Arberry, *The Koran Interpreted*).

The revelations that Muhammad received implied a radical reorganization of society. They envisioned a community based on faith rather than family relationships, and they emphasized justice and concern for others rather than profit and self-interest. As a result, they evoked considerable opposition from the powerful members of Meccan society. After the death of Abu Talib in 619, the opposition to Muhammad became outspoken and menacing. In the year 622, Muhammad and his followers were forced to flee secretly from Mecca to Medina, a town roughly 300 miles to the north. There they allied with the previous inhabitants, who agreed to recognize Muhammad's prophethood. This emigration, known as the *hijra* (also spelled *hegira*), marks the beginning of the Islamic community. Accordingly, Muslims date events A.H., "in the year of the hijra" (*anno Hegirae*).

From the Meccan point of view, Muhammad's alliance with Medina was an act of treason. In turn, the Medinas raided Meccan caravans, and war ensued. The fortunes of battle were uneven, but the Medinas won a major victory at the battle of Badr in 624. By 628 the warring parties had established a truce. In 630 the Meccans violated the truce, and in that year Muhammad finally entered Mecca in victory. He proclaimed a general amnesty, purified the KAABA (the central shrine in Mecca) of the many idols that it contained, declared Mecca off-limits to all but Muslims, and established PILGRIMAGE to Mecca as a major Islamic RITUAL.

Muhammad died in the year 632 shortly after making a final pilgrimage to Mecca. He was buried in Medina. At the time of his death, the Islamic community was already beginning to expand by establishing relations with peoples in other parts of the Arabian Peninsula.

TEACHINGS

Muslims call the time before the prophet Muhammad *al-Jahiliya*, "the times of ignorance." During that period Mecca society was characterized by POLYTHEISM and social disorder. The disorder was due to the disruption of traditional patterns of life, which were more suited to desert herding than to a thriving mercantile city.

The messages revealed to Muhammad and preserved in the Qur'an had as their bedrock an insistence upon the absolute oneness of God (Arabic, *tawhid*). As one reads in the Qur'an: "Say: He, Allah, is One. Allah is He on Whom all depend. He begets not, nor is He begotten. And none is like Him." (Qur'an 112, Muhammed Shakir). Verses such as these rejected more than polytheism. In insisting on the absolute unity of God, Muhammad rejected any notion that implies plurality, like the Christian notion of God as a TRINITY. In insisting that God could neither beget nor be begotten, he rejected any claim that JESUS was the son of God. Indeed, he insisted on keeping God and human beings in their respective places: God is the creator upon whom the entire universe depends; it is the duty of human beings to submit to God's will (Arabic, *islam*).

Given this relationship, it follows that every human being must avoid two sins above all: the denial of the truth (Arabic, *kufr*) and mistaking the created for the creator (*shirk*). The latter is best seen in a very broad sense. It refers to letting anything, such as money or clan loyalty or tradition, guide one's life in violation of God's will. In this context Muhammad emphasized concern for the less advantaged as well as the avoidance of destructive social practices, such as drinking, gambling, prostitution, and usury, that is, charging exorbitant interest on loans. The RESURRECTION of the dead and a final judgment (*see* JUDGMENT OF THE DEAD) also played a great role in Muhammad's ethical outlook. These notions had not been prevalent earlier in the indigenous religions of Arabia.

SIGNIFICANCE

For Muslims, Muhammad was only a human being chosen by God to be a messenger. Muslims teach that Muhammad was born like every other person, that he died, and that he is buried in Medina.

At the same time, Muhammad is supremely important as the last of a long line of prophets to whom God has revealed his truth. That line begins with ADAM, the ancestor of all people, and includes many figures familiar to Jews and Christians, such as NOAH, DAVID, SOLOMON, ELIJAH, and Jesus, as well as figures from other traditions. Muslims hold that while all previous revelations were distorted or changed by various communities, the revelation to Muhammad preserved its purity. Thus, with Muhammad God's revelation of divine truth became full and complete. Initially the community preserved these revelations orally along with some written fragments, but within 25 years of Muhammad's death an authoritative compilation of the Qur'an had come into existence.

As the culmination of prophetic tradition or, as Muslims say, the seal of the prophets, Muhammad represents more than the vehicle for God's revelation. He also exemplifies the ideal way of responding to it. This conviction gave rise to the practice of collecting accounts of his sayings and deeds, known as HADITH. The Hadith provide guidance on religious matters, but they also establish the way one should go about many daily activities.

Islam does not separate religion from other areas of life but sees every facet of human existence as subject to God's commands. It is appropriate, then, that Muhammad's significance extends far beyond the narrowly religious. For example, the Qur'an is the highest standard in Arabic poetry. Of even broader significance, the community established through Muhammad united the various peoples of the Arabian Peninsula for the very first time. In doing so it changed the face of the world's political, cultural, and military history.

Further reading: Martin Forward, *Muhammad: A Short Biography* (Rockport, Mass.: Oneworld, 1997); Maxime Rodinson, *Muhammad: Prophet of Islam* (New York: I. B. Tauris, 2002); Ibn Warraq, ed., *The Quest for the Historical Muhammad* (Amherst, N.Y.: Prometheus Books, 2000).

music and religion   The attitudes to and use of patterned, humanly created sounds in the various religions.

THE VALUE OF MUSIC

Music plays a major role in most religions, but not in all. Some religions have rejected it, at least in part. Some orthodox Muslims forbid the religious use of music, although for others it has played an important role in cultivating the spiritual life. Traditional JAINISM rejects religious music, too. Jains consider it too sensual for religious purposes. The BIBLE refers to instruments used in the JERUSALEM Temple, but for centuries it has been traditional for Jews not to use instruments in SYNAGOGUE services. In the ancient and early medieval periods, Christians also allowed vocal music but rejected the use of instruments. They saw them as pagan. During the REFORMATION, John CALVIN limited church music to the singing of psalms without instrumental accompaniment. Following Calvin's lead, some early Calvinists destroyed many church organs. Today, some Christians, such as the more conservative AMISH and MENNONITES, still allow only vocal music.

Many religions, however, have warmly embraced music. They give different reasons for doing so. In India sound carries the power that generates the universe. This is especially true of the sacred syllable, "OM." Many peoples have thought that music was created by gods or ancestors. For example, shamans receive their songs from spirits or ancestors during their journeys to the other worlds. Other peoples have heard the voice of gods or spirits in musical sounds. A good example is the bull-roarer, a piece of wood attached to some sort of string and whirled in the air. Indigenous peoples in Africa, Australia, Oceania, and North America have considered the sound of the bull-roarer to be the voice of a religious being.

Religions also value music for its effects. When a BON priest plays the drum, Tibetans believe that he ascends to heaven. In the Hebrew Bible, DAVID, the future king of Judah and Israel, played music to calm King SAUL's spirits. Some Buddhists say that music puts the mind in a state in which it is receptive to enlightenment. In Europe during the 19th and early 20th centuries many people said that musical experience was very similar to the experience of God's presence. A good example is the theologian and philosopher of religion, Rudolf OTTO.

Religious music is often performed by individuals for their own purposes or by the community as a whole. Many societies also have religious musical specialists. A shaman's songs are often an integral part of his special role. In JUDAISM, musicians known as cantors, not rabbis, often lead synagogue services (see RABBI, RABBINATE). Music has been an important tool in establishing new religious communities, too. Among European Christians Martin LUTHER, who sparked the REFORMATION, and Charles Wesley, who played an important part

in the founding of METHODISM, composed notable hymns. In India Guru NANAK became the founder of the Sikh community (see SIKHISM), and Caitanya organized devotion to KRISHNA in Bengal in large part because they composed and sang devotional songs.

KINDS OF RELIGIOUS MUSIC

It is possible to divide music into two broad classes: music primarily made with the human voice, and music primarily made with some other instrument. In general, religions have valued vocal music more highly than instrumental music. Indeed, as noted above, some religions have refused to allow the use of musical instruments.

In antiquity, songs—one type of music—played major roles in SACRIFICES and temple observances. A good example of the first is the collection of ancient Indian texts known as the VEDA. The Veda contains hymns and songs that BRAHMINS used in performing elaborate sacrifices. The Hebrew Bible provides good examples of songs sung before a god in a temple: the book of PSALMS. The Psalms formed the basis for worship in Jewish synagogues and Christian churches. During the Reformation, Calvinists cultivated the singing of the Psalter. Lutherans used songs known as hymns that were specially written for congregations to sing. Since the Reformation many Protestant churches have developed rich traditions of hymnody.

Indigenous peoples in Africa, the Americas, Australia, and Oceania have beautiful and complex traditions of religious songs. Not only do shamans have their special songs, but songs also figure prominently in very many rituals. In HINDUISM, singing to God is a major component of BHAKTI. Devotees meet in small groups at night and sing God's praises. Some Bengali devotees concentrate simply on singing the names of Krishna as God. As a result, their American converts became commonly known as "Hare Krishnas."

Many religions have a special kind of singing known as chanting. In Judaism and Islam, chanting is often called cantillation. Chanting is musical recitation, for example, musical reading from the Bible. The basic idea is that the voice one uses in ordinary speech is inadequate for reciting sacred words, so one intones them instead. Chanting is often done by religious specialists: cantors, priests, reciters of the Qur'an, monks. Some Tibetan Buddhist monks have developed an intriguing manner of chanting whereby a single voice can produce two pitches simultaneously, a fifth or a sixth along with a deep tonic.

Some forms of chant are relatively simple. Each syllable receives a note or two. Other forms of chant are very ornate. Each syllable receives a large number of notes. The first kind of chant is called syllabic, the second melismatic. Chants in which syllables receive a moderate number of notes are called neumatic. In the Gregorian chants of the Roman Catholic Mass, chants that aim to instruct are syllabic, those connected with ritual action are neumatic, while those that aim to provide a basis for contemplation and reflection are melismatic.

At one time or another, religious people also have used musical instruments of very kind: instruments that are solid and vibrate, such as bells; instruments that have "heads" that vibrate, such as drums; instruments in which air vibrates, such as flutes; and instruments in which strings vibrate, such as zithers. Instruments are most often used to accompany singing. For example, indigenous North Americans often accompany their singing with drum beats or flute music. Instrumental music may mark the beginning and end of rituals. In many temples people ring bells to attract a deity's attention before they pray. It is relatively rare for purely instrumental music to be by itself the central RITUAL activity.

Religions may give rise to special musical performances. These performances may focus on music, especially vocal music, or they may combine music with other arts, such as dance or drama.

African religions often combine music and dance. So does Japanese SHINTO, in an event known as *kagura*. Performances in which Indonesian *gamelan* orchestras accompany the telling of traditional myths such as the *Ramayana* (*see* RAMA, RAMAYANA) are well-known. Religion has also inspired some of the masterpieces of European music. Johann Sebastian Bach's cantatas, passions, and *B-minor Mass*, Georg Friedrich Handel's oratorios, including the *Messiah*, Franz Joseph Haydn's *The Creation*, Ludwig van Beethoven's *Missa solemnis*, Gabriel Faure's *Requiem*, and Johannes Brahms's *German Requiem* are just a few examples.

SIGNIFICANCE

There is a close relationship between religion and music. Music has contributed significantly to most, if not all, religious traditions. At the same time, religion has inspired the creation of musical masterpieces throughout the world.

Further reading: Albert L. Blackwell, *The Sacred in Music* (Louisville, Ky.: Westminster John Knox Press, 1999); David W. Stowe, *How Sweet the Sound: Music in the Spiritual Lives of Americans* (Cambridge, Mass.: Harvard University Press, 2004); Lawrence E. Sullivan, ed., *Enchanting Powers: Music in the World's Religions* (Cambridge, Mass.: Harvard University Press, 1997).

Muslim   *See* ISLAM.

Muslim, Black   *See* Islam, Nation of.

mystery religions   Esoteric religions in the ancient Mediterranean world. Those who practiced mystery religions promised not to speak with outsiders about the central RITUALS of these religions. As a result, the rituals were called "mysteries."

In the ancient Mediterranean world, people often practiced religions defined by the specific social and political communities to which they belonged. Families, villages, and states all had their own religious observances. Mystery religions were different. People practiced mystery religions apart from families, villages, and states. As single persons they joined special "associations." These associations were formed solely in order to practice the mysteries.

People joined mystery associations in a special way: They underwent an INITIATION. As part of the initiation, they promised never to reveal the content of the secret rites and teachings. The ancient initiates kept their promises very well. We do not know nearly as much as we would like to know about any of the mystery religions. Scholars often suppose, however, that these religions claimed to provide a blessed existence for souls after death.

Some mystery religions began with the Greeks. The most important of them were celebrated at the town of Eleusis near Athens. They were called the Eleusinian mysteries. Already in the "golden age" of Athens, the fifth century B.C.E., these mysteries were becoming famous.

The mysteries of Eleusis had a specific mythology: the story of Demeter and her daughter Kore, sometimes called Persephone. The seasonal rhythms of growing grain seem to have provided the Eleusinian mysteries with an important symbol. Kore was said to spend half of the year above ground, and half of the year in the underworld. About the central rituals, we know only that they consisted of three components: things said, things done, and things shown.

Beginning about 200 B.C.E., other mystery religions developed in the ancient Mediterranean world. They used elements from places like Egypt, Turkey, and Persia. One set of mysteries centered on the Egyptian GODDESS ISIS and her slain husband, OSIRIS. A second centered on the goddess Cybele, also known as the Magna Mater, "Great Mother," and her younger male attendant, Attis, who came from the region of what is now Turkey. The god Mithras seems distantly related to the Persian god MITHRA. For a time toward the end of the third century C.E. the WORSHIP of Sol Invictus, the "Unconquered Sun," became the official religion of the Roman Empire.

Each of these mysteries had its distinct teachings, rituals, and communities. For example, the mysteries of Mithras appealed especially to Roman soldiers. They practiced the mysteries in special buildings known as "mithraea." Every "mithraeum" contained a picture of the god Mithras killing a bull. The exact meaning of this picture is unclear. Other pictures depicted stars and constellations.

In many ways ancient CHRISTIANITY took the form of a mystery religion. Members joined the Christian community through an initiation ritual (BAPTISM) after careful preparation. Non-Christians were forbidden to observe the central ritual act, the celebration of the EUCHARIST. In addition, Christianity provided a way to ensure that one's soul lived a blessed existence after death. Indeed, the Greek word for the most important Christian rituals, the SACRAMENTS, is *mysteria,* "mysteries."

mysticism States of consciousness interpreted as profound religious experience, or teachings about them or derived from them. In common usage, the word mysticism can mean many different things. For some it means that which is irrational, or vague and "misty." For some it suggests the arts of OCCULTISM AND ESOTERICISM, like ASTROLOGY or black MAGIC. For others it means psychic powers such as telepathy. In religious studies, mysticism generally refers to deep, intense states of religious consciousness, such as those attained by persons like the BUDDHA, the Sufi (*see* SUFISM) mystics of ISLAM, the great masters of the KABBALAH or HASIDISM in JUDAISM, or in CHRISTIANITY, SAINTS on the order of FRANCIS OF ASSISI or St. Teresa of Avila.

For people like these mysticism indicated a direct, personal experience of GOD or divine reality. Often the experience is described in the language of oneness: The mystic will say, "I became one with God." There also will be a sense of deep inwardness about it; "I felt God deep in my heart"; "I knew enlightenment in every fiber of my being." It can also be put in the terminology of love: "I felt the love of God sweep over me like the waves of the sea."

The precise words in which mystical experience is put will, of course, vary from one religion to another. For those religions based on an impersonal monism, like BUDDHISM or VEDANTA Hinduism, it will be realizing enlightenment, NIRVANA, or BRAHMAN as *Satchitananda,* "Being-knowledge-bliss," within one's true and ultimate nature. For those religions like Judaism, Christianity, and Islam that see God in terms of personal MONOTHEISM, and stress that a created being like a man or woman can never be absolutely the same as God the Creator, they will speak of the mysticism of love, and of being united with God in the same way as a lover yearns to be united with the beloved.

However, it is important to realize that the speech and writings of mystics, even the greatest, are always an attempt to describe and interpret an experience that many of them nonetheless say is beyond words. The words of description are not the experience itself.

Two people may have an experience of deep joy and rapture. One may take it to be just a psychological experience, the other a religious encounter with the divine. Even the second will probably interpret it in terms of a religion with which that person is familiar, whether it is monistic or monotheistic. Even so, the great mystics East and West have greatly enriched their languages and literatures with beautiful and evocative attempts to communicate their deep and subtle encounters with divine grace.

Many spiritual traditions teach techniques that help one to have mystical experiences. These include, first of all, PRAYER and especially MEDITATION. Prayer is believed to bring one into contact with God, while stilling the mind through meditation can allow the divine love or divine presence to well up deep within. Preparation for meditation like YOGA, sitting in the lotus posture, deep slow breathing, focusing the eyes or the mind on a single point, and chanting a mantra or sacred set of syllables are all among the methods used. Others say that music, especially the beat of a drum, and dance like that done by Muslim Sufi and Jewish Hasidic practitioners, among others, can include mystical states.

However, thoughtful teachers of mysticism warn that it is something far more subtle than a state that can be automatically brought about by practices or techniques. They can help, but in the end mysticism is more of an art than a science. Even the greatest artists sometimes have better days than others, times when the streams of creativity seem to flow well and others when they run dry. So it is with the mystics.

Teachers of mysticism in fact describe various stages of the mystical path. One of the best-known books on the subject is Evelyn Underhill's *Mysticism*. Combing reports of numerous mystics, she outlines five basic stages. First is the Awakening, when—sometimes in a powerful conversion or "born-again" kind of encounter with the divine—one awakens to the reality of the spiritual life. This initial stage tends to be very emotional and erratic, though, and needs to be stabilized in the Purgative or Preparative stage, when the wise practitioner will deepen and stabilize the spiritual life with a disciplined life and regular prayer and meditation. This leads to the Illuminative stage, a basically happy time when God seems to be near, prayers answered, and the promises of religion fulfilled.

For some, however, it is followed by something distressing: the Dark Night of the Soul, as it was called by the great St. John of the Cross. Now God seems to have withdrawn his presence, and one is left as though on a desert at night without a compass. Many give up at this point in despair. But the Dark Night is really a time of deepening and of purging away even the subtlest kinds of attachment to good religious feelings and the like one may have, that one may come to know God alone. For the Dark Night finally leads into Underhill's supreme stage, the Unitive state, when one is united with God on so deep a level that the divine presence is always there, even when one is not thinking about it, and one is guided in all one's doings by love.

Religious traditions have evaluated mystical experience differently. Some, such as PURE LAND BUDDHISM and certain strands in Protestant Christianity, have emphasized simple FAITH and harbored suspicions that too much craving for mystical "states" gets in the way of reliance on faith alone. Others might accuse mysticism of being "escapist" and taking up time and attention that would be better spent in the doing of good works in the world, even though some of the greatest "do-gooders" from St. Francis to GANDHI have also been great mystics. Probably the majority of religionists in the world, though, would say that while being a mystic may not be necessary to SALVATION, some mystical experience can deepen and enrich one's spiritual life.

Further reading: Emilie Griffin, ed. *Evelyn Underhill: Essential Writings*, (Maryknoll, N.Y.: Orbis Books, 2003); Gershom Scholem, *Major Trends in Jewish Mysticism* (New York: Schocken Books, 1995); D. T. Suzuki, *Mysticism, Christian and Buddhist* (New York: Routledge, 2002).

myth and mythology   A story that is religiously important, and the study of such stories. For the average person, a myth is simply a story that is not true: "that's just a myth." In religious studies, though, the meaning is rather different. It is taken to be a story that expresses the basic world view of a culture or religion in narrative form. It says some very important things about the way in which the people telling the story think about GOD, human nature, the origin and destiny of the world, how we should live our lives now, and how we can get into right relationships with the divine. For a myth is basically a story, but it is a story about ultimate things. In this respect, in the eyes of students of folklore, a myth differs from a fable or legend or fairytale. Those may be entertaining, and reveal such information as how the fox lost his tail or a certain town got its name. But myths tend to tell how the world was made and how SALVATION came into it. Some people may believe the myth stories literally, others take them as poetic renderings of ultimate things that are otherwise hard to put into words or to understand.

Let us consider three types of religious myth: creation myths, hero / savior myths, and myths of ESCHATOLOGY, or the end of the world.

The creation myths tell how God or the gods made the world "in the beginning." People tend to believe that if you know where something came from, you know something very important about it and how to handle it. Thus whether the world came into being by divine design, or by accident, or

has just always existed, has important meaning for us living on it. For example, the creation account of JUDAISM and CHRISTIANITY found in the book of Genesis, at the beginning of the Hebrew Scriptures, tells us that God made the world as though it were something outside of himself, like a carpenter making a box, then looked on it and saw that it was very good. He then placed human beings—also made as, so to speak, the work of his hands—into that creation, and gave them instructions.

The creation story tells us that the world and the Creator of the world are not to be confused. The world is to be honored because it was made by God, but it is not the same as God. We humans can have a deep relationship of love, service, and obedience to God, but we must not say that we are God. All these very important ideas, central to Judaism and Christianity, are embedded in the creation myth.

Compare that account with one from the VEDAS of India, which tells us that the world is a sacrifice made by Prajapati, a Creator God who made the world by dividing up his body so that his bones became the mountains, his blood the rivers, and so forth. Here is conveyed something told in much more philosophical language in later HINDU-ISM, that God is not a Creator separate from the world, but the word *is* God, God in disguise, God playing hide-and-seek with himself, and to know God we do not look outside of the world, but into the depths of the world, into our own innermost nature.

All the many creation myths of the world doubtless bear some such important message about the true nature of the world as seen by their tellers. One thing they tell that is important is that at the beginning humans were close to their Creator, one way or another. But as time went on, they lost that closeness, falling into forgetfulness of it or, like ADAM and EVE, being expelled from the primal garden.

Next examine the role, in myth, of the hero, like RAMA or KRISHNA in India, or in Western lore St. George who slew the dragon, who defeats EVIL and perhaps establishes an ideal kingdom. In some ways even the divine prophets and saviors of the great religions have such a role as they show the way back to right relationships with God or the divine. These would be stories like that of the BUDDHA, who attained perfect consciousness through deep MEDITATION under the tree, or MOSES who received the divine law on Mount Sinai, or JESUS who reestablished the possibility of a right relationship with God for humans through his death on the cross and his rising again to renewed life. In these stories, the prophet or savior is, like the heroes of myth, a pioneer, a leader, with superhuman powers that help set the world right.

Finally, myths of the end may lead up to stories of the end of the world and the end of time, like those of the Last Judgment in Christianity, when it is said CHRIST will return to judge the living and the dead, or the coming of the future Buddha MAITREYA in Buddhism. Often the end in myth really represents a return to the paradise of the beginning.

Myths like these and many others continue to have a tremendous power in the world. There are the myths of nations, of political movements, of particular sects and denominations of religions that tell in mythic terms of their origins and their world view. There are also personal myths. Probably deep inside, most people in the world have a story they like to tell themselves that helps them understand who they are, what they are like, why they do the things they do, and what their role in the world is. Myths are powerful because at the profoundest level most of us respond better to seeing ourselves as actors in a story than as abstract ideas; the ideas and beliefs come alive when they are parts of a story, especially our own. Mythical thinking can also be dangerous, for it can tend to see everything as black and white, absolutely good like the hero or bad like the dragons against which he fights. It can stigmatize whole groups of people, and is not very good at working out all the nuances and degrees of good and bad that occur in the real world. But it also gives life to some of the profoundest of human insights, and can motivate new heroes for today.

See also HEROES AND HERO MYTHS.

Further reading: William G. Doty, *Myth: A Handbook* (Westport, Conn.: Greenwood Press, 2004); Phil Cousineau, ed., *The Hero's Journey: Joseph Campbell on His Life and Work* (Novato, Calif.: New World Library, 2003); Robert A. Segal, *Myth: A Very Short Introduction* (New York: Oxford University Press, 2004).

N

Nanak (1469–1539) *the first Sikh guru and founder of the Sikh religion* Nanak was born in the Punjab, the region of the five tributaries of the Indus river in northwest India and northern Pakistan. He grew up in a Hindu family. As a young adult he hosted evening gatherings for devotional singing. A Muslim musician accompanied him.

At the age of 30 Nanak disappeared for three days. On his return he proclaimed a religion that transcended the differences between Hindus and Muslims and worshipped the one true GOD. He also rejected distinctions between castes and the use of images in WORSHIP. The proper way to worship God, he taught, was through MEDITATION and the singing of hymns.

Nanak traveled, teaching and singing and becoming the GURU of a group of disciples (*sishyas* or *sikkhas*). He was the first in a lineage of 10 Sikh gurus. His sayings are preserved in the Sikh holy book, the ADI GRANTH.

See also SIKHISM.

nationalism, religious Movements that link the power and fate of a nation with a specific religion. In the second half of the 20th century and the beginning of the 21st century, religious nationalism was a major force in many areas. Some called religious nationalism "fundamentalism," an analogy with fundamentalist CHRISTIANITY in the United States, even though fundamentalism has not traditionally been active in politics (see EVANGELICAL CHRISTIANITY and FUNDAMENTALISM, CHRISTIAN).

The separation of religion and governments is relatively new. Throughout most of history governments have had their own religions. In Europe the idea of separating religion and government first arose among some Protestants. These Protestants were the Anabaptists of the 16th century (*see* MENNONITES) and the Baptists and QUAKERS of the 17th century (*see* BAPTIST CHURCHES). Before these movements, religion and nationalism went hand in hand. A good example is JOAN OF ARC who saw it as her mission from GOD to help the heir to the French throne become king. The first governments to separate themselves from religion—in technical terms, to "disestablish" religion—were North American colonies of Great Britain, such as Pennsylvania. The first nation that officially separated religion and government was the United States. Although the United States is officially secular, it often thinks of itself in Protestant terms. In the early 20th century, it added the words "In God we trust" to its money, and in 1954 it added the phrase "under God" to the Pledge of Allegiance.

The late 20th and early 21st centuries saw several powerful movements of religious nationalism. These movements did not all adopt the same political stance. Islamic movements in the Middle East, Hindu nationalism in India, and Christian nationalism in the United States were reactionary. They wanted to restore the past—or what they perceived the past to have been. At least one movement was revolutionary: the black nationalism proclaimed at various times by the Nation of Islam (*see* ISLAM, NATION OF) in the United States. And at least one movement—Jewish nationalists who settled on the west bank of the Jordan River—was colonizing. It wanted to appropriate land that had previously belonged to other people, and it used religion to justify that action. These movements generally used political action to try to achieve their ends. Some extremists also used physical violence.

Religious nationalists generally perceived themselves as embattled communities, even when, as in India, they claimed to speak for an overwhelming majority. They saw themselves as reasserting a necessary union between government and religion ("The United States should be a 'Christian nation'."). They also saw themselves as reasserting several other points: tradition and its values against modernity and its depravities; a religious view of the world over a secular one; the proper identity of a particular people over the homogenizing global culture created by multinational corporations and the mass media; national purity in the face of growing plurality; and power in the face of perceived powerlessness and disenfranchisement.

The rise of religious nationalism caught many observers by surprise. In their eyes, global communications and travel had held out great promise. The nationalist ambitions in World War II had produced grisly horrors. The force of secularism was supposed to be irresistible. In the second half of the 20th century a growing internationalism was supposed to take the place of nationalist loyalties.

At the beginning of the 21st century, it was impossible to predict the ultimate fate of religious nationalist movements. Were they the futile, last gasps of those dissatisfied with the irresistible march of a global civilization? Would the sparks of violence that religious nationalism had already occasionally ignited once again light the flames of full-scale violence? Or were religious nationalist movements genuine and convincing religious alternatives that would continue to attract followers in great numbers? It seems certain, at least, that the takeover of Iraq in spring 2003 by the United States and the United Kingdom has led to an increase in religious nationalism among some Muslims, including those associated with the radical group AL-QAEDA.

Native American religions The religions of the peoples whose ancestors lived in the Americas before Columbus. Separate entries discuss the religions of the major pre-Columbian civilizations: Maya religion, Aztec religion, and Inca religion.

The indigenous peoples of the Americas have never constituted a single group. They represent many languages, cultures, and religions. For example, before Columbus arrived, the Americas were home to civilizations in the Valley of Mexico, the lowlands of the Yucatan Peninsula, and the Andes Mountains. Some peoples in the eastern United States had large settlements near mounds that served as bases for temples. The Anasazi in the Southwest built impressive residential communities. Both the inhabitants of the Great Plains and the inhabitants of the Amazon basin lived by hunting and gathering. Nevertheless, they had significantly different ways of life. They also had significantly different religions.

General statements about Native American religions inevitably distort them. Such statements may, however, give some indication of their character.

Most traditional Native American religions aimed to further life in this world. They involved give-and-take relationships with persons who represented the powers of nature. Outsiders usually called these persons gods or spirits. When these beings had a particularly close relationship with one group of relatives (a lineage), they were sometimes called totems. The giving and taking took the form of offerings, SACRIFICES, and PRAYERS. It furthered traditional means of earning a living: hunting and agriculture. It also helped heal (see HEALING, RELIGIOUS). Outsiders often call religious healers shamans (see SHAMANISM).

Shamans played major roles in most of the traditional indigenous religions of South America. In addition, most South Americans traditionally told stories about a creator. But they did not worship this creator much because the creator had little to do with daily life. Twins figured prominently in the traditional religious stories and RITUALS of South America. For example, the Ge in eastern Brazil worshipped the sun and the moon, both male. Across northern South America, from the Atlantic

A religious figure among the Algonquian-speaking Native Americans was the shaman, or medicine man. This drawing shows an Algonquian shaman preparing his medicine. He sings sacred songs as he mixes various ingredients together while shaking a rattle. *(Library of Congress)*

to the Pacific, the jaguar received a great deal of religious attention.

Traditional religions of North America varied greatly. To the east of the Mississippi lived well-off agricultural communities as well as woodland hunters. In this region tribes and villages entered into larger confederations and alliances, notably, the Iroquois confederacy centered in what is now upstate New York and the Five Civilized Tribes of the American Southeast.

People in the northern part of the region worshipped spiritual realities known in different languages as *manitou* and *orenda*. Opinions differ over whether these terms always referred to super-

natural beings or sometimes also to a nonpersonal, supernatural power. Dreams provided an important source of communication with the supernatural. Houses, often big enough for several families, were thought to mirror the structure of the universe at large (sky, earth, directions, and so on).

In the southern lands east of the Mississippi people depended heavily on agriculture. As a result, Green Corn ceremonies figured prominently in their religions. These people told many stories and folktales, such as earth-diver stories about the creation of the world and stories about the antics of TRICKSTERS. Some of their communities were wealthy enough to have full-time priests. Especially important for their descendants is the memory of their forced resettlement west along the "Trail of Tears."

West of the Mississippi, in the region of the Great Plains, Native Americans had different lifestyles and religions. Some groups, such as the Hidatsa and Pawnee, lived in villages, but many others, such as the Comanche and Lakota, were nomadic hunters. Crucial to these people's religion was a VISION, which provided them with their personal spiritual helpers. Native Americans on the Great Plains often sought visions through practices such as prolonged fasting. Helpers would often appear in the form of birds or animals. These people often practiced elaborate rituals. An example of such a ritual is the Sun Dance, which some groups held every summer. It was common for participants to purify themselves in a SWEAT LODGE before the rituals.

In what is now the southwestern United States, people known as Pueblos had elaborate ceremonies to further growth and encourage rain. *Kachinas,* masked figures, played an important part in them. Also well-known are *kivas,* chambers partly underground in which Pueblo religious societies met. The Navajo hold elaborate series of rituals known as "sings," used to heal and create social and natural harmony. Their sand paintings and weaving work often illustrate their complex notions of the structure of the universe and the emergence of the Navajo people from the center of the Earth.

Among the Native Americans of California, as among many other Native Americans, shamans or medicine men played important roles as healers. These people also used religious means, as was common, to further the growth of crops. In addition, Native Americans in California had ritual societies into which people were initiated. In southern California one such society cultivated visions by ingesting a hallucinogen known as datura.

Perhaps the best-known feature of Native Americans of the Northwest coast is the totem pole. The images carved on totem poles represent superhuman beings. Particularly important supernatural beings for these people were the salmon, on which their lives depended. These people held elaborate ceremonies known as potlatches, in which the wealthy outdid one another in giving gifts or destroying their own property. Shamans, who acquired their powers through prayers or visions, performed the roles of healers. From visions, too, people learned about dances, an important kind of ritual performance.

In much of what is now Canada and Alaska, native peoples believed that spirits controlled the herds of animals on which their lives depended. They sought to ensure good relations with the animals through ritual. For example, they protected the remains of a slain animal from being eaten by dogs. In some cases they talked with the slain animal politely, offered it gifts such as tobacco, and held feasts in its honor. In the far north, Eskimos told stories about the person who controlled sea life. Some called her Sedna.

The European invasion of the Americas changed Native American life immensely and brought pressure to convert to CHRISTIANITY. Many Native Americans did adopt Christianity, but many also continued traditional practices at the same time. For example, the well-known Lakota figure Black Elk (c. 1863–1950) was buried holding both his sacred pipe and a rosary.

Native Americans have also used religion to resist European incursions. Many Native Americans had visions about resistance. They include such figures as Handsome Lake (1735–1815; Seneca), Smohalla (c. 1815–95; Wanapum), John Slocum (1841–97; Squaxin Island Tribe, Coast Salish), Wodziwob (d. c. 1872; Northern Paiute), and Wovoka (c. 1856–1932; Northern Paiute). The last two spurred on the GHOST DANCE.

In the past several decades religion has influenced militant indigenous resistance movements, such as the American Indian Movement, often known by the acronym AIM. Religion has helped motivate legal action to redress grievances, for example, the efforts to recover ceremonial lands. It has also played a major role in reviving indigenous culture. Examples include the Native American Church, well known for its use of peyote; the Sun Dance; teachings about the sacredness of the earth; and sweat lodges. Native American teachings, sometimes newly invented, have also figured prominently in New Age teachings in North America.

Further reading: Dee Alexander Brown, *Bury My Heart at Wounded Knee* (New York: Henry Holt, 2001); Vine Deloria Jr., *God Is Red,* 3d ed. (Golden, Colo.: Fulcrum, 2003); Sam Gill, *Native American Religions: An Introduction* (Belmont, Calif.: Wadsworth, 1981); Ake Hultkrantz, *Religions of the American Indians* (Berkeley: University of California Press, 1981); Clara Sue Kidwell, Homer Noley, and George E. Tinker, *A Native American Theology* (Maryknoll, N.Y.: Orbis 2001); Joel W. Martin, *The Land Looks After Us: A History of Native American Religion* (New York: Oxford University Press, 2001). Peter Matthiessen, *In the Spirit of Crazy Horse* (New York: Viking, 1991); John G. Neihardt, ed., *Black Elk Speaks: Being the Life Story of a Holy Man of the Oglala Sioux* (Lincoln: University of Nebraska Press, 2004).

nature and religion The significance of the natural world for religion. All religions must deal not only with humanity, but also with the environment in which we dwell. They must, in other words, have something to say about the plants and animals, the mountains and forests, the soil and sky and stars that are visible and tangible. They must deal with nature.

That is not always easy to do. Nature can be experienced in many ways. Sometimes it seems lush and beautiful and friendly beyond anything else imaginable, and we believe nature must be the very footstool of GOD or the manifestation of divine reality. Yet at other times, in the wake of floods or drought or earthquake, nature appears cruel and ruthless, the enemy of all human hopes and dreams. Yet again, there are times when we are struck by the heartlessness of nature, the suffering of so many creatures, and the hardness of the natural environment against which we must often struggle.

Religions have contented with all these perceptions. The members of some religions, like TAOISM and a few "nature mystics," have virtually been "pantheists," that is, people who have thought God and nature virtually to be identical. The harshness of nature, they say, is the harshness of God, yet to know the heart of nature is to get beyond that and into a profound sense of wonder at the ultimate beauty of what is in the world before and beyond humankind. All one can do, they say, is attune oneself with the essence of nature—the Tao, in Taoist language—and through it go beyond human concepts of good and evil.

At the other end of the spectrum are those who, as in the ancient GNOSTICISM and MANICHAEISM, have emphasized the EVIL in nature, and have said that nature could not have been created by a good God. Many Gnostics said that the world as we know it was created by a lower god than the supreme Lord, who botched the job and made the fallen natural and human world around us; we ourselves are sparks of light from a higher realm who have become entrapped in this evil realm and must escape from it.

The positions of most of the major religions are somewhere in between. HINDUISM and BUDDHISM would say that nature contains beings, animals, demons, and others who, like ourselves but with less capacity for understanding, are driven by ignorance and desire. Thus nature too is suffering, but also bears the divine spark or the BUDDHA-nature and can be freed through compassion. Some would say that the suffering of nature is at least in part a projection of our own twisted consciousness onto it.

The western MONOTHEISM of JUDAISM, CHRISTIANITY, and ISLAM would generally say that nature is good insofar as it was created, like us, by the one supreme God. Christianity would add that nature, also like us, has been touched by SIN and is "fallen," so that its original pure and true nature is hard to see. But, though it is generally said that animals (and other beings in nature) do not have immortal souls like humans, they suffer in fallen nature and as creatures of God deserve our compassion and help.

In many ways, then, nature remains a deep mystery for religion, but also an arena for the exercise of whatever love and VISION religion provides.

Nazarene, Church of the A church in the Holiness tradition, founded in the United States. The Holiness movement is an outgrowth of Methodism that emphasizes sanctification, that is, the development of moral perfection. The Church of the Nazarene resulted from mergers of several churches in this tradition, starting in 1907. It was originally named the Pentecostal Church of the Nazarene, but the word Pentecostal was dropped when the Pentecostal Church became associated with speaking in tongues (see Pentecostalism), which Nazarenes do not do. The name Nazarene refers to Jesus, who came from Nazareth.

Like many Protestants, Nazarenes accept the Bible as the Word of God and maintain that people are saved from sin by God's grace through Jesus rather than through anything people do. Beyond this, Nazarenes also believe that "entire sanctification" is possible. This sanctification comes after the regeneration of baptism, and it eliminates original sin and instills in the Christian a spirit of complete devotion to God.

In pursuit of this perfection or holiness, Nazarenes have embraced a strict lifestyle, outlined in their Covenant of Christian Conduct. The church's membership may alter this covenant in keeping with changing understandings of the Christian life. Among other things the covenant in effect in the summer of 2004 required Nazarenes to avoid any form of entertainment, such as radio, television, or cinema, that promoted socially dangerous values, such as violence, pornography, and the occult; gambling, including state run lotteries; dancing; and the use of tobacco, liquor, or hallucinogenic drugs. In keeping with these provisions, Nazarenes use only unfermented grape juice when they celebrate communion (see Eucharist). The church has also strongly condemned homosexuality and the legalization of abortion.

The churches that came together to form the Church of the Nazarene were active in overseas missions even before the mergers that created the church. At the beginning of 2006 the church reported a total membership of 1.6 million members, more than 60 percent of whom lived outside the United States.

Nehemiah (586–539 B.C.E.) *a governor of Jerusalem in the period after the Babylonian exile, and the name of a biblical book.* The Persian king Artaxerxes I (ruled 464–423 B.C.E.) sent Nehemiah, one of his cupbearers, as governor to Jerusalem in 445 B.C.E. Nehemiah rebuilt the city walls and made it safe to live in once again. Some time later—the date is not known with certainty—Artaxerxes sent Nehemiah to Jerusalem for a second term as governor. On this occasion he undertook religious reforms that emphasized a return to tradition and a rejection of intermarriage with non-Jews. The relationship of Nehemiah's activities to those of Ezra is uncertain. The Bible gives the impression that they were active at the same time, but many scholars argue that Ezra must have come after Nehemiah.

The book of Nehemiah is really the second part of the book of Ezra. It tells mostly of the events of Nehemiah's governorship. It does so in a first-person narrative that makes the book read as if it were the memoirs of Nehemiah himself.

New Age movement The term New Age or New Age Thinking is a general label used since the late 20th century and after to cover a number of interrelated spiritual interests. They include belief in "alternative healing" or "holistic health" (acupuncture, homeopathy, diet-based cures, etc.), astrology, crystals, a strong affirmation of the power of thought to change oneself and reality, the "channeling" of great teachers or "masters" through trance, reincarnation and karma, and a general sympathy with nature and ecology. Many speakers and best-selling books, tapes, and videos, such as those of the actress Shirley McLaine, have popularized the concepts.

Though one can find numerous groups and bookstores recognizable as New Age, the movement has produced no major, long-lasting organization. Nevertheless, several important centers reflect its spirit, such as the Findhorn community in Scotland and the Association for Research and Enlightenment in Virginia Beach, Virginia, established by the famous "sleeping prophet" Edgar Cayce (1877–1945), considered a precursor of the New Age.

The New Age movement has roots in the ancient world, especially Platonic philosophy. Some of its ideas, such as astrology and cosmic energy, have long enjoyed a sort of underground coexistence with the dominant religions of Europe and North America for centuries. Their outlook might be considered an alternative to the spiritual mainstream. This side surfaced strongly in the 19th century in New England Transcendentalism, SPIRITUALISM, and NEW THOUGHT, and in movements like THEOSOPHY. The term *New Age* itself goes back to that period. But its most immediate predecessor was the famous "counterculture" of the 1960s. Many New Age concepts and practices became popular in that era, and the New Age movement began in the wake of the 1960s.

For all its diversity, the New Age movement has certain common core ideas. Most basic is the concept of energy. Many philosophies, both Eastern and Western, have postulated a basic, universal energy, much like the "Force" in *Star Wars,* most intense in biological organisms, that drives and regulates all things. When it is balanced and flowing freely in a person, she or he is in good health. When it is not, there is disease. But there are processes, for example, acupuncture and YOGA, to remove blockages and restore the energy's proper flow. New Age approaches to healing and health generally are grounded on this energy concept. They are called "alternative medicine" because they differ in this respect from mainline medicine, which is centered more on fighting and destroying disease-causing organisms.

Some New Age adherents believe that energy can also be worked with in its universal aspect. Certain objects, such as crystals, may be particular sources or transmitters of it. Properly placed crystals can send cosmic energy to a person and help restore his or her own energy. Some New Age teachers have postulated "energy vortexes" or "power spots" on Earth, for example, Sedona, Arizona, and Mount Shasta in California, where the energy is especially accessible.

Others believe that cosmic energy also operates through what the ancients called "correspondences," subtle lines of force between phenomena in one part of the universe, including the heavens, and others, including human beings. Movement of the stars and planets can affect events on earth and the lives of its inhabitants. Gemstones or colors can be in harmony with various days of the week or organs of the body, and thus can affect the potency of healing energies.

No less important are New Age beliefs about consciousness. It is usually assumed that consciousness and matter are both universal forces, like two sides of the same coin, so one can always affect the other. New Age followers attempt to use meditation and concentrated thought to change health and even events in the outer world. New Age people accept what earlier thinkers called the "great chain of being" doctrine: Centers of consciousness can rise above humanity just as they can descend below it into animals and plants; the higher consciousness would be what we call spirits, saints, masters, angels, and demigods, up to God Supreme. For many New Age people these entities are important as companions and guides and can sometimes be "channeled" or enabled to speak through human mediums during trances.

Though perhaps perceived as less vogue than they were around the 1980s, New Age attitudes have continued to be powerful in popular culture in the 21st century.

Further reading: James R. Lewis, *The Encyclopedic Sourcebook of New Age Religions* (Amherst, N.Y.: Prometheus, 2003); Shirley MacLaine, *Out on a Limb,* Rpt. (New York: Bantam, 1999); J. Gordon Melton, *New Age Encyclopedia* (Detroit: Gale, 1990); Sarah Pike, *New Age and Neopagan Religions in America* (New York: Columbia University Press, 2004).

new religions Religions that have arisen recently, generally within the last few generations. Some religions are very old, but new religions are continually appearing as well.

Thousands have arisen in the 20th century alone, especially in rapidly changing societies such as Africa and parts of Asia. New religious movements typically center around remarkably charismatic personalities who believe they have seen VISIONS or had experiences that present a dramatically new teaching or practice to the world, although occasionally the new religion may be constructed without a single leader. However, a new religion must have not only a founding person or idea, but also an audience and a situation receptive to the novel perspective on ultimate truth. In changing times—and we must remember that most times are changing times for people actually in them—old religious teachings, practices, and institutions may seem out of step with the real world in which people live. Perhaps an old tribal religion may not seem to have the right tools to deal with a world of contact with European culture, with new ideas, economies, and technologies; this was the situation out of which CARGO CULTS arose. An old religion may seem hopeless in terms of a religious world view. Perhaps a religious language whose images are of camels, kings, and shepherds may not make contact with some people whose real world centers more around cars, congresses, and corporations.

A prophet may then arise to declare, here is a new religion revealed by GOD or a god who says the old ways are really true, but here are some ways of looking at the religion which show it is really compatible with the new science. Moreover, the central God of the old belief is now changing the world faster than before, and all the progress you see around you is really leading up to the KINGDOM OF GOD; have FAITH this is so. An example of this type in CHRISTIANITY would be SEVENTH-DAY ADVENTISM.

Note that the most successful new religions, like those in Japan (see JAPAN, NEW RELIGIONS OF), do not say everything in the former faith is false and bad. Rather, they will probably affirm the old, but put it all in a new light, so that people can say of the new teaching, "This was really true all the time, but we didn't realize it until now." It also must provide potent inward motivation for breaking with the past and meeting the new needs it has uncovered. This probably will be obtained through strong simplicity in leadership, organization, and practice. The new religion will likely have a single

powerful prophet and a close-knit organization, like a surrogate family, to counter-balance the natural inclination of people to remain with the old for the sake of family and community. It probably also will single out some simple, sure technique or practice—a method of PRAYER or MEDITATION, a dance or rite—that comes reassuringly out of the past, but also is strong enough to give people a powerful and immediate experience. Features like these will motivate people to spread the new teaching, and in a few cases the new religion will be successful enough to grow worldwide, like Mormonism (see LATTER-DAY SAINTS) or the Unification Church.

New religions are often controversial. Some have been regarded as dangerous "cults," (see CULTS AND SECTS, RELIGIOUS) a word that has come to suggest a religious movement that makes excessively high demands on its members' time, energy, and freedom of thought. At the same, most of the established religions of the world began with many of the characteristics of new religious movements.

New Testament   The second part of the BIBLE that Christians use; for Jews, the Bible consists of three parts, TORAH, PROPHETS, and Writings. Christians refer to the entire Hebrew scriptures as the Old Testament (see SCRIPTURES, HEBREW). To it, Christians add 27 books about JESUS and his earliest followers. These 27 books are called the New Testament.

THE FORMULATION OF THE NEW TESTAMENT

It took a little more than 300 years for Christians to put the New Testament into final form. The idea that some Christian writings were sacred seems to have arisen early. The book of 2 Peter (see PETER, EPISTLES OF) in the New Testament already refers to a collection of PAUL's letters. But the Gnostic teacher Marcion (mid-second century C.E.; see GNOSTICISM) seems to have been the first to suggest that there be an authoritative selection of Christian writings. As a Gnostic, Marcion rejected the Hebrew Bible because he thought that "the God of the Jews" was EVIL. He suggested replacing it with the letters of Paul and the gospel of Luke, both edited, however, because he thought they had been corrupted by pro-Jewish additions.

Christians who disagreed with Marcion responded by drawing up lists of books they accepted. The earliest known lists are the so-called Muratorian Fragment (late second century C.E.) and a list in the writings of Irenaeus, a bishop of Lyons, France (c. 200 C.E.). Both accept the four GOSPELS, the ACTS OF THE APOSTLES, thirteen letters of Paul, 1 and 2 JOHN, and REVELATION. They also accept books that were later rejected, such as 1 Clement and the Shepherd of Hermas.

The canon of the New Testament, that is, the authoritative list of accepted books, was first finalized in the Easter letter of bishop Athanasius of Alexandria in 367 C.E. He accepted the current set of 27 books. Other writers, such as bishop Eusebius of Caeserea, provide evidence that the inclusion of JAMES, Jude, 2 Peter, 2 and 3 John, Hebrews, and Revelation was questioned in the early fourth century. In the end, Christian authorities accepted into the canon only books that they thought were written by apostles and that were used in worship services by the major apostolic churches.

CONTENTS OF THE NEW TESTAMENT

The New Testament consists of several kinds of material: four gospels (Matthew, Mark, Luke, John); the book of Acts; letters from various apostles, especially the apostle Paul; and an apocalypse known as the Revelation to John.

Gospels

The gospels recount the words and deeds of Jesus. Strictly speaking, they are not biographies, for their purpose is to present not Jesus' life but the religious message about Jesus the MESSIAH. Matthew, Mark, and Luke are called "synoptic gospels" because they present in much the same way the story of Jesus' adult activities and his trial and crucifixion. They differ on Jesus' birth: Mark says nothing about it, while Matthew and Luke present two different stories. They also present the discovery of the empty tomb somewhat differently, and they differ a great deal in their accounts of Jesus' appearances after his RESURRECTION. John presents a different view of Jesus from those in the synoptic gospels. The events in John follow a different order, and John's Jesus reflects on large questions a great deal, especially questions about who he is. Famous examples include the "I am" sayings—for example, "I am the good shepherd"—and John 3.16: "For God so loved the world . . ." The names of the gospels are traditional. Many scholars think that Matthew, Mark, Luke, and John were not the actual writers of them.

Acts

The book of Acts is a sort of sequel. It continues the gospel attributed to Luke. It tells the history of the early church from the appearances of the risen Jesus to his followers, especially at Pentecost, to the arrival of the apostle Paul at Rome. The first part deals mainly with the disciples of Jesus at JERUSALEM. Among other things, it shows them wrestling with the question whether the messiahship of Jesus was just for Jews or whether it was for Gentiles, or non-Jews people, as well. The second part tells about Paul, who was not one of Jesus' disciples but who converted to CHRISTIANITY after persecuting Christians. Acts records several journeys that Paul made through Asia Minor (now Turkey) and Greece, spreading the message of Christianity farther and farther. Some passages in this part are in the first-person plural ("we") and may be from travel diaries that Paul's companion Luke kept.

Epistles of Paul

The apostle Paul wrote several letters to Christian churches in Asia Minor, Greece, and Rome. Tradition attributes 10 such letters to Paul. Scholars agree that most, if not all of them were written by him. Often Paul wrote to churches that he founded or visited. He gave them advice on what they should and should not do and answered their questions. For example, Christians at Thessalonika apparently wanted to know what happened to people who died before Jesus returned.

The letter to the Romans is a little different from the rest. Paul wrote it to Christians that he hoped to visit. It is extremely important, because in it Paul systematically presents his views, including those about the saving significance of Jesus' death and resurrection.

Other Epistles

Besides the epistles of Paul, the New Testament contains 11 other letters from the earliest years of Christianity. The letters to Titus and Timothy attributed to Paul are almost certainly not by him. They reflect how someone influenced by Paul would respond to situations that Paul himself could not yet have faced. Other letters include an anonymous letter to the Hebrews and letters attributed to James, Peter, John, and Jude. A major theme in these letters is how Christians should live.

The Revelation to John

The book of Revelation is an apocalypse (see APOCALYPTIC LITERATURE). The word *apocalypse* indicates that the book uncovers knowledge that is hidden. Early Christians wrote several apocalypses. The book of Revelation in the New Testament reports a vision received by John of Patmos. Opinions differ about whether this was the same John who wrote the gospel and the letters. In highly symbolic language Revelation tells of the heavenly struggle between the forces of God and the forces of Satan. Many of its images have become well known, such as the seven seals, the four horsemen, the whore of Babylon, the beast with the mark on its forehead, and the lake of fire. The book ends with an inspiring account of the new HEAVEN and new earth that God will create and a plea to Jesus to return soon.

THE TEXT OF THE NEW TESTAMENT

The books of the New Testament were originally written in Greek. None of the original manuscripts has survived, and the old texts that do survive are not all the same. Scholars known as textual critics try to reconstruct the lost originals as accurately as possible. The first person to do so was a Dutch scholar named Erasmus (1466–1536). He compared several Greek manuscripts to come up with what he considered the best reading. But the manuscripts Erasmus used were rather late. Discoveries within the past 200 years have helped scholars

do a better job. They include the oldest complete manuscripts of the New Testament, which date from the fourth and fifth centuries, as well as fragments of writing on papyrus, some of which are even earlier. In "critical editions" textual critics give their guess as to the best readings. They also provide the most important variations, telling which readings occur in which manuscripts. Most of the variations concern individual sentences. For example, some manuscripts add a sentence to the end of the Lord's Prayer in Matthew 6.13: "For yours is the kingdom, power, and glory forever, Amen." But the oldest complete manuscripts omit this sentence. A few variations concern entire sections. For example, two endings exist for the Gospel of Mark, but scholars think that neither of them was in the original.

Further reading: Raymond E. Brown, *Introduction to the New Testament* (New York: Doubleday, 1997); Michael D. Coogan et al., eds., *The New Oxford Annotated NRSV Bible with the Apocrypha,* 3d ed. (New York: Oxford University Press, 2001); Paula Fredriksen, *From Jesus to Christ: The Origins of the New Testament Images of Jesus,* 2d ed. (New Haven, Conn.: Yale University Press, 2000).

New Testament, apocryphal Books produced by early Christians that were not included in the NEW TESTAMENT. Early Christian communities produced a variety of books. Eventually, in the fourth century C.E., churches that stood in the tradition of Roman Catholicism and Eastern Orthodox Christianity came to agree on a standard list of authoritative books, known as a canon, for the New Testament. Books that they did not include make up the apocryphal New Testament. (Protestants [see PROTESTANTISM] also use the name Apocrypha for books in the Old Testament that they do not accept but that Catholics and Orthodox Christians do.)

The books in the apocryphal New Testament come from many sources. Some represent the views of the same communities that produced the books in the New Testament. Books like 1 Clement, the Shepherd of Hermas, and the Didache or

Teaching of the Twelve Apostles were once quite popular. They simply failed to meet the requirements for being included in the New Testament. For example, 1 Clement was written by an early pope (*see* PAPACY), not an APOSTLE.

Other books come from communities whose teachings are quite different from what we now consider CHRISTIANITY. Some represent views known as GNOSTICISM, an ancient religious movement that stressed salvation through secret knowledge, not FAITH. Others come from communities that we can no longer easily identify because they have been largely forgotten. Christians today may find the contents of these books odd, such as the stories they tell about JESUS and the sayings they attribute to him. Nevertheless, some people who considered themselves Christians at other times thought of these books as containing religious truth.

Like the New Testament itself, the New Testament apocrypha include many kinds of books: gospels, ACTS OF THE APOSTLES, epistles, sermons, apocalypses, and other kinds of writing thought to reveal divine truth. Many are ascribed to familiar apostles, such as James, John, Paul, Peter, Philip, and Thomas. Others are, unlike any of the books of the New Testament, associated with the names of prominent women: the Gospel of Mary (meaning MARY MAGDALENE), the Acts of Thecla (a companion of Paul), and even a gospel written by EVE. Still other books name the communities that used them, wrote them, or to whom they were addressed, such as the gospels of the Hebrews, the Egyptians, and the Ebionites and Paul's Letter to the Laodiceans and Third Letter to the Corinthians. Scholars today think that most if not all of these names are wrong. (That is true for many books in the New Testament, too.) They were most likely given by the writers to make the books seem authoritative. Most of the writings date to the second century C.E., although some scholars have placed the Gospel of THOMAS in the first century.

It is difficult to generalize about the content of all of these books. They allegedly recount the childhood of Jesus or the secret teachings of Jesus, or they simply portray a different Jesus than is described in the New Testament. The various books of Acts tell tales, some of them rather tall tales, about the apostles; among them, however, are traditions that are rather widely known, such as the story in the Acts of Peter that he was crucified upside down. One epistle, ascribed to Titus, urges Christians to avoid sexual relations altogether, even if they are married. (Sexual abstinence was, in fact, common among early Christians.) The Apocalypse of Peter contains vivid descriptions of heaven and hell.

Although Christian churches today do not accept these books as authoritative, they cast interesting light on the diversity of views that counted as Christian before Christianity defined itself officially during the fourth and fifth centuries.

New Thought movement

New Thought movement A popular American spiritual movement emphasizing the fundamental importance of the mind in creating what each of us sees as real and the power of thought to affect healing and success. Beginning as a distinctive movement in the late 19th century, New Thought had roots in the long-standing idealist tradition of philosophy, which says that mind or consciousness is the basic reality. What we call the world is, for the idealist, a projection out of consciousness, whether from the mind of God or from that of the individual. New Thought's immediate background was the 19th century revival of this tradition by German idealist philosophers and their counterparts in New England Transcendentalism, especially Ralph Waldo Emerson.

The New Thought spiritual movement, sometimes called "mind-cure" or "metaphysical" religion, went a step further. Its founders, including Phineas Quimby (1802–66) and Emma Curtis Hopkins (1853–1925), were not content just to say theoretically that mind is all but wanted also to show how the supreme power of mind can be employed on behalf of health, happiness, and prosperity. It was a time when America was changing, growing, and prospering as new technologies and new opportunities appeared. To some, it seemed that ways of thinking should change too, in order to be open to new endless possibilities and unleash the power to realize them. It was religion for an optimistic, confident society and for people who wanted to feel that way too.

New Thought stresses that God and his world are wholly good and that it is only our negative thinking that keeps us from seeing and appreciating this. But if we truly believe that we can be perfectly healthy or that our legitimate goals in life can be realized, then we are already well on our way to health and success. To focus thought in this way, advocates urge meditation or concentration, sometimes recommending chantlike affirmations as well.

New Thought produced several small religious denominations, including the Church of Divine Science, the Church of Religious Science, and Unity. Note the frequent use of the word *science* in New Thought; its practitioners say that their approach is based on a scientific knowledge of how thought works, not merely on blind faith.

CHRISTIAN SCIENCE, although obviously closely related to New Thought, does not consider itself part of the New Thought movement. It says that although New Thought teaches the power of thought to heal and change reality, the Christian Science teaching of Mary Baker Eddy (1821–1910) declares instead that there never was anything wrong with reality or ourselves; it is only our erroneous thoughts that were at fault.

Numerous other "inspirational" speakers and books, some of them best-sellers, clearly have sources in the movement. In the mid-20th century, Norman Vincent Peale (1898–1993) was widely known. Although he was a minister in mainline denominations, his books, such as *The Power of Positive Thinking, Guide to Confident Living, The Tough-Minded Optimist,* and *You Can If You Think You Can,* virtually sum up the New Thought message in their titles alone. Over and over, with the help of simple slogans and homespun anecdotes, Peale presented his method for successful living: Set goals, believe you can accomplish them, do not give way to the mental drainage of gloomy, defeatist thoughts. His tradition is continued in the "possibility thinking" of Robert Schuller of the Crystal Cathedral in California. Other important 20th-century New Thought teachers have been Emmet Fox,

Joel Goldsmith, and Charles and Myrtle Fillmore of Unity.

Further reading: Charles S. Braden, *Spirits in Rebellion: The Rise and Development of New Thought,* Rpt. (Dallas, Tex.: Southern Methodist University Press, 1987); Donald Meyer, *The Positive Thinkers* (New York: Pantheon, 1980); Norman Vincent Peale, *The Power of Positive Thinking,* Rpt. (New York: Simon & Schuster, 2003).

New Year festivals   Religious commemorations of the beginning of a new year. In virtually all traditional cultures, the change from an old year to a new year is a time of religious significance. Sometimes it is celebrated, as in the modern Western calendar, on the first of January, shortly after the winter solstice. Or it may come, as in the Chinese calendar, around the beginning of spring, or as in the Jewish calendar, in the fall. In any case, the commencement of a new year signifies something like a miniature recreation of the world, when the old dissolves and a fresh start is made. It may also be seen as a time of conflict between old and new, or between different kinds of fortune for the next year. The colorful ceremonies that mark New Year's Day around the world all reflect themes like these.

New Year's Eve may be seen as a time for partying and "letting go," because it is like the old year or world returning to chaos before being made again. It is also a time, as in traditional China, for paying debts, cleaning the house thoroughly, and sending off the kitchen god with a bit of honey on his painted lips to sweeten his mood as he goes to heaven to report to the supreme gods on the family's conduct over the past year. In China also, New Year's Day means honoring ancestors, reestablishing family bonds by paying calls, and a parade in which a great dragon weaves through the streets—the dragon being a symbol of *yang,* the male energy of sun and growth whose half of the year then begins. Elsewhere, New Year's Day may be symbolized by lighting a new fire, eating new foods, or (as in Wales) sprinkling fresh water on houses. In many cultures, from England to Japan, New Year's Day has been thought of as a time when—it being a time of turning—the gateways to the other world opened a bit, and mysterious gods and spirits could come through, and ancestors might return in spirit to visit. Sometimes costumes are worn to personify these entities by celebrators going from door to door. This may also be the ultimate ancestor of the tradition of new year parades, like the famous Rose Parade in Pasadena, California.

On a more serious note, the start of the new year is a time for repenting of things done wrong in the past, and for making resolutions to help one do better in the future. The theme of conflict between old and new, or between two sides, on New Year's Day is reflected in the practice of new year contests, whether tug-of-war as in some places in Japan, or the football bowl games in the United States. In all, New Year's Day is a time, though now often secularized, that has had deep religious meaning in its past.

Nichiren (1222–1282) *Japanese Buddhist priest and reformer* Nichiren was born to a poor fishing family in a village called Kominato, northeast of the present location of Tokyo. Despite his lowly background, he received an education in a local Buddhist temple. From the age of 16, he traveled widely from one temple and school of BUDDHISM to another, seeking truth. It was a time of much conflict and fighting in Japan, and of the rise of new, simplified forms of Buddhism. This caused Nichiren to be particularly worried about two questions: Why, in the civil wars then going on in Japan, did armies often lose despite all the PRAYERS and ceremonies offered on their behalf by Buddhist priests? and, How can I be sure that I am myself saved?

Nichiren finally decided that the answers lay in the power of the LOTUS SUTRA, a great Buddhist text, which had been regarded as the most important of all by the Tendai school of Buddhism in which he had been raised. But Nichiren said it was now the only scripture; all the others were outdated.

Trust in it and it alone would bring success here and now, he said, whether for armies and the nation or for individuals; that trust was also one's only sure hope for salvation. The *Lotus Sutra* was not just to be read, but chanted and worshipped for the power that lay in its very words. Nichiren taught people a recitation called the *Daimoku*. It consists of the words *Namu myoho renge-kyo* ("Hail the marvelous teaching of the *Lotus Sutra*") chanted rapidly. The chant is best done in front of a shrine called the *Gohonzon*, a rectangular sheet of paper bearing the words of the Daimoku and the names of some figures from the *Lotus Sutra*. Nichiren Buddhists today find this a very effective form of prayer.

Nichiren believed that all Japan must accept his FAITH in the *Lotus Sutra*. He denounced other religions as false, but said that if Japan as a whole would turn to the *Lotus*, it would be blessed and would be a center of light for the world. He believed that Japan's famous Mount Fuji represented the mountain on which the Buddha had originally delivered the *Lotus Sutra* as a sermon. On the other hand, if the nation rejected the *Lotus Sutra*, he said, many disasters would befall it. He pointed to a series of calamities around him: earthquakes, drought, famine, epidemics. He also predicted that Japan would be invaded from outside, and claimed to have been right when the Mongols came in 1268. But Japan was saved in that fateful year by a typhoon (called the *kamikaze*, "divine wind") that destroyed the enemy's fleet; Nichiren said this was because at least some Japanese had accepted his preaching.

Nichiren's teaching created much opposition. He was twice exiled and once sentenced to death; legend has it that he was spared the death sentence at the last minute, when the executioner's sword was struck by lightning. But he started a religious movement, Nichiren Buddhism, which has had an important role in Japanese history and has grown rapidly in the 20th century in the form of some of the largest of the new religions of Japan (*see* JAPAN, NEW RELIGIONS IN), especially SOKA GAKKAI.

nirvana Sanskrit for "blowing out"; in BUDDHISM, the blowing out of the flames of craving that are responsible for continued rebirth. Nirvana is the goal for which Buddhists strive. Paradoxically, it too can become an object of craving. In that case the craving for nirvana is an obstacle to be overcome.

THERAVADA BUDDHISM, the form of Buddhism common in southeast Asia, distinguishes two forms of nirvana. These are called nirvana with and nirvana without a "substrate" (roughly a base made up of mental and physical elements). Nirvana with a substrate is the nirvana of the person whose passions have been blown out but who remains in the body until the consequences of earlier, craving-motivated action (KARMA) work themselves out. It is described as a calm, cool bliss, beyond happiness and sadness. When the final flickers of karma go out, one enters parinirvana, that is, the ultimate nirvana, nirvana without a substrate.

Theravada Buddhism teaches that there is no permanent self, and this leads to a very pointed question: Does a person continue to exist after entering parinirvana? The Buddha refused to answer this question. He said it did "not lead to edification." It simply distracted the questioner from seeking nirvana.

Thinkers in the tradition of MAHAYANA BUDDHISM disagree with the Theravada analysis of nirvana. Following the lead of the great thinker Nagarjuna, they generally maintain that all distinctions are ultimately empty, including the distinction between nirvana and SAMSARA, that is, the realm of continued rebirth. That is to say that nirvana is not a separate state of existence that one enters; it is simply perceiving the world as it is, apart from our grasping and attachment. In addition, Mahayana Buddhists generally reject the idea that nirvana is a goal that individuals pursue for themselves. Rather, motivated by compassion, they stress nirvana's communal aspect. In the words of a BODHISATTVA vow: "I cannot be happy unless all sentient beings are happy."

Noah In the BIBLE and the QUR'AN, the patriarch who survived the universal flood together with his wife and family. All living human beings are said to be his descendants.

There are several parallels to Noah in the world's religions. The Sumerian Utnapishtim, the Akkadian Atrahasis, and the Indian MANU were also said to have survived a universal flood.

As the Bible tells the story (Genesis 6–9), GOD decided to destroy the Earth because of its wickedness. The barriers that kept the primal waters above the sky and below the Earth gave way, and a great flood ensued. But Noah, a righteous man, and his family had built an ark (boat) according to God's specifications. In it, they and representative animals survived.

When the waters receded, God made a COVENANT with human beings. He promised never to send another flood, and he sealed his promise with the rainbow. He also granted human beings permission to eat meat for the first time. Shortly thereafter, Noah planted a vineyard. At harvest time, he made wine, got drunk, and disgraced himself.

According to Jewish tradition, all human beings are to observe the covenant made with Noah. The later covenant made with MOSES is binding only on Jews. According to Christian tradition, Noah and his family in the ark prefigure the saving of Christians through the waters of BAPTISM (1 Peter 3.20–22). Muslims hold that Nuh (Noah) was the first prophet through whom God punished people for their SINS. They may recite his story when they begin a journey, for example, Mecca (see MECCA, PILGRIMAGE TO).

Nordic religion The pre-Christian religion of Scandinavia, including Iceland. Nordic religion was part of a larger religious complex known as Germanic religion that consists of the pre-Christian religious beliefs and practices of peoples who spoke languages known as Germanic. In the southern Germanic regions, such as England and Germany today, people converted to Christianity relatively early. Germanic speakers further north converted later: the Danes in the 900s, the Icelanders around 1000, the Norwegians slightly later, and the Swedes by 1100. As a result, more is known about their pre-Christian religious beliefs and practices.

Several sources provide information about Nordic religion. One of the most important is early Icelandic literature: the Eddas and skaldic poetry. The single most important early Icelandic writer is Snorri Sturluson (1179–1241). These early writings tell stories about the gods, but it is often difficult to separate pre-Christian from post-Christian elements. Other sources that provide information about Nordic religion include archaeological excavations, inscriptions written in runes, ancient artwork, and writings by outside observers such as Adam of Bremen and Saxo Grammaticus.

Nordic stories identify two groups of gods, the Aesir (generally military gods) and the Vanir (generally fertility gods). In the distant past these two groups fought with one another, but they then made peace. Another story tells how the trickster god, LOKI, engineered the death of the god Balder, the son of Odin (known as WOTAN further south). When Balder was born, his mother, Frigg, had made him invincible against all the weapons she named. She did not mention the wood of the mistletoe. Balder died from an arrow of mistletoe.

Nordic speakers told different stories about the creation of the world. According to one of these stories, which resembles one found in a famous hymn of the Rig VEDA, the world came from the killing and dismembering of a giant named Ymir. Perhaps best known of all Nordic stories, however, are those about the end of the world, called Ragnarok. At that time, the god Odin, the highest god, will die in battling against the wolf Fenrir. (The spirits of slain human warriors who have been living with him in his castle, Valhalla, will join him in the battle.) The god THOR will die battling the serpent who surrounds the world, Jörmungand. The cosmic ash tree, Yggdrasill, at whose foot the well of wisdom sits, will shake and perhaps fall. The sun will go out, the sky will go black, and the earth will sink beneath the ocean. This will not, however, be the true end. The earth will rise again and peace will be restored.

Animal and sometimes human SACRIFICE played a major role in Nordic religion. For example, a well-known carving in Sweden shows a man being hanged on a tree, apparently a sacrifice to Odin. Sacrifices originally took place at outdoor sanctuaries, such as rocks and waterfalls. Eventually Nordic peoples built wooden temples, perhaps because of Christian influence. A particularly fine temple is said to have been in the city of Uppsala in Sweden. No Nordic temple has survived, but perhaps they looked like wooden stave churches in the region today.

Archaeology tells us about Nordic burial practices. Particularly well-known are tombs that include ships. Some Nordic people may have thought that death involved a journey to the west across the sea. Others seem to have located the afterlife in the far north or in an underworld. Nordic people sometimes called the realm of the dead Hel. They did not, however, conceive of it as a place of punishment, the way Christians have traditionally conceived of HELL.

During the last 200 years there has been much interest in Nordic religion. Not all of this interest has been beneficial. For example, some Nazis studied Nordic religion because they saw it as the true religion of the Aryan peoples. Speakers of English are familiar with more benign survivals of Nordic religion. The names for Tuesday, Wednesday, Thursday, and Friday derive from the Nordic gods Tyr, Odin (Wotan), Thor, and Frigg, respectively.

See also ARCTIC RELIGIONS.

Further reading: Brian Branston, *The Lost Gods of England* (London: Constable, 1993); H. R. Ellis Davidson, *Myths and Symbols in Pagan Europe: Early Scandinavian and Celtic Religions* (Manchester, U.K.: Manchester University Press, 1988); Peter Berresford Ellis, *A Brief History of the Druids* (London: Robinson, 2002); E. O. G. Turville-Petre, *Myth and Religion of the North: The Religion of Ancient Scandinavia* (New York: Holt, Rinehart & Winston, 1964).

occultism and esotericism   Spiritual doctrines and practices that are considered secret. The word "occult" means hidden, and "esoteric" means within, in the sense of something concealed within something else. In the context of religious traditions, these more or less overlapping terms refer to teachings and practices that are not widely given out, but kept within a select circle. One example would be MANTRAS (sacred words) and mudras (sacred gestures) in HINDUISM and BUDDHISM, which are passed on from a guru or teacher to a disciple at the latter's initiation. Another would be in JUDAISM, the special symbolic meaning given Hebrew words and even letters in the scriptures by students of the tradition known as KABBALAH. Ancient GNOSTICISM is sometimes considered an esoteric version of CHRISTIANITY. There are also occult and esoteric systems of thought and practice not closely tied to any major religion; in the West, a group of ancient teachings such as ASTROLOGY, ALCHEMY, palmistry, and MAGIC are often collectively labeled occultism. What these and all so-called occult or esoteric teachings tend to have in common is a belief in subtle cause-and-effect relationships or "correspondences." These relationships are not easily understood until one is ready to understand them. In occultism, they may be between humanity and some aspect of the universe; for example, between a gemstone and a particular mood, or between the position of the planets and the course of one's life.

Teachings and practices can be occult or esoteric for several reasons. Sometimes, of course, a group wants to keep its secrets close for reasons of wealth and power. It may also be that it honestly believes a spiritual perception or technique is too powerful to be widely known; it would be dangerous in the wrong hands, and should be imparted only to one who has been carefully prepared through training and initiation. It may be considered that it could not really be understood by one who knows only the words, but has not had the experiences to go with it, just as a child cannot really understand what it is like to be adult until she or he has gone through some years of growth and change, or one cannot understand higher mathematics until one has studied the basics.

Thus, it may be claimed, occult secrets just cannot be grasped without background knowledge. Books on calculus are not exactly kept hidden; they can be found in any good library or bookstore. But if one has not had the necessary preliminary training in arithmetic and algebra, they might as well be hidden. Occultists would say that some inner teachings of the spiritual life are like that. In fact, today books on many things supposedly occult, from the lore of the stars to the lore of gemstones, are widely available, and occult orders offering initiations advertise in popular magazines. The consumer must cautiously decide what their teachings are worth. At the same time, deeper occult secrets about the relation of humanity to the universe may be hidden at the heart of all the great spiritual traditions.

Oceanic religion   *See* PACIFIC OCEAN RELIGIONS.

om   The most sacred syllable in HINDUISM. Hindus consider the syllable *om* a symbol of primal totality—the whole that contains all things—and the most important of all MANTRAS or sacred sounds. They intone or chant it at the beginning and end of prayers and religious recitations, among other occasions. It is known as *pranava*, "humming," and *ekakshara*, "the one syllable."

It is customary to say that the syllable *om* contains three sounds, *a, u,* and *m*. As a result, it is sometimes written "aum" in English. The three sounds stand for very many things, including the three parts of the universe (earth, atmosphere, sky) and the three major gods (BRAHMA, VISHNU, SIVA). The most philosophical interpretation says that the three sounds stand for the three states of consciousness: waking consciousness, dreaming consciousness, and sleep without dreams. It also says that the silence that follows the syllable stands for the fourth state, the indescribable source of all that exists (*see* BRAHMAN).

The symbol that Hindus use for *om* (ॐ) has become well known in North America. It is found on T-shirts, CD covers, skateboards, and tattoos, to name just a few places. Many Hindus, however, find the way that American popular culture uses this, their most sacred symbol, disrespectful. People using the symbol for *om* should remember that to many people it is a sacred symbol that should not be used just for fun.

ordination   A RITUAL that appoints a person to a religious office. North Americans usually associate ordination with Christian rituals that make someone a priest or minister. Roman Catholic and Orthodox Christians think of ordination as a SACRAMENT. But other religious groups ordain, too. Jews ordain rabbis. Some people speak of ordination when Buddhists become MONKS AND NUNS. Used broadly, ordination can be applied to virtually every religion.

In ancient times, Jews and Christians ordained in the same way, by "laying on hands." Those with authority would place their hands on top of the head of the person to be ordained. But Jewish and Christian ordination developed differently. Jews stopped laying on hands. They instead presented rabbis with certificates testifying to their office.

Then, in the 20th century, Jews revived the ancient practice. In the Middle Ages, Christians not only retained the ancient practice, they also elaborated on it. They presented the person being ordained with many symbols of office, such as special clothes and a staff. During the REFORMATION, Protestants simplified the ritual once again or eliminated it altogether.

In the past, Jews and Christians only ordained men to the rabbinate and ministry. In the 20th century, more liberal groups began to ordain women, too. At the end of the 20th and beginning of the 21st century many Buddhist women, too, were attempting to reestablish the order of nuns in areas where it had died out, such as the Theravada countries of southeast Asia.

Orphism   A religious movement in ancient Greece associated with the mythical singer Orpheus. Orphism seems to have arisen in the area around Athens in the sixth century B.C.E. It was also practiced in southern Italy and in the region of the Black Sea, regions in which the Greeks had colonies. Orpheus and Orphism are depicted in scenes painted on vases, mentioned in references in writers such as Plato and ancient poems that go by its name, and represented in a few recent archaeological discoveries. Although knowledge of Orphism is limited, these sources reveal some things about Orphic practices and teachings.

People who followed Orphism were strict vegetarians: They ate no meat (*see* DIET AND RELIGION). What is more, they refused to SACRIFICE animals to the gods. Such sacrifices were part of the festivals that held Greek states together, but according to Plato the Orphics gave the gods only honey-soaked cakes and fruit.

Orpheus, whom they followed, was said to have come from Thrace, that is, far northern Greece. A famed singer, he could charm wild beasts. When his wife Eurydice died of a snakebite, he went to the underworld and won her release. He was told not to look at her until they reached the surface of the earth. Unfortunately, he violated this instruction and lost her forever. It is said that, faithful to his dead wife, Orpheus rejected advances made by women of Thrace known as *Bassarae*. He died when, in wild rituals devoted to Dionysos, the *Bassarae* ripped him to pieces.

The Orphics also told a story about the origins of human beings. The Titans, who were wicked, ate the god Dionysos. In anger ZEUS slew the Titans with his thunderbolt and made human beings from the ashes. This story teaches that human beings have a divine core (Dionysos) trapped by evil (the Titans). Indeed, according to Plato the Orphics taught that the body was the prison of the soul. They may have also believed in rebirth. Orphic religious practices seem to have aimed at freeing the soul from its prison and at avoiding punishments in the underworld after death.

Osiris   A god of ancient Egypt identified with the dead Pharaoh or king. The worship of Osiris goes back to the third millennium (3000–2001) B.C.E.

Our best account of the stories of Osiris comes from the Greek writer Plutarch, who lived in the late first to early second century C.E. According to him, Osiris's wicked brother and rival, Seth, tricked Osiris, killed him, and eventually cut his body into 14 pieces, which he scattered here and there. Osiris's wife, Isis, searched for and managed to find all of the pieces except for the sexual organs. She reassembled them and brought Osiris back to life as the god of the underworld. Then the assembly of the gods decided that HORUS, the son of Osiris, should be king in his place. In accordance with the wishes of Isis, however, they did not put Seth to death.

In the earliest times that we know of, Osiris was identified with the dead king and so was the ruler of the dead. By about the year 2000 B.C.E., large numbers of Egyptians came to believe that ordinary dead people could also become Osiris and attain immortality after death. To do so, they had to perform the right RITUALS. These rituals prepared them for a test after death, when their hearts would be weighed in a balance against a feather, which stood for truth. Much later still, after Alex-

ander of Macedon's conquests (Alexander the Great, 336–323 B.C.E.), the cult of Osiris combined with that of Apis, a sacred bull that was kept in Memphis; when the bull died, it was mummified and a new bull was chosen. The result was a god known as Serapis. The worship of this god spread throughout the Mediterranean world as one of the MYSTERY RELIGIONS.

Artwork often shows Osiris as a mummy with arms crossed. Despite the connection with the bull, the later Serapis was imaged as a seated, majestic male, modeled on the image of Zeus. The most popular Osiris temple was at the Egyptian town of Abydos. There the road along which a procession traveled during the Osiris festival became a popular place to be buried.

Further reading: Ruth Schumann Antelme and Stéphane Rossini, *Becoming Osiris: The Ancient Egyptian Death Experience*, trans. Jon Graham (Rochester, Vt.: Inner Traditions, 1998); Plutarch, *Moralia*, vol. 5, Loeb Classical Library (Cambridge, Mass.: Harvard University Press, 1960); Ian Shaw, *Ancient Egypt: A Very Short Introduction* (New York: Oxford University Press, 2004).

Otto, Rudolf (1869–1937) *influential German theologian, philosopher, and historian of religions* Otto taught Protestant theology at the universities of Göttingen, Breslau, and Marburg. His major concern was to analyze the experiences that, he said, made all religion possible. He did so, especially in his best-selling book, *The Idea of the Holy* (1917).

According to Otto, religion depends upon a human experience that is unlike any other. To refer to this experience, he coined the word "numinous."

Otto analyzed the numinous experience in terms of three moments. As *mysterium*, it totally transcends human understanding and evokes a response of silent dumbfoundedness. As tremendum, it appears as overpowering and majestic and evokes a response of trembling and a feeling of creatureliness. As *fascinans*, the numinous appears as gracious and merciful and evokes a response of love.

P

Pacific Ocean religions The religions of the peoples who lived on Pacific islands before Europeans arrived. This area is sometimes called Oceania. Its religions are sometimes called Oceanic religions.

The Pacific Ocean contains more than 10,000 islands. Some are immense, for example, New Guinea and the islands of New Zealand. Others are extremely small. The islands stretch from New Guinea in the west to Easter Island in the east, from the Hawaiian Islands in the north to New Zealand in the south. The eastern half of this region is called Polynesia. The northwestern quarter is called Micronesia. The southwestern quarter is called Melanesia.

People first settled in New Guinea 20,000 to 30,000 years ago. They only began to settle Micronesia and Polynesia much later, perhaps around 2000 B.C.E. The islands at the far extremes—the Hawaiian Islands, Easter Island, New Zealand—were settled even later, roughly 500 to 1000 C.E. In general, the islands of Polynesia are more productive than those of Melanesia and Micronesia. As a result, Polynesians, unlike Melanesians and Micronesians, developed complex hierarchies of social classes. Chiefs and kings are very important figures in Polynesian religions. They are not so important farther west.

The islands have their own languages, cultures, and religions. Any attempt to describe "the religion" of the islands is bound to fail. But some features did appear in many different places.

Pacific Ocean islanders paid attention to a variety of spiritual beings, sometimes called spirits in English, and sometimes called gods. Some beings bore goodwill to people; others bore ill will. Some were the souls of the departed. Most islanders had elaborate ideas of what happened to the soul after death. It journeyed, sometimes to the underworld, sometimes to the upperworld, and sometimes to a distant island.

Pacific islanders provided scholars with classic examples of INITIATION rituals. They also had elaborate ceremonies for the dead. Some of the ceremonies involved beautiful artwork. The body of the dead received careful attention. Sometimes it was buried temporarily; sometimes it was exposed. The bones of the dead often became important RITUAL objects.

Most Pacific islanders used MAGIC of some sort in their daily life. Many societies also had magical specialists. These were often men. But in many places people sought out women for help in healing and in furthering love relationships.

Polynesia gave the English-speaking world the words mana and TABOO. Things as well as persons could have mana. The word referred to a powerful religious state. Such states were also *tabu,* that is, they required persons to observe special prohibitions.

Some Pacific Island societies were matrilineal and matrilocal, that is, people traced their descent through their mothers, rather than their fathers, and they lived with their mothers' families. Nevertheless, Pacific island religions remained strongly male-centered. That was true even of religions in which goddesses were prominent. In western parts of the region, religion was the secret preserve of adult men. They found the presence of women polluting and therefore threatening.

By the beginning of the 21st century, few if any Pacific Ocean religions survived in traditional form. Christian MISSIONARIES had converted the entire area. During the 19th and 20th centuries, Pacific Ocean islanders also developed distinct rituals known as CARGO CULTS. These cults sought to make their followers prosperous in material goods. They often taught that "white men," (their ancestors) were going to bring them material goods as gifts.

pacifism, religious Refusal, motivated by religious principles, to engage in acts of violence or war. Nonreligious people have embraced pacifism, too, and religious people may adopt pacifism for reasons other than religious ones. But the world's religions have given rise to some of the most important traditions of pacifism (*see, however,* WAR AND RELIGION).

Extremely influential traditions of religious pacifism derive from ancient India. Religious pacifism in its fullest form may be found in JAINISM. Jains advocate complete AHIMSA or noninjury. In pursuing this ideal, Jains avoid all violence against other human beings. They even refuse to consider any statements to be absolutely true. To do so, they say, would injure those who see the world differently than they do.

BUDDHISM arose at the same time as Jainism. It, too, embraces the ideal of ahimsa. Some claim that there is no justification within Buddhism for war of any kind. One well-known example of Buddhist pacifism from ancient times is the emperor ASOKA. Early in life he finished the conquest of India that his ancestors had begun. But the conquest was so bloody that in remorse, it is said, Asoka adopted Buddhism and renounced violence. Today Buddhists are very active in promoting peace. Organizations that do so in North America include the Buddhist Peace Fellowship and the Zen Peacemaker Order. Influential Buddhist spokespersons for peace include the Vietnamese monk Thich Nhat Hanh (b. 1926) and the DALAI LAMA (b. 1935).

JUDAISM, CHRISTIANITY, and ISLAM have also had pacifist movements. In one sense Judaism and Islam share an ideal of peace, known as shalom in Hebrew and salaam in Arabic. Their histories, however, have led them to pursue this ideal differently. Some parts of the Hebrew scriptures celebrate brutal, religiously motivated warfare (*see* SCRIPTURES, HEBREW). Rabbinical Judaism, however, has traditionally emphasized witnessing to God's truth in the face of oppression and not responding to violence with violence. Throughout much of history, then, Jews have been pacifists. One exception to this rule was the actions of some Jewish terrorists leading up to the founding of the state of Israel.

Unlike Jews, Muslims have often held political power. Furthermore, many have seen the QUR'AN as teaching that Muslims are required to defend Islam by military means, if necessary. This view of JIHAD has led some people, including scholars, to assert that Islamic pacifism is impossible. Nevertheless, Muslims known as Sufis (*see* SUFISM) have often taken jihad to be not a military but a personal struggle against temptation. Moreover, Abdul Ghaffar Khan (1890–1988), a leader in the movement that led to the creation of Pakistan, was a staunch Muslim, a close personal friend of Mohandas GANDHI, and an advocate of unconditional nonviolence. He saw no contradiction between pacifism and Islam. Today many Muslims, like many other people around the world, actively work for peace.

Among Christians pacifism has often characterized outsider movements—small groups that have broken away from the Christian mainstream. In the Middle Ages both the WALDENSIANS, members of a 12th-century movement in southern France condemned as heretics, and the followers of John Wycliffe (c. 1320–84) were pacifists. Anabaptist groups that arose during the Reformation and later, like the MENNONITES, AMISH, and Brethren, are pacifists. So, too, are members of the Society of Friends, often known as QUAKERS. A famous example was William Penn (1644–1718), who refused to use violence against native Americans. In the past 100 years Christian pacifists in the United States have opposed war, such as the war in Vietnam. They have also advocated that countries disarm. Many Christians, however, reject pacifism. They prefer a theory that justifies certain kinds of war, the "just war theory."

Perhaps the most prominent religious pacifist in the last 100 years was a Hindu, Mohandas K. Gandhi (1869–1948), often known as the Mahatma. Gandhi advocated what he called "soul-force" rather than "body-force." The goal, he said, was to persuade opponents of the truth, not to coerce them by using or threatening to use violence. Those who use soul-force, however, must be prepared to suffer or even die. Although he was a Hindu, Gandhi received inspiration from non-Hindu sources, such as the Sermon on the Mount in the gospel of Matthew and the writings of Leo Tolstoy (1828–1910). Gandhi's ideas profoundly influenced the American civil rights leader Martin Luther KING Jr. (1929–1968), among others.

Further reading: Peter Brock, *Varieties of Pacifism: A Survey from Antiquity to the Outset of the Twentieth Century,* 4th ed. (Syracuse, N.Y.: Syracuse University Press, 1998); *A Call to Conscience: The Landmark Speeches of Dr. Martin Luther King Jr.,* ed. Clayborne Carson and Kris Shepard (New York: Warner Books, 2001); Eknath Easwaran, *Nonviolent Soldier of Islam: Badshah Khan, A Man to Match His Mountains,* 2d ed. (Tomales, Calif.: Nilgiri Press, 1999); *The Essential Gandhi: An Anthology of His Writings on His Life, Work, and Ideas,* ed. Louis Fischer, 2d ed. (New York: Vintage Books, 2002); David R. Smock, *Perspectives on Pacifism: Christian, Jewish, and Muslim Views on Nonviolence and International Conflict* (Washington, D.C.: United States Institute of Peace Press, 1995); Thich Nhat Hanh, *Being Peace,* ed. Arnold Kotler (Berkeley, Calif.: Parallax Press, 1987).

Paganism, Modern Contemporary movements that have tried to revive or reconstruct in a way appropriate to today's world the religious style of the ancient or pre-Christian world. Modern Paganism, or Neo-Paganism, includes groups that base their spiritual practices on the religion of the ancient Egyptians, Greeks, Celts, and Nordic peoples. Increasingly, themes from non-European cultures, African, Asian, and Native American, have found their way into Modern Paganism as well. A substantial part of Modern Paganism is Wicca, or WITCHCRAFT, which tends to be eclectic, adapting ideas and RITUALS from many sources or creating its own. (Modern Wiccans emphasize that their witchcraft has none of the negative connotations sometimes associated with the word but is entirely a benign, nature-oriented faith.)

Modern Paganism has sources in folklore, romanticism, and a few early revivals, especially in England. But as a major movement it is essentially a product of the 1960s and the great spiritual upheaval of that era. Many people found themselves alienated from conventional Western religion and sought a way closer to nature and its cycles, sensitive to feminism and the spiritual equality of men and women, and bearing a romantic sense of identity with the distant past. The colorful participatory rituals characteristic of Modern Paganism, featuring circle dances, rich robes, and attractive offerings of fruit and flowers, appealed to dwellers in stark modern cities. These dramatic rites evoke an immediate sense of sacred space and time that makes religious reality more tangible for some than do the services of ordinary churches and temples.

What are some major themes of Modern Paganism? First, the desire to be in close touch spiritually with nature. Many rituals are outdoors, if possible in natural woodland settings, and harmonize with the turning of the seasons. The solstices and equinoxes are significant ritual times. Many Neo-Pagans are concerned with current ecological issues, seeing them as having an important spiritual dimension. Many believe deeply that nature is infused with divinity, perhaps with spirits still in trees, hills, and springs as in ancient times. They see their belief as a new cosmic religion oriented to the tides of nature rather than to events and persons in human history.

Second, they emphasize the importance of the feminine as well as the masculine in the divine. Some are worshippers of the GODDESS, the Great Mother, as well as of GOD. Some Wiccan groups, called Dianic (*see* DIANA), are entirely made up of women. Those that are composed of both men and women usually have equal parts for both genders, as priests and priestesses or as participants. To them this is an important corrective to the male-centered practices in many conventional religions.

Third, many Pagans, as they revive the gods and goddesses of ancient times, see them as representing parts of themselves and thus helping them understand themselves. Often deities are viewed as archetypes, as in the psychology of Carl Gustav JUNG. If Pagans accept POLYTHEISM, belief in many gods and goddesses, that belief reflects their sense of the divine's nuance and complexity both in nature and in themselves.

Modern Paganism has no central organization but is expressed through numerous local groups. Many are now linked through Pagan Internet sites. Estimates of the number of Modern Pagans in the United States vary widely.

Further reading: Margot Adler, *Drawing Down the Moon: Witches, Druids, Goddess-Worshippers and Other Pagans in America* (New York: Penguin USA, 1997); Sarah Pike, *Earthly Bodies, Magical Selves: Contemporary Pagans and the Search for Community* (Berkeley: University of California Press, 2001); Starhawk, *The Spiral Dance: A Rebirth of the Ancient Religion of the Goddess* (San Francisco: HarperSanFrancisco, 1999).

papacy, the The institution that governs the Roman Catholic Church. The papacy centers on a man known as the Pope. (Women are not allowed to hold this office.) The word comes from the medieval Latin word *papa*, which means "father." In ROMAN CATHOLICISM the Pope is the bishop of Rome. According to Roman Catholic teachings, he is superior to all other bishops. Therefore, he should govern the church throughout the world. The congregations that acknowledge his supremacy make up the Roman Catholic Church. In addition to governing this church, the Pope also rules a small territory in Rome known as Vatican City. He is assisted by an administrative unit, known as the Curia, and the College of CARDINALS, whose members he appoints. He also appoints the heads of the regional churches throughout the world. They are known as bishops.

The papacy's claims to power go back to the NEW TESTAMENT. There JESUS tells PETER that he is the rock upon which the church will be built (Matthew 16.18–19). He also gives Peter the power to forgive SINS on Earth, or not, as he chooses. According to Roman Catholic tradition, Peter was the first Pope. He passed down to future popes the powers that Jesus had given to him. In the view of the Roman Catholic Church, the Pope is the vicar of CHRIST on Earth. He sits on the throne of Peter. According to a controversial decree of the First VATICAN COUNCIL (1869–70), the Pope is infallible. That means that when he speaks on matters of church teaching or practice, he cannot make a mistake. His pronouncements must be accepted.

The actual powers of the popes has varied. When CHRISTIANITY first spread, Rome was the capital of an empire that ruled the entire region of the Mediterranean Sea. Early on, the Roman church was influential. But other churches were influential, too, for example, the churches at Antioch, Alexandria, and, from the fourth century, Constantinople.

During the fifth century C.E. invaders from northern and eastern Europe sacked Rome: the Visigoths in 410, the Vandals in 477. The papacy filled the political vacuum that was left. It spoke with unquestioned authority in the Latin-speaking, western half of the empire.

But the bishop of Rome claimed more. He claimed universal prestige. At the Council of Chalcedon, Leo I (pope, 440–461) mediated a dispute between two warring factions of Greek-speaking theologians. Gregory I (pope, 590–604) argued strenuously for the Pope's claim to rule the entire church. The Orthodox churches never accepted this claim. In 1054 the Pope and the Patriarch of Constantinople excommunicated one another. The schism remained until 1965, when each revoked his decree of excommunication.

In 1076 Gregory VII (pope, 1073–85) excommunicated and humiliated the Holy Roman emperor,

Henry IV. In doing so, he established the power of popes over kings and princes. From 1100 to 1300 the popes enjoyed unmatched power in western Europe. At the end of this period Boniface VIII (1294–1303) claimed complete supremacy over virtually all of creation. A document known as the Donation of Constantine supported papal claims. It stated that Emperor Constantine had given all of his power to the popes.

After Boniface the political power of the papacy gradually diminished. A number of events were responsible: a period during which the popes lived in Avignon, France (1309–77), followed by a period in which two, then three, men claimed to be pope (1378–1417); the demonstration that the Donation of Constantine was a forgery; the rise of national powers in Europe; and the Protestant REFORMATION.

In the 20th century John XXIII (pope, 1958–63) attempted to modernize the church. But successors such as John Paul II (pope, 1978–2005) took a more conservative line. That meant that the papacy was occasionally at odds with the more liberal North American Catholic Church. One presumes that Pope Benedict XVI (pope, 2005–), will continue the direction established by his predecessor, John Paul II.

Further reading: William J. La Due, *The Chair of Saint Peter: A History of the Papacy* (Maryknoll, N.Y.: Orbis Books, 1999); Philippe Levillain, ed., *The Papacy: An Encyclopedia* (New York: Routledge, 2002); Michael J. Walsh, ed., *Lives of the Popes: Illustrated Biographies of Every Pope from St. Peter to the Present* (London: Salamander, 1998).

Parsees Zoroastrians who live in India and their descendants. By 1000 C.E. Zoroastrians had emigrated from Persia (today Iran) to the region of Gujarat in western India (*see* ZOROASTRIANISM). Tradition says they did so in response to the conquest of Persia by Muslims, which began about 635 C.E. The name "Parsee" refers to Persia, their country of origin. Today a large number of Parsees live in Bombay. They have become influential in business, higher education, and the professions. In the 20th century significant numbers of Parsees also settled in London and Toronto.

Parsee priests are males who inherit their positions from their fathers. Five times a day they place fuel on the eternal fires that burn in their temples. As they do so, they recite PRAYERS from the Zoroastrian SCRIPTURES.

According to tradition a person is a Parsee if her or his father is a Parsee, it is not possible to convert to the FAITH. At the age of seven, Parsee children undergo a ceremony known as *navjot*. In that ceremony they receive a white shirt and a sacred thread. The faithful always wear these symbols of the Parsee faith except when they are sleeping and bathing.

Parsees are well known for their traditional funeral practices. They place bodies of the dead in "towers of silence." There the bodies are eaten by vultures. The idea behind this practice is that no element—earth, air, fire, or water—should be defiled by corpses.

In the 20th century some Parsees began to advocate electric cremation as an acceptable alternative to exposure. In a few places they even began to raise the possibility of converting to the faith.

Parvati The consort of the god SIVA in Hindu mythology. Parvati's name derives from a Sanskrit word for mountain (*parvata*). Indeed, she is said to be the daughter of Himavat, the lord of the Himalayas. As a GODDESS she is much less independent than DURGA or KALI. Her major role is as Siva's wife, but in this role she is indispensable. She tames the wild, limitless, austere energy of the god and makes it available to human beings. A famous line by the poet Kalidasa equates the necessary relation of Siva and Parvati with that of a word's meaning and its sound.

Parvati is the mother of both of Siva's sons: the elephant-headed god GANESA and the six-headed god Skanda. According to the *Siva-PURANA*, she gave birth to Ganesa all by herself. One day she wanted to take a bath, but Siva was away, so she created Ganesa from the dirt of her body and set him to stand guard.

Parvati is generally shown accompanying Siva. Certain religious texts known as TANTRAS take the form of a dialogue between Parvati and Siva (*see* TANTRISM).

Passover One of the most widely observed JEWISH FESTIVALS. The Hebrew name for Passover is Pesach.

Passover is celebrated from the 15th to the 23rd of the Jewish month of Nisan (in Israel, to the 22nd). This period occurs in late March or April. Because the Jewish calendar is partly lunar, Passover does not occur on any fixed date in the Gregorian calendar used in North America and Europe.

Passover combines two ancient festivals. One was the SACRIFICE of a lamb. This RITUAL was discontinued when the JERUSALEM Temple was destroyed in 70 C.E. The other was the feast of unleavened bread. At its most ancient, this feast seems to have been a spring harvest festival. In celebrating it, the inhabitants of ancient Canaan disposed of the previous year's grain products and used only grain from the new harvest. The products disposed of included the fermenting agent used in baking, something like the starter used to make sourdough bread. For about a week, they ate unraised or unleavened bread, because it took that long for the starter made from the new grain to ferment.

Passover also has roots in the early history of the Jewish people. It recalls the EXODUS from Egypt under MOSES. This is the freeing of the children of Israel who were living in Egypt as slaves. The name "passover" derives from an event recorded in Exodus 12. There it is said that GOD visited the Egyptians with one final plague to convince the king of Egypt to release the children of Israel from slavery. First he instructed the children of Israel to smear their doors with the blood of a sacrificed lamb. Then he sent the ANGEL of death to kill the first-born sons of the Egyptians. The angel is said to have "passed over" houses of the children of Israel, whose doors had been smeared with blood.

The reading of the Haggadah takes place at a Passover seder, like the one in the background of this picture. The Haggadah read here has been written completely in Hebrew, although many are written in both Hebrew and English. *(Ya'acov Sa'ar, Government Press Office, Israel)*

He killed only the first-born sons in the unmarked houses of the Egyptians.

The first two and the last two days of Passover are especially sacred for traditional Jews. On those days one is not allowed to work. (In Israel work is not allowed only on the first and the last day of Passover.) Jews observe the central ritual of Passover on the first two nights, generally at home with family members. This ritual is known as a *seder*, from the Hebrew word for "order." The seder "haggadah" or story recounts the events of the exodus. One of its best known moments comes when a young child asks, "Why is tonight different from all other nights?" During the answer, the participants refer to certain foods: *matzah* or unleavened bread; horseradish in remembrance of the hardships endured in Egypt; a lamb bone and a roasted egg, in memory of the Passover sacrifice and the offerings once given in the Temple; a mixture of apples, nuts, and wine known as *haroseth*, said to stand for the mortar that the children of Israel used as slaves in Egypt; a dish of saltwater that symbolizes the tears the slaves in Egypt shed; and some sort of green, usually parsley, to represent the emergence of new life in the spring. Special seder plates contain depressions to hold these symbolic items.

During the course of the seder the participants drink four cups of wine. They leave a cup of wine undrunk for the prophet ELIJAH in case he should return, as Jewish tradition says he will. Several features involve children. In addition to asking important questions during the recital of the haggadah, children may be asked to find a piece of matzah that has been hidden. When they do find it, they receive a reward. During the entire Passover period Jews eat special foods. The foods vary with how strict the Jewish family is in its practice. Some Jews simply eliminate leavened bread; the very strict eat only foods specially blessed for Passover.

Passover is one of three PILGRIMAGE festivals in JUDAISM. Shavuot (Pentecost or Weeks) and Sukkot (Huts) are the other two. The name "pilgrimage festival" derives from ancient Israelite practice. The ancient Israelites traveled or made pilgrimage to Jerusalem in order to offer the Passover sacrifice at the Temple. Today only the SAMARITANS observe Passover with a sacrifice. They make their sacrifice on Mt. Gerizim.

Paul, the apostle *also called Saul; the most influential early Christian missionary.* His letters make up a large part of the NEW TESTAMENT. Paul was born in the town of Tarsus, now in southern Turkey. From his writings it is clear that he had a good education in Greek. He was also an extremely observant Jew. When CHRISTIANITY first arose, he strongly opposed it. But on the way to Damascus, now in Syria, he had a VISION of JESUS in HEAVEN. As a result, he began to advocate Christianity. His message centered on the death and RESURRECTION of Jesus. His writings say virtually nothing about what Jesus taught or did during his lifetime.

Starting from Antioch on the Orontes River (far southern Turkey), Paul traveled throughout what are now Turkey and Greece, establishing Christian churches. On the basis of the book of Acts, it is traditional to say that Paul made four missionary journeys. Paul's own letters make this itinerary seem somewhat artificial. Paul's efforts sparked much unrest. During a visit to JERUSALEM, he was arrested. He was transferred to Caesarea and spent two years there in prison. Then he was transferred to Rome. It is presumed that he died in Rome under Emperor Nero (ruled, 54–68 C.E.).

Tradition attributes 14 books of the New Testament to Paul. These are letters that Paul allegedly wrote. Of these books, virtually all modern scholars accept seven as genuinely by Paul: Romans, 1 and 2 Corinthians, Galatians, Philippians, Philemon, and 1 Thessalonians. Virtually all modern scholars reject Hebrews as by Paul; it does not in fact claim that Paul wrote it. Most modern scholars also reject 1 and 2 Timothy and Titus as by Paul, because they address problems that did not yet exist when Paul died. Scholars have also questioned whether Paul wrote Ephesians, Colossians, and 2 Thessalonians.

Paul converted primarily non-Jews to Christianity. This sparked a major controversy, because the earliest Christians were all Jews. They observed the TORAH as a matter of course. The question became: Do people have to observe the Torah to accept Jesus as the MESSIAH? The APOSTLES at Jerusalem—Jesus' closest followers—answered yes; Paul and his associates answered no. Some went even further. They said that in the new age of Jesus, people could do whatever they wanted.

In addressing this situation, Paul developed his most distinctive ideas. Among other places, he summarized these ideas when he wrote to Christians in Galatia: "a person is justified not by the works of the law [observing the Torah] but by FAITH IN JESUS CHRIST" (Galatians 2.16). Paul's concern in this and other verses is JUSTIFICATION: What makes people acceptable in God's sight? In Paul's eyes, observing the Torah cannot do this, because no one keeps the Torah perfectly. Instead, all people SIN and therefore deserve God's punishment. Only the death and resurrection of Jesus can make people, both Jews and non-Jews alike, acceptable to God. In explaining these views, Paul talks about GRACE and faith. The saving work of Jesus shows God's grace because it is freely given (cf. the English word "gratis"). People receive that gift through faith in Jesus.

Christians began to make collections of Paul's letters very early. For example, 2 Peter, the latest book in the New Testament, refers to these letters (3.15–16). But people argued over who interpreted Paul correctly. The Gnostic teacher Marcion claimed to represent Paul's true teachings (*see* GNOSTICISM). The Catholic and Orthodox churches were more successful in claiming Paul's heritage. Paul's ideas of justification have been particularly important in ROMAN CATHOLICISM and PROTESTANTISM. In particular, they powerfully influenced thinkers like AUGUSTINE OF HIPPO, Martin LUTHER, and John CALVIN. These thinkers found in Paul's answers to specific questions about observing the Torah, more general principles upon which to build Christian teachings.

Pentecostalism   A variety of PROTESTANTISM that began in the United States at the beginning of the 20th century. By the beginning of the 21st century, many estimate, Pentecostals accounted for roughly one-fourth of all the world's Christians. The majority lived not in North America but in Latin America, Africa, and certain countries in Asia.

The name *Pentecostal* comes from "Pentecost," known in Hebrew as Shavuot, a JEWISH FESTIVAL that occurs seven weeks after PASSOVER. A remarkable event happened at Pentecost in the year of JESUS' execution. As the ACTS OF THE APOSTLES tells the story, the Holy Spirit came upon Jesus' follow-ers. Tongues of fire appeared on top of their heads, and they began speaking in languages they did not know. The apostle PETER gave a speech to Jews assembled for the festival that was the first public proclamation of the message of CHRISTIANITY.

Most Christians look on these events as wonderful but unusual. They do not expect them to occur today. Pentecostal Christians believe that all Christians can receive such gifts of the spirit. The most important gift is the one received at Pentecost: glossolalia, or speaking in tongues.

HISTORY

Pentecostalism began in the HOLINESS MOVEMENT. This movement was an offshoot of METHODISM. John WESLEY (1703–91), the founder of Methodism, taught that once someone had been saved, moral perfection was possible. The first American Methodists sought this perfection in a process they called sanctification. They also held energetic revival services, often in camp meetings. But by the middle 1800s, Methodism had become more restrained. Perfection became a topic most Methodists no longer talked about. Methodist services became subdued and more respectable to followers of other denominations.

Some Methodists longed for the old ways. They tried to remain within their churches and hold camp meetings and cultivate perfection on the side. But church officials became suspicious, and forced them to leave. They founded their own churches. One of the most prominent is the Church of the NAZARENE.

Charles Fox Parham (1873–1929) was a Holiness preacher and teacher. He ran Bethel Bible College in Topeka, Kansas. He was disturbed by the state of the church and the world, and he taught that only another outpouring of the Holy Spirit could renew the church. In 1901 a woman studying at his college began to speak in tongues, that is, to speak an unknown language. Others soon received this gift, too.

Parham and his students spread the word across the American Southwest. Then, in 1906, an African American named William Seymour (1870–1922) opened the Asuza Street Mission in

Los Angeles. Seymour, too, had been a Holiness preacher, but under Parham's influence he had become Pentecostal. People flocked to Seymour's mission. From there Pentecostalism spread to the rest of the country.

Pentecostalists had hoped to renew mainline Protestantism, but they were repudiated and had to found their own churches. In the United States Pentecostal Christianity has been most successful in the hill regions stretching from the southern Appalachians to the Ozark mountains, as well as in Northern and Western cities.

By 1910 converts had begun to bring Pentecostalism to Europe, Latin America, Asia, and Africa. Especially in Africa Pentecostalism resembled movements begun by indigenous African preachers. One such preacher was Isaiah Shembe (c. 1870–1935), who founded the amaNazaretha church in South Africa and thought of himself as the prophet of the Zulus. Another was Simon Kimbangu (1889–1951), a baKongo who began to receive revelations from Jesus and to heal in 1921. American Pentecostals have sometimes been reluctant to see the gifts of these indigenous preachers as genuine gifts of the Spirit. That is because these preachers have often included elements of indigenous religions in their teachings.

Soon after it arose, Pentecostalism began to split into different groups. Splits sometimes occurred because of arguments over proper teachings. Most Pentecostal groups also divided along racial lines. Such divisions were present at the very beginning. William Seymour had to sit in the hallways to listen to Charles Parham's classes because Parham, influenced by the Ku Klux Klan, would not let Seymour in the classroom.

In the 1960s a CHARISMATIC MOVEMENT began in other Protestant groups and then in ROMAN CATHOLICISM. In many ways this movement resembled the Pentecostal churches. Its adherents spoke in tongues and practiced faith healing. They managed, however, to integrate their experiences into the teachings of their own religious congregations. Other members of their denominations often looked on them with suspicion, but they were not forced to leave.

Although Pentecostalism arose in the United States, today its center of gravity is in the southern hemisphere. Especially starting in the 1950s it has thrived in Latin America, sub-Saharan Africa, and certain countries in Asia. These churches have even begun to send missionaries to Europe.

BELIEFS AND PRACTICES

In general, Pentecostal Christians' beliefs are fundamentalist (see FUNDAMENTALISM, CHRISTIAN). Pentecostals have tended not to adopt specific statements of faith, such as CREEDS. What distinguishes Pentecostal Christians is their emphasis on the gifts of the Spirit. Among these, the gift of speaking in tongues is the most important. Other gifts include healing, prophecy, and the interpretation of tongues.

Pentecostal churches differ on how to talk about these gifts. Some Pentecostals, for example, the Church of God in CHRIST, say that people receive God's GRACE in three different stages: conversion, sanctification, and the (Pentecostal) gifts of the Spirit. Other Pentecostals, such as the Assemblies of God, say that people receive God's grace in two stages: the work of Calvary (which includes conversion and sanctification) and the gifts of the Spirit.

Still other Pentecostals belong to the "Jesus Only" movement. Most Christians baptize in the name of the Father (or Creator), Son, and Holy Spirit (see BAPTISM). But these Pentecostals baptize only in the name of Jesus. They do not recognize the Father and the Holy Spirit as different persons of a TRINITY.

At first Pentecostal worship services were exuberant occasions at which the gifts of the Spirit—speaking in tongues, healing, prophecy, and energetic behavior—were highly visible. They still are in minority churches in North America and in many Pentecostal churches elsewhere. White American Pentecostal services have tended to become more subdued.

Pentecostal worship tends to be nonliturgical. It emphasizes singing—often simple melodies with lines repeated many times—fervent praying, preaching, and people giving testimonies about their religious experiences. The style of Pentecostal worship is contemporary. Pentecostals have been willing to adapt contemporary styles, musical instruments, and technology for use in worship.

The majority of Pentecostals are women. Some studies suggest that Pentecostal women are more open to religious experiences and talk about them in more detail than Pentecostal men. Official Pentecostal church leaders, however, continue to be men.

PENTECOSTALISM IN THE UNITED STATES

Pentecostal Christianity has been a visible part of American life. Almost from the beginning, Pentecostalism has produced public figures. A good early example is Aimee Semple McPherson (1890–1944), founder of the Foursquare Gospel Church. She captured headlines in the 1920s when, as it seems, she engineered her own kidnapping. Another prominent Pentecostal healer was Oral Roberts (b. 1918), who established a large complex in Tulsa, Oklahoma. In 1969, Roberts joined the United Methodist Church. In the 1980s Pentecostals Jim (b. 1939) and Tammy Faye (b. 1942) Bakker and Jimmy Swaggart (b. 1935) were some of the best-known television evangelists (see TELEVANGELISM). Eventually, however, they suffered public disgrace because of sexual indiscretions. Pentecostals have not traditionally been prominent in American government, but perhaps the most prominent American Pentecostal in the early years of the 21st century was John Ashcroft (b. 1942), the U.S. Attorney General 2001–2005.

People such as Oral Roberts and John Ashcroft may occupy prominent places in the public imagination, but they should not overshadow the importance of various Pentecostal groups. Such groups include University Christian Fellowship, Full Gospel Business Men's Fellowship, and—not to be overlooked—Pentecostal congregations themselves. Many of the latter remain unaffiliated with any denomination.

PENTECOSTALISM ELSEWHERE

Outside of North America, Pentecostalism has grown with tremendous speed since the 1950s.

Especially in Africa and Latin America people have found it attractive. There are a number of reasons for this. Unlike many other preachers, Pentecostal preachers have not hesitated to promise success and prosperity. Such promises echo the traditional concerns of religions in these regions, which often tried to help people achieve material well-being. They also appeal to needy people, as Pentecostalism seems especially to have done in Latin America.

Pentecostal preachers have also advocated a morally strict lifestyle. This lifestyle has often countered certain characteristics of male-dominated cultures. A good example is the culture of machismo in Latin America, which people in the region often associate with Roman Catholicism. Pentecostals preach against drinking and gambling. They deplore marital infidelity and male violence against women. They urge people to take responsibility for their actions, and they advocate values such as thriftiness and cleanliness. Women often find these emphases appealing. It is not surprising, then, that Pentecostalism in Latin America attracts about twice as many women as it does men. It is also not surprising that people who become Pentecostals often find that their lives improve. When they abandon a lifestyle that involves drinking, gambling, and spending a great deal of money, they have more resources at their disposal.

Pentecostalism has yet another advantage over more traditional forms of Christianity in these regions. Pentecostal organization is looser than the structure of the Roman Catholic Church and the various Protestant churches. As a result, Pentecostalism changes to fit local conditions more easily. It often spreads through the activities of an independent preacher, who can adapt to local conditions quickly without having to convince his or her superiors of the need to do so. Pentecostals have also been willing to improvise by using readily available materials—vacant storefronts, overhead projectors rather than hymnbooks, easily learned songs, informal and emotional worship—instead of insisting on traditions that come from other times and places.

Many have criticized Pentecostalism in the southern hemisphere as spreading not Christianity but capitalism and a lifestyle based on consuming material goods. Those who are attracted to liberation theology have expressed that criticism quite sharply. (Liberation theologians, influenced by Marxism, have seen the goal of Christianity as the elimination of poverty and oppression; some have favored bringing this about by violent means.) But liberation theology no longer enjoys the favor that it once did. Furthermore, Pentecostals counter that they are doing people more good than armed rebellion ever did. They are helping them integrate productively into the changing worlds in which they find themselves.

Some Pentecostal churches are churches founded by American missionaries, but local preachers have probably been most important in the spread of Pentecostalism. Their churches include the so-called AICs—an acronym whose first letter stands for *African,* whose last letter stands for *churches,* but whose middle letter has been rendered a number of different ways, including *independent, indigenous,* and *initiated.* Latin American Pentecostalism has been particularly strong in Brazil and Chile and in central American countries such as Costa Rica. In Asia it has done well in India, Indonesia, and Korea. Some claim great successes for Pentecostalism in Europe, too, including the former Soviet Union, but others argue that the successes there have really not been very large.

SIGNIFICANCE

When Pentecostalism first arose 100 years ago, many people looked down on it and expected it to be a passing fancy. Today outsiders still find much to reject in Pentecostalism. Nevertheless, Pentecostalism turned out to be one of the major Christian movements of the 20th century and is now a major force in Christianity around the world.

Further reading: *Between Babel and Pentecost: Transnational Pentecostalism in Africa and Latin America,* ed. André Corten and Ruth Marshall-Fratani (Bloomington: Indiana University Press, 2001); *The Century of the Holy Spirit: 100 Years of Pentecostal and Charismatic Renewal, 1901–2001,* ed. Vinson Synan (Nashville: Thomas Nelson, 2001); Elaine J. Lawless, *God's Peculiar People: Women's Voices and Folk Tradition in a Pentecostal Church* (Lexington: University Press of Kentucky, 1988); David Martin, *Pentecostalism: The World Their Parish* (Oxford: Blackwell Publishers, 2002); *The New International Dictionary of Pentecostal and Charismatic Movements* (Grand Rapids, Mich.: Zondervan Pub. House, 2002); Grant Wacker, *Heaven Below: Early Pentecostals and American Culture* (Cambridge, Mass.: Harvard University Press, 2001).

persecution, religious The mistreatment and deprivation of rights of people because of their religion. A disturbing feature of the history of religion is the way in which certain religions have often been considered unacceptable by the state, or by the dominant religion in collusion with the state, or even by independent "vigilante" groups within a society determined to take the law into their hands. These religions have suffered persecution. The nature of the persecution can range from the suppression of information about the unacceptable religion in books and other media, to the destruction or confiscation of its property, the arrest of its members, and finally the massacre of its adherents, often to the accompaniment of horrible torture. Examples are manifold. Christians were persecuted under the Roman Empire, and after the triumph of Christianity, Jews and those deemed "heretics," or holders of incorrect beliefs, were persecuted within Christendom. In early modern Europe and North America, "witches" were persecuted, tortured, and put to death. Comparable accounts could be given from the Islamic world, traditional China and Japan, and elsewhere. Even in the contemporary world, wars based on religion that amount to persecution take place, and even in countries supposedly recognizing freedom of religion, religious groups popularly regarded as "cults" or otherwise unacceptable have suffered various degrees of persecution.

At the same time, it should be realized that these and other persecutions did not take place equally at all times. Religious persecution tends to arise in times of crisis or rapid change in a society, when it seems important to the authorities or to popular opinion to maintain common symbols of community, and to draw sharp boundaries between who's "in" and who is excluded by the social order lest it self-destruct. If a society has a single generally accepted religion, as do the majority, religion naturally becomes a way of defining those boundaries and determining who is part of the social order and who is not. The temptation then is to try to get rid of the latter. Only when religious freedom becomes part of what is held to characterize the society and its values is this temptation averted.

Religious persecution, moreover, is often political as well as religious. It may be expressed in religious terms, but it is usually engaged in because the authorities or the community thinks the unacceptable religion is in some way a threat to its power and its ability to control things as well as false on some theoretical level. Religions have also been persecuted for economic reasons, such as the supposed wealth of the unpopular FAITH or its members. So long as some religions are considered more unacceptable than others, or more threatening to the state and the social order than others, forms of religious persecution are likely to persist.

See also HOLOCAUST, THE.

Peter, the apostle In the Christian NEW TESTAMENT, the most important of JESUS' disciples or messengers. The Roman Catholic Church appeals to Peter to support its claim that the Pope is supposed to govern the church throughout the world (see PAPACY, THE).

According to the New Testament, Peter was a fisherman by trade. He worked with his father and his brother Andrew. Peter was one of the first disciples Jesus called, and he was a member of an inner circle with James and John. His name was Simon or Simeon; according to the New Testament his byname, Peter, derives from Jesus himself. Peter is portrayed as brash, almost foolhardy. Among many famous incidents is an occasion when Peter tried to join Jesus as he walked on water. He sank. Peter's fallibility came to a climax the night Jesus was on trial. Peter denied knowing Jesus three times in a row.

After Jesus' crucifixion, Peter seems to have been the leader of the earliest church. Luke's GOSPEL makes him the first to see the empty tomb after the women discover it. Some New Testament passages mention him first among those to whom the risen Jesus appeared. According to the book of Acts, Peter preached the first public sermon at the Jewish festival of Pentecost (Shavuot; see JEWISH FESTIVALS). In PAUL's letters Peter appears first as the leader of the church in JERUSALEM, then as a missionary to the Jews. Paul may mean that Peter preached to the Jews in the diaspora, that is, Jews living outside Palestine. In the important early dispute over whether Christians of non-Jewish origin should be required to observe the TORAH, Peter seems to have taken a mediating position. He agreed with Paul against James that non-Jewish Christians did not need to observe the Torah. At the same time, he aroused Paul's anger when he was reluctant to associate fully with such nonobservant Christians.

Legend says that toward the end of his life Peter traveled to Rome. He became the first bishop of the church there and was executed, probably during the persecutions under Emperor Nero (ruled, 54–68). According to the nonbiblical *Acts of Peter*, he insisted on being crucified head downward. He felt that he was unworthy to be crucified in the same manner as Jesus.

Several ancient writings bear Peter's name. Two letters in the New Testament claim to be written by him. It is doubtful that Peter wrote the first. It is almost certain that he did not write the second; it simply expands the letter of Jude. Writings outside the BIBLE that bear Peter's name include the *Gospel of Peter*, the *Kerygma ("Preaching") of Peter*, the *Acts of Peter*, the *Acts of Peter and the Twelve Apostles*, the *Letter of Peter to*

Philip, and the *Apocalypse of Peter.* According to tradition, the biblical gospel of Mark was based on Peter's teaching.

In the later history of the church Peter has been most important in connection with the papacy. In Matthew 16.16–19, Jesus gives Peter his name and makes him the foundation on which the church will be built. The Roman Catholic Church rests the Pope's claim to primacy upon this saying. It claims that Peter passed down to the future bishops of Rome the position that he received from Jesus. The church remembers Peter on several different days. The most important is June 29, the festival of the apostles Peter and Paul.

Peter, epistles of   Two short books in the NEW TESTAMENT said to have been written by PETER, an APOSTLE of JESUS. In the early centuries of Christianity several writings circulated under the name of Peter. They include the Gospel according to Peter, the Acts of Peter, the Revelation to Peter, and several epistles or letters. Only two of the letters were later accepted into the BIBLE. By the end of the second century C.E., some, but not all, Christians considered 1 Peter to be an authoritative book. (There was no New Testament yet.) None of the sources for such topics include 2 Peter. By the early 300s, all churches had accepted 1 Peter, but they disagreed about 2 Peter. By the end of the 300s, however, the disputes about whether to accept 2 Peter had ended.

1 PETER

1 Peter claims to be written by Peter from Rome to churches in Asia Minor, now Turkey. But in the ancient world it was common, and not considered dishonest, to write books under someone else's name. Many scholars think that 1 Peter concerns a situation that came too late for Peter to have addressed it. If this is the case, the letter is another writer's attempt to explain what Peter would have said.

1 Peter seems to address Gentiles who have converted to CHRISTIANITY. They are being treated as outsiders; 1 Peter refers to them as exiles and aliens. It also refers to a "fiery ordeal" that they are suffering, presumably some form of persecution, perhaps from their neighbors (*see* 4.1–6), or perhaps from the government.

In this situation 1 Peter exhorts Christians to live properly. It gives general advice, such as to refrain from insincerity and slander, and it identifies the sufferings of Christians with the sufferings of Jesus. 1 Peter also gives more specific advice. It tells Christians to obey the government. It tells slaves to put up with being beaten, even if they are being beaten for no reason. And it tells wives to obey their husbands and seek spiritual rather than physical beauty. The advice to husbands is much shorter and assumes that they are in a position of power.

Many scholars suggest that 1 Peter urged persecuted Christians to be model citizens and not to arouse suspicion. This may have been much-needed advice at the time. For example, slave revolts were not uncommon in the Roman empire, and Jesus had been executed on the charge of insurrection, that is, rebelling against the government.

2 PETER

It may be doubtful whether Peter the Apostle wrote 1 Peter, but it is almost certain that he did not write 2 Peter. The book refers to a collection of Paul's letters that Christians were misinterpreting; a collection of Paul's letters was probably not available in Peter's lifetime. It also seems to assume that its readers know the first three GOSPELS, which were not written until after Peter died. In addition, part of 2 Peter (2.1–8) parallels the book of Jude (4–16). Finally, the specific issues that 2 Peter discusses are very different from those in 1 Peter.

Much of 2 Peter is invective against people who teach false things and entice Christians to behave in ways that the author considers immoral. The statements are very general, and readers can use them against many people with whom they disagree. The only specific issue that 2 Peter mentions is one that seems to have been a problem for many of the earliest Christians. Although the apostles proclaimed that Jesus was going to return soon for the last judgment, that had not happened. 2 Peter urges Christians to remember that GOD experiences time differently from human beings. He urges them to remain faithful until the day of judgment.

Further reading: Paul J. Achtemeier, *1 Peter: A Commentary on First Peter* (Minneapolis, Minn.: Fortress Press, 1996); John H. Elliott, *1 Peter: A New Translation with Introduction and Commentary* (New York: Doubleday, 2000); Jerome H. Neyrey, *2 Peter, Jude: A New Translation with Introduction and Commentary* (New York: Doubleday, 1993).

Pharisees   A prominent religious group in late Second Temple JUDAISM (roughly 200 B.C.E.–70 C.E.). The Jewish antiquarian Josephus (37–after 93 C.E.) wrote books on the Jews and their history. He identified several religious groups in Judaism during the late Second Temple period: the Pharisees, the Sadducees, the ESSENES, and the Zealots.

The Pharisees centered their religious life on the study of the TORAH and on the SYNAGOGUE rather than on the SACRIFICES of the Temple. Their primary constituency seems to have been shopkeepers and merchants, and their leaders were known as RABBIS. When the Temple was destroyed in 70 C.E., their descendants took charge of the community and tradition. They formulated rabbinical Judaism, the Judaism we know today.

The Pharisees appear frequently in the NEW TESTAMENT. The GOSPELS highlight their differences from JESUS, who preached to the poor, or from those who lacked the resources to maintain the Pharisees' style of Judaism. Many scholars have suggested that this portrayal is inaccurate. It may reflect a situation of competition between Pharisees and the earliest Christians for Jewish loyalty in the first century C.E.

pilgrimage   Travel for religious reasons, particularly to visit a site that is considered especially sacred and a source of blessings to those who approach it. Virtually all religions in the world, with the exception of Protestant Christianity (*see* PROTESTANTISM), have significant examples of pilgrimage as part of their tradition.

Medieval Christians went to JERUSALEM and the Holy Land; the alleged cutting-off of access to these sacred places was a principal reason for the CRUSADES. Modern Roman Catholics go to Jerusalem, Bethlehem, and Rome, and also in great numbers to shrines, especially where apparitions of the Blessed Virgin MARY are believed to have occurred: Lourdes in France, Fatima in Portugal, Guadalupe in Mexico, and others. Eastern Orthodox Christians travel to the Holy Land and also to famous shrines and monasteries in their homelands. Many Jews go to Israel in a pilgrimage mood, visiting such sacred places as the Wailing Wall in Jerusalem.

Hindus flock to the banks of the sacred GANGES RIVER, especially at such holy cities as BANARAS and Rishikesh, and to countless shrines of gods and SAINTS throughout the land. In China and Japan sacred peaks, like Taishan in China, Mount Kailas in Tibet, and the celebrated Mount Fuji in Japan, draw innumerable pilgrims; something about the clear, clean atmosphere of a mountain height suggests entry into a sacred realm. It is well known that all Muslims, once in their lifetime, try to make the hajj, the pilgrimage to the holy city of MECCA in Saudi Arabia. Islam also boasts many shrines of saints that draw spiritual travelers as well.

Pilgrimage is based on a common religious assumption that the geography of the Earth is not, so to speak, spiritually homogenous, but that some places are more open to contact with divine power than others. That may be because of association with a sacred person or event, which has there left its mark, or because of a divine VISION or revelation, or just because GOD has in some way blessed it. Thus to be there is to be close to sacred power.

Second, the very act of pilgrimage can be seen as a spiritual exercise, like PRAYER or MEDITATION or YOGA or going to a service, but with one's feet or by other means of travel. Many people want to express their religion by doing something active, and pilgrimage is one way of doing it. It combines religion with an activity many people find pleasant and educational.

Third, since pilgrimage is frequently done in a group, its religiously social meaning must not be overlooked. A pilgrim band can become a closely-knit set of people with a shared spiritual experience. Many commentators have noted that, on pilgrimage, ordinary barriers of rank and status and even gender fall away as the band gets farther from home and closer to the sacred site before which all are equal. Sometimes, as on the Muslim hajj, pilgrims of all backgrounds wear the same plain white garments in the holy city to symbolize this. The ideal goal of a pilgrimage is to reach a place both outward and within oneself where one can break down all barriers to complete openness between persons, and between the human and the divine. This is an ideal that may not always be reached. Like everything human, even the most religious things, pilgrimage can doubtless be corrupted and debased. But it is surely better for humans to set forth on pilgrimage than to set out on missions of pillage and war.

politics and religion   In the United States, as in many other countries today, religion and politics—church and state, as they are often called—are supposed to be separate. Indeed, most people agree that religious freedom is a good thing, although they disagree on what that means. It may seem surprising to Americans that in the history of the world, such a separation of religion and politics is a very recent development and an exception to a widely prevalent norm. In most places throughout most of history, religion and politics have been closely linked.

RELIGION AND GOVERNMENT BEFORE THE MODERN ERA

Until about 300 years ago, most people assumed that religion was necessary to good government. It would have been difficult to find a state that did not have a connection with religion.

The first cities arose in southern Mesopotamia (southern Iraq today). They grew up around temples, and the priests of the temples ruled them. Ancient Egyptians considered their king, called

Pharaoh, a god. On earth he was the god HORUS; after his death he became the god OSIRIS.

In south and east Asia, too, government and religion were closely connected. Starting in about 1100 B.C.E., Chinese emperors claimed to rule according to the Mandate of Heaven. Later, officials in the Chinese government spent a great deal of time performing the cult of CONFUCIUS. In India different rulers promoted different religions, such as HINDUISM and JAINISM. One famous emperor, ASOKA, promoted harmony among all religions but especially favored BUDDHISM. Buddhism provided the basis for government in other parts of south and southeast Asia, too, such as Sri Lanka, Burma, and Thailand.

In South America before the arrival of Columbus, the Inca emperor was said to be divine. Aztec state rituals at the Templo Mayor in Tenochtitlán (now Mexico City) are notorious for the human SACRIFICES that were performed.

Greek and Roman states had their official religious practices, while each of the "Abrahamic" FAITHS—JUDAISM, CHRISTIANITY, and ISLAM—has supported governments. In ancient Israel a close connection linked the kings with the Temple in JERUSALEM. Today, Israel is a Jewish state. In the early 300s C.E. the emperor CONSTANTINE made Christianity a legal religion; in the late 300s C.E. the emperor Theodosius made it the only religion allowed. Christianity remained the official religion of European countries and governments established by Europeans until the founding of the United States. Islam has not accepted the idea that religion and government are separate spheres. For most Muslims the best government is the government that observes God's laws.

People have given several reasons for such a close relationship between religion and government. One reason is that religion makes a government seem legitimate. For example, some Chinese thought that so long as an emperor ruled with the Mandate of Heaven, he was the rightful emperor. Another reason is that only religion can provide the morals society needs to survive. Even religious skeptics have believed this. For example, the Roman orator Cicero (106–43 B.C.E.) wrote that neither he nor other officials of the Roman Republic believed in the traditional Roman religion. Nevertheless, they believed that it was necessary for them to perform the traditional rituals to maintain proper order in the state.

SEPARATION OF RELIGION AND GOVERNMENT

Starting in the Protestant REFORMATION (16th century), Europe experienced devastating religious wars. People who favored different kinds of Christianity fought and killed one another. As a result, some philosophers began to claim that religion should be a private matter, not a matter for governments. Some Christians advocated this view, too, among them Anabaptists such as MENNONITES, members of BAPTIST CHURCHES, and QUAKERS. These groups argued that governmental support harmed religion. It meant that people adopted a religion because they had to, not because they were committed to it.

Like other governments at the time, most British colonies in North America began with official religions. For example, Massachusetts was a Puritan colony. In the early days it executed Quakers and sent Baptists into exile. But both Rhode Island, founded by exiles from Massachusetts, and Pennsylvania, chartered to William Penn (1644–1718), a Quaker, rejected the idea of an official religion. Some but not all of the founders of the United States also rejected the idea of an official religion. For example, Thomas Jefferson (1743–1826) and James Madison (1751–1836) did; George Washington (1732–99) and John Adams (1735–1826) did not. The First Amendment to the U.S. Constitution prohibits an "established" or official religion. Originally, however, it applied only to the federal government. Massachusetts was the last state to give up its official religion. It did so in 1833.

Today many other countries in the world have no official religions. Two notable examples are France and India. But opinions differ on what exactly separation of religion and government means. In the United States people interpret the First Amendment in two main ways. "Separationists" believe that the Amendment erects an absolute "wall of separation" between church and state or religion and government. "Accommodationists" believe that it prevents government from favoring one religion over another, but not from encouraging religion.

POLITICS AND RELIGION TODAY

The former Soviet Union considered religion dangerous. Until its fall in 1991, it and its Communist allies tried to eliminate religion entirely and promote ATHEISM among their people. Technically, the People's Republic of CHINA recognizes freedom of religion, but at some times, such as the Cultural Revolution (1967–77), it has tried to eliminate religion, too. Much more common today, however, are efforts to reintroduce religion into government and to strengthen its role in government.

Among Muslims the most famous example of such efforts is the Iranian Revolution. In 1979 Iranians overthrew the Shah, a secular ruler, and established an Islamic Republic, led by the Ayatollah KHOMEINI. In many other Islamic countries people have become frustrated with secular governments, too. They see these governments as too Westernized. They also see them as lacking moral standards, in part because they have been dictatorial and financially corrupt. Many insist that the only proper government is one set up in accordance with God's law, SHARIAH. Political parties in states with Muslim majorities that had been very secular have successfully pursued such goals. An example is the Refah Party in Turkey (see FUNDAMENTALISM, ISLAMIC).

The situation in India is a little different. To outsiders it often looks as if powerful movements—the Bharatiya Janata Party, the Vishwa Hindu Parishad, and the Rastriya Swayamsevak Sangh—are introducing religion into politics (see FUNDAMENTALISM, HINDU). Indeed, their policies have received strong support from some but not all sadhus and sadhvis (see SADHU, SADHVI). Perhaps the most famous such supporter has been Uma Bharati (b. 1959); she has held many high government positions, including the position of

Chief Minister (governor) of an Indian state. From the inside, however, these movements often see themselves as pushing not religion but traditional culture, *Hindutva* (Hindu-ness) rather than Hinduism. They want India to acknowledge that it is a Hindu state and to promote Hindu culture. Their activities have led to violence against Muslims and, to a lesser extent, Christians.

The United States has a long tradition of separating religion and government, but it also has strong traditions of mixing religion and government. As followers of John CALVIN (1509–64), the Pilgrims and Puritans believed that the state should obey and further God's law (*see* PURITANISM). More recent practices mix religion and government, too, such as printing the phrase "In God We Trust" on U.S. money since the 1920s, adding the phrase "under God" to the Pledge of Allegiance in 1954, and opening sessions of Congress with a prayer. Not everyone sees such acts as religious. For example, in 2003 the Chief Justice of Alabama, Roy Moore (b. 1947), lost his office. He had erected a monument to the Ten Commandments in the rotunda of the state's judiciary building and then refused to move it when ordered to do so. But Moore claimed his monument was not religious. It simply acknowledged the basis of all American law.

Some Americans want to see more religion in government. Prominent conservative Christians like Pat Robertson (b. 1930) and Jerry Falwell (b. 1933) subscribe to what some call "dominion theology." They want the United States to acknowledge that it is a nation under God's dominion or control and act accordingly. Since the 1980s many of their followers have tried to put these ideas into practice through activity in the Republican Party. Some have even said that the abbreviation G.O.P., from the party's nickname, "Grand Old Party," really means "God's Own Party" and that a vote for Republican candidates is a vote for God.

Like some people in other parts of the world, certain Americans with these views have abandoned political processes. They have sought to make their ideals reality through acts of violence.

For example, some Christians have bombed abortion clinics and killed medical personnel who provide abortions. However, most Americans realize that these people do not represent all Christians, though many Americans do believe that extremist Muslims and Hindus represent all people of their faiths.

Further reading: N. J. Demerath, *Crossing the Gods: World Religions and Worldly Politics* (New Brunswick, N.J.: Rutgers University Press, 2003); *One Electorate under God? A Dialogue on Religion and American Politics,* eds. E. J. Dionne Jr., Jean Bethke Elshtain, and Kayla M. Drogosz (Washington, D.C.: Brookings Institution Press, 2004); *Religion Returns to the Public Square : Faith and Policy in America,* Hugh Heclo and Wilfred M. McClay, eds. (Baltimore, Md.: Johns Hopkins University Press, 2003); Kenneth D. Wald, *Religion and Politics in the United States* (Lanham, Md.: Rowman & Littlefield, 2003).

Polynesian religion　*See* PACIFIC OCEAN RELIGIONS.

polytheism　Belief in many gods. Polytheism may be contrasted with MONOTHEISM or belief in one GOD, or with ATHEISM, belief in no god whatsoever. Most archaic religions, like EGYPTIAN RELIGION, MESOPOTAMIAN RELIGION, GREEK RELIGION, and ROMAN RELIGION were polytheistic, though they may have believed that somewhere there was a supreme god or principle. Religions like HINDUISM, MAHAYANA BUDDHISM, and TAOISM today may appear to be polytheistic, but many of their adherents would insist that the many gods or BUDDHAS and BODHISATTVAS one sees in their temples should be regarded more like, say, the SAINTS in ROMAN CATHOLICISM: glorified human beings who have attained near-divine holiness and so can help us, or else as personifications or aspects of the One. Some would say that SHINTO in Japan is the most nearly polytheistic religion found today in a major advanced society.

Polytheism has very ancient roots. In primal tribal societies, one can find belief in various spirits—ancestors, spirits of places like mountains and woods, or animals—as well as usually a ruling high god. Generally each tribe, and later each city, would have its guardian or patronal god too. But it was in the ancient empires like Egypt and Babylon that polytheism really grew. As many tribes and cities were combined into larger empires, all their local gods might become parts of a vaster pantheon of gods. At the same time, as human life became more complex, gods of specialized occupations came to be honored by their followers. Sometimes a heavenly bureaucracy paralleled that of the empires of Earth. It was against this greater and greater complexity of polytheism that monotheism finally rebelled.

But wherever found, in remaining tribal societies, in the archaic world, in Japan or elsewhere, polytheism is important because it communicates a different VISION of the sacred than monotheism. As the theologian Paul Tillich once put it, polytheism is a matter of quality as well as quantity. It is not just that the polytheist has many gods while the monotheist has one; it is that this makes the whole experience of God different. For the monotheist, the whole universe is unified under one rule and one will. For the polytheist, it is divided up, pluralistic, nuanced: There is a separate god for this sacred tree and that sacred waterfall, for love and for war, and each can be sovereign in his or her own time, but all are also finite and none can rule the whole show. Decisions in a polytheistic universe must be made by divine consensus, not fiat. A few people today, in Neo-Pagan movements, are attempting to recover something of the spirit of polytheism.

pope *See* PAPACY, THE.

prajna A Sanskrit word for "wisdom." In HINDUISM prajna is occasionally linked to the GODDESS of learning, SARASWATI. But prajna is most often associated with BUDDHISM.

In THERAVADA BUDDHISM, prajna, along with morality and MEDITATION, defines the path to liberation. In this context prajna means being persuaded that Buddhist teachings about the world, about the predicament of sentient or conscious beings, and about the means of release are true.

In MAHAYANA BUDDHISM prajna is one of the most important of the "perfections" that practitioners nurture. In general Mahayana emphasizes both compassion and wisdom as cardinal virtues. But in some schools, such as the school of Nagarjuna, prajna becomes supreme.

For Mahayana Buddhism, prajna is intuitive insight into the nature of all things. So important was this perfection that it became personified as Prajnaparamita, "the perfection of wisdom," and was said to be the mother of the Buddhas. Some of the most important Mahayana texts are the *Prajnaparamita Sutras*, such as the *Heart Sutra* and *Diamond Sutra*.

prana A Sanskrit word meaning "breath." The term has profound religious significance in HINDUISM.

In the UPANISHADS, *prana* stands for the vital energy. In this it resembles *pneuma* and *spiritus,* the Latin and Greek words for "breath" or "spirit." Occasionally the Upanishads even identify prana with BRAHMAN, reality itself.

Hindus have generally taken a different view of prana. They have taught that the vital breath circulates through the body and enlivens it. As a result, psychophysical disciplines have given much attention to breathing. For example, breath control (*pranayama*) is the fourth stage of the royal YOGA systematized by Patanjali in the *Yoga-sutras.*

prayer Communication with a religious being, such as a god, spirit, ancestor, or SAINT. Religion involves many forms of communication. Sometimes religious people are convinced that a religious being has communicated with them; this is revelation. Often religious people instruct and exhort; this is teaching or PREACHING. People may express religious desires. If such desires are not directed to beings such as gods or ancestors, these are wishes or spells. Prayer is communication addressed to a god or some other religious being. It is one of the most important forms of communication found in religions.

Prayers vary widely. Some prayers are extemporaneous. They arise from the needs and thoughts of the moment. Others are planned or written ahead of time. Some Protestants prefer extemporaneous prayers. They feel that people should address GOD directly in their own words, just as they would in a conversation. Other forms of CHRISTIANITY often use formal, written prayers, such as the prayers of the Mass in ROMAN CATHOLICISM or the Divine LITURGY in the Orthodox churches.

Individuals pray; so do groups. Any means by which human beings communicate can and has been used in prayer. Prayers can be spoken out loud. In the most sacred part of the Divine Liturgy in the Orthodox churches, the holiest prayers are muttered softly. Prayers can be danced. They can be acted out. Some prayers are silent. That may mean people recite words in their minds. It may also mean that they sit in silence, open their hearts, and wait for illumination.

Spoken prayers take a variety of forms. Some prayers are poems. For Jews and Christians, the supreme examples are the PSALMS in the Hebrew BIBLE. Prayers spoken by groups may be litanies: A leader recites various requests known as petitions; the rest of the group responds with a fixed formula. Some prayers involve the repetition of the same word over and over again, much like a MANTRA. One example is the JESUS prayer that some Orthodox Christians use; they repeat the name of Jesus. A similar example is the *nembutsu* that Japanese Pure Land Buddhists repeat: *Namu Amida butsu,* "Praise to the Buddha AMIDA" (*see* PURE LAND BUDDHISM). Still other prayers recite lists. On the DAY OF ATONEMENT Jews ask God collectively to forgive SINS. One prayer lists representative sins that begin with every letter of the Hebrew alphabet in succession. Hindus honor gods with prayers in which they praise their *sahasra-namas,* their "thousand [and eight] names."

Prayer may be a simple verbal act, but it also may involve the person's body. Muslims perform ablutions before the daily prayer known as SALAT. As they pray, they assume a series of postures, such as standing, bowing, and prostration. Hasidic Jews seem to bob back and forth as they pray; their movements actually are continual acts of bowing in the presence of God. Hindus may pray to a god with their hands in *pranjali.* They hold their palms together at their chests; their fingers and thumbs point upward. Christians adopted this gesture for prayer; they also use several others. Some mark out a cross on their foreheads, chest, and shoulders; some kneel. Some religions teach people to cover their heads when they pray.

Religious people have also invented external objects to help them pray. Many religions use rosaries—strings of beads used to count prayers repeated over and over again. Hindus who worship SIVA use rosaries made of large seeds known as *rudrakshas.* Tibetans use other devices: prayer flags and prayer wheels. The flags and wheels have prayers printed on them. Each time they blow in the wind or rotate, Tibetans say the prayer has been offered.

Thinkers of different religions have classified prayers in terms of their purposes, such as supplication, adoration, thanksgiving, and confession. In reality, people have used prayers for every purpose that requires them to address religious beings. One especially common form of prayer is a request.

Most requests would seem to leave the response up to the beings addressed. But some particularly interesting prayers actually fulfill their own requests. The eucharistic prayers that Catholic and Orthodox priests and some Protestant ministers recite do this. They ask the Holy Spirit to descend upon the bread and wine. But the very act of asking is said to consecrate these elements.

Some religions have particularly sacred prayers. For Jews, the most sacred prayer is the *Shema.* Observant Jews recite it two times a day. It begins with verses from Deuteronomy 4: "Hear [shema], o Israel; The Lord is our God, the Lord is one." That part of the service is followed by "Eighteen Benedictions." Another very important prayer in JUDAISM is the *Kaddish*. It is a doxology recited at the conclusion of sets of prayers during worship. Jews recite a special form of the Kaddish at funerals and for mourning.

For Christians the most important prayer is the one that Jesus taught, the LORD'S PRAYER. The NEW TESTAMENT presents two versions of this prayer. Christians generally use the fuller version in the GOSPEL of Matthew. Especially Roman Catholics use another prayer, the *Ave Maria:* "Hail, Mary [ave Maria], full of grace . . ."

Praying can be the central act of worship. This is true of the SYNAGOGUE service in Judaism and salat in ISLAM. It is also true of the many "ways" that the Navajo people in the southwestern United States observe. Many indigenous Americans hold prayers in a special building known as a SWEAT LODGE. In the sweat lodge, sweat-inducing steam and fragrant aromas such as sage combine with praying to produce a refreshing and renewing experience.

In American public life during the last half of the 20th century prayer, especially prayer in public schools, was one of the most controversial issues. The first amendment to the U.S. Constitution prohibits the government from supporting any religious act (*see* CHURCH AND STATE). Several Supreme Court rulings declared widespread practices of praying in school unconstitutional. Examples include having students recite a prayer in the morning before school, having a religious professional—priest, minister, or RABBI—offer a prayer at school ceremonies, and having a student say a prayer that he or she had written at the beginning of a sporting event.

In some areas schools violated the law until someone objected. At times conservatives attempted to amend the Constitution to allow school prayer. Many organized religious groups, from Baptists to Buddhists, spoke out against their efforts. The controversy illustrates at least this much: Whatever their preferences, prayer is a religious practice that Americans still take very seriously.

Further reading: Robert S. Alley, *Without a Prayer: Religious Expression in Public Schools* (Amherst,

N.Y.: Prometheus Books, 1996); Marcel Mauss, *On Prayer*, W. S. F. Pickering, ed. (New York: Durkheim Press/Berghahn Books, 2003); *Rehras = Evensong: The Sikh Evening Prayer*, Reema Anand and Khushwant Singh, trans. (New York: Viking, 2002); Christopher L. Webber, ed., *Give Us Grace: An Anthology of Anglican Prayers* (Harrisburg, Pa.: Morehouse, 2004).

preaching Religious speech-making. Preaching is a way to teach, to convert, to inspire, to exhort, to critique, and probably to do other things as well.

Many religions have had preachers. But preaching has been especially important to Protestant Christianity. At the time of the REFORMATION, Martin LUTHER raised the pulpit—the stand from which preachers speak—higher than the ALTAR. This act was a powerful sign. For many Protestants preaching is the center of WORSHIP. By contrast, for Catholic and Orthodox Christians worship centers on the celebration of the EUCHARIST.

Preaching may take place in many contexts. RABBIS, ministers, and IMAMS preach during weekly congregational services. On the American frontier, wandering preachers held meetings known as revivals just for the purpose of preaching. Some have preached, so to speak, on the streetcorners. DOMINICAN friars did this during the Middle Ages; John WESLEY did it during the 18th century. A much different style of preaching is the sermon that a Zen (*see* ZEN BUDDHISM) master gives to his disciples. He delivers it during prolonged sessions of Zen effort. His manner of delivery is formal and restrained and he often repeats the same sermon verbatim.

Many sermons are expository. That is, they comment upon sacred SCRIPTURES. For example, rabbis may expound the Hebrew BIBLE; Christian preachers may expound the Old and NEW TESTAMENT; imams may comment onn the QUR'AN; a Zen master may comment on Buddhist *sutras*. Preachers in liturgical traditions generally comment on assigned passages. Others choose their own topics. At times they may preach a series of sermons that explore, say, a book of the Bible or develop a complex theme.

In some religions preachers are those ordained to a special office. Rabbis, priests, some Christian ministers, and Zen masters fall into this class. Others preach because they feel they have a special calling to do so. Imams preach because the community recognizes their learning and stature.

Protestant preaching has often been strictly oral. But other preachers have made extensive use of visual aids. In the third century B.C.E. the Indian emperor ASOKA sent "ministers of DHARMA" throughout the countryside to teach BUDDHISM to the people. His *Edicts* indicates that these "preachers" based their "sermons" on drawings or paintings of Buddhist stories. In medieval Japan traveling Buddhist nuns used much the same technique.

At one time in the Protestant world, sermons were important elements of culture. People attended sermons for entertainment as well as edification. Respected preachers were public figures. They published their sermons in countless books. People bought and read these books the way people today buy and read science fiction and mystery novels.

Although preaching has become less important in American culture, it is not negligible, either. During the second half of the 20th century, many Jewish and Christian preachers abandoned the dogmatic and moralistic sermons that had been common. They tried to preach in the manner of a storyteller. Social reformers and revolutionaries found preaching to be a powerful tool. Two ideal examples are Martin Luther KING Jr. and MALCOLM X. Preachers also readily adopted powerful new means of communication, such as radio and television. Some conservative and fundamentalist Christian preachers have even become television personalities.

prehistoric religion   The religion of the earliest humans, before the invention of writing. Prehistoric religion had the same central concerns as all religion, but was different in significant ways from religion as we generally know it now.

It had, obviously, no written scriptures, and was not centered on a single pivotal historical event like the time of MOSES, CHRIST, or BUDDHA. Rather, it would have been "cosmic," meaning that its sacred time was based on the turn of the seasons, and its sacred places were perhaps mountains, caves, and shrines in the same locale where its followers dwelt. Its lore would have been told in remembered myths (*see* MYTH AND MYTHOLOGY), songs, and dances.

Much of the actual religion of people before history is now forgotten forever, but its general character can be estimated from two sources: remains recovered by archaeology and comparison with the religion of recent or contemporary nonliterate tribal people. Both must be used with caution, but they are all we have.

The first stage of human culture is what is called the Paleolithic Age, or Old Stone Age. Paleolithic people were hunters and gatherers using stone tools, but without metal or agriculture. Among the earliest remains that definitely suggest religious themes are burials and the famous cave paintings of up to 40,000 years ago. In some archaic burials, the bones of the dead are covered with red ochre, the color of blood and life, and are buried in fetal posture, suggesting thoughts of return to the womb and perhaps rebirth. This tells us that people were probably already confronting death through religion and may have been thinking of life beyond it—ideas always important to religion.

The great cave paintings from the Pyrenees region of France and Spain are even more suggestive and puzzling. Certainly they show distinctively human creativity and imagination. But what do they mean? Perhaps they were hunting MAGIC, designed to help take the animals they so vividly portray. Perhaps the cave art galleries—which are deep underground, far from any living areas and difficult to reach—were sacred temples and, if we could but crack their code, the pictures records of sacred events or myths. They may have been used for initiation too. In one cave, a soft area is covered with numerous small footprints, as though from the dance steps of youthful initiates into the mysteries of the tribe.

All these things suggest themes found today in the religion of many tribal peoples. There is the idea of soul, a life-principle separable from the body and having a separate destiny, perhaps going to another world, perhaps being reborn in this one. Hunting magic that wins the favor of the gods in opening and closing the forests and the goodwill of the animals important to the survival of the tribe, is essential. Some form of initiation of young men, and often of young women, into the tribe is also very common. For the tribe is a spiritual unity, a reality also reflected in its dances and stories. To become a true part of it is the most important thing in a person's life.

One or two of the early cave paintings have suggested to some observers another figure in much recent Paleolithic religion, but which may go back a very long ways indeed: the shaman (see SHAMANISM). A shaman is a religious specialist who typically has had a special call and initiation greater than the ordinary, and who is a special mediator between this world and the next. The shaman is a healer, driving out EVIL spirits or finding lost and strayed souls. Going into trance, she or he may communicate in the voices of gods or ancestors, or even travel to the other world. The shaman is the prototype of many later religious personalities: the priest, the prophet, the medium, the poet and bard.

The Neolithic or New Stone Age is basically stone age society after the discovery of agriculture. Beginning some 12,000 years ago, probably in Asia, it meant the onset of sedentary communities. Religiously, agriculture meant a revolution no less profound than was the social and economic impact of farming. Attention moved to the Earth, to the mother GODDESS who is often identified with the Earth, and to the cycle of seasons with seed-time PRAYERS and harvest festivals. All in all, agriculture meant a new emphasis on goddesses and the sacredness of the Earth. In some places it also meant a darker development in religion, for farming has its anxious side and brings a fuller realization of the relation of death and life: Like the seed, the seeming death of one thing can mean the life of another. Neolithic mythology often told that the coming of agriculture meant the death of a goddess, out of whose body came the abundant products of the field. In Neolithic religion, more than before, appeared animal and human SACRIFICE, headhunting, and perhaps cannibalism as a religious rite.

At the very end of prehistory comes an interesting development that seems a precursor of the large-scale building of ancient civilization—megalithism, or the making of megaliths like at Stonehenge and other sites in Britain, huge upright stones clearly with some sacred meaning. Parallel to them are the mazes of Malta and the large tombs of Japan. After this came the tiny marks by which engineers and merchants kept dimensions and accounts, and a little later historians kept records, and priests transcribed as scripture the words and deeds of their gods. At this point prehistoric religion became the religion of history. But many of the basic themes of religion—gods, temples, rituals, the role of religious specialists, myths, religion as the upholder of community values—had already been laid down.

Further reading: Cynthia Eller, *The Myth of Matriarchal Prehistory: Why an Invented Past Won't Give Women a Future* (Boston: Beacon Press, 2000); Marija Gimbutas, *The Living Goddesses,* Miriam Robbins Dexter, ed. (Berkeley: University of California Press, 1999); Timothy Insoll, *Archaeology, Ritual, Religion* (London: Routledge, 2004); Steven Mithen, *The Prehistory of the Mind: A Search for the Origins of Art, Religion, and Science* (London: Thames & Hudson, 1999).

Presbyterian and Reformed churches Protestant churches that follow the teachings of John CALVIN (1509–64). Technically, any churches that follow John Calvin's teachings are Reformed churches. Presbyterian churches are Reformed churches that are organized in a particular way. They are governed by assemblies of ministers and elected lay representatives. The name "Presbyterian" comes from the word "presbyter," which means "elder." The representatives at Presbyterian assemblies are often called presbyters or elders.

Churches of British, especially Scottish, origin use the name "Presbyterian." Churches that started in continental Europe use the name "Reformed," for example, the Dutch Reformed.

HISTORY

John Calvin led the REFORMATION in Geneva, Switzerland, from 1541 to 1564. He had a distinctive THEOLOGY and a distinctive VISION of what a Christian society should be like.

On the continent of Europe, Calvin's teachings came to dominate religious life in the Netherlands. Reformed churches became minority churches in France, Hungary, Bohemia, and Poland. After the Peace of Westphalia in 1648, some German princes decided to have Reformed rather than Lutheran or Catholic churches in their realms (see LUTHERANISM and ROMAN CATHOLICISM).

The Reformed tradition influenced Scotland very early in its history. An important leader there was John Knox (c. 1514–72). Eventually the Presbyterian Church became the established or official religion of Scotland. South of Scotland, in England, many people favored the Reformed tradition, too. They were called Puritans, because they wanted to purify the English church of Catholic influence (see PURITANISM and ANGLICANISM). The Puritans were not successful; the Church of England retained its Catholic heritage. Nevertheless, the Edict of Toleration (1689) permitted English Presbyterians and other English Protestants to form their own churches.

Reformed traditions came to North America very early. The Dutch Reformed Church was the established religion of the colony of New Netherland, which later became New York. The Puritans of New England were staunch Calvinists, but they favored CONGREGATIONALISM rather than Presbyterianism. Scotch-Irish immigrants brought Presbyterianism to the North American colonies. German immigrants from the region of the Rhine brought their own Reformed traditions. After the Revolutionary War, however, other Protestant churches dominated the American religious scene. As the frontiers expanded west, Baptists and Methodists were better able to meet the needs of the pioneers. They became the dominant churches of 19th-century America.

MISSIONARIES planted Presbyterian and Reformed churches in many parts of the world. Indonesia, formerly a Dutch colony, and Korea have very large Reformed churches. Presbyterian churches flourished among British immigrants in Canada, Australia, and New Zealand. Dutch settlers known as Boers brought the Dutch Reformed Church to South Africa. That church provided a religious sanction for apartheid. Apartheid was the legal separation of whites and blacks to ensure white rule.

In the 19th and 20th centuries, Reformed churches have pursued Calvin's twin interests—theology and the proper organization of society—in exemplary fashion. Prominent Reformed theologians have included the "father" of liberal theology, Friedrich Schleiermacher (1768–1834), the prominent "neo-orthodox" theologians, Karl Barth (1886–1968) and Emil Brunner (1889–1966), and the American brothers, Reinhold Niebuhr (1892–1971) and H. Richard Niebuhr (1894–1962). The Reformed traditions have also worked actively for social reform and improvement. Reformed theologians played prominent roles in the Confessing Church, some of whose members opposed Nazi policies in Germany.

BELIEFS

Like most Protestants, Calvinists recognize the BIBLE as the ultimate religious authority. Indeed, a strong current in Calvinism has insisted that Christians may only accept practices that are positively mandated in the Bible. Calvinists also recognize the ancient Christian CREEDS. They worship GOD as a TRINITY and confess that in JESUS two natures, divine and human, were joined in one person.

Calvin agreed with Martin LUTHER in emphasizing that human beings cannot earn their own SALVATION. They must be saved by God's GRACE. He also emphasized the absolute majesty and power of God. In doing so he taught that God chooses to save some sinners but to consign others to HELL. That teaching has led to some disputes in the past, but most Reformed thinkers have preferred to leave questions of salvation in God's hands. They have emphasized other themes instead: that God is the mighty lord of history, active in the world through his grace, and human beings should praise him and seek to follow the path that he has established—not to earn salvation but to express their recognition of God's glory and goodness.

PRACTICES

During the Reformation, Luther and his followers adopted the policy of rejecting only those Catholic traditions that they thought violated the message of the Bible. Calvin and his followers went further. They allowed only those practices that they thought the Bible directly commanded. The sermon became the central feature of Reformed WORSHIP (*see* PREACHING). Another prominent feature was singing Psalms rather than nonbiblical songs. Calvin himself produced a *Psalter*—Psalms set to simple music—and many others followed. The Reformed tradition has tended to shy away from weekly celebration of the EUCHARIST. It also disagrees with both the Catholic and the Lutheran ideas that Jesus' body and blood are really present in the bread and wine of communion. Calvin taught instead that the eucharist brings Christians into Jesus' presence.

Calvinists take very seriously their calling to do God's work in the world. As a result, the Reformed tradition has cultivated a particular attitude toward life in the world. That attitude is one of earnestness and seriousness rather than idleness and frivolity. The sociologist Max WEBER (1864–1920) suggested that this attitude came about because Calvinists needed to convince themselves that they belonged to God's chosen or elect. This, he said, was the origin of capitalism. Although Weber's idea about the origin of capitalism may be wrong, his characterization of the Calvinist way of life was correct. Calvinists believe that those who live an upright life will prosper.

ORGANIZATION

Not all Reformed churches have adopted a Presbyterian form of organization. Some have preferred Congregationalism. A few have even had bishops. But many Reformed churches are Presbyterian. This means that they see all ministers as having equal status; they do not allow bishops. It also means that assemblies made up of ministers and elected elders govern the church. Assemblies meet at different levels, from the local congregation to the national church. The Reformed tradition has taken particularly seriously one function of the elders: the maintenance of church discipline.

SIGNIFICANCE

The Reformed tradition is one of the oldest and most important forms of PROTESTANTISM. It played a major role in shaping the traditional outlook of the United States. It gave Americans the idea that their nation is special or chosen by God, an idea that is theologically questionable. It also provided the motivation for certain traditions, such as observing Sunday as a day of rest.

Further reading: Renée House and John Coakley, ed., *Patterns and Portraits: Women in the History of the Reformed Church in America* (Grand Rapids, Mich.: W. B. Eerdmans, 1999); Donald K. McKim, *Presbyterian Beliefs: A Brief Introduction* (Louisville, Ky.: Geneva Press, 2003); Jan Rohls, *Reformed Confessions: Theology from Zurich to Barmen* (Louisville, Ky.: Westminster John Knox Press, 1998); James H. Smylie, *A Brief History of the Presbyterians* (Louisville, Ky.: Geneva Press, 1996).

priests and priesthood A class of religious specialists in many religions. A priest differs in some ways from other specialists, like a shaman (*see* SHAMANISM), minister, or teacher, or like a Jewish RABBI or Muslim IMAM. The priest's work involves presenting a formal service of offering, commonly interpreted as a SACRIFICE; it is generally presented at a special place, most often a sacred table or ALTAR. The priest may well have special training in the teaching of the religion and have a role as instructor and pastor. She or he may also have had profound religious experiences that make one a mystic or an ecstatic, impart a charismatic personality, or even that make one a shaman or prophet. But that is not the essence of priestly office. It is understood to be a formal position, built into the formal institutional structure of a religion and imparted through ordination by an authorized person. In Christian priesthood, like that of ROMAN CATHOLICISM, EASTERN ORTHODOX CHRISTIANITY, or ANGLICANISM, ORDINATION is imparted by a bishop who is believed to be in a lineage of such ordinations going back to the APOSTLES themselves, who were appointed by CHRIST; this is called "apostolic succession." Services conducted by priests, whether the Catholic Christian EUCHARIST or mass, or the sacrifices of the temple in ancient Israel, or the offerings of the BRAHMINS of India, are usually performed in a predetermined, ritualistic way, with emphasis more on precise correctness of word and gesture than on feeling. A reverent, devotional mood on the part of the priest is certainly encouraged, yet it is usually said that the effectiveness of the rite for other believers does not depend on the feeling or worthiness of the priest, but simply on the correct doing of the rite by a duly authorized officiant.

Priesthood may be vocational or hereditary. In the former, persons enter it because they feel called to the office, and generally undertake formal training in preparation for ordination. In principle, that is the case with the Christian and Buddhist priesthood. In some cases, as with Roman Catholic priests and many Buddhist monks, priests practice CELIBACY, giving up marriage for the sake of the vocation. In others, such as Eastern Orthodox and SHINTO priesthood, and Buddhist priesthood in Japan, the priesthood often appears to be hereditary in practice though vocational in its ideal.

Strictly hereditary priesthood, like that of ancient JUDAISM and of the Brahmin priests in Hinduism, is restricted to certain families or castes as a matter of principle. These priests properly receive training before entering into the sacred office, but their ultimate authorization is transmitted by birth. Sometimes disparaged, the steady, faithful work of priests over the generations has kept many religions alive.

primal religion The religion of humans living in tribal societies before, or independent of, the invention of writing. This style of religion has been called "primitive religion," but that term now has the wrong connotations, suggesting it is elementary and unsophisticated. Actually, primal religion can be very sophisticated in its myth (*see* MYTH AND MYTHOLOGY) and SYMBOLISM. *Primal* is intended only to indicate that this form of religion was first and is the basis on which all other religion was built historically.

This collection of patterns of religious life was once presumably universal but has gradually given way to subsequent developments: the religions of the ancient empires like EGYPTIAN RELIGION or Chinese religion (*see* CHINA, RELIGIONS OF); the rise of the major religions founded in historical times, such as BUDDHISM and CHRISTIANITY; and finally the development of other ways of life in recent times. Now only small and scattered groups of peoples live in truly tribal, primal religion societies. But carryovers from primal religion can be found in all later faiths, and understanding it can illuminate much about human life today.

THEMES OF PRIMAL RELIGION

Primal religion today includes the traditional faiths as diverse as NATIVE AMERICAN RELIGIONS, AFRICAN RELIGIONS, ARCTIC RELIGION, PACIFIC OCEAN RELIGIONS, and the religions of tribal peoples in India. Some are hunters and gatherers; some practice early forms of agriculture. They are far from all the same. Nonetheless certain themes can be found widely, if not universally, throughout societies that practice forms of primal religion. These are themes related to cosmic religion, gods and spirits, INITIATION, SHAMANISM, hunting religion, and agricultural religion.

COSMIC RELIGION

The historian of religion Mircea ELIADE used the term *cosmic religion* to refer to religion centered on nature and the turn of the seasons rather than on historical events (as for example, JUDAISM centers on the EXODUS or Christianity centers on the life and death of JESUS). For cosmic religion, the location of the Sacred, as Eliade called the object of religion, is here and now, in nature and the temple—a sacred mountain, tree, or site where dances or sacrifices are performed—or in the "sacred time" of seasons and festivals. Every NEW YEAR FESTIVAL is like a repeat of the creation of the world. Virtually all primal religion is imbued with the cosmic religion outlook. Indeed, much of the cosmic lingers today just behind the historical perspective. In Christianity, for example, Christmas commemorates a historical event, the birth of Jesus, but the Christmas tree, and the holiday's close proximity to New Year's, are cosmic religion symbols.

GODS AND SPIRITS

Primal religion is religion of many spiritual forces: divine spirits, spirits of nature, ancestral spirits. But often there is a supreme GOD, or group of gods, who first made the world and placed human beings in it. There are many beliefs as to how the world came into existence. In some, the world was born of the mating of the deities of heaven and earth. Sometimes humans emerged out of the earth, or they came down from heaven. Sometimes they were taught the skills of civilization by a TRICKSTER deity, such as Coyote in Native American stories or the more tragic Prometheus of Greek myth, who stole fire from heaven to give it to humanity. Sometimes, in stories reminiscent of ADAM and EVE in the Garden of Eden, humans were at first close to the gods but through some error or rebellious act fell away from that intimacy. In some cases the FALL was associated with the discovery of agriculture. In response the supreme God may have withdrawn from daily interaction with the world, leaving the field to spirits of nature and ancestors.

The SOUL, or spirit within, may be thought of as a separable, undying part of oneself. In the AFTERLIFE it has its own destiny. It may go to another world underground, in a sacred mountain, or over the sea. Or it may remain around the hearth or family altar. Or again, it may become a powerful ancestral spirit (see ANCESTOR VENERATION) who guards descendents still in this life but also punishes them if they violate TABOOS or moral codes. Or different aspects of the soul may perform all three of these functions.

Related to belief in soul are the great dances (see DANCE AND RELIGION) and festivals that primal peoples often observe. In them they may take on the appearance of, and even feel themselves one with, gods or ancestors. For example, in AUSTRALIAN RELIGIONS, dancing festivals, which may continue for days, were considered participation in the Dreamtime, the other world of gods, ancestors, and mythic events. Dances held before hunting or planting, or in celebration of success in the field or harvest, may use costumes and symbols indicating identification with the mythic first hunters or farmers.

INITIATION

For many primal religion societies, life is a series of initiations (see INITIATIONS, RELIGIOUS). It is through them that members become more and more a part of the tribe and prepare themselves for the afterlife. The most important are usually those of young women and men who, at puberty or adolescence, become full members of the society. Imitation is often compared to a second birth, or a death and rebirth, and inevitably the way it is enacted contains symbolism suggestive of birth and death.

For example, among New Guinea societies, the young men were taken by the older men to a lodge deep in the jungle. The women would look on anxiously as they left, for they were told that the boys were to be eaten by a monster, who would release them only on the condition that they sacrificed a sufficient number of pigs. In the lodge, a great noise was made by a device called a bullroarer to emulate the growling of the beast, which frightened the boys. They then received CIRCUMCISION and, while in the lodge, learned the secret lore of the tribe.

Sometimes the young men ritually passed through the legs of the older men, in imitation of physical birth. When they returned, like newborn children they were first fed only soft food, but soon they were recognized as full-fledged men of the tribe. However, in some such societies further initiations were possible, like higher degrees, which gave members greater and greater status and prepared them for encounters with the gods at DEATH.

In some examples, the initiation was more individual, like that of the Native American Pawnee youth, who went on a "vision quest": He was expected to remain alone in the wilderness until he had received a dream or vision of his guardian spirit.

Initiation for girls often occurs individually rather than in a group as with boys, taking place at the onset of puberty. It may entail such practices as isolating the young woman in a special lodge, singing over her by other women of the tribe, and making marks such as tattoos. Sometimes the rite is part of a series that leads directly up to marriage, the wedding ceremony being the culminating initiation for a woman. Female initiation is just as important and common as male.

SHAMANISM

Some initiations are special to certain people. The most important is typically that of the shaman, an individual believed to have a special call from the gods enabling him or her to experience SPIRIT POSSESSION or to travel in spirit to the realm of the gods or ancestors. The shaman is therefore like a mediator between this world and the divine (*see* SHAMANISM).

RELIGION OF HUNTING AND GATHERING SOCIETIES

Among the first humans, and in some societies today, food and other necessities are obtained through hunting and gathering. (These are called Paleolithic, or "Old Stone Age," societies. *See* PREHISTORIC RELIGION.) Inevitably this quest involves a religious dimension, for it is essential to life itself. It is necessary to prepare spiritually for a hunt. Some hunters would prepare by FASTING or observing a special diet (*see* DIET AND RELIGION) and by remaining silent while leaving for the field. Sometimes a "master of animals," a divine spirit who

is able to "open" or "close" the forest, making the game easy or impossible to find, was invoked. This being favors hunters who approach the quarry with reverence, thank the animal for giving himself to them, and use every part of the kill.

Gathering, often the province of women, is no less important and in fact in many primal societies gathering produced a much higher proportion of sustenance than hunting. The gatherers had special knowledge of the earth spirit, who provided these "gifts" out of her bounty.

AGRICULTURAL RELIGION

It may have been women also who first "discovered" agriculture, if it was they who first noticed that discarded seeds from gathered crops could produce the same near to home and who may in time have learned to domesticate animals as well. (Early agricultural societies are called Neolithic, or "New Stone Age.") Nonetheless, in mythology, agriculture is often seen as a kind of forbidden knowledge, stolen by a human or divine rebel against the primal gods, perhaps by killing a deity and taking agricultural crops out of the divine body.

Agriculture brought hardships as well as benefits to societies. It can be more monotonous and labor intensive than hunting or gathering and, moreover, seems to involve the grim principle of life for life. It was in connection with early agriculture that extensive CANNIBALISM, human and animal SACRIFICE, and headhunting came into use, basically in the belief that they would increase the harvest. For example, sometimes parts of a sacrificial victim would be placed around a field or, like the shrunken heads made by the Jivaro of the upper Amazon, "danced" through the fields so that life-energy could flow from them into the crops.

In agricultural religion, often the Sky was a male god, perhaps of the Sun (*see* SUN AND RELIGION) or of the Moon (*see* MOON AND RELIGION), and the earth was a mother goddess. Many great goddesses of antiquity, such as ISIS, Demeter, Ishtar, KALI or AMATERASU (*see* GODDESSES), seem to be of this background. Because in agriculture the seasons of planting and harvest are so important, rituals and festivals connected with them became prominent landmarks of the year. These still continue in such popular spring celebrations as PASSOVER and EASTER, and Thanksgiving in the fall. Out of archaic agricultural religion emerged the ancient religions and religious founders (*see* FOUNDERS, RELIGIOUS) of literate societies.

Further reading: Mircea Eliade, *Cosmos and History* (New York; Harper Torchbooks, 1959); Mircea Eliade, *A History of Religious Ideas,* Vol. 1 (Chicago: University of Chicago Press, 1978); Sam D. Gill, *Beyond "The Primitive": The Religions of Nonliterate Peoples* (Englewood Cliffs, N.J.: Prentice Hall, 1982); Stephan D. Glazier, *Anthropology of Religion* (Westport, Conn.: Greenwood, 1997); Johannes Maringer, *The Gods of Prehistoric Man* (New York: Knopf, 1960).

prophecy Words spoken by a human being on behalf of GOD. In common English a prophecy tells something that will happen in the future, often in the distant future. Christians have often, but not always, looked upon prophecy in this way. They have taken the prophecies recorded in the Hebrew BIBLE as referring to JESUS. Some have also applied biblical prophecies to current events. In religion in general, however, prophecy also has a different meaning. It refers to messages that human beings transmit for a god or gods. Such messages may say something about the future, but they may not. Even when they talk about the future, they most often refer to events that are about to occur.

Prophecy was particularly important in the religions of the ancient Near East. It was one way by which people learned the wills of the gods who had power over events. Religions that derive from the ancient Near East—ZOROASTRIANISM, JUDAISM, CHRISTIANITY, MANICHAEISM, and ISLAM—have important traditions of prophecy. People sometimes speak of prophets in HINDUISM, BUDDHISM, and east Asian religions, too. An example is the Japanese "prophet" NICHIREN, although he was not a prophet in the sense that he communicated a message from a god.

People in the 19th and 20th centuries continued to claim to receive messages from gods. Prophets arose among the indigenous peoples of North America and Africa. Contact with European settlers and colonizers had produced hardships for these peoples; indeed, it had often destroyed their traditional ways of life, when it did not destroy the people themselves. Prophets spoke to these situations. They also addressed crises unrelated to European incursions. Prophets arose among European Americans, too. The best known may be Joseph Smith, who founded the LATTER-DAY SAINTS, commonly known as the Mormons. Pentecostal Christians claim that people today may receive the gift of prophecy (*see* PENTECOSTALISM). In 19th-century Iran a resurgence of prophecy gave rise to the BAHA'I faith.

Prophets generally deliver a message to a group or society rather than to a private individual. Some prophecies address the immediate concerns of a specific community, while others are more universal in scope. The prophets of ancient Israel relayed prophecies of the first kind. Earlier prophets—Miriam, Deborah, Samuel, ELIJAH, Elisha—only spoke their words. The words of important prophets from the eighth century on—AMOS, HOSEA, ISAIAH, JEREMIAH, EZEKIEL—came to be written down. Jewish tradition holds that prophecy ended in 400 B.C.E.

Other prophets have relayed messages that are universal. The most prominent examples are prophets who founded major religions: ZARATHUSTRA, Mani, and MUHAMMAD. Both Mani and Muhammad saw themselves as conveying God's final and complete revelation and therefore bringing the line of prophets to a close. Mani and Muhammad also saw Jesus as one of the prior prophets. Some may consider Jesus' activities to be closer to those of a charismatic healer or a moral teacher.

In the last half of the 20th century, psychologists carefully studied what happens "when prophecy fails." Many people choose not to abandon the prophecy. They deal with the "cognitive dissonance" that results in a number of ways. For example, William Miller had predicted that Jesus was going to return in 1844. He did not, but rather than surrender the prophecy, leaders of the

SEVENTH-DAY ADVENTISTS interpreted it in such a way that the prophecy had been fulfilled.

prophets, biblical The name of a group of religious specialists in ancient Israel, as well as of a collection of books in the Hebrew scriptures (*see* SCRIPTURES, HEBREW). Religious people have often wished for messages from their gods. In the areas around what is now Israel and Palestine during the second millennium B.C.E. (2000–1001 B.C.E.), special classes of people claimed to receive such messages. Similar people existed in ancient Israel and Judah (the northern and southern kingdoms, respectively), too. We now call them "prophets," although that word comes from ancient Greek rather than ancient Hebrew. Some of these prophets seem to have received their messages as words; others seem to have had visions. They were active in ancient Israel from before the monarchy (before 1020 B.C.E.) until about the year 400 B.C.E.

The BIBLE distinguishes between true and false prophets. This judgment reflects the views of later times, when it was clear which prophets had been correct and which had been wrong. At the time when the prophets were active, it would have been much harder to tell. Some prophets did speak for the GOD YHWH ("the Lord"), while others only spoke for other gods, such as BAAL and Asherah. But it was fairly common for people in ancient Israel to worship those other gods, and they took their prophets seriously. In addition, prophets of YHWH often argued with one another and gave contradictory messages.

A superficial reading of the Bible might suggest that prophets were lone figures who stood up to authority, spoke the word of God, and then vanished. However, a careful reading of the Bible shows that there were regular groups of prophets in ancient Israel and Judah, and at various times prophets seem to have been full-fledged members of the king's court.

Prophets often seem to have been called to prophesy as a result of extraordinary experiences. In this experience they are somewhat like SHAMANS in other religions, who also communicate with the unseen. The prophets in the biblical tradition talk a great deal about remaining loyal to God and making society more just. They often thought of justice as returning to the way things used to be. Prophets sometimes acted out their messages, as when ISAIAH walked naked through JERUSALEM and JEREMIAH wore a yoke. They also occasionally challenged their opponents to contests, as in the contest between ELIJAH and the prophets of Baal. But the most typical activity of the prophets was to speak messages from God. Often their prophecies took the form of poetry.

The earliest biblical prophets—those whom the Bible considers genuine—include figures such as Miriam, the sister of MOSES, and Deborah, the judge. The prophet Samuel helped set up the monarchy, while the prophet Nathan was an important and sometimes critical adviser of King DAVID. After the monarchy had split into northern and southern kingdoms, Elijah and Elisha were active in the northern kingdom. They called upon the people to remain faithful to the worship of YHWH. AMOS and HOSEA also opposed the worship of other gods, though few of these prophets' sayings are recorded. The prophets whose words were gathered into major books came a little later: Isaiah around 700 B.C.E., Jeremiah around 600 B.C.E., and EZEKIEL during the exile in Babylon (597–539 B.C.E.). The prophecies of two anonymous prophets became part of the book of Isaiah. "Second Isaiah" was active during the Babylonian exile, while "Third Isaiah" was active after the exiles returned home.

According to tradition, prophecy ceased in Israel about the year 400 B.C.E. Certainly after that time the inhabitants of Judea tended to favor writings known as APOCALYPTIC LITERATURE. These writings make the fate of God's people depend not so much on their return to YHWH and their seeking of justice but on the outcome of a cosmic struggle between God and forces opposed to God. But the ancient Judeans still respected the older prophets. By about 200 B.C.E. they had begun to collect, edit, and combine the sayings of Isaiah, Jeremiah, Ezekiel, and "the Twelve" to form the second part of the Hebrew scriptures, *Nevi'im*, "the Prophets."

Further reading: Rodney R. Hutton, *Fortress Introduction to the Prophets* (Minneapolis, Minn.: Fortress Press, 2004); David L. Petersen, *The Prophetic Literature: An Introduction* (Louisville, Ky.: Westminster John Knox Press, 2002); John F. A. Sawyer, *Prophecy and the Biblical Prophets*, rev. ed. (New York: Oxford University Press, 1993).

Protestantism   One of the three major branches of CHRISTIANITY. Protestantism resulted from the REFORMATION. That event produced several distinct churches and traditions: the Lutheran, the Reformed and Presbyterian, the Anabaptist, and the Anglican or Church of England (*see* LUTHERANISM, PRESBYTERIAN AND REFORMED CHURCHES, MENNONITES, AMISH, and ANGLICANISM). Later events added more churches to Protestantism. These include QUAKERS, Congregationalists, Baptists, Methodists, the Pentecostal churches, and groups about which "mainline" Protestants have some suspicion, for example, the LATTER-DAY SAINTS, also known as Mormons and the JEHOVAH'S WITNESSES (*see* CONGREGATIONALISM, BAPTIST CHURCHES, METHODISM, and PENTECOSTALISM). In the 19th century, Protestants became intensely interested in missionary work. As a result, many Protestants now live outside the traditional Protestant homelands of northwestern Europe and nations made up of European settlers. In the 20th century, Pentecostals were especially successful in spreading their faith in Latin America and Africa.

Protestants differ widely in their beliefs, practices, and ways of organizing churches. That is why there is no single Protestant church. But they share some general features.

During the Reformation, Protestants rejected the PAPACY. They insisted that the ultimate authority in religion was the BIBLE. Some insist that the Bible is entirely without error, but others disagree. Many Protestant churches also acknowledge the ancient Christian CREEDS. With the creeds, they conceive of GOD as a TRINITY, Father (or Creator), Son, and Holy Spirit. Many Protestant groups have also written specific summaries of their own beliefs. These summaries are known as "confessions."

During the Reformation, Martin LUTHER insisted that human beings could not earn their own SALVATION. Salvation was a gift given freely by God. This may be the central Protestant insight. But interpretations of it vary. Strict Calvinism teaches that God chooses to save some people but condemn others (*see* John CALVIN). Methodism stresses that all may be saved; once saved, a person should pursue moral perfection.

Almost all Protestants gather for WORSHIP on Sunday. But there are exceptions. Seventh-Day Adventists worship on Saturday (*see* SEVENTH-DAY ADVENTISM). The heart of Protestant worship has always been the sermon (*see* PREACHING). During Protestant services congregations sing psalms or hymns together. They also listen to readings from the Bible and recite PRAYERS. Most but not all Protestants recognize two SACRAMENTS: BAPTISM, or the RITUAL for joining the church, and the EUCHARIST, a sharing of bread and wine or grape juice. Unlike Sunday services in the Catholic and Orthodox churches, Protestant Sunday services do not always include the Eucharist.

Protestants organize their churches in many different ways. Some churches have bishops. Presbyterian churches are governed by assemblies of elders. Congregationalist churches insist that each individual congregation be self-governing. Most Protestant churches have ordained clergy. The more liberal churches ordain women.

During the 20th century, many smaller Protestant churches merged to form larger bodies. Some mergers joined different groups who shared a common heritage. Examples include the Presbyterian Church in the United States and the United Pentecostal Church. Other mergers joined Protestants who had different heritages. Examples include, in the United States, the United Church of Christ, which combined Congregationalist and Reformed churches, and the Church of South India, which combined Anglican, Methodist, Presbyterian, Dutch Reformed, and Congregationalist churches.

During the 20th century, many Protestants also took part in the "ecumenical movement." This movement tried to overcome the divisions separating not just Protestant groups but all Christians. In

1948 Protestants and Orthodox Christians created the World Council of Churches. Individual Protestant churches also entered into DIALOGUE with Catholics, Jews, and members of other religions. Not all Protestants approve of these activities. Some see them as abandoning God's revealed truth. Another powerful movement within Protestantism during the last 100 years has been FUNDAMENTALISM (*see* FUNDAMENTALISM, CHRISTIAN).

Further reading: Karl Barth, *Protestant Theology in the Nineteenth Century: Its Background and History* (Grand Rapids, Mich.: W. B. Eerdmans, 2002); John Dillenberger and Claude Welch, *Protestant Christianity: Interpreted through Its Development*, 2d ed. (New York: Macmillan, 1988); Martin E. Marty, ed., *Varieties of Protestantism* (New York: K. G. Saur, 1992).

Protestantism in America   The practice of PROTESTANTISM, one of the three major branches of CHRISTIANITY, in the Western Hemisphere. This entry focuses on Protestantism in the United States.

At the end of the 20th century, the largest single Christian body in the United States was the Roman Catholic Church. In fact, it had been the largest American religious body for roughly 150 years. Nevertheless, the public culture of the United States and its defining ideals have traditionally been Protestant in character.

The 13 British colonies that became the United States were overwhelmingly Protestant. Nine of the 13 had a kind of Protestantism—or Protestantism in general—as their "established" or official religion.

American Protestantism developed several distinctive characteristics. These include an emphasis on experience, activism, and millennialism. These traits do not characterize all Protestant bodies. For example, sacramental traditions, such as ANGLICANISM and LUTHERANISM, are considerably different. But these traits characterize the Protestantism that has had the most impact on American public life.

The New England Puritans emphasized experience (*see* PURITANISM). At first only those who could give evidence of a conversion experience could be full-fledged members of their community. The emphasis on a personal experience of SALVATION continued through many later movements. It sparked the First Great Awakening in the mid-1700s; the Second Great Awakening on the frontier in the early 1800s; Holiness movements in the latter part of the 19th century; Pentecostal Christianity in the 20th century (*see* PENTECOSTALISM); and, of broader appeal, a tradition of revivals. The revival tradition in turn inspired many 20th-century preachers as they began to use the new media of radio and television. Given this continued emphasis on a religion of experience, it is perhaps fitting that William James wrote the first important American book in religious studies on just this subject: *The Varieties of Religious Experience*.

American Protestantism has also been activistic. That is, it has sought to create a better society. The largest reform movements of the 19th century were the movements to abolish slavery and the use of alcohol. At the end of the century, liberal Christians pursued the "Social GOSPEL." More conservative Christians, such as the SALVATION ARMY, preferred the work of "rescue missions." In the 20th-century, Protestant activism continued with the civil rights movement of the 1950s and 1960s and, for more conservative Christians, the crusade to end legalized abortion of the 1970s through the 1990s. By the beginning of the 21st century the activism of conservative Evangelical Christians was making its presence felt in support of conservative Republican candidates in elections at various levels.

Protestant activism looks to the future. So does Protestant millennialism. Millennialism emphasizes that JESUS is going to return soon and usher in a golden age. The Adventist groups of the 1840s are textbook examples of millennialist movements (*see* SEVENTH-DAY ADVENTISM). Millennialism also became a common feature of fundamentalism (*see* EVANGELICAL CHRISTIANITY and FUNDAMENTALISM, CHRISTIAN).

By the beginning of the 21st century, the Protestant character of American public life was threatened. The population of the country was becoming more plural religiously, and its public culture was becoming increasingly secular. These changes sparked a large response from conservative, evangelical Protestants. They sought to recall the United States to its moral roots. In doing so, they were active in American politics from the local to the national level. In effect, many called for a return to the situation in which Protestantism was the "established" or official religion of the United States in fact, if not in law.

Further reading: Sydney E. Ahlstrom, ed., *Theology in America: The Major Protestant Voices from Puritanism to Neo-Orthodoxy* (Indianapolis: Hackett, 2003); Randall Balmer and Lauren F. Winner, *Protestantism in America* (New York: Columbia University Press, 2000); Douglas Jacobsen and William Vance Trollinger Jr., ed., *Reforming the Center: American Protestantism, 1900 to the Present* (Grand Rapids, Mich.: W. B. Eerdmans, 1998); Mark A. Noll, *Protestants in America* (New York: Oxford University Press, 2000).

Psalms   A book of the BIBLE that contains ancient Hebrew poems or hymns; more broadly, the kind of hymns or poems that this book contains. Psalms is the first book in the part of the Hebrew Bible known as *Ketuvim,* "writings." In Hebrew it is called *Tehillim,* "Praises." It contains 150 psalms, divided into five groups called "books." Some of the psalms are among the best-known parts of the Bible.

THE COMPOSITION AND CONTENT OF PSALMS

By the time of JESUS it was already customary to refer to King DAVID as the author of the book of Psalms. In actuality, however, the psalms in this book seem to have many different authors. Psalms itself refers to different groups of PRIESTS as the authors of some psalms.

The book of Psalms does not contain the only psalms that were written in ancient Israel. There are similar poems in other books of the Bible. Compare, for example, Psalm 18 with 2 Samuel 22. There is also an ancient collection of psalms known as the Psalms of SOLOMON. Psalms are not considered poetry because they rhyme. Instead, they put together two or occasionally three short statements in a single verse. Often the statements parallel one another. For example, Psalm 145 begins:

> *I will extol you, my GOD and King,*
> *and bless your name forever and ever.*
> *Every day I will bless you,*
> *and praise your name forever and ever.*

Scholars have tried to group psalms according to their content, but they have come up with different groupings. It may be helpful to say that Psalms includes, among other kinds of poems, hymns of praise, laments, songs of thanksgiving, psalms that recount events from the past, and songs that reflect on the nature of God.

The book of Psalms seems to name certain melodies that should be used in the singing of specific psalms. For example, apparently Psalm 56 was to be sung to the tune of "The Dove on Far-Off Terebinths." It also contains other terms whose meaning has been forgotten but that may be directions for singing. One example is the word *selah,* which appears frequently in Psalms. Some people speculate that it marks spots for musical interludes.

No one knows when the Psalms were first collected. Guesses range from the 400s to the early first century B.C.E. The DEAD SEA SCROLLS— roughly from the time of Jesus—include many scrolls containing psalms. These scrolls show that people at the time still disagreed on the exact number of poems to include in the book. In addition, although the scrolls agree on which psalms belong in Books 1 and 2 (Psalms 1–72), they disagree about which psalms belong in the last three books. But although the text of Psalms may not have been entirely fixed, people at the time still seemed to recognize the book of Psalms as having special status. For example, Jesus refers to the TORAH, the PROPHETS, and Psalms (Luke 24.44).

THE USE OF THE PSALMS

Long before the time of ancient Israel, it was common for priests in the Middle East to recite poems in praise of the gods as part of daily worship in temples. This is certainly the way the Psalms were used in the Second Temple in JERUSALEM (fifth century B.C.E. to 70 C.E.). Scholars presume that this is also the way the Psalms were used in the First Temple (mid 900s to 587 B.C.E.).

Later Jews and Christians have used the Psalms in worship, too. The standard Jewish liturgies use 84 of the psalms. In the Middle Ages, monks recited the entire book of Psalms once a week. During the Protestant REFORMATION, some of the strictest Protestant churches, such as the Reformed Church in Switzerland, allowed Christians to sing nothing but Psalms in church. The tunes that they used for these Psalms, such as "Old Hundredth" (used for Psalm 100), later became used for newly written hymns.

Many Psalms are famous, but perhaps the most famous of all is the Twenty-third Psalm. It has provided comfort to countless suffering people. It begins, "The Lord is my shepherd, I shall not want."

Ptah A god of ancient Egypt. At first Ptah was simply the god worshipped at the town of Memphis. Around 3000 B.C.E. Menes unified Egypt. He made Memphis his capital, because it stood at the place where Upper and Lower Egypt met. Ptah became a god important for all of Egypt. He was often shown standing rigidly upright, a cloth wrapped tightly about his body, holding a scepter directly in front of him in both hands.

Ptah is best known for his role in the so-called Memphite THEOLOGY. This is the story of creation that the priests of Memphis told. It is known today from a document that dates to roughly 700 B.C.E. Most scholars assume the original story is much older.

In the Memphite theology, Ptah creates by thinking in his heart and speaking words from his mouth. In other words, he creates an ordered world in the same way that the kings of Egypt created an ordered world: by giving commands. This method of creation reminds some scholars of the way in which GOD creates the world in Genesis 1.

puja Sanskrit for "honor," or WORSHIP; the common way of worshipping gods in HINDUISM for roughly the last 1,500 years.

Puja is generally directed toward the divine in image form. The underlying idea is that GOD, who is far beyond human approach, has consented out of GRACE and favor to take up residence in a particular image. One treats the image as one would treat God if God were present in his or her proper form.

Puja is performed both at home and in temples. It has three parts: giving, viewing, and receiving. Either directly or through a *pujari* (priest), the worshipper presents various ministrations to the god. These may include bathing the image in water, milk, or coconut milk, dressing it, perfuming it, ornamenting it with flowers, powders, and jewels, offering it food, waving lights and burning incense before it, and chanting SCRIPTURES and reciting PRAYERS. *Darsana*, viewing the image, is also an important act of worship. It gives the worshipper a glimpse of what is in reality beyond all sight. Finally, the worshipper receives the god's blessings. This *prasada* is generally symbolized physically in water, a spoonful of which may be sipped and sprinkled over one's self, or food. The latter may be the family's meal, offered to the god before eating, or the bits of coconut, nuts, or flowerettes of sugar often dispensed at temples.

See also IMAGES, ICONS, IDOLS IN RELIGION.

Puranas From the Sanskrit word for "ancient, old." Puranas are the chief mythological books in contemporary HINDUISM.

Tradition assigns the Puranas, like the *Mahabharata*, to an author named Vyasa, literally, "the compiler." Each Purana is supposed to discuss five topics: creation, dissolution, the genealogies of gods and ancestors, the ages of the worlds, and the history of the solar and lunar dynasties. In fact, the Puranas discuss much more.

Although the number of Puranas is large, 18 are singled out as major. Some divide them into three groups of six, identified with the gods BRAHMA, VISHNU, and SIVA. The most loved of all Puranas is the *Bhagavata*. It recounts in full the tales of the youthful KRISHNA.

Pure Land Buddhism An important movement in East Asian BUDDHISM; also called Amidism. In contrast to the emphasis on MEDITATION in some other forms of the religion, Pure Land may be called a Buddhism of SALVATION by FAITH alone. For the central idea is that the BUDDHA called Amitabha (Emiduo-fo in Chinese, AMIDA in Japanese) ages ago vowed out of compassion for all suffering sentient beings that all who called upon his name in faith would be saved by being brought after death into his HEAVEN, called the Western Paradise or Pure Land.

The teaching began in India, where it was first taught that great buddhas like Amida (not to be confused with the historical Buddha, the founder of the Buddhist religion) have a paradisal universe extending around them as a kind of aura. Persons deeply attuned to one of these buddhas can enter this paradise through faith. Amida, out of infinite love for all creatures, made his paradise accessible simply by faith. His heaven or Pure Land is a wonderful place in itself, described in the old Indian Pure Land scriptures as filled with trees covered with jeweled nets and beautiful music played by angelic beings. Furthermore, in the Pure Land it is easy to do the final meditations that will lead to the ultimate liberation, NIRVANA.

Coming to China in the early centuries C.E., and thence to Korea, Japan, and Vietnam, Pure Land was influenced by Taoist ideas of paradise (*see* TAOISM) and also by a Chinese perception that salvation cannot be divided up into stages but must be realized all at once, just as one cannot leap over a canyon in several jumps, but must

do it in one bound or not at all. Hence salvation is attained by a simple act of faith. In China (*see* CHINA, RELIGIONS OF, KOREAN RELIGION, and VIETNAMESE RELIGION), Pure Land is the characteristic Buddhism of ordinary laypeople, while Chan or Zen is the practice of monks.

In Japan, Pure Land eventuated into two main denominations started in the Middle Age: Jodo-shu (Pure Land sect), founded by Honen (1133–1212), and Jodo-shinshu (True Pure Land sect), founded by his disciple Shinran (1173–1262). Both stress the importance of chanting the Nembutsu (*Namu Amida Butsu*, "Hail Amida Buddha") as the act of faith, and say that this faith is what is really important. Salvation, Honen and Shinran taught, comes from the GRACE or power of Amida, not from one's own efforts. This is true Buddhism, they said, because to depend on the grace of another rather than on oneself is real egolessness, and the whole point of Buddhism is to realize the emptiness of the ego and the continuity of one's whole being with the universe as a whole. Amida, some say, can be thought of as a personification of that universe.

Shinran was even more radical than Honen. Sometimes called the Martin LUTHER of Japan, he understood that if Pure Land is true, faith alone is what matters, not rites or priesthood or anything else. Therefore, though a monk, like Luther he gave up monastic CELIBACY to marry and have children. He emphasized that even the greatest sinner can be saved by simple faith expressed through the Nembutsu. Jodo Shinshu temples have married priests and relatively simple temples with only an image of Amida and a statue of Shinran in front. Pure Land became particularly popular among Japan's peasant population and its growing class of merchants and craftsmen. Often it took the form of colorful Nembutsu dances, performed while singing the sacred chant. In all of East Asia, it has made Buddhism and the hope of salvation accessible to high and low alike. In the United States Pure Land Buddhism has been present since the late 1800s. During World War II it organized itself as the Buddhist Churches of America.

purification, religious Making oneself clean or pure in a religious sense. Virtually all religions have some concept of that which is pure—that is, which is as it should be, and which is of the same pure nature as the soul and the divine—and of that which is polluted, in other words, the opposite: dirty, dangerous, of a nature that separates one from the divine.

Pollutants may be inward: EVIL, "impure" thoughts, sinful ideas, bad attitudes. They may be expressed in behavior: sinful deeds, the violation of TABOOS, doing RITUALS incorrectly. Or they may be external or occasional. Many societies, for example, have notions that such things as feces, blood, childbirth (see BIRTH RITUALS), sickness, the presence of death or a corpse, are inherently polluting and may require ritual purification before the person exposed to them can be considered pure and perform certain religious acts, or even be accepted in society. Sometimes certain animals are considered impure, either inherently or as foodstuffs, as in the traditional dietary rules of Orthodox JUDAISM and ISLAM, which forbid eating the flesh of the pig. Sometimes, as in the Hindu caste system, some human beings, and their occupations, are regarded as impure to those of higher status, and so contact between them must be limited.

Ritual ways of removing impurity are very common. Often a person who has indulged in inward pollution or SIN should confess and do penance to make up for it, as in ROMAN CATHOLICISM. External and other kinds of pollution may be removed by such acts as ritual bathing, ritual sweeping gestures, the ritual use of water, salt, or fire (all widely regarded as purifying), and the like. Frequently religious services begin with ritual gestures purifying the area and the persons present, like the sprinkling of holy water in the Catholic traditions of CHRISTIANITY or the waving of an evergreen branch in SHINTO. Even when ritual expressions of purity versus pollution are not present, they are often felt and dealt with inwardly.

Purim Hebrew word meaning "lots"; the name of a Jewish festival. Purim celebrates the deliverance of the Jewish people from a planned massacre in ancient Persia. The date of the massacre had been set by casting lots—thus, the name.

Purim is celebrated on the 14th day of the Jewish month of Adar, generally in March. It is preceded by a fast on the 13th day. At the heart of the celebration is a festive reading of the book of ESTHER in the SYNAGOGUE. Esther tells the story of the plot against the Jews and how it was thwarted. The name of the person responsible for the plot was Haman. Whenever his name is read, congregations often use loud noisemakers to keep his name from being heard.

Jews celebrate Purim with other lighthearted activities. These often include costume parties and the performance of plays. Purim is also a time to give gifts to friends and charity to the poor.

Puritanism A movement within Protestant CHRISTIANITY. Puritanism was active in England and its North American colonies in the late 16th and the 17th centuries. It took its name from its program: It wanted the Church of England (see ANGLICANISM) to be purely Protestant (see PROTESTANTISM).

King Henry VIII began the English REFORMATION as a political rather than a religious move. Henry's only objection to the Catholic Church was that it would not grant him a divorce. Therefore, he nationalized the church in his realm (see NATIONALISM, RELIGIOUS). By the time of Queen Elizabeth I the Church of England had assumed a compromise form. Its beliefs, practices, and structures were neither Roman Catholic nor Protestant but somewhere in between.

The Puritans opposed this compromise. They favored Protestantism. They first objected to the Catholic vestments that the Church of England required its ministers to wear. But this objection was only a symptom of a much more profound disagreement. At issue were central features in THEOLOGY and church organization as well as WORSHIP practices. Some Puritans left the Church of England. Indeed, some had to flee England itself. But most stayed in England and its church. Puritanism was a movement, not a separate Christian body.

In theology the Puritans followed John CALVIN. They emphasized the majesty and power of GOD. They also emphasized that all human beings were born into a state of SIN. No one, they taught, was capable of earning God's favor. Nevertheless, God in his mercy has chosen to save some sinners. He gives FAITH to those whom he chooses to save. The Puritans analyzed the process of coming to faith in detail. It centered on an experience of being born again through God's GRACE. American Puritans expected the elect to be able to give evidence of this experience.

Before 1649 the Puritans had little actual effect on the Church of England. They did, however, contribute significantly to the Civil War that pitted the English Parliament against the king. After the execution of King Charles I in 1649, the Church of England moved in a Puritan direction. But in 1660 the monarchy returned. The old church came back with it. In 1689 the Act of Toleration ended the dispute. The Church of England as formed in Elizabeth's day was the official church. But those who favored other options could establish legally recognized churches. Depending upon their particular views, Puritans formed Presbyterian, Congregationalist, or Baptist congregations (*see* PRESBYTERIAN AND REFORMED CHURCHES, CONGREGATIONALISM, and BAPTIST CHURCHES).

The story of Puritanism in the United States is more eventful. In the early 1600s, some Puritans gave up the attempt to reform the Church of England. They decided instead to establish a model Puritan commonwealth in North America. Eventually, Puritan churches appeared in each of the North American colonies.

In England Puritans had mostly been outsiders. In New England Puritanism was the established or official religion. As an official religion, it showed a repressive side. Orthodox Puritans expelled people like Roger Williams and Anne Hutchinson, who had different religious ideas. In 1659 and 1661 they executed four people because they were QUAKERS. In 1692 some Puritans held the infamous Salem witchcraft trials, which cost 20 people their lives.

But Puritanism has also greatly influenced the way Americans think of themselves. Some American politicians, such as Ronald Reagan (president, 1981–89), provide a good example. When they speak of the United States as a model to the rest of the world, they essentially reflect the self-image of the American Puritans.

Q

qabbalah   *See* KABBALAH.

Qaeda, al-   Arabic expression meaning "the base"; a loose organization founded in the early 1990s by Osama bin Laden (b. 1957) and other mujahideen who fought in Afghanistan against the Soviet invasion. It is best known for attacks against the World Trade Center and the Pentagon in the United States on September 11, 2001.

In 1979 the Soviet Union occupied Afghanistan. In response, fighters (mujahideen, people engaged in JIHAD) came to the region and fought to expel the Soviets with the help of the United States. Among them was Osama bin Laden from Saudi Arabia, the son of a wealthy businessman.

After the Soviets were expelled, bin Laden and his fellow mujahideen were dismayed at the influence the United States was exercising in the Middle East, especially on countries like Saudi Arabia and Egypt. They founded al-Qaeda to struggle against this influence by force. Some say they simply replaced the Soviet Union with the United States and its allies as the object of their antagonism. Originally based in the Sudan, al-Qaeda moved to Afghanistan in 1996, where it ran training camps for its members.

Al-Qaeda is a loose connection of cells. Each cell is a small group of people, perhaps, three, joined together to accomplish a specific task. Because it is a secret organization, some details are not known. It seems certain, however, that al-Qaeda has associates in as many as 60 countries around the world in such diverse places as the United States, Great Britain, and the Philippines.

The principal targets of al-Qaeda are the United States, its interests, and its allies. Notorious al-Qaeda attacks include the August 1998 truck bombings of American embassies in Kenya and Tanzania and the attacks in Riyadh, Saudi Arabia, in 2003, as well as the attacks of September 11, 2001. It has alliances with other groups, such as the Jemaah Islamiyah, which carried out bombings in Bali in 2002 and Jakarta in 2003.

The goals of al-Qaeda are often defined in negative terms. A statement issued by bin Laden in 2003 reads: "We—with God's help—call on every Muslim . . . to comply with God's order to kill the Americans and plunder their money wherever and whenever they find it." Understandably, this attitude repels people in the United States and other Western countries. In traditionally Islamic countries, some people admire bin Laden for standing up to the United States, which they see as inappropriately interfering with their lives. Most Muslims, however, strongly disapprove of al-Qaeda's tactics.

Q source (New Testament)   A document that scholars have hypothesized is a source used by the authors of the GOSPELS of Matthew and Luke. "Q" refers to the German word *Quelle*, "source." The hypothesis that this source existed helps scholars explain the "synoptic problem" (described later). They use the first letter of a German word because German scholars first came up with the idea.

The synoptic problem is this: Matthew, Mark, and Luke are called "synoptic Gospels" because, although their accounts of JESUS' birth and RESURRECTION differ, they tell the story of Jesus from his baptism to his crucifixion in much the same way. In fact, they repeat many of the same words, phrases, and sentences. That raises the synoptic problem: How can these similarities be explained?

The most common explanation is that Matthew and Luke both used the Gospel of Mark as their basis; the Gospel of Mark is simpler and appears to be older. But Matthew and Luke also contain a large number of sayings of Jesus that are not in Mark. Because Matthew and Luke use these sayings in very different ways, many scholars prefer to think that they used a common source rather than, say, that Luke used Matthew as a source. They call that source "Q."

No one has ever seen Q, but in the 1940s another book, the Gospel of THOMAS, was discovered that contains only sayings of Jesus. That discovery made the Q hypothesis more plausible. Some scholars have even tried to use the sayings that Q would have contained to reconstruct the "Q community," that is, the group of early Christians who would have used and preserved these sayings of Jesus.

Further reading: Mark Goodacre and Nicholas Perrin, eds. *Questioning Q: A Multidimensional Critique* (Downers Grove, Ill.: InterVarsity Press, 2004); Burton L. Mack, *The Lost Gospel: The Book of Q and Christian Origins* (San Francisco: HarperSanFrancisco, 1993); James M. Robinson, ed., *The Sayings of Jesus: The Sayings Gospel Q in English* (Minneapolis, Minn.: Fortress Press, 2002).

Quakers Members of a Christian group that is more properly known as the Society of Friends. Traditionally Quakers do not rely on SCRIPTURE or church teachings. They rely on the Inward Light of GOD.

The Society of Friends was organized in England in the 1650s. The name Quaker comes from the way in which early members of the society reacted to the experience of God's Light. They met outdoors in groups and waited for God's

George Fox, the preacher considered to be the founder of the Society of Friends *(Library of Congress)*

Light to illumine their hearts; when it did, they trembled.

The Friends met under the inspiration of a preacher named George Fox (1624–91). He is considered to be the founder of the movement. Because Quakers believed that God stirred in every human heart, they had little use for the ordinary trappings of CHRISTIANITY: scriptures, CREEDS, doctrines, BAPTISM, the LITURGY, ordained ministers. They also rejected the then common practice of an established religion, that is, a religion that the government legally recognized. In the spirit of JESUS' teachings, they dressed plainly. They also refused to take oaths, bear arms, or use titles when addressing people. In their regular meetings, they met—and still meet—in silence, waiting for God's revelation to come to someone present. That person then shared God's revelation for discussion. Because God's Light is found in every heart, Quakers never forbade women to hold positions of leadership, as many branches of Christianity have. Quakers have also been active in social causes.

The oldest tradition in the Society of Friends is quietistic. It emphasizes a passive waiting upon the Inward Light of God. In the early 1800s some Quakers found the tenets of evangelical Christianity attractive (see EVANGELICAL CHRISTIANITY and FUNDAMENTALISM, CHRISTIAN). These tenets emphasized the BIBLE as God's revealed word and Jesus as savior. As a result, the society split. In the early 1900s, the Quaker teacher Rufus Jones added another strand to the tradition. He taught a form of ethical MYSTICISM.

Because Quakers often rejected practices that their neighbors considered normal or normative, they have been persecuted. In 1659 and 1661, the authorities of Massachusetts Bay Colony executed four Quakers for practicing their religion. Other colonies, such as Virginia, had equally harsh laws against Quakers, although in Virginia Quakers were never executed. During the Revolutionary War American Quakers were persecuted because they refused to fight. In the late 1700s Quakers emancipated their slaves. In the 1800s they became active in the abolitionist movement and the Underground Railroad.

Quakers have made other prominent contributions to American and British life. As is well known, a Quaker, William Penn (1644–1718), founded Pennsylvania. The colony followed Quaker principles in its concern for religious toleration, pacifism, and respect for indigenous Americans. British Quakers founded prominent financial institutions, including Lloyd's of London and Barclay's Bank. The early champion for women's rights, Susan B. Anthony (1820–1906), and the American presidents Herbert Hoover (1874–1964) and Richard Nixon (1913–94) were of Quaker background. In the 19th century American Quakers founded several institutions of higher learning, including such colleges and universities as Earlham, Haverford, Swarthmore, Bryn Mawr, Cornell, and Johns Hopkins. The spirit of Quakerism finds expression in the philanthropic activities of the American Friends Service Committee. In 1947 the committee, along with its British counterpart, received the Nobel Prize for Peace for its relief activities following the devastations of World War II.

Further reading: Hugh Barbour and J. William Frost, *The Quakers* (Richmond, Ind.: Friends United Press, 1994); Brent Bill, ed., *Imagination and Spirit: A Contemporary Quaker Reader* (Richmond, Ind.: Friends United Press, 2002); Eleanor Nesbitt, *Interfaith Pilgrims: Living Truths and Truthful Living* (London: Quaker Books, 2003).

Qur'an Also spelled Koran; the sacred book in ISLAM. The Arabic word "Qur'an" means recitation. Muslims believe that the Qur'an is the supreme revelation of GOD to human beings. It consists of Arabic poetry received from God and recited by the prophet MUHAMMAD (570–632 C.E.). In theory the book governs every aspect of Islamic life.

HISTORY

Muhammad was accustomed to retire occasionally to the desert for spiritual retreats. On one such occasion in the year 611, Muslims believe that God spoke to him. This event is known as the "night of power."

Islamic tradition associates this event with a particular *surah* or chapter of the Qur'an. The angel Gabriel appeared to Muhammad and commanded him, "Recite." Muhammad asked, "What shall I recite?" The angel answered in the words of surah 96:

Recite in the name of your Lord Who created.
He created man from a clot.
Recite: your Lord is Most Honorable,
Who taught (to write) with the pen
Taught man what he knew not.
(96.1–5, M. H. Shakir, altered)

Page from the Qur'an written in Kufic writing in the 11th century. Surah al-Rum (XXX, The Romans), verses 24 and 25: ". . . after it (the Earth) is dead: verily in that are signs for those who are wise. And among his signs is this, that heaven and earth stand at his command. Then when he calls you by a single call from the Earth . . ." *(Victoria & Albert Museum, London/Art Resource, N.Y.)*

At first Muhammad doubted the reliability of his experiences. The doubts became more intense when the messages from God stopped briefly. But the messages resumed, and until the end of his life Muhammad continued to receive messages that Muslims attribute to God. Sometimes these messages came as a ringing in Muhammad's ears. Sometimes the ANGEL Gabriel delivered them. And sometimes Muhammad heard the voice of God himself.

Muhammad did not write the Qur'an, either in the sense that he composed it as an author or that he recorded it as a scribe. According to tradition, Muhammad could not write. During the prophet's lifetime people recorded portions of the revelations on scraps of material that happened to be available: bits of leather, papyrus leaves, ribs of animals. They also committed the revelations to memory.

Tradition attributes the work of compiling the Qur'an to Zaid ibn Thabit. Indeed, it attributes it to him twice. During the term of Abu Bakr (caliph, 632–634), the first caliph or leader of the Islamic community after Muhammad's death, many people who had memorized the revelations were killed in a great battle. Abu Bakr was worried that the revelations might be lost. Therefore, he commissioned Zaid to gather into a book as many of the revelations as he could find. The resulting work was passed down to the next caliph, Umar (caliph, 634–644), and then to Umar's daughter.

Uthman (caliph, 644–656), the caliph after Umar, became concerned that there were many different versions of the Qur'an, and that these might cause confusion. Therefore, he commissioned Zaid to assess the various versions and add verses that were genuine to his earlier work. When Zaid was finished, Uthman ordered that all competing versions be destroyed. In fact, all other versions of the Qur'an were not destroyed, but for all intents and purposes they were. Uthman's version is simply considered the Qur'an today.

CONTENTS

The Qur'an consists of poetic verses revealed to the prophet Muhammad at various times during a period of 22 years. It does not tell connected stories, the way parts of the BIBLE do. It also does not systematically present the teachings of Islam, in the way, for example, that a CREED or a confession might. Rather, it contains distinct verses on a large variety of topics. Many of them addressed concerns that were pressing in the Arabic community at the time they were given. Muhammad reported to the community what he received from God. Because he did so, when the Qur'an speaks in the first person ("we"), the pronoun refers not to Muhammad but to God.

The Qur'an is Arabic poetry. Indeed, those who speak Arabic insist that it is a form of poetry whose beauty is incomparable. Translating poetry is difficult in any case. One can reproduce the literal meaning, but not the allusions and effects upon which poetry depends. Muslims have been reluctant to translate the Qur'an at all. The Qur'an preserves the very words of God, and any translation would no longer present God's own words.

The verses of the Qur'an are gathered into 114 units known as surahs. It is a little misleading to call surahs "chapters." Some of them are extremely long; others consist of only four lines, more like a stanza than a chapter. In general, the longer surahs are toward the beginning of the Qur'an; the shorter ones are toward the end. Muslims also distinguish between those surahs that the prophet received when he was living in Mecca, and those he received after he had immigrated to Medina. The Medinan surahs tend to be longer than the Meccan ones. Therefore, the revelations of the Qur'an run roughly in reverse chronological order. The latest revelations come first, the earliest ones come last.

All surahs except the ninth begin with a phrase known as the *Basmalah: "Bismillah al-Rahman al-Rahim,"* "In the name of God [ALLAH], the Merciful, the Compassionate." Muslims use the first surah, known as the Fatihah, very frequently in their WORSHIP. It reads:

In the name of Allah, the Merciful, the
Compassionate.
All praise is due to Allah, the Lord of
the Worlds.
The Merciful, the Compassionate.
Master of the Day of Judgment.
Thee do we serve and Thee do we
beseech for help.
Keep us on the right path.
The path of those upon whom Thou
hast bestowed favors. Not (the path) of
those upon whom Thy wrath is brought
down, nor of those who go astray.

(Shakir tr., altered)

The central themes of the Qur'an are the fundamental teachings of Islam. God is one, and God is unique; there is no other like him. He created all that is, including human beings. The duty of human beings, as of all creatures, is to serve their Creator. They do this by following his commandments. These commandments cover every sphere of life, not simply RITUAL or religious observances. At the end of time God will raise all people from the dead. He will welcome the righteous into the gardens of paradise, but the evil he will dispatch to HELL.

SIGNIFICANCE

It is almost impossible to overestimate the significance of the Qur'an in the Islamic world. It embraces all of life. The first words a baby hears should come from the Qur'an. So should the last words that a dying person hears. Between birth and death the Qur'an provides guidance and comfort. Some even ascribe to it magical power.

Muslim thinkers have tried in several ways to describe the special status of this book. The Qur'an itself refers to a heavenly book of which the earthly revelations are copies. Many say that the Qur'an is an attribute or characteristic of God, namely, his speech. Some have insisted further that that speech is not something external to God. For them the heavenly Qur'an is itself an essential part of God.

Further reading: Michael Cook, *The Koran: A Very Short Introduction* (New York: Oxford University Press, 2000); Farid Esack, *The Qur'an: A Short Introduction* (Oxford: Oneworld, 2002); *The Koran: With a Parallel Arabic Text*, N. J. Dawood, trans. (New York: Penguin Books, 2000); Kristina Nelson, *The Art of Reciting the Qur'an* (New York: American University in Cairo Press, 2001).

R

rabbi, rabbinate From a Hebrew word meaning "my master, my teacher"; the leader of the Jewish community, and the office of leadership, respectively. The office of rabbi—the rabbinate—has assumed different functions and structures at different times and places. Today's rabbis perform functions that ancient and medieval rabbis did not perform. Furthermore, the rabbinate in the United States differs considerably from the rabbinate in Israel. Nevertheless, the rabbi has been the chief religious leader of JUDAISM since the destruction of the Temple in 70 C.E.

The rabbinate—and with it modern rabbinical Judaism—grew out of the branch of ancient Judaism known as the Pharisaical movement. PHARISEES were people whose religion centered on the study of TORAH. According to tradition, the term "rabbi" was first used in Palestine after the destruction of the Temple.

Originally, rabbis were experts in both written and oral Torah—the first five books of the BIBLE and the discussions that were eventually recorded in the TALMUD. Because Torah contains instructions on how to live, the rabbis became judges. When other forms of leadership died out, the rabbis gradually became the leaders of Jewish communities. In the Middle Ages the rabbinate became a full-time occupation. It also became common for each locality to recognize one, and only one, rabbi. During the 19th century most European countries gave Jews full civil rights. Among other things, that meant that they were subject to the laws of the state and could use state courts to pursue their legal claims. As a result, rabbis stopped acting as judges. Instead, they began to perform many new duties that were pastoral and social in nature.

In the United States today rabbis resemble Protestant ministers and Catholic priests. They attend seminaries, are ordained, and are then hired by congregations. As leaders of congregations one of their chief responsibilities is to lead SYNAGOGUE services on the Sabbath and holidays. That includes preaching sermons on a regular basis, something traditional rabbis did only twice a year. Other responsibilities of American rabbis include performing weddings and funerals, teaching, especially teaching the youth, visiting the sick and performing other pastoral duties, organizing and leading the social life of the congregation, and—not an insignificant role—representing the Jewish community to its non-Jewish neighbors.

The rabbinate in Israel is considerably different. In Israel, unlike the United States, the rabbinate is a state-controlled institution. HALAKHAH (Jewish law) is the official law in most civil matters, and one of the primary functions of rabbis is to act as judges in civil, but not criminal, proceedings. Another is to ensure that halakhah is observed in, for example, the preparation of food. Only rarely if ever is being the rabbi of a synagogue in Israel a full-time job.

One of the most important changes to the rabbinate in the 20th century was the admission of women. Although halakhah permitted women to teach and to preach, it did not traditionally allow them to serve as witnesses or judges. Therefore, women had been excluded from ordination. Reform Judaism rejected this restriction and, in 1972, became the first group to ordain women to the rabbinate. By the mid-1980s, Reconstructionist and Conservative Judaism had also begun to ordain women.

Rama, *Ramayana* Legendary hero of ancient India, and the most important account of his story. Although ancient Indians told many stories about a hero named Rama, the *Ramayana* was the most important. In it, Rama, a young prince of the city of Ayodhya, must go into exile in the forest for 14 years at the command of a greedy stepmother. While there, his wife Sita, who had accompanied him, is carried off by the chief of demons, Ravana. Rama enlists the help of the forest monkeys to search for Sita. A monkey general, Hanuman, finds Sita in Ravana's fortress, Lanka, which some traditions identify with the island of Sri Lanka. Together with his brother, Lakshmana, and armies of monkeys, Rama lays siege to Lanka, rescues Sita, and defeats and kills Ravana. He then returns to Ayodhya to rule and ushers in a golden age.

The first version of the *Ramayana* was a poem of 24,000 Sanskrit couples written at least 2,000 years ago by a sage known as Valmiki. (The exact date is disputed.) Most Hindus today use other, more recent renditions of the story, such as Tulsi Das's Hindi version or Kamban's Tamil one. The events of the *Ramayana* have provided the subject for very many works of art not only in India but also throughout south and southeast Asia. In recent years comic books and an extremely popular television series have also told the story.

Hindu tradition identifies Rama with an AVATAR of the deity, Lord VISHNU. In addition, Hindus—and other Indians as well—see the characters of the story as ideals of how to live one's life. For example, Rama is the ideal ruler and husband; Sita is the ideal wife; Hanuman is an exemplary religious devotee. Festivals such as Ramanavami and Dussehra celebrates the events and characters of the *Ramayana,* and Hindus often invoke Rama's name. Indeed, *He Ram!* ("Oh Rama!") were the last words that Mahatma GANDHI spoke. As a powerful symbol of Hindu identity, the *Ramayana* has also been important to Hindu nationalists (*see* FUNDAMENTALISM, HINDU). On December 6, 1992, partisans of Hindu nationalism destroyed a mosque at the alleged site of Rama's birth, touching off anti-Muslim violence throughout India.

Ramadan The ninth month of the Islamic calendar, during which Muslims fast from sunup to sundown. The fast during Ramadan is one of the five pillars of ISLAM.

Because Muslims use a lunar calendar that is not adjusted to the solar year, Ramadan cycles throughout the months of the Gregorian calendar used in North America and Europe. When Ramadan falls in December, the days of fasting in the northern hemisphere are relatively short; when it falls in June, they are relatively long. Muslims make adjustments for people living in the far northern or southern portions of the globe, where at some times of the year the sun never rises, and at other times it does not set.

Fasting during Ramadan, known in Arabic as *sawm*, is a full fast. Muslims should not eat, drink, smoke, or engage in sexual intercourse from sunup to sundown. The purpose of the fast, however, is spiritual discipline, and it should not endanger a person's health. Those who are sick, traveling, pregnant, nursing, or too old to undertake the fast without danger are exempt from the fast. Some who are exempt, such as travelers, must make up the fast at a later date. The end of the fast comes when a reliable person sights the crescent of the new moon, which marks the start of the next month. That is the occasion for a feast known as the *Id al-Fitr,* the "festival of fast-breaking."

Muslims give a variety of meanings to the Ramadan fast. Above all they fast because GOD commanded them to do so in the QUR'AN. In addition, the "Night of Power," that is, the night in which God's revelations to his messenger MUHAMMAD first began, falls toward the end of Ramadan. Therefore, Muslims use this month as an opportunity to reflect on God's revelation. During the course of the month many Muslims recite the entire Qur'an.

Muslim women pray facing Mecca, on the first day of Lebaran or Id al-Fitr, the end of Ramadan. *(Getty Images)*

The fast has other meanings, too. For example, some say that voluntary fasting teaches them compassion for the poor, who may have no choice but to fast all the time.

Ramakrishna (1836–1886) *a very influential Hindu* SAINT He is often referred to as Ramakrishna Paramahamsa. The second name means "the supreme ascetic."

Ramakrishna was a priest at a temple of the GODDESS Kali near Calcutta. From an early age, he experienced trances when he was overcome with religious emotion. Later, he experienced similar trances in visions of the goddess Kali as Mother.

After several years of spiritual struggle and searching, Ramakrishna came to develop an inclusive vision of reality in the nurturing arms of the Mother as supreme Godhead. Into this vision of personal deity he integrated the impersonal BRAHMAN of SANKARA's Advaita VEDANTA. He also had visions of and worshipped ALLAH and CHRIST, whom he saw as manifestations of the Mother. All religions, Ramakrishna taught, were different paths to the same goal.

Eventually, Ramakrishna became the catalyst for a Hindu revival movement in eastern India. His disciple VIVEKANANDA was the most influential of those who spread his ideas.

Rapture In popular Christian APOCALYPTIC LITERATURE, the Rapture (from Latin for "taken up" or "caught up") refers to a belief that, before openly coming for the Last JUDGMENT OF THE DEAD, CHRIST, will secretly return to take those who truly believe in him directly up to heaven. From the perspective of the world, these persons will simply disappear as society otherwise continues on its course. But the raptured persons, now in heaven with Jesus, will be spared the chaos and wars of the subsequent "Tribulation" on earth, the horrific Last Days leading up to the Final Judgment and the "new heaven and earth."

The concept of the Rapture is based on certain biblical passages, especially I Thessalonians 4:16–17 ("Then we who are alive and remain shall be caught up . . . in the clouds to meet the Lord in the air, and thus we shall always be with the Lord."). But the Rapture was not a distinct part of Christian belief until around the middle of the 19th century, when a traveling preacher named John Nelson Darby used the term and made it an important part of his message. For him, one significant aspect of the teaching was that true believers constituted an "invisible church," known only to God, that might well cut across denominational lines but would be made known on the day of Rapture. Darby's ideas were then adopted by Cyrus I. Scofield, whose *Scofield Reference Bible* (first published 1909), widely consulted in the first half of the 20th century, made the Rapture concept well known. The bestselling Left Behind series of novels by Tim LaHaye and Jerry Jenkins, beginning in 1995, gave the idea a new burst of popularity.

Rastafarians

Rastafarians Members of a religious movement that began in Jamaica among people of African descent. They are also called Rastas.

The name *Rastafarian* comes from *Ras* (prince) *Tafari*, the name of the former emperor of Ethiopia, Haile Selassie (1892–1975), before his coronation. The Rastafarian movement was inspired in part by a movement led by another Jamaican, Marcus Garvey (1887–1940). Garvey preached black pride and advocated the return of black people to Africa. The coronation of Haile Selassie in 1930 filled many black people with hope for political and economic independence. Indeed, many Rastafarians have seen him as God's messenger on earth.

The best known Rastafarian aspects are the wearing of dreadlocks, the use of *ganja* (mari-juana), and reggae music. Dreadlocks, with roots in the Nazarite vow in the BIBLE (Numbers 6), mark the Rastafarians as distinctive; they have a number of symbolic resonances, starting with the beauty of a black person's hair. The sacramental use of marijuana, Rastafarians believe, allows them to connect with one another and their deeper selves. Much reggae music incorporates Rastafarian themes and as a result has been important in spreading the movement.

These symbols (*see* SYMBOLISM IN RELIGION) receive their meaning from a deeper vision. Rastafarians see themselves as living in exile in Babylon. Forces of the surrounding society—the former British rulers, the cultural and economic dominance of the United States, the structures of Jamaican society, and traditional Christian churches—oppress black people. Rastafarians reject those forces and celebrate Africa, especially Ethiopia. Traditionally, they have seen Africa as a paradise to which black people will one day return. That return will mark the end of their suffering.

Like Jews and Muslims, Rastafarians do not eat pork. Some of them are vegetarians. They have been active in promoting black political and economic power. Although they first arose in Jamaica, today Rastafarians are found in most places where people of African ancestry live.

Further reading: Leonard E. Barrett, *The Rastafarians* (Boston: Beacon Press, 1997); Ennis Barrington Edmonds, *Rastafari: From Outcasts to Culture Bearers* (New York: Oxford University Press, 2003); Noel Leo Erskine, *From Garvey to Marley: Rastafari Theology* (Gainesville: University Press of Florida, 2005); *Chanting Down Babylon: The Rastafari Reader,* Nathaniel Samuel Murrell, William David Spencer, and Adrian Anthony McFarlane, eds. (Philadelphia, Pa.: Temple University Press, 1998).

Rebekah

Rebekah The wife of ISAAC in the BIBLE. In order to ensure that his son Isaac did not marry a Canaanite woman, ABRAHAM sent a servant to the region where his brother Nahor lived. The servant brought back Rebekah, the daughter of Abraham's nephew Bethuel. As portrayed in the Bible, she is a woman who can influence the course of events. Sometimes she must resort to deception to do so.

Like her mother-in-law SARAH, Rebekah had difficulty conceiving children. She eventually gave birth to twins, Esau and JACOB. According to the Bible, these two were the ancestors of the Edomites and the Israelites, respectively. Rebekah favored Jacob, the twin born second. She helped deceive the old and blind Isaac, so that he gave the blessing for the first-born son to Jacob rather than to Esau. Then she helped Jacob flee from his enraged brother.

redemption   *See* SALVATION.

Reformation, Protestant   A movement in western European CHRISTIANITY in the 1500s. During the Reformation many Christians broke away from the Roman Catholic Church (*see* ROMAN CATHOLICISM) and formed their own, independent churches. They were known as "Protestants" (*see* PROTESTANTISM). They protested against the teachings, practices, and institutions of the Catholic Church. The movement itself is known as the Reformation because it aimed to reform, that is, to correct abuses and errors in the church.

But Protestants did not disagree only with Catholics. They also disagreed with each other. As a result, the Reformation produced a variety of Protestant churches: Lutheran churches, especially in Germany and Scandinavia (*see* LUTHERAN-ISM); Reformed (Calvinist) churches, especially in Switzerland, the Netherlands, France, and Scotland (*see* PRESBYTERIAN AND REFORMED CHURCHES); the Church of England (*see* ANGLICANISM); and Anabaptist churches such as the MENNONITES and the AMISH. Each made its own contribution to the story of the Reformation. So did the Catholic reaction, known as he Counter-Reformation.

LUTHERAN REFORMATION

The Reformation began in Germany on October 31, 1517. On that date a university professor, Mar-tin LUTHER, posted on a church door 95 "theses" or propositions that he wanted to debate. Luther objected to the manner in which a Dominican friar was raising money nearby (*see* DOMINICANS). The friar promised that if people gave him a certain amount of money, all their SINS would be forgiven.

The issue quickly grew beyond an academic discussion. Copies of Luther's theses appeared in many places and helped stir up dissatisfaction with the church. Meanwhile Catholic authorities tried to silence Luther. In 1521 the church excommunicated him. The rift between the church and Luther's supporters had grown too wide to bridge.

Luther and his followers organized their own churches. In doing so, they altered many Catholic practices. They eliminated whatever contradicted the BIBLE, as they read it. They translated the Bible and the Mass from Latin into the language people ordinarily used. They eliminated MONKS AND NUNS. They allowed clergymen to marry. Above all, they rejected the authority of the Catholic Church and looked to the Bible as their only authority. As they read it, the Bible taught that human beings received GOD's forgiveness freely (*see* GRACE). They did not have to do good works to be saved. They only had to have FAITH.

CALVINIST REFORMATION

Luther's example inspired others. Soon religious rebellion had broken out in many different cities and regions of the Holy Roman Empire. Another important center was Switzerland. There the reformers eliminated not only what contradicted the Bible, but also whatever the Bible had not actually commanded.

In the early 1520s a parish priest named Huldrich Zwingli (1484–1531) held religious debates before the town council of Zurich. He convinced the council that certain common practices, such as using images in worship, were unbiblical and should be abolished. He also convinced the council that the Catholic view of the EUCHARIST was wrong. Zwingli's view of the Eucharist differed from Luther's, too. The two reformers met in 1529 but could not come to any agreement. Two years later Zwingli was killed. Much more politically active than Luther, he died helping to defend Zurich against the armies of Swiss Catholics.

The most influential leader of the Swiss Reformation was actually French: John CALVIN. Having fled from France, Calvin eventually settled in Geneva. His own religious views emphasized the overwhelming majesty of God. Calvin picked up on Luther's teaching that human beings cannot do anything to save themselves. Calvin reasoned that since not all are saved, God must predestine some for salvation and others for damnation. Something like Zwingli, Calvin saw himself called to act politically as well as religiously. He reformed the laws and educational system of Geneva, attempting to make it into a Christian commonwealth.

CHURCH OF ENGLAND

In England the Reformation was almost entirely a political movement. When the trouble with Luther first broke out, King Henry VIII attacked Luther's views and defended the Catholic Church. The Pope called him "defender of the faith." Henry always preferred Catholic teachings and practices. But later he wanted a divorce that the Pope would not grant. In response, Henry declared the English church independent and got his divorce.

After Henry died, the Church of England experienced a stronger move to Protestantism under those who ruled on behalf of Edward VI, who was still a child. Edward's stepsister, Queen Mary, tried to reestablish the Catholic Church. Her cruel measures earned her the nickname "Bloody Mary." Under Queen Elizabeth the English church reached a compromise position between Catholicism and Protestantism.

ANABAPTIST CHURCHES

During the 1520s some Europeans thought changes were coming too slowly. Many of these people felt that it was wrong to baptize infants (see BAPTISM). Only those people should be baptized who could decide for themselves that they wanted it. As a result, they rebaptized adults who had been baptized as infants. This earned them the name Anabaptists, "rebaptizers."

The earliest Anabaptists were inspired by utopian visions, that is, visions of how to create a perfect society on Earth. Some of them led armed uprisings. In the early 1530s they took over the town of Münster in Germany. When Catholics and other Protestants retook the town after a siege, the results were disastrous. Such events managed to give the Anabaptists a very bad name.

In the early 1530s, however, a Dutch priest named Menno Simons (1496–1561) began to teach a different form of Anabaptism. Simons noted that it was impossible for Anabaptists to take control of the political structures. Therefore, they should withdraw from political life and practice nonviolence. Simons's spiritual descendants, the Mennonites and the Amish, still cherish these ideals.

COUNTER-REFORMATION

Once the Reformation began, it could not be reversed. Its momentum was too great. But the Catholic Church did respond.

The most important element in the Catholic response was the Council of Trent (see TRENT, COUNCIL OF), which met from 1545 to 1563. Reformers like Luther had originally called for a council to mediate the dispute between the Catholics and the Protestants. But only firm Catholics participated in the Council of Trent. The council reaffirmed the authority of the Catholic Church and maintained Catholic teachings in the face of Protestant opposition.

The Society of Jesus (see JESUITS) also worked vigorously for the Counter-Reformation. Baroque art was an important tool, too. Many Protestants had rejected art as idolatry. The Catholic Church sponsored art as a way to make itself more attractive.

SIGNIFICANCE OF THE REFORMATION

The Reformation was much more than just a theological dispute. It changed the face of Europe. It produced a Europe that was much more divided politically as well as religiously. It was an important step in the development of European nations as we know them today. It also encouraged the development of national literatures and styles of art.

Further reading: Madeleine Gray, *The Protestant Reformation: Belief, Practice, and Tradition* (Portland, Ore.: Sussex Academic Press, 2003); Diarmaid MacCulloch, *The Reformation* (New York: Penguin Books, 2005); Lewis W. Spitz and William R. Kenan, eds., *The Protestant Reformation: Major Documents* (St. Louis, Mo.: Concordia Publishing House, 1997).

reincarnation   The idea that a person is reborn when he or she dies. Reincarnation goes by many different names. Sometimes it is called "metempsychosis," from the Greek words for "soul" and "change of place." Sometimes it is called "transmigration," because the person is said to wander to a new body. Sometimes people call reincarnation "rebirth." Some Hindu texts actually speak of redeath. In discussions of reincarnation, one often encounters the Sanskrit word SAMSARA. One scholar has aptly translated this word for the cycle of births and deaths as the "run around."

Jews, Christians, and Muslims do not usually talk about reincarnation. When they talk about what happens after death—and Jews tend to focus on this life—they talk about eternal life, a RESURRECTION of the dead, and a final judgment (*see* JUDGMENT OF THE DEAD). But many other peoples believe that persons are reborn when they die. Some indigenous peoples in the Americas, Australia, the Pacific Ocean region, and Africa have complex ideas about rebirth. For example, some believe that every child is an ancestor returning to Earth. Many ancient Greek philosophers believed in reincarnation. The most famous example is the "myth of Er" at the end of Plato's greatest work, *The Republic*. Many people whose religions began in India—Hindus, Buddhists, Jains, and Sikhs—simply accept reincarnation as a fact of life. During the late 19th, 20th, and early 21st centuries some North Americans also believed in reincarnation. They included people who subscribed to THEOSOPHY and Asian religions like HINDUISM and BUDDHISM. They also included people in the public eye, such as the movie actress Shirley MacLaine.

Not every religion that teaches reincarnation teaches the same views. The religions that arose in ancient India have very complex ideas about how reincarnation occurs. These religions stress the operation of KARMA: The actions of this life determine the conditions of the next one. A good person will have a good rebirth, a bad person a bad rebirth. But each religion and school has a different way of explaining how the process works. For example, many Hindus say that an eternal, unchanging ATMAN or self is reborn. Buddhists teach rebirth, but they deny that there is any eternal, unchanging atman. Some books describe in detail what happens between death and rebirth. An ideal example is the Tibetan book of the dead, the BARDO THODOL. A Sanskrit scholar of some standing once taught an editor of this encyclopedia how to recognize dreams and imaginings that were memories from a previous life. He had himself identified the place and approximate time of one of his more recent lives.

North Americans who believe in reincarnation often find the idea comforting. They see it as a reprieve from the black, empty night of eternal death. Peoples who believe that children are reborn ancestors basically see reincarnation as positive, too. But religions originating in India often view samsara as being in the end negative. The ultimate goal of religious practice is to escape from an endless series of rebirths or reincarnations. The most common names for this goal are moksha ("liberation") and NIRVANA.

relics   Objects "left over" from a holy person or SAINT. These may be body parts or personal items, such as clothing.

Religions that use relics insist that their practitioners do not actually WORSHIP them. They venerate them and use them as aids to reflection. They also often expect relics to heal and grant favors.

At times Muslims venerate relics. An example is hair from the prophet MUHAMMAD. But relics have been especially important in BUDDHISM and ROMAN CATHOLICISM. Buddhists have built monumental structures known as STUPAS to house relics of the BUDDHA. Similarly, the Second Council of Nicaea (787) required ALTARS in all Christian churches to contain relics.

Buddhists have tended to venerate parts of the Buddha's cremated body. A particularly important part has been the Buddha's tooth housed in Kandy, Sri Lanka. Whoever owned it ruled the country Christians have venerated relics of the saints, the Virgin MARY, and JESUS. Christian relics were especially common in the Middle Ages.

With the high demand for relics, unscrupulous people have traded in fakes. The pious have also made honest mistakes. An example of the latter is the Shroud of Turin. Tradition said Jesus was buried in it. Some scientific tests date it to the late medieval period.

religion, definition of Explaining what religion is. Religion is one of those words people tend to feel they know the meaning of until it comes to providing a precise definition that covers all cases of what one wants to call religion, excluding everything else. Then it can be surprisingly difficult to define—first of all, because religion embraces so much.

Religion can range from one's innermost and subtlest feelings to large and powerful institutions that can seem as much political as religious, to folk customs that appear on the borderline between religion and culture. Many traditional societies, in fact, do not clearly distinguish between religion and the social order or popular culture; indeed, the religion scholar W. Cantwell Smith has argued that the notion most of us have of a religion as a separate, detachable area of human life apart from the political, economic, social, and cultural spheres is a quite modern idea that would be meaningless to many people in the Middle Ages and before.

At the same time, attempts at definition can and have been made. Some people, especially in the Christian West, from Enlightenment Deists (believers in GOD but not in "supernatural" religion) like Thomas Jefferson and Voltaire, to the pioneer anthropologist E. B. Tylor, have wanted

to define religion as those ideas and practices that have to do with belief in God, gods, or spirits. Others, however, have contended that some Eastern examples of the sort of practices that "look like" religion, such as Confucian RITUALS or even Buddhist MEDITATION, do not necessarily involve the Western concept of God. They have therefore expanded the idea to anything that gives one a sense of awe, wonder, or of connectedness to the universe: Friedrich Schleiermacher called it that which produces feelings of dependence on something greater than oneself. Rudolf OTTO saw as the ground of religion a sense of a reality tremendous, yet fascinating and "wholly other"; this could be the Buddhist NIRVANA as well as God. Paul Tillich said religion is the state of being grasped by one's "ultimate concern."

Others have preferred a definition based more on religion's social or ritual role. Émile DURKHEIM saw religion mainly in "totems," festivals, dances, and other symbols or practices that both represented and created the unity of a tribe or society. Mircea ELIADE made fundamental to religion the experience of "sacred space" and "sacred time," that is, places and occasions that are separate, "nonhomogeneous," demarcated off from the ordinary or "profane" world. He recognized, however, that these can be interior as well as out there; the experiences of PRAYER or meditation can make for an inward sacred space and time even in the midst of everyday life.

Perhaps it must be acknowledged that any definition of religion can only be fairly complex. It might be possible to start with the idea that religion does, in fact, need to deal in some way with whatever is seen as ultimate, unconditioned reality, call it God, Nirvana, or even the absolutely ideal social order. Then one could take into account the three forms of religious expression as put forward by the sociologist of religion, Joachim Wach. These are: the theoretical, that is, the beliefs and stories of a tradition having to do with ultimate reality or its manifestation in gods and revelations and the like, answering to the question "What do they say?"; the "practical," practices or forms of WORSHIP with the same object, answering to the question

"What do they do?"; and third, the sociological, dealing with issues of leadership, organization, institutions, and relations with the larger society. All real religions, by this understanding, have both an ultimate point of reference and an expression in all three of these forms. If there is only the theoretical, it is philosophy rather than religion. If only practices, it is MAGIC rather than religion. If only the sociological, it is a club. But put them all together with a reference to some understanding and experience of ultimate reality, that which one cannot go beyond in comprehending the meaning of the universe, and it is religion in the sense the word is used in speaking of the traditional religions, such as JUDAISM, CHRISTIANITY, ISLAM, HINDUISM, or BUDDHISM. While this approach may not coincide with everyone's personal definition of religion, it may be useful for looking at and distinguishing religion socially or historically.

religion, history of   A way of studying religions that arose in Europe and North America in the late 19th and early 20th centuries. The name is somewhat misleading. The books and articles that "historians" of religion wrote did not all deal with history. Other names sometimes used for this way of thinking about religions include the comparative study of religions and the phenomenology of religion, an unusual term that is discussed below.

THE BASIC APPROACH

Most people are familiar with theology, even if they do not use that word. Theology attempts to say what religious truth is, which is a topic of great interest to many religious people. Other people try to explain how it is that people come to have religions. Some, but not all, who try to do this consider religion to be false. Still other people try to engage in what is known as interreligious dialogue, sharing their religious views with one another. They may want to learn about and develop respect for other people, and they may also hope to discover an ultimate truth that all religions share.

Historians of religion take yet a different approach. They seek to understand what religious people claim and what religions are about, partly by talking to religious people, partly by studying religions historically, and partly by comparing religions with one another. They put the question of religious truth to one side and consider religion simply as something human beings say and do. (However, many historians of religion have hoped eventually to discover religious truth as well.) Historians of religion sometimes say that in putting aside the question whether the claims of religion are true, they are "bracketing" it. They borrow this term loosely from a field in philosophy known as phenomenology, which talks about "phenomena"—that is, about "what appears" to the senses and the mind—rather than about whether those appearances are true. (The British-American scholar of religions Ninian Smart [1927–2001] once referred to this attitude as "methodological agnosticism": Scholars are free to believe what they will, but as scholars they think as if they were agnostics.)

In treating religion this way, historians of religion generally claim that there is something called religion which is sui generis, a Latin phrase meaning "in a class by itself." These scholars mean that just as it is possible to study society as society, literature as literature, and music as music, so it is possible to study religion in and of itself, rather than as belonging to some other field such as psychology or sociology. The Rumanian-born French-American historian of religion, Mircea Eliade (1907–86), once put it this way: "a religious phenomenon will only be recognized as such if it is grasped at its own level, that is to say, if it is studied *as* something religious. To try to grasp the essence of such a phenomenon by means of physiology, psychology, sociology, economics, linguistics, art or any other study is false; it misses the one unique and irreducible element in it—the element of the sacred" (*Patterns in Comparative Religion*, p. xiii). A word that is often used in these discussions is *reductionism*. Historians of religion reject any approach that tries to "reduce" religion to something that is not religion. Many people find that this position makes sense, but many scholars find it debatable.

Historians of religion are interested in any way of understanding religion that adopts this position. One way that does so is the study of history. For example, when and where did BUDDHISM arise? What did the BUDDHA do? What did he teach? Who were his followers, and how did they guide Buddhism after his *parinirvana* (what non-Buddhists call his death)? That is all useful historical knowledge. Another approach is sometimes called phenomenology, and the use of that word a second time makes for some confusion. This approach can also be called typology, morphology, or perhaps even just comparative study. It tries to identify what is common among religions and what is unique to each. For example, what are the basic patterns of SACRIFICE practiced in religions? What are the basic kinds of MYTH?

Most historians of religion have also been interested in psychology, sociology, and anthropology. What they have meant by the psychology and sociology of religion has, however, often been somewhat different from the kinds of psychology and sociology taught in American high schools and universities.

PROMINENT HISTORIANS OF RELIGION

It is not possible to name all of the historians of religion who have made important contributions. Mentioning a few prominent names may give a further idea of what this way of studying religions is about.

Rudolf OTTO (1869–1937) was a Christian Protestant theologian and philosopher who provided some basic ideas in the history of religion and also inspired many scholars to pursue it. He is best known for claiming that religion is the result of a unique kind of experience that human beings have. In a famous book, *The Idea of the Holy,* he called this experience "numinous." He said that the experience of the numinous, which Jews and Christians might think of as the direct experience of God, is totally unlike any other experience that human beings have.

Another early scholar was Gerardus van der Leeuw (1890–1950). He developed the phenomenology of religion, in both senses of the term. At the heart of religion he placed power, and he discussed the basic forms of religion in terms of the religious object (e.g., GOD), the religious subject, and the interaction between the two.

Otto and van der Leeuw were Europeans. Important for the development of the history of religion in the United States was a scholar named Joachim Wach (1898–1955). He sought refuge in the United States from Nazi Germany because of his Jewish ancestry. Wach talked about religion as an expression of the experience of "ultimate reality." That experience, he said, expresses itself in three basic forms: "theoretical," that is, in beliefs and stories; "practical," that is, in RITUALS and ETHICS; and "sociological," in the structures of religious communities.

Somewhat different was Mircea Eliade, who has already been mentioned. He was particularly interested in the patterns according to which the Sacred, as he called it, manifested itself in human consciousness. Important for his thinking is the idea that religious people define their lives by reference to patterns established at the creation of the world. He called these patterns "archetypes."

Ninian Smart, among his many contributions, suggested that religion had six dimensions: ritual, mythological, doctrinal, ethical, social, and experiential. He also often talked about "worldviews" rather than religions. He did so because, although communism presented itself as scientific and antireligious, it actually had many of the same features as religions.

Eliade and Smart taught in the United States starting in the 1960s and 1970s. They trained many scholars. One weakness that their students noticed in their teachers' work was that it was too general and superficial. As a result, historians of religions trained since the 1960s have tended not to think in such grand terms. Instead, they have focused on specific topics within a religious tradition, such as the stories and worship of the Hindu god GANESA or the practices of female shamans in Japan (*see* SHAMANISM).

CRITICISM

At the beginning of the 21st century many scholars had expressed strong doubts about the history of religion. They doubted whether it makes sense to talk about religion as a single thing that exists across cultures. They asked whether it makes sense to fault scholars for trying to explain religious thought and behavior in terms of human psychology or sociology, and whether this prohibition is not opposed to the ideals of scholarly work. Furthermore, they have accused Otto, van der Leeuw, Wach, and Eliade of presenting Jewish and Christian ideas as if they were found in all religions everywhere.

These criticisms raise important questions. At the same time, events in the early 21st century such as the September 11, 2001, attacks, point out just how important it is for people to know about the world's religions. Work by historians of religion who study specific religions and religious topics can play a crucial role in providing that knowledge.

Further reading: Mircea Eliade, *Patterns in Comparative Religion* (Lincoln: University of Nebraska Press, 1996); Charles H. Long, *Significations: Signs, Symbols, and Images in the Interpretation of Religion* (Aurora, Colo.: Davies Group, 1999); Russell T. McCutcheon, *Manufacturing Religion: The Discourse on Sui Generis Religion and the Politics of Nostalgia* (New York: Oxford University Press, 1997); Ninian Smart, *Worldviews: Crosscultural Explorations of Human Beliefs*, 3d ed. (Upper Saddle River, N.J.: Prentice Hall, 2000); Jonathan Z. Smith, *Map Is Not Territory: Studies in the History of Religions* (Chicago: University of Chicago Press, 1993).

religion, study of Careful reflection, writing, and speaking about religions, generally within the context of an educational institution.

HISTORY

For centuries thinkers have carefully formulated and elaborated the teachings of their own religions. This kind of thinking includes Jewish, Christian, and Islamic theologies, as well as Hindu, Buddhist, Jain, Confucian, and Taoist philosophies. All of these movements have to some degree influenced the study of religions in North America. But the most influential tradition has been that of Europe.

In Europe critical reflection on religion arose in ancient Greece. Ancient writers known as mythographers compiled myths and legends. Geographers and travelers described the religions of the people they visited. Above all, Greek and Roman philosophers like Xenophanes, Euhemerus, Lucretius, and Cicero strongly criticized the gods of mythology, without necessarily denying some higher GOD or force altogether.

In the fourth century C.E. CHRISTIANITY became the official religion of the Roman Empire. For more than a thousand years it defined the setting with which Europeans studied religions. Theologians worked out Christian teachings in great detail. They also took up topics in the philosophy of religion. For example, they tried to prove that God exists (*see* GOD, THE EXISTENCE OF). But despite some rich cultural exchanges among Jews, Christians, and Muslims, knowledge of other religions generally remained marked by profound antagonism.

In the 17th and 18th centuries the movement known as the Enlightenment gave rise to a search for "natural religion." "Natural religion" meant the few propositions that all religions were (falsely) thought to share: belief in God, in the soul, and in rewards and punishments after death. At the same time, the growth of European colonialism meant that Europeans became more aware of the outside world and scholars had more material at their disposal. At this time, too, thinkers like David Hume began to write accounts of religious history that diverged from the story found in the BIBLE.

During the 19th century historical approaches to religions, including Christianity, flourished. At times the tension with orthodox theologians was severe. By the end of the century people had begun to study religions comparatively and as facets of human society, personality, and culture. During the 20th century these approaches to religion—humanistic, sociological, psychological, and anthropological—flourished. In addition, the old attitude of missionary conquest gave way. Many theologians became interested in learning about others, not converting them. A preferred method was interreligious DIALOGUE. By the beginning of the 21st century, many scholars had begun to explore the roots of religion in the human brain (*see* BRAIN, MIND, AND RELIGION).

WAYS TO STUDY RELIGIONS

It is possible to study religions in several ways: from within a religious tradition, from a perspective that treats all religions equally and on their own terms, and from a perspective that analyzes religion as a part of society or the human personality. One may call these three standpoints theological, humanistic, and social scientific approaches to the study of religions, respectively.

Theological

JUDAISM, Christianity, and ISLAM have traditionally claimed that they have grasped religious truth better than other religions. Indeed, they have at times claimed to be the sole source of religious benefit. A standard Christian formula runs, *Extra ecclesia nulla salus,* "there is no SALVATION outside the church." Furthermore, Christians have seen Christianity as the true continuation of ancient Judaism. Muslims have seen Islam as the culmination of Judaism and Christianity. These religions certainly have a right to their claims to truth. But when other religions are seen as threatening or mistaken, the typical approach to them is "heresiology" and "apologetics." That is, it becomes common to list the errors of other religions and defend the truth of one's own. The danger, too often realized, is misrepresentation, distortion, and ill-will.

In China and Japan it has been traditional for people to practice more than one religion. In such an environment, one religion may suggest that it is a more perfect statement of another religion. Japanese BUDDHISM and SHINTO have made this claim about each other. Many Hindus—and others as well—have taken a different approach. They have seen all religions as different paths to the same goal. This viewpoint is certainly well-intentioned.

It may also make it difficult to recognize the distinctive characteristics of other religions.

In the course of the 20th century, representatives of many religions have come together for interreligious dialogue. The goal of this enterprise is not to convince others of one's own religious truth. It is to listen to another person in order to learn about that person's beliefs and practices. Advocates say that if dialogue is to work, all participants must share their beliefs and practices openly and honestly. By the beginning of the 21st century, however, strong movements often known as FUNDAMENTALISM were reasserting traditional teachings of such religions as Christianity, HINDUISM, and Islam, often from an exclusionist position.

Humanistic

In contrast to THEOLOGY, which openly adopts a specific religious perspective, the humanistic study of religions tries to take each religion on its own terms. Some have suggested that this approach requires a stance of "methodological agnosticism." That is, for the purposes of study, one refuses to make a judgment about the truth of various religions. This approach has taken two major forms: historical studies and comparative studies.

Conceived narrowly, the historical study of religions studies how religions change over time. More broadly, this approach studies a religion or one of its elements. Examples would be books about specific features of HINDUISM, Buddhism, or Christianity. In the last half of the 20th century historians were especially interested first in religious symbols and meanings, then in the ways religions exercised or undercut power and domination.

In the late 19th century the goal of the comparative study of religions was to rank religions from the crudest to the most advanced. During the 20th century, scholars generally rejected this approach. Throughout much of the century they studied what religions shared. For example, Rudolf OTTO described how human beings experienced the sacred. Mircea ELIADE tried to identify the fundamental patterns by which the sacred showed itself to human beings. During the last quarter of the 20th century scholars became less interested in what religions shared and more interested in how they differed.

Social-scientific

Some social scientists have been very critical of religion. For example, the psychologist Sigmund FREUD thought religion was a psychological illusion. Sociologists influenced by Karl MARX have seen religion as a force by which those with wealth and power dominate the poor and powerless.

Other theorists have seen the contributions of religion more positively. The psychologist Carl Gustav JUNG thought religion was a powerful force leading to an integrated personality. The sociologist Émile DURKHEIM thought religion reinforced society's most important values and thus helped it function. The anthropologist Claude LÉVI-STRAUSS thought myths embodied fundamental codes (*see* MYTH AND MYTHOLOGY). These codes defined how the people who told the myths conceived of the world.

In the United States there has been a strong emphasis on studying religions "empirically." This kind of study carefully constructs hypotheses and then tries to test them. Those who follow this approach gather data through such means as questionnaires and surveys. Then they analyze the data with the help of statistics. At the beginning of the 21st century, two approaches in particular attracted social scientists in North America: an economic study of religious groups and a neuro-scientific study of religious experiences and ideas (*see* BRAIN, MIND, AND RELIGION).

CONCLUSION

There is probably no single best way to study religion. People have different questions about religion that they want answered. The approach that they take depends at least in part upon the questions that they have.

Further reading: Peter Connolly, ed., *Approaches to the Study of Religion* (London: Cassell, 1999); William E. Paden, *Interpreting the Sacred: Ways of Viewing Religion* (Boston: Beacon Press, 2003); Daniel L. Pals, *Seven Theories of Religion* (New York: Oxford University Press, 1996).

religion, theories of origin of   For many people, the origin of religion (*see* RELIGION, DEFINITION OF), or at least of their own religion, is obvious. It began with the special revelation of divine truth to the founders of the religion (*see* FOUNDERS, RELIGIOUS), or with a special experience of enlightenment, such as that of the BUDDHA (*see* RELIGIOUS EXPERIENCE). Others, however, have sought to understand religion in more natural ways (*see* RELIGION, STUDY OF). Even some who accept the basic truth of religion may acknowledge that human beings came to the realization of those truths through slow and natural historical processes. Still others may perceive a combination of natural development and special revelation in the origin and progress of faith from the first humans to the present. There are also those who consider all religion to be a human invention.

THEORIES FROM ANCIENT TIMES TO THE ENLIGHTENMENT

Such theories of the origin of religion go back to ancient times. Prodicus of Ceos (fifth century B.C.E.) and Euhemerus (c. 330–260 B.C.E.) argued that the gods were really heroic humans who were later considered divine; this doctrine is called euhemerism. Critias (fifth century B.C.E.) said, like many later skeptics, that religion was devised to frighten people into morality. Plato (427–347 B.C.E.) thought that religion, or at least religious myth, could be a "noble lie" used to promote morality and good social order. In China at about the same time, Hsun Tzu (c. 300–228 B.C.E.) taught that Confucian religious rites (*see* CONFUCIANISM) were not really for the sake of dubious gods but were performed as models of the social order and of "safe" ways of expressing emotion.

By and large, though, the ancient and medieval worlds accepted religion as based on divine revelation and authentic human experience, to be received by faith and interpreted by reason. In modern times, beginning with the 18th-century Enlightenment, alternative naturalistic views again arose. Philosophers such as Voltaire (1694–1778), while not entirely denying the existence of religious reality, regarded most of the superstructure of religion—its churches, RITUAL, and doctrine (*see* DOGMA AND DOCTRINE)—as superstition, probably crafted by PRIESTS to keep the masses subservient.

THE 19TH AND EARLY 20TH CENTURIES

In the 19th century, theories about religion abounded, now aided by far more actual anthropological fieldwork than previously. The great pioneer anthropologist Edward B. Tylor (1832–1917) theorized that religion started in ANIMISM, or belief in the SOUL separable from the body. He thought this concept must have been first suggested by the experience of dreams, in which the sleeper apparently left the body to travel to far places where he or she could meet souls of the deceased. It was no great extrapolation to develop a doctrine of the AFTERLIFE from animism. Souls could be found in other entities as well, in animals or the moving wind and sun, which could be made into gods. This further step led to POLYTHEISM (belief in many gods) and finally to MONOTHEISM (belief in one GOD).

However, Andrew Lang (1844–1912), a distinguished Scottish folklorist, was disturbed by reports that, contrary to animist theory, some undeveloped peoples nonetheless believed in a quasi-monotheistic "high god." He proposed a primal monotheism whose deity was the creator and first lawgiver.

On the other hand, R. R. Marett (1866–1943), an English anthropologist, traced religion back past animism to a pre-animist state of "animatism," sheer divine energy known by such names as *mana* or *wakan*. Sir James Frazer (1854–1941), in his much-cited *The Golden Bough*, put magic in first place, saying religion began with sorcery and only gradually conceived of gods.

Also in the 19th century, but adopting a different perspective, Karl MARX (1818–83) put religion in the context of his fundamentally economic concept of the evolution of human society. In the feudal and capitalist stages of society, which depended on the exploitation of one class by another, religion provided sanctions and explanations for injustice, offered emotional release for the exploited (through devotion to gods and expectation of reward after death), and salved the consciences of the exploit-

ers. In the perfect society to come, religion would not be necessary.

Early-20th-century views of religion tended to emphasize social and psychological factors. Émile DURKHEIM (1858–1917) pointed to the societal origins of religion in the "social effervescence" of a tribe or group in dance and festival. The father of psychoanalysis, Sigmund FREUD (1856–1939), viewed religion as the relic of an unspeakable primal crime for which religion atones: the primal patricide, or killing of a father by his sons. Freudianism tends to see all of religion as a "projection" of childhood experiences: all-powerful parents made into gods, childish guilt needing punishment and wanting expiation, desire for "magical" ways to deal with intractable life situations.

A disciple of Freud who later broke with him, C. G. JUNG (1875–1961) viewed religion as stemming from the almost infinite world of the unconscious, whose nameless but powerful currents could be named and crystallized by means of "archetypes," figures familiar from MYTH and religion. These include the Great Mother (ISIS, KALI, MARY), the Wise Old Man (ZEUS, God the Father), the Hero, the Divine Maiden, and the Shadow (SATAN, Mara).

Other thinkers, more strictly in the history of religion tradition, looked for the origin of religion in a single psychological capacity. For G. van der Leeuw (1890–1950) religion was the quest for power. For the influential Rudolf Otto (1869–1937), it was the sense of the "numinous," that which is "wholly other" to humans and is both terrifying and fascinating. Mircea ELIADE (1907–86) made basic the experience of the Sacred, which can be thought of in terms of the special feeling a believer has in a great cathedral, temple, or any place long hallowed by belief in the presence of a god or in a time of religious festivity. The Sacred is set against the Profane or ordinary world, and religion involves the interaction of these two realms of human experience.

RECENT THOUGHT

More recent thought has tended away from seeking the origin of religion in any single key experience or idea and more toward seeing it as just a part of human culture generally. Religion's development goes along with the emergence of memory, language, art, and story. Certain features of religion clearly have roots extending far back to early human ancestors: ritual behavior, and by some reports the ability to express awe in a particularly "numinous" place. But such attitudes could not become fully religious until the awakening of what the Nobel Prize winner Gerald Edelman (*Bright Air, Brilliant Fire*, 1994) has called higher-order consciousness, which includes the notion of a personal self, an ability to imagine long-term past or future possibilities, and a view of the self as an actor with various possible choices. Edelman argues that this kind of consciousness appeared with *Homo sapiens*, the kind of human we are, who emerged perhaps 50,000–100,000 years ago. Among the early expressions of this distinctive human self-awareness may have been the famous cave art.

David Lewis-Williams (*The Mind in the Cave*, 2002) linked cave art, SHAMANISM, and religion in an interesting way. He says that *Homo sapiens* may first have entered the new higher-order consciousness using drumming, rhythmic actions, and intense concentration to induce trances in which they might recall memories, dream, and see VISIONS—and possibilities—outside the present. These practices are all characteristic of shamanism, which Lewis-Williams, among others, suggests was the first form of what is now called human religion (*see* PREHISTORIC RELIGION).

Shamans were adepts of the new kind of consciousness. Art, including cave art, was, in Lewis-Williams's view, a way of recording what they saw, as it were to keep the visions alive. That was undoubtedly also the purpose of early religious practices like dancing, telling stories that became myths, and making special sacred places. Religion, in this view, began as a kind of expanded language to convey a new human consciousness. At the same time, religion would also have acquired social functions, giving communities symbols of their cohesion and enforcing moral norms.

Another recent theory is that of sociobiologists like Edward Wilson. They argue that altruism, the ability to act for the benefit of others in a community even to the point of self-sacrifice, had survival value for early humans and therefore was sanctioned by religious myths and symbols.

In the end, though, it is important to realize that human religion is a complex thing. Probably all that now goes under the name of religion does not have a single common origin, and no one theory explains it all.

Further reading: Paul A. Erickson, *A History of Anthropological Theory* (Peterborough, Ont.: Broadview, 2003); David Lewis-Williams, *The Mind in the Cave* (New York: Thames & Hudson, 2004); Eric Sharpe, *Comparative Religion: A History* (LaSalle, Ill.: Open Court, 1986); Edward O. Wilson, *Sociobiology* (Cambridge, Mass.: Harvard University Press, 1975).

religious experience Feelings, often intense, that are associated with a sense of religious awareness and interpreted religiously. They are various in type. The term mystical experience is often used for profound, peaceful, timeless states that are thought to be experiences of oneness, of unity with the divine without separation. They may, as in BUDDHISM or VEDANTA Hinduism, be considered to be realizations of the impersonal divine essence that is already within; or, as in religions with a personal GOD, such as CHRISTIANITY, ISLAM, or BHAKTI Hinduism, occasions of drawing very close to God in love, so that the two become one in the way that two lovers might. PRAYER can produce a rich sense of communication with God but not oneness in the mystical sense. Even guilt can be a religious experience, less pleasant perhaps, of sinfulness and the way it separates one from God; it can lead to amendment through confession, penance, and a change in one's way of life. Intellectual religious experience can be a mainly mental realization of a religious truth, perhaps stimulated by sermon, lecture, or reading, accompanied by the exaltation one feels at such understanding in an important matter. Aesthetic religious experience is the feeling of being deeply moved that one may have from religious music, art, or poetry; it is not in itself unity with God, though it can lead to that and in any case have a significant impact one one's life. Conversion experiences are those of any nature, though often highly emotional, that produce a major change in one's religious outlook and commitment.

A sense of divine guidance, though perhaps not always intensely felt, can be regarded as experiential religion, especially when it occurs at critical moments in one's life. So is an overall steady sense of divine presence. Experiences of the presence of religious entities, less than the Ultimate, such as ANGELS or SAINTS, may also be religious experiences, for they partake in the sacred world and such beings certainly share in the divine power. Visionary experiences, which appear to be given to some people, are religious experiences presented before the eyes, and perhaps also the ears if one hears sacred or divine voices. Usually they are accompanied by strong feelings of wonder and awe as well. (Terrifying visions from within the religious world view, as of demonic figures or the fires of HELL, are also possible and may have a strong admonitory effect.) Miracles, whether "psychic" phenomena like telepathy or clairvoyance (seeing things far away) or precognition (seeing the future), or physical miracles like healings or the biblical walking on water, are often regarded as divine gifts. They can evoke a sense of wonder and gratitude, which certainly is religious experience as well as is the confirmation of divine reality. (They are also, however, sometimes taken to be deceptive lures of the devil.) Most religions would insist that a truly authentic religious experience, in contrast to one that is deceptively induced by psychological factors or the wiles of demonic forces, must result in both true belief and a moral and godly way of life.

It must finally be noted that religious experience is an interpretive category, not necessarily one built into the experience itself. Two people may have very similar experiences of rapture and joy while walking in the woods. One may interpret it in a quite natural way, as a psychological response to the beauty and peace of the surroundings. The other may interpret it as a sense of the presence of God, based on prior beliefs about God and how and where he may be felt. Only the second would, strictly speaking, be a religious experience. For religious beliefs can induce religious experience, but they also are what interprets experience as religious. At the same time, religion without experience would be a paltry thing and probably not long endure.

restoration movement A movement in the early 1800s among Protestants in the United States that led to the formation of the Christian Church (Disciples of Christ), the Christian Churches/Churches of Christ, and similar churches. It is sometimes called the "Stone-Campbell movement" after the last names of its instigators, Barton W. Stone and Thomas Campbell.

Barton Stone was a Presbyterian minister who sponsored the Cane Ridge Revival in Cane Ridge, Kentucky (1801). Afterward, he became convinced that Christians should abandon the CREEDS that they had formulated and follow only the BIBLE as authoritative. He and a small number of fellow ministers who shared his ideas formed what they called the Springfield Presbytery. In 1809, however, they dissolved the Presbytery and issued a document titled "The Last Will and Testament of the Springfield Presbytery." It is an important milestone in the history of the restoration movement. From that point on, Stone and his associates called themselves "Christians." They saw themselves as in unity with all Christians everywhere.

Thomas Campbell had come to the United States from Scotland and served as a Presbyterian minister in western Pennsylvania. Like Stone, he rejected all creeds. In 1808 he and like-minded followers founded the Christian Association of Washington, Pennsylvania. It took as its motto, "Where the scriptures speak, we speak; where the Scriptures are silent, we are silent." At first Campbell aligned himself with Baptists in the area, but eventually differences forced them to separate. In 1830 he and his fellow believers became known as Disciples.

Stone, Campbell, and their associates met in Lexington, Kentucky, in 1832. They determined that they agreed on basic teachings and decided to unite. From that date the Christian Churches and the Disciples of Christ formed a "brotherhood." Because their ultimate goal was to restore the original unity of the Christian church, the name *restoration movement* arose. Today many scholars within the tradition do not like this name. In retrospect, it seems to reflect views about Christian unity that were unrealistic.

Despite the hopes for unity, the development of the movement was largely characterized by division. Very conservative churches accepted Campbell's dictum of speaking only when the Bible spoke and rejected the use of instruments in worship. They officially separated themselves from the other churches in 1906 as the Churches of Christ (Non-instrumental). These churches have since divided into smaller units over issues such as the use of a common cup in communion (*see* EUCHARIST) and the holding of Sunday School. With the rise of the CHARISMATIC MOVEMENT Churches of Christ with a Pentecostal orientation arose from this tradition (*see* PENTECOSTALISM). They sometimes allow the use of music.

Another split came in the 1930s. Some member churches favored the so-called higher criticism of the Bible and a more unified church structure. Others opposed that criticism and favored a looser church structure. The two groups split. Those who favored a looser structure call themselves Churches of Christ and Christian Churches. They tend to be found among rural churches in the Midwest. The others eventually constituted themselves as the Christian Church (Disciples of Christ) in 1968. Disciples tend to be found among urban, northern churches. They also tend to emphasize issues such as diversity and social justice.

At the beginning of the 21st century, the Churches of Christ (Non-instrumental) had roughly 1,500,000 members in the United States, the Churches of Christ and Christian Churches about 1,072,000 members, and the Christian Church (Disciples of Christ) about 805,000 members.

resurrection   The notion that the bodies of the dead will rise and regain life. This notion is found especially in CHRISTIANITY and ISLAM but also in JUDAISM. Of the three, only Christianity teaches that resurrection has already happened once in the person of JESUS.

The idea of resurrection does not figure prominently in the Hebrew BIBLE (Old Testament). In fact, it appears only in the very late book of DANIEL. It is anticipated in EZEKIEL's VISION of dry bones coming together again (Ezekiel 37:1–14), but this vision foresees not a resurrection of the dead but a change in fortune for the nation of Israel. For the most part the Hebrew Bible envisions a dry, dreary existence for the dead in a place it calls "Sheol."

In the so-called intertestamental period (roughly 200–1 B.C.E.) the notion that the dead would be raised at the end of time seems to have become fairly common among Jews (*see* 2 Maccabees 7.14, 12.43; 4 Ezra 2:23). It became so possibly under the influence of the Persians, who liberated the Jews from captivity in Babylon. From them it passed into Judaism, Christianity, and Islam.

Within Judaism the notion of resurrection appears, for example, in Maimonides's famous summary of Jewish teaching known as the "Yigdal," a poetic version of which is often used in SYNAGOGUE services. While affirming the resurrection of the dead, however, traditional Judaism has focused on sanctifying this life, not anticipating a future one. The Reform movement, influenced by the European intellectual movement known as the Enlightenment, has been reluctant to affirm that the dead will be raised. It prefers to speak instead of "eternal life," a phrase that can be interpreted in various ways.

The resurrection of the dead is much more important within Christianity and Islam. It figures in the notion of a final judgment that both religions share. In addition, Islam as well as Christianity connects the resurrection of the dead with the return of Jesus. In 1 Corinthians 15, PAUL develops a particularly detailed scenario for the resurrection. He teaches that at the sound of the last trumpet, the dead, along with those still living, will assume a spiritual, imperishable body, in contrast to the physical, mortal bodies that they had in life. The QUR'AN teaches that those who are found righteous at the final judgment will enter the gardens of paradise, whereas those who are not righteous will suffer torment.

Muslims believe that Jesus did not die. Therefore, he was not raised from the dead; he was taken up into HEAVEN without dying, as Enoch and ELIJAH were. But Christians believe that the final resurrection of the dead has been foreshadowed in the resurrection of Jesus. Indeed, the resurrection of Jesus is the pivotal event on which all of Christianity rests. Among other things, it provides the concept that even in this world religious life means dying to SIN and rising to new life.

It is impossible to establish Jesus' resurrection as an historical event. As a matter of principle, academic history knows no way to establish the occurrence of MIRACLES. The earliest Christians appealed to two types of evidence in proclaiming the resurrection of Jesus. The first comprises reports of finding Jesus' tomb empty. The second comprises the testimony of those who claimed to have seen the risen Jesus, for example, PETER, James, and Paul (*see* 1 Corinthians 15.5–8). After dating the writings of the New Testament and carefully assessing what was proclaimed at different periods, some scholars have come to the conclusion that the earliest Christians testified to Jesus' resurrection on the basis of encounters with the risen Jesus alone.

Revelation, book of Also called the Apocalypse; the last book of the NEW TESTAMENT. The book of Revelation belongs to a kind of writing known as APOCALYPTIC LITERATURE. This kind of writing was especially common in late Second Temple JUDAISM (roughly 200 B.C.E.–70 C.E.), early CHRISTIANITY, and ancient GNOSTICISM. Apocalyptic literature communicates hidden knowledge. Writers receive this knowledge in one of two ways. Either they have VISIONS or they make a journey to the HEAVENS. Apocalyptic literature generally sees the world as a battle between warring forces, good and EVIL. It provides hope that the forces of evil will be defeated in the near future.

Many examples of apocalyptic literature are "pseudonymous." That means that although they were written more recently, they were attributed to a famous person of the past: ADAM, Enoch, ABRAHAM, MOSES. Even the biblical book of DANIEL is pseudonymous. The book of Revelation is unusual in that it reveals the name of its actual author: John, imprisoned on the island of Patmos. It is not clear how this John relates to John the APOSTLE of JESUS, to the GOSPEL of John, or to the letters of John in the New Testament.

In the first three chapters, John addresses seven churches in what is now Turkey. He encourages them to be faithful in the practice of Christianity. The other 19 chapters contain visions of heaven and heavenly events. These visions are equal to any science fiction fantasy. They use many images from the Hebrew BIBLE. For example, the "four living creatures" with different faces (4.6–8) closely resemble creatures described in ISAIAH (6.1–3) and EZEKIEL (1.5–11). The visions are organized according to series of sevens: seven seals (6.1), seven trumpets (8.6), seven plagues (15.1). Mixed in with these "sevens" are visions of a woman and beasts. At the climax of the book, the armies of CHRIST defeat the forces of SATAN. When that happens, a new heaven, new Earth, and new JERUSALEM replace the world that now is.

Christians have discussed the meaning of these visions for centuries. Many images clearly allude to the city of Rome and its empire (for example, 17.9 and 18). Modern scholars see the book as comforting early Christians at a time of severe persecution by Roman authorities. Many think that the book was written during the persecution by Emperor Domitian (ruled, 81–96 C.E.). Some favor an earlier persecution under Nero (ruled, 54–68 C.E.). The letters of Nero's name add up to the famous sum 666, associated with the idea of Satan or evil (13.18). (In ancient Greek the same symbols were used for letters and for numbers.)

Some suggest a practical reason for the elaborate symbolism of the book: It helped the author and readers avoid being detected by the empire. The visions are also appropriate to the author's goal of encouraging the persecuted. They tell in wondrously graphic terms that what the churches experience is not the ultimate reality. In the end, their tormentors will be defeated by much greater forces.

Throughout history Christians have tried to read Revelation in terms of the events of their own time. Some still do. In the last half of the 20th and beginning of the 21st centuries some Christians in the United States saw political enemies such as Muammer El-Qaddafi of Libya, Saddam Hussein of Iraq, Osama bin Laden, the Soviet Union, and even such an apparent friend of the United States as Mikhail Gorbachev as the figures behind the book's symbols. Many also expected the "millennium," a thousand-year period in which Jesus will reign with the martyrs (20.1–6).

These interpretations may strike some as unfounded and even bizarre. For those who cultivate them, however, they define the shape of contemporary history.

revivalism A form of religious practice typical of PROTESTANTISM in the United States. Characteristics of revivalism include an emphasis on powerful religious emotions; large, infrequent meetings led by visiting ministers rather than ministers residing where the meetings are held; and an emphasis on conversion, rededicating oneself to moral behavior, and sometimes healing.

Religions often experience movements of renewal and revitalization. Examples include HINDUISM in the mid-19th century, BUDDHISM at the end of the 19th century, and ISLAM toward the end of the 20th century. In ROMAN CATHOLICISM a period of increased religious excitement often follows special occurrences such as Marian apparitions (see MARY, APPARITIONS OF). Among people in Melanesia, millenarian movements such as CARGO CULTS can count as revival movements (see OCEANIC RELIGIONS and MILLENARIANISM).

Protestantism in the United States has a long tradition of renewal movements in the form of revivalism. This tradition extends back to the First Great Awakening before independence.

By the first half of the 18th century, American Protestantism had come to seem stale and routine.

The intensity and fervor with which the Puritans had once pursued their faith had diminished. They had been forced to take various measures, such as the "half-way COVENANT," to keep family members in the church who could not testify to personal experiences of conversion.

In this context, an itinerant (wandering) preacher from England, George Whitefield (1714–70), toured the colonies, drawing large crowds and instilling religious excitement. Local preachers, such as Jonathan Edwards (1703–58), also contributed to the movement. The Great Awakening was part of a broader movement in European Protestantism that emphasized "heart-felt" religion. It produced METHODISM in England and America and a movement known as Pietism in the Protestant regions of the European continent.

The enthusiasm of the Great Awakening eventually died down, but a succession of other movements followed. The Second Great Awakening began shortly after the United States achieved independence. It addressed the situation of people living on the frontier, far away from urban life and any established churches. Wandering preachers visited these people from time to time and held "camp meetings." These meetings were enthusiastic affairs with catchy songs, bodily gestures such as clapping, and an emphasis on accepting JESUS and joining the church.

Successive waves of revivalism adapted their techniques and messages to the changing situation of the American population. In the 1830s Charles G. Finney and other revivalists dealt with urgent moral issues of the day, such as slavery and women's rights. A revival in the late 1850s also helped people in cities deal with strain caused by a financial crash. In the decades around and after 1900 revivalists such as Dwight L. Moody and Billy Sunday adapted emerging techniques of business and advertising for spreading the message of Christianity in a revival setting. In the years after the Second World War, Billy Graham's crusades, as his revivals were called, presented revivalism in a form that respectable, middle-class Americans could appreciate. A couple of decades later, televangelists adapted revival forms to the possibilities of communication created by television (*see* TELEVANGELISM).

Because of their emphasis on moral rededication, revivals have fostered a kind of Christian activism. The camp meetings of the Second Great Awakening sowed the seeds of the temperance (no-alcohol) and women's suffrage (right to vote) movements. They also fostered abolitionism. By the beginning of the 20th century, however, the moral activism of revivals had become largely associated with a conservative emphasis on tradition. Moody and other revivalists at the time were instrumental in the rise of Christian FUNDAMENTALISM (*see* FUNDAMENTALISM, CHRISTIAN). Billy Graham's crusades promoted a moderate conservatism, but the revivalism of the 1980s and beyond, in the era of Ronald Reagan, Newt Gingrich, and others, became militantly antiliberal.

Revivalism remains a factor on the religious scene of the United States. Many local Protestant churches hold periodic revivals as a means of regenerating enthusiasm in their members. Those who cannot or choose not to attend revivals now have ready access to them on religiously oriented television stations. In the late 1990s a revival movement known as the Promise Keepers addressed what it saw as the deteriorating situation of the American family by appealing specifically to men. At its large, men-only meetings held in sports stadiums, participants dedicated themselves not only to being better husbands and fathers but also to reclaiming their biblical roles as head and final authority in the family.

rites of passage RITUALS that take place at important junctures in a person's life. A Belgian anthropologist named Arnold van Gennep identified rites of passage for the first time in 1909. They are one of the most important kinds of rituals. They define the different stages through which human life proceeds, such as childhood, adulthood, and parenthood. They also transfer a person from one stage to another. For example, the rite of marriage transforms two single people into a married couple (*see* MARRIAGE AND RELIGION).

People sometimes look upon these transitions with anxiety. Therefore, rites of passage are sometimes called "life-crisis rituals." Rites of passage routinely occur at birth, puberty, marriage, and death. Almost every religion has rites of passage for these occasions, although there may be some exceptions. For example, Protestants who use BAPTISM as a puberty rite may not observe religious rituals in conjunction with birth. In North America, however, the broader society provides rituals for marking the occasion. These include baby showers, sending out birth announcements, in earlier days passing out cigars, and perhaps a welcome-home party.

Rites of passage mark biological changes and developments: birth, physical maturity, and death. But they do not take place only on the day of one's birth or death. That is because the stages and transitions marked by rites of passage are just as much social and cultural. Indeed, in the minds of the participants, social and cultural changes may be the most prominent. For example, Protestants who baptize at an age of accountability might be shocked to hear baptism described as a "puberty rite." For them physical maturation has little or nothing to do with the ritual. The biological terms remain, however, the most convenient ones to use.

There are many important birth rituals. Some Christians baptize infants and anoint them with oil. Jews circumcise boys on the eighth day after birth as a sign of their covenant with God (*see* CIRCUMCISION). Muslims circumcise, too. Traditional high-caste Hindus have an elaborate series of rituals focused on male children. It extends from the conception of the child to the child's first haircut at the age of three. Many societies require mothers and newborn children to observe a period of seclusion immediately after birth.

Puberty rituals are often called INITIATIONS. As already noted, some Christians practice baptism as a puberty ritual; others practice confirmation. In JUDAISM the standard puberty ritual is bar mitzvah for boys and, in more liberal congregations, bat mitzvah for girls (*see* BAR/BAT MITZVAH). In some Buddhist countries boys take the initial vows of a monk for a short time. It is part of their growing up as adult members of the Buddhist community. According to tradition, highcaste Hindu boys went through a prolonged period of religious study in conjunction with maturing intellectually and spiritually. In the best known rite, a boy between the ages of eight and 12 was "invested with" or given a sacred thread to wear draped over his left shoulder. In traditional HINDUISM, it became common for girls to be married before menstruation. As a result, the wedding was their puberty ritual.

Funeral practices are equally varied. Jews and Muslims bury the dead in a simple wooden casket and white shroud. Hindus bury especially holy people, but they cremate most corpses and deposit the ashes in water, such as in the sacred river GANGES. Parsees have traditionally washed the corpse and then solemnly exposed it so that birds of prey could devour the flesh. The above examples simply talk about what to do with the corpse. They do not begin to note the rituals associated with the process.

Van Gennep proposed a scheme that is helpful in understanding rites of passage. He identified three clusters of rituals: "liminal" rites, that is, rituals that take place at the boundary (cf. *limen,* Latin for threshold) between two stages of life; "pre-liminal" rites, rituals that occur before that time; and "post-liminal" rites, those that occur afterward. Each set of rites has distinct purposes: Pre-liminal rites separate the person concerned from the old state of life; liminal rites bring about a change; post-liminal rites integrate the changed person into the community and restructure it.

A "typical" North American wedding (shaped a great deal by PROTESTANTISM) illustrates each of these stages. Before the wedding, various actions separate the bride and groom from their previous state: announcing the engagement in the newspaper, the gift of an engagement ring, wedding showers for the prospective bride, a bachelors' party for the prospective groom. The wedding itself is held in a special, ritual space that functions as a threshold: a church or chapel, a garden or a place of special significance to the persons being married. The rituals by which the bride enters this space also mark separation: a grand procession and, in very traditional settings, the father giving the bride away. (What does it say about the relative importance of this ritual for men and women that the entrance of the groom is not so elaborate?)

The liminal rites—the rites at, say, the ALTAR—mark the transformation in any number of ways. The bride and groom usually make vows. They often exchange rings. They may receive special blessings. In the last half of the 20th century many couples created rituals of transformation that had special meaning to them. Many others adopted innovations that they saw at the weddings of relatives and friends.

A number of post-liminal rites incorporate the new married couple into the community. These may include a line in which the newly married couple greets all the guests, photographs of the couple taken in that special period just after the ceremony, eating and drinking together, throwing the bouquet and the garter, and dancing. It is also customary in North America for the newly married couple to observe a period of seclusion. It is called a honeymoon.

More recent scholars have added to our understanding of rites of passage. A psychologist has noted that the ordeals that are sometimes associated with puberty rituals help make these rituals seem more special afterward. The anthropologist Victor Turner found the concept of the liminal or "liminality" useful in many other settings as well.

In many parts of the world today, people have been abandoning traditional rites of passage. But as a class, rites of passage remain important. They mark special occasions, such as graduations. They make people members of special societies, such as sororities and fraternities. By the beginning of the 21st century, some women in North America had developed rites of passage to celebrate other important moments in their lives, such as the onset of menopause. Indeed, the phrase "rites of passage" is an example of a scholarly term that has passed into popular or general use.

Further reading: Jean Holm and John Bowker, eds., *Rites of Passage* (New York: St. Martin's Press, 1994); Ronald L. Grimes, *Deeply into the Bone:*

Re-inventing Rites of Passage (Berkeley: University of California Press, 2000); Victor Turner, *The Ritual Process: Structure and Anti-Structure* (New York: Aldine de Gruyter, 1995); Arnold van Gennep, *The Rites of Passage* (Chicago: University of Chicago Press, 1961).

ritual   The deliberate repetition of conventional and stylized words and actions with special significance. Ritual is very important to religion, where such acts may seem to be meaningless apart from the religious context and interpretation. Ritual may vary from the highly stylized acts of a Vedic rite or the colorful drama of the Eastern Orthodox LITURGY to the simple silence, with a handshake at the end, of a QUAKER meeting.

But it must be realized that virtually all religion, from the most elaborate to the simplest, has ritual in the sense that things are done in a conventional, traditional way, and with words and movements that make no sense apart from the religion. This is as true of a plain Protestant service as of a high mass or an ancient SACRIFICE. It is as true of a highly formal service choreographed like a dance as of an emotional and seemingly spontaneous devotional or Pentecostal type of event, so long as much of it is done—as such things as hymns and hand-raising inevitably are—in customary and conventional ways. Even private PRAYERS and MEDITATION are often done ritually, in a customary manner.

What kinds of rituals are there and what messages do they convey about the divine and about humans and their ways of WORSHIP? If it is a rich, ancient, formal ritual, it tells us the best way to reach the divine is by getting outside of ourselves through participation in something old, close to our roots, and aesthetically beautiful. If it is free and seemingly spontaneous, it says we get in touch with the divine by losing inhibitions and giving vent to inner feelings. Similar questions about religious leadership, symbols, and communities can also be asked about ritual events.

Most religious rituals have some features in common. First, they set apart a sacred time and place for the rite. Participants inwardly expect their experiences there to be different from those in daily life. They can expect to be in close touch with the divine, because the time and place are particularly open or "transparent" to the sacred. Second, the time and place usually also hark back to the great sacred times of the religion, as the Jewish PASSOVER recalls the EXODUS or the Christian Holy Communion the Last Supper of JESUS, or in general recalls the times and places of sacred story when the divine presence was strongly felt in the world. Rituals often present what may be called "condensed symbols" of those events, like the ritual bits of bread and wine in Christian Communion, which for believers "trigger" thoughts of the whole story, just as the sight of an old photograph may recall a whole episode in one's life. Ritual acts can release religious feelings precisely through their routine nature, in that if well practiced and interiorized they come more or less automatically, like dancing or playing the piano when well accomplished, and this can produce an inner reduction of tension and feeling of peace, allowing one's thoughts and feelings to move easily to the religious object. Finally, ritual, as a religious act done together, reinforces the cohesion of religious communities, the authority of the religious leaders performing them, and the institutional structure of the religion making them available.

See also SYMBOLISM IN RELIGION.

Roman Catholicism   One of the three main branches of CHRISTIANITY. The word "catholic" means universal. Roman Catholicism is universal in two senses. It extends around the globe, and more important, it sees itself as the proper bearer of the universal Christian tradition. It is called Roman because it considers the bishop of Rome to be the supreme leader of Christianity. The bishop of Rome is called the Pope (*see* PAPACY, THE).

HISTORY

For much of the past, the history of Roman Catholicism is the history of Christianity, then of Christianity in western Europe. The Roman Catholic Church—the church of western Europe—did not break officially with the Orthodox churches—the churches of eastern Europe (*see* EASTERN ORTHODOX CHRISTIANITY)—until 1054 C.E. The Protestants left the Catholic Church only during the REFORMATION in the 16th century.

Nevertheless, the roots of a distinct Roman Catholicism are very old. They go back to a general cultural split in the Roman Empire. The language and culture of the eastern half of the empire were Greek. Those of the western half of the empire were Latin. The bishop of Rome claimed very early to be supreme among bishops. According to tradition he was the successor of PETER, the most important of JESUS' disciples and the first bishop of Rome. Bishops in the eastern half of the empire never recognized this claim. Jesus' APOSTLES had founded their most important churches, too.

By roughly 500 C.E., east and west were going their separate ways. Political institutions in the west had largely collapsed. The Pope maintained order. Under his direction, Christianity was brought to northern Europe, for example, to England and Germany. By 800 C.E. the Holy Roman Empire ruled central and western Europe. When the Pope and the head of the Orthodox churches excommunicated each other in 1054, the dispute was between distant cousins, not brothers.

The Middle Ages were a formative period for Roman Catholicism. Pope Gregory I (pope, 590–604), the Emperor Charlemagne (742–814) systematized the LITURGY of the Mass. A long line of thinkers, stretching from AUGUSTINE OF HIPPO to Thomas AQUINAS, formulated Catholic teachings. Builders constructed impressive churches in the Romanesque style, then churches in the Gothic style that still take one's breath away (*see* CATHEDRAL). Monks, nuns, and friars practiced a way of life rooted in religious devotion. Mystics, many of them women such as Julian of Norwich and Hildegard of Bingen, reported intense VISIONS of the divine. But this was also the time of the INQUISITION and the CRUSADES.

When the Protestants revolted in the Reformation, Catholics responded with the Counter-Reformation. At the Council of Trent (*see* TRENT, COUNCIL OF) they reformed certain practices but reaffirmed central Catholic teachings. While many Protestants were rejecting the works of human hands as idolatry, the Catholic Church was commissioning masterpieces of baroque art. Especially with the help of the newly founded Society of Jesus (*see* JESUITS), Catholic MISSIONARIES preached Christianity in Asia and the Americas.

Among the British colonies of North America, Catholics had the closest ties to Maryland. A Catholic, Cecil Calvert, received the first charter for Maryland. The first Catholic bishop in the United States was the bishop of Baltimore, John Carroll (elevated 1789). Bishop Carroll was a cousin of Charles Carroll, a signer of the Declaration of Independence. During the 19th century the American Catholic Church grew tremendously as people emigrated from Catholic countries such as Ireland, Italy, and Poland.

During the 19th and 20th centuries, Catholics in the Protestant countries of Europe as well as the United States were objects of persecution, sometimes vile and severe. In this context the election of a Catholic, John F. Kennedy, as president of the United States was a major, positive event. During the same period, the church wrestled with modern, scientific thought. The First VATICAN COUNCIL (1869–70) rejected modern ideas and asserted the supreme position of the Pope. The Second Vatican Council (1962–65) took a more conciliatory position. By the beginning of the 21st century strong conservative currents were flowing through the church.

BELIEFS

Catholics affirm the truths of Christianity as formulated not only in the ancient CREEDS and councils but also in all councils of Catholic bishops and in pronouncements of the Pope. They maintain that God is a TRINITY, Father, Son, and Holy Spirit, and that Jesus is both fully divine and fully human.

In formulating the truths of Christianity, Catholics have tended to use different terms than Orthodox Christians. The Orthodox churches have tended to talk about human beings becoming sacred or divine. Catholic thinkers have tended to use the more legal language of original SIN, atonement, and redemption. These are, however, only tendencies.

Catholics differ from Protestants on any number of points. Protestants accept only the BIBLE as the source of religious truth; Catholics accept church traditions as well. Protestants have tended to emphasize that God's GRACE saves, not human works; Catholics insist that grace works together with human effort. Protestants have tended to see ritual actions only as signs of religious truth; Catholics teach that God imparts his grace in the SACRAMENTS. Protestants have tended to focus exclusively on Jesus; Catholics venerate Jesus' mother MARY, too, as the vehicle by which God became flesh. They also venerate past SAINTS.

PRACTICES

Catholics recognize seven sacraments: BAPTISM, confirmation, the EUCHARIST, penance (confession of sins), marriage (*see* MARRIAGE AND RELIGION), ORDINATION, and the anointing of the sick.

The centerpiece of Catholic WORSHIP is the Mass. This is a traditional, liturgical celebration of the eucharist. Since the Second Vatican Council, Catholics have celebrated the Mass in local languages rather than in Latin. They have also placed a greater emphasis both on congregational participation, such as singing, and the homily (sermon) as a way of instructing the participants.

ORGANIZATION

Catholics actually recognize two supreme authorities: meetings of bishops known as councils, and the Pope. The relation between these two has changed throughout history.

The Pope governs the church from Rome. He is assisted by an administrative staff, known as the Curia, and a select group of bishops, known as the College of CARDINALS. The Catholic Church divides the world into territories known as dioceses. A bishop administers each diocese. Within dioceses priests and deacons serve parishes. The church strictly reserves its offices for unmarried men.

In addition to bishops, priests, and deacons, the Catholic Church has a long tradition of MONKS AND NUNS, people who devote themselves to a religious life instead of marrying.

SIGNIFICANCE

Roughly one-sixth of the world's population is Roman Catholic (in 2004 roughly 1,098,000,000 people). Roman Catholicism has made immense contributions to the cultural heritage of Europe. It is also an important part of life for many people around the globe.

Further reading: Thomas Bokenkotter, *A Concise History of the Catholic Church* (New York: Doubleday, 2004); James T. Fisher, *Catholics in America* (New York: Oxford University Press, 2000); Richard P. McBrien, *Catholicism* (San Francisco: HarperSanFrancisco, 1994); Richard P. McBrien et al., eds., *The HarperCollins Encyclopedia of Catholicism* (San Francisco: HarperSanFrancisco, 1995).

Roman Catholicism and Eastern Orthodoxy in America   The practice of the religion centered on JESUS in the Western Hemisphere. This entry focuses on only two of the three major branches of Christianity, ROMAN CATHOLICISM and EASTERN ORTHODOX CHRISTIANITY. A separate entry discusses PROTESTANTISM IN AMERICA.

CATHOLICISM IN NORTH AND SOUTH AMERICA

Columbus brought Catholicism to the Western Hemisphere. He captained a ship named the *Santa Maria* (Saint Mary). He named the first island he encountered San Salvador (Holy Savior). His discoveries began an era of Spanish and Portuguese colonization that had a well-formulated religious policy: Make the Indians Christians.

As a result, indigenous Americans from Mexico to Tierra del Fuego became Catholic Christians. But they did not simply surrender their own religious traditions. They developed a rich Catholicism that combined earlier religions with Christianity. A good example is the cult of the Virgin of Guadalupe. At Guadalupe in 1531 the Virgin Mary appeared to an indigenous Mexican in indigenous form.

The Roman Catholicism of Central and South America remained allied with the colonial government and the small minority who, after Spanish and Portuguese colonization, owned the land. Those who sought independence often opposed the church. After independence, the church generally allied itself with the wealthy and powerful. It seemed to have little compassion for those who worked the land. In the 1960s this stance changed. Liberation THEOLOGY identified economic justice as the proper work of the church. The hierarchy in Rome, however, had suspicions about this politically oriented theology.

Like the Spanish and Portuguese MISSIONARIES in Central and South America, French Catholic missionaries were active in North America. As a result, Roman Catholicism is now the majority religion in CANADA, by a slim margin. It is especially important in Quebec. There people have preserved their Catholic heritage along with their French identity.

Roman Catholicism was present in Florida as early as 1514 and in the American southwest from the 1580s. Nevertheless, the dominant religious culture of the United States has been Protestant. Catholicism, however, has been very important in more localized regions, such as the state of Maryland. The first American Catholic bishop was John Carroll of Baltimore, who became a bishop in 1789. His diocese was the entire country.

During the 19th century many Catholic immigrants came to the United States from countries such as Ireland, Italy, Germany, and Poland. They made the Catholic Church the largest single religious body in the United States. Catholic immigrants often encountered hostility from Protestant neighbors. But by the second half of the 20th century anti-Catholic sentiment and behavior had largely disappeared. Thus, in 1960 a Catholic, John F. Kennedy, could be elected president.

The American Catholic Church has tended to be more innovative and less traditional than Catholic churches in other areas. This stance has led at times to conflict with the hierarchy in Rome over such issues as the place of women in the church and the practice of birth control.

ORTHODOXY IN THE UNITED STATES

Russian missionaries first brought Orthodox Christianity to the United States. In the late 1700s they worked in Alaska. In time the Alaskan church moved its headquarters to San Francisco. In 1970 the patriarch of Moscow declared the Orthodox Church of America independent.

Not all Orthodox Christians accepted this church. Immigrants from many Orthodox countries, especially Greece, maintained their own national churches. They adopted some features from religious life in America, such as pews in church buildings and the use of some English in the Divine LITURGY. In general, however, the different national churches have remained resolutely separate.

Roman religion The religion of the Roman people before CHRISTIANITY became the official religion of Rome. Much Roman religious activity took place in the home. Households presented offerings to many gods. These gods included the Lar familiaris (perhaps associated with the fields), the Penates associated with the storeroom), Vesta (the cooking fire), the genius (the spirit of the family's patriarch), and Janus (the two-faced god of the entryway). Some of the gods received offerings every day. The purpose was not to win HEAVEN or achieve enlightenment. It was to ensure that the household thrived. Ultimately, the patriarch of the family (paterfamilias) was responsible for all household worship.

The purpose of the religious observances of the Roman state was the same: to ensure that the state flourished. The strategy was basically the same, too: Maintain good relationships with the gods through performing various RITUALS, often by celebrating festivals. Some of the state gods corresponded to the household gods. Rome had its hearth—served by special priestesses known as vestal virgins. It had Penates, Lares, and a Janus, too. Communities also worshipped the ancestors (Manes).

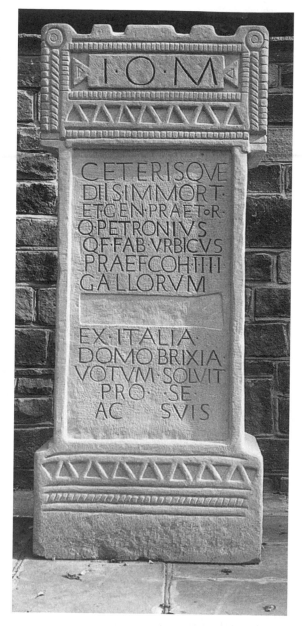

Copy of an altar dedicated to Jupiter *(Lesley and Roy Adkins Picture Library)*

on the Capitoline Hill: the supreme god, Jupiter Optimus Maximus, along with JUNO and Minerva. In early times, Roman gods lacked personality and mythology. Many seem to have been simply abstract powers: Victory, Harmony, the Boundary Stone.

From a small settlement on the Tiber River, Rome came to rule all the lands surrounding the Mediterranean Sea. As its power grew, its religion grew, too. From neighbors in Italy known as the Etruscans Romans learned to worship images of gods and to house them in roofed buildings, that is, temples. From the Greeks they borrowed mythologies. By 200 B.C.E. many Roman gods had Greek alter-egos: Jupiter was ZEUS, Juno was Hera, Mars was Ares, and so on.

The Romans did not simply identify traditional gods with foreign ones. They also imported foreign gods. During the republic they began to worship the Greek healer Asklepios, the "Great Mother" from Anatolia (ancient Turkey), and Bacchus. During the empire (began roughly 30 B.C.E.) they learned to WORSHIP ISIS of Egypt, MITHRA of Persia, and Sol Invictus of Syria. When the empire was established, the emperor also became the object of a cult. That does not mean, however, that he became a god. The imperial cult took many forms. Emperors were declared gods when they died, or they were worshipped along with the goddess Roma when alive, or portrayed as the supreme priest, or designated as specially chosen by the gods.

Priests supervised Roman religious practices, but they rarely did so as a full-time job. Important priests included the "King of Rituals" (*rex sacrorum*), the "Highest Priest" (*pontifex maximus*), ancient priests known as flamens, the vestal virgins, the salii who danced at festivals of Mars, and the augurs, who determined whether times were right for conducting state business, including war.

Toward the beginning of the fourth century C.E., it became legal for Romans to practice Christianity. By the end of the century, it had become mandatory. Some Romans continued traditional worship for a time. But in the end, Christianity replaced the old Roman religion.

The Roman state worshiped other gods too. The earliest known include JUPITER, MARS, and Quirinus. At the beginning of the republic (traditionally 509 B.C.E.), Romans worshiped a triad of gods

The exterior of the tomb of Jalal ad-Din ar-Rumi, the founder of the Mawlawiyah order of mystics (SEF/Art Resource, N.Y.)

Rosicrucianism From Latin for "rosy cross," a collective label for teachings and groups that developed in the tradition of European ALCHEMY and OCCULTISM. The Rosicrucian name began with the publication in 1614 of a booklet called *Fama Fraternitatis* (Fame of the Fraternity), presenting the legend of a certain Christian Rosenkreutz who had sought for wisdom in the East and brought it back to his native Germany. The book claimed that a secret fraternity was based on his teachings. Although most seekers were unable to find the group, several orders, including modern ones, teaching esoteric lore have taken the name.

Rumi (1207–1273) *very influential Sufi (Muslim mystic)* Rumi's full name is Jalal al-Din Rumi. His followers call him Mawlana, "our master." His poems in Persian are masterpieces, and his religious insight was the ultimate inspiration for an order in SUFISM often called Whirling Dervishes.

Rumi, the son of a teacher of theology, was born in what is now Afghanistan. For political reasons his family moved to a town called Konya, now in Turkey. In 1244 he met a mystic named Shams al-Din, and his life changed completely. After the meeting, various events in daily living would evoke in him a profound sense of love. He expressed this sense spontaneously in poetry. Eventually followers made two collections of his poems, named the *Divan-i Shams* and the *Mathnavi*. According to those who know Persian, translations do not begin to capture the beautiful language of these books. They celebrate love and the loss of oneself in the beloved, the rebirth that follows death, and prayer as communication with the ultimate beloved, God.

After Rumi's death his son organized his followers into a Sufi order. It is technically known as the Mevlevi order, but members of the order are sometimes called Whirling Dervishes. They do a slow, twirling dance. In the process, they lose themselves in the experience of God.

Further reading: Philip Dunn, Manuela Dunn Mascetti, and R. A. Nicholson, *The Illustrated*

Rumi: A Treasury of Wisdom from the Poet of the Soul: A New Translation (San Francisco: HarperSanFrancisco, 2000); Shems Friedlander, *Rumi and the Whirling Dervishes*, music by Nezih Uzel, foreword by Annemarie Schimmel (New York: Parabola Books, 2003); Annemarie Schimmel, *Rumi's World: The Life and Work of the Great Sufi Poet* (Boston: Shambhala, 2001).

Russia, religion in Religion in Russia and the former Soviet Union. EASTERN ORTHODOX CHRISTIANITY was formally introduced into Russia and accepted by the Principality of Kiev, then the major Russian state, in 988 C.E.

Since then, religion in Russia has been chiefly associated with the Russian Orthodox church, still the traditional faith of the great majority of the population. This church was intimately connected with the state in the days of the czars, and for most people Russia and Orthodoxy were one and the same thing. The church has long been noted for its lengthy but beautiful LITURGY, rich musical heritage, onion-domed churches, and colorful painted icons (pictures of JESUS and the SAINTS). It also has a tradition of deep spirituality, centering around identification with the suffering and RESURRECTION of CHRIST and the ideal of the "fool for Christ," or saint indifferent to the outward circumstances of life. At the same time, the predominance of Russian Orthodoxy in czarist times often led to persecution of Jews and other non-Orthodox minorities.

With the Communist revolution of 1917, ATHEISM was officially imposed on Russia and, in principle, religion was left to wither away as a premodern, outmoded institution. In practice, however, the situation was more complex: The Communist Party and the state sometimes viciously attacked and persecuted religion and sometimes (especially during World War II) befriended it in order to rally the loyalty of both believers and nonbelievers and present a favorable image to the outside world. At all times, however, the governance of religious bodies, especially the Russian Orthodox church, was closely controlled, and religious leaders who stepped out of line were severely punished.

After the collapse of communism in 1989, the picture changed dramatically. During the 1990s religious belief, under the new regime, appeared to increase greatly. Churches were reopened, religious leaders were involved in public life, and religion was highly visible in the media. Minority movements new and old endeavored to take advantage of the novel openness to spiritual life in all its varieties.

Despite czarist and Soviet oppression, Russia has long harbored dissident and minority religious groups. An early example is the Old Believers, a group formed in the late 1600s by those who opposed reforms introduced into the Russian Orthodox church by the Patriarch (chief bishop) and the czar. Other early dissidents were Russian varieties of radical Protestants, such as the Doukhobors, strict pacifists (see PACIFISM, RELIGIOUS) and followers of the "inner light" who rejected SACRAMENTS and other outward forms of religion, and the Molokans, also pacifists and followers of inner guidance, some of whose practices resemble those associated with PENTECOSTALISM.

In the 19th century Western missionaries introduced other forms of PROTESTANTISM, especially the BAPTIST CHURCH, the JEHOVAH'S WITNESSES, SEVENTH-DAY ADVENTISM, and PENTECOSTALISM. SPIRITUALISM also appeared in Russia, and two major figures in modern OCCULTISM AND ESOTERICISM, Helena P. Blavatsky (1831–91), cofounder of THEOSOPHY, and Georges Gurdjieff (c. 1872–1919), were from regions that were then parts of the Russian Empire.

Under the new religious freedom of the 1990s, still more new religions arose in Russia, and others, like the Hare Krishna movement (see KRISHNAISM IN THE WEST), were introduced. One result was a controversial new law on religious freedom in 1997 that put firm restrictions on the activities of new religions and groups brought in from outside Russia.

Traditional ethnic minorities include Muslims (see ISLAM), some 7.6 percent of the population in 2000, and a smaller number of Jews and Buddhists (see JUDAISM and BUDDHISM). Relations between them and the Christian majority have often been painful. Jews suffered from discrimination and persecution under both czarist and communist rule. In the early 21st century, Chechnya, mostly Muslim, attempted to secede from Russia, with violent results.

Russia, a vast land with newfound freedom but a tradition of religious policy imposed from above, remains in a spiritual ferment that holds possible consequences for the world as a whole.

Further reading: John Anderson, *Religion, State, and Politics in the Soviet Union and Successor States, 1953–1993* (New York: Cambridge University Press, 1994); Jane Ellis, *The Russian Orthodox Church: A Contemporary History* (Bloomington: Indiana University Press, 1986.); Jane Ellis, *The Russian Orthodox Church: Triumphalism and Defensiveness* (New York: St. Martin's Press, 1996); Shireen Hunter, *Islam in Russia* (Armonk, N.Y.: M. E. Sharpe, 2004).

S

Sabbath *See* JUDAISM.

sacraments The most important RITUALS for Catholic, Orthodox, and most Protestant Christians. Orthodox Christians also call sacraments "mysteries."

Not all Christians acknowledge sacraments. For example, QUAKERS do not. But all of those who do, accept at least two sacraments. These two are BAPTISM and the EUCHARIST. Baptism—either immersion in or sprinkling with water—is the ritual by which people enter the Christian church. The eucharist is the sharing of bread and wine that is somehow linked to the body and blood of JESUS. Over the last 2,000 years Christians have disagreed strongly over the proper way to perform these rituals as well as their proper meaning. These disagreements played a large part in the splintering of CHRISTIANITY into many different groups.

For the first thousand years of Christianity, the term "sacrament" was somewhat fluid. It designated other rituals besides baptism and the Eucharist. In the Middle Ages, a Catholic thinker named Peter Lombard (c. 1100–60) identified seven sacraments. The great medieval theologian, Thomas AQUINAS, followed him. This became the standard teaching of the Roman Catholic Church. In the 16th century the Protestant Reformers universally rejected the seven sacraments. They generally favored only two. In the 17th century, however, the Orthodox churches accepted the teaching of seven sacraments (*see* EASTERN ORTHODOX CHRISTIANITY). They practice them somewhat differently than the Catholic Church does.

In addition to baptism and the Eucharist, the seven sacraments include: confirmation or chrismation, penance, marriage (*see* MARRIAGE AND RELIGION), holy orders (*see* ORDINATION), and anointing. Both the Catholic and the Orthodox churches baptize infants. The Catholic and Anglican Church recognize a sacrament of confirmation. In this ritual baptized persons reaffirm their acceptance of Christianity once they are old enough to speak for themselves. The Orthodox churches recognize instead a sacrament of chrismation. This ritual, which preserves the most ancient practice, occurs immediately after baptism. It is an anointing with oil and a laying on of hands.

In penance Christians confess their SINS, either individually before a priest or as a group, and receive words of forgiveness. Marriage joins two people together as husband and wife. The sacrament of anointing is a ritual performed for spiritual and physical healing. At various times it has been practiced as a ritual for the dying. Holy orders sets aside men for special offices within the church. The most prominent of these are the offices of bishop and priest. Both Catholic and Orthodox churches limit ordination to men. The Catholic Church ordains only unmarried men. The Orthodox churches ordain married men as well, but they do not permit an unmarried man who is ordained to marry later. They also do not allow married priests to be bishops.

Different churches emphasize different aspects when they talk about the sacraments. The Orthodox churches have generally spoken of sacraments as providing a foretaste of HEAVEN on earth. The Catholic Church has traditionally emphasized the validity of sacraments as conveying God's GRACE, quite apart from the qualities of the person performing them. Lutherans say that sacraments convey God's grace when they are received in FAITH (*see* LUTHERANISM). Calvinists say sacraments are signs of God's grace, but they do not convey it (*see* PRESBYTERIAN AND REFORMED CHURCHES).

Some writers use the term "sacrament" for important rituals in other religions, but the word has too many Christian connotations. Applying it to non-Christian rituals almost always results in misunderstanding.

sacrifice One of the most important religious RITUALS. Sacrifice is the giving up of objects or the killing of animals or persons for religious purposes.

The most common form of sacrifice is the religious killing of animals. Indeed, animal sacrifice is in some sense the ruler by which scholars measure all other sacrifices. If a ritual act resembles animal sacrifice, it is a sacrifice. In the course of history human beings have made sacrifices of virtually anything and everything at their disposal: plants; smoke; dairy products; material products such as cloth, paper, statues, money, alcohol, drugs, and cooked food; rocks and minerals; speech; human blood and body parts; even entire human beings.

THE PRACTICE OF SACRIFICE

No one knows exactly when the practice of sacrifice began. Most animal sacrifices involve domesticated animals. Therefore, some scholars have suggested that sacrifice began when people first domesticated animals. In this view, sacrifice was the proper way to kill such animals for meat. Evidence for this view is scanty. It requires several controversial assumptions: that human culture went through a single series of developmental stages; that the culture of, say, prehistoric hunters closely resembled that of hunters today; and that rituals of the Paleolithic period cannot properly be called sacrifices.

There is no such thing as a typical sacrifice. Sacrifices vary in a number of ways. They vary in terms of what is sacrificed, who performs the sacrifice, who or what allegedly receives it, who benefits from it, what occasions it, where and when it is performed, and how it is supposed to work. Examples can only begin to hint at this variety.

In ancient Greece festivals to the Olympian gods were something like barbecues to which both gods and mortals were invited (*see* GREEK RELIGION). The community led the victims in procession to an elevated open-air ALTAR. The gods descended from the sky. The sacrificers slaughtered, butchered, and cooked the animals. Only the gods received some portions. Mortals received the rest. Sacrifices known as "hecatombs" were the largest feasts. At them the Greeks killed and cooked a hundred (or more) oxen.

The priests of ancient India known as BRAHMINS developed an elaborate complex of sacrifices. They sacrificed animals, dairy products, and an intoxicating liquid called soma. Wealthy patrons sponsored major sacrifices and received their benefits. In time brahmins gathered the chants, rules, and explanations for the sacrifices into sacred books known as the VEDA. They suggested that the sacrifice worked because of connections between elements of the rituals and elements of the universe.

Peoples who lived in urban Mesoamerica before the arrival of Columbus also had well developed sacrificial systems. The sacrifices of the Aztecs are notorious (*see* AZTEC RELIGION). People often offered their own blood to the gods. At times—it is very difficult to say just how often—they offered entire human beings. They either cut off their heads, cut out their hearts, or drowned them. (Ancient Greeks and Indians occasionally sacrificed human beings, too.)

Some religions and religious movements have rejected sacrifice. The Aztecs looked back to a mythological Toltec leader, Topiltzin Quetzalcoatl, who eliminated many sacrifices, including human sacrifice. In India during the sixth century B.C.E. BUDDHISM and JAINISM rejected sacrifice entirely. Some Hindus, too, came to deemphasize sacrifices in favor of ascetic exercises. The Persian prophet ZARATHUSTRA eliminated animal sacrifice; he retained only the sacrifice of the sacred liquid known as *haoma*. Some Jewish prophets insisted that justice and a pure heart were more important than sacrifices. When the Romans destroyed the Second Temple in JERUSALEM in 70 C.E., JUDAISM gave up sacrifices altogether. During the PILGRIMAGE to MECCA Muslims offer a sacrifice in memory of ABRAHAM's faithfulness when GOD asked him to sacrifice his son. A major feast marks this day.

Christians do not sacrifice animals, but they have often used the image of sacrifice in talking about JESUS. The Catholic and Orthodox churches teach that the EUCHARIST makes present the sacrifice of Jesus on the cross. Protestants often use the language of sacrifice to talk about personal morality instead.

THEORIES OF SACRIFICE

People who sacrifice have many different ideas about how sacrifices work. Scholars do, too. Their theories are suggestive, insightful, and sometimes outlandish. None are definitive.

One common theory has maintained that sacrifice is a gift to gods or spirits. A formula that the Romans addressed to their gods sums this theory up nicely: *do ut des*, "I am giving to you, so that you will give to me." Another theory has seen sacrifice as an occasion for human beings to commune with the sacred; this communion brings all sorts of benefits. Adolf Jensen, an anthropologist, once suggested that sacrifice originally reenacted events that certain myths ascribed to the beginning of the world. Walter Burkert, a scholar of Greek religions, derived sacrifice from the need to cope with the anxiety that comes from killing animals. Rene Girard has argued that sacrifice was a way to deflect violence that threatened to destroy society from within; sacrifice directs that violence onto the sacrificial victim instead. In a much different vein, some have suggested that Mesoamericans sacrificed human beings in order to make up for a lack of protein in their diet.

SACRIFICE TODAY

At the beginning of the 21st century animal sacrifice was a controversial practice in North America. Some North Americans objected to it on religious grounds. Others objected to it because they favored animal rights, or at least the humane treatment of animals. A few religions, however, did sacrifice animals. An example is SANTERÍA, a religion with African roots. True to its heritage, Santería requires its adherents to sacrifice chickens.

Toward the end of the 20th century the town of Hialeah, Florida, was disturbed that adherents of Santeria were sacrificing chickens. So it made animal sacrifice illegal. In June 1993, the U.S. Supreme Court overturned the law. The court found that Hialeah's law had only one purpose: to prohibit a religious practice. That violates the First Amendment to the U.S. Constitution (*see* CHURCH AND STATE). The First Amendment guarantees all Americans the right to practice their religions freely and without government interference. That guarantee extends to practices that may be unpopular, such as animal sacrifice.

Further reading: Maurice Bloch, *Prey into Hunter: The Politics of Religious Experience* (New York: Cambridge University Press, 1992); Jeffrey Carter, ed., *Understanding Religious Sacrifice: A Reader* (New York: Continuum, 2003); *The Girard Reader*, James G. Williams, ed. (New York: Crossroad, 1996).

sadhu, sadhvi Hindu holy men and women, respectively. There are considerably more sadhus than sadhvis.

The names sadhu and sadhvi denote people who are pursuing a *sadhana*, a way of life that leads to some ultimate goal. According to Hindu tradition (*see* HINDUISM), during the last stage of life a man renounces his possessions, family, and identity and wanders while pursuing spiritual liberation. In actual practice, sadhus and sadhvis adopt a life of renunciation at many different ages, some of them very young.

It is virtually impossible to count or classify the many different kinds of sadhus and sadhvis. Some are entirely independent and live off by themselves. Many others belong to organized groups. These groups are distinguished from one another by their teachers, teachings, gods, dress, body-marks, and other factors. The relative rank of sadhus and sadhvis emerges at festivals like the Kumbh Mela. There holy men and women line up in order of rank to proceed to the RITUAL bath.

Not all Indians respect sadhus and sadhvis. Some see them as freeloaders. Some sadhus are in fact con artists or criminals on the run. They have given those who are genuinely religious a bad name. During the course of the 20th century sadhus and sadhvis became very active in Indian politics. In general they are confirmed traditionalists, so they often opposed the government's policy of neutrality toward religion. They also tended to champion reactionary causes. Groups of sadhus and sadhvis were important supporters of the Bharatiya Janata Party (BJP), a pro-Hindu political party that governed India during the 1990s and early 2000s.

saints Holy people. Especially Christians use the term "saint." In the NEW TESTAMENT, PAUL the APOSTLE calls all Christians "saints." Most Protestants use the word in the same way. They do not recognize a special class of Christians known as saints.

Catholic and Orthodox Christians, however, call special Christians saints. They have a position in the church similar to the position of heroes in the army. They are special because of their personal characteristics, not simply because they hold an office.

Martyrs are saints (see MARTYRDOM). So are Christians who perform MIRACLES—often after death. Catholic and Orthodox Christians venerate—but do not WORSHIP—saints. They preserve their RELICS and visit their shrines. They also dedicate special days to each saint. Christians celebrate the lives of saints in literature known as "hagiography." Orthodox Christians venerate pictures of saints known as icons (see IMAGES, ICONS, IDOLS IN RELIGION).

Other religions have persons similar to saints. These include especially the *wali* or "friend [of God]" in ISLAM, and also the tsaddiq in Hasidic JUDAISM, the GURU and SADHU in HINDUISM, the sage in CONFUCIANISM, and the ARHAT, the BODHISATTVA, and the lama in BUDDHISM.

sakti, Saktism The manifestation of GOD in female form in HINDUISM and the groups that worship it. *Sakti* is a word in Sanskrit, an ancient language of India, that means "power" or "energy." It is a female divine principle and the power of all the gods. At a higher level of abstraction, some Indian schools of thought distinguish between spirit and nature. Spirit is male, nature is female. Spirit is also eternal and unchanging—inactive and inert. Nature is active, energetic, and creative. As such, some people consider it better to worship the active principle or *sakti*. People who worship *sakti* in its various forms are called *saktas*. Taken together, their beliefs and practices are called Saktism.

Sakti is as much an abstract principle as a divine being. It may refer to the highest god or to the consort of a god, especially SIVA. In personal form *sakti* is most generally known as Devi, "the Goddess." Hindus know many GODDESSES, whom they usually revere as mothers. They may think of all of them as different forms of Devi or as different, independent goddesses. Some goddesses have fierce characters; others are benign. Two well-known fierce goddesses are DURGA and KALI. Benign goddesses include Annapurna, Gauri, and PARVATI. In addition, most villages have their own goddesses. A common goddess at this more popular level is the goddess of smallpox. She is worshipped in order to keep the disease away.

Many Saktas worship the goddess through PUJA. They pray and offer gifts to her with the help of images and sacred symbols, such as the Sri-cakra-yantra. This yantra consists of a series of five triangles pointing down and four pointing up, surrounded by stylized lotus petals, which are themselves surrounded by a rectangular border. One distinctive feature of such worship among forms of Hinduism is that saktas' gifts may include the SACRIFICE of animals, such as goats. Animal sacrifice especially characterizes the worship of Kali and the village goddesses. Saktas also sometimes engage in practices that show special devotion or the possession of special powers, such as walking on fire or entering into trances.

Saktism is closely associated not only with devotional worship but also with tantric YOGA (see TANTRISM). Through this yoga Saktas seek ultimate realization and release. Tantric yoga aims to awaken the internal life force. This force is a form of *sakti*, and it is often envisioned as KUNDALINI, that is, a coiled serpent sleeping at the base of the spinal column. When awakened, the kundalini is visualized as moving upward through the *sushumna*. In this school of thought, people possess not only a body made up of coarse matter but also a subtle body made up of fine matter or energy. The *sushumna* is a part of the subtle body. It is situated along the spinal column and serves as a channel for energy. The kundalini moves through seven centers of the subtle body known as CAKRAS, "circles." The uppermost cakra is located at the top of the skull. When the kundalini reaches it, the practitioner experiences ultimate realization and release.

Saktas use many techniques to achieve these results. Their techniques tend to emphasize the use of feminine and material elements. Some practitioners belong to groups that are called "left-handed." Their activities violate normal social conventions. These activities include the use of intoxicants, the eating of meat, and the ritual practice of sexuality—all in search of ultimate realization.

The worship of goddesses is very old on the Indian subcontinent. It appears to have been prevalent in the Harappan or Indus Valley period, almost 5,000 years ago. From these roots Saktism came into being by about the year 500 C.E. Today, right-handed Saktas, those who observe normal conventions, are prevalent in southern India. Left-handed Saktas are prevalent in northern and especially eastern India. Perhaps the most famous Sakta was RAMAKRISHNA Paramahamsa, a priest of the goddess Kali in Kolkata (Calcutta). An ecstatic, he had visions not only of Mother Kali but also of JESUS and MUHAMMAD.

Further reading: Wendell Charles Beane, *Myth, Cult, and Symbols in Sākta Hinduism: A Study of the Indian Mother Goddess* (Leiden: Brill, 1977); Agehananda Bharati, *The Tantric Tradition* (Westport, Conn.: Greenwood Press, 1977); Georg Feuerstein, *Tantra: The Path of Ecstasy* (Boston: Shambhala, 1998); Sir John Woodroffe, *Sakti and Sākta: Essays and Addresses,* 8th ed. (Madras: Ganesh, l975).

salat The Arabic word for formal PRAYER; the second pillar of ISLAM. Salat is not informal petition of GOD, which Muslims may do at any time as need arises. It is formal, prescribed prayer. For devout Muslims salat defines the rhythms of daily life. It brackets and interrupts one's daily activities. It therefore helps to consecrate one's whole life to the service of God.

Adult Muslims follow the example of the prophet MUHAMMAD and pray five times a day: in the early morning, at noon, in mid-afternoon, in the evening, and at night. In cases of special need, the noon and midafternoon prayers may be combined. So may the evening and night prayers. In Muslim countries businesses routinely make allowances for salat during the workday. Employers in non-Muslim countries may make allowances, too. Afternoon prayers do not take any longer than a coffee break. In any case, Muslims are not to pray at the precise moment of sunrise or sunset or when the sun reaches the zenith. That might give the impression that they are worshipping the sun.

All the prayers may be done in any place that is quiet and clean. One may not wear shoes. It is best to pray with at least one fellow Muslim, if possible, but if necessary individuals may pray alone. The only exception to these rules is the Friday noon prayer. Men are to perform that prayer with a congregation in a MOSQUE. Women may join them there, but they may also perform the Friday noon prayer at home instead. At the Friday prayer service, the prayer leader, known as an IMAM, gives a sermon.

Before salat, Muslims must clean themselves. One should not present oneself before one's creator in an impure state. In most cases cleaning involves washing one's hands and forearms, face, and feet, rinsing the mouth and nose, and wiping one's head, neck, and ears. Because of this requirement one generally finds pools of water in mosques. At the same time, Islam arose in a desert climate, and it makes a special provision for that climate. If no water is available, going through the motions of washing will satisfy the requirement.

Muslims recite the actual prayers themselves facing the direction of the KAABA in MECCA. In a mosque this direction is noted by a niche on the wall. Some Muslims carry specially adapted compasses to allow them to find the *qiblah,* as the direction of Mecca is called. The prayers are recited in Arabic, and they must be recited from memory. When prayers are done in a group, a respected and capable member of the group stands in the front as imam. A man must lead groups of men or mixed groups. A woman may lead groups of women in prayer.

Muslims pray two or more sets of prayers at a time. Each set consists of prescribed prayers accompanied by prescribed postures and gestures. It begins by reciting the first *surah* or section of the QUR'AN while standing, for most Sunnis with hands crossed, for Shi'ites with hands at one's sides (*see* SHI'ITE ISLAM and SUNNI ISLAM). Other postures include leaning forward in a bow, prostrating by placing one's forehead and hands on the ground, and sitting. With each change of posture, the person recites "God is most great." When prayer is ended, the person praying recites a greeting to the right and to the left: "Peace be upon all of you and the mercy and blessings of God."

Children may begin to observe this duty at age seven. They should do so by age 10. But they are not absolutely required to do so until they reach puberty. Children may join the adults in the Friday prayer service. When they do, the boys stand behind the men. Girls pray with the women.

salvation   Rescue in a religious context. Salvation presupposes that there is a situation from which persons or things need to be saved or res-

cued. CHRISTIANITY calls this situation SIN. The myth of the FALL tells how sin began. In dualistic religions, such as ZOROASTRIANISM, GNOSTICISM, and MANICHAEISM, the problem is that good and EVIL, light and darkness have been mixed together. In HINDUISM, BUDDHISM, and JAINISM, the problem is that people are bound in SAMSARA, that is, they are continually reborn. This bondage is often traced to a more basic problem: ignorance.

Some religions save individual human beings. Christianity often saves individual sinners. Other religions save communities. Perhaps the best example of salvation in JUDAISM is the EXODUS, in which the whole people was saved. Some religions, such as Zoroastrianism, teach that an element of the cosmos, such as light or goodness, will be saved. Some Christians expect the salvation of the entire universe.

Many religions teach their followers how to help bring about salvation. But many religions also emphasize that people need help from the outside. They teach about saviors, such as JESUS or perhaps the Buddha AMIDA and the bodhisattva AVALOKITESVARA.

Salvation Army   An organization to spread CHRISTIANITY. Its structure imitates that of an army.

William Booth (1829–1912) was a Methodist minister (*see* METHODISM). He and his wife worked among the poor in London. In 1878 he hit upon the idea of organizing his mission as an army for GOD. Booth became general for life. Ministers became officers of various rank. Converts signed Articles of War and became soldiers. They were organized into groups called corps. A group of corps makes a division; a group of divisions makes a territory.

These military images appealed to the militaristic and nationalistic spirit of the late 19th century, and Booth's idea of a Salvation Army proved very successful. It quickly spread overseas. It now has centers throughout the globe. It has had its greatest success in the United States.

The teachings of the Salvation Army are fundamentalist (*see* EVANGELICAL CHRISTIANITY and FUNDAMENTALISM, CHRISTIAN), but the group refuses to discuss issues that might confuse the uneducated. Its WORSHIP services are designed for popular appeal. What is most distinctive of the army is the thorough way in which it carries out the military image. Its officers wear uniforms. Its members play Christian hymns in military-style bands. Its publication is *The War Cry*.

The Salvation Army continues to be very active in "rescue mission" work. It seeks not just to convert the poor but also to assist those who, for whatever reason, need material support. Unlike more liberal branches of PROTESTANTISM, it has shied away from social reform—that is, the attempt to reorganize society in a way that eliminates the causes of poverty and other evils.

Samaritans   A people in central Israel who claim to be descended from the Israelite tribes of Ephraim and Manasseh; indeed, they call themselves Israelites as well as *Shamerim,* "keepers of the law." The English name comes from Samaria, the name of the capital of the ancient kingdom of Israel. According to Jewish tradition, the Samaritans are not Israelites but are descended from peoples transplanted to the region when Assyria conquered Samaria in 721 B.C.E.

Samaritans are strict monotheists. They WORSHIP God under the name YHWH ("the Lord"). Their SCRIPTURES contain only the TORAH or Pentateuch, that is, the first five books of the BIBLE. They also revere MOSES and look forward to a final day in which God will restore their claims and take vengeance on the wicked.

The most sacred site for Samaritans is Mount Gerizim. They built a temple there in the late 300s, but it was destroyed by the Jewish priest and ruler John Hyrcanus in 128 B.C.E. The Samaritans still celebrate PASSOVER at Mount Gerizim. They also strictly observe the Sabbath.

In the ancient world there was considerable animosity between Samaritans and Jews. Those who returned from exile in Babylon saw the Samaritans as interlopers and refused Samaritan help in rebuilding the Temple in JERUSALEM. JESUS' well-known parable of the good Samaritan recognizes the hostile relations between the two groups (Luke 10.29–37).

Today only about 650 Samaritans survive. Roughly half live near Tel Aviv and are citizens of Israel. The other half live in the area of Nablus, near Mount Gerizim, a strongly Palestinian area. The Israeli-Palestinian Peace Agreement of September 28, 1995, guaranteed all Samaritans freedom of religion and access to holy sites. The Palestinian Elections Law approved in December 1995 reserved one seat on the 83-seat Palestinian Council for the Samaritans living near Nablus.

samsara   Sanskrit word for the continuous cycle of redeath and rebirth in which all beings live; thus, ordinary existence. The notion of samsara is shared by both HINDUISM and BUDDHISM.

Notions of rebirth are probably age-old on the south Asian subcontinent, but the idea of samsara came to prominence in both Hinduism and Buddhism roughly in the sixth century B.C.E.

For centuries priests who performed the sacrifices described in the VEDA had detailed the benefits of the sacrifices to their wealthy patrons. The primary benefit was a long number of blissful years spent in *svarga,* heaven. Around the sixth century B.C.E. certain sages began to speak of what happened when those benefits ran out: redeath, followed by rebirth. The conditions of rebirth were determined by the qualities of one's action (Karma).

About the same time, the BUDDHA was analyzing the condition of all sentient or conscious beings. On his analysis, all beings experience a continuing process of rebirth as a result of their craving-motivated acts, acts characterized by hatred, greed, and ignorance.

Hindus explain the process of rebirth in a variety of ways, but key to all of them is the notion of an eternal, unchanging self, sometimes called the ATMAN, which undergoes the various births. The situation in Buddhism is more difficult, because Buddhists deny that there is any eternal, unchanging self. They tend instead to speak of samsara in terms of a continuity of causality, a continuous series in which each craving-motivated event is both the result of a prior event and the cause of a future one. It is thought that this causal chain is not interrupted even by death.

Both Hinduism and Buddhism have developed schools of thought that downplay the significance of samsara. Like KRISHNA in the BHAGAVAD-GITA, many Hindus have taught that since the self is eternal and unchanging, it can experience neither birth nor death. The cycle of samsara occurs, then, only on the less real level of appearances. Mahayana Buddhists have tended to follow the great teacher Nagarjuna in asserting that NIRVANA, release, is not separate from samsara. Rather, nirvana is simply a manner of living within samsara.

sangha   "Group" in Sanskrit and Pali; the name for the religious communities of BUDDHISM and JAINISM. The sangha is one of the three "jewels" in which all Buddhists take refuge.

Sometimes sangha refers to the entire religious community of monks, nuns, laymen, and laywomen. It often refers more narrowly, however, to the community of MONKS AND NUNS. No centralized authority oversees the entire sangha in either Buddhism or Jainism. Instead, the sangha consists of self-governing local groups. This arrangement has led to dissension and division, so that different communities follow different traditions of "discipline."

In the earliest days members of both the Jain and Buddhist sanghas wandered the countryside begging. They settled in one place only during the rainy season when travel was difficult and hazardous. With time wealthy patrons endowed monasteries and convents. The life-style changed drastically, but the distinction between lay and religious remained. In some Buddhist schools, however, this distinction has almost completely broken down. For example, in several schools of Japanese Buddhism, it is no longer meaningful to speak of the sangha.

Sankara (eighth century C.E.)   *also spelled Shankara. Also known as Sankaracarya; the most influential Indian philosopher*   During his short

life (he died around the age of 30) Sankara systematized the Advaita (non-dualist) school of VEDANTA—with profound consequences. He developed his views in commentaries on the UPANISHADS, the BHAGAVAD-GITA, and the Vedanta-sutras; he traveled throughout India, debating the leaders of rival schools and converting them to his point of view; and he founded four monasteries, one in each of India's regions. These monasteries are among the most respected of India's religious institutions today. In doing all this, he helped to revive HINDUISM and contributed to the decline of BUDDHISM and JAINISM in India.

Central to Sankara's position is the insistence that BRAHMAN, the ultimate reality underlying all that we perceive, is not dual. Sankara developed this view by identifying four levels of reality. From lowest to highest, these are the self-contradictory (for example, a square circle), the illusory (for example, a mirage), the pragmatic (in which we ordinarily live), and the ultimate (brahman). Sankara teaches that we "superimpose" lower levels of reality on the next higher level. For example, at night a person may step on a rope and mistake it for a snake. That person superimposes the illusion of a rope onto the pragmatic reality of a snake. Similarly, Sankara says, we superimpose the perceptions of pragmatic reality onto brahman.

Santería   A popular religious movement originating in Cuba that combines African and Roman Catholic themes. Santería, "The Way of the Saints," developed among African slaves in Cuba, and has spread throughout the Caribbean and the United States. In it, Catholic SAINTS are identified with traditional African deities (*see* AFRICAN RELIGIONS), mainly Yoruba from the area that is now Nigeria and Benin, and worshipped in colorful rites that include vegetable and animal SACRIFICES. Santería ALTARS and costumes are often magnificent works of art. The most impressive ceremonies are those in which the deities, called *orishas,* "mount" or possess initiated devotees. The possessed one will then speak and act in ways characteristic of that god. The rites by which a devotee becomes an initiate of a particular deity, able to mediate that god through possession, are long and elaborate, involving a lengthy period of isolation and instruction. On the other hand, many people use simple everyday Santería practices for divination and luck.

Santería has flourished in the late 20th and early 21st centuries, both in Cuba (despite the revolution of 1959) and in the United States, where Cuban exiles have made it a presence in most major metropolitan areas. Although it has occasionally been controversial in the United States because of its use of animal sacrifice and alleged magical practices, it appears to be well established and has drawn some non-Cuban adherents.

Sarah   Also spelled Sarai; in the BIBLE the wife of ABRAHAM and also his half-sister (*see* Genesis 20.12). Sarah is best known for her difficulties in becoming a mother. She did not become pregnant for many years, and it was assumed that she could not have children. As the Bible tells the story, Abraham then had a son with her servant, Hagar. The son's name was Ishmael. In jealousy, Sarah eventually drove Hagar and Ishmael away. Arabs recognize Ishmael (Arabic, Ismail) as their ancestor. Stories of Hagar (Arabic, Hajar) and Ishmael are especially connected with the region of MECCA.

After the birth of Ishmael, Abraham and Sarah were visited by messengers from GOD. The messengers promised Abraham a son by Sarah. Because Sarah was past menopause and, therefore, beyond child bearing, she laughed. Nevertheless, she became pregnant, and the child was named ISAAC, after a Hebrew word related to laughter.

Saraswati   The Hindu GODDESS of learning and the arts. Saraswati is usually said to be the consort of the god BRAHMA. She is often shown with a stringed instrument known as vina. Sometimes she is accompanied by a goose, her vehicle or animal attendant.

Unlike Brahma, Saraswati is actually worshipped. Students invoke her as the goddess of learning. So do various Sanskrit texts. Musicians

present their instruments to her in the hope of obtaining her blessings during a performance.

Satan   The chief EVIL being in JUDAISM, CHRISTIANITY, and ISLAM. In the Hebrew BIBLE Satan appears most prominently in the book of JOB. There he is not the familiar figure of later times. He is an ANGEL in GOD's court. His function is to make accusations against human beings to God.

A little before the time of JESUS, Satan took on more familiar form. He became an adversary of God who tempts human beings to SIN. In the NEW TESTAMENT he constantly opposes Jesus. He appears as a tempter in the QUR'AN, too. There he is also called Iblis. Jewish, Christian, and Islamic images of Satan and his functioning differ in detail. All three, however, associate Satan with the serpent. The image of Satan common in North America—a horned being with pitchfork and tail—seems to derive from medieval Christian folklore.

Neither Judaism, Christianity, nor Islam makes Satan equal in power to God. All of them insist that God will ultimately vanquish Satan. Indeed, for Christians that victory has already been won in the death and RESURRECTION of Jesus. But some have taken a more positive view of Satan. For example, the Sufi al-Hallaj (c. 857–922: *see* SUFISM) took Satan as his model. As he saw it, Satan faithfully fulfilled the role God had assigned him, despite the consequences.

sati (suttee)   The practice in which a Hindu widow immolates herself (burns herself to death) on her husband's funeral pyre. It is, understandably, one of the most controversial practices in HINDUISM.

Sati is a Sanskrit word that means "good woman." It is also the name of a wife of the Hindu god SIVA, who burns herself to death. The British rulers of India often spelled it suttee. It was never universally required for a widow to commit or, more properly, "become" sati. The most authoritative ancient lawbook, the *Laws of MANU*, says more than once that a widow is expected to submit to the authority of her son and says nothing about sati. Nevertheless, the position of widows in traditional Hindu society was often not good, and in some places the practice of sati developed. It was particularly widespread in the western Indian state of Rajasthan, famed for its warrior traditions, and in the eastern Indian state of Bengal.

Feminist thinkers have often taken sati as a sign of the broader ill treatment of women in traditional India. They find a model for it in the story of Sita, the wife of RAMA in the *RAMAYANA*. Many Indian women consider Sita to be the ideal woman. To prove to her husband that she was pure, Sita threw herself into a fire prepared for ritual sacrifice, although according to the story the fire did not harm her in any way. Feminists have also suggested that women have been forced to immolate themselves against their will; traditional Hindus often reject this suggestion.

The British first outlawed sati in 1829. The last legal incident occurred in 1861. But although sati is not common today and offends many, perhaps most, Hindus, it still occurs. One recent incident was the sati of Roop Kanwar in Deorala, Rajasthan, on September 4, 1987. Pilgrims now visit the town to worship at the site where she committed sati.

Further reading: Lindsey Harlan and Paul B. Courtright, eds., *From the Margins of Hindu Marriage: Essays on Gender, Religion, and Culture* (New York: Oxford University Press, 1995); John Stratton Hawley, ed., *Sati, the Blessing and the Curse: The Burning of Wives in India* (New York: Oxford University Press, 1994).

Saul (11th century B.C.E.) *the first king of ancient Israel* In the 11th century B.C.E. the tribes of Israel lived in the hill country between the Jordan River and coast of the Mediterranean Sea. They were banded together into a loose confederation. But they were weaker than the Philistines, people who lived along the Mediterranean coast. As the BIBLE tells the story, they decided that they needed a king. They did so despite opposition from Samuel, the prophet of their god YHWH ("the Lord").

Samuel anointed Saul as the first king of Israel. Initially Saul's military efforts met with success. But the fighting was difficult, and Saul seems to have suffered emotionally. As the Bible tells it, he also became obsessed with a younger rival named DAVID. Saul and his sons lost their lives in battle at Mount Gilboa. After this event, the much more successful David became king.

science and religion The relationship of scientific knowledge to traditional religion. No issue has more profoundly disturbed the modern world than conflict between science and religion. Not only do the two use different methods for the ascertaining of truth, in their pure forms they also end up with radically different views of the ultimate nature of the universe, with consequent conflicting views of the origin, nature, and destiny of humans. These conflicting views in turn produce contrasting ideas on how human life should be lived, above all in its moral and psychological dimensions. Or so many spokespersons for each side have declared, though there have also been important attempts to mediate the two.

Science in the West, since its origins in the 16th century, has sought to determine the truth of nature through careful empirical observation, including precise measurements, induction from what is observed to general hypotheses, deducing other possible consequences of the principle, then testing them and the original law through repeated observation, in controlled experiments when possible. Its overall picture of the world develops through consensus among persons qualified to do such work, and in theory is always prepared to change its views in light of new evidence. Religion on the other hand characteristically bases its teachings on divine revelation or nonrational inner experience, presented through authoritative books and teachers, though revelation and doctrine may certainly be supported and amplified through rational means like those of science. Nonetheless, the resulting pictures of the world have contrasted greatly in recent centuries: Science has overwhelmingly offered a material, impersonal, mathematical universe—though one in which these terms must be qualified at the most advanced reaches of physics and psychology. The religious worldview, though not in conflict with science on some levels, is one in which mind and consciousness are much more important, with a Divine Mind as Creator or Sustainer, and the human soul or spirit of central significance.

The conflict began with the new astronomy of Copernicus, centered on the Earth revolving around the sun rather than being the center of the system as in the older view accepted by most religions, though in time virtually all religionists concluded that a flat or central Earth was not really crucial to religious truth and came to terms with it. More traumatic was the 19th-century conflict between Darwin's evolution and the biblical account of creation in Genesis, climaxing in the direct creation of ADAM and EVE by GOD. Here the two views of human beings seemed to many irreconcilable: Either humans are creations of God and the BIBLE is true, or they are natural, evolved over time as are the animals, and God is not necessary.

To some the issue seems still to be in those opposing terms. But many more liberal religionists were able to conclude that the Bible is only a book of principles, not a textbook in science; God can still be the ultimate creator, while science just tells us how it was done over previously unimaginable spans of time. At the same time, spokespersons for other religions, especially BUDDHISM and Vedanta HINDUISM, and in some ways also JUDAISM and ISLAM, claimed that their FAITHS were "more scientific" than the CHRISTIANITY dominant in the West, since they ordinarily do not require a literal reading of the old creation story. In the case of VEDANTA and Buddhism, there are also some similarities between their views of karmic cause and effect and the interrelatedness of all things and Albert Einstein's scientific theory of relativity and the more advanced frontiers of cosmology.

Moreover, in the 20th century, new issues have arisen, especially in connection with bioengineering and "artificial intelligence." These are often as much ethical issues important to religion as theoretical challenges to religion. Do humans have the right to "play God" by altering lifeforms, or making computers that practically think? And does this suggest that the originals of body and mind also could have come into being without the traditional God?

On the other hand, could it be that such works are simply exercises of the power God gave humanity over the Earth, but we still need God to keep from going too far? Unfortunately, another feature of modernity has been the terrible discovery that science can be abused to produce EVIL as well as good, from the alleged depersonalization of human life in the industrial or technological city to the atomic bomb and other refined weapons of destruction. In the eyes of many, even the great advances in medicine and agriculture have led to crises of overpopulation and the prospect of ecological disaster. Can we resolve such issues without the help of religious values? These are problems whose solutions may await further developments in the conflict, or harmonization, of science and religion.

Scientology A religious movement founded in 1952 by the science fiction writer L. Ron Hubbard, on the basis of his best-selling book *Dianetics*. Its fundamental practice is individual counseling, which enables individuals to discover the cause of their problems in "engrams" or conditioned responses caused by occasions of fear and suffering, implanted in this or previous lives. One can then "go clear" by removing them by Scientological means. The tightly organized and economically active movement has been controversial in the United States and several other countries. It remains, however, prosperous and successful.

scripture In all major living religions, a body of words or writings declared to have been revealed by the highest authority and containing the fullness of spiritually important truth: the BIBLE of JUDAISM and CHRISTIANITY, the QUR'AN (Koran) of ISLAM, the Sutras of BUDDHISM, the VEDAS of HINDUISM, the Confucian Classics, and so forth. In Hinduism, the

Vedas were not committed to writing until comparatively modern times, having been, because of their great sacredness, transmitted orally from father to son, or master to disciple, for many generations. Otherwise the written form of the scripture came early as the sacred text is considered important *as* a book or set of books, though the spoken word is always in the background, and scriptures are often considered most powerful when spoken or chanted aloud, sometimes in the original tongue, like Hebrew in Judaism, Arabic in Islam, or Sanskrit in Hinduism. But the background, content, and role of scriptures in different religions varies considerably.

First, it must be noted that the existence of written scripture obviously depends on the invention of writing, and could not have come into being before that event two or three millennia or so before the common era. Before then, the lore of religions was oral, passed on by word of mouth in the form of myths and traditions. Thus scriptures were made possible by the invention of writing. Scriptures came into being in a time of gathering empires, of a growing sense of individualism, and of awareness that we live in historical time—that is, that things change and do not change back. Above all, it was the time of the great religious founders: Moses, the Buddha, Confucius, Lao-Tzu, Jesus, and Muhammad. All these men had messages to help people contend with the new world of writing, empires, history, and individualism. Scriptures were part of that message, and vehicles of it.

Scriptures contain many things: histories, as in the Hebrew scriptures and the Kojiki of Shinto Japan, to help people see that God or the gods are working in history and so one need not be afraid of change; laws and rituals, as in parts of the Hebrew scriptures and the Confucian books, to help people keep alive traditions of the past in the face of change; rules and attitudes for right living, as in the Qur'an; wisdom and poetry for the sake of fullness of life and praise to God; philosophy as in the Upanishads part of the Vedas and the Buddhist Sutras to help people realize the timeless in the midst of time. The scriptures of Judaism, Christianity, and Islam show that there is a God sovereign over the world of change, and that this God has revealed himself in the world in particular times. In the Christian New Testament, this revelation is in the person of Jesus Christ. Responding to the growing individualism of the times, the scriptures of these then-new religions emphasize ways to individual salvation and living an individually responsible life.

The establishment of the "canon" of scripture, that is, which books are officially regarded as part of the sacred list and which are excluded, was not always an easy task. In early Buddhism and Christianity, for example, it was decided in the end by councils of monks and bishops respectively centuries after the founding of the religion; while some books had been long accepted by general consensus, others, like the epistle to the Hebrews and the Revelation of St. John in Christianity, were long disputed. By now, however, the tradition of the whole religion has long since approved an accepted canon.

Scriptures have many functions in religion besides being regarded as a source of authoritative truth, and even their truth can have different meanings. Some conservative Christians regard the Bible as literally true, even on historical and scientific matters; others recognize it as containing important principles but accept that its books were written in the context of the world view of ancient times and may contain myth, poetry, and outdated ideas as well as relevant truth. Many Buddhists regard their more philosophical texts as suggestive of insights beyond words that must be then realized in MEDITATION. Scriptures are studied, meditated on, preached out of, read aloud in services, chanted (in Hinduism and Buddhism, the very sounds themselves are key seeds of religious experience), sung as hymns, used as sources of folk wisdom.

Scriptures are also important as symbols of the identity of religious communities; members are people who have this in common. They promote the spread of literacy. They seal the authority of religious leaders, who are their proper interpreters, and validate the religion's paths to individual SALVATION. Yet they also can legitimate independent prophets and reformers, who can go back to the original scriptures to find their new ideas, perhaps ideas that they say the established leaders have set aside, and challenge their authority with them. Scriptures can stir things up as well as keep them under control. Scriptures are basic to the life of religion as we know it.

scriptures, Buddhist The sacred books of BUD-DHISM are unlike the sacred scriptures with which readers may be familiar. For one thing, most North Americans associate sacred scriptures with a closed canon, a "rule" of authoritative writings that does not make room for any additions. For another, they imagine scriptures as being long, perhaps, but still relatively manageable. For example, it is possible to bind the BIBLES that Jews and Christians use as well as the QUR'AN into single volumes. These characteristics do not describe Buddhist scriptures. One school of Buddhism, the Theravada (see THER-AVADA BUDDHISM), does have a canon that is officially closed. The Tibetan canon, in the tradition of VAJRAYANA BUDDHISM, is closed in fact, if not officially. But the canon of MAHAYANA BUDDHISM is not closed. Books can still be added to it. Furthermore, all Buddhist schools have many more sacred books than could ever be bound into a single volume, at least a single volume with readable print. Finally, different schools of Buddhism differ much more about which books are sacred than do, for example, Protestant and Catholic Christians, who differ on the APOCRYPHA, or Sunni and Shi'ite Muslims, who accept the same Qur'an.

Like JESUS and MUHAMMAD, the BUDDHA, known to Mahayana and Vajrayana Buddhists as Sakyamuni, taught orally. He did not write any books. Tradition records that, after his *parinirvana* (which non-Buddhists see as his death), his disciples gathered in India in a place called Rajagriha. The Buddha's cousin and secretary, Ananda, led them in reciting the Buddha's teachings. In theory, at least, these teachings constitute the sacred scriptures of Buddhism. Within about two centuries, however, different schools of Buddhism had arisen, and each was developing its own set of scriptures.

All schools recognize three basic kinds of sacred scripture. These kinds are called *pitakas* or baskets. The scripture as a whole is called the *Tripitaka* or "Three Baskets," a name particularly associated with the Theravada canon. (Theravada Buddhists usually write *Tipitaka*, the name in Pali, the language in which their sacred books are written.) The three baskets contain the rules for MONKS AND NUNS, known as the *vinaya;* sermons preached by the Buddha, known as sutras or, in Pali, *suttas;* and philosophical texts, known as *abhidharma* or, in Pali, *abhidhamma.* The individual books that each basket contains are too numerous to list here, but some important components include the *Theragatas* and *Therigatas* (poems by ancient monks and nuns), *jatakas* (stories of previous lives of the Buddha), and *apadanas* (the lives of remarkable Buddhists told as examples). The Theravada canon was allegedly closed around the time of Jesus. That may not be historically accurate. The collections associated with different regions, such as Sri Lanka and Burma, differ somewhat.

Buddhism came to China in the early centuries C.E., and Buddhists actively translated Buddhist texts into Chinese. As a result, several Chinese versions of the *vinaya* for monks and nuns exist. The Chinese did not translate the sutra and *abhidharma* texts completely. But more important for the practice of the religion, Mahayana Buddhism in East Asia has recognized a number of sutras that the Theravada does not recognize. These texts allegedly record the secret teachings of the Buddha. They were written relatively late and contain distinctive Mahayana teachings, such as teachings about buddha nature and the Pure Land. The most important Mahayana sutras include the *Diamond Sutra* and *Heart Sutra* (see DIAMOND SUTRA), part of a group called the "perfection of wisdom" sutras; the *Lankavatara Sutra,* particularly important for Ch'an or ZEN BUDDHISM; the *Lotus Sutra,* a major text for a school known as Tendai as well as for NICHIREN Buddhism; and three sutras particularly important to PURE LAND BUDDHISM: the shorter and the longer *Amitabha Sutra* and the *Meditation Sutra.*

Like Mahayana Buddhists, Tibetan Buddhists recognize many texts as authoritative that are not in the *Tipitaka* of the Theravada. Their canon has two parts. The Kanjur or "Word of the Buddha" contains the *vinaya,* many sutras, and texts known as *tantras.* The Tenjur or "Teachings" contains a wide variety of texts, including *tantras* and commentaries on the sutras and the *abhidharma.*

Readers may wonder how Buddhists deal with such a large and varied set of sacred scriptures. It is impractical, perhaps impossible, for anyone to be familiar with all of the texts. Indeed, since the Mahayana canon is not closed, no one can ever know all of the Mahayana sacred scriptures. The Theravada claim to base their teachings solely on the *Tipitaka.* Different Mahayana schools tend to emphasize different scriptures. Sometimes the most important text will not even be a sacred scripture. A school of Zen Buddhism known as Soto pays most attention to the writings of its founder, Dogen. Nichiren Buddhists consider the *Lotus Sutra* the perfect revelation of the Buddha, superior to all others. Their chief practice is not, however, to study the text, as Muslims might study the Qur'an. Instead, they simply recite its praises with the phrase *"Namu Myoho-Renge-Kyo"* ("Hail to the marvelous teaching of the *Lotus Sutra*").

Further reading: *Buddhist Scriptures,* Donald S. Lopez, ed. (New York: Penguin Putnam, 2004); *The Dhammapada,* John Ross Carter and Mahinda Palihawadana, trans. (New York: Oxford University Press, 2000); *The Essential Lotus: Selections from the Lotus Sutra,* Burton Watson, trans. (New York: Columbia University Press, 2002); *Perfect Wisdom: The Short Prajñāpāramitā Texts,* Edward Conze, trans. (Totnes, England: Buddhist Pub. Group, 1993); *Songs of the Sons and Daughters of Buddha,* Andrew Schelling and Anne Waldman, trans. (Boston: Shambhala, 1996).

scriptures, Hebrew The Bible used by the Jews, which Christians call the Old Testament. Jews use a Bible written in Hebrew that consists of 24 books. In content these books are identical with the 39 books in the Protestant Old Testament (*see* Protestantism) They are simply divided and counted differently. The Catholic and Orthodox churches have several other books in their Old Testaments (*see* Roman Catholicism and Eastern Orthodox Christianity). Protestants place these other books in the Apocrypha.

THE FORMULATION OF THE HEBREW SCRIPTURES

Perhaps the best name for the Hebrew scriptures is Tanakh, an acronym derived from the three parts into which Jews divide the Bible: Torah (teaching), *Nevi'im* (prophets), and *Ketuvim* (writings). For Jews this is the order of the importance of each part: Torah is most important; *Ketuvim* is least important. (For Christians all three parts have equal authority.) Torah, *Nevi'im,* and *Ketuvim* is also the order in which Jews accepted the books as authoritative.

Most modern scholars believe that Torah combines several sources. One source appeared in the southern kingdom, known as Judah, perhaps during the ninth century B.C.E. It uses a proper name for God: YHWH, which out of respect is usually simply rendered in English as "the Lord." A second source appeared in the northern kingdom around the eighth century B.C.E.; it refers to God generically as "Elohim" (God). The book of Deuteronomy constitutes a third source, discovered in the temple during the reign of King Josiah (640–609 B.C.E.), while priests during the Babylonian Exile (587–539 B.C.E.) or afterward systematized legal procedures to provide the last source. Torah as a whole seems certainly to have come into existence by the time of the priest Ezra (late fifth or early fourth century B.C.E.).

At the same time that Torah was being formulated, various religious leaders in ancient Israel, known as prophets, were making their pronouncements. According to tradition, prophecy continued in ancient Israel until around 400 B.C.E. The sayings of some of the prophets were collected into books. It seems certain that a collection of books known as the Prophets existed by around 200 B.C.E.

By the time of JESUS, the Hebrew Bible was not yet complete. Jesus refers to Torah ("the law") and the Prophets and sometimes the Psalms (for example, Matthew 5.17; 22.40; Luke 24.44) but never to Torah, the Prophets, and the Writings. Instrumental to the collection of the Writings and the closing of the "canon" or authoritative list of books was a council of rabbis led by Johannan ben Zachai at Jamnia in the year 90 C.E. Although not all of the rabbis wanted to include all of the books now in the Writings, they eventually decided on a canon of 24 books because there are 24 letters in the Hebrew alphabet.

CONTENTS OF THE HEBREW SCRIPTURES

Torah

Torah means "teaching"; it has sometimes also been translated as "law." The books of Torah are called teaching, because in them God teaches his people how he wants them to live. These teachings are given in *mitzvot*, commandments. The rabbis have identified 613 *mitzvot* in Torah.

Torah comprises the first five books of the Bible, traditionally attributed to MOSES. The first book, Genesis, provides a universal prehistory or mythology, followed by stories about ancestors of the people of Israel: ABRAHAM and SARAH, ISAAC and REBEKAH, and JACOB, his wives, and his children. The other four books, Exodus to Deuteronomy, center on Moses. They tell of the freeing of the people of Israel from slavery in Egypt, the giving of the commandments on a mountain that Exodus calls Sinai and Deuteronomy calls Horeb, and the wandering of the Israelites in the desert for 40 years.

Nevi'im

Judaism recognizes two kinds of prophets. The first, called "Former Prophets," include the books of Joshua, Judges, Samuel, and Kings. Christians often refer to these books as "historical." Calling the books prophets highlights how they differ from history as we know it: Their goal is not to record human deeds and events but to identify how God was active in the past. Modern scholars often refer to the perspective of these books as "deuteronomistic" because they view the history of Israel in terms of distinctive ideas in the book of Deuteronomy, especially the idea that God will bless Israel for keeping the covenant but punish and even destroy it for violating the covenant.

The second kind of prophets are called "Latter Prophets." These include the books known as ISAIAH, JEREMIAH, EZEKIEL, and the Twelve. From a Jewish perspective these prophets describe how God was active in their time. Christians have generally seen them as foretelling the future, especially events concerning Jesus. A verse from Isaiah can provide a good example of the difference. The Jewish Publication Society's translation of Tanakh renders Isaiah 7.14: "Assuredly, my Lord will give you a sign of His own accord! Look, the young woman is with child and about to give birth to a son. Let him name him Immanuel." The King James version translated the same verse, "Therefore the Lord himself shall give you a sign; Behold, a virgin shall conceive, and bear a son, and shall call his name Immanuel." Modern scholars tend to agree that at the time Isaiah was giving a sign of hope by referring to a pregnant woman in the king's court, perhaps the queen.

Ketuvim

The Writings comprise a variety of sacred books, such as PSALMS, Proverbs, Ezra-Nehemiah, Chronicles, JOB, and DANIEL. Of these, perhaps the most important is the book of Psalms; the psalms or poems that it contains have been used by Jews and Christians in worship since ancient times. Chronicles retells the story of Israel's history down to the exile in Babylon, while Ezra-Nehemiah tells about the return from Babylon and the rebuilding of the Temple in Jerusalem. Proverbs and Job are examples of WISDOM LITERATURE. Proverbs gives advice for living, while Job wrestles with the problem of undeserved suffering. The book of Daniel is a well-known story written in the time of the Maccabean revolt (168–164 B.C.E.) but set in the time of the Babylonian exile. It urges Jews to remain faithful to the covenant and predicts that the Maccabees will be successful in their revolt.

THE TEXT OF THE HEBREW SCRIPTURES

One characteristic of the Hebrew scriptures that may seem peculiar is the wide variety of versions that exist for many of the books. The text that Jews consider authoritative, also used by Christians, is known as the Masoretic text. That is because scholars known as Masoretes finally established it as authoritative around the year 1000 C.E. But there are also very different versions for many of the books. For example, the Samaritans have a version of the Torah, or Pentateuch, that differs considerably from the Jewish version. The Greek text of the Hebrew scriptures known as the Septuagint contains very different versions of the Latter Prophets, for example, the prophet Isaiah, as well as of some of the writings, such as Esther and Daniel.

In the past people saw different versions of the Hebrew scriptures as corruptions of the original text. Discoveries of ancient manuscripts such as the DEAD SEA SCROLLS have tended to change that view. They seem to show that for many of the Hebrew scriptures there never was an original text, written by a single author, from which all the others diverged. Instead, various people seem to have collected various materials together under the same name, for example, Isaiah. As time went on, different religious communities established standardized versions of these books.

Further reading: Lawrence Boadt, *Reading the Old Testament: An Introduction* (New York: Paulist Press, 1984); *The Complete Dead Sea Scrolls in English*, Geza Vermes, trans., new ed. (New York: Penguin Books, 2004); *The New Oxford Annotated NRSV Bible with the Apocrypha*, 3d ed., Michael D. Coogan et al., eds. (New York: Oxford University Press, 2001); *Tanakh: The Holy Scriptures, The New JPS Translation According to the Traditional Hebrew Text* (Philadelphia: Jewish Publication Society, 1985); Joseph Telushkin, *Biblical Literacy: The Most Important People, Events, and Ideas of the Hebrew Bible* (New York: William Morrow, 1997).

seasons and religion Religions celebrate environments, make them meaningful, and help people live in them. They do so, among other ways, by giving attention to seasons. The seasonal dimension of religion is often especially important for people like hunters, gatherers, and farmers, whose livelihood makes them aware of the rhythms of nature.

One way religions pay attention to the seasons is by telling stories. A well-known story from the ancient Greeks tells about Kore or Persephone, who was abducted by Pluton and eventually had to spend six months a year below ground and six months above. Most people connect this story in some way with the seasons and the rhythms of plant life.

A more visible way of celebrating the seasons is through public RITUALS. Public RITUALS often mark important points in the agricultural calendar. Two important SHINTO FESTIVALS take place at the time of planting in spring and harvesting in autumn. But the agricultural calendar is not always defined by spring and autumn. Two HINDU FESTIVALS, Dussehra and Divali, mark the end of the rainy season and the planting of winter crops.

Still other seasonal festivals mark events in the solar year. The ancient Romans celebrated the rebirth of the sun at the time just after the winter solstice on December 25. European folklore preserves memories of celebrations of the summer solstice on Midsummer Night's Eve. During the summer, although not on a specific date, Native Americans on the Great Plains often celebrated Sun Dances (*see* NATIVE AMERICAN RELIGIONS).

Many religions mark the beginning of the NEW YEAR, although the dates on which they do so vary considerably. One common feature of New Year festivals is excess. Some scholars connect this excess with a disappearance of the old order, followed at the end of the festival by the establishment of a new order.

The conditions of modern life often distract people from the rhythms of the seasons. Nevertheless, many rituals common in North America have a seasonal dimension, even if it is not always very apparent. The JEWISH FESTIVALS of PASSOVER, Shavuot, and Sukkot correspond to important times in the agricultural year of ancient Canaan. CHRISTMAS falls on the date of the old celebration of the rebirth of the sun, and EASTER is a spring celebration of new life.

Seventh-Day Adventism

Seventh-Day Adventism An American Christian group best known for worshipping on Saturday rather than Sunday. Adventists expect the immediate return ("advent") of JESUS. A Baptist minister named William Miller (1782–1849) predicted that Jesus would return to Earth in 1843 and then in 1844. He did not, but a few remained convinced that Miller got the date right. Instead of returning, they taught, Jesus had entered the heavenly sanctuary to examine the Book of Life.

These people became Seventh-Day Adventists. They took this name because, unlike other Adventists, they decided that Christians were supposed to WORSHIP on Saturday, not Sunday. They were also convinced that one of their early leaders, Ellen Harmon White (1827–1915), had the gift of PROPHECY. Although the community began in the United States, it has been very successful overseas.

Seventh-Day Adventists have emphasized vegetarianism and a good diet. They indirectly made a very important contribution to American life: breakfast cereal. The head of an Adventist health institute in Battle Creek, Michigan, Dr. J. H. Kellogg, experimented with cereals for his patients. Eventually he and his brother, W. K. Kellogg, went into business making corn flakes. One of Dr. Kellogg's patients also went into the cereal business: C. W. Post.

sexuality and religion The relation of religion to the sexual nature of human life. Human sexuality has always raised issues for religion and been viewed many different ways. Sexuality can be viewed as a source of temptation that leads one away from GOD.; on the other hand, it is a source of a powerful energy that some have been bold enough to say can be redirected and used in the quest for God. As for religion, its two main functions, maintaining the social order and offering a means to SALVATION, can be at odds on the question of sexuality. The social order is fundamentally based on marriage and the family, and so requires a morality in which sexuality is affirmed but kept within wedlock. However, the quest for salvation, in some eyes, may call for CELIBACY, or at the other extreme, the use of sexual RITUALS outside of marriage.

The conventional view is that sexuality is a sacred gift to be used within marriage for procreation, since a fundamental human obligation is, in the words of the book of Genesis, to "be fruitful and multiply." Fertility is a common religious theme; just as there are prayers for rites on behalf of the fertility of fields and animals, so wedding rites are likely to contain veiled sexual symbols like the wedding ring, and PRAYERS for children. Some gods, like the Hindu SIVA and his companion, Nandi the bull, or the SHINTO Inari, have clear fertility meaning. Some primal societies have had orgiastic festivals to promote fecundity, and obvious sexual symbols can still be seen in some Shinto celebrations. Nonetheless all major religions strongly uphold marriage as the way of life for most people, holding that sexuality is to be expressed fully only within it. Often in practice, however, there is a double standard between men and women. Some religious cultures are very particular that brides be virgins, but seem less concerned about males.

At another extreme there is TANTRISM in HINDUISM and BUDDHISM, which uses sex or its symbols as a sacrament or sign of the divine. In the Hindu Tantric ritual called *maithuna* or "union," the male identifies with Siva, the female with his sakti or energy and the creation; thus they enact the union of HEAVEN and Earth, God and the world. This is a common theme of the art of Vajrayana of TIBETAN RELIGION, though there the rites are usually done symbolically. Similar usage can be found in TAOISM.

There is also the widespread practice of celibacy, or forgoing active sexual expression for the sake of spirituality. It is followed in ROMAN CATHOLICISM by priests, and by celibate MONKS AND NUNS within the Catholic traditions of CHRISTIANITY, and in Buddhism, Hinduism, and Taoism.

See also HOMOSEXUALITY AND RELIGION.

Shakers An American communitarian movement. The Shakers were an offshoot of the QUAKERS. They began in England in 1747. They got their name because their WORSHIP services involved much energetic activity, including shaking. This was taken to be a sign that the Holy Spirit was present.

In 1774 the Shakers came to the United States under the leadership of Ann Lee (1736–84). They considered her a prophet and eventually a personification of the female aspect of God. "Mother Lee" taught that people who remained celibate could achieve perfection.

The Shakers formed several communities from Maine to Indiana. Their communities stressed celibacy and the equality of the sexes. The residents of the communities held all property in common.

The Shakers were most numerous in the middle 1800s, when they had around 6,000 members. By the end of the 20th century they were virtually extinct. Though small in number, the Shakers made important contributions to American society. These include their music, crafts, and distinctive, simple but elegant furniture.

shamanism The practice of religious specialists who have been specially trained and initiated to go into trance and contact the spiritual world directly. The shaman is an important fixture of religious life in PRIMAL RELIGION, preliterate tribal cultures, and traditional societies of many parts of the world. The word shaman and classic examples come from Siberia and central Asia. But shamans can also be found throughout the Americas, where they have sometimes been called "medicine men," in China, Korea, and Japan (where they are most often female), and elsewhere. Significant traces of shamanism can be seen in the background of most of the major religions of history.

One becomes a shaman in two ways: through heredity or special vocation. In the latter case, the prospective shaman often displays highly bizarre behavior, as though going mad; this is a sign the gods have singled out this person. The future shaman may go out into the wilderness until he or she sees a VISION or has another sign that a guiding spirit has come who then will help the novice control and use spiritual powers. The prospective adept next may seek training from a senior shaman. In Japan blind girls have sometimes become shamanesses. Shamans often have elaborate dress and accoutrements. They may wear robes and ornate hats, and beat drums to help them go into trance. Their performances may include dance and drama as they go about their two main duties, to speak to the gods and heal the sick.

There are two main kinds of shaman: "possession" shamans and "traveling" shamans. The former stay in one place, so to speak, in their ecstatic trance, but call down gods and spirits to possess them and speak through their lips. Such shamans can receive the spirits of the departed and so let their loved ones hear their voices again. They also communicate the instructions of gods, and do healings with the help of the gods who have entered them.

"Traveling" shamans are believed, in trance, to be able to fly through the air or dive into the Earth to visit the land of the dead, recover lost or stolen souls, or speak to the gods above. Sometimes these scenarios are quite dramatic public performances. The Altaic shaman would climb an upright tree trunk representing the way from Earth through the various heavenly spheres above. On each level the shaman would call down to the audience of his tribespeople, describing the particular paradisal realm he was now entering. Eskimo shamans, in a crowded but darkened room, would enact a vivid ritual, with sound effects, of going into the Earth to seek the central realm of their deities.

Shamans have often been associated with healing. Sickness was frequently believed to be caused by the loss of one's soul. Shamans in North America's Pacific northwest, in the presence of sick persons and the family, would dramatically enact their journey to the other world in search of the lost soul, including the crossing of treacherous rivers and combat with guardian demons. When they had found the strayed spirit, they would bear it back in triumph, singing its song. One can imagine how such a performance would revive and perhaps even heal the patient! Another view of sickness was that it was the result of invasion of the sick person by EVIL spirits. Other shamans would heal the sick by sucking out or driving out the malevolent entity. In any case, the shaman tends to diagnose and then treat the illness in terms compatible with the world view of his culture.

Shamanism also had a profound impact on the early development of human culture. One could say that shamans were the first physicians, psychologists, poets, and prophets. Shamanism also had a deep relationship with the beginnings of art and story, for the shamans created or used these in their costumes and performances to a greater degree than anyone else. They could also serve as magicians and priests, and custodians of tribal lore. To be sure, shamans have sometimes been sleight-of-hand artists, resorting to trickery to achieve their effects. Yet, all in all, they greatly expanded the horizons of human experience and ability.

The rise of science, modern medicine, electronic communication, and global business has not meant the end of shamanism; it has produced new forms of shamanism instead. In a country with a strong shamanistic tradition like Korea, shamanism continues to thrive, but the concerns of the people who seek a shaman's assistance have changed. Formerly people sought healing. Today they are just as likely, or more likely, to seek help and advice in uncertain business dealings.

In North America and Europe, a different approach to shamanism has arisen, sometimes called "neoshamanism." More critical of capitalism and business practices, it provides an alternative sense of meaning in the modern world for people who find traditional JUDAISM and CHRISTIANITY no longer effective.

Starting in the 1960s North Americans and Europeans began to take a great deal of interest in anthropology. In the process they discovered shamanism. An early, influential popularizer of shamanism was Carlos Castaneda (1925–98). The most influential such anthropologist today may be Michael Harner (b. 1929).

Neo-shamanism uses rhythmic techniques such as drumming and dancing to induce special mental states. (Some have suggested that the electronic dance music known as techno that is played at raves has this effect, too.) Practitioners believe that in these states they come into contact with the spirit world or more broadly with the whole world of nature. Their spirit helpers, along with the knowledge of plants and crystals that they have learned in their altered states, give them the ability to heal. Some movements calling themselves shamanic make use of a wide range of healing techniques, such as aromatherapy, rain drop therapy, and Reiki (a healing practice based on touch) as well as shamanic journeying and soul retrieval.

Neoshamanism rejects sharp boundaries between human beings and animals and often seeks to restore wholeness on a cosmic as well as an individual level. In this respect it has a strong ecological character.

Modern medicine attributes whatever healing benefits neoshamanic practices have to psychological factors. Many medical professionals are also suspicious that many claims about healing are unproved and overstated. At the same time, a patient's psychological state does contribute to healing, and shamanic techniques may have some demonstrable positive effects.

Further reading: Mircea Eliade, *Shamanism: Archaic Techniques of Ecstasy* (New York: Bollingen Foundation, 1964); Michael Harner, *The Way of the Shaman: A Guide to Power and Healing* (New York: Bantam Books, 1982); I. M. Lewis, *Ecstatic Religion: A Study of Shamanism and Spirit Possession,* 3d ed. (New York: Routledge, 2003); *Shamanism: A Reader,* Graham Harvey, ed. (New York: Routledge, 2003); Margaret Stutley, *Shamanism: An Introduction* (New York: Routledge, 2003); Piers Vitebsky, *Shamanism* (Norman: University of Oklahoma Press, 2001).

Shariah An Arabic word meaning path; in ISLAM GOD's revealed law for human beings. Islam holds that God, as creator, desires human beings to live in certain ways, and that he has revealed those ways to humans (*see* ALLAH). That revealed law is known as Shariah. It is distinct from *fiqh*, human attempts to formulate God's law.

God has revealed Shariah through two sources, the QUR'AN, God's revelations to the Prophet MUHAMMAD, and the HADITH, reports about what the Prophet said and did that have been carefully scrutinized to ensure their accuracy. According to these sources there are some actions that God requires human beings to perform and some that God absolutely forbids. Other actions fall somewhere in between, as being either preferable to do, preferable to avoid, or neutral.

Although the Qur'an and Hadith contain Shariah, human beings must interpret them. In SHI'ITE ISLAM the proper interpretation is associated especially with the descendants of the Prophet, the Shi'ite IMAMS, and in practice today with religious authorities known as AYATOLLAHS. In SUNNI ISLAM interpretation is the job of legal scholars or jurists. These jurists endeavor to determine precisely what the texts mean. They also reason from analogy, in part because situations arise today that could not have been anticipated in Arabia at the time of God's final revelation. An individual jurist may issue a fatwa, a statement of what the law requires. Such a legal opinion is instructive, but it is not binding. More binding is the unanimous consensus of jurists. A verse in the Qur'an says that the community of the faithful will never agree on error.

Ideally, Shariah constitutes the law of a Muslim state. In practice, most Muslim states have used Shariah in some areas, such as personal law, and made their own laws in other areas, such as criminal law. In recent decades Muslim feminists have argued that many traditional rules that disadvantaged women are not Shariah but improper interpretations on the part of past legal scholars (*see* FEMINISM). Fundamentalist Muslims take a different position. They condemn the secularism that they see around them as an abandonment of God's revelation and advocate the application of Shariah in most or all spheres of life (*see* FUNDAMENTALISM, ISLAMIC).

Shi'ite Islam A variety of ISLAM practiced by about 15 percent of all Muslims. The name "Shi'ite"

derives from the Arabic phrase, *Shi'at 'Ali*, "the party of Ali." It refers to those who support the claim that Ali, a cousin and son-in-law of the prophet MUHAMMAD, and his descendants are the rightful rulers of the Islamic community. A large majority of Muslims reject Shi'ite claims and practice SUNNI ISLAM. Sunni and Shi'ite Islam differ somewhat with regard to beliefs and practices, but the major difference concerns who is the rightful ruler of the Islamic community. The dispute goes back to the time of the prophet's death.

HISTORY

During his lifetime, the prophet Muhammad led the community of Islam both religiously and politically. He was the ultimate religious authority. He also supervised the life of the community and led its armies against its enemies.

When the prophet died, the question of who should succeed him remained unsettled. According to Sunni Islam, Muhammad died without appointing a successor. The community entrusted its political affairs to a political leader, and it allowed scholars to decide religious issues. By contrast, Shi'ite Islam maintains that a single person was to exercise both religious and political leadership, as the prophet had done. Indeed, Shi'ites claim that before the prophet died, he appointed such a leader, his cousin Ali.

Ali's connections to the prophet were particularly close. He was the son of Abu Talib, who had raised Muhammad and protected him from his enemies within the Quraysh tribe. He was also the prophet's son-in-law, the husband of Muhammad's daughter Fatima. He was the father of the prophet's only grandsons, Hasan and Husayn. And he was the first male who accepted God's revelations to Muhammad.

When the prophet died, Ali did not succeed him. The community selected three successive leaders known as caliphs: Abu Bakr (caliph, 632–634), Umar (caliph, 634–644), and Uthman (caliph, 644–656). These caliphs were social, political, and military leaders, but not religious ones. Shi'ites do not acknowledge them as legitimate. Ali did rule as fourth caliph from 656 to 661, but there was much unrest at the time. His grasp on the government was never firm.

Upon Ali's death, his son Hasan abdicated in favor of the powerful, ambitious, and militarily successful Muawiyah (caliph, 661–680). He lived the rest of his life in retirement and died in 669. At that point Hasan's brother Husayn became the rightful IMAM, the name Shi'ites give the leader of the community. Muawiyah died in 680, and Husayn saw an opportunity to assert his claims. But while he was traveling to gather supporters, he and his family were intercepted at a place in southern Iraq called Karbala. Negotiations failed, and a massacre followed. Husayn's head was sent to the new caliph, Yazid, in Damascus. Only one of his sons survived. Throughout the world Shi'ites remember this event every year with mourning in an observance known as Ashura.

During the next several generations the Shi'ite community split over who was the rightful imam. Three major groups emerged. They are commonly called "fivers," "seveners," and "twelvers."

Fivers favor the claims of a grandson of Husayn named Zayd to have been the fifth imam. He and his followers insisted that it was their duty to overthrow illegitimate rulers with force. They had limited success. In the late ninth century they established a state in Yemen, where fivers continued in power until 1963.

Seveners and twelvers differ over the question of who was the seventh imam. Seveners say it was Ismail, the older son of the sixth imam. His father had appointed him imam, but he died before his father did: Seveners insist that Ismail's appointment stands anyway, and they followed Ismail's son. In the 10th century a sevener established the Fatimid dynasty, and seveners ruled Egypt for roughly 200 years. From the Fatimids came the Nizari Ismailis, a group known in the Middle Ages as the ASSAS-SINS, and a small community with its own religion known as the DRUZE. Today the Nizari Ismailis are a peaceful and peace-loving community. They recognize the AGA KHAN as their imam.

The twelvers are the largest Shi'ite group. They recognize the 12th imam as the last. In 873 C.E., they say, the 12th imam went into hiding.

Eventually he will emerge from hiding and restore true Islam. In the meantime he inspires religious scholars, known as *mujtahidin* or AYATOLLAHS, who lead the community. In the 16th century a twelver Shi'ite dynasty, the Safavids, took control of Iran. The Shi'ite community was instrumental in bringing about the Iranian revolution of 1979.

BELIEFS, PRACTICES, AND ORGANIZATION

Like all Muslims, Shi'ites practice the five pillars of the FAITH. They accept the QUR'AN as authentic. They also recognize the authority of the prophet's words and deeds as recorded in the (Shi'ite) HADITH.

The major difference between Sunni and Shi'ite Islam is over who should govern the community and how. As already noted, the Shi'ites say a single person known as the imam should rule both politically and religiously. For them, the imam is God's own witness on Earth. He possesses perfect religious knowledge.

As a result, Shi'ites also differ from Sunnis on how the Muslim community learns what is right. According to Sunnis, the Qur'an and the Hadith of the prophet teach what is right. The consensus of religious scholars determines what they mean. When one confronts situations not found in the Qur'an and the Hadith, as happens today, religious scholars determine what is right by reasoning from analogy.

Shi'ites reject both the consensus of scholars and reasoning from analogy. They add to the Hadith of the prophet the pronouncements of imams. To determine what is required today, some communities, such as the Nizari Ismailis, consult their imam; others, such as the twelvers, consult a recognized religious scholar, who reasons independently. This reasoning results in the issuing of a legal pronouncement known as a *fatwa*. One of the most notorious fatwas of the 20th century was pronounced by the leader of Iran, the Ayatollah Ruhollah Khomeini. He called upon Muslims to kill a novelist, Salman Rushdie, because, Khomeini claimed, Rushdie had blasphemed God and the Qur'an in one of his books. One should emphasize that this particular fatwa is extreme, unusual, and controversial, even in Shi'ite communities.

Shi'ites have often lived as a persecuted minority. They have seen "dissimulation" as an appropriate response. That is, they may outwardly act like their neighbors and practice Shi'ite Islam in secret. The most distinctive Shi'ite observance is Ashura. It commemorates the assassination of Husayn on the 10th of Muharram, often through the performance of "passion plays."

SIGNIFICANCE

At the beginning of the 21st century, Shi'ite Islam was familiar to North Americans as the official religion of Iran and the majority religion of Iraq. It was often associated with reports of violence in the news media. But in all ages, including the present, the vast majority of Shi'ites have practiced their religion in peace, sometimes despite severe persecution. They have also made major contributions to global culture. Examples include the famous al-Azhar University in Cairo, Egypt, founded by the Fatimids in 970 C.E., and the glorious architectural monuments of Isfahan, Persia (now Iran).

Further reading: Michael M. J. Fischer, *Iran: From Religious Dispute to Revolution* (Madison: University of Wisconsin Press, 2003); Heinz Halm, *Shi'ism*, 2d ed. (New York: Columbia University Press, 2004); Etan Kohlberg, ed., *Shi'ism* (Burlington, Vt.: Ashgate, 2003).

Shinran   *See* PURE LAND BUDDHISM.

Shinto   Japanese religion of the indigenous gods of the country. The word Shinto means "the way of the gods." This is to distinguish it from the way of the BUDDHA, or BUDDHISM, the other great religious tradition of Japan (*see* JAPANESE RELIGION). Shinto is the WORSHIP of the KAMI, or ancient Japanese gods. Many of those worshipped now were there long before Buddhism arrived in Japan in the sixth century C.E. and are still honored in the Shinto shrines of Japan today.

HISTORY

In the Middle Ages kami and buddhas were often worshipped together. The kami were considered guardians of the buddhas, or sometimes special Japanese forms of the same spiritual power seen in Buddhism as a Buddha. But in modern times Shinto shrines and Buddhist temples have been kept separate. This is largely because the nationalistic governments that ruled Japan from 1868 up until the end of World War II in 1945 wanted to make Shinto a separate patriotic cult, untouched by anything of foreign origin like Buddhism (*see* NATIONALISM, RELIGIOUS). The extreme nationalists emphasized that the emperor of Japan was himself a kami and descended from Amaterasu, kami or goddess of the sun. He was therefore worthy of all honor and sacrifice (*see* KINGSHIP AND RELIGION).

However, Shinto as a religion is much more than an example of religious nationalism. The kami of most shrines are peaceful deities, protectors of families and local communities, honored in festivals that have their roots in the agricultural year. They were there long before the extreme nationalists, and have outlasted them. Though the emperor of Japan is still installed with very ancient Shinto rites, his religious and political role is now almost always seen as purely symbolic.

BELIEFS AND PRACTICES

The visitor to present-day Japan will see evidence of Shinto on every hand. In most places one is not too far from a Shinto shrine or *jinja* large or small. Large city shrines are on parklike grounds, with grass and one or two old trees. In the countryside, shrines are often in places of striking natural beauty: on a mountainside, by a waterfall, beside the ocean or a lake or a rushing stream. Wherever situated, the entry to a Shinto shrine is marked by the distinctive gateway called a *torii*, which has become a symbol of Shinto as recognizable as the Christian cross or the Jewish Star of DAVID. Passing under the torii, the visitor will approach the shrine itself, a small wooden building. In the front will be a sort of porch, perhaps containing such characteristic Shinto symbols as a drum beaten during sacred dance, *gohei* or zigzag strips of paper fastened to an upright pole, and in the center a mirror indicating the presence of divinity. In a section behind the porch an eight-legged offering table may be seen. Behind it, steep steps lead up to massive closed doors. These doors, usually closed, open into the *honden* or inner sanctuary of the shrine, where a special token of the kami presence is kept.

Persons passing a shrine often pause to pray. They will come to the front of the shrine, clap their hands twice or pull a bell-rope, bow, and whisper a PRAYER. Priests present offerings at shrines periodically. The great occasions of a shrine, however, are its annual *matsuri* or festivals. Then the shrine really comes to life. Festivals are planned and prepared for weeks, and usually draw large crowds. They have a happy, holiday atmosphere, but begin with solemn worship and prayer.

First the priests enter the shrine in their white or pastel robes and black *eboshi* or high rounded hats. The chief priest next purifies the shrine and the assembled crowd through a gesture like waving an evergreen branch. Then the offerings are slowly and carefully advanced and placed on the offering table. Offerings are usually beautifully arranged dishes of rice, seafood, fruit, vegetables, salt, water, and sake or rice wine. When they are all in order, the chief priest stands behind the table and chants a *norito* or prayer. Then the offerings are slowly removed.

After that, the *matsuri* changes to its festive mood, kept a little differently in each shrine according to local tradition. A carnival may open on the shrine grounds. Maidens may perform sacred dance. The kami may be carried vigorously through the streets in a palanquin called a *mikoshi*, borne on the shoulders of young men. Many shrine traditions are famous and draw spectators to the pageantry of their *matsuri* from afar. Celebrated attractions include grand parades, bonfires, horse or boat races, dances, and much else, all usually in colorful traditional costumes.

SIGNIFICANCE

For many Japanese, Shinto is important because it provides links to the rich traditions of their nation's past. Spiritually, it emphasizes the importance of purity, for the kami and their shrines are thought to be very pure places, and one can purify one's own mind and heart by closeness to them. As a polytheistic religion, one affirming many gods and goddesses, Shinto suggests that the divine can be found in many different local forms, and by this means is close to the lives of communities and people.

Further reading: Thomas P. Kasulis, *Shinto: The Way Home* (Honolulu: University of Hawaii Press, 2004); C. Scott Littleton, *Shinto: Origins, Rituals, Festivals, Spirits, Sacred Places* (New York: Oxford University Press, 2002); John K. Nelson, *A Year in the Life of a Shinto Shrine* (Seattle: University of Washington Press, 1996); Inoue Nobutaka, ed., *Shinto, A Short History* (New York: RoutledgeCurzon, 2003).

Shinto festivals Celebrations held at SHINTO shrines in Japan. The Japanese celebrate a great number of festivals, many of them connected with Shinto, the indigenous Japanese religion. Some are celebrated nationwide; others are festivals specially celebrated at a particular shrine.

As the ancient religion of Japan, Shinto has many connections with farming. Two very common Shinto festivals are the festival to pray for a good harvest, held in the spring, and the harvest festival, held in the fall. Shinto is also connected with growth on the human level, and some festivals celebrate the growth of children into adults. They include a festival on November 15, at which parents present at a shrine sons aged three and five and daughters aged three and seven; a festival for girls on March 3, a festival for boys on May 5, and a festival at which people who turned 20 years old in the preceding year visit a shrine on January 20.

Shinto festivals are both solemn rituals and joyous, even ribald affairs. At the shrine itself priests purify the sacred area; worshippers then bow, present offerings to the KAMI, pray, and entertain the *kami* with music and dance. Offerings include water, salt, sake (rice wine), vegetables, and seafood products, but nothing that has blood, such as meat. Worshippers commune with the *kami* by drinking sake that has been presented at the shrine.

Festivals also resemble great fairs. It is very common to celebrate festivals with a procession in which several worshippers carry portable shrines for the *kami* in parades through the streets. Other common events at festivals include plays, sumo wrestling, and feasting. Some festivals have events that are peculiar to them. Examples include kite battles at the Hamamatsu Kite-Flying Festival (May 3–5), dances performed by unmarried women holding lilies for the Lily Festival at the Isakawa Shrine (June 17), and various forms of horse races at the Soma Wild Horse Chase Festival (July 23–25).

Sikhism A religion from northwest India that traces itself back to 10 CURUS, beginning with Guru NANAK (1469–1539). Today the Sikhs venerate above all a book of writings known as the ADI GRANTH or Guru Granth Sahib.

HISTORY

Guru Nanak lived in the Punjab, "the region of the five rivers" in northwest India. At the age of 30 he had an extraordinary religious experience. Afterward, he began to preach a distinct religious path

From the *Illustrations to* One Hundred Poems by One Hundred Poets: Emperor Sanjo (r. 1012–1016). A ritual for the full autumn moon; a priest holds a *gohei*, a paper or cloth offering used in Shinto rituals, and an acolyte offers a cup of sake. Courtiers kneel in prayer. *(Erich Lessing/Art Resource, N.Y.)*

This miniature portrait made on ivory shows Guru Nanak, founder of the Sikh religion *(Victoria & Albert Museum, London/Art Resource, N.Y.)*

that went beyond the differences between Hindus and Muslims. Nanak was followed in succession by nine other gurus or teachers. The fifth guru, Arjun, began building the most sacred shrine of the Sikhs, the Golden Temple at Amritsar in northwest India. He also collected writings from his predecessors into a book known as the Adi Granth.

From 1526 northern India was ruled by the Mughal dynasty. The Mughals were Muslims. At first relations between the Sikhs and the Mughals were good. But in 1605 Jahangir came to the throne. He tortured and executed Guru Arjun, because he thought Arjun had adulterated Islamic teachings. In response, the Sikhs saw themselves as called to be soldiers as well as saints. In the face of continuing persecution, the last guru, Guru GOBIND SINGH (1666–1708), established a Sikh community known as the *khalsa*. He also ended the line of human gurus and transferred his authority to the Adi Granth.

In the 19th century the Sikhs decided British rulers were preferable to Muslim ones. Many Sikhs became soldiers in the British army. Others became prosperous in business and agriculture. With the establishment of India and Pakistan in 1947 and 1948, some Sikhs began to agitate for the establishment of a separate Sikh state to be called Khalistan. In the 20th century a modest Sikh community also began to grow in North America and Europe, especially in the southwestern United States. In the aftermath of the September 11, 2001, attacks Sikhs in the United States experienced discriminatory treatment and violence because some people wrongly associated their distinctive appearance with Osama bin Laden and AL-QAEDA.

BELIEFS

Every morning Sikhs pray a PRAYER known as the *Japji*. It summarizes Sikh teachings about GOD: He is one and true; he is the creator; he is present in all the universe but is not subject to the laws of rebirth. Sikhs believe that God cannot be found in images. Instead, they find God in his name, in the 10 gurus, and in the Guru Granth. Sikhs believe that by following God's path people can become pure and, over a succession of rebirths, eventually unite with the eternal.

PRACTICES

Sikhs WORSHIP together in a building known as a *gurdwara*. There the Guru Granth rests upon an elevated platform, where it is decorated with flowers and fanned. During worship Sikhs listen to and participate in singing from the Guru Granth. They also present gifts to the Guru Granth and receive a sweet in return. Sikh holidays include the birthdays of Guru Nanak and Guru Gobind Singh and the anniversary of Guru Arjun's martyrdom.

ORGANIZATION

Most Sikhs are members of the *khalsa*. They observe what are known as the "five k's" (in the Punjabi language each stipulation refers to a word beginning with "k"): They do not cut their hair, including beards in the case of men; they carry combs; they wear special steel bracelets; they carry swords; and they wear a special kind of pants. Male Sikhs generally wear turbans over their hair.

Sikhism has no formally ordained priests, although certain sects recognize living gurus. A committee known as the SGPC oversees Sikh shrines in India, where the vast majority of Sikhs still live. Its members are elected.

SIGNIFICANCE

Once considered a sect of HINDUISM, Sikhism has come to be recognized as a religion in its own right. At the beginning of the 21st century, it claimed roughly 20 million adherents.

Further reading: Gurinder Singh Mann, *Sikhism* (Upper Saddle River, N.J.: Prentice Hall, 2004); W. H. McLeod, *Sikhs and Sikhism* (New York: Oxford University Press, 2004); Patwant Singh, *The Sikhs* (London: John Murray, 1999).

sin A violation of GOD's instructions. Although the idea of sin is important in JUDAISM, it is especially so in CHRISTIANITY.

The goal of Judaism is to sanctify life, that is, to make life holy by following God's instructions. Judaism recognizes that people are tempted to act in ways that violate God's instructions. In other words, they are tempted to sin. Indeed, at some time or other every person sins. Even MOSES, who received the TORAH from God personally, was not without sin.

The RABBIS, or those who made Jewish law, have classified sins. Some sins are sins of commission: People do something that violates God's instructions. Some sins are sins of omission: People fail to do something that God has instructed. People do some sins intentionally. But people can also sin without intending to do so or even being aware that they have sinned. In any case, Jews believe that, like a compassionate parent, God forgives persons who sincerely repent. On the DAY OF ATONEMENT Jews fast, pray, and collectively ask God's forgiveness for their sins. Jews do not, however, see SALVATION from sin as the most important goal of Judaism.

For traditional Christians, sin has created a condition from which all people need to be saved.

As a result, God sent his son JESUS to die on the CROSS. Some Christians view this act as a "substitutionary atonement." In dying on the cross, Jesus paid the penalty that human beings owed to God because of their sin.

Like Jews, Christians distinguish sins of omission and commission and intentional and unintentional sins. Protestant and especially Roman Catholic thinkers have classified sin in other ways.

In the fourth century C.E. a British monk named Pelagius taught that children were sinless. They resembled ADAM before the FALL. In response, AUGUSTINE OF HIPPO developed the idea of original sin. It says that human beings are from the start born into a condition that is corrupted by sin. As a result, it is inevitable that all human beings will sin in thought, word, and deed. These sinful acts are called actual sins, to distinguish them from inherited original sin.

Roman Catholic thinkers also classified sins as more and less severe: mortal and venial sins, respectively. According to Thomas AQUINAS, a mortal sin turns a person away from God. Therefore, mortal sins must be forgiven in the SACRAMENT of penance. A venial sin only disturbs a person's relationship with God. Tradition speaks of seven deadly sins: pride, envy, anger, sloth, avarice, gluttony, and lust. Protestant thinkers reject the distinction between mortal and venial sins. For them, all sins equally disrupt one's relationship with God. Only God's GRACE can restore this relationship.

Most religions recognize that human beings are less than perfect, but they do not think of this imperfection as sin. The classical scholar E. R. Dodds once distinguished two types of culture, "shame-cultures" and "guilt-cultures". According to Dodds, some cultures, like the early Greeks, emphasize public shame at failure. Others emphasize guilt that results from improper actions. In Judaism and Christianity, guilt may be seen as a psychological counterpart to sin.

Just as important, not all religions have conceived of ethical injunctions as instructions from God. In HINDUISM, BUDDHISM, and JAINISM, bad actions do not offend a creator who has

Statue of the Hindu god Siva *(Getty Images)*

commanded human beings how to act. The criteria of good and bad are simply given, and the consequences of action (KARMA) usually result from the operation of natural processes.

Siva Also spelled Shiva. One of the most important gods of HINDUISM. In Hinduism, BRAHMA, VISHNU, and Siva are thought of as the gods of creation, preservation, and destruction, respectively. Siva, the god of destruction, is commonly known by several other names. These identify his important characteristics: Mahadeva, "the great god"; Nilakantha, "the blue-throated god"; Pasupati, "the lord of animals"; Bhairava, "the terrifying god"; and Trimukha, "the three-faced god." Worshippers of Siva are known as Saivas or Saivites.

In Sanskrit, the name Siva means "auspicious." It gracefully links this god to a fierce god of the VEDA, Rudra, "the howler." Some have found evidence of Siva WORSHIP in seals from the Indus Valley Civilization (*see* INDUS VALLEY RELIGION). South India, too, may be a significant source of Siva worship. The Tamil name Sivan, "the red one," closely resembles the Sanskrit name Siva.

Siva is especially associated with religious austerities and YOGA. His mythology moves back and forth between extremes of severe renunciation and sexual excess. He is easily recognized by his matted hair, his trident, his animal-skin cloak, the third eye in the middle of his forehead, and his blue throat. Siva's throat turned blue when he drank poison that was spreading on the surface of the primal ocean. Siva is also associated with ash. His followers smear ash on their foreheads and sometimes their bodies in imitation of the god.

Siva's special abode is Mount Kailasa in the Himalaya range. His consort is PARVATI. Siva beheaded her father Daksa when he failed to invite Siva to a sacrifice. Siva has two sons, Skanda, who was early identified with the south Indian god Murugan, and the elephant-headed god GANESA, the remover of obstacles. Siva's vehicle, the massive bull Nandi, often stands in front of his temples. The *rudraksha,* a large, coarse, beadlike seed, is also sacred to Siva. From it Saivas construct *malas* or rosaries to use when reciting the god's names or MANTRAS.

Several kinds of Siva image are famous worldwide. One depicts Siva as Nataraja, "king of the dance." In it Siva dances on top of a demon and within a circle of flames. With two hands he creates and destroys the universe. With two other hands he calms the viewer's fears and points to the means of release. Another well-known image is Siva Ardhanari, half man and half woman. The image emphasizes the intimate connection between the male god and his female sakti or power. The most famous Siva image of all is the image enshrined in temples. It is an upright cylindrical shaft known as a lingam. The lingam rests in a yoni or basin, which catches libations. Originally the lingam and yoni depicted the human sexual organs in stylized form. Polished egg-shaped stones, such as stones from the Narmada River, are particularly popular as lingams.

There are several different subgroups of Śaivas. The Pasupatas, now extinct, took their name from the cattle that they associated with the god. Saiva-Siddhanta is especially popular in the far south of India. It insists that the theology of Siva is the ultimate truth (*siddhanta*). Another southern movement, Vira-Saivism (heroic Saivism), emphasizes social reform. It is also called Lingayat (lingam-wearing), because its adherents wear lingams on necklaces. Kashmir in the far north was also home to several distinct subgroups of Saivism.

The most important Saiva text may be the *Svetasvatara* UPANISHAD. It identifies Siva with all reality. Saivas also have distinctive collections of mythology and RITUAL (PURANAS and Agamas). According to tradition the great Indian thinker SANKARA was a Saiva. So were the great Kashmiri philosophers Abhinavagupta and Srikantha, who formulated a special form of VEDANTA philosophy.

The major Saiva festival is Sivaratri (*see* HINDU FESTIVALS). During this festival worshippers bathe the decorated lingam.

Soka Gakkai

Considered the largest of the "new religions" of Japan, claiming some 16 million members, Soka Gakkai ("Value-creation Society") began as a lay organization of the NICHIREN Shoshu denomination of BUDDHISM. It was founded by Makiguchi Tsunesaburo in 1937 as an educational society emphasizing the importance of human benefit as well as abstract truth in education. But Makiguchi was also a devout Nichiren Buddhist, and saw the relation between his educational philosophy and Nichiren's emphasis on benefits from religious practice here and now. He died in prison during the war because of his refusal to participate in SHINTO worship. But the movement was revived in postwar Japan by Toda Josei, who reorganized it on religious lines. Practice consists chiefly of chant-ing the formula *Nam Myoho Renge Kyo* ("Hail the marvelous teaching of the LOTUS SUTRA"), called the Daimoku, and recitation of the Lotus Sutra. Toda also emphasized benefits, like healing and prosperity, from chanting here and now. He encouraged aggressive recruiting practices, and also popular cultural activities. Soka Gakkai was criticized for its aggressive tactics, but grew very rapidly during the 1950s.

After Toda's death in 1958, Soka Gakkai mellowed a bit, but remains both powerful and controversial. A related political party was founded, and in the 1970s the movement built a vast new temple at the foot of Mount Fuji. Beginning in the 1960s, the movement also spread successfully to the United States and other countries outside Japan. In the 1990s a bitter dispute between the lay leadership of Soka Gakkai and the priests of the religious organization led to a split between Soka Gakkai and Nichiren Shoshu. Soka Gakkai is now a vigorous, independent international organization. It promotes a colorful, streamlined, well-organized form of Buddhism, which its followers say is the Buddhism of the future.

Solomon

Solomon (10th century B.C.E.) *a son of DAVID and king of Israel and Judah; revered in CHRISTIANITY and ISLAM as well as JUDAISM* The BIBLE tells of Solomon's reign in 1 Kings 1–11 and 2 Chronicles 1–9.

Solomon was the son of David and his wife Bathsheba, whose first husband David had killed. After winning the struggles to succeed his father, Solomon ruled over an extensive empire in relative peace.

He is remembered for his building program. The most important of his buildings was the Temple in JERUSALEM. This was the first Temple to be built on the site. Its plan, which the Bible describes in detail, followed Phoenician models.

Solomon is also famous for his wisdom. One famous story tells how he decided which of two competing women was really a baby's mother. He ordered the baby to be cut in half. One woman pleaded with the king to let the baby live and give it to the other woman. The other woman agreed that the baby should be cut in two. Solomon realized that the first woman must be the baby's mother.

Recognizing Solomon's wisdom, Jews and Christians have traditionally attributed to him three books in the Bible: Proverbs, Ecclesiastes, and the Song of Songs, sometimes called the Song of Solomon. (*See* WISDOM LITERATURE.)

At the end of his reign, Solomon's empire split into two parts, Israel in the north and Judah in the south, with much of the discontent coming from forced labor on Solomon's building projects.

soul, concepts of Ideas about the spiritual essence of a person. In most religious traditions, there exists some concept of a soul or spirit in human beings, which is distinct from the physical body and has religious importance. The soul is invisible to ordinary eyes, though words for it in several languages associate it with the breath. Being nonphysical, the soul is commonly believed to survive the death of the body (*see* AFTERLIFE IN WORLD RELIGIONS). It then may receive the reward or punishment earned in its earthly life, whether in a spiritual HEAVEN or HELL, in a new REINCARNATION, or in a resurrected body. Some traditions have also believed in the preexistence of the soul in a heavenly realm or in previous INCARNATIONS before its coming into the present life.

Beliefs about the exact nature of the soul differ. In HINDUISM it is in essence divine as the atman or divine within. BUDDHISM rejects the idea of a separate, eternal soul, though it believes in reincarnation. The Western monotheistic religions, JUDAISM, CHRISTIANITY, and ISLAM, generally believe that each soul is a new creation of GOD, rather than itself divine, infused into each person at conception or soon after. Some PRIMAL RELIGIONS believe in multiple souls, perhaps reflecting a person's different moods, and perhaps with different after-death destinies: reincarnation within the family or tribe, hovering around the grave, going to the heavenly world. Nonreligious persons, on the other hand, reject the idea of a soul, believing that all the mys-

teries of consciousness can be explained through the brain and its psychology.

spirit possession An altered state of consciousness, usually producing unusual behavior, interpreted within its religious culture to be the result of a spirit entering the subject and taking control over his or her mind and body. It can be either benign or malevolent, depending on whether the possession is by good or demonic spirits. In the former case, possession can be deliberately induced by chanting, drum-beating, ecstatic trance, or RITUAL as a part of religious activities. Examples can be found in PRIMAL RELIGION, SHAMANISM, Haitian VOODOO, Afro-Brazilian religions like Macombo, Spiritualism, and elsewhere. In Voodoo, for example, in the context of religious services persons may dress in the part of a god, dance or otherwise go into trance, and, undergoing impressive personality changes, "become" that deity for a time. During this time the possessed one is treated like the deity, made much of and even prayed to by the congregation. Divine possession can also happen spontaneously, as a religious experience.

Cases of malevolent spirit possession call for a different religious response, that of the exorcist or specialist in driving out EVIL and demonic spirits. Traditional and even contemporary accounts of demonic possession make hair-raising reading as they describe the horrible grimaces and bizarre behavior of the afflicted one. The process of EXORCISM is said to be a difficult and grueling one, for the demon struggles and will not go out easily. In TAOISM priests use ritual swords, in ROMAN CATHOLICISM holy water is employed in this spiritual warfare, but in the end it is a battle of wills and the relative power of good and evil.

Spiritualism A religious movement based on communication with the spirits of the departed through persons called mediums. Typically the medium goes into trance and speaks words believed to be from the spirit, although other means, such as the Ouija board or rappings, may be used. The spirits are often of deceased loved ones but may also be of great teaching figures on "the other side."

Modern Spiritualism began in 1848, when the two young Fox sisters, Margaretta (aged 11) and Kate (8) in upstate New York reported hearing mysterious rappings in their house, which they ascertained to be a departed spirit attempting to communicate in something like the newly invented Morse Code. News of this event spread rapidly, and before long such communications by rappings, and soon enough by voice mediumship, spread across the country. In the 1850s Spiritualism became a vogue. "Home circles" gathered around mediums, Spiritualist lecturers drew large crowds, and controversy concerning the authenticity of the phenomenon filled the pages of the press.

Despite its newness, Spiritualism also claimed, with some reason, to be "the oldest religion in the world," going back to ancient SHAMANISM. Yet it had a special appeal for a new age that considered itself scientific and democratic. Spiritualists declared that now for the first time religious tenets concerning the spiritual world and the afterlife could be tested scientifically, by experiments and firsthand experience, and did not have to rely merely on FAITH. The new religion also saw itself as democratic, since anyone with the talent for it could become a medium; the role did not depend on education or church appointment. Many women, who certainly could not hope to exercise comparable spiritual leadership in a mainline church in the 19th century, became prominent Spiritualist mediums and speakers. Early Spiritualists also tended to support the progressive social and political causes of the time, such as the abolition of slavery, the rights of women, new methods of education, and prison reform.

Spiritualism quickly developed a general doctrine of the afterlife, largely based on teachings like those of the Swedish mystic philosopher Emanuel Swedenborg (1688–1772) and the Viennese developer of hypnotic trance Anton Mesmer (1734–1815). It saw life after death as educative more than punitive. After death the spirit enters the "Summerland" and from there advances to higher and higher planes, guided by lofty teaching spirits.

Spiritualism declined somewhat in the 1860s, hurt by fraudulent mediums and national preoccupation with the Civil War, but revived afterward, as it often has following wars as bereaved survivors seek to contact loved ones lost in battle. Spiritualism also spread around the world from the United States, taking root in England, France, Australia, New Zealand, and Latin America especially. The first Spiritualist churches and denominations, in contrast to home circles and study groups, appeared around the 1890s. Spiritualist "camps" and then communities, like Lily Dale in New York state and Cassadaga in Florida, appeared and survive today. During the 1920s Spiritualism had another revival, sparked in part by the convert and tireless lecturer on its behalf Arthur Conan Doyle (1859–1930), the creator of Sherlock Holmes.

In the second half of the 20th century traditional Spiritualism seemed in decline. But its place has largely been taken by the NEW AGE MOVEMENT, which has shown many similar attitudes and ideas. What the New Age calls channeling seems similar to mediumship, although it is usually more concerned with communications from ancient teachers of high wisdom than messages from loved ones. The view of the afterlife presented by near-death experiences, a characteristic New Age interest, as well as by various teachers associated with the movement, is not very different from that of Spiritualism.

Many large and important new religious movements around the world, especially in Latin America, Africa, and East Asia, give important place to shamanistic or mediumistic communication with spirits and have clearly been influenced by 19th century Spiritualism as well as by local cultures. They respond to what is clearly a universal need.

Further reading: Ann Braude, *Radical Spirits: Spiritualism and Women's Rights in Nineteenth-Century America* (Bloomington: Indiana University Press, 2001); Arthur Conan Doyle, *The Wanderings of a Spiritualist*, Rpt. (Oakland, Calif.: Ronin,

1998); R. Laurence Moore, *In Search of White Crows: Spiritualism, Parapsychology, and American Culture* (New York: Oxford University Press, 1977); Christine Wicker, *Lily Dale: The True Story of the Town That Talks to the Dead* (San Francisco: HarperSanFrancisco, 2003).

stupa A Buddhist shrine that contains a relic of the BUDDHA. Stupas are also known as *dagobas* (southeast Asia), pagodas (east Asia), and *chortens* (Tibet).

When the Buddha died or, as Buddhists say, entered the parinirvana, his body was cremated. Eight kings received his remains and enshrined them in mounds known as stupas. In the third century B.C.E. the Indian emperor ASOKA is said to have dug up the remains and built 84,000 stupas. Many other stupas were built later.

Stupas take different shapes. In India and Sri Lanka stupas are often large hemispheric mounds surrounded by a fence. A good example is the ancient stupa at Sanchi, India. The stupa at Borobudur, Indonesia, is a massive, terraced mound, each terrace smaller than the one below it. Its carved decorations depicting the life of the Buddha are world-famous. In east Asia stupas are towers of as many as 13 layers.

The Great Stupa from the south, located in Sanchi, Madhya Pradesh, India *(Borromeo/Art Resource, NY)*

The stupa is not generally a place for congregational WORSHIP. Instead, worshippers may circumambulate the stupa, leave offerings, reflect on Buddhist truths, and meditate there.

Sufism MYSTICISM in ISLAM. The word Sufism seems to derive from the Arabic word *suf*, which means "wool."

The prophet MUHAMMAD died in C.E. 632. By the year 700 the Islamic world stretched from Spain in the west all the way to Persia, where Iran is today, in the east. Many Muslims, including the rulers known as caliphs, enjoyed wealth well beyond anything available to Muhammad and his companions. But this wealth offended some, who thought it led to dissolute living. They adopted an austere life-style that they considered more fitting to servants of God. Among other practices, they wore clothes of wool (*suf*) and perhaps for that reason were called Sufis.

Sufis turned very early to the cultivation of mysticism. They were led in this direction by several persons who had intense, personal experiences of GOD's reality and presence. These early Sufis often did and said things that offended traditional Muslims. For example, al-Bistami (d. 874) was fond of the phrase, "Glory be to me!" He wanted to emphasize that God dwelled at the very core of a human being. Two hundred years later thinkers such as al-Ghazali (1058–1111) formulated Sufism in a way that the orthodox could accept.

Early Sufism was not tightly organized. In general, masters passed down secret teachings to their disciples. But by the 13th century Sufis had organized themselves into brotherhoods. At the head of each brotherhood stood a leader known as a *shaykh* or *pir,* whose office was inherited. Some shaykhs were thought to work miracles. At the same time the brotherhoods began to attract "lay" followers—people who were interested in Sufism but did not devote their lives to it.

Sufism cultivates the experience of a profound closeness between God and the soul. Some Sufis talk about a union of God and the soul. Others say that personal identity dissolves in God altogether.

Rabia (d. 801), one of the greatest of the early Sufis, was so filled with love for God that she lost all concern for whether she went to paradise or hell. Jalal al-Din RUMI (1207–73) celebrated the joy of union with God and the anguish of separation from him in renowned Persian poetry. Other Sufis have likened the soul to a moth that is drawn to the flame of a candle, that is, to God—with inevitable consequences.

One common Sufi practice is *dhikr.* This is the continual chanting of a verse containing one of the names of God (*see* ALLAH). The chanting aims to produce an intense awareness of God's presence. A more controversial practice is the use of music. Overwhelmed by the music, some may break into dance. The Mevlevis, the order founded by Rumi, practice a kind of dance that has won them the name Whirling Dervishes. The disciples stand in a circle around the master. Each twirls around, and as he does so the entire circle of disciples revolves around the master. (Think of the planets rotating as they revolve around the sun.) On a more popular level, laypeople may make PILGRIMAGE to the tombs of powerful SAINTS. Many believe that the saints work MIRACLES after death as they did in life.

In the 20th century, Sufism was an embattled institution. Muslims who wanted to "modernize" Islam considered Sufism to be outmoded superstition. Others saw "modernization" as abandoning Islam for foreign practices and wanted to reassert Islamic tradition. In their eyes, Sufi assertions of a union between God and human beings violated the fundamental principles of Islam. Nevertheless, some Muslims continue to find inspiration and spiritual depth in Sufi teachings.

suicide and religion Because most religions have much to do with death and morality, it is not surprising that they also have much to say about suicide. Several dramatic instances of religiously motivated suicide in the second half of the 20th and the beginning of the 21st century have especially brought the topic to the attention of North Americans.

Some ancient Greeks and Romans considered suicide an honorable and appropriate way to die, if done properly and under the appropriate circumstances. Exemplary figures who committed suicide include Socrates (c. 470–399 B.C.E.), Lucretia (a legendary heroine of early Rome, traditionally sixth century B.C.E.), and the Roman philosopher Seneca (c. 4 B.C.E.–65 C.E.). There are examples of noble suicides in the BIBLE, too. The best-known is probably Samson. Later, however, Jews and Christians came to condemn suicide. The most influential thinker to do so was AUGUSTINE OF HIPPO. In his *City of God* (fifth century) he argued that suicide is always a SIN, regardless of the circumstances, and must always be avoided. MUHAMMAD, too, taught that people who commit suicide are condemned to HELL. At the same time, JUDAISM, CHRISTIANITY, and ISLAM praised martyrs, that is, people who were killed for their faith. In early Christianity martyrdom was seen as a "baptism by blood." Islam teaches, as some early Christians did, that martyrs reach paradise before the final judgment. What some people consider martyrdom, however, others may consider suicide.

HINDUISM, BUDDHISM, and JAINISM have generally condemned wanton suicide as well. Nevertheless, they have permitted suicide under certain circumstances. Jains in old age who wish to end their life in the best way possible do so by a process called *sallekhana*. They stop eating and drinking and eventually die. Some spiritually developed Hindus also end their lives at an advanced age. Much more controversial has been the practice of SATI. In this practice a widow, often but not always a Hindu, burns herself on her husband's funeral pyre. Probably not every case of sati has been voluntary, and many Hindus condemn the practice, as do many non-Hindus.

Although Buddhism generally condemns suicide, it allows it in certain cases. One example is as a self-sacrifice that benefits other people. In the LOTUS SUTRA a BODHISATTVA known as the Medicine King offered his own body to alleviate the suffering of all beings. Some Chinese Buddhists seem to have imitated him by burning themselves to death, sitting in perfect calm. To the shock of many North Americans, Vietnamese Buddhist monks did the same thing in 1963 to protest the war that was ravaging their country. Somewhat different is the Japanese practice of seppuku, a way in which members of the Japanese warrior class, the samurai, sought an honorable death in the face of defeat or disgrace. They did so by ritually disemboweling themselves. An assistant would also decapitate them, that is, cut off their head.

In North America media attention has focused recently on two kinds of religious suicide. One kind is represented by the suicide attacks by Muslims in the Middle East and elsewhere. The September 11 attacks on the World Trade Center and the Pentagon are dramatic examples of this kind of suicide. It is important to remember that many Muslims, as well as non-Muslims, find these acts reprehensible. Those who perform them probably do not see them as suicide but as acts of ultimate devotion in the service of GOD. This view might seem a little more understandable, though still not acceptable, if it is compared to the practice of honoring soldiers after death for having undertaken suicide missions.

The second kind of religious suicide that has received media attention is mass suicides, such as those committed by members of the People's Temple in 1978 and the Solar Temple and Heaven's Gate in 1997. Such suicides are equally shocking, but they are not completely unique. Previous mass suicides have included the suicides of Jews at Masada in 74 C.E. and in Worms, Germany, in 1096. What seems unusual about the 1997 suicides, however, is that they were not directly responding to perceived persecution.

Further reading: Kenneth Cragg, *Faith at Suicide: Lives Forfeit: Violent Religion—Human Despair* (Portland, Ore.: Sussex Academic Press, 2005); Arthur J. Droge and James D. Tabor, *A Noble Death: Suicide and Martyrdom among Christians and Jews in Antiquity* (San Francisco: HarperSanFrancisco, 1992); S. Settar, *Inviting Death: Indian Attitude towards the Ritual Death* (New York: Brill, 1989).

Sun and religion, the   The religious role and significance of the Sun. The source of the Earth's light and heat, and the most prominent feature of the unclouded daytime sky, the Sun has had an important role in religion. It is a natural as a god or symbol of light, day, sovereignty, and consciousness. Many ancient sacred kings have claimed descent from the Sun, including those of Egypt, Japan, and the Incas. While the Moon is no less important in ancient mythologies, it represents changing and cyclical things, together with rain and fertility, while the Sun is steadiness and power, like the Sol Invictus, the "Invincible Sun" of an ancient Roman cult. Often the Sun is masculine, though sometimes, as in the case of the Japanese Amaterasu, it is associated with a goddess. In the major historical religions, the Sun may continue to have a symbolic meaning. In CHRISTIANITY it has been associated with CHRIST, and CHRISTMAS, his birthday, was earlier the birthday of both Sol Invictus and the god MITHRA.

See also MOON AND RELIGION, THE.

Sunni Islam   The branch of ISLAM to which the vast majority of Muslims belong. Islam has two main branches. About 15 percent of all Muslims practice SHI'ITE ISLAM. They live throughout the Islamic world, but especially in Iran, Iraq, Lebanon, and Yemen. Most of the remaining Muslims are Sunnis.

The name "Sunni Islam" comes from the Arabic word *sunnah*. It means "tradition" or "custom." In Arabia before the time of the prophet MUHAMMAD, sunnah referred to the tradition and customs of each tribal group. Islam replaced those customs with a sunnah of its own. Actually, Sunni and Shi'ite Islam each have their sunnah or customs. Each also traces this sunnah back to the same two sources. One is the QUR'AN. The other is the example of the prophet (*see* HADITH) and, for Shi'ite Islam, of its IMAMS.

Sunni and Shi'ite Muslims have much in common. They disagree, however, on how the community of Islam should have been organized. Shi'ite Muslims maintain that the prophet Muhammad designated his cousin and son-in-law, Ali, to be the leader of the Muslim community. Leadership of the community should then have passed down to descendants of Muhammad and Ali. Shi'ite Muslims know these descendants as their Imams.

Sunni Muslims took a very different approach. They maintain that the prophet Muhammad died without designating a successor. Instead, he indicated that the community should itself come to a consensus on who would lead it. The community chose in succession four leaders called the "rightly guided caliphs." After them, several dynasties claimed the caliphate (rule over the Islamic world), among them the Umayyads of Damascus (ruled, 661–750, in Spain until 1031), the Abbasids of Baghdad (ruled 750–1258), and the Fatimids of Egypt (ruled 909–1171). The caliphate was abolished when the Ottoman Empire collapsed after World War I.

Shi'ites expected their imams to be both political and religious leaders, but Sunnis assigned to the caliphs only the political role of preserving unity, law, and order. Caliphs protected the community against threats from abroad and disorder from within. Sunnis assigned to religious scholars the task of preserving and applying the revelation given through Muhammad. These scholars, known as the *ulama* or the "educated," work in harmony with the political authorities. They serve as judges and legal consultants, teachers, prayer leaders, and in other positions as well.

Members of the Sunni ulama belong to one of four different legal schools. The Hanafi school, founded by Abu Hanifah (699–797), is dominant in the Near East and in south Asia. The Maliki school, founded by Malik ibn Anas (715–795), is dominant in north and west Africa. The Shafi'i school of Muhammad ibn Idris al-Shafi'i (d. 820) is dominant in east Africa and southeast Asia. The Hanbali school of Ahmad ibn Hanbal (780–855) is very small. Today it is mostly found in central Saudi Arabia.

All of these schools use several sources to determine what Muslims should do: the Qur'an, the Hadith of the prophet, the consensus of legal scholars, and reasoning by analogy. According to tradition, the period in which scholars needed to think independently ended in the 14th century. During the 20th century, the Islamic community faced new situations and challenges. Some Muslims who had received a secular education rejected traditional Islamic learning. But many legal scholars took active roles in independence movements. In most places, their advice is still valued.

Further reading: Donna Lee Bowen and Evelyn A. Early, ed., *Everyday Life in the Muslim Middle East* (Bloomington: Indiana University Press, 2002); Huseyn Hilmi Isik, *The Sunni Path* (Saddle Brook, N.J.: Hizmet Books, 1993); Garbi Schmidt, *Islam in Urban America: Sunni Muslims in Chicago* (Philadelphia: Temple University Press, 2004).

The Star of David, or Magen David (Hebrew for "shield of David"), is a conventional symbol of Judaism and the Jewish people, consisting of two overlapping triangles that form a six-pointed star. *(Getty Images)*

sweat lodge   An important RITUAL structure for most of the native peoples of North America. A sweat lodge is more or less a religious sauna. It is an enclosed structure in which water is poured on hot rocks to make steam. Those inside the structure sweat from the heat. They also pray and sing. Participants find the experience purifying, healing, and refreshing.

A sweat lodge is often a dome-like frame covered with canvas, bark, or skins. The entrance is low to the ground. Participants enter on their hands and knees. Some sweats are for men only. Many sweats allow women, provided they are not menstruating. In mixed sweats participants wear light clothing. In traditional ones they sweat naked.

Rocks are heated in a fire outside the lodge. They are brought in at regular intervals and piled up in a pit in the center. The symbolism of the lodge alludes to the four directions, the Earth, and the sky. Indeed, some see the sweat lodge as a miniature universe. The "floor" is the Earth's surface; the dome is the sky. Others interpret the lodge in sexual terms. The lodge itself is the womb of the world. It is impregnated by the heat of the sun, symbolized by the heated rocks.

See also NATIVE AMERICAN RELIGIONS.

symbolism in religion   The use of concrete objects to point to religious meaning. Few things are more important to religion than symbols. This is because religion always points toward that which is invisible, even beyond human understanding, and which can be indicated only by something less than the ultimate. This is the role of symbols, to stand in for the ultimate.

To understand symbols, we need to distinguish them from signs. A sign just indicates something is there, like a roadsign telling how many miles it is to the next town. But a symbol in some way is part of that which it symbolizes, and calls up the feeling associated with it. Thus the cross on a Christian church, the Star of DAVID on a SYNAGOGUE, or the star and crescent on a MOSQUE, for believers in the religion is not just a sign indicating what kind of building this is. The symbol also suggests the whole range of associations that go with the FAITH it symbolizes: the sacrificial death of CHRIST, the sufferings and hopes of Jews, the romance of MUHAMMAD's journey from MECCA to Medina when he was guided only by the light of the crescent moon and a star. Symbols are ways of entry into the culture of a religion: the other churches, synagogues, and mosques in which one has worshipped, friends and relatives of the faith—the chain of associations can go on and on. Religious people moreover feel comfort in the fact that they will see many of the same familiar symbols in all houses of their religion.

Symbols are numerous. Today each religion seems to have a "main" symbol, like those just mentioned. But enter a religious edifice and you will see many more. In Hindu temples each of the gods is not only a symbol in his or her own right of spiritual lines of force, but also is surrounded by more symbols, like the moon and serpents of SIVA or the conch shell and discus of VISHNU. Even the deity's hand gestures are symbols in their own right. In CHRISTIANITY the SAINTS and APOSTLES have

their particular symbols. Lights and candles, vestments worn by religious leaders, sacred books on the ALTAR—all these are symbols as well as just what they are, for they evoke associations that lead one deeper into the faith. It is not always necessary to know a one-to-one meaning for each symbol in a religion. These kinds of things can have meanings special to each person, and the main point anyway is not to put it into words but to let the symbol lead one beyond words.

This is particularly true of what might be called general symbols. Certain things seem to appear over and over in the world's religions as symbols: things like sun, moon, water, tree, heroic figures

The interior of an Ashkenazim synagogue in Jerusalem *(Library of Congress)*

and mother figures. The specifics may vary: In one tradition the tree may be the tree of the knowledge of good and evil in the garden of Eden and a poetic name for the cross on which CHRIST died, in another it may be the central pillar connecting HEAVEN and earth, or a place where gods descend. But always it is connected with life, wisdom, and reaching to heaven, as water is with purity and rebirth. As the theologian Paul Tillich said, a symbol participates in that which it symbolizes.

See also MOON AND RELIGION, THE; SUN AND RELIGION, THE; WATER AND RELIGION.

synagogue   Jewish place of WORSHIP. Reform and occasionally Conservative Jews may call a synagogue a temple.

In the late Second Temple period (200 B.C.E.–C.E. 70) Jews worshipped in two different kinds of place. One was the Temple, where GOD's presence dwelled. The other was the synagogue, where one studied the TORAH. But in C.E. 70 the future Roman emperor Titus destroyed the Temple in JERUSALEM. From that time on, the synagogue has been the main worship place in JUDAISM. It is a place of PRAYER, a place of study, and a place of fellowship.

No hard and fast rules prescribe what a synagogue must look like, but synagogues tend to have several features.

On the far wall, opposite the doorway, is an elevated chest called the ark. It contains Torah scrolls. Above the ark is an eternal flame, traditionally an oil lamp.

Another feature of the synagogue is the *bimah*, an elevated place from which the Torah is read. Traditionally it is in the center of the room. In more liberal congregations it is against the wall where the ark is. In that case, the bimah looks something like a stage.

Although in some respects synagogues may resemble churches, there are many features often found in churches that would never be found in a synagogue. For example, a synagogue would never contain symbols of CHRISTIANITY, such as a CROSS or crucifix.

In more traditional synagogues, men and women sit separately. Women sit either in balconies or in the back.

T

taboo A prohibition. The term *taboo* derives from the Polynesian word *tapu,* which means "forbidden." In Polynesia, objects are tapu because they contain *mana.* Mana is a sacred, effective energy that one needs to treat with care.

At the end of the 19th century, anthropologists generalized these Polynesian notions. They theorized that religion—and MAGIC—began when people recognized mana in objects and established taboos. These ideas influenced important thinkers like Sigmund FREUD and Émile DURKHEIM.

Scholars now recognize that tapu and mana are specific to Polynesia, not universal. But people continue to use the word taboo for prohibitions, especially religiously significant ones. All societies have a taboo against incest, although not every society defines incest the same way. Many societies have taboos against certain foods (*see* DIET AND RELIGION). And by tradition, many indigenous Australian men were never allowed to meet their mothers-in-law.

People often try to explain taboos in terms of natural causes. Thus, one forbids incest to avoid genetic defects. Sociologists also see taboos as important ways to create order in society.

Talmud (with Mishnah) In JUDAISM, the authoritative codification of and commentary on the oral TORAH. In 70 C.E., Roman troops destroyed the Temple in JERUSALEM. This event made it impossible to practice the religion of ancient Israel and Judah. That religion centered on presenting offerings and SACRIFICES to GOD at the Temple. Then in 135 C.E. Bar Kokhba's attempt to create an independent Jewish state failed. As a result, Jews were barred from even entering the city of Jerusalem.

These events posed a challenge: how to synthesize from traditions that could no longer be practiced a religion for those living in exile. The challenge fell to the RABBIS, who specialized in the study of the TORAH. In response, they created Judaism as we know it today. Their efforts are preserved in writings known as the Mishnah and the Talmud.

Mishnah is a Hebrew word meaning teaching or repetition. According to the rabbis, MOSES did not write down all of the instructions he received from God on Mount Sinai. Rather, he memorized some instructions and handed them down orally. It is this oral Torah that was recorded in the Mishnah. Tradition says that the Mishnah was recorded around the year 200 C.E. by the leader of the Jews in Palestine, Judah ha-Nasi (c. 135–c. 220).

The Mishnah has six "orders" or parts. These are further divided into 63 tractates and 531 chapters. The six orders discuss (1) agriculture, (2) appointed times, such as festivals and Sabbaths, (3) women, especially in relation to marriage and divorce, (4) damages, that is criminal and civil law, (5) ordinary Temple procedures, and (6) regulations concerning purity. As the North American scholar Jacob Neusner has pointed out, a good deal of the Mishnah discusses the Jerusalem Temple, even though the Temple was in ruins and Jews could not set foot in Jerusalem. These portions of the Mishnah do not describe how one should live today. Rather, they preserve the heritage of the past and stand as a sign of hope for the future. Other portions of the Mishnah discuss the repeated occurrences of ordinary life. Unlike the BIBLE, the Mishnah has very little to say about historical events.

After the Mishnah was compiled, rabbis discussed and debated its meanings. The Talmud—Hebrew for "study"—contains the results of their discussions. It follows the organization of the Mishnah, taking up and exploring each topic in turn. At times it seems as if the rabbis are entirely off the subject. At others it seems as if they are trying to split the finest of hairs. In any case, their discussions testify to an intense, intellectual ethos in which it was just as religious to study the law as to observe it.

There are two "recensions" or versions of the Talmud. The Jerusalem Talmud was compiled in Galilee, despite its name, during the fifth century C.E. It comments on 39 of the 63 tractates in the Mishnah. The Babylonian Talmud was compiled in Babylonia, today Iraq, around 600 C.E. It comments on 37 tractates. The two overlap considerably, so not every tractate of the Mishnah has Talmudic commentary associated with it. The Jerusalem Talmud limits itself more narrowly to explaining the Mishnah and resolving apparent contradictions in it. The Babylonian Talmud also contains essays that comment on the Bible. Since about the year 1000 the Babylonian Talmud has been considered authoritative. As a result, scholars have studied the Jerusalem Talmud less.

In the 18th century, legal restrictions against Jews began to be eliminated, and Jews began to participate in the life of the broader societies in which they live. As a result, Talmudic study no longer has the impact it did when the rabbis were the legal experts and judges for self-sufficient Jewish communities. Nevertheless, Talmudic study remains an important means of communing with God.

Tantrism A movement in HINDUISM, BUDDHISM, and to a lesser extent JAINISM. The basic goal of Tantrism is to appropriate the creative energies of the universe. To reach this goal, practitioners visualize cosmic powers and ritually participate in cosmic processes. Tantrism often deliberately transgresses limits and inverts established orders. As a result, other traditions have at times looked upon it with disdain.

HISTORY

It is generally difficult to write a history of religions in India. It is even more difficult to write a history of Tantrism. Tantrism has generally been practiced in secret.

Tantrism may have its roots in local, popular practices. Hindu and Buddhist Tantrism seem to have come into existence in India by the end of the sixth century C.E. During the next one thousand years, Hindu Tantrism was at its height. Its practitioners wrote important Tantric texts, such as Tantras (handbooks of doctrine), Agamas (RITUAL manuals), and Samhitas (collections). These texts use Sanskrit, the language of learned BRAHMINS. Therefore, Tantrism probably developed among the religious elite. Temples built during this period also reveal prominent Tantric influence. The famous temples at Khajuraho (950–1050 C.E.) are good examples.

By about 1500 Tantrism was beginning to lose its creativity. But in the late 19th and early 20th centuries, Europeans and North Americans started taking an interest in Hindu Tantrism. Their interest stimulated a minor revival in India.

In Buddhism, Tantrism is seen as a specific *yana* or "vehicle," the Vajrayana, "Diamond Vehicle," or Mantrayana, "Mantra Vehicle." Vajrayana was common in India during the eighth century when Buddhism spread from India to Tibet. It became the dominant religion of Tibet (*see* TIBETAN RELIGION). That country eventually housed a vast store of Buddhist Tantric texts. Vajrayana was also exported to China. In fact, some of the earliest Buddhist Tantric writings are in Chinese. From China Kukai took Tantric Buddhism to Japan. There it became Shingon, a school still popular today.

BELIEFS

Because it is a movement found in several different religious contexts, Tantrism does not have a single coherent body of thought. Furthermore, many Tantric texts are written in what is known as "twilight language," a symbolic language whose full significance cannot be understood except with the help of a code revealed only to the initiated.

There are, however, some common Tantric themes. One theme deals with the creative duality between male and female. Tantrism often gives the female the higher place. Another theme concerns the links between the macrocosm or structure of the universe and the microcosm or structure of the human being. Finally, Tantrism often conceives of liberation as reuniting the male and the female into one.

In Hindu Tantrism the ultimate Godhead is formless. But on a less than ultimate level the Godhead is sexually dual, having both a male and a female form. The female form, known as Sakti or the god's power, is responsible for the creation of the world. At the same time, Sakti is the source of liberation. When Sakti reunites with the male principle, the original unity is restored.

According to Hindu Tantrism these macrocosmic processes find their reflections on the microcosmic level. In the human person Sakti is generally imaged as a coiled serpent asleep at the base of the spine (KUNDALINI). When the serpent is aroused, it rises and eventually unites with the masculine principle at the top of the skull. When it does so, the result is liberation.

VAJRAYANA BUDDHISM uses different ideas. Before Vajrayana arose, MAHAYANA BUDDHISM had developed a pantheon of Buddhas and BODHISATTVAS. Vajrayana carried this process further. It identified even more Buddhas and bodhisattvas, assigned them feminine consorts or counterparts, and delighted in images of the wrathful and the horrific. Vajrayana also linked the macrocosm and the microcosm. It identified the various Buddhas and bodhisattvas with different parts of the body. A person followed the path to liberation by visualizing these various beings and thereby acquiring their powers. In fact, one might say that in Vajrayana, Buddhists imagined themselves as enlightened beings in order to achieve enlightenment and do so more quickly.

At a more abstract level. Vajrayana sees liberation as a union of male and female. In Buddhist Tantrism the female in PRAJNA, "wisdom." The male is *upaya*, "skill is means," that is, a person's ability to practice the Buddhist path. The union of the two, wisdom and the ability to practice, eventually produces enlightenment.

PRACTICES

Both Hindu and Buddhist Tantrism make heavy use of ritual diagrams (YANTRAS and MANDALAS), ritual sounds (MANTRAS), and ritual gestures (MUDRAS). These diagrams, sounds, and gestures vary from tradition to tradition, but they are all thought to embody the powers of the universe. In both Hindu and Buddhist Tantrism the diagrams, sounds, and gestures allow practitioners to acquire sacred power and ultimately to achieve release. Practitioners acquire the power of these diagrams, sounds, and gestures by meditating on them.

To construct and use a mandala is a relatively benign act. Tantrism is also known, however, for a variety of rituals that deliberately invert established order and transgress normal bounds. Such acts require special control, for the goal is not to enjoy forbidden fruits. It is to use the things of the world to conquer the world, to overcome desire by acting out what desire demands and yet remaining untouched by desire.

Perhaps the best known system of such rituals are "the five elements" found in Hindu Tantrism. These elements are also called "the five m's," because the Sanskrit word for each starts with the letter "m." The five are wine (*madya*), meat (*mansa*), fish (*matsya*), parched grains (*mudra*), and sexual union (*maithuna*). Like Hindu Tantrism, Buddhist Tantrism recognizes sexual rituals. Such rituals call for extreme concentration. If they are performed to fulfill carnal desires, the consequences are drastic.

ORGANIZATION

Tantrism is a religion of small, private, secret groups. For that reason, it is difficult to know how many people practice it. The basic organization is that of a teacher (GURU) and disciples.

The first ritual is initiation. In initiation, members join the group. They swear to maintain secrecy, and they begin their training in the secrets of Tantrism. In the course of Tantric practice they allegedly attain various supernormal powers.

There have been many attempts to classify different Tantric groups. Perhaps the most common classification distinguishes right-handed and left-handed Tantrism in Hinduism. Right-handed Tantrism limits itself to the use of mandalas, yantras, mantras, and mudras. Left-handed Tantrism practices ritual acts that are otherwise forbidden.

SIGNIFICANCE

Although Tantrism strictly speaking is confined to small groups, its influence has been great. Much of present-day Hinduism contains some Tantric elements. For example, all Hindu temples are built on mandalas. In Tibet, Vajrayana produced a vibrant national religion. Its leader, the DALAI LAMA, won the Nobel Peace Prize in 1989.

Further reading: Agehananda Bharati, *The Tantric Tradition* (Westport, Conn.: Greenwood Press, 1977); Georg Feuerstein, *Tantra: The Path of Ecstasy* (Boston: Shambhala, 1998); David Kinsley, *Tantric Visions of the Divine Feminine: The Ten Mahavidyas* (Berkeley: University of California Press, 1997); Reginald A. Ray, *Secret of the Vajra World: The Tantric Buddhism of Tibet* (Boston: Shambhala, 2001); David Gordon White, ed., *Tantra in Practice* (Princeton, N.J.: Princeton University Press, 2000).

Taoism A Chinese religion; pronounced with an initial "d," and therefore also spelled Daoism. Taoism teaches that by living in harmony with the Tao (pronounced and sometimes spelled Dao) or the way of nature, it is possible to prolong life and even become immortal.

Scholars have often distinguished two different trends in Taoism: philosophical Taoism and religious Taoism. Philosophical Taoism refers to ideas put forth roughly from 600 to 200 B.C.E. Religious Taoism refers to movements and practices like ALCHEMY (transforming metals into medicines that were thought to grant immortality) and MEDITATION that began around the first century C.E. These two trends help to distinguish two major stages in the history of Taoism. But it would be incorrect to think that philosophical and religious Taoism were entirely separate movements.

HISTORY

The founder of Taoism is known as LAO-TZU, "Old Master." He may have lived in the sixth century B.C.E., or he may be only legendary. It is said that Lao-tzu dictated the classic book of Taoism, the *TAO TE CHING*, as he was leaving China in old age. In any case, by the fourth century B.C.E. a book in 5,000 Chinese characters had come into existence that advocated yielding to the way of nature in all things. It called the prime characteristic of that way *wu-wei*, action that lacks deliberate intention. A later book developed these insights further. It was named CHUANG-TZU after the person who supposedly wrote it.

In the first century C.E. several movements used these figures and books to develop rituals and institutions. Some looked for a golden age to come in the future. This age was known as the great peace. Those who followed Taoist principles were expected to rule during that peace. Inspired by such teachings, many secret movements tried to usher in the golden age. Among them was an attempt to overthrow the Han dynasty in 184 C.E.

Another Taoist movement that began in the same period is known as "the way of the heavenly masters." Its founder claimed to have received revelations from Lao-tzu, whom he considered to be a god. Among other things, the movement promised to heal the sick. It also provided its members with a series of books or "registers" in which to record their spiritual progress.

The first millennium (1–1000) C.E. was the golden age of Taoism. Taoists developed elaborate RITUALS. They also perfected many techniques that were said to lead to long life and, if done just right, immortality. Occasionally Taoism became the official religion. Different kingdoms required their subjects to perform Taoist practices, for example, to celebrate the birthday of Lao-tzu.

The first millennium C.E. was also the time when BUDDHISM came to China. Taoists often opposed Buddhism, and they convinced several rulers to outlaw it. The two religions did, however, influence one another. Taoist ideas helped transform Buddhism. This can be seen especially in the school known in China as Ch'an and in Japan as ZEN BUDDHISM. Perhaps under Buddhist influence, Taoists developed monasteries and convents funded by the state.

Throughout most of the second millennium (1001–2000) C.E. Confucianism dominated official Chinese religion. The official outlook promoted the unity of the three religions, Confucianism, Taoism, and Buddhism. During this period Taoism developed forms more suited to the needs of private individuals than of the official cult.

With the victory of communism in mainland China in 1949 and especially the Cultural Revolution of the late 1960s, Taoism suffered tremendously. Because the government objected to both old traditions and religion, it opposed Taoism. In the 1980s some Taoist institutions were rebuilt and Taoist WORSHIP resumed. Meanwhile, Taoist practice flourished in Chinese communities elsewhere, especially on Taiwan.

TEACHINGS

The earliest Taoist texts celebrate the Tao. According to the beginning of the Tao te Ching, it is impossible really to give the Tao a name. It is simply indescribable. At the same time, the Tao is the mother of all things. It produces everything in the world, including ourselves.

The earliest texts advocate that human beings should live in harmony with the Tao. Consider, for example, water flowing in a stream. What does it do? Strictly speaking, it does nothing. It simply yields to the forces exerted on it. It falls because of the force of gravity; it moves out of the way when it hits a boulder. Yet in simply yielding, water proves to be stronger than the boulder. It wears the boulder away. Taoists find this example instructive. The best human action, they say, is action that

is not forced by deliberate intention. The earliest Taoist texts also apply these ideas to government. That government is best whose subjects are hardly aware of the government's activities at all.

Later Taoism develops a full range of mythological ideas. It teaches that there are many immortals. Some immortals are connected with the world at large. Others are connected with the human body. Taoism has other teachings, too: about islands of the immortals in the eastern ocean, where elixirs of immortality may be found; about the five sacred mountains in China, the most sacred of which is T'ai Shan in the eastern province of Shantung; and about the life-giving properties of various substances, such as gold. In addition, Taoism analyzes the human being in detail. For Taoism, the most important life-force is the original breath known as *chi*. Chi and other life-forces concentrate in three centers: the head, the heart, and the navel. These three "fields" are where the three "holy ones," the three most important immortals, dwell. They are also home to three beings known as "worms" that devour the vital energy and bring about death.

PRACTICES

There are two main kinds of Taoist practice: exercises to prolong one's life and large, elaborate rituals for the well-being of the community.

The exercises to prolong life try to preserve or restore the vital energy with which a person is born. Certain practices, called the "external elixir," involve eating and drinking, especially the eating and drinking of metals. For the ancient Chinese, gold symbolized the state that all Taoists sought. It could neither be destroyed nor corrupted. The "external elixir" attempted to synthesize gold from baser substances, especially lead and mercuric sulfide (cinnabar). In theory one acquired long life either by using vessels made with synthesized gold or eating and drinking it. These practices are the source of what came to be known in Europe and North America as alchemy.

Around 1000 C.E. the "external elixir" was replaced by an "internal elixir." In these practices Taoists do not eat or drink physical substances. They perform rituals instead. The rituals include meditation and breathing and gymnastic exercises.

Like the two "elixirs," the great public rituals, known as *jiao*, provide long life to the priests who perform them. They also give peace, health, and protection to the community as a whole. In these colorful festivals, the three "holy ones" are invited to a feast. Technically, only the Taoist priest offers the feast, but members of the community also participate with rituals of their own.

ORGANIZATION

Taoism has had both MONKS AND NUNS. But the number of nuns has always been extremely small, and the majority of Taoist priests are not monks but live in families.

In Taiwan today there are two orders of priests. Those with red headbands perform only rituals of EXORCISM. Those with black headbands also perform the major public festivals.

Some Taoist communities, such as "the way of the heavenly masters," have been carefully structured. Today the head of the community, sometimes called a pope, still claims to be a descendant of the original founder. At times Taoists have also formed secret societies dedicated to the overthrow of the Chinese government.

SIGNIFICANCE

In addition to its immense contribution to Chinese society, Taoism attracted the attention of Europeans and North Americans in the 20th century. Ideas from the early Taoist texts became popular. So did physical exercises such as T'ai Chi and Taoist-influenced martial arts (*see* MARTIAL ARTS AND RELIGION).

Further reading: Russell Kirkland, *Taoism: An Enduring Tradition* (New York: Routledge, 2004); Catherine Despeux and Livia Kohn, *Women in Daoism* (Cambridge, Mass.: Three Pines Press, 2003); Jennifer Oldstone-Moore, *Taoism: Origins, Beliefs, Practices, Holy Texts, Sacred Places* (New York: Oxford University Press, 2003); N. J. Girardot, James Miller, and Liu Xiaogan, ed., *Daoism and Ecology: Ways within a Cosmic Landscape* (Cambridge, Mass.: Harvard University Press, 2001).

Tao Te Ching (Daodejing)   The most important book in TAOISM. The book is also called LAO-TZU after the person who, tradition says, wrote it. Modern scholars are reluctant to say who compiled the book or when. Some date it as late as the third century B.C.E.

Tao Te Ching literally means "Way Power Classic." It contains 5,000 Chinese characters. They make up two parts that together contain 81 "chapters." The first part is supposedly about the Tao or way. The second is supposedly about the *te* or power of the way. The chapters are actually short, enigmatic paragraphs whose precise interpretation is difficult. Despite that difficulty, or perhaps because of it, the *Tao Te Ching* has been translated into English more times than any other Chinese book.

The famous opening words of the *Tao Te Ching* announce its central theme, the Tao. They also say that it is impossible to talk about the Tao:

> *The Tao that can be spoken of is not the eternal Tao;*
> *The name that can be named is not the eternal name.*
> *The nameless is the origin of heaven and earth;*
> *The named is the mother of all things.*
> *Always rid yourself of desires in order to observe its secrets;*
> *Always allow yourself desires in order to observe its manifestations.*
> *These two are the same, but they have different names as they are produced.*
> *Being the same, they are called mysteries: profound mystery, the mystery of mysteries*
> *—the gateway of all mysteries.*
>
> (*Translated by Witter Bynner*)

Another passage that expresses that the Tao is beyond words runs as follows: "whoever knows does not speak; whoever speaks does not know."

There is a good reason, then, for the puzzling language that the book uses. No one can express directly what the book is trying to say.

The Tao is not only nameless. It also has no intentions or purposes. Thus, the *Tao Te Ching* insists that the Tao never acts. Nevertheless, the Tao is "the mother of all things." The *Tao Te Ching* uses many different images to express the creative power of the Tao. One is mathematical: "The Dao produced the one, the one produced the two, the two produced the three, and the three produced the ten thousand." Another image appeals to nature: "There is nothing softer and weaker than water, and yet there is nothing better for attacking hard and strong things."

According to the *Tao Te Ching*, the Tao should be our guide in life. The book rejects CONFUCIUS and his emphasis on proper behavior. In carefully prescribing behavior Confucius carves blocks of stone, so to speak, and thus destroys them. According to the *Tao Te Ching*, one should simply accept the stone as it is, uncarved. Governments, too, should imitate the Tao. The best rulers do not govern with iron fists. "The best leaders value their words, and use them sparingly. When they have accomplished their tasks, the people say, 'Amazing: we did it, all by ourselves!'"

The above quotes and observations only begin to reveal the contents of this remarkable book. It bears careful rereading and calm reflection.

Tara A Buddhist GODDESS worshipped for protection. Tara is the female counterpart of the BODHI-SATTVA known as AVALOKITESVARA. Although her cult arose in India, she is most popular in Tibetan Buddhism (*see* TIBETAN RELIGION). There, monks and laypeople alike WORSHIP her as a deity who protects them from all sorts of dangers. It is sometimes said that Tara gives protection from eight dangers: elephants, lions, serpents, thieves, vampires, sea monsters, fire, and chains. Artists have been particularly fond of depicting the eight Taras who save worshippers from these threats.

By tradition, traveling troupes of players acted out tales of Tara and her deliverances, By tradition, too, the inhabitants of eastern Tibet held great summer festivals in her honor.

Tathagata A Sanskrit word meaning "having gone [*gata*] or come [*āgata*] thus [*tathā*]." The term is designation for the BUDDHA. It applies especially to the Buddha after his parinirvana (*see* NIRVANA).

In the oldest traditions of BUDDHISM the Buddha is not a god whom Buddhists WORSHIP. He is a human being who is venerated because he blazed the path to ultimate release from SAMSARA or rebirth. To achieve release, human beings must follow him.

As a result, the Buddha was called the Tathagata, "the one who went that way." Buddhists also read the term as "the one who came thus," referring to the Buddha's teaching of the dharma in the world. The title is said to date back to the Buddha himself.

televangelism The use of television to spread religious messages. The word "evangelism" refers specifically to spreading the message of Christianity, but other religions, too, have begun to use television for similar purposes.

Television first became widespread in the United States in the 1950s. At that time, several mainline churches experimented with television broadcasts. For example, in 1958 the United Lutheran Church of America began work on a cartoon series, "Davey and Goliath." In 1960, however, the federal government ruled that broadcasters did not have to give nonprofit organizations such as churches a certain amount of their airtime without charge. As a result, interest in such programming among producers fell off.

In the 1980s, televangelism came into its own, largely among conservative Protestants (*see* PROTESTANTISM). These people formed their own broadcasting networks, such as the Christian Broadcasting Network, founded by Pat Robertson (b. 1930), and the PTL network, founded by Jim Bakker (b. 1939). In addition, many Christian televangelists emerged as well-known personalities, among them Robertson; Bakker and his wife, Tammi Faye (b. 1942); Jerry Falwell (b. 1933); Jimmy Swaggart (b. 1935); and Rex Humbard (b. 1919). According to some estimates, in the mid-1980s these televangelists were reaching 15 million households each week and attracting 25 million viewers.

After the mid-1980s, however, public interest in televangelism had begun to drop off. Then, in the late 1980s, the movement suffered tremendous shocks when it was learned that two leading televangelists, Jim Bakker and Jimmy Swaggart, were both guilty of sexual misconduct. People became more suspicious of people whom they knew only from television images. They also began to ask serious questions about the money-raising and money-managing practices of televangelists.

Many predicted in the late 1980s and the early 1990s that televangelism was doomed. As readers with access to cable television probably know, those predictions have not come true. The audience for televangelists did drop off. Televangelists have also found it more difficult to raise the money they need to keep their enterprises on the air. Nevertheless, televangelism has continued into the early 21st century. It also has developed new formats. Besides broadcasts of revivals, prayer meetings, Bible studies and discussions, and interviews, conservative Christian networks also have experimented with, among other formats, game shows. Such programs have drawn audiences who find the values of programming on the major secular networks unacceptable.

According to a study done in 2000, the major televangelists in the United States tend to be white (90 percent) and male (80 percent). They also tend to be Protestant, although one prominent exception was a Roman Catholic woman, Mother Angelica (b. 1923) of the Eternal Word Television Network. Many people, at least those who do not watch televangelists regularly, have the idea that evangelists spend a large percentage of their time raising money. It is true that some do. The 2000 study showed that Jerry Falwell spent 22 percent of his airtime raising money and another 27 percent promoting products; Oral (b. 1918) and Richard (b. 1948) Roberts

spent 27 percent of their airtime on fundraising. Yet other televangelists, such as Mother Angelica and the programs "Days of Discovery" and "Tomorrow's World" spent virtually no airtime raising money. Televangelists tend to support political candidates from the Republican Party, but most do not spend a significant amount of airtime discussing politics. An important exception is Pat Robertson's 700 Club, which in 2000 devoted 34 percent of its broadcast time to discussing politics.

Although people in the United States are most familiar with televangelists who are English-speaking Protestants, the phenomenon extends more broadly. Programs in Spanish have begun to appear for the large number of Spanish-speaking people in the United States. Jewish groups (see JUDAISM) and ISKCON, the "Hare KRISHNA" movement (see HINDUISM), have also begun television broadcasts.

Christian televangelism has also appeared outside the United States, for example, in many African and Latin American countries. In these countries it sometimes encounters problems that it does not face in the United States. For example, laws in Great Britain do not allow religious groups to raise money through television broadcasts. They also do not allow people to broadcast claims of miracles; in the eyes of British authorities, that amounts to fraud. In 1998 Muslims in Nigeria objected to the airing of televangelistic programming. They managed to prevent the broadcasts from airing in Muslim regions.

temples in world religions   See ARCHITECTURE, RELIGIOUS.

Ten Commandments   A set of biblical precepts, recorded in Exodus 20.1–17 and Deuteronomy 5.6–21, sacred to both Jews and Christians. Jews and Christians revere many different guides to behavior, for example, "you shall love the Lord your GOD with all your heart and soul and might" (Deuteronomy 6.5 cf. Mark 12.30); "you shall love your neighbor as yourself" (Mark 12.31); and "do to others as you would have them do to you" (Matthew 7.12). Indeed, according to rabbinical tradition there are 613 *mitzvot* (commandments) in TORAH, the first five books of the BIBLE. But the Ten Commandments are the most important.

According to the Bible, the Ten Commandments were the first instructions given to the people of Israel at Mount Sinai (or Horeb) when they entered into a COVENANT with God. As such, they can be seen as analogous to the stipulations that rulers in the ancient Near East passed down whenever they took charge of a people. For Jews and Christians today, however, they are of universal significance.

The commandments may be divided into two "tables" or parts. The first part deals with obligations human beings have to God. They are not to WORSHIP any God but YHWH ("the Lord"); they are not to make any images for worship; they are not to use the name YHWH improperly; and they are to observe the Sabbath rest. As a result of the third commandment, it has become common in JUDAISM never to utter the name YHWH. When the SCRIPTURES are read, the word Adonai, roughly, "the Lord," is substituted for God's name. In accordance with the fourth commandment, observing the Sabbath is one of the major practices of Judaism.

The second table or part of the Ten Commandments deals with relationships between human beings. It is similar to prescriptions found in other religions, for example, the Five Precepts in BUDDHISM: Respect your parents; do not murder; do not commit adultery; do not steal; do not testify falsely; and do not covet or desire what belongs to someone else. Although certainly not a complete and sufficient guide on how to act, these six commandments provide basic guidelines for life in society.

The Ten Commandments are an important symbol of Judaism. They are often depicted in the form that recalls the two tablets that MOSES received from God (Exodus 31.18): as two rectangles, taller than they are wide, with rounded tops on which are inscribed in Hebrew the first letters of each commandment. In this form, the commandments can often be seen in SYNAGOGUES, displayed above the doors of the ark where the Torah scrolls are kept.

Tenrikyo One of the "new religions" of Japan. Tenrikyo was founded by Nakayama Miki (1798–1887) as a result of a commission she received while in trance in 1838 to serve as herself the shrine of "the true and original GOD," also called Oyagami, "God the Parent." Tenrikyo emphasizes the story of the creation of the world received through the Foundress, and says that God is trying to call human beings back to himself through revealing this story to the world through her. The worship is based on attractive dances enacting the creation story, and sweeping away "dusts" that have accumulated since then. It is headquartered in Tenri City, a large town near Nara that is centered on the religion and where one finds a striking temple, university, hospital, hostels for pilgrims, and administrative buildings. The religion is widespread in Japan and has been brought to other countries, largely within communities of Japanese immigrants. (*See* JAPAN, NEW RELIGIONS IN.)

theodicy An attempt to answer a theological question: If GOD is good, omnipotent, and omniscient, why is there EVIL and suffering in the world? Theodicy has been one of the most persistent and troubling questions in JUDAISM and CHRISTIANITY. That is because Jews and Christians want to say several things about God: God desires good for creation, including human beings; God is all-powerful; and God knows everything. If all three of these statements are true, it becomes difficult to explain why evil and suffering exist. Archibald Macleish expressed this difficulty cleverly in his play, *J.B.:* "If God is God he is not good; if God is good he is not God; take the even, take the odd." The same difficulty confronts a child whose mother or father is killed in an automobile accident: "Why did God let Mommy—or Daddy—die?"

One response says that, despite our experiences of suffering and evil, God has in fact made the best world possible. This was the position of the German philosopher G. W. Leibniz (1646–1716). But this position is not without its critics. In his book *Candide* the French writer Voltaire mercilessly attacked the idea that "all is arranged for the best in this best of all possible worlds."

Many have tried to show, however, why evil and suffering must exist in the best possible world. Many Jews and Christians have explained evil and suffering in terms of free will (*see* FREE WILL AND DETERMINISM). God wanted, they say, to create human beings, not robots. Therefore, he gave them the opportunity to make choices. It is inevitable that some people choose to do evil. The traditional objection to this view is that not all suffering results from human actions. What about a child who dies of cancer? The ancient Christian thinker AUGUSTINE OF HIPPO had an answer. He said that natural catastrophes and hardships entered the world when human beings first sinned.

Another explanation says that evil and suffering are actually good for people. They help people grow and mature. If people lived in paradise, they would remain childish and never develop their full potential. The ancient Christian thinker, Irenaeus, developed this view.

There is, however, a problem with the responses given above. They basically tell people that they cannot expect God's help when they most desperately want it. If evil and suffering are an inevitable part of the world, or a necessary consequence of free will, or part of "growing up," what good is God in the midst of evil and suffering?

Faced with the question "why?" in the midst of human tragedy, many RABBIS, priests, and ministers simply answer, "We do not know." Another option says that God is good but cannot do everything, Rabbi Harold Kushner took this position in his popular book, *When Bad Things Happen to Good People* (1981). A third view emphasizes that God suffers with people and sustains them. Christians look to JESUS suffering on the cross; Jews speak of God suffering along with his people. During the 20th century, the HOLOCAUST raised the issue of theodicy very forcefully. Some found that in the face of such immense evil, they could no longer believe in God. The Nobel Prize-winning novelist Elie Wiesel expressed this position in his moving novel, *Night*.

Theodicy has not been so large a problem outside Judaism and Christianity. Most Muslims insist that human beings should not question God's judgments. Zoroastrians, Gnostics, and other dualists see the universe as a battleground between the forces of good and evil. Hindus, Buddhists, and Jains attribute evil and suffering to KARMA, that is, acts done in previous life.

theology   A subject of study, especially within CHRISTIANITY. The word "theology" comes from a Greek word that means "talk about GOD" As a definition of theology, this phrase is too narrow. Theology talks about many other topics, too. Classical theological topics include the nature of God, God's relation to the world and to human beings, and SALVATION.

In general, theology tries to state the truths of a particular religion, most often Christianity, from the perspective of someone who practices that religion. But theology does not simply assert basic beliefs. CREEDS and confessions do that. Theology tries to state a religion's truths in ways that stand up to careful examination.

DO ALL RELIGIONS HAVE THEOLOGY?

Theology has been extremely important for Christians. During the medieval period, western Europe developed universities. In these universities theology was the most important subject of study. People called it "the queen of the sciences." Today theology no longer holds this position. But the Christian heritage has strongly influenced what the word "theology" means.

Many cultures have developed traditions of thinking that use abstract propositions. In such cultures some people try to state the truths of their religion in rigorous and sophisticated ways. But it is questionable whether these efforts are "theology."

It is possible to speak of Jewish and Islamic theology. But one must be careful. Christianity has tended to define itself in terms of beliefs. By contrast, JUDAISM and ISLAM have tended to define themselves in terms of practice. Rigorous, intellectual thinking in these two traditions has often had a different focus from theology: in Judaism the study of the TORAH, both written and oral, and in Islam the study of jurisprudence (*fiqh*).

Hindu traditions of thought about the self and the world are usually called "philosophy." "Orthodox" schools accept the authority of the sacred books known as the VEDA; other schools reject it. Some schools of both varieties are actually atheistic. Others give God or the gods little or no attention. BUDDHISM has sophisticated traditions of thought, but it is better to call them philosophy or even buddhalogy than theology. To label Confucian, Taoist, and SHINTO thinkers "theologians" would be odd.

TOPICS IN THEOLOGY

Christians and others use the word "theology" in both a broad and a narrow sense. In the broad sense, theology includes any and every subject taught in a school of theology or a seminary. Different schools organize their curricula differently, so there is no single list of such subjects. Some identify four areas of theology: biblical, historical, systematic, and practical. Biblical theology deals with the BIBLE. Historical theology deals with the history of the religious community, for example, the church. Systematic theology deals with the community's beliefs and morality. Practical theology teaches people how to meet the needs of a community, for example, PREACHING, teaching, WORSHIP, and pastoral care.

In a narrow sense, theology refers to the study of systematic theology, especially to the study of beliefs. (The study of morality is called "ethics.") Here again, there is no standard list of topics that all theologians address. Theologians choose and arrange topics in ways that will best allow them to express their views and insights. Some topics, however, are fairly common.

Theologians often identify the sources of knowledge that they consider valid or binding. Protestant theologians usually depend upon the Bible. Roman Catholic theologians depend upon traditional teachings of the church as well as the Bible. Orthodox theologians see their task as explaining the Bible as understood by the Fathers of the church.

Theologians also take up many particular topics. They often discuss what God is like, how people can know about God, and, in Christianity, the TRINITY and INCARNATION. Other topics include God's relationship to the world (COSMOLOGY), God's relationship to human beings (anthropology), how salvation takes place (soteriology), and what will happen at the end of time (ESCHATOLOGY).

THEOLOGY TODAY

After World War I, the dominant school of theology was Neo-orthodoxy. Its primary spokespersons were two Swiss theologians, Karl Barth and Emil Brunner. According to this school, a theologian's task is to expound the Word of God. But for Barth and Brunner the Word of God meant something different from the Bible. It meant the self-revelation of God, especially in JESUS. Influential thinkers related to this school but not strictly Neo-orthodox include Paul Tillich and the American brothers Reinhold and H. Richard Niebuhr.

Beginning in the 1960s, other currents of theology became extremely influential. One of them was "liberation theology." It addressed the situations of oppressed peoples, especially Latin American peasants, women (*see* FEMINISM), and African Americans. Other theologians became acutely aware of religious plurality. Some of them entered into DIALOGUE with representative thinkers of other religions. Some also began work on comparative or global theologies.

More recently, some theologians have been exploring the implications of research into the structures of the mind and brain for religion. They call their work "neurotheology" (*see* BRAIN, MIND, AND RELIGION).

Before World War II, American schools, colleges, and universities that taught about religion generally taught theology. They offered courses in Bible, in the history of Christianity, in theology narrowly conceived, in ethics, and in "comparative religion." Schools affiliated with a religion often still teach religion this way. Many Catholic schools are good examples.

After World War II some American schools, colleges, and universities began to teach religion in a different way. This approach has come to be called "religious studies." Theology recognizes special, religious sources of knowledge (revelation, tradition); religious studies does not. Theology also attempts to state religious truth for members of a religious community; religious studies attempts to state truths about religion that do not require membership in a specific religious community.

At the end of the 20th century, there was no agreement on whether theology should have a place in religious studies. In addition, some conservative religious people felt that religious studies did in fact state religious truth for a specific "religious" community. It stated truths for a secular community that rejected religion.

SIGNIFICANCE

Past theologians—AUGUSTINE OF HIPPO, Thomas AQUINAS, Martin LUTHER, and John CALVIN—have produced masterpieces of European thought and literature. Even theologians who are not so famous make an important contribution to their religions. They state those religions in ways that thinking people find both religiously and intellectually compelling.

Further reading: Helen K. Bond, Seth D. Kunin, and Francesca Aran Murphy, eds., *Religious Studies and Theology: An Introduction* (New York: New York University Press, 2003); Gary B. Ferngren, ed., *Science and Religion: A Historical Introduction* (Baltimore, Md.: Johns Hopkins University Press, 2002); Daniel L. Migliore, *Faith Seeking Understanding: An Introduction to Christian Theology,* 2d ed. (Grand Rapids, Mich.: W. B. Eerdmans, 2004).

theosophy A modern spiritual movement. The word, meaning divine wisdom, refers generally to schools of religious thought that emphasize mystical knowledge of the inner workings of the divine. More specifically, however, it is the name of a modern spiritual movement founded as the Theosophical Society in New York in 1875 by a Russian woman, Helena P. Blavatsky, and an American, Henry Steel Olcott. This movement has spread throughout the world, and has been particularly instrumental in introducing Eastern religious and spiritual ideas to the West. Its basic premise is that there is an "ancient wisdom" underlying all existing religions as well as much of science and philosophy, and its object is to recover and study that wisdom. The ancient wisdom teaches the oneness of all things, the PILGRIMAGE of the soul through many lives and worlds, and the coming and going of lives and universes according to great cycles. The headquarters of the largest theosophical society is in Adyar, India. It has had an influence on modern art and the New Age movement.

Theravada Buddhism The "Way of the Elders," the form of BUDDHISM predominant in Sri Lanka, Myanmar (Burma), Thailand, Cambodia, and Laos. Theravada is understood by its adherents to be a conservative, traditional style of the religion. It follows as its scriptures the Tripitaka, the oldest Buddhist texts. These books give what are undoubtedly the earliest extant versions of the BUDDHA's words and teachings. Theravada thus emphasizes such foundational precepts of Buddhism as the FOUR NOBLE TRUTHS, the Eightfold Path, and the FOUR UNLIMITED VIRTUES. Theravadins stress the difference between the SANGHA (the monastic order) and laypeople, and Theravada MONKS AND NUNS are expected to follow strictly the ancient Buddhist monastic rule.

A monk can hope, after many lifetimes perhaps, to become an arhat, that is, a liberated being, by meditation, especially vipassana meditation, the meditation of analysis. Vipassana helps the meditator realize that life as ordinarily lived is full of suffering, always changing, and without a separate individual self at its center. Beyond that level of experience lies NIRVANA the opposite of everything changing, suffering, and individual.

Nonetheless, having been the religion of the five countries above for many centuries, Theravada Buddhism has popular and folk religion aspects as well. Theravada countries have a striking number of ornate temples, each containing a gilded image of the Buddha. Rather than meditate like monks, laypeople typically try to make good KARMA, or merit, by such practices as gilding images of the Buddha, giving support to the monks, performing acts of everyday charity and compassion to all beings. They may then in time win REINCARNATION as a monk on the way to arhathood. They may also gain rebirth in one of the Buddhist heavens, splendid places even if short of NIRVANA, but their time there lasts only as long as the good karma they have obtained holds out.

In all Theravada lands except Sri Lanka young men ideally enter a monastery for a year or so. They learn the basics of the religion and experience another way of life than that of the outside world. Most do not remain monastics, but those who do become elder monks and revered spiritual teachers, highly honored by laypeople and junior monks alike.

BUDDHIST FESTIVALS are important to popular Buddhism in Theravada lands. The chief annual festival is Wesak in the spring, commemorating the Buddha's birth, enlightenment, and entry into nirvana. On this day, trees are watered, candles and incense are burned, and rockets are set off. A month later, the rainy season begins, which for Theravadins is a time of special religious discipline, rather like Lent for some Christians. The monks remain in retreat in monasteries. Many laypeople resolve to follow Buddhist morality more strictly than otherwise. At the end of the retreat, another great festival is held with traditional dances and the formal presentation of gifts to the monks.

In the 20th century, the Theravada world suffered considerably from war and rapid change. When Sri Lanka and Burma (later Myanmar) won freedom from Britain, monks played a leading role in the independence movements. Subsequently Sri Lanka was shocked by internal conflict between the Buddhist Singhalese and the Hindu Tamil minority, and Myanmar has experienced political repression. Cambodia and Laos were caught up in the devastating Vietnamese War; subsequently Cambodia suffered under the particularly brutal regime of the communist Khmer Rouge (1975–79). Thailand has been spared the worst but has undergone the traumas of rapid modernization. Through all these vicissitudes, Theravada Buddhism has offered the peoples of these nations a place of inner refuge and symbols of continuity with the culture of their past.

Further reading: Winston King, *Theravada Meditation* (University Park: Pennsylvania State University Press, 1980); Winston King, *A Thousand Lives Away* (Cambridge, Mass.: Harvard University Press, 1964); Robert Lester, *Theravada Buddhism in Southeast Asia* (Ann Arbor: University of Michigan Press, 1973).

Thomas, gospel of An ancient collection of sayings of JESUS allegedly recorded by Thomas the Apostle. The BIBLE contains four GOSPELS (books about what Jesus said and did), but many more gospels have survived from antiquity. Two of them are said to have been written by an apostle of Jesus named Thomas. According to one of them, the Gospel of Thomas, Thomas was Jesus' twin brother. (In Aramaic, the language of Palestine in the time of Jesus, *Thomas* means "twin.")

THE INFANCY GOSPEL OF THOMAS

The "Infancy Gospel of Thomas" tells about Jesus as a boy, a topic about which the NEW TESTAMENT says very little. It ends with a story that the Gospel of Luke tells, too: how Jesus stayed behind in the temple at Jerusalem and worried his parents. But other stories present a Jesus who is quite different from what most Christians imagine. When playmates made fun of birds Jesus was making out of clay, he brought them to life. When a boy kicked open a dam and drained a pond that Jesus had made, Jesus cursed the boy, who then shriveled and died. At one point Jesus got into an argument with his teacher; he cursed the teacher, who seems to have died, too. Apparently, the people who preserved this gospel were most interested in Jesus' powers to work wonders, not in his virtue.

THE GOSPEL OF THOMAS

The other gospel supposedly written by Thomas is simply known as the Gospel of Thomas. From the point of view of scholars who study Jesus, it is much more important. In 1945, a complete manuscript of this gospel turned up in the desert of Egypt as part of the Nag Hammadi Codices. (Codices are ancient books; Nag Hammadi is the place in Egypt where they were found.)

The Gospel of Thomas contains 114 sayings of Jesus—or at least sayings attributed to Jesus. Some of them are familiar from the Bible. For example, in Thomas Jesus says, "Blessed are the poor, for theirs is the kingdom of heaven," and he tells a parable about a man who goes out to sow seed. Other sayings, however, are cryptic: "Lucky is the lion that the human will eat, so that the lion becomes human. And foul is the human that the lion will eat, and the lion still will become human" (verse 7; scholar's translation). The last saying in the gospel, which some scholars think was added later, even presents salvation as for men only. The apostle PETER questions MARY's right to be among the apostles, because she is a woman. Jesus assures him that he will first make Mary into a man, for women who become men can participate in the kingdom of God.

The Gospel of Thomas is important for several reasons. First, scholars long thought that ancient Christians had made collections of Jesus' sayings (see Q SOURCE). Now they have evidence for that idea. Second, some of the material in Thomas appears to be very old. For example, scholars had long expected that Jesus' parables were at first remembered only as parables and that the explanations in the Bible came later. Thomas contains one simple version of the parable of the sower and no explanation. In fact, some sayings in Thomas may record what Jesus said more accurately than the Bible does.

Perhaps Thomas is most important, however, because it tells something about the earliest Christians. After several centuries the Christian church eventually came to adopt certain books and ideas and to reject others. But Thomas shows, Christians originally had many ideas about who Jesus was, what he taught, and what it meant. In other words, there were originally a great variety of different Christianities. The Gospel of Thomas is sometimes said to be a book belonging to Christians known as Gnostics (see GNOSTICISM). According to one scholar, Elaine Pagels (b. 1943), its basic message is not that Jesus is God but that God dwells in all of us. As Jesus says in Thomas, "There is light within a person of light, and it shines on the whole world" (verse 24).

Further reading: *The Gospel of Thomas: The Hidden Sayings of Jesus,* Marvin Meyer, trans. (San Francisco: HarperSanFrancisco, 1992); Elaine Pagels, *Beyond Belief: The Secret Gospel of Thomas* (New York: Random House, 2003); Stephen J. Patterson and James M. Robinson, *The Fifth Gospel: The Gospel of Thomas Comes of Age,* Hans-Gebhard Bethge et al., trans. (Harrisburg, Pa.: Trinity Press International, 1998); *Thomas at the Crossroads: Essays on the Gospel of Thomas,* Risto Uro, ed. (Edinburgh: T & T Clark, 1998).

Thor   A god of ancient Germanic and Scandinavian mythology. Thor was associated with thunder, rain, and farming, and was a champion warrior. He personified the values of the warrior class: He was hospitable, a defender of the weak, and quick to respond to any slights to his honor. He rode a chariot drawn by goats through the sky, and wielded the hammer that was his symbol. Rough and redbearded, Thor was robust though not as profoundly wise as WOTAN (Odin); perhaps for this reason he was the most popular of gods among ordinary people who saw in him a divine figure more like themselves. His name is perpetuated in our day Thursday.

Tibetan religion   The religions traditionally practiced in the cultural expanse of Tibet. Besides the political territory known as Tibet today, this area includes territories to the east annexed by China in the 1950s along with adjacent regions in Bhutan; Mongolia, and the former Soviet Union.

Mahakala (Mgon po) is one of the protective deities of Bhutan and of the Drukpa Kagyupa school. *(Erich Lessing/Art Resource, N.Y.)*

BUDDHISM is the dominant Tibetan religion, but BON and popular practices are also important.

HISTORY

Little is known of Tibetan religion before the eight century C.E. Tradition calls this early religion Bon, but if that is right, the Bon religion has clearly changed between then and now.

At least from the sixth century C.E. the ancient Tibetan religion glorified kings as the sons of god. The first king was said to have descended from HEAVEN. Early kings were thought to have returned bodily to heaven. Later kings most definitely died. They received elaborate funerary RITUALS that included the SACRIFICE of horses, sheep, and yaks. The ancient Tibetans believed in sacred beings who dwelled in the sky. They also knew less kindly beings of the underworld. They thought the underworld consisted of water.

In the seventh century C.E. Tibet was unified for the first time. In the next century Tibetan kings imported Buddhism, presumably to provide their newly unified realm with a "world class" religion. In the battle for supremacy that followed, the Tantric Buddhism of India, known as VAJRAYANA, won out over the Chinese Ch'an tradition, known in Japan as Zen (*see* TANTRISM and ZEN BUDDHISM). An important event in the struggle was the council held in Lhasa 792–794 C.E. (*see* COUNCILS, BUDDHIST). Tibet became the leading center of Vajrayana Buddhism.

In the middle of the ninth century the Tibetan monarchy collapsed. Tibetan Buddhism collapsed along with it. But within a hundred years a Buddhist revival began. Another hundred years later Bon was beginning to take the form that it has today. Perhaps because it was a minority religion, it developed teachings and practices that closely resemble Buddhism.

Tibetan Buddhism modeled itself on the Indian Buddhism of the time. That is, it developed large monastic institutions. Tibetan monks belonged to one of four schools: Kadampa, Kagyupa, Sakyapa, and Nyingmapa. Tibet also became a repository for a large number of Buddhist texts. The two groups of texts became known as Kanjur and Tenjur. The Kanjur (Word of the BUDDHA) contain canonical texts. The Tenjur ("Translation of Teachings") contain later commentaries and other works. Bon texts, too, were divided into these two groups.

During the 14th century, the important Gelukpa school of Buddhism arose as a reform movement within Kadampa. It is known as the "yellow hat school," because its members wear yellow hats, as distinct from the red hats of their early political rivals, the Karmapa (a sect of Kagyupa) and the black hats of Bon priests. Eventually the leader of the Gelukpa sect received the title DALAI LAMA.

In the mid-17th century, the fifth Dalai Lama acquired full political control of Tibet. He did so because his patron, a Mongol leader, defeated the patron of the rival Karmapa school in battle. The fifth Dalai Lama built Potala Palace in Lhasa. From there subsequent Dalai Lamas ruled Tibet until 1950. In that year, the Chinese took control of Tibet. In 1959 the Dalai Lama fled to exile in India.

From the 1950s to the 1970s, Tibetan monks and their institutions suffered tremendously at the hands of the Chinese government. The Chinese forced many monks to leave the order and destroyed their monasteries. From the 1960s on, Tibetan Buddhist centers have been active in North America and Europe. In the 1980s, rebuilding began in Tibet itself on a small scale.

BUDDHISM AND BON

Tibetan Buddhism and Bon share many characteristics. Both are centered on large monasteries. Both revere teachers who revealed the truths of KARMA, rebirth, enlightenment, and release—for Buddhists the Buddha, for Bon, Tonpa Shenrap. Both religions possess scriptures divided into two collections, Kanjur and Tenjur. Both also make heavy use of Tantric features such as MANDALAS and MANTRAS. Typical Tibetan paintings known as *thangkas* illustrate the use of mandalas. A common Buddhist thangka shows a circle divided into the various worlds into which one may be reborn. Clutching the circle on all sides is a hideous demon with long, fang-like teeth.

Tibetan religion also includes popular or "unnamed" practices. These are RITUALS that all laypeople as well as Buddhist and Bon monks observe. For example, it is common for Tibetans to write PRAYERS on the perimeters of wheels or on flags. When worshippers spin the wheels or the wind blows the flags, each revolution or movement is equivalent to saying the prayer. Tibetans also work to acquire merit—spiritual credit that will benefit them in future births. One important way to do so is for laypeople to give gifts to monks. This important act sustains the monastic institutions.

Another common Tibetan practice is PILGRIMAGE. Worshippers traditionally traveled to destinations such as Lhasa, the seat of the Dalai Lama, and Mount Kailasa, the most sacred Tibetan mountain. There they circumambulated the sacred places and objects, Buddhists in a clockwise direction, Bonpos counterclockwise.

In addition to worshipping Buddhist or Bon deities, Tibetans have preserved from pre-Buddhist days the idea that aquatic spirits live beneath the Earth. When human activity disturbs these spirits, they must be pacified. Tibetan legends tell of an earthly paradise in the snowy regions to the north, hidden by the mountains and known as Shambhala. They also tell of a mythical king named Geser. Tibetans locate him in the past, present, and future, all three. In the remote past, Tibetans say, Geser descended from heaven to Earth to restore order. In the present he protects his worshippers from danger and provides advice. Tibetan Buddhists say that he will come in the future to drive out enemies and institute a golden age.

SIGNIFICANCE

In earlier years, Europeans and North Americans found it difficult to travel to Tibet. As a result the region evoked images of magic, mystery, and a mythical paradise. During the 20th century, a more realistic image of Tibetan religion began to emerge. There are still aspects of Tibetan religion, however, that scholars know little about.

Further reading: Per Kværne, *The Bon Religion of Tibet: The Iconography of a Living Tradition* (London: Serindia Publications, 1995); Donald S. Lopez, ed., *Religions of Tibet in Practice* (Princeton, N.J.: Princeton University Press, 1997); John Powers, *Introduction to Tibetan Buddhism* (Ithaca, N.Y.: Snow Lion Publications, 1995).

Torah Hebrew meaning "teaching"; the most revered part of the Hebrew BIBLE. The first five books of the Hebrew Bible, traditionally said to have been written by MOSES, are known as the Torah. The first book, Genesis, tells the story of the creation of the world and the lives of ABRAHAM and his immediate descendants in Canaan. The last four tell of the freeing of the people of Israel from bondage in Egypt (*see* EXODUS) and

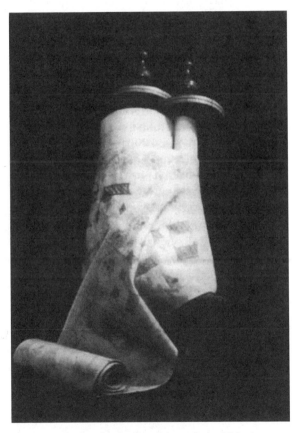

The Torah, the first five books of the Hebrew Bible, is used in the form of a scroll in synagogues and prayer services. *(Image Bank)*

their wanderings in the wilderness. Moses is the central figure of the last four books.

The Torah received its name because it contains instructions on how to live. The most famous instructions are the TEN COMMANDMENTS, which God gave to Moses on Mount Sinai. In all, the RABBIS identify 613 *mitzvot* or commandments in the Torah.

These commandments always require interpretation. For example, when exactly does the Sabbath begin? As a result, rabbinical tradition holds that there is an oral Torah, which was also received by Moses on Mount Sinai. It was codified in books known as the TALMUD.

The Torah that is used in WORSHIP is written by hand on scrolls of parchment. The precious scrolls are kept in the front of the SYNAGOGUE in a chest known as an ark. In more liturgical congregations, the Torah scrolls are removed and paraded through the congregation when they are to be read.

totemism

totemism   A religious complex that many once thought was the earliest form of religion. Late 19th-century anthropologists "identified" totemism. It was allegedly found among the peoples of Australia, Oceania, and North America. But they could never agree on what totemism was. Common characteristics included: a society organized into exogamous groups (people could not marry within the group), the notion that each group descended from a "totem" or animal ancestor, a prohibition on eating or using one's totem, and a ritual in which the group ate the totem.

Two scholars made the idea of totemism popular: William Robertson Smith, who saw it as the earliest form of SACRIFICE, and James George FRAZER. The sociologist Émile DURKHEIM and the psychologist Sigmund FREUD used the idea in developing their theories of religions. Later, the anthropologist Claude LÉVI-STRAUSS transformed totemism as he developed his own ideas about social classification.

American anthropologists took the lead in showing that totemism (but not totems) was a figment of the scholarly imagination. In 1912 Robert Lowie wrote: "any ethnologist who identifies . . . totemism [in America] with totemism in Melane-

sia, sinks to the level of a zoologist who [classifies] whales with fishes, and bats with birds."

Trappists   The popular name for the Order of Cistercians of the Strict Observance, a branch of the larger order of Cistercian MONKS AND NUNS in ROMAN CATHOLICISM. The Cistercians were founded at Citeaux, France, in 1098; the Trappist wing of the movement derives from reforms instituted by Armand-Jean Le Bouthillier de Rancé, who became abbot of a monastery at La Trappe, France, in 1664, hence the name *Trappist*. Cistercians are enclosed contemplatives who live austere lives devoted to ASCETICISM, PRAYER, and MEDITATION. The Trappists have practiced this way of life more rigorously than most other orders. Until changes were made in the late 1960s following the second VATICAN COUNCIL of the Roman Catholic Church, Trappists ordinarily lived in complete silence, communicating by a system of hand signs when necessary, and fasted strenuously (*see* FASTING), abstaining from meat, fish, and eggs. Now, although their lives are certainly simple and disciplined by ordinary standards, some speech and other forms of individual expression are allowed.

Traditionally, Trappist monasteries have been located in rural areas and have striven to be self-sustaining agricultural communities. Many today still specialize in producing and selling agricultural products. At the same time, study and writing have not been neglected. Undoubtedly the most famous modern Trappist was Thomas Merton (1915–68), a convert to Catholicism who entered the Trappist monastery of Our Lady of Gethsemane in Kentucky in 1941. His autobiography, *The Seven Storey Mountain* (1948), excited great interest in the Trappist life and caused the numbers of Trappists to grow dramatically in the 1950s. Merton wrote many other books, including *The Waters of Siloe* (1949), a history and description of the Trappist movement.

Trappists continue their life today. Many Trappist monasteries, noted for their hospitality and spiritual guidance, are popular places for pilgrimage and retreats. There are also Trappist nuns, called Trappistines.

Trent, Council of

A council of the Roman Catholic Church convened in the 16th century in reaction to the Protestant REFORMATION. In CHRISTIANITY a council is a meeting of bishops from all over the world to make decisions on teaching and practice. From 1545 to 1563 bishops of the Roman Catholic Church met in council at Trent, a town in northern Italy. The purpose was to respond to the threats posed by the Protestant Reformation. The Holy Roman Emperor also hoped that the council would reunite Catholics and Protestants. The most influential participants were Spanish and Italian.

Even before the Protestant Reformation Catholics like Erasmus (1466–1536) had criticized many of the practices of the Catholic Church. The bishops took steps to rectify these abuses.

At the same time, the bishops stood by Catholic tradition on the points to which Protestants had objected. Among other points, the council defined which books Catholics considered to be part of the BIBLE. It also insisted that the bread and wine of the EUCHARIST changed into JESUS' body and blood, that priests could not marry, that the church determined the correct interpretation of the Bible, and that a person needed to perform good works in order to be saved.

tricksters

Amusing, antiheroic heroes. Tricksters are comic figures in traditional stories. They are called tricksters because they often attempt to gain advantage by tricking others. As often as not the tricks backfire upon the tricksters themselves. People most often see tricksters in stories told by indigenous Americans and Africans.

Tricksters take a variety of forms. They are often animals. Common animal tricksters include Coyote and Raven among indigenous North Americans, Rabbit and Spider among indigenous Africans, and Fox among indigenous South Americans. Tricksters may also take human form. South American stories tell about tricksters who are twins.

Both human and animal tricksters may have exaggerated or incongruous features. In keeping with the light-hearted nature of trickster stories, these are often features that would appear indecent in a more serious context. For example, in some stories the North American Coyote has a male sexual organ so large that he must carry it in a backpack.

Tricksters are characterized by excess. They are extremely clever—so clever that they often outwit themselves and appear incredibly stupid. As already noted, their physical features may exceed what is generally considered proper. These features may be too large, of the wrong shape, or attached at the wrong place. Above all, tricksters violate the conventions of proper behavior. Sometimes they wear clothes properly reserved for the other sex or another species. Sometimes they make public, creative use of bodily substances—feces, flatulence—that are properly disposed of privately. Tricksters often mock the activities of more proper RITUAL specialists. They may change shape, eat to excess, engage in acts of incest, steal, boast—do just about anything that is ludicrous, outlandish, or offensive. In behaving in this way, tricksters are not EVIL; they are funny. Indeed, tricksters tales often contain messages about how one ought to act.

At times tricksters are involved in creating the world and human culture—precisely because they violate convention (see MYTH AND MYTHOLOGY). This is true of both Raven and Coyote in indigenous North American stories. According to one common story Raven manages to steal the sun from a chief who had been hiding it. He returns it to the world and restores light. In California stories Coyote often creates the world in conjunction with a creator whose behavior and demeanor are more socially acceptable and admirable, for example, Eagle or Wolf. He may provide a humorous counterpart to the activities of the other creator, as he does for example in an Earth-diver story once told by the Yokuts of California. Or he may be responsible for the creation of sickness and death.

Africans who came involuntarily to North America as slaves brought elements of their traditional culture with them. One element seems to have been trickster stories with a rabbit as a central character. That would appear to be the ultimate origin of stories Joel Chandler Harris published in the late 19th century. He attributed them to an old African-American storyteller he called "Uncle Remus."

trinity The Christian teaching of one GOD in three persons. The BIBLE presents JESUS as having a particularly close relationship with God, whom he called "Father." It also speaks of God's "spirit," and according to the GOSPEL of Matthew the risen Jesus instructed his followers to baptize "in the name of the Father and of the Son and of the Holy Spirit" (28.19). The word "trinity," however, never appears in the Bible.

Later, in the fourth and fifth centuries, Christians formulated with great precision the teaching of one God in three persons: Father, Son, and Holy Spirit. (In earlier English the Holy Spirit was called the Holy Ghost. Some now prefer the term Creator for the first person of the trinity.) They asserted that these three were distinct persons, equal in glory and majesty and alike in being uncreated, unlimited, eternal, and omnipotent. At the same time, these ancient Christians insisted that there was only one God, not three. They used the metaphors of "begetting" (fathering a child) and "proceeding" (coming out of) to describe how the three persons related to one another. The Son, they said, is "begotten" by the Father, while the Holy Spirit "proceeds" from the Father. Roman Catholics and Protestants, but not Eastern Orthodox Christians, add that the Spirit also proceeds from the Son.

In the 18th century, some people began to adopt a "unitarian" view of God. These Christians denied the teaching of the trinity and taught that God is one. Other Christians admit that the notion of a trinity strains logic, but they feel that the logical difficulties reflect the mystery of God.

U

UFO religions Religious movements based on messages believed to be communicated by visitors to Earth who have arrived on UFOs (unidentified flying objects, also called flying saucers). Such religions began with reports of "flying saucers" in 1947 and the following years. Before long, "contactees"—those claiming to have had personal contact with UFO visitors—came forward, delivering messages to Earth they said they had received from spacemen. Typically, the messages warned the people of Earth that they must stop atomic testing and warlike behavior; if they did so, the space people, far in advance of earth both morally and technologically, would help humans make Earth into a paradise and would welcome Earth into the fellowship of advanced worlds across the galaxy.

The first important contactee was George Adamski, who said he had met a man from Venus in 1952. But though Adamski was a popular lecturer and writer on this and other UFO encounters, only small and short-lived groups appeared around him. Another 1950s contactee, Daniel Fry, was more successful in forming a group. After a claimed UFO encounter at White Sands, New Mexico, including a half-hour ride from there to New York and back in 1954, Fry founded Understanding, Inc. His contacts professed to be the remnants of a past supercivilization on earth that had destroyed itself through war, and they did not want that disaster repeated. Understanding, Inc., comprised informal discussion "units" based on Fry's talks and writings. As many as 60 such groups were listed at the movement's heyday in the 1950s and 1960s, but by century's end Understanding, Inc., was in serious decline.

More substantial was the Aetherius Society, founded in London, England, in 1954, by George King, when a voice told him he was to become "the voice of the Interplanetary Parliament." The Aetherius Society has established churches in several countries to promulgate these messages from other worlds. It has been particularly interested in performing ritual "operations" intended, under higher guidance, to defend Earth against evil assailants.

Also founded in 1954 under UFO influence, the Unarius Society, headquartered near San Diego, emphasizes reincarnation and the impending return of the visitors. Colorful rituals have been developed to express its UFO-given teachings and to greet friends from outer space.

The Raelian movement, established in France in 1973, attracted attention around the end of the 20th century because of its emphasis on biotechnology and its claim to have achieved successful cloning. This was understandable, for a basic teaching of Raelianism is that human life on Earth was created by scientists from another planet who want to return to Earth to meet their creations. But whether they do so is up to Earth; the religion is intended to spread this news and help make preparations.

More ominous than these was the Heaven's Gate movement, known for its mass suicide on March 27, 1997. Its adherents apparently believed that a spaceship was coming in the wake of Comet Hale-Bopp to meet the faithful, and that by means of death they could attain the "next level" and be ready to enter a new world. Misguided religious belief can have tragic consequences.

The famous psychologist Carl Gustav JUNG (1875–1961) has said that, for believers, UFOs represent "technological angels." That is, they present modern, space-age equivalents to ancient religious motifs: angels, gods, saviors, departed spirits descending to Earth from above. For a few people, the UFOs widely reported in the second half of the 20th century have taken on this role.

Further reading: George Adamski and Desmond Leslie, *Flying Saucers Have Landed* (New York: British Book Centre, 1953); Douglas Curran, *In Advance of the Landing: Folk Concepts of Outer Space* (New York: Abbeville, 2001); Carl G. Jung, *Flying Saucers: A Modern Myth of Things Seen in the Sky* (New York: Signet, 1969); Susan Palmer, *Aliens Adored: Rael's UFO Religion* (New Brunswick, N.J.: Rutgers University Press, 2004); Christopher Partridge, ed., *UFO Religions* (New York: Routledge, 2003).

Unitarianism A liberal PROTESTANT movement in Europe, Britain, and the United States originally based on denial of the TRINITY. Unitarian means emphasizing just the unity or oneness of GOD. Characteristically, Unitarianism likewise rejects other traditional doctrines related to the trinity, such as the divinity of JESUS CHRIST and SALVATION exclusively through him, in favor of a view of Jesus as simply a great moral teacher and exemplary human being.

Modern Unitarianism began with radical REFORMATION anti-Trinitarian movements in 16th- and 17th-century Poland and Transylvania, but these were eventually suppressed. The Enlightenment spirit of the 18th century, stressing the importance of reason and ethical conduct in religion while discounting supernaturalism, produced a revival of Unitarianism. The distinguished minister and scientist Joseph Priestley (1733–1804) advocated a liberal religion he called Unitarian Christianity in both England and America. Many eminent Americans of that era, such as Benjamin Franklin and Thomas Jefferson, have been considered Unitarians in all but name.

Unitarian churches appeared in England and the United States in the late 18th and early 19th centuries, largely as an outgrowth of, and in reaction against, Calvinist (*see* CALVIN, John) PURITANISM. In North America, Unitarianism arose chiefly in New England, where the Puritan heritage was strong. The new outlook initially retained the Calvinist Creator-God and the Puritan's stress on the importance of a good life while rejecting Calvinism's gloomy notions of human depravity and of God's "irrational" election of only some to salvation. The great Boston preacher William Ellery Channing (1780–1842), often considered the theologian and father of American Unitarianism, proclaimed a rational Christianity based on the fatherhood of God, the essential goodness of humans despite SIN, and the example of Jesus as a perfect human being to be emulated. A number of once-Calvinist churches, largely in eastern Massachusetts, adopted this kind of theology. In 1825 they formed the American Unitarian Association as a separate denomination. Across the Atlantic, a British Unitarian Association was formed on the same day.

As the 19th century advanced, Unitarianism in America spread westward with the frontier. At the same time, in both Britain and the United States, Channing's rational, biblical Unitarianism was challenged by the more intuitive, mystical vision of the English romantics and of New England Transcendentalists like Ralph Waldo Emerson (1803–82). In the 20th and 21st centuries, some Unitarians no longer call themselves Christians or believers in God but proponents of religious HUMANISM. While not endorsing a deity or anything supernatural, they consider churches and worship of the Unitarian type to be good settings for the celebration of the joys of human life and the affirmation of the highest human ideals.

Unitarian churches are congregational; that is, each congregation has the authority to call its own minister and determine its own forms of worship and life. All advocate complete freedom of belief. In 1961 the American Unitarian Association joined with the Universalist (*see* UNIVERSALISM) church, another liberal body of New England background, to form the American Unitarian Universalist Association.

Further reading: John A. Buehrens, *Our Chosen Faith: An Introduction to Unitarian Universalism* (Boston: Beacon Press, 1989); Earl Morse Wilbur, *Our Unitarian Heritage: An Introduction to the History of the Unitarian Movement* (Boston: Beacon Press, 1956); Conrad Wright, ed., *A Stream of Light; A Sesquicentennial History of American Unitarianism* (Boston: Unitarian Universalist Association, 1975).

United Church of Christ   A mainline Protestant denomination in the United States. The United Church of Christ (UCC) came into existence 1957. It brought together two groups: the General Council of Congregational Christian Churches and the Evangelical and Reformed Church (*see* CONGREGATIONALISM *and* PRESBYTERIAN AND REFORMED CHURCHES). The history of these groups shows just how complicated Christian life in the United States has been. Their union into a single body defines the character of the UCC: "In essentials unity, in non-essentials diversity, in all things charity."

The roots of the General Council of Congregational Christian Churches extend back to the founding of New England. Both the Pilgrims who settled at Plymouth in 1620 and the Puritans who settled at Massachusetts Bay in 1630 were Congregationalists. They believed that individual congregations or local Christian groups should be free to make their own decisions. This belief contrasts with the hierarchical model of ROMAN CATHOLICISM, in which the Pope and the bishops oversee all Catholic parishes. For many years Congregational churches in North America remained separate, but in 1871 they formed the National Council of Congregational Churches. At the same time, several churches that had broken away from the Baptists, Methodists, and Presbyterians formed a second group known as the General Convention of the Christian Church (*see* BAPTIST CHURCHES *and* METHODISM). In 1931 the National Council and the General Convention merged to form the General Council.

The Evangelical and Reformed Church united two churches with different backgrounds. One was the Reformed Church in the United States. Immigrants from Germany and Switzerland had established it in Lancaster, Pennsylvania, in 1793. As Reformed Christians, they accepted a statement of faith known as the Heidelberg Confession. The second group was the Evangelical Synod of North America. Immigrants from Germany, including both Reformed and Lutheran (*see* LUTHERANISM) Christians, founded it in 1840 near St. Louis, Missouri. In addition to the Heidelberg Confession, they accepted important Lutheran documents: Luther's Small Catechism and the Augsburg Confession. In 1934 these two groups merged to form the Evangelical and Reformed Church.

The United Church of Christ brought all of these churches together into a single denomination. It continues the tradition of the Evangelical and Reformed Church by having a Statement of Faith, but it also continues the tradition of the Congregational Churches by not forcing individual congregations to follow that statement. In other words, the UCC does not insist on a unity created by excluding those who disagree with a particular vision of Christianity. Instead, it seeks unity by celebrating different Christian visions. It takes as its motto the words of Jesus: "That they may all be one."

The UCC is perhaps best known for its commitment to social justice. The traditions it inherited in 1957 include the movement to abolish slavery and a movement known as the social gospel to help people impoverished by industrialization. It has continued these traditions, among other ways, by emphasizing inclusiveness. Through Andrew Young (b. 1932), a UCC minister, it contributed a prominent voice to the civil rights movement. It ordained the first openly gay minister in the history of Christianity in 1972. In 1976 it became the first church body in the United States to have an African-American president. And in 1995 it issued a hymnal that referred to God as female as well as male. Because these steps characterize a very liberal Protestantism, it is important to recognize that the UCC also includes members who are conservative evangelicals.

In the early 21st century more than 6000 congregations within the United States belonged to the United Church of Christ. In addition, the UCC had official partnerships with churches in 70 countries around the world.

United States, religion in

As a religious society, the United States is in many ways unique in the world. While the nation is predominantly Christian (*see* CHRISTIANITY), virtually every religion in the world can be found in America, practiced by both immigrants and converts. Statistics at the beginning of the 21st century show the population of 280 million to be about 85 percent Christian—20 percent Roman Catholic (*see* ROMAN CATHOLICISM) and the remainder Protestant (*see* PROTESTANTISM), EASTERN ORTHODOX, LATTER-DAY SAINTS, and others. Of the total population 2 percent are Jewish (*see* JUDAISM), 1.5 percent Muslim (*see* ISLAM), 1 percent Buddhist (*see* BUDDHISM), and 0.4 percent Hindu (*see* HINDUISM); there are also members of NEW RELIGIONS, of other Asian religions, and of NATIVE AMERICAN RELIGIONS and people who are nonreligious.

Moreover, the Protestant part of the Christian population is divided into many DENOMINATIONS, including such well-known bodies as METHODISM, BAPTIST CHURCHES, EPISCOPALIANISM, PRESBYTERIAN AND REFORMED CHURCHES, LUTHERANISM, UNITED CHURCH OF CHRIST, and others. Indeed, the United States has been called a "denominational society." Unlike most Christian (and other) countries, where one church, often traditionally a state church, is likely to embrace the great majority of the population, like Lutheranism in Scandinavia or Roman Catholicism in Spain, in America the leading role is taken by a collection of churches.

Behind this reality lies the traditional and constitutional separation of church and state. In principle, no religion is favored over any other, and each must fend for itself without assistance outside its own membership. In the early days of the Republic, there were those, including Thomas Jefferson, who thought that without state support, religion might wither away. Instead, the opposite effect has occurred. There is far greater religious participation in the United States than in Europe, which has state church traditions, or in most other comparable developed countries.

This is partly because "pluralism," or a wide diversity of groups, all officially equal and without state support, has created a competitive, "free enterprise" situation in religion, so that many feel responsible for supporting their own church or temple over others. It must also be recalled that America is a nation of immigrants, and that the tradition of supporting churches and temples stems in large part from times when a familiar religious institution was a vital anchor, a spiritual and social center alike, for newcomers to a strange and often baffling land. For African Americans, churches were virtually the only institutions they truly controlled, so they took on important cultural significance.

Moreover, the United States is virtually the only immigrant society in which the majority of immigrants were at odds with the religious and political power structure of their native lands: Dissident Puritans (*see* PURITANISM), Baptists, and Methodists from England; Roman Catholics from Ireland and Poland, where they once lived under discriminatory non-Roman Catholic regimes; Jews escaping persecution in Russia, Germany, and elsewhere. All these and many others sought freedom to practice their religion. There is thus an inner tradition of independence, of honoring the right to dissent and freedom of religious thought, which, though sometimes threatened, persists throughout American life. In practice, even religions with very different ways of operating elsewhere have had to accept the "ground rules" of a pluralistic, equal, free enterprise religious society in America, and they have often found that they flourished better in it than ever before.

Because of its heritage and the nature of the groups that have made it up, American religion as a whole tends to be distinctively centered on inner, subjective experience as opposed to social and cultural bonding. The strong Evangelical and

Pentecostal (*see* Evangelical Christianity *and* Pentecostalism) churches make much of personal conversion and expression. So in their own ways do Spiritualism, New Thought, the New Age movement, and many other characteristic American movements that emphasize a subjective, mind-and-feeling basis for religion. All these features have kept many Americans highly committed to religion and, so long as personal freedom is maintained, its institutions.

Further reading: Catherine Albanese, *America: Religions and Religion* (Belmont, Calif.: Wadsworth, 1981); Harold Bloom, *The American Religion* (New York: Simon & Schuster, 1992); Andrew Greeley, *The Denominational Society* (Glenview, Ill.: Scott, Foresman, 1972).

universalism The belief that all souls, however sinful, will eventually be saved. Within Protestant Christianity (*see* Protestantism), this view had its first modern institutional expression in the 18th century. People affected by the liberal, rational attitudes of the Enlightenment looked again at traditional ideas and decided that eternal damnation to hell was incompatible with a loving, fatherly God. In North America, worship groups were formed by those who had left other churches, or been expelled from them, because of their universalist persuasions. In 1790 they formed the Universalist Church of America in Philadelphia under the leadership of Hosea Ballou (1771–1852). This denomination flourished in parts of the United States in the 19th century, largely in rural areas, but eventually declined. In 1961 the Universalist Church combined with the equally liberal American Unitarian Association (*see* Unitarianism) to form the Unitarian Universalist Association.

The term *universalism* is also used to refer to a general belief that there is validity in all religions, or that the universal religious impulse ought to be given priority over particular expressions of it in our understanding of religion. Ethically, it can mean regarding the needs of humanity as a whole, and obligation to all persons, to be more important than particular nations or communities.

Upanishads Sanskrit for "sit at the feet of"; the name given to more than a hundred separate texts that make up the last part of the Veda, the most sacred of Hindu writings. Their most important themes are two notions central to Hinduism, the self or Atman and the Brahman or universal reality.

The Upanishads are also known as the Vedanta, Sanskrit for "the end of the Veda." They preserve esoteric knowledge, originally shared with only selected groups of gifted students. Eventually these writings became the foundational texts for the most significant schools of orthodox Indian philosophy, the Vedanta schools.

The Upanishads may be seen as records of conversations and discussions about the most basic questions of existence. To judge from the texts themselves, these discussions were not limited to priests but included both nobles for whom the priests performed Rituals and prominent women. Given their origin, the texts cannot be expected to have a tight structure or a uniform perspective.

As Vedic literature, the Upanishads were occasioned by the performance of Vedic rituals. They stand in a tradition that sought to explain how Vedic Sacrifices could affect the world and thus benefit the sponsor of the sacrifice. But most Upanishads have very little concern for the actual rituals themselves. They concentrate instead on the topics of the self and the world, or rather, the realities that underlie the self and the world that we consciously perceive, atman and brahman, respectively.

The sages of the Upanishads use several different methods in exploring these topics. They operate with a rich and complex series of classifications and draw numerous correlations between the self and the world. They also construct series in which each item presumably requires or depends upon the next; the eventual goal is to work back to what all items require. Another technique is to develop special interpretations of sacred formulae and syllables. For example, the relatively brief *Mandukya Upanishad* contains reflections on the parts of the sacred syllable "om"—in Sanskrit, a + u + m. The first element is the state of being awake, the second the state of dreaming, and the third the state of deep, dreamless sleep. Beyond these three is a fourth state, pure atman or self, which is the word "om" in its entirety.

Because the Upanishads are compilations, they support many different points of view. Different schools of thought have tried to give a systematic presentation of Upanishadic teachings, but in doing so they have given opposite interpretations of even the very same verse. A good example is the famous saying, *tat tvam asi* (*Chandogya Upanishad* 6.8–16). For nondualists, such as the philosopher SANKARA, this saying has three words, *tat tvam asi*, "you are that." The reality that underlies the self that we experience (the atman) and the world that we experience (brahman) are the same. For dualists, however, this verse has only two words, *tattvam asi*, "Indeed, you are." On their reading, the verse asserts that a self or soul (atman) exists distinct and independent of universal reality (brahman). The most common view interprets the Upanishads from a nondualist perspective.

V

Vajrayana Buddhism   Literally, the "thunderbolt or diamond vehicle," an esoteric or partly secret school of BUDDHISM, forming the basis of Mongolian and TIBETAN RELIGION and the Shingon school of JAPANESE RELIGION, among other expressions. It arose in the sixth and seventh centuries C.E. within Indian Buddhism as the Buddhist form of TANTRISM. Fundamentally, Vajrayana emphasizes the presence of the Buddha-nature, that is, the pure principle realized by a BUDDHA at his enlightenment, in all beings here and now. Enlightenment for all is just a matter of recognizing that inner natural power and presence. This, according to Vajrayana, can be achieved by various ritual and experiential means, especially MANTRA, MUDRA, and visualization MEDITATION.

Vajrayana recognizes a great number of "cosmic" buddhas and BODHISATTVAS beyond the "historical" Buddha. They represent centers of consciousness within and beyond the individual that can be activated to help in the quest for enlightenment. These beings are usually arranged in mandalas, or significant patterns. In Vajrayana, the masculine buddha and bodhisattva figures are often portrayed embracing a female figure, who represents wisdom. The figures can also appear in peaceful or terrifying forms, indicating different aspects of their nature; however, both are ultimately good and the contemplation of both leads to ultimate enlightenment, though by different psychological dynamics.

A further characteristic of Vajrayana is the importance it places on the role of a GURU or spiritual guide, called a LAMA in Tibet. Typically the bond between a student and the guide is very close, and the student believes that obedience to that mentor is essential.

The guide may assign the student a particular figure from the mandala who represents his personal buddha-nature or ideal and transmits its secrets to him. The novice then, by reciting that figure's mantra, making its mudra, and visualizing its form as portrayed in sacred art, endeavors more and more to identify with it and recognize it as his own true nature. In some cases the figure's union with the female wisdom has been enacted by rituals of the Tantric type, but more often in Buddhist Vajrayana the union has been mental and meditative.

Undoubtedly the best-known classic work of Vajrayana Buddhism is the BARDO THODOL (Tibetan "Book of the Dead"). A guide to the after-death journey, it vividly exemplifies key aspects of Vajrayana. On that pilgrimage, the traveler encounters the buddhas of the central Vajrayana mandala, in both peaceful and terrifying aspects, and must recognize in them his own true nature. He will do so it he has practiced visualization and so realizes he has, as it were, put them there by his own mind. Vajrayana ultimately depends on an idealistic or "mind-only" philosophy, which says that human beings create their own world, and their own heaven and hell, out of their minds, through their desires, fears, angers, and moments of enlightenment; this is the final meaning of the peaceful and terrifying buddhas.

Vajrayana Buddhism, especially in its Tibetan form, has become increasingly popular in the United States and other Western countries. This popularity is partly due to the influence of the highly respected DALAI LAMA, its best-known exponent, but also to the subtle psychological insight it seems to many to employ.

Further reading: John Blofeld, *The Way of Power* (London: Allen & Unwin, 1970); Miranda Shaw, *Passionate Enlightenment: Women in Tantric Buddhism* (Princeton, N.J.: Princeton University Press, 1994); Robert A. Thurman, *The Tibetan Book of the Dead* (New York: Bantam, 1994).

Vatican Councils　Two councils of the Roman Catholic Church held in Vatican City about a hundred years apart. In CHRISTIANITY a council is a meeting of bishops from all over the world to make decisions on teaching and practice. Vatican City is a small, independent state that the Pope rules within the city of Rome. The Roman Catholic Church has held two councils in the Vatican. They contrast sharply.

The first Vatican Council (1869–70)—Vatican I—rejected much of the social, political, and philosophical thinking of modern Europe. Its most important single act was to establish the doctrine of papal infallibility. According to this doctrine, when the Pope makes religious pronouncements, he cannot be mistaken.

The second Vatican Council (1962–65)—Vatican II—took just the opposite approach. It emphasized the need for the Catholic Church to modernize. For example, Vatican II encouraged Catholics to say the Mass in the language that they used in everyday life. Until that time Catholics had said the Mass in Latin. Vatican II also encouraged congregations to participate in the Mass rather than simply observing it. Catholics around the world have widely adopted these recommendations.

Veda (or Vedas)　Sanskrit for "wisdom"; the collection of the most sacred texts in HINDUISM. The position of the Veda is unlike that of the BIBLE in JUDAISM and CHRISTIANITY or the QUR'AN in ISLAM. Although all Hindus respect the authority of the Vedas, other texts, such as the EPICS and PURANAS,

usually play a much larger role in their religious lives.

HISTORY

The Veda is known as *sruti,* "what is heard." Traditional Hindus believe that it contains the sounds that arose at the very moment of creation, heard, remembered, and repeated by the sages.

The Veda as we know it is an entire library of literature that rose in conjunction with the practice of public sacrifices in ancient India. Its oldest portions are written in a distinctive language, Vedic, which is an older relative of classical Sanskrit. On some interpretations the oldest portions of the Veda reveal evidence of migration and conquest. European and American scholarship has tended to associate these passages with the "Aryan invasion" of India around 1500 B.C.E. Some today dispute whether this invasion ever occurred and date the Veda much earlier.

The Vedic texts were preserved orally for centuries. Indeed, they were written down for the first time only within the last 500 years. Indian scholars developed very elaborate methods for preserving the texts unchanged. The reliability of these methods seems to have been confirmed by modern scholarship. For generations students memorized certain Vedic phrases that seemed to be meaningless. Historical linguists have now recovered their meanings by coming to understand the process of linguistic development. The Veda has been preserved by several different *sakhas* or schools of priests, each of which looks to a sage as its founder. As a result, there are different versions of the major texts.

CONTENTS

Leaving aside the many kinds of supplementary literature, we may say that there are four main strata or chronological layers of Vedic literature. The oldest texts are the *samhitas* (roughly 1500–1000 B.C.E.). They are collections of RITUAL formulae that were used by the priests in performing the public sacrifices. Because different priests had different ritual tasks, there are four major samhita collections. The oldest of all, the Rig-Veda(-samhita), is a collection of hymns in praise of the gods who were invited to attend the sacrifice. The Sama-veda is a collection of songs. The Yajur-veda is a collection of ritual formulae. The Atharva-veda is actually a collection of spells and chants used for domestic purposes, since its priests had nothing in particular to say at the public sacrifices. The later parts of this literature, especially the relatively late last book of the Rig-Veda, contain hymns that begin a tradition of profound speculation on the nature of the universe.

The next layer of Vedic literature consists of the Brahmanas (roughly 1000–800 B.C.E.). These are commentaries on each of the Vedic samhitas. They explain the meaning of the rituals, give instructions on how to perform them, and relate stories that were loosely inspired by sacrificial practices. In general, they explain the effect of the sacrifice as resulting from intimate connections between the SACRIFICE and the universe at large. The Aranyakas (roughly 800–600 B.C.E.) and the UPANISHADS (600 B.C.E.–200 C.E.) continue the tradition of commentary that the Brahmanas began. But especially in the Upanishads the sacrificial ritual has withdrawn into the background, and reflection concentrates on the nature of the self (ATMAN) and the world (BRAHMAN).

SIGNIFICANCE

The Veda is a splendid, full collection of ancient religious literature that includes moments of profound insight. All Hindus respect its authority, and Hindu priests still occasionally perform large Vedic sacrifices.

Vedanta A Sanskrit word meaning "the end of the Veda." Vedanta is the most important of the six "orthodox" philosophical schools in HINDUISM.

Actually, there are several different Vedantas. All of them rely upon the same sources: the UPANISHADS, the Vedantasutras, in which an ancient author named Badarayana systematized the teachings of the Upanishads, and the BHAGAVAD-GITA. Vedanta thinkers concentrate on two topics: the BRAHMAN, which is the reality that underlies the universe, and the ATMAN, which is the reality that underlies human beings.

The most widely known form of Vedanta is called Advaita, "nondualist." It was developed by the great Indian thinker SANKARA (eighth century C.E.). Advaita Vedanta maintains that there is ultimately no distinction between the brahman and the atman. The reality that underlies the universe is the reality that underlies the human person. On the other extreme is the Dvaita or "dualist" school of Madhva (13th century C.E.). Madhva argued that brahman and atman are two distinct realities. He also taught, unlike Sankara, that each person has a separate atman.

The other Vedanta schools occupy positions somewhere between these two extremes. The most important is the Visishtadvaita or "qualified nondualism" of Ramanuja (11th century C.E.). The name comes from Ramanuja's disagreement with Sankara. Sankara says that we can know brahman apart from any qualities or characteristics. But Ramanuja insists that we know brahman only as "qualified" or having characteristics. That is, we know brahman only as GOD.

Venus An ancient Roman GODDESS. The most ancient Romans did not WORSHIP Venus, but their "cousins," the Latins, did. Some scholars say she was originally a goddess of fertile fields. In the 200s B.C.E., the Romans identified Venus with the Greek goddess Aphrodite. In later mythology, she became the goddess of the sexual attractiveness and fertility of women. She often assumed this form in Renaissance art. At the same time, the Romans worshiped Venus as "Verticordia." In this personification, Venus "diverts the hearts" of young women from illicit sexual activity.

According to the Greek poet Homer, Aphrodite was the mother of the Trojan hero Aeneas. At Rome, the Julian family claimed that it descended from Aeneas and therefore from Venus. Julius Caesar built a temple to Venus as his ancestress. This Venus appears in Vergil's famous epic poem, the *Aeneid*.

Vietnamese religions   Religion in Vietnam is a complex mixture that includes many different traditions. This complexity is due in part to the country's history. China ruled Vietnam for more than a thousand years (111 B.C.E.–939 C.E.). Then, after centuries of independence, the French conquered the country and made it into a colony (1883–1939). A Communist government officially opposed to religion took control of Vietnam in 1974.

Most Vietnamese have been farmers living in villages. They have worshipped the protecting deity of their village. Each village has had a different protector. Some villages have worshipped heavenly gods, but others have worshipped thieves, prostitutes, or rebels—whatever being the inhabitants thought would assist and protect them. Villagers traditionally maintained an ALTAR for this deity in a public building where members of the village met to make decisions.

Besides worshipping village deities, the Vietnamese have known many other religious traditions. Vietnam is sometimes considered a Buddhist country, but its BUDDHISM is unusual. The Chinese brought Buddhism into northern Vietnam. As a result, the Buddhism that traditionally prevails there is MAHAYANA BUDDHISM in two forms: Thien Buddhism, related to Chinese Ch'an and Japanese ZEN BUDDHISM, and Tinh-do, the Vietnamese form of PURE LAND BUDDHISM. In the south, however, Buddhism came from Khmer people living in the Mekong delta. Their Buddhism was the rather different THERAVADA BUDDHISM, the Buddhism of Cambodia and other Southeast Asian countries.

The Chinese brought more than just Buddhism to Vietnam. They also brought CONFUCIANISM and TAOISM. During the Chinese period Confucianism, which emphasizes propriety and learning, formed the worldview of the ruling elite. After independence in 939, Confucianism suffered a temporary setback, but later Vietnamese rulers returned to it. The religion of the court also had some important protecting deities of its own: the dragon king and the turtle god.

Taoism was more a religion for ordinary people. In Vietnam as in China, it did not emphasize the ideas that most Americans associate with it,

the ideas of LAO-TZU and CHUANG-TZU. It emphasized such practices as communicating with spirits through seances, HEALING by religious means, laying out tombs and houses through the art of FENG SHUI, and telling the future by such means as using the Chinese book the I CHING.

All of these religions existed together. The educated elite favored Confucianism, the farmers favored village religion and Taoism, and people looked to Buddhism to deal with death and beyond. But all formed part of a loose association. The coming of ROMAN CATHOLICISM, favored by the French colonial rulers, changed that. Many Vietnamese converted to Roman Catholicism. Indeed, Roman Catholicism was more successful in Vietnam than anywhere else in East Asia, except the Philippines. Catholics were supposed to reject all other religions. Not everyone did so, but those who did made life in the villages difficult. They refused to cooperate in village worship. Some of their non-Catholic neighbors also saw them as disloyal.

Vietnam has also known several new religious movements. In the 19th century an apocalyptic movement known as Buu Son Ky Huong became popular in the south. It developed around the idea that the Buddha MAITREYA was going to appear soon and restore pure Buddhism. In 1939 a new movement, Hoa Hao, arose when a 20-year-old man claimed to be the reincarnation of the founder of Buu Son Ky Huong. In 1926, another new religious movement, Cao Dai, appeared after an experience that its founder had at a seance. Organized like the Catholic church—it even has a pope (*see* PAPACY)—Cao Dai recognizes not only Buddhist, Taoist, and Confucian deities but also JESUS, MUHAMMAD, and such unlikely figures as Pericles and Victor Hugo as gods. Both Hoa Hao and Cao Dai were active militarily in the war between North and South Vietnam that followed World War II.

Today, the situation of religion in Vietnam is uncertain. The government has taken some steps to ensure that religions will not threaten it. At the same time, Vietnamese who have left Vietnam have brought their religions with them. The most famous is probably the Buddhist Zen monk, Thich

Nhat Hanh (b. 1926). An advocate for global peace, he is widely popular with Buddhists of North American and European ancestry.

virgin birth   Birth from a woman who has never had sexual relations. It is especially important in CHRISTIANITY.

Virgin birth is a special form of a very common myth (*see* MYTH AND MYTHOLOGY): birth from mothers who have become pregnant by supernatural means. Indigenous Americans tell several virgin birth stories. For example, the Inuit tell how Raven was conceived when his virgin mother swallowed a feather. In the *Mahabharata*, a Hindu epic (*see* HINDUISM), a virgin named Kunti has a son, Karna, after Surya, the sun, impregnates her and then restores her virginity. Although the BUDDHA's mother, MAYA, was not technically a virgin, she is said to have had no sexual relations at the time when she became pregnant with the Buddha.

The virgin birth of JESUS is a central dogma (*see* DOGMA AND DOCTRINE) for most Christians. For them Jesus' mother, MARY, became pregnant through the agency of the Holy Spirit. This activity is not thought of as sexual. The NEW TESTAMENT sees the virgin birth of Jesus as fulfilling a prophecy of ISAIAH (Matthew 1.23), but only the Greek text of Isaiah refers to a virgin. The Hebrew text simply refers to a "young woman" (Isaiah 7.14).

Roman Catholics have deduced that Mary remained a virgin all of her life. Protestants generally reject this idea and say that Mary had children through ordinary means after Jesus was born. In the last two centuries more liberal Christians have taken the virgin birth not as a biological fact but as a metaphorical expression of the special character of Jesus.

Vishnu   One of the most important gods of HINDUISM. In Hinduism, BRAHMA, Vishnu, and SIVA are thought of as the gods of creation, preservation, and destruction, respectively. The BHAGAVAD-GITA captures Vishnu's character well. It states that whenever DHARMA wanes and EVIL waxes, Vishnu

Vishnu from Konarak, Orissa, created in the Ganga dynasty in the 13th century *(Scala/Art Resource, N.Y.)*

takes form on Earth to restore order. Vishnu's large number of worshippers are known as Vaishnavas.

The name Vishnu appears as early as in the VEDA. Worshippers also call upon Vishnu under several other names, such as Narayana, Vasudeva, and Hari. Some scholars think that these names probably refer to non-Vedic gods who were once independent. Later these gods were brought into the Vishnu cult. Vishnu is said to take form on Earth in several AVATARS, meaning "descents." The standard number of avatars is 10, but traditions vary on the identity of the 10. The two most prominent avatars are the well-known heroes RAMA and KRISHNA. These two have become objects of WORSHIP in their own right. Indeed, some worshippers of Krishna see him, not Vishnu, as the supreme GOD.

Vishnu's special abode is the HEAVEN known as Vaikuntha. He has several consorts or female counterparts, among whom the most important are Sri, LAKSHMI, and Bhu. Sri and Lakshmi are GODDESSES of prosperity and wealth. Their symbol is the LOTUS. Bhu is the Earth. Vishnu's vehicle or animal counterpart is Garuda, a mythical bird. His sacred plant is tulasi, a variety of basil. Worshippers offer its leaves to the god. A kind of black stone is also sacred to Vaishnavas. It is called Salagrama, from the name of the village where many specimens have been found.

There are several ways to portray Vishnu. One common image shows him standing. His skin is dark-blue. His four arms hold a conch, a discus, a mace, and a lotus, symbols of his power to protect and govern. In addition, Vishnu wears an age-old jewel known as Kaustubha. He also sports a twist of hair on his chest known as the *sri-vatsa*. It attests to the presence of Sri or Lakshmi.

Another common image of Vishnu shows him asleep on the cosmic serpent Sesha. According to mythology, Vishnu sleeps on Sesha during the time between the end of one universe and the beginning of the next. When he awakes, a lotus sprouts from his navel. On it sits the god Brahma, creator of the world.

There are several different subgroups of Vaishnavas. The most encompassing classification divides them into Bhagavatas and Pancaratrins. On some accounts, Bhagavatas stress the avatars of Vishnu, while Pancaratrins speak instead of four *vyuhas* or emanations from Vishnu. A group known as the Sri-Vaishnavas is especially prominent in South India. They take their name from the emphasis they place on Vishnu's consort Sri. The prominent VEDANTA philosopher Ramanuja

belonged to this sect. Other prominent Vedanta philosophers have also worshipped Vishnu, among them Madhva.

Vaishnavas have produced many masterpieces of Indian religious literature. Their writings include India's two major EPICS, the *Mahabharata* and the *Ramayana* (*see* RAMA, *RAMAYANA*), the philosophical poem known as the Bhagavad-Gita, several collections of myths, especially the *Bhagavata-PURANA*, and poems by important devotees such as Nammalvar, Kabir, Surdas, Tulsidas, Mirabai, and Tukaram.

visions   Visual images, generally of gods, SAINTS and other religious beings. Visions appear suddenly before the eyes and seem to have no natural explanation. Visions have been reported in virtually all ages and within all religious traditions. In the West, Roman Catholic visions of the Blessed Virgin MARY, as at Guadalupe, Lourdes, or Fatima, or of the ANGEL who showed himself to Joseph Smith, the founder of the LATTER-DAY SAINTS (Mormonism), are well known. Native Americans, especially those who lived on the Great Plains, deliberately sought visions as an important step in becoming an adult. Whatever their explanation in religion or in psychology, visions have had a profound impact on religious history. Like the visions of Mary, they have often served to confirm the FAITH of those within a tradition. But like Smith's vision, they have also served as impetus for the visionary to found a new religion (*see* SHAKERS). For many religious persons, seeing is believing.

Vivekananda (1863–1902)   *the chief disciple of the Indian saint, Ramakrishna Paramahamsa* Vivekananda founded the VEDANTA Society and the Ramakrishna Mission. He was also the first advocate of HINDUISM to have a major impact on North America and Europe.

Vivekananda taught the Advaita school of Vedanta combined with devotion and social concern. He gained wide attention in 1893 when he addressed the World's Parliament of Religions in Chicago. The address brought Vivekananda speaking engagements, much media attention, and many Western followers.

Vivekananda's influence was not limited to spreading Hinduism abroad. When he returned to India, he founded the Ramakrishna Mission. In doing so, he did much to advance the cause of social reform at home.

Voodoo A religion practiced by people of African descent in Haiti, and by people who have emigrated from Haiti. Haiti is a country that occupies the western third of the island of Hispaniola in the Caribbean. The Dominican Republic occupies the other two-thirds.

The name comes from *vodun*. This word means spirit in a language spoken in the nation of Benin, West Africa. Outsiders coined the name. They have also spread many rumors about the religion. The origin of the name does, however, indicate something important. Voodoo preserves and adapts many African religious beliefs and practices. Those who practice the religion say they are "serving the spirits."

Haiti was a French colony (established in 1697) that produced sugar. It was home to a large number of slaves originally from West Africa. Inspired by the French Revolution (1789), the

Ceremony Couzin Zaka (a Voodoo scene) by A. Pierre, Haiti, 20th century *(Manu Sassoonian/Art Resource, N.Y.)*

slaves revolted. In 1804 they established their own country, the first republic ever established by Africans. Records from this time are scarce. Nevertheless, it seems that Voodoo played a part in the slave revolt. The religion combines African spirit worship with aspects of ROMAN CATHOLICISM, the official religion of Haiti.

Those who practice Voodoo believe in a supreme GOD. They call that God *Bondye,* from the French phrase for "good God." But Voodoo practitioners consider Bondye distant and inaccessible. Their religious life centers instead on various spirits. These spirits are above human beings, but not so high as Bondye. Some spirits are ancestors; others are associated with natural phenomena. They are organized into "nations." One common system speaks of two nations of spirits: sweet spirits, which are kindly, and hot ones, which are powerful and energetic. People serve spirits that their mothers and fathers served. They also serve the spirits of the areas where they live.

At its simplest, one serves spirits by lighting candles, saying PRAYERS, and giving offerings. But Voodoo knows larger observances, too. The RITUALS at major festivals include the sacrifice of an animal (often a chicken), feasts, drumming, dancing, and singing. The goal of the drumming, dancing, and singing is to bring about spirit-possession. A spirit takes control of a human body, uses it as its "horse," and in that way communicates with human beings. Major spirits have their counterparts among the Catholic SAINTS, and Voodoo festivals often take place in conjunction with Catholic festivals. At times the Catholic Church has attempted to suppress Voodoo, because it found the mingling of African spirits and Christian saints offensive.

Although it is possible to serve the spirits on one's own, Voodoo also has its own religious specialists. A male priest is called a *houngan;* a female priest is called a *mambo.* They oversee festivals, practice divination, bless, and heal. Voodoo also has its anti-social side. Those who practice Voodoo call that side the "work of the left hand." It involves serving spirits that one has bought and using the bodies of the recently deceased for slave labor (zombies).

Toward the end of the 20th century economic deprivation and political instability forced many people to flee Haiti for North America. As a result, Voodoo spread to Miami, New York City, and other places in the United States.

W

Waldensians A group of Christians expelled from the Roman Catholic Church in the 12th century. The Waldensians originated from the teachings of a man named Peter Valdes or Waldo. In the 1170s Waldo began preaching at the town of Lyons in southern France. His preaching resembled that of Francis of Assisi in stressing simplicity and poverty (*see* Francis of Assisi and Franciscans).

Waldo and his followers got into trouble with the church authorities. That was because they used the Bible in the ordinary language of the people, rather than Latin, and preached even though they were not priests. The Waldensians were excommunicated in 1184. In 1211 80 of them were burned to death in Strasbourg, now in France. After these events, many Waldensians became highly critical of practices in the Catholic Church and of a few Catholic beliefs.

The Waldensians settled in the Alps at the border of France and Italy. During the time of the Reformation they adopted many Reformation beliefs. Beginning in the mid-1800s members of the community immigrated to South America, especially Uruguay. Some also immigrated to the United States. Most Waldensians in the United States have been accepted into the Presbyterian Church (*see* Presbyterian and Reformed churches).

war and religion War is organized, violent conflict between two opposed, unified groups. According to some people, religion has been responsible for more wars than any other social force. According to others, religion leads to peace and therefore is opposed to war.

Both of these views reflect important aspects of our experience. In the period after the Protestant Reformation, rival Christian groups fought some of the most devastating wars in European history. Today there are seemingly unresolvable conflicts between Protestants and Catholics in Northern Ireland, Muslims and Jews in the Middle East (note that not all Palestinians are Muslims), and Hindus and Muslims in South Asia. At the same time, these conflicts may seem to contradict what the religions involved really stand for, whereas people who oppose war, like Mohandas Gandhi, the Dalai Lama, and Martin Luther King Jr., seem to represent their religions better.

This last view is overly idealistic and unrealistic. All religions have produced advocates for peace, but they have also produced advocates for war. At the same time, it cannot be demonstrated that religion has caused more wars than any other social force. First of all, it is impossible to catalogue all of the wars that human beings have fought. It is also impossible to determine which wars religion is responsible for and which ones it is not. Most wars have many causes.

Three topics can help illuminate the complicated relations between religion and war: some ways in which religion has taken important symbols from war, some ways in which religion has legitimated or justified war, and some ways in which religion has limited, or tried to limit, war.

WAR IN RELIGIOUS SYMBOLISM

Religions have often taken symbols from warfare. In the 19th century Great Britain was the major military power in the world, so perhaps it is not surprising that British Christians used military symbols. Examples well known to most Protestants include the hymns "Onward, Christian Soldiers" and "Stand Up, Stand Up, for Jesus, Ye Soldiers of the Cross." An earlier example from the time of the Reformation is the famous hymn "A Mighty Fortress Is Our God." An important hymn from the American Civil War is the Battle Hymn of the Republic: "Mine eyes have seen the glory of the coming of the Lord." Although these hymns use military imagery, Christians who sing them may distinguish between spiritual battle and physical combat.

In JUDAISM, CHRISTIANITY, and ISLAM the tradition of using military symbolism reaches back into antiquity. Some scholars think that the GOD YHWH ("the Lord") was originally the war god of the twelve tribes of Israel. Ancient ZOROASTRIANISM saw the universe as a cosmic struggle between the forces of good, headed by Ahura Mazda, and the forces of evil. APOCALYPTIC LITERATURE took up the theme of cosmic warfare. It appears prominently, for example, in the NEW TESTAMENT book of REVELATION. Islam does not see God as engaged in combat with any rival, but among human beings on earth it does distinguish between "the house of Islam" and "the house of conflict," that is, non-Muslim regions.

Military symbols have played a prominent role in HINDUISM, too. Perhaps they are nowhere more prominent than in the BHAGAVAD-GITA. In this classic text the god KRISHNA urges the reluctant warrior Arjuna to fight. As a warrior, Arjuna should fulfill his DHARMA—do his duty—and let God worry about the consequences. It is possible to interpret this text in a nonviolent, spiritual manner, but not everyone has read it that way.

BUDDHISM celebrates the path discovered by the BUDDHA, who abandoned the possibility of world conquest to pursue NIRVANA or ultimate release. Nevertheless, militaristic styles have inspired some forms of Buddhist practice, such as ZEN BUDDHISM in Japan.

In the case of the Aztecs of ancient Mexico, religion seems to have done more than drawn symbols from warfare (*see* AZTEC RELIGION). Aztec SACRIFICES were part of a military complex, and vice versa. The Aztecs needed to sacrifice human victims to nurture the forces of the universe, and these victims were people whom they had captured in war.

RELIGIOUS LEGITIMATION FOR WAR

Religion is a powerful force for uniting a group of people. In fact, social science research has consistently shown that religion sharpens the boundaries between people who belong to a group and those who do not. In doing this, religion helps create conditions in which warfare can erupt.

Religion does more than help create conditions for warfare, however. Because warfare has such a prominent role in religious symbolism, religious people can see their own wars in terms of what the religion teaches. In this way, religion can legitimate or justify war. It makes war seem desirable and necessary. For example, it allows a warring party to imagine that it is participating in the cosmic struggle between God and evil.

One prominent Christian example is the CRUSADES. Pope Urban II (1042–1099; pope, 1088–1099) called the first Crusade in 1096 to "free" the "Holy Land"—the land of ancient Israel and Judah, where JESUS and his disciples lived—from Muslim rulers. This and other Crusades were terribly brutal. Christians justified them, however, by referring to the struggle of God against the forces of evil. They similarly justified the wars to reconquer Spain.

Muslims use the notion of JIHAD in much the same way. Technically, jihad refers to the struggle against evil. Muslims can and do take jihad to refer to the struggle of individual Muslims against temptation. Some organizations, however, like AL-QAEDA, HAMAS, and Islamic Jihad claim that armed acts of terrorism, as well as full-scale wars, are acts of jihad.

One scholar of religions, Mark Juergensmeyer (b. 1940), has suggested that the identification of human war with the grander warfare celebrated in a religion's symbols has several consequences. Among others, it promises religious rewards to those who fight. For example, Pope Urban promised the Crusaders that all their sins would be forgiven. It provides a social network that can be used to motivate people to support the war. It also turns enemies into demons. Doing that may allow people to commit atrocities that they would otherwise find unthinkable.

RELIGIOUS ATTEMPTS TO LIMIT WAR

Although religions can legitimate war, they may also act as a brake on war. Since the time of AUGUSTINE OF HIPPO, Christians have tried to identify the conditions that make war just or proper. They have commonly said that (1) the war must be fought for a just purpose; (2) all other alternatives must have been tried and have failed; (3) the warring party must carefully distinguish between people who are fighting (combatants) and those who are not, although inevitably some people will die as "collateral damage;" and (4) the amount of force used must be proportional to the threat, that is, it must not be excessive. Such a "just-war" theory may limit the kinds of wars in which people engage. Unfortunately, warring parties can also use just-war theory in their wartime propaganda.

Religions have also developed traditions of PACIFISM, that is, traditions that reject war and violence either in whole or in part. Religious pacifists in North America today include the so-called peace churches, namely, the MENNONITES, the AMISH, the Brethren, and the QUAKERS. They also include Buddhist organizations such as the Buddhist Peace Fellowship and the Zen Peacemaker Order, as well as people inspired by the teachings of Dr. Martin Luther KING Jr. on nonviolence.

Further reading: J. Harold Ellens, ed., *The Destructive Power of Religion: Violence in Judaism, Christianity, and Islam* (Westport, Conn.: Praeger, 2004); Mark Juergensmeyer, *Terror in the Mind of God*, 3d ed. (Berkeley: University of California Press, 2003); Oliver McTernan, *Violence in God's Name: Religion in an Age of Conflict* (Maryknoll, N.Y.: Orbis Books, 2003); John P. Reeder Jr., *Killing and Saving: Abortion, Hunger, and War* (University Park: Pennsylvania State University Press, 1996).

water and religion The religious symbolism and significance of water. Water is one of the richest and most prevalent of religious symbols. Like most symbols, it can have many meanings, not all consistent: Water can be chaos, destruction, life, purity, and rebirth.

Water first of all can represent the primordial chaos before the world completely took form: "In the beginning," the first chapter of Genesis tells us in the BIBLE, "the earth was without form and void . . . and the Spirit of GOD was moving over the face of the waters." In Japanese mythology the primal parents first came down upon an endless ocean, and out of it congealed the first island (*see* IZANAGI AND IZANAMI). Water is the raw material, or the formless context, out of which real creation commences. Returning to the waters, then, as in RITUAL bathing and BAPTISM, can be like a return to the beginning so that one can, as it were, start off life again fresh, as though newly made.

Because it is shapeless and spreads out to cover everything, water can also be destructive. In the Bible, the Great Beast in the book of REVELATION came out of the sea. When God wished to destroy what he had made, he sent a great flood. Many FLOOD STORIES can be found in world mythology (*see* MYTH AND MYTHOLOGY). But the flood is not truly the end. The stories also contain as account of SALVATION *out* of the waters: NOAH's Ark, for example, and the great Hindu sage MANU who, by means of power gained through PRAYER and fasting, was able to survive a universal flood and, in the form of a great fish, rescue other beings.

Thus life can come out of water, as it does in rain, a great gift of HEAVEN. Water is also in the womb and so is a symbol of birth. The Christian rite of baptism, consisting of washing or immersion with water, represents new birth by a symbolic return back to the womb and the primordial chaos in order that one may come out again, clean and renewed (*see* SYMBOLISM IN RELIGION). Indeed, water is widely spoken of as a source of immortality. The River of Life was said to water the Garden of Eden, and the QUR'AN speaks of the rivers of paradise. The prophet Jeremiah called GOD "the fountain of living waters," and the book of Revelation says that the new, heavenly JERUSALEM contains "the river of the water of life, bright as crystal." Ponce de Leon sought for the Fountain of Youth in Florida, and the quest for an elixir of life based on water has been a staple of MAGIC and ALCHEMY everywhere.

Water is also purifying, as the flood of Noah purified the world, and rites of purification involving water are very common. After ritual or other pollution, bathing is recommended as a sacred as well as practical act. SHINTO priests bathe before a sacred ceremony, and shrines are often located by the purifying waters of a rapid stream. In the Catholic mass, the priest ceremonially washes his hands.

Symbolically, water is often linked with the moon because of the tides, and with women because of their related cycles (see MOON AND RELIGION, THE). In psychology, it is also often taken to represent the unconscious out of which come dreams and intuitions. Water is thought to be as pervasive and mysterious as God, and the prophet Isaiah foresaw a time when the glory of God would cover the Earth, "as the waters cover the sea."

Weber, Max (1864–1920) *German scholar who helped found the area of study known as sociology* Weber's contributions to the study of religion were immense. His most famous book is *The Protestant Ethic and the Spirit of Capitalism.* There he argued that PROTESTANTISM and its values were responsible for the rise of capitalism. As capitalist structures had begun to arise before the Protestant REFORMATION, this particular thesis is probably wrong. Nevertheless, many still find Weber's ideas significant tools for studying religions.

One powerful set of ideas concerns the authority on which religions depend. Weber identified three different kinds of authority: charismatic (the personal authority of particularly striking individuals), traditional, and legal-rational. He also identified a typical historical progression from one type to another. Many religions, he suggested, begin with striking individuals, that is, they depend at first upon charismatic authority. Think of the BUDDHA

for BUDDHISM, JESUS for CHRISTIANITY, and MUHAMMAD for ISLAM. When these figures die, authority shifts. It may shift to people whom tradition recognizes as authoritative, for example, Jesus' APOSTLES. Or it may shift to certain legal-rational procedures for ordering the community, such as councils or meetings of bishops. Each type of shift to another authority is called "routinization."

Wesley, John (1703–1791) *a minister in the Church of England who founded Methodism* John Wesley was the son of a priest of the Church of England (see ANGLICANISM). He studied for the ministry and was himself ordained a priest in 1728. At the time he was also a fellow of Lincoln College, Oxford.

John's brother Charles had started a study group among Oxford students. Members of this group met regularly to study Christian devotional literature; they took communion frequently; and they fasted on Wednesdays and Fridays. In time they also took an interest in working among the poor. Other students labeled them "Methodists," because they went about their religion so methodically. The name was meant to be a putdown. John Wesley eventually became leader of the group.

In 1735 Wesley was appointed to minister to settlers in the colony of Georgia. He spent almost two years there, but his ministry was not effective. He discovered that the settlers had little interest in his own "high church Anglicanism." At the same time, Wesley became impressed by missionaries of the Moravian Brethren. The Brethren emphasized a personal experience of the certainty of salvation.

Back in England in 1738, Wesley had such an experience. He was listening to a reading from Martin LUTHER's writings, and he became convinced of Luther's fundamental teaching that people are justified by GRACE through FAITH apart from anything they might do. At the same time, his heart was touched by the feeling that JESUS had indeed died for him. Wesley traveled to the continent to confer with the head of the Brethren, Nikolaus von Zinzendorf. Then he started out on his own mission.

Wesley's religious outlook differed from the Calvinism that was dominant in England at the time (*see* CALVIN, John). Calvinists taught that GOD elected some people for SALVATION and others for damnation. Wesley taught that God's grace had the power to save all human beings. He also taught that it was possible to be certain that one was saved.

Wesley's religious practice also differed from common practice. Wesley refused to acknowledge the boundaries of the parishes within which ministers were supposed to preach. He traveled from place to place preaching. He often preached among industrial workers who had no religious home. Although Wesley hoped to win other ordained ministers for this type of ministry, the demand was greater than the supply, so he enlisted the help of lay preachers.

Wesley's teaching, his traveling, and his use of lay ministers aroused considerable opposition. It also won followers. In 1784 Wesley incorporated a Methodist Conference that was independent of the Church of England. It was to carry on his work after his death. Wesley also left behind many influential writings, including his *Sermons* and his *Journal*. He also wrote, translated, and published hymns.

Wesley never wanted to found a new church. He always wanted to renew the Church of England. Nevertheless, his innovations and his manner of working placed him squarely outside the established church. After his death, the Methodist Conference split from the Church of England. Methodism became one of the dominant forms of CHRISTIANITY in the United States after the Revolutionary War. It also gave rise to offshoots like the Holiness Churches (*see* PENTECOSTALISM and SALVATION ARMY).

wisdom literature   Sacred literature that emphasizes how to live daily life. Wisdom literature is a modern category, unlike TORAH and PROPHETS, which are ancient names for parts of the BIBLE. Scholars generally consider three books in the Hebrew scriptures (*see* SCRIPTURES, HEBREW) to be wisdom literature: Proverbs, JOB, and Ecclesiastes. Two apocryphal or deuterocanonical books (books found in the Greek Old Testament but not in the Hebrew scriptures; *see* APOCRYPHA) belong to this class, too: the Wisdom of Solomon and Ecclesiasticus, also known as the Wisdom of Jesus Son of Sirach, or simply Sirach for short. Scholars sometimes discuss PSALMS and Song of Songs along with wisdom literature, but these are more properly poetic books.

During the 19th and 20th centuries, scholars unearthed and deciphered massive amounts of literature from the ancient Near East. Among other writings, they found works similar to the biblical books of Proverbs, Job, and Ecclesiastes. Parts of the Bible's wisdom literature seem to be based on these other works. For example, a section in Proverbs called the "Words of the Wise" (22.17–24.34) reflects teachings of an Egyptian wise man named Amenemope.

It is difficult to say who wrote most of the wisdom books or when. The books talk about everyday life, so they make little reference to history. Some portions claim to derive from King SOLOMON (Proverbs 1.1; Wisdom of Solomon); one collection claims to have been gathered by scribes working for King Hezekiah (Proverbs 25.1). Sirach may be the exception to the rule. It presents itself as the work of a specific author: Jesus, son of Eleazar, son of Sirach, a biblical scholar who lived and taught in JERUSALEM. It also contains an introduction by the author's grandson, who lived in Egypt after 132 B.C.E. and translated the book into Greek.

Modern scholars suggest several sources for wisdom literature: royal courts, families, and schools (*see* Sirach 51.23). Most wisdom literature seems to have been written after the Babylonian exile (586–539 B.C.E.). The students also seem to have been male; wisdom is personified as female, and they are urged to pursue her.

Each wisdom book has its own character. Proverbs contains many brief sayings known as aphorisms. It takes a generally positive attitude toward life in the world: GOD rewards those who are prudent and work hard; those who are foolish and lazy suffer. The book personifies Wisdom as the first of God's creations. Indeed, it says she helped God create the universe (Proverbs 8). It also teaches that "the fear of YHWH ("the Lord") is the beginning of wisdom" (Proverbs 9.10).

Job is much less complacent about prosperity and suffering. SATAN, the accuser (not the devil), appears in God's heavenly court. He questions whether Job is simply praising God because he is rich and enjoying life. God and Satan decide to check this out. Job loses his wealth, his children and grandchildren, and his health. The book then relates speeches by Job, several of his friends, and eventually God. These speeches raise the classic problem of THEODICY; Why do good people suffer? The book does not answer this question. It simply shows that when Job is confronted with the majesty of God, he is struck speechless.

Ecclesiastes is even more pessimistic. It teaches that all is vanity, all must die. But this pessimism makes many passages in the book profound. Probably the most famous passage begins: "For everything there is a season, and time for every matter under heaven: a time to be born, and a time to die; a time to plant, and a time to pluck up what is planted . . ." (Ecclesiastes 3.1–2).

The Wisdom of Solomon seems to present Jewish perspectives on Greek ideas. For example, some Greeks believed that the SOUL is immortal. The Wisdom of Solomon talks about immortality, too, but it links it to righteousness and unrighteousness. "The righteous live forever, and their reward is with the Lord" (5.15). That is true even of righteous people who die young. The unrighteous, however, those who pursue riches and fine living and oppress the poor, widows, orphans, and the old, will find that their good things simply vanish. They have made a covenant with death (1.16).

Sirach resembles Proverbs, although it is less aphoristic. The section headings in the Greek text give an indication of its content: "Self-control" (18.30), "Discipline of the Tongue" (23.7), "The Praise of Wisdom" (24.1), "Concerning Children" (30.1), "Concerning Foods" (30.18), "Hymn in Honor of Our Ancestors" (44.1), and "Prayer of Jesus Son of Sirach" (51.1). Not all of the advice translates well today. The section on children begins: "He who loves his son will whip him often, so that he may rejoice at the way he turns out." Not all of Sirach is so brutal: "The whole of wisdom is fear of the Lord, and in all wisdom there is the fulfillment of the law" (19.20).

Psalms is a collection of 150 hymns. According to tradition, King DAVID wrote them, but their true authorship is obscure. Some relate more specifically to wisdom themes than others. A good example of one that does is the first Psalm: "Happy are those . . . [whose] delight is in the Torah of YHWH, and on his Torah they meditate day and night."

Song of Songs is sometimes known as Canticles or Song of Solomon. It got the last name because tradition suggested that Solomon wrote it, as he allegedly wrote Proverbs, Ecclesiastes, and the Wisdom of Solomon. Song of Songs is a collection of love poetry. In much of it, one lover celebrates the beauty of the other. Jews have sometimes said that the book really celebrates YHWH's love for his people, Christians that it celebrates the relationship of CHRIST and his church.

Images and concepts in the wisdom books influenced JUDAISM and CHRISTIANITY. The books were also used in worship. For example, Song of Songs is used in the celebration of PASSOVER, Ecclesiastes in the celebration of Sukkot or "Tabernacles" (see JEWISH FESTIVALS). Wisdom literature also influenced GNOSTICISM. For Gnostics Sophia (Greek for "wisdom") was no longer a creature who helped the creator god. She was his superior. She also provided the divine insight that would undo the mess that the creator had made of the world.

Further reading: Dianne Bergant, *Israel's Wisdom Literature: A Liberation-Critical Reading* (Minneapolis: Fortress Press, 1997); H. Wayne Ballard Jr. and W. Dennis Tucker Jr., eds., *An Introduction to Wisdom Literature and the Psalms,* (Macon, Ga.: Mercer University Press, 2000); Roland E. Murphy, *Wisdom Literature and Psalms* (Nashville: Abingdon, 1983).

witchcraft The use of MAGIC or sorcery by persons or groups outside the mainstream of society. But the term "witchcraft," like "witch," has been used in different ways in different times and places. Witchcraft has often been regarded with suspicion by the social mainstream. But in modern times, it has also referred to a religious movement. Here the topic will be discussed in three parts: witchcraft in primal and ancient religion (*see* PRIMAL RELIGION), alleged witchcraft and the witch persecutions in medieval and early modern Europe, and witchcraft today.

In early, ancient and peasant societies everywhere, there is much use of simple magic and sorcery, such as charms and humble offerings to produce rain or fertility, assure successful childbirth,

or ward off enemies. Such practices are like the well-known burning of candles of different auspicious colors by some people today, or the use of "love potions." Performed independently of the official religion by ordinary people or by local specialists like a village "wise woman," these practices are sometimes called witchcraft. In primal societies, disasters also are often blamed on the work of malevolent witches, known or unknown, and their EVIL spells can be countered by other specialists, sometimes called witch doctors.

In Europe, with the rise of CHRISTIANITY, such practices continued, but at a fairly low level. Often they were regarded tolerantly by the Christian church. But around the 15th century, in an atmosphere of anxiety engendered by the rise of

This German woodcut, dated 1533, shows the execution of an arsonist witch by burning at the stake. *(Foto Marburg/ Art Resource, N.Y.)*

modernity, and, in the 16th century, by the REFOR-MATION, a wave of hysteria about witchcraft swept over Europe, lasting till about 1700. In both Catholic and Protestant countries, persons—almost all women—were accused of witchcraft, unjustly tried, and killed, most commonly by burning (*see* JOAN OF ARC). Children were encouraged to inform against parents, husbands against wives, relatives and neighbors against one another. Witnesses were paid to testify, and professional witchfinders received fees for each suspect they brought in. Then the alleged witches' confessions were obtained through horrible tortures. Witches were accused of making pacts with the devil, flying through the air on broomsticks, gathering in diabolic covens, having animal "familiars," and the like. Almost all of this, though it lives on in the popular imagination about witches, was undoubtedly a figment of the witchfinders' imaginations. The whole dreadful witchhunting mania, which may have numbered a million or more victims, was certainly the result of serious social sickness and mass delirium. One of the last major outbreaks was the famous witch-trials in Salem, Massachusetts, in 1692. Nineteen persons were executed after a group of young girls became hysterical while playing at magic, and the suggestion was made that they had been bewitched.

Turning to modern witchcraft, we may note that belief in traditional witchcraft in the sense of ancient magic remains alive in many parts of the world, including India, Africa, and Latin America. Occasionally there are sill accusations of evil witchcraft, associated with Satanism or devil WOR-SHIP, even in the United States.

At the same time, a revival of Paganism has grown remarkably as a new religious movement in the United States, Europe, and elsewhere in the last half of the 20th century (*see* PAGANISM, MODERN). One important wing of this movement is called Witchcraft or, in a term many of its adherents prefer, "Wicca." It is a benign movement having nothing to do with Satanism or anything evil. It is centered on belief in the spiritual importance of nature, the equality of men and women, and the power of magic (often interpreted as good thoughts). It has colorful RITUALS for the seasons and for getting in touch with nature's gods and GODDESSES. being closely aligned with the ecological and feminist movements, Wicca has found a place in the spiritual world of the early 21st century, and many of its adherents identify with the persecuted witches of three or four centuries ago.

worship Religious activities directed toward or done in the service of a superior being, such as GOD. Some have defined worship as the human response to an encounter with the "holy" or "sacred."

Worship is an idea and practice that is limited in its application. To start with, some religious acts are not directed toward a superior being, so they are not forms of worship. A good example is Buddhist MEDITATION. It simply seeks to cultivate an awareness of the way things are (*see* ZAZEN). Furthermore, the term "worship" seems to imply a certain serious, concentrated attitude of mind. But people often perform religious actions as a matter of rote. For example, a baseball or softball player may make the sign of the cross when she or he comes up to bat. It would be difficult to talk meaningfully about that action as worship, but it is religious.

As a result, scholars of religion often avoid the term worship. They prefer to speak of RITUALS instead. But for many who practice religions, worship is the best word to describe the most intense and intentional form of religious action.

WHO WORSHIPS?

People worship privately as individuals. They also worship in a variety of communities. In North America, Jews and Christians form special congregations that meet on a weekly basis. In many times and places, worship has been largely a family activity, for example, in ancient Greece and Rome and in HINDUISM today. In some countries, religious observance has been a matter of the state; these are countries with established or official religions. For Muslims, the worshipping community is the

House of ISLAM, which goes beyond any political boundaries.

Most worship communities have leaders: RABBIS, cantors, priests, ministers, deacons, IMAMS—in family worship, fathers or mothers. Many worship communities also have subcommunities that perform special tasks. Many congregations in North America have choirs. The structure of worship communities may also reflect gender and racial exclusiveness, sometimes despite an egalitarianism in the general society. In Orthodox JUDAISM, a worshipping community must have at least 10 men (males). In Catholic and Orthodox CHRISTIANITY, only men may be priests. Hindus do not allow non-Hindus to enter certain temples.

WHAT IS WORSHIPPED?

Religions often reserve the term "worship" for activities done in relation to the supreme being or beings. Other worshipful activities may be called "veneration."

Some Christians venerate MARY, the mother of JESUS. Buddhists often venerate accomplished beings known as BODHISATTVAS. Christians, Muslims, and Jains, among others, venerate SAINTS. Especially Christians and Buddhists venerate RELICS. Ancient Romans were required to venerate the emperor. These acts may resemble worship strictly speaking, but they often differ from it in subtle ways.

Many religions also identify certain forms of worship as improper. In Judaism and Christianity, the first commandment forbids the worship of any god but YHWH ("the Lord"). The second commandment forbids the use of cult images. In Islam, *shirk* is a cardinal SIN. It means giving any created object the respect and adoration that only the creator deserves.

WHERE DO PEOPLE WORSHIP?

Some forms of individual worship can take place anywhere. But human beings often set aside special areas for the performance of rituals, including worship. Some speculate that the European caves painted in prehistory were areas where ancient initiation rites took place (*see* INITIATION, RELIGIOUS).

Roughly in 6000 B.C.E. a community at Catal Huyuk in modern Turkey apparently dedicated many rooms to the worship of a GODDESS. Sacrificial worship often takes place at an ALTAR. Ancient Greeks, like other peoples, performed some acts of worship in sacred groves or woods. Among the Mayans and Aztecs as among ancient Babylonians some important altars sat on top of tall pyramids. Much worship has taken place at temples—places where a divinity is present, often in the form of a statue. Congregations often meet in special buildings for worship, such as SYNAGOGUES, churches, and MOSQUES.

WHEN DO PEOPLE WORSHIP?

Some worship activities take place every day. Muslims formally pray five times a day in the direction of MECCA (*see* SALAT). Some traditional Hindu householders perform rituals at the "twilights," dawn and dusk. Some Christian MONKS AND NUNS perform a series of daily services: vigils, matins, prime, tierce, sext, nones, vespers, and compline.

In addition, many religions have calendars of special festivals. The Islamic calendar is strictly lunar. As a result, Islamic observances, such as the Ramadan fast, move throughout the year. The Jewish calendar is partly lunar, partly solar. As a result, PASSOVER and Shavuot occur in the spring, Rosh ha-Shanah and the DAY OF ATONEMENT in the fall. Other festivals, such as CHRISTMAS, occur on specific dates in a solar year. Finally, some festivals take place only after several years. For example, the Aztecs performed the New Fire Ceremony after every 52 years.

IN WHAT WAYS DO PEOPLE WORSHIP?

There is practically no limit to the actions that worship can include. Worshippers speak to religious beings in PRAYER. They sing to them in songs and hymns. They offer them gifts. They kill animals and sometimes people in SACRIFICE. Religions that use images often treat the images as honored guests: They wake them, bathe them, clothe them, perfume them, feed them, entertain them, and put them to bed. Some worshippers eat and drink; consider the EUCHARIST in Christianity. Some worshippers preach and teach (*see* PREACHING). Ordinary life may also be seen as worship. In Judaism study of the TORAH is a profound act of worship. Many Christians see a life lived in service to others as a life of worship.

SIGNIFICANCE

A worshipper may give different reasons for worship than someone observing it from the outside. Worshippers may say that they worship because they will get some reward in return or because it refreshes them. They may worship to give visible expression to their inner feelings. They may also say that they worship to give God, for example, the honor and praise that God deserves. Others may worship simply because they feel it is the right thing to do.

Outside observers may note how worship helps create and maintain the identity and solidarity of a group. They may talk about how worship contributes to psychological integration and well-being. They may suggest that worship reinforces basic beliefs and values. They may also see worship doing less admirable things, for example, reinforcing the superior status of a specific class, gender, or race.

The word "worship" excludes many important religious activities. But for religious people who interact with superhuman beings, worship may well be the most important activity in human life.

Further reading: Thomas F. Best and Dagmar Heller, ed., *Worship Today: Understanding, Practice, Ecumenical Implications* (Geneva, Switzerland: WCC Publications, 2004); Stephen P. Huyler, *Meeting God: Elements of Hindu Devotion* (New Haven, Conn.: Yale University Press, 1999); Susan J. White, *A History of Women in Christian Worship* (Cleveland, Ohio: Pilgrim Press, 2003); Terry W. York, *America's Worship Wars* (Peabody, Mass.: Hendrickson Publishers, 2003).

Wotan The father and chief of the gods in Germanic and Scandinavian mythology. Also called Odin, Wotan represented fate. He presided over Valhalla, the home of the gods, and rode through the sky gathering the souls of the dead. In many ways he was like a great shaman (*see* SHAMANISM), magician, and poet. He was worshipped with SACRIFICES. The name of the day Wednesday is derived from *Wotan*.

Y

Yama The god of death in Hindu mythology. In the VEDA Yama is known as the first person who died. In the PURANAS his mythology takes on full form. There Yama rules the underworld from his palace Subhavati. He is also the judge of the dead.

Artwork often shows Yama holding a noose and a mace. Myths say that he has two four-eyed dogs, Syama and Sabala. The water buffalo is his vehicle; the crow and pigeon are his messengers. Yama is also associated with the south, the direction of the dead.

yantra A sacred diagram in India. Hindus and Buddhists who practice TANTRISM use yantras as objects of MEDITATION.

In Tantrism yantras provide emblems of sakti, the divine, creative energy. They are two dimensional diagrams, made up of lines, primary shapes, and arcs organized around a central point. Yantras are associated with MANTRAS, sets of powerful sounds. Large, elaborate yantras are also known as MANDALAS.

Perhaps the most famous yantra is the Sriyantra. It consists of nine triangles of gradated size, arrayed around a central point. Five triangles point downward; they symbolize the feminine power of sakti. Four triangles point upward; they symbolize the masculine power of SIVA. The triangles are surrounded by concentric LOTUS petals, which are surrounded in turn by concentric circles. The whole complex is set within a more or less square border. It symbolizes four walls with gates at the cardinal directions.

yin/yang theory A specific philosophical school in China, but more broadly a manner of conceiving of the world in terms of the harmonious interaction of complementary opposites. This article discusses the latter.

Prehistoric Chinese used various techniques of divination that may have influenced the development of the yin/yang theory. In one technique, hot iron rods were applied to the shoulder blades of deer and tortoise shells. The cracks that resulted revealed how the forces of nature were disposed at the time of the test. In another technique, diviners would cast sticks and notice which sticks broke and which did not. Originally, though, yin and

© Infobase Publishing

Yin/Yang symbol

481

yang referred to the weather. Yin was a cloud-covered sky; yang was a clear, sunlit sky.

According to the developed yin/yang theory, the world results from the harmonious interaction of opposites. Neither opposite can exist by itself; for example, the word "black" would be meaningless without "white." Moreover, neither opposite is ever encountered in pure form; and the opposites are constantly intermingling. A well-ordered world, as opposed to chaos, results when yin and yang intermingle harmoniously. An example would be the relationship between black and white in the words on this page.

It is possible to see the opposition between yin and yang in a wide variety of contrasts: black and white, blue and orange, cold and hot, moist and dry, valley and mountain, earth and sky, female and male, even and odd, passive and active, receptive and aggressive, soft and rigid. It would be wrong, however, to view good and EVIL as a similar opposition; both yin and yang are good. Evil results from a disruption in their harmony.

As a way of ordering the world, the yin/yang theory is supplemented by the theory of the five elements (*wu hsing*): wood, fire, earth, metal, and water. For example, in classifying the cardinal directions east is associated with wood, south with fire, west with metal, north with water, and the center with earth. The five elements relate to each other in several ways. For example, they give rise to each other (for example, wood produces fire); they also overcome each other (for example, water overcomes fire).

A common way to represent the yin/yang theory is as a circle divided in half by an S-shaped line, one side dark, the other light, but with a disk of the opposite color in the thickest part of each half. The diagram represents the continuous interpenetration of yin and yang and their perpetual admixture. Yin and yang can also be seen underlying many Chinese cultural products, such as paintings and drawings, gardens, and literary works.

China's two major, indigenous religious traditions, CONFUCIANISM and TAOISM, also reflect the interaction of yin and yang. Confucianism is a "rigid" and active tradition—yang. It emphasizes the careful observance of the rules of propriety within the bounds of social relationship. Taoism is a softer, more passive tradition—yin. It emphasizes lack of deliberate intention and harmony with natural processes. Thus, the central Taoist text, the Tao te ching, advises: "Know the male, but keep to the way of the female" (1.28).

yoga Literally, Sanskrit for yoke; by extension, any of a number of spiritual disciplines and religious paths in India, especially the "royal yoga" of Patanjali. In its broadest usage, the term "yoga" becomes virtually synonymous with religion. For example, the BHAGAVAD-GITA uses yoga for several spiritual paths that are often said to define the options available to Hindus. It identifies jñana-yoga, the yoga or path of insight, KARMA-yoga, the yoga or path of RITUAL and ethical action, and BHAKTI-yoga, the yoga or path of devoting oneself and one's actions to a god.

Usually, however, yoga refers to any number of different psychophysical exercises designed to achieve some ultimate end, such as liberation from continuous rebirth. Hatha-yoga is the yoga most commonly practiced outside of India. Its focus is on maintaining various physical postures, combined with breath control. Its goal is physical health and mental relaxation.

Tantric yoga is a set of meditative practices characterized by a distinct set of ideas (*see* TANTRISM). Practitioners of Tantric yoga conceive of the energy of the universe as a serpent resting at the base of the spine (KUNDALINI). Through their practices, the adept practitioners seek to awaken this energy and steer it through the six CAKRAS or regions through which the spine passes. Ultimately the aroused energy enters the cakra of the skull, and a blissful enlightenment ensues.

Yoga was systematized as a philosophical school in the Yoga-sutras of Patanjali (probably second century C.E.). The practices with which Patanjali worked may be age-old. Engravings on seals found at sites of the Indus Valley civilization (fl. 2500–1500 B.C.E.) seem to show a figure sitting in a meditative posture (*see* INDUS VALLEY RELIGION).

In any case, Patanjali gave the royal yoga its ultimate form as a path with eight "limbs" or stages.

The basic idea behind the royal yoga is concentration. The practitioner concentrates successively on different elements of the personality, calming them until they are at a state in which they require no attention. The process of concentration moves progressively inward, until the practitioner reaches the very core of his or her being.

An extended metaphor helps make sense of applying the term "yoking" to these practices. The self is envisioned as a passenger in a chariot running out of control. The driver of the chariot, the intellect or ego (there is no good translation) takes hold of the reins of the mind and uses it to bring the chariot to a halt. Then the self may step off and be in isolated purity.

The first two limbs of Patanjali's yoga—*yama* and *niyama*—deal with what is most external to the self: the way in which it acts in the world. These "restraints" and "observances"—like not injuring, not stealing, studying the SCRIPTURES, and turning over the fruits of one's actions to GOD—prepare the practitioner for the steps to come. It is said that they must not be observed simply in waking consciousness but in every form of consciousness that a person experiences, dreams included.

The next two limbs deal with the body: posture (*asana*) and breath-control (*pranayama*). The stage of posture does not aim at contorting the body into marvelous shapes. Rather, a practitioner should adopt a posture that is stable and that can be maintained for a long period of time with a minimum of discomfort. In traditional India, where European-style chairs were not used, the well-known LOTUS position met those goals perfectly.

As concerns the act of breathing, Yoga theory identifies at least three phases: inhaling, retaining the breath, and exhaling. The second phase is extremely important, because Indian tradition thought that at this point the breath circulated throughout the body and animated it. The goal of breath-control is twofold: first, to regulate the breathing so that it is rhythmical, that is, so that the three phases of breathing each take the same amount of time; second, to prolong these equal phases, so that the retained breath can circulate as much as possible.

When one's posture is stable and one's breathing is rhythmic, one's sense of awareness of one's surroundings is heightened. The next stage addresses these heightened senses. Using the metaphor of a turtle, Patanjali suggests that we must withdraw our senses from the world. This involves more than simply closing one's eyes. Rather, one must learn how to turn one's senses on and off, so that, for example, one can turn off one's sight even though one's eyes are open.

The goal of the sixth stage is to dissolve the mind. The practitioner learns to concentrate the mind solely on a single point. He or she meditates on a MANTRA (saying) or YANTRA (diagram) that has been given by one's teacher, analyzing its constituent parts and the role of the mind in conceiving the object.

The seventh stage moves beyond the analytical mind to a continuous awareness of the object of MEDITATION as a whole. At this stage practitioners are said to receive special powers. An example is the ability to project a lotus, have it levitate in the air, and to sit upon it. Practitioners are urged to try these powers to test the quality of their meditation.

Finally, practitioners enter a state in which consciousness of a distinction between subject and object disappears. What is ultimately left is pure self (ATMAN), without distinctions. This state, known as *samadhi*, is the goal of yoga practice. It is equivalent to ultimate release (*moksha*).

The state of samadhi does not at first persist indefinitely. Those who have attained samadhi but remain in the body are known as *jivanmukta*, liberated but still living (*see* JIVANMUKTI). They teach others who wish to achieve the same results.

When liberated persons die, there is no need to cremate their bodies. Cremation signals purification in preparation for rebirth, which the liberated do not experience. Indeed, it is questionable whether one should describe these liberated beings as being dead at all. Throughout their careers as teachers liberated beings go into meditative states as a lesson to their students. In some views, what we take as death may simply be a prolonged lesson in breath-control—a lesson in liberation that lasts an eternity. In any case, the bodies of the jivan-muktas are buried, and their tombs become places of PILGRIMAGE.

Further reading: Elizabeth De Michelis, *A History of Modern Yoga: Patañjali and Western Esotericism* (New York: Continuum, 2004); Ian Whicher and David Carpenter, eds., *Yoga: The Indian Tradition* (New York: RoutledgeCurzon, 2003); *The Yoga-sutra of Patañjali: A New Translation with Commentary*, Chip Hartranft, trans. (Boston: Shambhala, 2003).

Z

Zarathustra (first half of first millennium B.C.E.) *the founder of* ZOROASTRIANISM As a historical personage, Zarathustra (also known as Zoroaster) remains shrouded in mystery. He was Persian, but the time when he lived and his precise activities are known only vaguely. Scholars generally date him sometime between 1000 and 500 B.C.E. His religious poems, known as *Gathas,* provide the major evidence for his teachings.

In contrast to the then dominant polytheism, Zarathustra attributed the creation of the world to a single being, Ahura Mazda, the "wise lord." He is attended by seven lesser spirits, the Amesha Spentas. These in turn are opposed by EVIL spirits known as daevas. The world in which human beings live is the site of the struggle between these two forces, but Zarathustra taught that in the end good would triumph and the current world would be destroyed by fire.

Iranian religion derived from the same heritage as the VEDA in India. Prior to Zarathustra it had focused, as Vedic religion did, on animal sacrifice. Zarathustra may have eliminated the sacrifice of animals as defiling and therefore unworthy of Ahura Mazda and replaced it with a pure SACRIFICE of fire. At least that was later Zoroastrian practice.

zazen Seated MEDITATION in ZEN BUDDHISM. Buddhism cultivates an awareness of things as they are. Many activities can foster this awareness. The most specifically religious is sitting in meditation. It is the Zen practice that people living in North America are most likely to encounter.

There are two major traditions of Zen. The Soto school stresses zazen more. In the Soto tradition meditators sit around the perimeter of an enclosure, facing the outside wall. They adopt a comfortable posture with spine straight, shoulders hanging, and the hands resting in the lap, palms up and the tips of the thumbs touching. Ideally, the knees touch the floor and the feet rest, soles up, on the opposite thighs. (Other leg positions are available for the less limber.) Practitioners are encouraged to attend to their posture and breathing. DOGEN, the founder of Soto, considered zazen more than a means of achieving enlightenment. He considered just sitting, if done properly, to be enlightenment.

The other school of Zen, known as Rinzai, uses riddles called KOAN as well as seated meditation. In the Rinzai tradition, meditators face the interior of the room and thus each other. During meditation, they attend to their koan.

Zen Buddhism A variety of BUDDHISM found especially in Japan. It attempts to recover a person's "original mind" through MEDITATION. The word Zen is the Japanese version of the Chinese word *Ch'an,* which in turn reproduces the Sanskrit word *dhyana,* "meditation."

HISTORY

The "founder" or first patriarch of Zen was an Indian Buddhist named BODHIDHARMA. An expert in a scripture known as the Lankavatara Sutra, Bodhidharma was brought to China around the sixth century as part of a campaign to nurture Buddhism.

A story from his life illustrates the Zen emphasis on meditation. It tells how, upon arriving in China, Bodhidharma spent nine years in meditation facing the wall of a cave.

Another important figure in early Ch'an was Hui Neng (638–713). The Platform Sutra of the Sixth Patriarch tells how Hui Neng defeated a rival for the position of sixth patriarch. He did so in a contest to write a poem that most exhibited the mind of enlightenment.

For years the Ch'an school was divided between partisans of the two rival patriarchs. Eventually Hui Neng's branch won out, but it, too, split. Its two forms were known in Chinese as Lin-chi and Ts'ao-tung.

Lin-chi used enigmatic riddles (in Japanese, KOAN) in the hopes of provoking a sudden enlightenment. Ts'ao-tung cultivated a gradual enlightenment through the practice of sitting in meditation without any purpose or goal (in Japanese, ZAZEN). In the early 13th century two monks brought these schools to Japan. Eisai received training in Lin-chi, known in Japanese as Rinzai, while DOGEN received training in Ts'ao-tung, known in Japanese as Soto. In Japan both schools flourished.

During the Middle Ages the aristocratic-military classes who ruled Japan took a particular interest in Zen. Warriors were especially fond of the attitude of mind that Zen cultivated. As a result, Zen contributed to the strict martial ethic known as bushido. Somewhat later, the great Zen master Hakuin (1686–1769) systematized the *koan* or riddles that Rinzai Zen uses.

Eventually the influence of Zen extended to many Japanese arts. That is because, according to Zen, the original mind can be cultivated in any human activity. Zen arts of swordsmanship and archery recall the special relationship between Zen and the military class. The poet Basho (1644–94) developed haiku, a type of poem now well-known in North America, as a means of cultivating Zen mind. Other prominent Zen arts include gardening, especially waterless gardens of rock and gravel, the tea ceremony, Noh drama, calligraphy, and flower arranging.

Portrait of Bodhidharma (Daruma) from the late 16th century *(Erich Lessing/Art Resource, N.Y.)*

In the 20th century, Zen spread to North America and Europe, where it found devoted followers. An important early figure in this movement was the lay writer D. T. Suzuki (1870–1966). In the second half of the 20th century, Japanese businesses found it helpful for their employees to attend retreats at Zen monasteries.

BELIEFS

It violates the spirit of Zen to talk about Zen beliefs. Zen believes that words, thought, and reason always distort reality. They distort reality because they attempt to "grasp" it instead of simply observing and accepting it. Zen practice helps one relinquish this mental grasping.

The experience of relinquishing or release is known as satori. Satori is not a state of "no thought," which is achieved by deliberately forcing the mind to cease. It is simply the not-so-simple act of "not thinking," the recovering of one's original mind.

Given these attitudes, Zen could hardly have a set of beliefs or propositions to which its practitioners subscribe. Instead, Zen tries to use words and ideas to subvert the way we ordinarily use words and ideas. One typical Zen strategy is to pose a riddle that can have no solution. This is the strategy of the koan. The most famous koan reads, "Show me the sound of one hand clapping." A second Zen strategy is to write poetry that exhibits simplicity and a profound, aesthetic acceptance of things as they are. This is the strategy of the haiku, such as Basho's famous poem: "The old pond, ah! / A frog jumps in, / The water's sound." Yet a third strategy is to tell stories that somehow illustrate Zen mind. D. T. Suzuki tells of a father who taught his son the family business—thieving. He took his son out one night and, deceiving him, locked him in a nobleman's safe. The son's creative mental effort in escaping from the locked safe is similar to the efforts of a Zen practitioner in cultivating the mind of Zen.

PRACTICES

The most distinctive Zen practice is zazen, seated meditation. The preferred position is to sit with both legs crossed, the soles of the feet pointed up, the hands resting one on top of the other in the lap, the tips of the thumbs gently touching. In the Soto school, mediators face a wall and strive for a mind devoid of purpose. In the Rinzai school, they face one another and contemplate koan. Zen practice supplements zazen with *kinhin*, a walking meditation that helps to circulate the blood. At intervals of, say, twice a year, communities hold intense periods of meditation, perhaps a week long, known as *sesshin*.

In the Rinzai school zazen is punctuated by visits to one's master (*roshi*). These strictly private, one-on-one interviews are a sort of mental wrestling match. The disciple must answer the assigned koan in a way that shows insight but that is spontaneous and unpremeditated. Upon hearing an inadequate answer, the master curtly dismisses the disciple by ringing a bell.

Although the above are Zen practices, Zen does not recognize a hard and fast distinction between religious and nonreligious practices. As already noted, it is possible to realize the original mind through various arts. In addition, all Zen practitioners must work. Indeed, in monasteries kitchen work is said to be more important than zazen. Zen may also characterize a manner of living. That way of living definitely does not involve incessantly puzzling over koan.

ORGANIZATION

The basic relationship in Zen Buddhism is the relationship between the master and the disciple. Strictly speaking, masters are not teachers, because Zen cannot be taught. They are more like experienced guides. Masters put their disciples in situations in which the disciples may spontaneously experience the mind of Zen. Traditionally, master and disciples live in a monastery or, less commonly, a convent. Novices, known as *unsui*, include both those who are pursuing satori and those who are training to manage Zen temples. Besides meditating and working, disciples in a monastery must also beg. In keeping with the Buddha's insistence on a middle way, they also enjoy periods of exuberance and relaxation.

In North America and Europe most Zen practitioners are laypersons rather than resident monks and nuns. Ideally they visit meditation centers on a regular basis, including weekend retreats of intense meditation and work. Traditionally, Zen has been male-oriented, but especially in North America and Europe women, too, have assumed prominent roles.

SIGNIFICANCE

Although Zen is not the most popular form of Buddhism in Japan, its influence on Japanese life has been profound. During the 20th century Zen also became one of the most popular schools of Buddhism in North America.

Further reading: Soko Morinaga, *Novice to Master: An Ongoing Lesson in the Extent of My Own Stupidity* (Boston: Wisdom Publications, 2002); Eshin Nishimura, *Unsui: A Diary of Zen Monastic Life,* drawings by Giei Satō (Honolulu: University Press of Hawaii, 1973); Shunryu Suzuki, *Zen Mind, Beginner's Mind* (New York: Weatherhill, 2003).

Zend Avesta Also called simply the Avesta; the sacred collection of writings in ZOROASTRIANISM. The texts of the Zend Avesta are very old. Some seem to go back to ZARATHUSTRA himself. But the written collection did not come into existence until the middle of the first millennium (1–1000) C.E. The Zend Avesta that we have today preserves only a portion of the original.

The most important part of the Zend Avesta is a collection of poems known as *Gathas.* Many say that Zarathustra himself wrote them. They resemble the hymns of the Rig VEDA in India.

The *Gathas* make up part of a section known as the *Yasna,* "Sacrifice." When a Zoroastrian priest performs the SACRIFICE, he recites this section.

Other sections of the Zend Avesta include the *Yashts,* hymns to different *ahuras* (good spirits), and the *Vendidad,* laws that someone who wishes to remain pure must observe.

Zeus In Greek religion the most powerful of the Olympian gods. Zeus seems to be descended from a god of the sky whom Indo-Europeans worshipped. At least his name is related to a Sanskrit name for a sky god, Dyaus. Zeus's weapon is the thunderbolt. He looks after those who require special protection: suppliants and travelers. He also punishes those who break oaths.

According to Homer, Zeus is "the father of gods and men." His dwelling is on Mount Olympus. There he presides over a somewhat dysfunctional divine family. Hesiod tells how Zeus came to power by deposing his father Kronos. A few myths hint that Zeus himself may one day be deposed. Zeus's adventures in marital infidelity became, quite literally, legendary.

In classical times (600–350 B.C.E.) Zeus was the highest god of the Greek states. His major sanctuary was at Olympia. There the Greeks celebrated their common identity in a great Panhellenic festival. According to tradition, the Olympic games held every four years in conjunction with this festival began in 776 B.C.E.

Artwork showed Zeus as a bearded man, with bulging muscles and at times unclothed.

Zionism A Jewish movement in the late 19th and 20th centuries. Its goal was the founding of a Jewish state.

In late-19th-century Europe many judged the worth of a people by whether or not they had their own nation-state. Theodor Herzl (1860–1904), a newspaper reporter, wanted Jews to receive full respect among Gentiles and escape the dangers of European ANTI-SEMITISM. He argued that these goals required Jews to have their own state. In 1897 he founded the World Zionist Congress to work for a Jewish state.

Zionists overwhelmingly favored the ancient homeland of Israel as the proper site for a Jewish state. In the early 20th century Zionists began settling in Palestine, which was then part of the Ottoman Empire. During World War I Great Britain's Balfour Declaration promised that, if the Allies won, territory would be set aside for a Jewish state. But it was only after World War II, the murder of millions of European Jews in the HOLOCAUST, and considerable Zionist agitation that the state of Israel was established on May 14, 1948.

At first many Jews were sceptical of Zionism. The sceptics included ultraconservative Hasidic Jews as well as very liberal Reform Jews. After the Holocaust, Zionism became common in all forms of JUDAISM except HASIDISM. Later, although Zionism generally implied support for Israel, some radical Zionists are considered overly zealous.

Zoroastrianism

Zoroastrianism A religion begun in Iran by the prophet ZARATHUSTRA. Its followers WORSHIP only one GOD, Ahura Mazda. Zoroastrianism teaches that the world is the site of a struggle between good and EVIL. It also maintains that there will be a final judgment after death.

HISTORY

No one knows when Zarathustra lived. Some date him close to 1000 B.C.E. Others date him in the sixth century B.C.E. In any case, he lived in eastern Iran and reformed the traditional Iranian religion. He advocated the worship of Ahura Mazda (Lord of Wisdom) as the one true God. He also conceived of the traditional daevas—a word related to the English word "deity"—not as gods but as evil spirits. He eliminated the SACRIFICES that the daevas originally received.

Zoroastrianism flourished under the Persian emperors known as the Achaemenids. The emperors Darius (ruled, 522–486 B.C.E. and Xerxes (ruled, 486–465 B.C.E.) made it the official religion of their empire. The precise relations between Zoroastrianism and the traditional Persian priests known as MAGI are disputed.

After the conquests of Alexander the Great (356–323 B.C.E.), Zoroastrianism adopted a very low profile. Little was heard of it again until the Sassanids came to power in Persia (ruled, 224–636 C.E.). At that time, Ahura Mazda became known as Ormazd; the evil spirit opposing him became Ahriman. Several offshoots of Zoroastrianism also appeared. These included MANICHAEISM, a once prominent religion whose adherents were spread from the Atlantic coasts of Europe and North Africa all the way to the Pacific coast of China.

Beginning about 635 C.E. Muslim armies invaded and then conquered Persia. The vast majority of Persians converted to Islam. As a result, perhaps only 25,000 Zoroastrians, known as Gabars, remain in Iran today. They are concentrated in the remote cities of Yazd and Kerman.

By 1000 C.E. Zoroastrians from Persia began settling in the western Indian region of Gujarat. There they are known as PARSEES, because they came from Persia. For centuries the Parsees practiced agriculture, but under British rule in the 19th century they entered business, education, and the professions and became very influential. In the 19th century Parsees began to leave India and settle in trading outposts of the British Empire. In the period after Indian independence in 1947 significant Parsee communities were established in London and Toronto.

BELIEFS

The sacred collection of writings of the Zoroastrians is known as the Avesta or ZEND AVESTA. Among other writings it contains hymns by Zarathustra known as *Gathas*. Because Zoroastrianism has suffered throughout its history, only part of the Avesta survives today.

The central figure of Zoroastrian worship is Ahura Mazda, also known as Ormazd. He is eternal and uncreated and is said to have seven heavenly attendants, led by Spenta Mainyu, sometimes translated as "Holy Spirit." Opposed to Ahura Mazda is Angra Mainyu, "Evil Spirit," also known as Ahriman.

Zoroastrians think of the world as a battleground between these two sides. The heavenly attendants of Ahura Mazda have chosen to follow Truth. Angra Mainyu and the daevas have chosen to follow the Lie. Human beings are now called upon to choose Truth over the Lie, goodness over evil.

Zoroastrians also teach that there will be a final battle at the end of time. In that battle Ahura Mazda will defeat Angra Mainyu once and for all. They also teach that human beings are judged after death. They must walk across the Bridge of Recompense, which traverses an abyss. For a deceased person who has followed the Truth, the Bridge is wide. He or she crosses easily and enters the presence of Ahura Mazda. But if the deceased has followed the Lie, the Bridge becomes as narrow as a razor's edge, and he or she falls into the abyss.

PRACTICES

The most common symbol of Zoroastrianism is fire, for Zoroastrians think that fire is supremely pure. Indeed, Zoroastrian temples are known as fire temples. They contain fires that burn continuously in large metal vessels. Five times a day priests tend the fires. They add fuel and recite prayers from the Avesta.

Observant Zoroastrians bathe ritually for purposes of purity. Their daily life is also divided into five different PRAYER periods. The most important Zoroastrian festival is New Year's. Known as No Ruz or "New Day," it is a joyous celebration held around the time of the spring equinox.

At the age of seven for Parsees, 10 for Gabars, boys and girls become members of the community through a ritual known as *navjot,* "new birth." On this occasion they receive a white shirt and a sacred thread. They wear them for the rest of their lives.

The Zoroastrian practice best known to outsiders is probably the funeral, although it is simply one facet of a rich religious life. Zoroastrians believe that it is wrong to pollute any of the four elements, earth, air, fire, or water. Therefore, they have traditionally not buried or cremated their dead. Instead, they have placed the corpses in specially constructed wells known as "towers of silence." Relatively quickly, vultures eat the fleshy parts of the corpse. The bones are then dried by the sun and gathered into special holding areas or ossuaries.

In recent decades this practice has been the subject of some discussion within Zoroastrian communities. Those who live in areas where there is not a large concentration of Zoroastrians find it difficult to maintain the tradition. Some bury the dead. Others advocate electric cremation as a viable alternative to exposure.

ORGANIZATION

One can be a Zoroastrian only if one's father is a Zoroastrian. The community does not accept converts. Parsees say that they had to agree not to accept converts in order to gain permission to live in India.

A man may become a priest if his father was a priest. He receives special instruction, traditionally from his father. He also undergoes special RITUALS to invest him with the office of the priesthood.

SIGNIFICANCE

The number of Zoroastrians in the world is not large, perhaps 150,000. Nevertheless, Zoroastrianism is a major and ancient religion. In addition, significant elements of JUDAISM, CHRISTIANITY, and ISLAM may be of Zoroastrian origin. These elements include beliefs in ANGELS, in the devil, in a final judgment, and in a RESURRECTION of the dead.

Further reading: Mary Boyce, *Zoroastrians: Their Religious Beliefs and Practices* (London and New York: Routledge, 2001); Peter Clark, *Zoroastrianism: An Introduction to an Ancient Faith* (Portland, Ore.: Sussex Academic Press, 1998); Sooni Taraporevala, *Parsis: The Zoroastrians of India: A Photographic Journey* (London: Overlook Duckworth, 2004).

TOPICAL OUTLINE

The outline that follows groups the entries in
The Encyclopedia of World Religions under these main headings.
(All headings are also entries, except for headings in square brackets [].)

[Ancient Religions]
Buddhism
Christianity
[Comparative Topics]
Confucianism
[East and Central Asian
    Religions]

Hinduism
[Indigenous and Cross-
Cultural Religions]
Islam
Jainism
Judaism
New Religions

[Selected Nations,
    Religion in]
Shinto
Sikhism
The Study of Religions
Taoism

[Ancient Religions]

Aztec religion
Canaanite religion
    Baal
Egyptian religion
    Akhenaton
    Amon
    Horus
    Osiris
    Ptah
Gnosticism
Greek religion
    Adonis
    Apollo
    Athena
    Diana
    Hermes
    Orphism
    Zeus
Inca religion
Indus Valley religion

Manichaeism
Maya religion
Mesopotamian religions
    Gilgamesh
    Inanna
mystery religions
    Eleusis
    Isis, Isaic religion
    Mithra
Nordic religion
    Celtic religion
    druids
    Loki
    Thor
    Wotan
prehistoric religions
primal religion
Roman religion
    Juno
    Jupiter
    Mars
    Venus

Zoroastrianism
    Parsees
    Zarathustra
    Zend Avesta

Buddhism

Amida
arhat
Asoka
Avalokitesvara
Bardo Thodol
Bodhidharma
bodhisattva
Buddha, the
Buddhism in America
Buddhist festivals
councils, Buddhist
Dalai Lama
dharma in Hinduism and
    Buddhism
Diamond Sutra
Dogen

four noble truths
four unlimited virtues
koan
Lotus Sutra
Mahayana Buddhism
Maitreya
mappo
Mara
Nichiren
nirvana
prajna
Pure Land Buddhism
samsara
sangha
scriptures, Buddhist
Soka Gakkai
stupa
Tara
Tathagata
Theravada Buddhism
Vajrayana Buddhism
zazen
Zen Buddhism

Christianity

Acts of the Apostles
Amish
Anglicanism
Anselm
Antichrist
apostles
Aquinas, Thomas
Armenian Church
Assemblies of God
Augustine of Hippo
baptism
Baptist churches
Benedictines
Calvin, John
Canterbury
cardinals
Carnival
cathedral
charismatic movement
Christ
Christian Science

Christianity in America
Christianity, independent
Christmas
Congregationalism
Constantine, Emperor
Coptic Church
councils, Christian
creeds
cross
Crusades
dogma and doctrine
Dominicans
Easter
Eastern Orthodox
   Christianity
ecumenical movement
Episcopalianism
epistles
Eucharist
Evangelical Christianity
Fall, the
Francis of Assisi and
   Franciscans
fundamentalism, Christian
gospels
grace
Grail
Halloween
heresy
Holiness movement
incarnation
India, religions in
inquisition, the
James
Jehovah's Witnesses
Jesuits
Jesus
Joan of Arc
justification
King, Martin Luther, Jr.
kingdom of God
Latter-day Saints
Lent
liturgy
Lord's Prayer
Luther, Martin

Lutheranism
magi
Mary
Mary, apparitions of
Mary Magdalene
Mennonites
Methodism
Nazarene, Church of the
New Testament
New Testament, Apocryphal
ordination
papacy, the
Paul, the apostle
Pentecostalism
Peter, epistles of
Peter, the Apostle
Presbyterian and Reformed
   churches
Protestantism
Protestantism in
   America
Puritanism
Q source (New Testament)
Quakers
Rapture
Reformation, Protestant
restoration movement
Revelation, book of
revivalism
Roman Catholicism
sacrament
Salvation Army
Seventh-Day Adventism
Shakers
televangelism
Thomas, Gospel of
Trappists
Trent, Council of
trinity
Unitarianism
United Church of Christ
universalism
Vatican Councils
virgin birth
Waldensians
Wesley, John

[Comparative Topics]

abortion and religion
afterlife in world religions
alchemy
altar
ancestor worship
angels
animals and religion
apocalyptic literature
archaeology and religion
architecture, religious
art, religious
asceticism
astrology
atheism
Bible, biblical literature
birth rituals
brain, mind, and religion
cannibalism and religion
cats and religion
celibacy
charms and amulets
children, religion of
church and state
cinema and religion
circumcision
clothing, religious
clowns, religious
computers and religion
cosmogony
cosmologies
creation and world cycles
cults and sects, religious
dance and religion
death and religion
denomination
devils and demons
devotion, devotionalism
diet and religion
drama, religious
dreams and religion
drugs and religion
epics, religious
eschatology
eternity

ethics and religion
evil
evolution and religion
exorcism
fairies
faith
family and religion, the
fasting
fire and religion
flood stories
folk religion
founders, religious
free will and determinism
fundamentalism
games, play, and religion
ghosts
God
God, existence of
goddesses
guru
healing, religious
heaven
hell
heroes and hero myths
holy, idea of the
homosexuality and religion
humanism, religious
humor and religion
images, icons, idols in religion
incense
initiation, religious
judgment of the dead
kingship and religion
lotus
magic
marriage and religion
martial arts and religion
martyrdom
masks and religion
May Day
meditation
messiah
millenarianism
miracles
missionaries
monks and nuns

monotheism
mountains and religion
music and religion
mysticism
myth and mythology
nationalism, religious
nature and religion
New Year festivals
occultism and esotericism
pacifism, religious
persecution, religious
pilgrimage
politics and religion
polytheism
prayer
preaching
priests and priesthood
purification, religious
reincarnation
relics
religion, theories of the origin
   of
religious experience
resurrection
rites of passage
ritual
sacrifice
saints
salvation
Satan
science and religion
scripture
seasons and religion
sexuality and religion
sin
soul, concepts of
suicide and religion
Sun and religion, the
symbolism, in religion
taboo
theodicy
theosophy
visions
war and religion
water and religion
wisdom literature

SELECTED

❧ BIBLIOGRAPHY ❧

Although the writers and editors of this encyclopedia and the members of the editorial board are all original scholars in their own right, the ideas in this book are not entirely original or new. The writers have regularly consulted a variety of basic sources in preparing this volume, and we list them here.

Encyclopedias and Dictionaries

The Concise Oxford Dictionary of World Religions, John Bowker, ed. Oxford: Oxford University Press, 2005.

Encyclopaedia Judaica, Cecil Roth, ed. New York: Macmillan, 1972.

The Encyclopedia of Religion, 2d ed., Lindsay Jones et al., eds. Detroit: Thomson/Gale, 2005.

HarperCollins Dictionary of Religion, Jonathan Z. Smith et al., eds. San Francisco: HarperSanFrancisco, 1995.

New Catholic Encyclopedia, 2d ed. Detroit: Thomson/Gale, 2003.

The Oxford Classical Dictionary, 3d rev. ed., Simon Hornblower and Antony Spawforth, eds. Oxford: Oxford University Press, 2003.

Sacred Texts

Buddhist Scriptures, Donald S. Lopez, ed. New York: Penguin Putnam, 2004.

Charles, R. H. *Apocrypha and Pseudepigrapha of the Old Testament.* Oxford: Oxford University Press, 1998.

Ehrman, Bart D. *Lost Scriptures: Books That Did Not Make It into the New Testament.* New York: Oxford University Press, 2003.

The Koran: With a Parallel Arabic Text, N. J. Dawood, trans. New York: Penguin Books, 2000.

Narayan, R. K. *Gods, Demons, and Others.* New York: Bantam Books, 1986.

The New Oxford Annotated NRSV Bible with the Apocrypha, 3d ed., Michael D. Coogan et al., eds. New York: Oxford University Press, 2001.

Tanakh: The Holy Scriptures, The New JPS Translation According to the Traditional Hebrew Text. Philadelphia: Jewish Publication Society, 1985.

Tao te ching: A Literal Translation with an Introduction, Notes, and Commentary, Chichung Huang, ed. Fremont, Calif.: Asian Humanities Press, 2003.

Upanishads, Patrick Olivelle, trans. New York: Oxford University Press, 1998.

General Surveys

Eliade, Mircea. *The Sacred and the Profane.* New York: Harper Torchbooks, 1961.

Ellwood, Robert, and Barbara McGraw. *Many Peoples, Many Faiths: An Introduction to the Religious Life of Humankind,* 8th ed. Upper Saddle River, N.J.: Prentice Hall, 2005.

The Study of Religions

Eliade, Mircea. *The Sacred and the Profane: The Nature of Religion.* New York: Harper & Row, 1961.

Ludwig, Theodore M. *The Sacred Paths: Understanding the Religions of the World.* 3d ed. Upper Saddle River, N.J.: Prentice Hall, 2001.

Paden, William E. *Interpreting the Sacred: Ways of Viewing Religion.* Rev. and updated ed. Boston: Beacon Press, 2003.

Sharma, Arvind, ed. *Our Religions.* San Francisco: HarperSanFrancisco, 1993.

Smith, Huston. *The World's Religions.* San Francisco: HarperSanFrancisco, 1991.

Specific Studies

Balmer, Randall. *Religion in Twentieth Century America.* New York: Oxford University Press, 2001.

Braude, Ann. *Women and American Religion.* New York: Oxford University Press, 2000.

Burkert, Walter, *Greek Religion,* John Raffan, trans. Cambridge, Mass.: Harvard University Press, 1985.

Bushman, Claudia Lauper, and Richard Lyman Bushman. *Mormons in America.* New York: Oxford University Press, 1999.

Butler, Jon. *Religion in Colonial America.* New York: Oxford University Press, 2000.

Capps, Walter H. *Religious Studies. The Birth of a Discipline.* Philadelphia: Fortress Press, 1995.

Carrasco, Davíd. *Religions of Mesoamerica: Cosmovision and Ceremonial Centers.* San Francisco: Harper & Row, 1990.

Diner, Hasia R. *Jews in America.* New York: Oxford University Press, 1999.

Gaustad, Edwin S. *Church and State in America.* 2d ed. New York: Oxford University Press, 2003.

Joselit, Jenna Weissman. *Immigration and American Religion.* New York: Oxford University Press, 2001.

Kepel, Gilles. *The Revenge of God: The Resurgence of Islam, Christianity, and Judaism in the Modern World,* Alan Braley, trans. University Park: Pennsylvania State University Press, 1994.

Mann, Gurinder Singh, Paul David Numrich, and Raymond B. Williams. *Buddhists, Hindus, and Sikhs in America.* New York: Oxford University Press, 2002.

Markman, Roberta H., and Peter T. Markman. *The Flayed God: The Mythology of Mesoamerica.* San Francisco: HarperSanFrancisco, 1992.

Martin, Joel W. *Native American Religion.* New York: Oxford University Press, 1999.

Pals, Daniel L. *Seven Theories of Religion.* New York: Oxford University Press, 1996.

Robinson, Richard H., et al. *The Buddhist Religion: A Historical Introduction,* 3d ed. Belmont, Calif.: Wadsworth, 1982.

Rudolph, Kurt. *Gnosis: The Nature and History of Gnosticism,* Robert McLachlan Wilson, trans. San Francisco: HarperSanFrancisco, 1987.

Stein, Stephen J. *Alternative American Religions.* New York: Oxford University Press, 2000.

Thompson, Laurence G. *Chinese Religion,* 5th ed. Belmont, Calif.: Wadsworth, 1996.

Zaidman, Louise Bruit, and Parrel, Pauline Schmitt. *Religion in the Ancient Greek City,* Paul Cartledge, trans. Cambridge: Cambridge University Press, 1992.

ANCIENT RELIGIONS

Boyce, Mary. *Zoroastrians.* London: Methuen, 1985.

Godwin, Joscelyn. *Mystery Religions in the Ancient World.* New York: Harper, 1981.

Morenz, Siegfried. *Egyptian Religion.* Ithaca: Cornell University Press, 1973.

Ross, Anne. *The Pagan Celts: The Creators of Europe.* New York: Barnes & Noble, 1986.

EAST ASIAN RELIGIONS

Bahm, Archie J. *The Heart of Confucius.* New York: Harper & Row, 1971.

Earhart, H. Byron. *Japanese Religion: Unity and Diversity.* Belmont, Calif.: Wadsworth, 1982.

Ellwood, Robert S., and Richard Pilgrim. *Japanese Religion: A Cultural Perspective.* Englewood Cliffs, N.J.: Prentice Hall, 1985.

Hoover, Thomas. *Zen Culture.* New York: Random House, 1977.

Thompson, Laurence G. *Chinese Religion. An Introduction,* rev. ed. Belmont, Calif.: Wadsworth, 1969.

Thomson, Harry. *The New Religions of Japan.* Tokyo and Rutland, Vt.: Charles E. Tuttle, 1963.

Welch, Holmes. *The Practice of Chinese Buddhism.* Cambridge: Harvard University Press, 1964.

———. *Taoism: The Parting of the Way.* Boston: Beacon Press, 1957.

PRIMAL RELIGIONS

Eliade, Mircea. *Shamanism: Archaic Techniques of Ecstasy.* New York: Pantheon, 1964.

Maringer, Johannes. *The Good in Prehistoric Man.* New York: Knopf, 1960.

Turner, Victor. *The Ritual Process.* Ithaca: Cornell University Press, 1977.

INDEX

Locators in **boldface** indicate main entries.
Locators in *italic* indicate illustrations.
Locators followed by *m* indicate maps.
Locators followed by *t* indicate tables.

A

Aaron **1**
abortion and religion **1**
Abraham **1–2**
    Genesis 172
    Isaac 217, 218
    Jacob 228
    Joseph 244
    Kaaba 251
    Mecca, pilgrimage to 287
    monotheism 299
    Moses 301
    Rebekah 374–375
    Sarah 408
Abu Bakr (caliph) 369, 419
Abulafia, Abraham 252
Abu Talib 304, 419
Acts of the Apostles **2**, 105, 229–230, 320, 336
Adam **2**, 140, 145, 172
Adamski, George 457
Adi Granth **2–3**, 176, 252, 312, 424
Adonis **3**
Advaita Vedanta 59, 284, 407, 465, 468
Africa, new religious movements in *3*, **3–5**, 7, 89, 338–340, 444
African-American religions **5–6**, 93, 260–261. *See also* Islam, Nation of
African Methodist Episcopal Church 292
African religions **7**, 193–194, 407, 455–456, 469–470
Afro-Brazilian religion 61
afterlife in world religions **8–9**, 137, 173, 248–249, 428
Against Jews and Their Lies (Luther) 22
Aga Khan **9**
Agni **9**, 150–151
agriculture 351, 355–357, 422
ahimsa **10**, 19, 121, 229, 273, 331
Ahriman 116, 136, 140
Ahura Mazda
    devils and demons 116
    eschatology 136

    evil 140
    war and religion 472
    Zarathustra 485
    Zoroastrianism 489, 490
AIM (American Indian Movement) 315
Akbar (emperor of India) 118
Akhenaton (king of Egypt) **10**
alchemy **10**, 262, 441
Alexander III the Great (king of Macedon) 131, 329, 489
Ali (cousin and son-in-law of Muhammad) 212, 419–420
Ali, Muhammad 226
Ali, Noble Drew 226
Allah **10–11**
Alta Khan (Mongol king) 111
altar **11**, 479
altrusim 385
Amaterasu **11**, 219, 227
Ambedkar, B. R. 214
Ambrose 38
American Indian Movement (AIM) 315
American Muslim Mission 225, 226
Amida **11**, 40, 234, 274, 278, 363
Amidism. *See* Pure Land Buddhism
Amish **11–12**, 288
Amitabha. *See* Amida
Amman, Jakob 11
Amon 10, **13**, 131
Amos **13**
amulet. *See* charms and amulets
Anabaptists
    Baptist churches 46
    Christianity, independent 89
    Eucharist 138
    Mennonites 288
    nationalism 312
    politics and religion 345
    Protestant Reformation 376
Analects of Confucius **13–14**, 101
ancestor worship **14–15**, *15*, 69, 100
angels **15–17**, *16*
Anglicanism *3*, **17–18**
    Canterbury 74
    Christianity 88
    Episcopalianism 134–135
    Methodism 292
    Puritanism 364, 365
    Protestant Reformation 376
    John Wesley 474

Angra Manyu 116, 489
animal sacrifice 92, 401–402, 407, 408, 470
animals and religion **18–20**, *19*, 31
animism **18**, 126–127, 384
Anouilh, Jean 74
Anselm **20–21**, 144, 176, 178
anthropology
    James George Frazer 158
    Claude Lévi-Strauss 265
    Bronislaw Malinowski 276
    religion, theories of origin of 384
    sacrifice 402
    taboo 437
    totemism **454**
anti-Catholic persecution 393
Antichrist **21**
antifoundationalists 180
anti-Semitism **21–22**, 226, 247, 488. *See also* the Holocaust
Anurdhapura, council at 105
apartheid 352
aphorisms 475–476
apocalyptic literature **22–24**
    Daniel 112
    millenarianism 293
    New Testament 321
    prophets, biblical 358
    Rapture 373–374
    Revelation, book of **388–389**
    war and religion 472
Apocrypha **24–25**, 52, 142, 475
Apocryphon of John 175
Apollo **25–26**
apostles **26**. *See also* Acts of the Apostles
    Eastern Orthodox Christianity 128
    epistles **135**
    James **229–230**
    Mary Magdalene 283
    missionaries 295–296
    Paul (apostle) **336–337**
    Peter (apostle) **341–342**
Apostles' Creed 107
apostolic succession 17–18, 128, 354
Aquinas, Thomas **26–27**
    anti-Semitism 22
    faith 144
    Francis of Assisi and Franciscans 158
    God, existence of 180